Mao Against Khrushchev

DAVID FLOYD

Mao Against Khrushchev

A SHORT HISTORY
OF THE SINO-SOVIET CONFLICT

FREDERICK A. PRAEGER, *Publishers*

New York • Washington • London

Frederick A. Praeger, *Publishers*
111 Fourth Avenue, New York 3, N.Y., U.S.A.
77-79 Charlotte Street, London W. 1, England

Published in the United States of America in 1964 by
Frederick A. Praeger, Inc., Publishers

Second printing, 1964
All rights reserved

© 1963 by David Floyd

Library of Congress Catalog Card Number: 64-13362

This book is Number 142 in the series of
Praeger Publications in Russian History and World Communism

Printed in the United States of America

71262

CONTENTS

INTRODUCTION

This book is primarily an account of relations between the two largest Communist countries in the world, Russia and China, since the establishment of a Communist régime in China in 1949. It is an attempt to describe the development of their relations from the beginning of 1950, when the Soviet and Chinese governments concluded what appeared to be a natural and almost unbeatable alliance, to the moment in mid-1963 when their relations in every sphere had been reduced to the barest minimum and the leaders of both countries were denouncing each other in the strongest terms.

I have tried to tell the story in two ways. In the first part of the book I have described the various stages of the dispute in my own words with a certain amount of necessary interpretation and comment. In the second part will be found the essential documents on which the story is based, arranged in chronological order. The verbosity of Communist leaders made it impossible to include their complete outpourings. I think I have retained the essential passages from the main documents and speeches that will enable the student of the Communist world to read the story in the original, so to speak, and will provide the general reader with all the necessary references.

This is, however, not only an account of relations between Communist Russia and Communist China; it is also to a certain extent a study of the situation in the international Communist movement, of the present state of affairs in the camp of those who proclaim themselves to be the enemies and gravediggers of the democratic world. This was inevitable, because any study of the deterioration of relations between the two main Communist powers must also be a study of the failure of Marxism or Communism to provide a sure basis for their relations or for the 'unity' of the world Communist movement. But in the text and in the documentation, I have been able only to touch lightly on this much wider subject.

Why should we bother to study Sino-Soviet relations and the break-up of the Communist movement? Partly because the relationship between two great nations like Russia and China is a part of history which we must understand if we are to form opinions about the world we live in. But of more immediate importance, in my opinion, is the light which the Sino-Soviet dispute throws on the workings of the Communist mind. Despite their efforts to conceal the existence of their dispute and the nature of their differences, the polemics between Moscow and Peking in the last few years have told us more about the real problems that occupy the minds of Communist leaders and about their attitude to the main issues in the world today than we were able to learn from Communist publications in the previous quarter of a century. With each new contribution to the war of words a little more light has been thrown on the way the high priests of the Communist world are approaching their problems of policy-making.

In Stalin's day the making of policy in the Kremlin was a closed book. Today, under Khrushchev, some at least of the pages are open. But not all of them, by any means. There are many questions still to be answered. Thus, for example, in the Russians' final Open Letter in July 1963, there are the first hints of a quite new element in the dispute. Discussing the Chinese Communists' attitude to the questions of war and peace, the Russians ask whether the Chinese are not pursuing 'some quite different aims', distinct from the 'struggle for the destruction of capitalism', and they refer in this connection to the Chinese use of the slogan hailing the prevalence of the 'East Wind' over the 'West Wind'. This is obviously a deliberately imprecise comment. But it can only mean in the context that the Russians suspect the Chinese of hoping to exploit the mutual destruction that would be wrought by a nuclear war between Russia and America for their own, Chinese, advantage. This fearful thought is in itself sufficient reason for following as closely as possible the course of the Sino-Soviet dispute, and it should remove the impression that Moscow and Peking are just arguing about something called 'ideology'.

Mao Against Khrushchev

PART ONE

I

RUSSIANS AND CHINESE

Russian Far Eastern policy during this period offers a nearly perfect example of shameless duplicity. On the one hand, St. Petersburg professed to uphold the territorial integrity of China and the principle of the Open Door; on the other hand, it worked for the dismemberment of the Chinese Empire and the exclusion of non-Russian foreign influences from the territory north of the Great Wall.*

MICHAEL FLORINSKY

1. Tsarist Russia and Imperial China

The history of Russia from its origins as the little state of Muscovy in the fifteenth century has been one of almost continuous outward expansion. Pressure from a rapidly multiplying population, hungry for land and food, led successive Russian rulers to seek territorial acquisitions in every possible direction. By the end of the eighteenth century, Russia had already forced her way through to Siberia, had acquired more than a foothold on the Pacific coast, and had begun to encroach on Chinese territory. The nineteenth century saw Russian colonisation extend down the Pacific coastline. The process of expansion to east and south was facilitated by the relative weakness of the Chinese government in Peking.

By the end of the 'fifties of the last century, the Russians were in control of all territory on the left bank of the river Amur down to its mouth. The city of Khabarovsk was founded in 1854, the city of Vladivostok (meaning 'Ruler of the East') in 1860. The Treaty of Peking of 1860 recognised Russian sovereignty over all the territory north-east of the Amur and down the coast to Vladivostok, and gave the Russians extensive

---

* Michael Florinsky: *Russia, A History and an Interpretation*, Macmillan, New York, 1958.

trading rights in Mongolia and Chinese Turkestan. In 1875 the island of Sakhalin was taken over by the Russians.

An important part in the extension of Russian power in the Far East was played by the construction of the Trans-Siberian railway, which was started in 1891. The Russians took advantage of the relative weakness of the régime in Peking to extract the right to build the railway across the territory of Manchuria and to dominate the management and financing of the enterprise. The Chinese Eastern Railway, as it was called, became an important means of asserting Russian influence in Manchuria.

The Russians also continued, at the end of the nineteenth and beginning of the twentieth centuries, to press their interests in the two other border areas, Mongolia and Sinkiang. They supported the Mongols' resistance to Chinese domination and established special rights for themselves in Outer Mongolia. Similarly, by exploiting autonomous tendencies and its remoteness from Peking, the Russians established for themselves a special position in Sinkiang.

The story of Russia's relations with China throughout the nineteenth century and right up to the 1917 revolution in Russia was one of constant pressure, sometimes by force of arms, more often by commercial penetration and intrigue, on the border areas of Manchuria, Mongolia and Sinkiang. The Chinese resisted the pressures as best they could, by population transfer to the threatened areas, by diplomatic means and by force. Russian diplomacy sometimes played with Japan at the expense of China, sometimes backed the Chinese in resistance to Japanese and Western incursions.

At no time was there any love lost between Imperial China and Imperial Russia. Their relations were dominated by a battle for territorial acquisitions in which most of the spoils went to the Russians. The Russian Tsars and their ministers made no secret of their ambition to be a power in the Far East and Asia.

Count Muraviev-Amursky, who did more than any other Russian to extend Russia's influence to the Far East, said in 1854: 'to preserve Siberia it is necessary now to preserve and strengthen for us Khamchatka, Sakhalin and the mouths and navigation of the Amur and to obtain a solid influence over neighbouring China.'

Neither the replacement of the Tsarist régime by a Communist government in 1917 nor the establishment of a republican régime in China in 1912 affected the basic conflict between the two powers dominating Eurasia. If the Bolsheviks were less frank about their ultimate objective, they revealed themselves to be no less determined in practice to secure a 'solid influence' over China, and they were able to employ, in addition to the traditional means of imperial expansion, more subtle weapons for influencing China's internal policies.

2. Revolutionary Russia and Republican China 1917–1949

The immediate effect of the Bolshevik seizure of power in Petrograd was severely to reduce the impact of Russia in the Far East and to encourage Chinese efforts to restore control of the border areas. But the period of respite was short and, with the final defeat of the White Guard defenders of Tsarism and the departure of the interventionists, the new Soviet authorities found themselves in just as strong a position in the Far East as their Tsarist predecessors. By 1925 the Soviet government had regained all the positions which Russian imperial power had held in the Far East. In Manchuria, on the Chinese Eastern Railway, on Sakhalin island, in Sinkiang and outer Mongolia, while publicly rejecting 'imperialism' and the aims and methods of Tsarism, the Bolsheviks succeeded in at least maintaining and in some places improving their country's position. Whether they exploited Chinese fear of outside, notably Japanese, intervention and influence, or turned internal conflict in border areas to their own advantage, or encouraged the forces of revolution inside China itself, the dominant purpose of Moscow's policy remained to extend Russian influence as far into China as possible while at the same time keeping other powers out of China.

When in 1929 the Chinese under Chiang Kai-shek took steps to reduce Russian control of the Chinese Eastern Railway, the Soviet authorities did not hesitate to invade Manchuria and reaffirm their monopoly position. In the 'thirties the Soviet authorities took advantage of internal weaknesses in Sinkiang to establish a monopoly over trade and penetrate the administration in that area. Soviet control of Outer Mongolia was reaffirmed in 1924 and has not been seriously shaken since.

While pursuing these efforts to nibble away at the peripheral regions of the Chinese empire and thus to reduce its power, Stalin's policy towards Peking appears to have been based on support for a strong and united central Chinese government, so long as it was friendly to Russia and amenable to Russian influence. A weak China would only invite intervention in the Far East by powerful outsiders, and Stalin presumably considered that Russia's interests lay in supporting those forces inside China that appeared to have the best chance of forming a stable administration. This meant in practice Soviet support for the Nationalist Kuomintang, inspired by Sun Yat-sen and later led by Chiang Kai-shek. While Stalin was always ready to make use of the Chinese Communists to influence China's internal affairs, it does not appear he ever believed that a Communist government in China was either possible or desirable. Quite apart from his inherent distrust of indigenous and independent Communist leaders, he may well have believed that the spread of Moscow-inspired revolution across China might invite the very intervention by the West which he most wished to avoid.

Stalin's dual policy of using both the Kuomintang and the Communist party to further his ends in China had painful results for the Communists. It was not simply that they were obliged to play second fiddle to the Nationalists and submerge their organisation in the Kuomintang from 1923 to 1927. In the latter year Chiang turned on the Communist and left-wing elements in his movement, expelled them from all positions of power, reducing Communist influence in China almost to nil, except in some rural areas. Despite this rejection of Communist participation in the Kuomintang and despite the conflict between Russia and KMT forces over the Chinese Eastern Railway in 1929, Stalin continued to maintain contact with the KMT, though Soviet influence over Chinese affairs was greatly reduced in the 'thirties. At the same time the policy which Moscow urged on the Chinese Communists – of peasant risings in the countryside and insurrection in the towns – proved a failure, for which the blame was laid on Li Li-san, who had enjoyed Moscow's backing. From this time Chinese Communism, under the leadership of Mao Tse-tung, began to pursue policies which were not only independent of Moscow but often directly contrary to Stalin's advice.

The Japanese occupation of Manchuria in 1932 and the threat to the rest of China brought the Chinese Communists and the Kuomintang together again in an uneasy partnership aimed at defeating the invader. This 'united front' apparently had the blessing of the Russians, who were ready to back any combination that promised to prevent further Japanese penetration of the Chinese mainland. But when the 'axis powers' later appeared to be irresistible, Stalin did not hesitate to appease the Japanese by selling them the Chinese Eastern Railway in 1935 and by recognising the Japanese puppet state of Manchuria in 1941. He was even ready to exploit the relative strength of Japan to obtain from it a guarantee of Mongolia's independence of China.

For the greater part of the Second World War, the Russians were too involved in Europe to pursue an active policy in China. The truce between the Chinese Communists and the KMT in China continued, while the Russians and the world Communist movement continued to back Chiang Kai-Shek as the leader of Chinese resistance to Japanese imperialism. Within the framework of this situation Mao Tse-tung was steadily building up an independent Communist force.

As the end of the war approached and the ultimate defeat of Japan became inevitable, Stalin hastened to turn the wartime alliance to Russia's advantage in the Far East. At Yalta in 1945 he extracted from Roosevelt and Churchill (in return for a promise of Russian participation in the war against Japan), a guarantee of the status quo in Mongolia, the promise of the return to Russia of the whole of Sakhalin, a guarantee of Russian rights in the port of Dairen and Port Arthur and in the Chinese Eastern Railway, and the transfer to Russia of the Kurile islands.* This deal was arrived at without consultation with the Chinese, Nationalist or Communist. Thus, in return

* *See* Chronology: February 11, 1945.

for what in the event was a nominal contribution to the defeat of Japan, Stalin secured the return of all Chinese concessions which the Tsarist régime had lost to Japan in 1904.

In August 1945 the Soviet government concluded the treaty of friendship and alliance with the Nationalist government of China which secured to Russia what had already been promised at Yalta. Supplementary agreements established the rights of the Soviet military in Manchuria and Outer Mongolia's independence of China. The clear purpose behind these agreements and behind Soviet actions at the time was to exploit the Japanese defeat and China's weakness so as to restore and if possible extend Russian influence in the Far East. While continuing to support the Nationalist government of Chiang Kai-Shek, which he apparently expected to enjoy reasonable stability and control in the post-war period, Stalin set out to turn Soviet military occupation of Manchuria into political and economic control of the area. For the purposes of this particular intrigue it suited Stalin better to have a Nationalist rather than a Communist government in China itself, and, although the Chinese Communists benefited from the Russian presence in Manchuria, Stalin showed no desire to help them to oust the Kuomintang from power.

On the contrary, he himself admitted in 1948 that he had advised 'the Chinese comrades' after the war to abandon their independent effort to achieve power.*

Since relations between Russian and Chinese Communists have become more strained in recent years, the Chinese have also hinted at the resentment they felt at Stalin's lack of enthusiasm for their cause. One document attributed to the Chinese Communist Party contains the complaint that the Russians deliberately withheld military aid to Mao's forces.†

Within a remarkably short space of time, however, Mao had pushed ahead to defeat the Kuomintang and, in 1949, to proclaim the Chinese People's Republic, the first Communist power in the Far East. In so doing he did more than demonstrate the superiority of his judgement over Stalin's: he laid the foundations of a strong, stable, centralised government of China

* *See* Chronology: Autumn, 1945.
† *See* Chronology: December 1962.

which Stalin and his successors would have, for political reasons, to treat with respect. For, if the Russians could hope to control, limit and nibble away at a China governed by a relatively weak Nationalist régime, they would find much greater difficulty in pursuing such a policy towards a Chinese Communist government with which they would be linked not only by formal alliances but by bonds of Marxist 'ideological' fraternity. Henceforward ideology was going to prove an obstacle to the advancement of Russia's imperialistic aims in the Far East.

This brief review of Russia's relations with pre-Communist China is sufficient to suggest the fundamental rivalry existing between these two great nations which is the essential historical background to the present conflict. Moreover, there was little in the later relations between the Russian and Chinese Communist parties to suggest that 'ideology' or a common faith in the teachings of Marx was stronger than the deep national and historical factors. Like Tito, though in a country incomparably vaster, Mao had come to power through his own efforts and relying on his own judgement, often in the face of advice from the Russians. He had also been able to observe that Russian policy under Stalin's rule had not been noticeably better disposed towards China's national ambitions than it had been under the Tsars. Moscow's treatment of China's interests in the post-war years gave Mao little reason to trust the Russians to look after his interests.

II

STALIN AGAINST MAO, 1949–53

Comrade Stalin loved the Chinese people dearly and considered that the forces of the Chinese revolution were tremendous.

MAO TSE-TUNG*

Whatever Stalin thought privately about the victory in China of a revolution which owed relatively little to Russian aid and which was led by a man who was in no sense Moscow-trained, he had no choice in public but to welcome the development. The People's Republic of China was proclaimed in Peking on October 1, 1949, and on October 2 it was formally recognised by the government of the USSR. Russia's East European and Asian satellites quickly followed suit. Moscow and Peking rang with pledges of friendship and co-operation between the two peoples, governments and parties.

Even if Stalin may have harboured some doubts about his capacity to handle his enormous new ally in the East (he had, after all, just lost a battle to retain a much smaller one – Yugoslavia – in Europe), the entry of so numerous a people and so vast a territory into the Communist camp opened out tremendous prospects. So long as he could remain in indisputed command of the whole Communist camp, Stalin would now be able to speak for nearly a third of the world's population occupying a fifth of its land surface. Had not Lenin promised that the future of the world revolution lay in a firm alliance between Russia, China and India? Moreover, however Mao regarded Stalin and the Russian Communists' treatment of China, the simple fact was that Russia was the *only* possible source of the considerable financial and economic aid China must have if the new régime was to consolidate its grip on the

* Mao Tse-tung: 'The Greatest Friendship', *Pravda*, March 12, 1953.

country. It was natural, therefore, that two months after the People's Republic was proclaimed Mao should go to Moscow to negotiate a new alliance with Stalin.

He arrived in the Soviet capital in December 1949. He remained there for two whole months. The resulting thirty-year Treaty of Friendship, Alliance and Mutual Assistance was not signed until February 14, 1950.*

On paper at least, the Treaty and the supplementary documents signed as a result of the Moscow talks represented a retreat by Stalin from some of the positions taken up with regard to China in 1945, and it was so interpreted by Communist writers interested in raising the prestige of both Chinese and Russian Communism. But in practice Stalin gave away precious little that mattered.

The basic alliance was directed specifically against Japan and 'states allied with it' and provided for the rendering of 'military and other assistance' in the event of a Japanese attack: not a very heavy commitment, coming immediately after Japan's defeat. The Treaty also provided for 'consultation' between the Soviet and Chinese governments on all major international issues: a provision which the Russians had used to impose their policies on other potential and actual satellites.

Over the traditional points of friction between Russia and China the situation after the 1950 Treaty was as follows:

(i) *Manchuria*. The Chinese-Changchun railway was to be handed back to the Chinese by the end of 1952 at the latest (instead of by 1975) and without compensation, and the Russians were to hand over to the Chinese property seized from the Japanese. This was an apparent Russian retreat from Manchuria, though there were signs of friction over the staffing of the railway administration.

(ii) *Port Arthur*. The Russian command was to be replaced by a Soviet-Chinese commission pending its transfer to the Chinese by the end of 1952. But the Chinese were to pay for 'installations'.

(iii) *Dairen* (*Dalny*). No change was agreed in the status of this port, which the Russians had established as a naval base. But the civil administration, as well as some Japanese property,

* *See* Chronology: February 14, 1950.

was to be handed over to the Chinese. A mixed Soviet-Chinese company was to be set up for shipbuilding.

(iv) *Sinkiang*. The Russians recognised *de facto* Peking's sovereignty over the area, but secured agreement to the creation of joint companies for the exploitation of Sinkiang's oil and mineral resources, under direction of Soviet experts – one of Stalin's favourite devices for penetrating neighbouring territories.

(v) *Outer Mongolia*. The Chinese had no choice but to recognise the 'independent status' of this area, in which the Russians were firmly entrenched. But the Chinese managed to extract certain rights of immigration into Mongolia.

Even on paper, therefore, Stalin showed no excessive inclination to abandon Russian pressure on China. Mao Tse-tung came off only slightly better in 1950 than Chiang Kai-shek had in 1945. He was presumably too recently set in the saddle to press his demands on Stalin too far, and he was in any case in great need of economic aid, for which he had to make concessions. It is all the more surprising, therefore, that the amount of aid promised by the Russians under the 1950 treaty was so niggardly. All Stalin would offer at the end of the two-month negotiations was a loan of $300,000,000 at 1 per cent interest to be spread over five years. It was not much to offer a country the size of China, just recovering from two years of occupation and war and about to embark on a programme of major industrialisation. It was about a tenth of the amount Mao is rumoured to have asked for.

It would be difficult to overestimate the significance for the later development of Sino-Soviet relations of Mao's encounter with Stalin at the end of 1949 and the beginning of 1950. It cannot fail to have had a deep influence on the formation of Mao's policies and his attitude to the Russians. 1949 was for Mao what 1917 had been for the Russian Communists: the victory of the revolution; and in his case it had come about as the result of fifteen years of bitter struggle in the face of enormous physical and political obstacles. When he went to Moscow in 1949 he was leading some 500,000,000 people into the Communist world. Having proved the correctness of his policies, he could afford to forget and forgive the lack of enthusiasm that Stalin had shown for his cause in the past, and he could be forgiven himself for expecting that the Russians would pay generously for China's accession to the 'socialist camp'. There can be no doubt but that he was disappointed and it seems probable that this first and only meeting between Mao and Stalin was not of the happiest, though no details of their talks have ever emerged. All we know is that it took them two months to complete an agreement that ought to have been concluded in a few days. Mao left Moscow a wiser and probably a sadder man.

As the Russians began to put their new alliance with China into practice, it soon became apparent that Stalin intended to use the same tactics with regard to China as he had used with such success in Eastern Europe. No one knew better than he how to turn an alliance of 'friendship, alliance and mutual assistance' into an instrument for creating and controlling a satellite country.

Whatever military equipment the Chinese may have received under the treaty, it certainly served as an excuse for the arrival of a veritable flood of military advisers, amounting to not less than 20,000 and possibly reaching 25,000. Their nominal function was to modernise and train the basically peasant Chinese army. In practice they acted as a means of Russian control and intelligence at every level of the Chinese armed forces. As in the case of Yugoslavia (whence many of the advisers were probably transferred), the behaviour of the Soviet personnel led to friction and eventually to requests for their withdrawal.

Similarly, the commercial and cultural agreements served as an excuse for the despatch to China of many thousands of Russian engineers, technicians, scientists, professors, teachers and students who penetrated into every section of Chinese society. The number of strictly civilian advisers was probably not less than 50,000 and may have been much higher. Many of them, of course, brought with them technical knowledge of which the Chinese were in great need and many doubtless made a useful contribution to the Chinese economy. But there was no disguising the fact that they represented above all a vast army of Russian agents in strategic positions throughout China who were potentially a means of Russian influence and control over the direction of China's policies. At the same time the rapid reorientation of China's trade towards Russia and the Communist countries of Eastern Europe and her entry upon a programme of large-scale industrial development meant inevitably a steadily increasing economic dependence on the Communist world.

In Manchuria the Russians dragged their heels and showed no eagerness to abandon their positions. A conference between Chou En-lai and the Russians held in Moscow in September 1952 resulted in a 'request' by the Chinese for Soviet troops to remain in Port Arthur, which, according to the 1950 Treaty, they should have left by the end of 1952. There was no mention either of Soviet troops leaving Dairen, and it seemed as though the Russians were delaying the handing over of the Changchun Railway.

By 1952, however, the Russians had an excellent excuse for delaying their departure from China, for by then the Chinese were deeply involved in the war in Korea. This was an event which had far-reaching effects on Sino-Soviet relations, though very different from what Stalin had hoped for.

Ever since the Second World War, North Korea had been an outpost of Soviet influence in the Far East. The government was in the hands of Moscow-trained Korean Communists, many of them of Russian origin, and with Soviet citizenship. North Korea was bound to the Soviet Union by economic and military agreements which in effect gave the Russians absolute control of the North Korean armed forces. Stalin undoubtedly regarded Soviet control of North Korea as one of his most effective instruments, along with Soviet positions in Manchuria and Port Arthur, for the domination of China. It was to strengthen his position there, and possibly at the same time to weaken China, that he launched the Korean war.

From Stalin's point of view, the situation in Korea was ideal for the conduct of his operation. The Americans were about to abandon South Korea; North Korea had a large army, recently re-equipped and trained by Russia; Mao Tse-tung had agreed to transfer some 50,000 Chinese-trained Koreans to the North Korean forces. With what seemed to be ample military superiority, the North Koreans would be able to win a quick victory over the South without apparent Russian or Chinese involvement. Stalin saw the prospect of establishing a new Soviet satellite state in a dominating position on the Pacific. It would consolidate Russia's position as a Pacific power and make control of China easier.

Stalin's plans went awry. Swift American aid for the South Koreans made it quickly clear that there would be no easy victory for the North. Stalin was forced to appeal to Mao urgently to intervene in the war to prevent the complete rout of the North Korean forces. He apparently thought he would still be able to achieve his victory by exploiting Chinese manpower equipped with Russian arms. Mao Tse-tung was by no means eager to accept this thankless task and is said to have agreed to Stalin's request only after being promised considerable military and economic aid. The details of their bargain are not known; but the debt which the Russians incurred to the Chinese over the Korean war is said to amount to many hundreds of millions of dollars and the Russians' failure to settle accounts with the Chinese is not the least of the causes of the later conflict.

But, however much the Korean war cost the Chinese in men and money, their performance in it repaid them well in terms of prestige. The mighty Stalin was seen to have had to turn to Mao for help and Mao was seen to have saved the day. Moreover, through their intervention in North Korean affairs, the Chinese established positions there from which they were not to be dislodged.

Before the Korean conflict was resolved, however, and before its full effects on relations between Moscow and Peking became apparent, an event of far greater importance shook the whole Communist world: the death of Stalin in March 1953. He had been the sole architect and had dominated every aspect of Soviet policy at home and abroad and he had been primarily responsible for the shape which Sino-Soviet relations had taken. His death inevitably threw every aspect of policy into the melting pot. In particular it opened up for the Chinese the possibility of putting their relations with Russia on to a basis more approaching equality.

One of the differences that later emerged between the Russian and Chinese Communists was the latter's reluctance to join in Khrushchev's denunciations of Stalin. They continued to revere Stalin's memory when it had been almost erased from Soviet records. Yet it is difficult to believe that Mao Tse-tung cherished any sincere respect for Stalin's memory.

In truth, Mao had very little to thank Stalin for. Stalin had encouraged the Chinese Communists to enter into an alliance with the Kuomintang which turned out to be almost fatal for the Communist Party in China. He had opposed Mao's leadership of Chinese Communism. He had disagreed with Mao's policy of basing his movement on the peasantry. His advice to Mao in the final stages of his victorious march to power had proved wrong. He had badly miscalculated the Korean situation and led the Chinese into a situation which cost them very dear. After having been thus misled by Stalin, Mao can hardly have cherished any great respect for his judgement or affection for his character. In fact, Stalin's alienation of the Chinese Communists was by no means the least of the disservices he did to Russian Communism. He may well be held responsible for a dispute which was to become his successors' major preoccupation within a few years.

It may, of course, be argued on the other hand that Stalin's treatment of Mao Tse-tung reflected his political realism and foresight. He had never placed much faith in the 'international' spirit said to animate the Communist movement. His suspicion of other nations and peoples, whatever their religion or political beliefs, had been reflected in his early scorn for the Communist International and the brutal steps he took to bring it under Russian control. It seems probable that, from the earliest days of the Chinese Communist Party, he had seen that a victorious Communist revolution in China might produce for the Russians as many problems as it might produce benefits. That was doubtless why he set out to clip Mao's wings in the early years of the Chinese Communist régime.

III

POST-STALIN HONEYMOON, 1953–56

Soviet aid plays an extremely important part in enabling us to carry on our present construction work on such a large scale, at such high speed, on such a high technical level and at the same time to avoid many mistakes.

LI FU-CHUN,
Chairman of China's State Planning Commission*

The immediate reaction of Stalin's colleagues to his departure from their midst in March 1953 was to take steps to soften the impact of his policies on the Soviet population and on the world outside, and to retreat with as much dignity as possible from the more exposed and tense positions into which he had led them. This policy of relaxing tensions and reducing friction was not dictated by Marxist doctrines, but by considerations of elementary common sense. Stalin's death meant that there was less sureness in the grip of the hand, or hands, on the Kremlin's helm. His successors realised that it would take several years to recover from the shock of his sudden departure. It was essential, during such a period of internal weakness and uncertainty, that the Soviet Union should not be faced by a major crisis in foreign affairs. Whatever other differences there may have been in the Kremlin, there was general agreement on this.

Nothing could demonstrate more clearly the degree of strain that had existed in relations between Moscow and Peking before Stalin's death than the speed with which Stalin's successors moved to improve relations with the Chinese Communists and to appease Mao Tse-tung's wounded pride. The Russians' anxiety to make amends became apparent in the first few days following Stalin's death.

Unlike the majority of the other Communist rulers, Mao

* Li Fu-chun, speech on the First Five Year Plan, 1955.

Tse-tung did not go to Moscow for Stalin's funeral. The Chinese Communist Party was represented by Chou En-lai, Prime Minister and one of the inner circle of Chinese rulers. It was all the more striking, therefore, that he was singled out by the protocol-conscious Russians for most favoured treatment. On the balcony on Lenin's tomb, from which the funeral orations were made on March 9, Chou En-lai stood among the members of the Soviet Party Presidium and not among the other foreign leaders. In the funeral procession he walked immediately behind the gun-carriage bearing Stalin's coffin, side by side with Malenkov, Beria and Khrushchev. Even more significant was the appearance on March 10 in *Pravda*, the official newspaper of the Communist Party of the Soviet Union, of a picture of Mao Tse-tung flanked on the one side by Stalin and on the other by Malenkov. That this picture was intended to convey an important political message was evident from the fact that it had been reconstructed from a photograph taken in 1950 which did not show the three men in close company. What the purpose was is not difficult to divine. It was not merely to associate Malenkov, then apparently Stalin's successor, with Stalin; there were many other pictures of the two men together which could have been, and were, used by the Soviet press to stress the continuity of rule. The point was rather to link Malenkov with Mao Tse-tung, to identify Mao and the Chinese Communists with the succession to Stalin and to accord Mao a position in the leadership of world Communism which he had hitherto been denied. It is difficult to think of any other explanation for the faking of the Stalin-Mao-Malenkov picture, even if there had not been other evidence that the Chinese Communists had been promoted almost overnight to joint leadership of the Communist camp. The Chinese for their part responded sympathetically to the situation in which the Russians found themselves and joined harmoniously in the chorus of adulation for Stalin and of loyalty to the Soviet Union. Mao Tse-tung himself was among the loudest in praise of the departed leader.*

Another immediate sign of the Russians' anxiety to improve relations with China and raise the status of the Chinese in the Communist world was their replacement of the Soviet ambassa-

* *See* Chronology: March 12, 1953.

dor in Peking before the end of March 1953. Until then the Soviet mission in Peking had been headed by Alexander Panyushkin, a senior military officer believed to be more closely linked with the Soviet intelligence service than with diplomacy and a man who had had much to do with putting Stalin's China policy into practice. He was replaced by V. V. Kuznetsov, a former trade union official of less sinister reputation and more flexibility in dealing with foreigners, who later became one of Russia's most capable professional diplomatists. China was no longer to be treated as a satellite.

There were other signs of the improved status of the Chinese in Communist councils. The Chinese Communist Party, which ranked third after the Polish Party at the Nineteenth Congress of the CPSU in 1952, was after Stalin's death raised to second place. Similarly, in all public references to the Chinese People's Republic, it was henceforward given priority over all the other 'people's democracies'.

It was not only in matters of Communist protocol, however important they may be, that the Russians moved to appease the Chinese. They quickly agreed considerably to increase the scale of their economic aid to China. By the time Stalin died at the beginning of 1953, which was when the first Chinese Five Year Plan had been due to come into force, very little of the aid which he had promised in 1950 had found its way to China. Within three months of his death, the Russians promised to undertake the design and construction of 91 industrial plants in addition to the 50 which they had undertaken to equip under the 1950 agreements. The promises of May 1953 were written into formal agreements in September of the same year and supplemented by further agreements in October 1954, when another 15 industrial plants were added to the operation. Not only did these undertakings represent a considerable augmentation of Soviet aid; there is also reason to believe that the Russians were much more punctilious in their fulfilment of them than they had been in the case of the promises made in 1950. Khrushchev was even able to claim, in a speech to the Supreme Soviet in May 1957, that the Russian technicians were building more up-to-date plants in China than their own industry had at home.

The agreements of October 1954 were negotiated by a delegation of Soviet leaders which went to Peking for the celebration of the fifth anniversary of the People's Republic. It included Nikita Khrushchev, already First Secretary of the Soviet Communist Party, and Anastas Mikoyan, who had long handled Russia's major foreign trade negotiations and who is by far Russia's shrewdest and most capable diplomatist. This was Khrushchev's first meeting with Mao as leader of the Soviet Communist Party. Mao had no apparent reason for dissatisfaction with the encounter, which resulted in an additional long-term loan of 520 million roubles, the dissolution of the objectionable Soviet-Chinese 'mixed companies' and a firm undertaking that Soviet troops would leave Port Arthur and Dairen on May 14, 1955.* (The management of the Changchun railway had been handed over to the Chinese on February 1, 1953, after further pressure by the Chinese.)

In less than two years after Stalin's death, therefore, there had taken place, both in relations between the two Communist parties and between the Soviet and Chinese governments, a sharp swing in favour of the Chinese. China's prestige and weight inside the 'socialist camp' had been greatly enhanced, and she was beginning to receive the sort of material aid by means of which she could hope eventually to add economic and military power to the political influence she had already achieved. Moreover, with the exception of Mongolia and Korea, Mao had succeeded in ousting the Russians from all the positions in the border areas which Stalin and his Tsarist predecessors had regarded as essential for the containment of China. Whether they chose to continue to revere Stalin's memory or not, Mao Tse-tung and his colleagues in the leadership of Chinese Communism had no reason to be displeased with the post-Stalin changes in Soviet poicy. The Russians, for their part, appeared to realise that if they wanted to enjoy China's friendship and support they would have to offer something more than promises, and they seemed genuinely ready to do so. The Moscow-Peking axis appeared to have gained in strength.†

It was not only inside the 'socialist camp' and not purely

* *See* Chronology: September 29, 1954.
† *See* Chronology: October 12, 1954.

through Russian encouragement that the post-Stalin years saw an increase in the prestige and influence of the government in Peking. There were other clear signs that the Chinese Communists intended to restore China to her position as a great power and themselves to play a corresponding part in world affairs. In this ambition they seemed to be quite uninhibited by the parlous state of their own economy and their dependence on the Russians for aid.

The admission of the Chinese Communist government to the Geneva conference on Korea and Indochina in 1954, despite the bitterness engendered by the Korean war and America's refusal to recognise the new régime in Peking, was an opportunity for the Chinese to shine on the world's stage, an opportunity of which they took full advantage. Their delegation to Geneva was headed by Chou En-lai, Prime Minister and Foreign Minister, and considerably outnumbered every other delegation. The Chinese took over one of the largest hotels in the city and engaged a fleet of cars to carry them around. Chou En-lai installed himself, like the other great power delegations, in a villa and proceeded to receive and be received by British and French statesmen. There was no mistaking the concern of the Chinese to demonstrate that they knew as well as any government how to behave as a major power.

There was never any likelihood that the conference would find a solution to the problem of a divided Korea. Having fought to maintain the non-Communist régime in the South, the Western Powers could not abandon it now, any more than the Russians and Chinese could abandon the Communist régime they propped up in the North. Their intention in attending the conference was presumably no more than to obtain recognition for the status quo. It was the indirect results that mattered, especially to the Chinese, for whom it provided both access to world powers independent of the Russians and an opportunity to demonstrate to the Asian peoples, and especially the North Koreans, their skill and persistence in negotiation. Though Chou En-lai generally supported the line taken by Molotov, who headed the Soviet delegation, there were signs in their public statements that their tactical approach and even their aims were not identical with Russia's. Chou En-lai showed, understandably, greater anxiety than Molotov to keep the talks going even when it was apparent that agreement was impossible. In private conversations Chinese delegates and journalists did not hesitate to speak apologetically about Russian 'obstinacy' and to suggest that the Chinese approach was more flexible.

The Geneva experiment was not repeated and when the big powers met again in the same city to discuss East-West issues, Communist China was not represented. The Western powers were not ready to admit the Peking government to discussions of world issues which were primarily their concern and that of the Soviet government. The Russians, though perhaps no more anxious than the West to bring the Chinese in, and in any case unable to overcome Western resistance to China's intervention in world issues, took refuge in statements insisting that these issues could not be solved satisfactorily without Chinese participation. A specific demand was that the Peking government should take over the Chinese seat in the United Nations from the Nationalists. But the Russians never showed any excessive enthusiasm for this aim, and the Chinese Communists were later* to complain that Russian efforts to secure their entry into the United Nations were half-hearted.

In 1954 and 1955 there were other signs, if not of conflict, certainly of rivalry between the Russian and Chinese Communists in foreign affairs. It concerned their respective influence over the peoples of Asia. The Chinese had begun their thrust southwards into South-East Asia even before Stalin died. The Soviet leader, confident of his ability to turn China into a satellite, may well have encouraged this extension of Chinese influence southwards into Asia. In any case, by the end of 1950 the Chinese had seized control of Tibet by force, and in April 1954 the Indian government concluded an agreement with Peking involving the withdrawal of Indian influence from Tibet.

In June 1954, on his way home from the Geneva Conference, Chou En-lai stopped in New Delhi for talks with Nehru, the Indian Prime Minister. They reaffirmed the 'five principles' of peaceful coexistence, first enunciated at the signing of the Tibetan agreement, which were to govern Sino-Indian relations, and they agreed on the desirability of joint consultation on

* See Chronology: December (late) 1962.

Asian problems and with other Asian governments. In some of Chou En-lai's public pronouncements could be detected Peking's plans to make use of India's goodwill to extend Chinese influence in Asia and develop an 'Asia for the Asians' policy. 'Asia today is no longer the Asia of yesterday. The age when outside forces could decide at will the fate of Asia has gone for ever . . . I hope that China and India will co-operate even more closely in the noble aim of safeguarding peace in Asia.' In saying this, it may well be that Chou included the Russians among the 'outside forces' he wanted to exclude from Asian affairs.*

His talks in Delhi were followed in October 1954 by an official visit by Nehru to China. The visit resulted in further declarations of friendship between the two countries and the signature of a number of trade agreements. The Indian government seemed more than ready to accept the Chinese protestations of friendship, though it cannot have been unaware of pressure already being exerted by the Chinese in Burma and Vietnam.

China's efforts to assume leadership in Asia found their clearest expression in the Conference of Asian and African states held in Bandung (Indonesia) in April 1955. The formal conveners were the five 'Colombo powers', but the inspiration and initiation came almost exclusively from Peking. Twenty-five governments were represented at the conference, including all the principal nations of Asia and the Middle East, embracing one-third of the world's population. It was an exclusively Asian occasion in which the Russians played no part either as participants or as observers. The actual business conducted and the various resolutions passed were of little lasting significance except for their assertion of a community of 'Asian' interests clearly opposed to those of the 'imperialist' powers, and for their demand for an end to all 'colonisation'. The really important feature of the conference was the role played in it by Chou En-lai. In the most conciliatory and understanding of moods, he dominated the proceedings and made a deep impression on many of the leading delegates.

The Russians had no choice but to welcome the Bandung

* *See* Chronology: June 22, 1954.

meeting and its conclusions, and to derive what public satisfaction they could from this success of their Chinese ally. But
it is very doubtful if in their inner councils they found much
cause for satisfaction in Bandung. For the Chinese had
demonstrated all too clearly that they were quite capable,
without Russian support, without representation in the United
Nations and without recognition by America, of playing a
major role on the world stage. Within a year of Stalin's death,
the Chinese Communists had gone a long way towards seizing
the leadership of the Asian peoples.

Russian concern at the prospect of declining influence in Asia
soon became apparent in the efforts they made to improve
relations with India. In June 1955 Nehru went to Moscow on an
official visit during which he was accorded honours never
before granted to a foreign non-Communist statesman. Hasty
steps were taken to eliminate from Soviet textbooks and
reference books the earlier, Stalinist, assessment of Nehru as a
'lackey of imperialism', and his book, *The Discovery of India*,
full of non-Marxist ideas, was brought out in a Russian edition.
He was also permitted the unprecedented honour of addressing
a mass open-air meeting in Moscow. In talks with the Soviet
leaders, he agreed to an increase in Soviet-Indian trade and
the Russians undertook to construct a steel mill in India.

In the last two months of 1955, Khrushchev and Bulganin,
who was then Soviet Prime Minister, made a long tour of Asia,
including official visits to India, Burma and Afghanistan. The
importance they attached to maintaining and extending Soviet
influence in Asia was thus demonstrated by the fact that these
two leaders absented themselves from Moscow for six weeks
at a time of considerable internal strain and on the eve of the
critical Twentieth Congress of the Soviet Communist Party.

Khrushchev's colourful personality and lively denunciations
of Western misdeeds in Asia appear to have made a considerable impression in the three countries to which he directed his
attention. His public declarations and private diplomacy were
back up by a timely demonstration of Soviet military power,
in the form of the explosion of a hydrogen bomb while he was
touring India, and of Soviet economic wealth, through various
promises of trade and aid. Finally, Khrushchev also subscribed

to the 'five principles' which Chou En-lai had proclaimed as the basis of relations between states of all kinds even before the Soviet leader had formulated his own conception of 'peaceful coexistence' which was later to be one of the main issues in the Sino-Soviet dispute.

Khrushchev received much publicity on his tour of Asia, established personal ties with Asian leaders and did much to remind Asian governments that Russia was ready and eager to step into the vacuum left by the departure of the Western 'imperialists'. But his appeal was found to be less impressive than that of the Chinese, who had the advantage of being Asians themselves and who had a deeper understanding of the Asian mind and Asia's needs. The Russians could offer trade and aid and military might with which to champion the Asian countries against encroachments from the West. But they were outsiders, too, whereas the Chinese could speak with conviction of the prospect of 'Asia for the Asians'. And, if they had no H-bomb, they had certainly demonstrated, in Tibet and elsewhere, that they were a military power to be reckoned with. On the whole, Khrushchev's excursion into Asia was not a serious set-back to Chinese plans.

Khrushchev made one other important trip abroad in the immediate post-Stalin period. In May 1955 he went with a delegation, again including Bulganin and Mikoyan, to Belgrade to restore relations with Marshal Tito, the Yugoslav Communist leader who had defied Stalin successfully in 1948. This visit marked the beginning of a Khrushchevian pursuit of Tito that was to play an important, if only indirect, part in the later dispute between Khrushchev and Mao Tse-tung.

It seemed to be generally agreed among the Soviet leaders that an essential step in the post-Stalin relaxation would be an improvement in relations with Yugoslavia, or at least a reduction in the tension created by Stalin between Moscow and Belgrade.* As early as June 1953, the Soviet government had restored diplomatic relations with Yugoslavia to normal with the appointment of an ambassador after a break of over two years. But Khrushchev, if not some of his more rigidly minded

* See Chronology, passim 1953, 1954.

colleagues, wanted to go beyond 'normalisation' to the restoration of Yugoslav Communism to full membership of the 'socialist camp'. That was presumably why he accepted Tito's demand that he should go first to Belgrade as a visible sign of Russia's repentance for Stalin's treatment of Yugoslavia. In the event, Khrushchev's public apology* fell short of complete withdrawal and Tito refused to resume satellite status. Despite this, relations between the two parties were re-established and the Russians promised substantial trade and credits to aid the Yugoslav economy. While backing most Soviet objectives in foreign affairs, Tito still preserved a considerable degree of independence in his conduct of policy at home and abroad and began to exert pressure on Moscow for reforms in Eastern Europe.

There were to be many ups and downs in relations between Moscow and Belgrade following this first post-Stalin resumption of relations in 1955.† Even today (1963) Tito has still not succumbed entirely to Russian blandishments and has maintained his country's position somewhere between East and West. Nevertheless Khrushchev has continued to pursue the Yugoslav leader and at the end of 1962 accorded him the exceptional honour of addressing the Supreme Soviet in Moscow. Since this relationship between the Soviet and Yugoslav leaders and their Communist parties was later to become one of the central issues between Moscow and Peking, it is of importance to consider at this point the reasons which underlay it and which have tended to be ignored.

It was, as has been pointed out above, quite natural for Stalin's successors to wish to restore normal governmental relations with the Yugoslav government and so remove one of the centres of tension which Stalin had created in Europe. It was not so much a matter of ideology as of good practical politics. It was also understandable that those of Stalin's successors who were bent (as Khrushchev apparently was) on demonstrating their determination to lead Russia and the Communist movement away from Stalin's methods to something better should want to undo what was one of Stalin's most

* *See* Chronology: May 26, 1955.
† *See* Chronology: July 4, 1955.

spectacular blunders. He had driven Tito, one of the best-known and admired of Communist leaders, out of the Communist camp. Khrushchev and those who shared his views would bring him back.

Stalin's excommunication of the Yugoslav Communist Party had been the first major schism in the Communist bloc and it was understandable that Khrushchev should want to mend the break as quickly as possible and restore the 'monolithic unity' to which Communist leaders had always attached so much importance. This was especially important at a time when the Soviet leaders were faced with the problem of relaxing to some extent their controls over Eastern European countries, and when an independent but Communist Yugoslavia might well serve as a powerful centre of attraction for other dissident Communist leaders. Apart from the influence which an independent Yugoslavia might exert on other Communist governments and parties, there was also to be considered the significance which the Soviet Union's relations with Yugoslavia might have for the many newly independent 'non-committed' nations of Asia and Africa which the Russians were anxious to swing in their direction. If the Kremlin could not maintain friendly relations on a basis of equality with another professedly Communist country, what weight could be attached to its promises to respect the newly emergent nations?

All these considerations seemed at the time, and still seem today, good and legitimate reasons why the Russians should seek to restore friendly relations with the Yugoslav government and at least tolerable relations with the Yugoslav Communist Party. There was perhaps one other, less generally accepted, factor to be found in the character and personality of Marshal Tito himself. He was not only the best-known Communist leader after Stalin: far better known to the world at large in 1953 and even 1955 than Khrushchev himself; he was the only one who had a clean record of resistance to Stalin. Others might claim to have disapproved silently of Stalin during his lifetime: Tito's record was plain for all to see. It was clearly important for anyone setting out on the path of de-Stalinisation of the Communist movement to have Tito on his side. It seems very likely that Khrushchev saw in Tito's colourful, if independent, personality a valuable asset in his forthcoming battles with the dreary, unimpressive men whom Stalin had left behind in Moscow and the capitals of Eastern Europe.

For all these, and possibly other, reasons Khrushchev became committed to a rapprochement with Tito and the Yugoslav Communists. But, however reasonable this was, it seems that, in the course of the pursuit, the importance of the quarry became exaggerated out of its true significance. It became a point of honour with Khrushchev to maintain good relations with Tito even when it was clear that his efforts to do so would never be crowned with Tito's complete submission and that they were already causing bigger rifts in Moscow's relations with other parties. It would, of course, be ingenuous to believe that the Chinese Communists would make their alliance with Russia dependent on Moscow's relations with Belgrade or that the Russians would give their relations with a backward Balkan state priority over their alliance with the country which held the key to Asia. The truth probably is that both Russians and Chinese regarded Yugoslavia primarily as a convenient medium through which to conduct their dispute without directly confronting one another. Yugoslavia's neighbour Albania later came to be exploited in the same way by the two giants of Communism.

In 1955, however, Moscow's relations with Belgrade were not an issue between Moscow and Peking. The Russians were able to pursue, without interference from the Chinese, their efforts to improve relations, not only with the dissident Yugoslavs, but with the Western powers themselves. In June 1955 the heads of government of the United States, Britain, France and the Soviet Union met in Geneva for a discussion of East-West problems. The Soviet delegation was headed by the Prime Minister, Bulganin, and included both Khrushchev and Molotov. It was Khrushchev's first serious encounter at the conference table with Western statesmen. The meeting appeared to have its origins on the Western side in an unreasoning faith among the public, probably deriving from memories of wartime 'summit' meetings, in the ability of the world's top leaders to resolve problems if they met face to face. The motives on the Russian side were probably to disarm the West by an apparent willingness to negotiate major issues, to take some of the dangerous tension out of East-West relations, and to conduct a reconnaissance into Western thinking on major issues. Neither side came to the conference with the intention of making any serious concessions to the other, and in particular the Russians made it absolutely clear that their desire for better relations with the West did not mean they intended to abandon Stalin's post-war acquisitions in Eastern Europe.

The conference was a failure in that it brought the solution of none of the major East-West issues any closer, though the Russians chose to laud the emergence of what they called the 'Geneva spirit'. It is possible that the only important result of the conference was that it persuaded Khrushchev that, given a freer hand and without the dead weight of Molotov to hinder him, he could handle Western statesmen to the advantage of the Soviet Union and Communism generally. It was this belief, engendered at Geneva, that was to lead him into further 'summit' meetings and further disappointments and to earn him the disapproval and suspicion of the Chinese.

The Chinese showed little interest in the proceedings at Geneva in 1955, beyond mildly approving of the easing of tensions. Though the Russians demanded Communist China's admission to the United Nations and stressed the importance of its participation in future East-West discussions, this produced no result and the Chinese had no reason for gratification. But the question of the desirability of direct, top-level negotiations with the West and the possibility of advancing the Communist cause by those means was later to become a major issue in the dispute between Moscow and Peking. There was nothing in the Geneva Conference of 1955 to support the Russian view on this matter.

There were thus a number of important developments in relations between Moscow and Peking in the three years from the death of Stalin in 1953 and the Twentieth Congress of the Soviet Communist Party in 1956. They threw a great deal of light on the nature of Sino-Soviet relations and provided useful pointers for their future development.

In the first place, it was clear that the Russians had made an immediate and substantial effort to appease the Chinese and to reassure them about Russia's basic goodwill towards them and her willingness to extend practical assistance for China's industrial expansion. While Stalin had been able to hold the Chinese at arm's length and delay the provision of aid for China, his successors went out of their way to help, to the point of committing themselves to bearing the brunt of the task of turning China into an industrial power. In their anxiety to please the Chinese in this respect it may well be that the Russians overstretched themselves. It was their later withdrawal of aid that cause some of the bitterest feelings between the two countries.

Secondly, the Chinese received a considerable accession of status within the Communist movement, so that Molotov went so far on one occasion as to describe them as the joint leaders of the 'socialist camp'.* The Chinese themselves revealed no reluctance to step into this position, to which their size and their revolutionary record, if not their economic or military power, seemed to qualify them.

Thirdly, the Chinese made an immediate bid for the leadership of the Asian peoples. There is even reason to suppose that there was Russian acceptance of a division of 'spheres of influence' with the Chinese, in which the latter assumed prime responsibility for the Far East and South-east Asia.

Fourthly, it must be said that there was at this time no evidence of conflict between Moscow and Peking. The Russians appeared eager to maintain the best of relations, and the Chinese appeared quite happy to accept Russian leadership. They had everything to gain from these relations, through which alone they could hope to build up their backward economy. The Chinese later claimed that they began to disapprove of some aspects of Soviet policy in 1956 and even earlier. If they did, it was not apparent.

Finally, the period between 1953 and 1956 saw the evolution of a new Russian strategy in foreign policy, which was ultimately to provide most of the material for the dispute between the two parties. But it had not been sufficiently clearly defined by 1956 to evoke any opposition from Peking.

* *See* Chronology: February 8, 1955.

In short, at the beginning of 1956 it was reasonable to regard the Moscow-Peking axis as a powerful factor in world politics, which was likely to grow stronger rather than to break up. Both Russians and Chinese seemed to have every reason for maintaining a close alliance and none at all for quarrelling. Yet the seeds of conflict were already there, and, with the benefit of hindsight, it is clear that the Chinese Communists were already behaving primarily as Chinese and not as Communists. Their policies can be seen to have owed as much, if not more, to Chinese nationalist ambitions as they did to Marxism, and there was certainly no indication that they were intending to become obedient members of a Communist camp run by the Russians.

IV

THE BEGINNING OF THE TROUBLE, 1956–57

It is impermissible to impose the programme resolutions, line or policies of any one party on other fraternal parties.
'People's Daily', January 27, 1963

The Twentieth Congress of the Communist Party of the Soviet Union, which met in Moscow in 1956 from February 14 to February 25, was an event of the utmost importance to the Soviet Union itself and to the whole Communist movement. It was the first occasion since 1953 on which the leaders of world Communism were able to take breath and consider their long-term plans. Most of the steps taken by the Soviet leaders at home and abroad since Stalin's death had been in the nature of emergency measures calculated to ease tensions and eliminate the worst features of Stalin's rule. But towards the end of 1955, the Soviet leaders began to feel the need for a Party Congress which would lay down the general lines along which they expected Russia and the Communist world to advance. It was also the occasion for the first changes in the leadership of the Soviet Communist Party and in relations with the Communist movement as a whole.

The Twentieth Congress is remembered in the world at large mainly for the speech denouncing Stalin which Khrushchev made to a closed session of the Congress before it ended. This speech certainly had the dramatic effect throughout the Communist world it was no doubt intended to have. By destroying at one blow the sacrosanct image of the man who had ruled Russia and the whole Communist camp with an iron hand for so many years, Khrushchev and those who supported him presumably hoped to administer the sort of shock which would commit the movement irrevocably to the path of de-Stalinisation. It was also, and above all, his first body-blow to those

Communist leaders who continued to think in Stalin's way and to hope for a reversion to his methods.

But, important though Khrushchev's anti-Stalin speech was in its impact and implications, the contents of the report which he made in public at the opening of the Congress were of greater fundamental importance in the long run, especially for the development of relations between the Russian and Chinese Communists. In so far as it can be termed 'ideological', the Sino-Soviet dispute can be seen to have originated at the Twentieth Congress. The policy-makers in the Kremlin had been doing some hard thinking on fundamental issues of foreign policy and the application of Communist theory to a world increasingly dominated by atomic weapons, and they had come to some far-reaching conclusions. Since much of the subsequent dispute between Moscow and Peking centred around those policy innovations and their interpretation, it is necessary to set them out in some detail.

Khrushchev devoted one whole section of his report* to 'certain questions of principle affecting international development in the present day', which, he said, defined 'not only the course of current events but also further perspectives'. The questions concerned were: 'the peaceful coexistence of the two systems, the possibility of averting wars in the present epoch and the forms of transition to socialism in various countries.' His ideas on these three subjects ran as follows:

'Peaceful coexistence' had always been and would remain 'the general line' of Soviet foreign policy; it was 'not a tactical move, but the basic principle of Soviet foreign policy'. If there was a threat of war it did not come from the Soviet side. Russian Communists did not like capitalism but that certainly did not mean that they had any intention of interfering in the internal affairs of capitalist countries. If they hoped for a victory of the Communist system in its competition with capitalism, that did not mean that victory would be achieved through armed intervention in the internal affairs of capitalist countries. The principle of peaceful coexistence, Khrushchev claimed, had already become the keystone of the foreign policy of the Chinese People's Republic, of the 'people's democracies'

* *See* Chronology: February 14, 1956.

of Eastern Europe, and of the Indian, Burmese and other governments.

So far this was no more than the classical definition of 'peaceful coexistence' as already enunciated by Stalin. It was not new. But Khrushchev carried the concept further. Countries with different systems could not only exist side by side, he said. 'We must go further, towards an improvement of relations, a strengthening of trust between them and collaboration.' And in the midst of his argument he revealed the main reason for his extension of the concept. There was no other way out in current conditions. 'In fact there are only two paths: either peaceful coexistence, or the most devastating war in history. There is no third way.'

However sceptically the West was forced to view the Soviet leader's assurances, there can be no doubt that his words carried the concept of peaceful coexistence an important stage further and that they represented a major development in Communist thinking. Khrushchev was in fact outlawing war, not because of a conversion to pacifism, but out of a recognition that a major war with modern weapons would mean the end of Communism as well as capitalism, that you could not reasonably set out to advance a cause by means which would involve the destruction of yourself and your cause. Hitherto, while mouthing pacifist slogans, Communists had welcomed wars for the revolutionary situations they tended to produce. Were not the Russian revolution and the 'revolutions' in Eastern Europe the by-products of world wars? But now Khrushchev was saying that wars were outlawed and that the Communist world must even think in terms of 'collaboration' with the capitalists.

Khrushchev then had to face up to the objection that, from the Marxist point of view, it did not depend upon the Communists whether there would be war or not. Marxism taught that, so long as 'imperialism' existed, wars were inevitable. Khrushchev disposed of this objection, not very convincingly, by arguing that although, so long as imperialism existed, there would continue to be an *economic* basis for war, social and political forces in the world opposed to war had acquired such moral and material strength that they could either prevent the imperialists from launching a war or could 'deliver a crushing blow to the aggressors and upset their adventurist plans'. There was therefore, he said, no 'fatal inevitability' of war. He did not explain how a 'crushing blow' delivered against the West would differ from war.

There remained the question of the extension of Communism through revolution. The Communists had long been nominally opposed to war but not averse from the promotion and support of the forcible seizure of power in other countries. The 'imperialists' might well be forgiven for seeing little difference between the extension of Communist influence by open force of arms and its extension through covert or real aid to Communist movements in the free world. To deal with this objection, Khrushchev announced that 'new perspectives' were opening up in the matter of the transition of other countries and nations to 'socialism'. The transition, he said, would not necessarily be associated with civil war. There were now possibilities of peaceful, even parliamentary, transition to socialism, even if in some cases a 'sharp class, revolutionary struggle' might still be necessary.

Such was the message of the Twentieth Congress to the Communist movement on matters of basic principle: however unconvincing some of Khrushchev's arguments may have sounded and however many questions he left unanswered, there could be no mistaking the basic fear that had motivated his revision of the doctrine. Nothing was more important to Communism, or at least to the Soviet Union, than to avoid war, which would probably mean the end of everything. Khrushchev and his advisers had faced up to and answered as best they could a question that had been bedevilling all their pronouncements on foreign affairs since Stalin died and since Russia acquired atomic weapons. They had done their best to adjust Communist strategy to the realities of the atomic age without abandoning the cause of revolution. If their answers were not entirely satisfying it was not their fault, but the fault of an impossible situation: that of trying to be militant revolutionaries in the nuclear age.

The significance of Khrushchev's doctrinal reforms was missed in the fuss that followed leaked reports of his secret attack on Stalin and in the more dramatic events in Poland and

Hungary that disturbed the Communist world later in 1956. The public reaction by other Communist parties was the customary one of uncritical praise for Moscow's latest pronouncement. It seems likely, however, that the significance of Khrushchev's revisions was not lost on the other leaders. The Chinese Communists subsequently claimed* that from the very beginning they had had reservations about the questions of principle dealt with by Khrushchev. The Twentieth Congress of the CPSU, they said, had 'both positive and negative aspects'. And, with their usual bland arrogance, they went on:

> We have expressed our support for its positive aspects. As for its negative aspects, namely, the wrong viewpoints it put forward on certain important questions of principle relating to the international Communist movement, we have held different views all along. In talks between the Chinese and Soviet parties and at meetings of fraternal parties we have made no secret of our views and have clearly set forth our opinions on many occasions.

Whatever views they expressed in private, the Chinese Communists' public reaction to the Twentieth Congress of the CPSU was largely, but not entirely, approving. It took the form of an editorial article in the Peking *People's Daily* (April 5, 1956) entitled 'On the Historical Experience of the Dictatorship of the Proletariat'. The article was based on a discussion at an enlarged meeting of the Political Bureau of the Central Committee of the Chinese Communist Party and the Chinese summing up of the Congress. It dealt almost entirely with the exposure of the Stalin cult and its consequences.†

The Chinese agreed that Stalin had made 'erroneous decisions on certain important questions, which led to serious consequences'. Amongst other things, he had given 'certain wrong advice on the international Communist movement, and, in particular, made a wrong decision on the question of Yugoslavia'. The article recalled indirectly that some of Stalin's 'errors' had concerned relations with the Chinese Communists.

* 'Whence the Differences?', *People's Daily*, February 27, 1963.
† *See* Chronology: March 30 and April 5, 1956.

But their judgement of him was much more measured and far less emotional than Khrushchev's secret denunciation. It was, they said, a 'grave error' to think that Stalin had been wrong in everything.

On the whole, the Chinese appeared to approve the downgrading of Stalin and to be firmly behind Khrushchev's new line. This may have caused him some satisfaction. But it would be surprising if the Russian Communists were especially pleased by the patronising tone of the *People's Daily* article, which 'congratulated' the Russians on having exposed Stalin's mistakes, or by the self-satisfied way in which the article described how the Chinese Communist Party had had the wisdom and foresight to avoid the traps Stalin had fallen into. However this may be, for the time being the Chinese were not discussing questions of principle in public, though they claim to have been airing their views without inhibition behind the scenes.

There is one important general aspect of Khrushchev's pronouncement on Communist principles that certainly did not escape Mao Tse-tung and the Chinese Communist leaders. It was that, without prior consultation with the rest of the Communist movement, Khrushchev, the leader of *one* party, had proclaimed fundamental changes in basic Marxist doctrine and apparently taken it for granted that they would be accepted automatically by the other parties. Just as it appears that the Chinese delegate to the Twentieth Congress had not been forewarned about the impending downgrading of Stalin, so it seems that Khrushchev, who had yet to be credited with the authorship of a single work on Marxist theory, had not bothered, before revising Marx's teachings, to consult Mao Tse-tung, who was already credited with original contributions to Marxist thought. While rejecting Stalinism, Khrushchev was behaving as though he and his party could still legislate for the whole Communist movement. This attitude undoubtedly contained the seeds of conflict with Peking and was later to be the source of bitter complaint by the Chinese.

On the other hand, Khrushchev and his closest advisers seemed in 1956 to lose no opportunity of consulting with Tito and the Yugoslav Communists.* Side by side with a considerable

* *See* Chronology: June 2, July 21, September 19, September 27, 1956.

increase in Soviet trade with Yugoslavia and financial assistance for the Yugoslav economy, the Soviet leaders appeared to be seeking Tito's advice and support on matters affecting relations between Russia and the satellite governments of Eastern Europe. Tito paid an official visit to Moscow in June 1956 which resulted in the restoration of normal and friendly relations between the Russian and Yugoslav Communist parties, and of apparently cordial personal relations between Khrushchev and Tito. In the course of September and October 1956, delegations from the Polish, Bulgarian, Hungarian and Rumanian parties made the pilgrimage to Belgrade to restore good relations with the Yugoslavs. Meanwhile Mikoyan and Khrushchev both made flying visits to Tito and the latter flew to Russia for talks about the changes in the leadership of the Hungarian Communist Party. Although he had successfully resisted pressure to restore formal links with the Soviet bloc, either on the governmental or the party level, Tito had quickly resumed a very influential role in Communist councils—more influential than that accorded to Mao Tse-tung.

One of the results of the readmission of the Yugoslav leaders to the company of good Communists was the dissolution of the Cominform, the consultative body which Stalin had set up in 1947 to exert Russian control over the Communist parties of Europe. Since the Comintern, the original expression of the 'international' nature of Communism, had been abolished by Stalin in 1943, there was now no overt organisation through which Communist parties could consult and meet together to agree on common policies. Thus the question of how policy for the Communist movement as a whole was devised was left in abeyance; for the time being it was laid down in Moscow, with or without consultation with other parties. This was also to become one of the main issues in the Moscow-Peking dispute.

In the first nine months of 1956 there were, however, no overt signs of Chinese resentment at Tito's enhanced prestige. In January Peking agreed to establish relations with Yugoslavia and in June Wu Hsiu-chuan arrived to take up his post as ambassador. Along with his credentials, he presented Marshal Tito with personal gifts from Mao Tse-tung. In his report to the Eighth Congress of the Chinese Communist Party, which met in Peking in the second half of September 1956, Liu Shao-chi described the 'socialist camp' as 'a big family of fraternal, socialist countries headed by the Soviet Union'.* He reported:

> The Soviet Union and other socialist countries have established friendly relations with the Federal People's Republic of Yugoslavia. Our country has also established diplomatic relations and developed friendly intercourse with the Federal People's Republic of Yugoslavia.

There was, it is true, no reference to relations with the Yugoslav Communist Party. But this could be explained by the fact that the establishment of relations of any kind was so recent a development.

As far as could be seen, the whole Communist world, from Peking to Belgrade, was in general agreement with the line laid down by the Twentieth Congress of the CPSU. Events at the end of 1956 were to upset this apparent unity, and reveal the Chinese as anything but meek followers of the Moscow line.

At the end of October 1956, the Russians found themselves faced with open revolt in Poland and Hungary. The basic causes of the revolts were clearly to be seen in the crudity and brutality of Stalin's post-war handling of Eastern Europe, and in the lack of assurance which both the Soviet leaders and their proconsuls in Eastern Europe revealed in the post-Stalin period. The inevitable demands for a loosening of Moscow's grip and for a liberalising of Communist rule were doubtless encouraged by Khrushchev's denunciation of Stalin, and by the acceptance of the 'free-thinking' Yugoslav Communists back into the fold.

The stories of both the Polish and the Hungarian revolts against Moscow have been told elsewhere.† The Polish Communists succeeded in ousting their Stalinist leaders and persuading the Russians to grant them a substantial measure

---

* *See* Chronology: September 15, 1956.
† On Poland: Konrad Syrop: *Spring in October–The Polish Revolution of 1956*, Weidenfeld and Nicolson, London, 1957. Flora Lewis: *A Case History of Hope*, Doubleday and Co., New York, 1958.
On Hungary: Tibor Meray: *Thirteen Days that Shook the Kremlin*, Thames and Hudson, London, 1958; and Frederick A. Praeger, New York, 1958. George Urban: *The Nineteen Days*, Heinemann, London, 1975.

of internal autonomy without their having to resort to armed resistance. It was a bloodless operation. In Hungary passions were more inflamed and the alternative leaders were less in command of the situation, with the result that the Russians fell back on military force to ensure the maintenance of a Communist régime loyal to Moscow.

These events sent shock-waves right through the Communist movement. They also had an important effect on relations between Moscow, Peking and Belgrade. In particular, they marked the beginning of the hostility between the Chinese and Yugoslav Communists which was to remain so important a feature of the Sino-Soviet dispute.

There is good reason to believe that the Chinese leaders were initially enthusiastic supporters of a loosening of Moscow's control of the satellites. On November 1, 1956 they formally approved* the statement issued by the Soviet Communist Party on October 30† acknowledging (though too late to avoid a crisis in Hungary) equality of status for all Communist parties. Earlier in the year they had been offering encouragement to the Polish Communists in their resistance to Moscow, and it seems certain that during the crisis in Warsaw the Chinese used their influence to defend the Poles and restrain the Russians. Less is known about the part played by Chinese in the Hungarian events, though they later claimed responsibility for persuading Khrushchev to suppress the revolt by force. It was only after the situation in Eastern Europe had been restored at the beginning of 1957 that Chou En-lai visited Warsaw and Budapest and gave Peking's blessing to the settlements that had been reached.‡ His public speeches were notable for the stress laid on loyalty to Russian leadership of the bloc and his approval of the Soviet Declaration of October 30, 1956, on the new form relations between Communist parties should take. Meanwhile the Russians' enthusiasm for Tito had been seriously damped by events in Eastern Europe and relations between Moscow and Belgrade began to deteriorate.

Peking's considered judgement of the events of October and

* *See* Chronology: November 1, 1956.
† *Ibid.* October 30, 1956.
‡ *Ibid.* January 7, 1957

November 1956 was delivered in an editorial article in the *People's Daily* on December 29. It was the result of a discussion in an enlarged meeting of the Political Bureau of the Chinese Party and was clearly intended to be, and was subsequently used as, a basic statement of policy for the whole Communist camp. The article* was entitled 'More on the Historical Experience of the Dictatorship of the Proletariat', a title which suggested it was a development of the ideas expressed in the *People's Daily* editorial of April 5, 1956.

The article was prompted by Tito's speech† at Pula on November 11, in which he had given his judgement on the Hungarian revolt, and by reactions to it in the Communist press. In that speech Tito condemned the first Soviet intervention in Hungary, mainly on the grounds that it had resulted from the Russians' failure to take Tito's advice on Hungarian affairs, but approved the second intervention on the grounds that it was the 'lesser evil' to full-scale war. Perhaps more important for their effect on the Chinese, however, were Tito's views of Yugoslavia's future role in the Communist world.

> Together with the Polish comrades, we shall have to fight such [Stalinist] tendencies as crop up in various other parties, whether in the Eastern countries or in the West. This struggle will be difficult and long, for what is actually involved is whether the new trend will triumph in the Communist parties – the trend which really began in Yugoslavia – or whether the Stalinist course will prevail again.

In words which seem mild in comparison with their more recent comments on Yugoslav Communism and even with their later interpretation of this period, the Chinese declared that the views expressed by Tito and other Yugoslav leaders 'cannot be regarded by us as well-balanced or objective'. Though agreeing with much that he said and did, the Chinese were 'amazed that he attacked almost all the socialist countries and many of the Communist parties'. His views on the need for backing the *Yugoslav trend* against the *Stalinist course* 'can only lead

* *See* Chronology: December 29, 1956.
† *Ibid.* November 11, 1956.

to a split in the Communist movement', said the article. Summing up their views, the Chinese said:

> Clearly the Yugoslav comrades are going too far. Even if some part of their criticism of brother parties is reasonable, the basic stand and the method they have adopted infringed the principles of comradely discussion.

Though they pointed to real differences of opinion with the Yugoslavs, these comments were noticeably milder than those made by the Russians in their press in November. *Pravda* had accused Tito of 'interfering' in the affairs of other parties and had likened some of his analysis of the situation in the Communist world to the 'fabrications of reactionary propaganda'. It had also accused Tito of trying to spread his influence beyond the borders of Yugoslavia.

Later, in 1963, when their dispute with the Russians was in the open, the Chinese traced the origins of the dispute back to this intervention by Tito in the East European crisis. 'The current great debate', they then said, 'was first provoked by the Tito clique of Yugoslavia through its open betrayal of Marxism-Leninism.' They explained this statement thus:

> The Tito clique had taken the road of revisionism long ago. In the winter of 1956 it took advantage of the anti-Soviet and anti-Communist campaign launched by the imperialists to conduct propaganda against Marxism-Leninism on the one hand and, on the other, to carry out subversive activities within the socialist countries in co-ordination with imperialist schemes. Such propaganda and sabotage reached a climax in the counter-revolutionary rebellion in Hungary. It was then that Tito made his notorious Pula speech. The Tito clique did its utmost to vilify the socialist system, insisted that 'a thorough change is necessary in the political system' of Hungary, and asserted that the Hungarian comrades 'need not waste their efforts on trying to restore the Communist Party'.

This is a far less sympathetic interpretation of Tito's part in the Hungarian crisis than the Chinese gave at the time. Whether they were really so incensed in 1956 or whether their later interpretation is just a Chinese Communist rewriting of history is not clear. Nevertheless, it is not difficult to believe that, within the framework of the Communist world as early as 1956, the Chinese resented Tito's high-handed pronouncements and his apparent intention to impose his views on the Communist world.

The main purpose of the *People's Daily* article of December 29, 1956 was in fact to object to the manner in which other parties were behaving and to lay down the form which relations between Communist parties should take. The Chinese recognised the Soviet Union as 'the centre of the international Communist movement' by virtue of its seniority and its material resources (but not, be it noted, because of its superior knowledge of Marxism). 'We must continue to strengthen international proletarian solidarity with the Soviet Union as its centre.' There were bound to be difficulties about maintaining this unity, but:

> If the Communist parties maintain relations of equality among themselves and reach common understanding and take concerted action through genuine, and not nominal, exchange of views, their unity will be strengthened. Conversely, if, in their mutual relations, one party imposes its views upon others, or if the parties use the method of interference in each other's internal affairs instead of comradely suggestions and criticism, then unity will be impaired.*

This question of the unity and cohesion of the Communist camp was thus from the start the main issue involved in the dispute between Moscow and Peking and it has remained the central issue throughout. But, because on the surface both sides to the dispute appear to be equally enthusiastic about the

* 'More on the Differences between Comrade Togliatti and Us . . .', *Red Flag* article published in instalments in *People's Daily*, March 1–4, 1963.

'unity' of the camp, the real differences have been obscured. They will be examined briefly here.

The essence of the Chinese position is that they want to keep the Communist camp, and the Communist movement as a whole, united and at the same time they themselves want to have at least an equal say with the other parties, and especially the Soviet Party, in the direction of policy. Thus they support the apparently contradictory demands for unity in the camp and greater autonomy for its members. They are prepared to regard the Soviet Party as the 'centre' of the movement, but not as the 'leader'. There was therefore no necessary inconsistency between Peking's encouragement of Polish autonomy within the camp and its condemnation of the Hungarian revolt which finally threatened to remove Hungary from the Soviet orbit and perhaps begin the dissolution of Communism's European empire. Equality within a united and tightly knit bloc, and not disintegration, was what the Chinese wanted. And their reasons are not difficult to guess: the Communist countries must be held together so that the resources, both economic and military, of its richer members may be available for the poorer ones, notably China. But there must be equality and autonomy among the member countries to ensure that the needier members may have a say in the disposition of the bloc's wealth. Thus it was that the Chinese came to regard Tito, who was the first advocate of equality between Communist parties, as the arch-enemy, presumably because he insisted on preserving his position *outside* the Communist bloc and had appeared ready at the time of the Hungarian revolt to see the East European countries break away from Moscow.

At the beginning of 1957, Chou En-lai interrupted a tour of Asia to visit Moscow, Warsaw and Budapest and give Peking's blessing to the settlements arrived at in Poland and Hungary. A repeated theme in all his statements was the need for equality between 'socialist' countries, which was best expressed in a statement* issued jointly by the Chinese and Soviet governments on January 18, 1957, which said: 'it is fully possible in their relations to combine the unity of socialist countries and the independence of each individual country.' But the significance

* *See* Chronology: January 7–18, 1957.

of Chou En-lai's excursion to Eastern Europe lay not so much in the fact of Peking's approval of the changes there as in the new role it appeared to give to China in an area which had hitherto been a Soviet preserve. It is difficult to believe that the Soviet leaders, and Khrushchev in particular, welcomed this Chinese incursion and Chou's demonstration in practice of the principle of 'equality' between Communist countries. Russian satisfaction at having Chinese backing for their settlement of the Hungarian revolt must at least have been tinged with alarm at China's intervention in European affairs. But, if it was, the Russians kept their thoughts to themselves.

There were few significant developments in relations between Russia and China for the greater part of 1957. The attention of the leaders of both countries was mainly taken up by internal political conflicts which were resolved only in the summer and autumn. In Russia it appeared that Khrushchev had been forced to yield somewhat to the more conservative elements who could depict the Polish and Hungarian crises as the result of his 'revisionist' policies and in particular of his over-eager wooing of Yugoslavia. At the beginning of the year Khrushchev, the denouncer of Stalin, declared that he was 'proud of being a Stalinist', and in March Bulganin, then Soviet Prime Minister, declared that the Yugoslav assessment of the Hungarian revolt 'does not differ essentially from that of the imperialists'. This ascendancy of the Stalinists in the Kremlin was, however, short-lived; at the end of June Khrushchev and his supporters brought about the defeat of the 'anti-party group'* in the Soviet leadership and established his own personal ascendancy and that of his policies.

Khrushchev's victory was followed *immediately* by the resumption of intimate relations between the Soviet and Yugoslav leaders. The meeting of the Central Committee of the CPSU which ousted the Stalinists ended on June 29, and its decisions were announced on July 3. Only four days later, on July 7, Edward Kardelj and Alexander Rankovich, Tito's two

---

* Molotov, Kaganovich, Malenkov and Shepilov were then named; the group later included a majority of members of the post-Stalin leadership of the CPSU.

closest colleagues, left Belgrade for a 'holiday' in the Crimea which included, however, official talks in Moscow with the Soviet, Bulgarian and Albanian leaders. This meeting was followed by an unannounced and entirely secret meeting in Rumania on August 1 between Khrushchev and Mikoyan on the Russian side and Tito, Rankovich and Kardelj on the Yugoslav side. A statement issued after these talks affirmed in the strongest terms the determination of both sides to improve relations between their governments and their Communist parties 'on the basis of equality, mutual assistance and co-operation, respect for sovereignty, independence and non-interference'. The leaders of the two countries had also, the statement said, discussed the world situation, on which they had found themselves in substantial agreement, and 'problems of the international workers' movement'. From this it appeared that relations between Tito and Khrushchev had been restored to where they had been in the summer of 1956. But once again it was not easy to understand why Khrushchev should be so eager to have Tito's support, especially since the Yugoslavs had made it clear that he had no intention of rejoining the camp. The Chinese certainly eyed the return of the Yugoslavs to inner Communist councils with considerable suspicion.

But the Chinese leaders also had their internal problems. In 1957 they found themselves faced with a serious economic crisis as well as a wave of opposition and criticism which had been released by Mao Tse-tung's 'hundred flowers' experiment. This situation led to a conflict between left and right in the Chinese Party which was not resolved until the late summer when the left emerged the victors. Thus before they confronted each other in Moscow in November, a sort of polarisation of the Russian and Chinese parties had taken place: the Russians moving towards the right and the Chinese towards the left. The touchstone of their attitude to world problems had become their relations with Tito's Yugoslavia, with which Khrushchev was increasingly and persistently friendly and which Mao Tse-tung was eyeing with growing suspicion.

Before the November meeting there were important developments in another sphere, which was also to have an important effect on the policy debate in the Communist movement. In

August the Russians announced that they had carried out successful tests of an intercontinental ballistic rocket, and in October they launched the first artificial earth satellite. The effect of these two achievements, along with the Russians' known nuclear capacity, was to persuade the world at large that Russia was at least the equal of, and was probably ahead of, America in military power. Within the Communist world this did much to restore Russian prestige on the eve of the fortieth anniversary celebrations of the Revolution.

V

A UNITED MOVEMENT? 1957

We conducted a necessary struggle against certain wrong tendencies detrimental to unity and also made necessary compromises on certain matters, thus contributing to the unanimous agreement reached.

'People's Daily', January 27, 1963*

The celebration in Moscow of the fortieth anniversary of the October Revolution in November 1957 was an occasion of immense importance in the Communist world and above all to the two greatest parties, the Russian and the Chinese. Invitations to attend were sent to the leaders of all the ruling parties and governments in the Communist camp, to the leaders of the rest of the world's Communist parties, and to many near-Communist leaders. Altogether sixty-four Communist parties were represented in Moscow.

From the Russian point of view, it was an excellent opportunity to restore Moscow's prestige in the international Communist movement. The death of Stalin, the crises in Poland and Hungary, and the conflicts in the Kremlin itself had all tended to weaken Moscow's authority as the centre from which world Communism was directed. The fortieth anniversary of the Revolution was a good occasion to impress on Communism's proconsuls and foreign agents Russia's seniority and experience in the business of revolution and to remind them, by means of lavish entertainment, elaborate military parades and impressive sputnik-launchings, that Russia was still the centre of Communism's material power and sustenance.

For the Chinese the occasion was no less important, as the arrival of Mao Tse-tung himself at the head of China's delegation demonstrated. But he had other objectives than the

* From an article in this issue entitled 'Let us Unite . . .'

elevation of the Soviet Union in the Communist world. For him it was an opportunity to establish the right of the Chinese Communist Party to a say in the evolution of Communist strategy and the direction of Communist policy on a world scale. It was in fact Mao's *first* opportunity to do so since he had become one of the acknowledged leaders of world Communism.

Although the Twentieth Congress of the Soviet Communist Party in 1956 had also been well attended by foreign Communist leaders, it had not been made the occasion for an international meeting. It appears, indeed, that the foreign delegates received no prior warning of the general anti-Stalinist direction the Congress was to take and, as we have seen, it was several weeks before the Chinese were able to give their views on Khrushchev's innovations. In 1956 the Russians appear to have made no pretence of consultation; Khrushchev suddenly proclaimed a new course for world Communism and, as in Stalin's day, the foreign agents of Communism were left to take note and make the necessary adjustments in their own policies however awkward an operation this might prove. There is no doubt that the Chinese resented this.

Moreover, for an understanding of the Chinese attitude to the 1957 meeting, it is important to remember that there was no other means by which the Chinese leaders could exert an influence on the whole Communist movement. The Comintern and the Cominform were gone;* there was no international Communist organisation or forum in which the Chinese could exert an influence. The 'international Communist movement' existed solely through direct, sometimes only underground, ties between the parties and Moscow. The only formal organisations existing were the Warsaw Pact, which was primarily military and specifically aimed at the 'defence' of Eastern Europe, and the Council for Mutual Economic Aid (Comecon), which was again a specifically European body. But Chinese eagerness to play a part in international bodies was already apparent from the fact that they were sending 'observers' to both Warsaw Pact and Comecon meetings and were on the record as offering their military support if the Warsaw Pact

* *See* Chronology: May 15, 1943 and April 18, 1956.

countries became involved in war in Europe. We have already
seen how ready Chou En-lai was to play the role of arbiter in
Eastern Europe after the crisis of 1956. In these circumstances,
the presence in Moscow of the leaders of the Communist camp
and of world Communism was something which Mao Tse-tung
had to exploit to the full if he wanted to make China's prestige
and size effective in terms of policy. His attendance was not a
sign of esteem for the Russian Communists and their forty-
year-old revolution, but a first determined bid for a say in
world Communist strategy.

His presence was all the more necessary since it was known in
advance that the consultations were expected to produce an
agreed statement of Communist policy, which was in fact intended to be an application of Khrushchev's Twentieth Congress
ideas to the whole of the camp and to confirm Communism's
'new general line'. The Chinese also had good reason to expect
that the debates in Moscow would not be easy. A draft of the
'Declaration' which it was hoped to approve had apparently
been circulated to leaders in the Soviet bloc and had also been
submitted to the Yugoslavs. Disputes about the contents of the
Declaration were probably going on long before November.
The main purpose of Khrushchev's secret meeting with Tito
in August was presumably to reassure the Yugoslav leader
about the contents of the policy statement and secure his support
for it and his attendance at the November meeting. This would
in fact have signified Tito's formal reassociation with the
Soviet bloc and have been a substantial victory for Khrushchev.
But Tito did not in the end attend the Moscow celebrations (on
account, according to the official Tanjug agency, of an attack of
lumbago): a decision which this most extrovert of Communist
leaders must have found difficult to take, since it was to be an
occasion when he too might hope to spread his influence again
in the Communist world. Some time between the beginning of
August, when Tito and Khrushchev had proclaimed their
'identity of views' on all subjects, and the onset of Tito's lumbago at the end of October, the Yugoslavs must have become
convinced that the proposed statement of policy would not be
to their liking, and they took steps to keep Tito out of a situation which might have proved embarrassing. (Tito appears on

this and subsequent occasions to have been more wary than other Communist leaders of the dangers involved in accepting invitations to Moscow.) Despite the absence of direct evidence of what was going on behind the scenes, it is reasonable to assume that the Chinese were already letting their 'anti-revisionist' views be known. And Mao Tse-tung decided to use his own not inconsiderable weight to see that the final statement reflected Chinese views.

In public the leaders of the Communist world presented at Moscow in 1957 a convincing façade of friendship and unity. In his speech to a jubilee session of the Supreme Soviet, Khrushchev boasted of the growing strength of the Soviet state and rejoiced in the declining power of 'imperialism'. He appeared to retreat somewhat in his assessment of Stalin, who, he said, would yet 'occupy a worthy place in history', and he was at pains to stress that 'peaceful coexistence' did not mean that there could ever be 'complete harmony' between socialism and capitalism. But little is known in the West of the debates that went on behind the scenes. What is known is that Mao Tse-tung behaved in the grand manner, alone of the foreign leaders occupying an apartment in the Kremlin and receiving only selected representatives of other parties in audience. The Chinese delegation was intensely active, conducting talks on all sides. Many East European Communists were taken aback by this first encounter with Communism in its Oriental form.

The negotiations behind the scenes had their climax in a meeting of the twelve ruling Communist parties* from November 12 to 14. The meeting issued a 5,000-word Declaration† setting forth the party leaders' views on the world at large and in particular on the form which relations between their parties should take.

The Declaration was the first of the two documents around which the Sino-Soviet dispute was later to rage, and a word is necessary here on the nature of such documents and the role they play in Communist political life. They seem to originate

* USSR, China, Poland, Czechoslovakia, East Germany, Hungary, Rumania, Bulgaria, Albania, North Korea, North Vietnam, Mongolia.
† See Chronology: November 6, 1957.

in a peculiarly Communist demand for 'unity' and an assumption by Communist leaders that it is possible and necessary always to produce statements of common and agreed aims. It has often appeared in recent years that the Communists considered it of more importance to produce such a statement than to achieve actual agreement. Consequently, when faced with a real conflict of views, they have often tended to produce documents which were either little more than an ambiguous collation of differing views or which represented a weak and unworkable compromise between conflicting opinions. The Communist leaders often give the impression of believing that the mere existence of a document is in itself a factor capable of inducing 'unity'.

It is this that accounts at least in part for the extreme length, verbosity and imprecision of the documents with which we have to deal. They often appear calculated to evade and confuse rather than to clarify. But the imprecision and obscurity of the documents is also a result of another factor: the curious dilemma with which the Communist leaders find themselves confronted. On the one hand, they are compelled to proclaim to the world and their followers an agreed policy; on the other, the nature of their movement and its revolutionary aims compel them to conceal the true nature of the issues they discuss, the differences they have and the real purpose of their policies. The result of these conflicting demands is that Communist policy statements are drawn up in a sort of Marxist code-language which can be properly understood only by the initiated. It is easy to see that, far from clearing up differences, such documents are likely only to provide material for a multitude of interpretations. This was the case with the Declaration of 1957 and the later 'Statement' of 1960.

A reading of the whole of the Declaration suggests that it is, for the greater part, the work of Russian minds. Much of the general assessments of the state of capitalism and Communism was, of course, equally acceptable to Russians and Chinese. But the conclusion that 'the question of war or peaceful coexistence is now the crucial question of world policy', that forces now commanded by Communism could 'prevent the outbreak of war', and that the decisions of the Twentieth Congress of the CPSU had 'further developed and brought up to date' Lenin's ideas on peaceful coexistence were all primarily Khrushchevian ideas. So was the affirmation that it might prove possible to 'win state power without civil war' in some capitalist countries.

It was mainly in the section of the Declaration dealing with the situation *inside* the Communist movement that the influence of the Chinese was apparent. After the usual assertion of the unity of ideas characterising the movement, the Declaration declared:

> Of vital importance in the present stage is intensified struggle against opportunist trends in the working-class and Communist movement. The meeting underlines the necessity of resolutely overcoming revisionism and dogmatism in the ranks of the Communist and Workers' parties.

Dogmatism and sectarianism, the Declaration said, 'hinder the development of Marxist-Leninist theory and its creative application in the changing conditions', led to 'isolation from the masses' and could not bring victory to the working-class. At the same time the Communist parties believed:

> the main danger at present is revisionism or, in other words, right-wing opportunism, which as a manifestation of bourgeois ideology paralyses the revolutionary energy of the working class and demands the preservation or restoration of capitalism.

But, having come down thus firmly against revisionism as the 'main danger', the Declaration took a step back again with the statement that 'dogmatism and sectarianism' could also be the 'main danger' at one time or place or another and that it was 'for each Communist party to decide what danger threatens it more at a given time'. Here was a typical piece of evasion and ambiguity, and Communist leaders could be forgiven if they were left in some doubt about where the 'main danger' really lay!

The Declaration had still another paragraph, however, denouncing the evils of 'modern revisionism' as 'smearing' and rejecting the whole of Marxist teaching. And this section ended with a call for the defence of the unity of the ranks of Communism and the 'banning of factions and groups sapping unity'. There is every reason to suppose that these paragraphs were the work of the Chinese and that they were directed primarily against the Yugoslavs, though they would later also find application to Khrushchev himself, and could later still be turned against the Chinese.

There was sufficient Chinese inspiration in the Declaration to permit Mao Tse-tung to put his signature to it and to provide the Chinese with documentary support in their later battles with the 'revisionists'. That they were not completely satisfied with the document emerged only later when, discussing the 1957 meeting, they could say only that it 'eliminated *certain* differences among the fraternal parties'. But they continued to insist throughout that it was the 'common programme' of the international Communist movement. It was at any rate the only document that could be so described!

The Yugoslav delegates, however, refused to subscribe to the Declaration, seeing in it no doubt a weapon to beat them with. The understanding between Tito and Khrushchev of August 1957 had come to nothing. Tito had avoided the trap of the Moscow meeting; Khrushchev felt let down by the Yugoslavs; and Mao had scored a substantial victory on his first appearance as a Communist statesman on the world scale. While insisting on what he considered the 'main danger', he had been ready to compromise on issues that appeared less important, such as the interpretation of 'peaceful coexistence'.

Surprise was caused among both Communists and Western observers by Mao's reported stress on the leading role of the Soviet Union in the Communist camp. This was reflected in the Declaration by a reference to 'the camp of socialist countries headed by the Soviet Union', which had previously been the standard formula, and by a description of the Soviet Union as 'the first and mightiest socialist power', which was indeed no more than a statement of fact. But Mao was also reported to have insisted on Soviet leadership in other statements, notably to Moscow University students on November 17 and in his address to the Supreme Soviet. This apparent elevation of

Moscow did not necessarily represent a reversal of Mao's earlier attitude towards the Soviet Union. His emphasis on Soviet leadership was entirely consistent with views earlier expressed, notably by Chou En-lai, in January 1957. Mao wanted equality, and especially equality for himself, within a closely knit Communist camp; it was exactly this which prompted his opposition to Tito, in whom he saw the breaker up of the bonds holding the Soviet bloc together. Soviet power and prestige were by far the most effective unifying forces in the camp, and so long as he could persuade the Russians to concede to his wishes, Mao was quite content to back Soviet 'leadership'. Perhaps he might one day himself succeed to that position, though that was not on the cards in 1957. What was then important was to preserve a united camp with a recognised centre and an agreed programme over which the Chinese could exert their growing influence. That was, in effect, Peking's short cut to world power.

The Moscow meeting of 1957 ended in a clear victory for the Chinese over the Yugoslavs and a no less clear assertion of Chinese influence within the camp. And since Khrushchev had made no secret for some years of his desire to bring the Yugoslav Communists back into the fold, Tito's absence from the meeting was also a defeat for Khrushchev and must have been so interpreted in informed Communist circles. Indeed, it must be presumed that Mao's success in securing the inclusion of what was in fact a condemnation of Yugoslav Communism in the 1957 Declaration owed something to support from other Communist leaders in the camp. There was apparently still sufficient latent Stalinism and suspicion of Tito among East European Communists to enable the Chinese to carry the day. Many of the leaders still in power, notably those in Albania, Bulgaria and Czechoslovakia, had been too enthusiastic in their denunciations of Tito in Stalin's lifetime to support – with much conviction – Khrushchev's effort at a rapprochement. Mao Tse-tung undoubtedly exploited this situation for his own ends.

Khrushchev's immediate reaction to this defeat was to retreat on the question of Yugoslavia. The Moscow meeting must have convinced him that he faced too much opposition in the camp to force through the Yugoslav issue without risking a split.

He therefore decided to drop it for the time being. However much he wanted Tito back in the camp, it was not, in 1958 at least, worth risking the disintegration of the camp itself. It could wait until Khrushchev felt surer of his position.

So that there should be no doubt about where they stood, the Russians reverted to public criticisms of Yugoslav policy, though not in quite the same abusive terms as they had used in Stalin's day. The Yugoslav Communists made their task easier by drawing up for submission to the Seventh Congress of their party, to be held in Ljubljana in April 1958, a new programme embodying their revised views on the nature of Communism and its policies. The fundamental 'revisionist' element in the programme was the neutral attitude it took up towards both the Communist and capitalist camps. On the one hand, the programme declared that Communists 'should no longer be concerned primarily with questions relating to the overthrow of capitalism'; on the other hand, it described Stalin's treatment of Yugoslavia in 1948 as an example of 'hegemonistic aims put above the actual interests of Socialism'. The programme appeared to draw no real 'Marxist' distinction between the Warsaw Pact which, in Communist parlance, was 'defensive', and the Western alliances which were invariably 'aggressive'. It regarded them as equally militaristic, and equally to be avoided.

The programme was apparently communicated to the Russians before the Congress, and the Yugoslavs made an attempt to meet some of the objections the Russians raised to it. But these proved insufficient, and on the eve of the Congress, Moscow condemned the Yugoslav programme in firm but measured terms. The Soviet Communist Party withdrew its agreement to attend the Ljubljana Congress, and so did the other eleven parties in the camp. The Communist countries were, however, allowed to send their diplomatic representatives in Yugoslavia as 'observers', though all of them, with the notable exception of the Polish ambassador, withdrew during a speech in which Alexander Rankovich replied to Russian criticisms. These had come on the eve of the Ljubljana Congress from the mouth of Khrushchev himself. Arriving in Moscow after a visit to Hungary, and apparently under the influence of good food and wine consumed aboard his aircraft, Khrushchev spoke scathingly of leaders who 'grovelled for the friendship of those who would like to throw them some of their stale goods in order to entice them to their side', and who 'adapted themselves to the imperialists'. In what was certainly a reference to Tito, he said: 'Nobody can sit on two stools at the same time. He will inevitably come a cropper on a certain part of his anatomy, and rightly so.' These remarks were hotly resented by the Yugoslavs.

In their speeches at the Ljubljana Congress, Tito and Kardelj made clear the Yugoslav attitude to relations between the parties which was presumably the reverse of the Chinese view at the time and the main cause of Chinese opposition to Tito. Commenting on the meekness with which the other parties had accepted direction from Moscow right up to the Twentieth Congress of the CPSU in 1956, Tito said: 'It is particularly important that the old forms of co-operation are being gradually abandoned and that bilateral relations are being adopted.'

He added that it was because of these views that the Yugoslavs had not been able to sign the Declaration of 1957. The question of whether the Communist camp was to be closely knit and disciplined was at the centre of the dispute. Kardelj spelt out the Yugoslav view in greater detail:

> The [Yugoslav] programme provides that co-operation [between Communist parties] should be completely voluntary and based on equality; that it should preclude the imposition of an attitude by a majority; and that it should recognise the exclusive right of each individual party to appraise the suitability or the ideological or tactical correctness of any action.

He added that the Yugoslav Communists' views on this subject were not unaffected by their memories of how Stalin had used the Cominform as an 'instrument of pressure on Yugoslavia'.

The implication of the Yugoslav statements was that there were already moves afoot inside the Communist camp to set up a new international organisation. There were other, independent hints of this, though the question was nowhere discussed in public. Since it was the issue upon which the Yugoslavs dug in their heels, it may well have been the central issue of the 1957 meeting. But, if so, it is significant that, even without the Yugoslavs' being present, the advocates of a new international did not succeed in having their way. Very few of the leaders of the twelve ruling parties at the beginning of 1958 were well disposed towards Yugoslavia. Yet no new organisation was created and it was, apparently, only in the face of some opposition that agreement was reached to publish a single periodical for the whole Communist movement.*

It is difficult to avoid the conclusion that some of the opposition to new 'organisational' measures came from the Russians themselves. Had they been in favour of such moves they would scarcely have had any difficulty in pushing them through. If Khrushchev disapproved of Tito's fence-sitting between East and West, he did not therefore necessarily disagree with Tito's views on relations within the camp.

The Chinese, however, left no one in any doubt about their views. On May 5, the Peking *People's Daily* declared flatly that the Cominform Resolution of 1948, expelling Yugoslavia from the 'socialist camp', had been 'basically correct'. The new Yugoslav programme was an attempt to lead the working-class to 'surrender to capitalism', the Chinese said. This article was immediately reproduced in the Soviet press, and on May 9 *Pravda* published an editorial condemning the Yugoslav Communists for 'kow-towing to American ruling circles', adding that if the Yugoslavs regarded their economic ties with the Soviet Union as a form of 'exploitation', it would be possible to 'free Yugoslavia from such exploitation'.

The Russians quickly followed their words with deeds. A visit to Yugoslavia by Marshal Voroshilov, the Soviet President, due to take place on May 11, was cancelled at the last moment. Far more serious from the Yugoslav point of view was the Soviet decision, announced at the end of May, to suspend the credits and other economic aid promised to Yugoslavia in

* Under the editorship in Prague of a senior Soviet party official, the first issue of the *World Marxist Review* appeared in September 1958. It was published in eighteen languages of the Communist bloc and Western Europe, including Chinese. From November 1962, however, it ceased to be printed in Chinese.

1956. The Yugoslavs reported in June that the Russians had even refused to complete the delivery of 200,000 tons of wheat due under the trade agreement.

The clearest and certainly the most dramatic indication of the swing in Soviet policy and perhaps also of the extent to which the more conservative or Stalinist elements in the camp had regained influence was the execution in June of Imre Nagy, the Hungarian Communist leader who had tried unsuccessfully to establish Hungary's independence of the Soviet bloc. Though he was not its inspirer, Nagy had become the symbol of the Hungarian revolt and had, by taking refuge in the Yugoslav embassy in Budapest, become closely identified with Tito and Yugoslavia. His execution, which was a case of pure political murder without any practical justification, was clearly intended also as a blow at the Yugoslav Communists. It served to reactivate all the dormant Stalinist elements in Eastern Europe, and even Gomulka, who had been more moderate than any other leader in his comments on the Yugoslav programme, felt constrained to describe Nagy's execution as 'an internal Hungarian affair'. Those who, like the Albanian and Bulgarian Communist leaders, had long resented Tito's position, were delighted at Khrushchev's swing to the left.

Khrushchev's abandonment of Tito appeared to be complete and clearly reflected a major and sudden change of Kremlin policy decided at the time of the 1957 meeting. It was all the more striking in view of the efforts Khrushchev had made to improve relations with Yugoslavia between 1955 and the end of 1957. But, once having made up his mind to banish Tito, Khrushchev did not pull his punches. At the congress of the Bulgarian Communist Party in June 1958, he described Yugoslav 'revisionism' as a Trojan horse in the Communist camp.* At a congress of the East German Communist Party in July 1958, he sneered at the Yugoslav leaders for accepting American aid, of which he said they were ashamed to tell their people and for which they would later pay dearly. In his report to the Twenty-first Congress of the CPSU in January 1959, Khrushchev criticised Yugoslavia for being a member of the (already defunct) Balkan Pact which, he said, was part of NATO.

* *See* Chronology: June 3, 1958.

It is impossible to determine the extent to which the Russians believed these charges. They all were, in fact, charges which could have been levelled against the Yugoslavs before 1957, at the time when Khrushchev was lavishing aid on them. They were also charges which were quickly forgotten by the Russians a few years later when it again suited their book to establish good relations with Yugoslavia. The controversial programme of the Yugoslav Communist Party, which Khrushchev described in 1959 as 'revisionist' and 'anti-Marxist', and which the Yugoslavs have resolutely refused to modify, proved no obstacle to a resumption of cordial relations between the Russian and Yugoslav parties in 1962. This episode of the Yugoslav 'deviation' demonstrates more clearly than any other the secondary nature of the 'ideological' issues to which the two sides in the Sino-Soviet dispute devote so many words. Khrushchev's switches over Yugoslavia force us to look elsewhere for the real motives for his actions.

In this case, a possible explanation is that he was surprised by the degree of opposition he met with at the 1957 meeting and by the long-term aims which he detected behind Mao's attitude. He probably decided that he must postpone his own plans for the camp and reassure the other leaders by making an unmistakable swing to the left. The immediate victim of this swing was Marshal Tito, who learnt for the second time in a decade the risks involved in becoming economically dependent on Russia.

Another possible reason for Khrushchev's sudden retreat over Tito was that it was not until the 1957 meeting that he realised the nature and size of the problem that was emerging in the East. In November 1957 he may have realised clearly for the first time that Mao Tse-tung was playing for far bigger stakes than he had realised and that, if he did not turn his attention eastwards, he ran a risk of losing the leadership of the whole camp. He could not deal with all problems at once, and it was better to postpone reforms in Eastern Europe, at the expense of Tito's friendship, and to try and bring China under control. It was to this great problem that the Russians devoted much attention and effort in the next two years, 1958 and 1959.

VI

WHO'S BOSS? 1958, 1959

The truth is that the international differences among the fraternal parties were first brought into the open . . . in September 1959 – on September 9, . . . to be exact.
'People's Daily', February 27, 1963

The years 1958 and 1959 were critical in the history of Sino-Soviet relations, packed with events, starting with an apparent rapprochement between Moscow and Peking and ending with relations so strained that a conciliation between Mao and Khrushchev had become practically impossible. The events of these two years determined the whole future course of the Sino-Soviet dispute.

From the beginning of 1958, Khrushchev's China policy appears to have had two main elements: to increase the scale of Soviet economic, and possibly military, aid to China, thus reassuring the Chinese of Russian friendship and support and increasing Russian penetration of China's economy; and to oust Mao Tse-tung and the leftist elements from the Chinese leadership. Khrushchev made a desperate and expensive effort in these years to bring Communist China under Moscow's control. He failed.

There can be no doubt that the question of economic aid to assist the Chinese Communists' ambitious plan for industrialisation loomed large in all Sino-Soviet talks and was also an issue in the dispute within the camp. Even while insisting on the need for equality and respect in relations between the Communist countries, the Chinese had always added that there should also be mutual aid. They took the convenient view that the Communist camp was a single unit which had the common aim of 'bringing about a common upsurge in the economies and cultures of *all* the socialist countries with the Soviet Union at their head'. They expected the more advanced countries to help the less advanced, and China was certainly as backward and in need of help as anyone.

We have seen how one of the first signs of a more yielding Soviet policy towards China after Stalin's death in 1953 was a substantial increase in aid. This continued to increase over the years, so that between 1950 and 1956 the Russians were committed to providing the bulk of the equipment and technical aid for the construction of 211 industrial plants, estimated to cost a total of 2.5 billion roubles. Though the exact amount of Soviet aid has never been given, the Chinese have admitted receiving loans from Russia totalling $2,200 million between 1949 and 1957.

In 1958 and 1959 the scale of Soviet aid increased sharply. Khrushchev's visit to Peking in August 1958 resulted in a Russian agreement to construct an additional 47 industrial plants. Chou En-lai visited Moscow in February 1959 and extracted an undertaking from Khrushchev to build a further 31 plants and to grant the Chinese a loan of $1,250 million.

By this time, aid to China represented a very heavy burden even for an economy of the size of Russia's, which was in any case not without its own shortcomings and troubles. How burdensome it must have been, and how demanding the Chinese must have been, is suggested by a claim later made by Khrushchev that the Russians were building more up-to-date factories in China than they were at home. What proportion of the Soviet economic effort was absorbed in China we cannot tell; nor do we know how much more was consumed in military aid or what part of their aid was repaid in useful commodities by the Chinese. What is certain, however, is that without Soviet aid the Chinese could not have embarked on their ambitious economic plans. In the words of an authority on China's economy: 'Without the economic assistance provided by the USSR, Peking's First Five-Year Plan would have failed and there could not have been a Second Five-Year Plan.'* There can also be little doubt that the aid they gave to China seriously affected the ability of the Russians and their allies in East

* Dr. Sidney Klein: 'Sino-Soviet Economic Relations, 1949–62', *Current Scene*, Vol. II, No. 15, June 15, 1963.

Europe to extend aid and win friends in the rest of the world. Such an effort was worth making only so long as it brought equivalent economic or political returns, which meant in effect so long as Peking was ready to behave as a loyal, obedient satellite of Moscow. This was what Khrushchev set out to achieve in 1959.

In the latter part of 1958, the Chinese challenge to Soviet leadership of the Communist world assumed another, quite different shape. It centred around the concept of the 'people's commune'. The idea, worked out in the early part of 1958 and announced in a resolution of the Chinese Communist Party of August 29, was to reorganise the 500,000,000 people of the Chinese countryside into units, or 'communes', in which everything would be shared equally and everyone would give freely of his labour. Part of the plan was the development by each commune of small industrial units which would in the mass considerably raise China's industrial output. In so far as the scheme made economic sense at all, it could be seen as an attempt to deal with the pressing problems of food shortage and lagging industrial plans by exploiting the one resource of which China had no shortage: unskilled manpower.

Even before they had had any real opportunity of trying out the reform, the claims put forward by the Chinese leaders for the effectiveness of the commune were extravagant in the extreme. The Party's resolution itself announced that the communes would 'accelerate socialist construction, complete the building of socialism ahead of time, and carry out the gradual transition to Communism'. It now appeared, said the resolution, that 'the realisation of Communism in our country is not something distant'. Later in 1958 the *People's Daily* already saw China moving forward with 'lightning speed', so that even eighty and ninety-year-old people would live to see the advent of Communism. One leader was reported in October to have said: 'In about three years our people will live a happy life, disposing of an abundance of food and clothing'. To judge from these and similar statements, the Chinese Communists appeared sincerely to believe that they had found a short cut to Communism and plenty. Along with these exaggerated claims there went increasingly fulsome praise of Mao Tse-tung as an original contributor to Marxist thought.

The significance of the commune reorganisation for the Sino-Soviet dispute lay not in whether they were really capable of providing the answer to China's economic backwardness so much as in the far-reaching political conclusions the Chinese drew from their reform. Less than ten years after taking over a backward country largely devastated by war they were claiming to be within sight of Communism. This was a goal which the Russians, for all their industrial achievements over the previous forty years, had only just dared to name, and even then in the vaguest terms. This was a very serious challenge to the Russians' primacy in the camp, which they owed, in the Chinese view, to an accident of history rather than to superior skill or knowledge. Hitherto they had been forced to acknowledge Russian economic superiority and accept Russia's dominating say in the disposition of Communism's major wealth. But now they were saying that, in a few years' time, China would have caught up with the rest of the camp and all the Communist countries would enter Communism together. In that case there was no need for the Chinese to take a back seat in Communist councils.

There was all the less reason for them to do so since they were led by Mao Tse-tung who was a 'prophet' and an original Marxist thinker. Who else could compete with him? Khrushchev was by comparison a petty party official, with no 'works' to his name.

The Russians were slow to recognise the challenge which the communes represented. But when they did, they were firm in their rejection of the idea. For the most part they avoided a discussion of the commune reform itself and ignored the changes taking place in China, though Khrushchev was reported to have told the American Senator Humphrey in December 1958 that communes were 'old-fashioned' and 'reactionary'. The main Soviet reaction came, however, at the Twenty-first Congress of the CPSU at the end of January 1959, which may well have been summoned specifically for the purpose of putting the Chinese in their place. The Congress, significantly named the 'Congress of the Builders of Communism', dealt primarily with the new Seven-Year Plan, which provided speakers with ample opportunity to remind the world of Soviet economic achievements and plans. It also provided Khrushchev with an opportunity to indulge in some 'creative Marxism' on the issues raised by the Chinese. He declared that there could be no skipping of stages in the progress from capitalism to Communism; that the process would inevitably be long and gradual; and that the only sure way of speeding the advent of Communism was to increase the production of material goods. Finally Khrushchev, while reminding his listeners of Russia's long start along the road to Communism, avoided a discussion of priorities by producing the vague dictum that all the countries in the camp would enter Communism more or less at the same time.

At the Twenty-first Congress, Khrushchev said nothing directly about the communes themselves. But in July 1959, in a speech in Poland, he suddenly made a sharp and apparently carefully timed attack on the whole concept. Dismissing the communes with contempt, he said people who advocated them 'had a poor idea of what Communism is and how it is to be built'. At this point the Chinese themselves had already retreated somewhat on the commune issue, and a more tolerant attitude had been apparent in the Soviet press. The sharpness of Khrushchev's comments appear, therefore, to have been prompted by some additional factor. It may have been the fact that pro-Chinese elements in Eastern Europe, notably the Bulgarians and Albanians, were seizing on the commune idea themselves. Or it may have been that Khrushchev was more concerned with a bitter conflict going on inside the China Communist Party itself.

In 1959 the Chinese Communist Party was living through an internal crisis comparable to that which raged in the Soviet Communist Party in 1957. There was widespread discontent in the ranks of the Party, deriving from the swing against the 'rightists' in 1958, the failure of the communes and the 'great leap forward' and the bad harvest of 1958. The Wuhan plenum in December 1958 had seen a modification of claims made for the communes and Mao's withdrawal from the Chairmanship of the Republic to the post of Chairman of the Party. Conditions were ripe for latent opposition to show its head.

The opposition finally took shape at the eighth plenum of the Central Committee of the Chinese Party held in Lushan in August 1959. From subsequent reports, it has been clearly established that at Lushan Marshal Peng Teh-huai, Minister of Defence, a member of the Politburo and a man of considerable influence in the Chinese Communist Party, made a direct attack on the prevailing political and economic policies of the leadership. He was supported in his criticisms by Chang Wen-tien, a Vice-Minister of Foreign Affairs, and by General Huang Ko-cheng, the Chief of Staff of the Army, as well as by less important figures composing what was later denounced as an 'anti-party group'. Peng submitted a resolution condemning current policies and a memorandum explaining his criticisms. As far as is known from later reports, Peng's criticisms were mainly directed at the lack of thought which had gone into the formation of economic policies and the ridiculously exaggerated claims that had been made for them. But it seems certain that the dispute in the Central Committee, which lasted for a fortnight, at one point brought the matter of Mao's leadership into question and that Mao had to bring his personal prestige into play to rout the opposition. Peng and his followers were defeated and dismissed from positions of influence and a campaign of denunciation was undertaken inside the Party. It was not, however, until September 16 that the dismissals were made public.

This incident would have little significance for the dispute between Moscow and Peking had it not been established that the Russians were at least privy to Peng's plans and may well have given him encouragement and assistance to carry them through. Peng's opportunity for contact with the Russians was extensive. Between April and June 1959, he spent seven weeks travelling in Russia and Eastern Europe and was in Albania at the same time that Khrushchev made an inexplicably long visit there at the end of May. That he was likely to have apprised the Russians of his plans is suggested by the fact that his main supporter, and possibly inspirer, was Chang Wen-tien, a former ambassador in Moscow and Chinese member of the Comintern, who may well have had links with the Russians, was also in Eastern Europe at the end of April, attending a Warsaw Pact meeting. Moreover, one of the charges later made against Peng was that he had communicated his views to the Russians in a 'secret letter'. Finally, Khrushchev was reported at the Bucharest meeting in June 1960 to have protested at Peng's dismissal and to have said that his only offence was to have taken the Soviet Party into his confidence.

Until passions run even higher between Moscow and Peking and more is revealed of the case of Peng Teh-huai, it will not be possible to determine how much Russian inspiration was behind his action. All that can be said is that, as Sino-Soviet relations were in 1958 and 1959, it would have been very agreeable to the Russians if the leftists had been defeated and replaced by Chinese leaders more willing to come to terms with Moscow and to consider Russian interests. But Mao proved too experienced a politician to be easily unseated and the incident apparently served only to consolidate his position and further embitter his relations with Khrushchev.

It was in 1958 also that it first became apparent that the Chinese were out to exert an influence over Soviet policy on a world scale. Mao's efforts to upset Khrushchev's attempts to reach an understanding with the West brought the conflict to a state of high tension.

It was not until the beginning of 1958 that Khrushchev had firmly established his position in command of the Soviet ship of state and put himself in a position to determine the general course of its foreign policy. There had been general agreement between him and the Soviet 'anti-party group' on the need in the post-Stalin period for a retreat from the most exposed and delicate positions. But there had been no agreement about the further course of Soviet foreign policy, and there had been heated disputes in the Kremlin on this subject. Now, with his defeat of the 'anti-party group' in mid-1957, his removal of Marshal Zhukov at the end of the year, and his assumption of the Premiership in addition to the post of First Secretary of the party in February 1958, Khrushchev was in a better position to put his ideas on foreign policy into practice; and this he proceeded to do.

In January 1958 the Soviet leader delivered to prominent
farm workers in Byelorussia a long speech, half of which had
nothing to do with the prospects of the Byelorussian potato
crop and was obviously intended for foreign consumption. It
was, in effect, a persuasive appeal to the Western powers to
hold a 'summit' meeting and come to terms on major East-
West issues. Though couched in his usual provocative manner
and rejecting any suggestions that Russia should retreat from
Eastern Europe the speech was conciliatory in tone and purpose,
and marks the beginning of Khrushchev's excursions into
'summitry' on his own account. He wanted to give 'peaceful
coexistence' his own special meaning, welcoming face-to-face
meetings with the leaders of the West, and notably of America.

Before the year had far advanced, an opportunity occurred
for Khrushchev to test the effectiveness of his 'summit'
approach. A crisis over the Lebanon led to a voluminous
exchange of letters between Khrushchev and Western statesmen
which centred finally around a proposal to hold a 'summit'
meeting at the United Nations Security Council. Despite much
haggling about the precise nature of the meeting, Khrushchev
appeared to be eager to see it take place, and on July 28 sent a
note to America, Britain and France suggesting that they, with
India and the USSR, should meet and end the Middle Eastern
crisis.

On July 31, however, Khrushchev made an unplanned visit
in conditions of complete secrecy to Peking, from which he
returned to Moscow on August 3.* On August 5 he sent notes
to the Western heads of government abruptly withdrawing his
agreement to a summit meeting. It was generally assumed that
his sudden change of front was directly connected with his
visit to Peking. This assumption seemed to be supported by his
condemnation of the Security Council for the presence in it of
the representative of the Chinese Nationalist government.

But it seems unlikely that the Middle Eastern crisis was the
only, or even the main, reason for Khrushchev's sudden
departure for Peking and his talks with Mao. The preparations
for the bombardment of the off-shore islands of Quemoy and
Matsu in the Straits of Formosa which began almost immedi-

* See Chronology: July 31, 1958.

ately after Khrushchev returned to Moscow, and the campaign of intensive shelling that started on August 23, must also have been discussed between the Chinese and Russian leaders. Indeed, news that the Chinese were about to test American strength in the Far East in this way may well have been the reason for the secrecy and speed of Khrushchev's trip. The probability that matters of major strategic significance were discussed was strengthened by the fact that Khrushchev was accompanied by his Defence Minister, Marshal Malinovsky, and that the Chinese Defence Minister, Marshal Peng Teh-huai, was also involved in the talks. It is very likely that Khrushchev and Mao had on this occasion a critical and possibly not very amicable discussion of their joint strategy in the nuclear age, a question which underlay many of their differences.

Mao had already let it be known that he attached great significance to the striking advances the Russians had made in nuclear capacity and in missiles in 1957. The Russians were also gratified at the progress they had made, but they were more restrained in the conclusions they drew from it and showed signs of recognising that the nuclear race would be a long one which was far from being won. But the Chinese, and Mao in particular, were inclined to draw the most far-reaching conclusions from what they regarded as Russia's – and therefore the Communist camp's – clear military superiority over the West. It was this that had led Mao, at the Moscow meeting of November 1957, to make his portentous statement about the superiority of the East wind over the West wind. It was a logical development of this point of view that the Communist camp should seek to exploit its superiority as soon as possible and wherever possible, safe in the knowledge that the West would fear to resist. Mao appears to have been surprised at Khrushchev's failure to take more vigorous action over Anglo-American intervention in the Middle Eastern crisis, and appears to have set out to demonstrate the correctness of his own thesis over Quemoy and Matsu.

By 1958, however, Khrushchev was already as impressed by the dangers involved in nuclear armaments as he was by the possibilities of exploiting them, and there is reason to suppose that the Russians and Chinese had already found themselves at odds over nuclear strategy at the Moscow meeting in 1957. The arrival of a top-level Chinese military delegation in Moscow on the eve of that meeting showed that other topics besides Yugoslav 'revisionism' had been under discussion. It was not unreasonable to suppose that the Chinese, as Russia's major allies, should want to know how the Russian break-through in nuclear weapons was going to affect their own military arrangements. Was the Communist camp's nuclear capability going to remain under exclusively Russian control, or were Russia's allies to have a say in its direction? Were the Russians going to share nuclear weapons with other members of the camp, and in particular with China? If so, in what form: the actual transfer of weapons to the Chinese army, the stationing of nuclear missiles on China's territory under Russian control, or assistance to China to develop her own nuclear capacity? These and similar questions were of considerable importance to the Chinese, and without answers to them they could not easily plan their own military affairs. Were they, after all, to continue to maintain a vast army of many millions of men equipped with conventional weapons, or could they now rely on Soviet nuclear power? It must be presumed that it was questions like these that Mao and his military advisers raised in 1957 and again in July 1958, and it must also be presumed that these were the questions which the Russians wanted least of all to face up to. Though we cannot know what arguments were used by the two sides in this debate, since neither Russians nor Chinese have ever discussed the question of their military collaboration publicly, we know that neither in 1957 or subsequently did the Russians enter into any nuclear commitment to the Chinese. As far as is known the Chinese have received no aid in nuclear armaments from the Russians, nor have they granted the Russians rights to station nuclear bases in China. There can be no doubt that this is one of the main sources of friction between the two powers.

The Chinese started their all-out bombardment of the off-shore islands on August 23. Later developments suggested that they did so without having the wholehearted approval or any firm backing from the Russians in their enterprise, beyond the impression of agreement and unity that was created by the Peking talks and the resultant communiqué which spoke of the 'complete accord' reigning between the two governments. After it had been made clear that the Americans were preparing to support the Chinese Nationalists, possibly with tactical nuclear weapons, the first Soviet reaction was to declare on August 31 that 'anyone who tries to threaten an attack on the Chinese People's Republic must not forget that he is also threatening the Soviet Union', and to promise 'the necessary moral and material aid' to China. This was a very cautious statement, committing the Russians to very little. It was only a week later on September 7, after Chou En-lai had already taken the heat out of the situation by hinting at a readiness for talks, that Khrushchev was ready to declare roundly that 'an attack on the People's Republic of China is an attack on the Soviet Union'. There was at this point comparatively little danger that the Chinese People's Republic would be attacked. Khrushchev subsequently made even firmer and tougher statements but they played little part in the solution of the crisis, which dissolved as the Chinese Communists eased their pressure on the off-shore islands.

The crisis over the off-shore islands in July and August 1958 threw a good deal of light on the state of relations between Moscow and Peking. It pointed to a complete lack of co-ordination between their plans in foreign affairs. It pointed to an apparent lack of any clear military commitments between the two governments. It drew attention to the Russians' reluctance to commit themselves in a military sense to support for the Chinese Communists' aspirations. It made it clear that the Chinese Communists had not received nuclear weapons from the Russians, nor even the latest forms of aircraft. There was even a suggestion that the Chinese had mounted the whole operation deliberately to force a decision on the question of nuclear co-operation between the two powers. If so, it was an unsuccessful operation from the Chinese point of view, from which they quickly withdrew when they realised it was not producing the results they wanted from Russia. The next time they embarked on a military adventure (on the Indian frontier in 1959), they did so without any reliance on Soviet support. For the Russians, the off-shore islands affair must have served as a clear warning of the dangers of allowing their Chinese allies to juggle with the Communist world's 'nuclear supremacy', and they reacted accordingly.

In 1959 the Chinese carried out two further military operations which played an important part in the development of Sino-Soviet relations. In March a revolt of the people of Tibet against Chinese domination of their land was brutally suppressed by Chinese armed forces, and the Dalai Lama was forced to flee to India, where he was granted asylum. This, and the wave of indignation that swept over India at the Chinese action, led to fierce denunciations of the Indian government by Peking and a serious cooling-off in relations between China and India. It was noticeable, however, that the Soviet press carefully avoided reporting this dispute between China and India, and in particular refrained from repeating the charges the Chinese made against the Indian government. At the same time the Russians avoided comment on the Chinese action in Tibet by saying that it was an 'internal affair' of the Chinese people.

The Russians' unwillingness to commit themselves in this issue or to identify themselves with Chinese criticisms of the Indian government followed naturally from the pains they had taken to restore friendly relations with India in the post-Stalin period. They had no intention of undoing the results of years of diplomatic and economic effort for the sake of China's southward expansion. Indian neutrality was a delicate flower.

In the summer and autumn of 1959, however, the Chinese caused the Russians even greater embarrassment by their military moves on the Indian frontier in which they sought to occupy two areas claimed by India. The dispute dragged on from August to November with a steady deterioration in relations between China and India and with the Russians apparently striving to avoid involvement in the affair. In so far as it touched on the subject, the Soviet press recorded Indian and Chinese statements but without offering any comment. On September 9, however, the official Soviet news agency TASS issued a statement on the dispute 'deploring' the frontier incidents, stressing the friendly relations which the Soviet government maintained with both India and China, and hoping that the two countries would settle their differences peacefully.

This apparently harmless statement by TASS,* which attracted little attention at the time, seems to have caused the Chinese Communists much pain. They were later to declare that it was this declaration of Russian neutrality as between China and India which first brought the Sino-Soviet dispute into the open for all the world to see. In February 1963 an article in the *People's Daily* said:

> The truth is that the internal differences among the fraternal parties were first brought into the open, not in the summer of 1960, but on the eve of the Camp David talks in September, 1959 – on September 9, 1959, to be exact. On that day a socialist country, turning a deaf ear to China's repeated explanations of the true situation and to China's advice, hastily issued a statement on a Sino-Indian border incident through its official news agency. Making no distinction between right and wrong, the statement expressed 'regret' over the border clash and in reality condemned China's correct stand. They even said it was 'tragic' and 'deplorable'. Here is the first instance in history in which a socialist country, instead of condemning the armed provocations of the reactionaries of a capitalist country, condemned another fraternal socialist country when it was confronted with such armed provocation.

The Chinese went on to say that the 'imperialists' exploited the TASS statement to sow discord in the Communist world. Though they exaggerated the extent to which the non-Communist world appreciated the significance of the TASS statement, the Chinese were obviously right, from a Communist point of view, in their criticism of the Russians. Whatever the right and wrongs of the frontier incidents, China was a 'fraternal' Communist country bound to Russia by a treaty of alliance, while India was at best a neutral country only recently

* *See* Chronology: September 9, 1959.

liberated from British rule. The laws of 'proletarian internationalism' demanded that the Russians should back their
Chinese comrades through thick and thin.

Chinese intransigence over the off-shore islands and India
had the additional effect, possibly intentional, of upsetting
Khrushchev's progress towards a 'summit' meeting with the
West. It was particularly embarrassing for him, at a time when
he was out to convince the leaders of the West of his reasonableness and eagerness to settle disputes by direct negotiation, to
have the Chinese deciding matters by force of arms. Khrushchev's need to dissociate himself from Chinese actions may well
have accounted in part for his non-committal attitude on Tibet
and the Sino-Indian frontier incidents. It may not have been
entirely fortuitous that it was only after the announcement at
the beginning of August that Khrushchev was to visit President
Eisenhower in America that the Chinese provoked a serious
conflict on the Indian frontier. This did not, however, prevent
Khrushchev's American tour and his meeting with Eisenhower
at Camp David from taking place.

For all the publicity they attracted, Khrushchev's tour of
America and his talks with President Eisenhower did not resolve
any East-West problems. But the excursion seemed to play an
important part in Khrushchev's plans at the time and was the
subject of an extensive propaganda campaign inside Russia
and the Communist camp calculated to demonstrate the power
of Khrushchev's personality to resolve international differences.
Though this particular episode was later erased from the
official Khrushchev biography, there was no doubt at the time
that Khrushchev believed Camp David was an important step
forward in East-West relations.

There can be equally little doubt that the Chinese did not
share Khrushchev's hopes or optimism. His tour of America
began on September 15, 1959. On September 19, the *People's
Daily* delivered one of its standard attacks on 'American
imperialism'. Though the Chinese refrained from public
criticism of Khrushchev himself, they made it quite clear that
they did not think 'imperialism' changed its spots because its
leaders had agreed to talk.

Khrushchev arrived back in Moscow from America on September 28, and on the next day he left for Peking to attend the celebration of the tenth anniversary of the People's Republic. He was accorded all the honours demanded by protocol, including a banquet attended by 5,000 guests, and Chou En-lai went so far as to congratulate him on the success of his mission to America. The talks which went on behind this polite façade between the Soviet delegation (which included Mikhail Suslov, one of the secretaries of the CPSU, and Andrei Gromyko, the Foreign Minister) and the Chinese delegation (consisting of Mao Tse-tung, Liu Shao-chi and Chou En-lai), can have been anything but cordial. This was apparent even at the time from the brief reports of what took place.

Even in his public speech at the banquet, Khrushchev felt himself constrained to issue a warning which appeared to be directed at the Chinese leaders and the arguments they had been using in their talks with him. After reaffirming the strength of the Communist world compared with the 'imperialist aggressors', Khrushchev said:*

> But this certainly does not mean that since we are so strong we should test the stability of the capitalist system by force. That would be wrong; the peoples would never understand and would never support those who took it into their heads to act in this way . . . Even such a noble and progressive system as socialism cannot be imposed by force of arms against the will of the people.

These remarks seemed to make sense only if someone, presumably the Chinese, was advocating the spread of 'socialism' by force, and it was reasonable to suppose that Khrushchev's words were an echo of what he had been saying to Mao Tse-tung about the latter's excursions into Tibet and India and his views in general about the use to which Soviet nuclear power should be put. That this was the case was confirmed later by the Chinese when they discussed the origins of the dispute in 1963. They then said:†

* *See* Chronology: September 30, 1959.
† 'Whence the Differences?', *People's Daily*, February 27, 1963.

After the Camp David talks the heads of certain comrades were turned and they became more and more intemperate in their public attacks on the foreign and domestic policies of the Chinese Communist Party. They publicly abused the Chinese Communist Party as attempting 'to test by force the stability of the capitalist system' and as 'craving for war like a cock for a fight'. They also attacked the Chinese Communist Party for its general line of socialist construction, its big leap forward and its people's communes, and they spread the slander that the Chinese Party was carrying out an 'adventurist' policy in its direction of the state.

From this Chinese version it sounds very much as if Khrushchev took advantage of his 1959 meeting with Mao and the other Chinese leaders to speak his mind. Still flushed with what he believed to be the success of his American tour, and still smarting from the way the Chinese had tried to upset his applecart with their actions over the off-shore islands and India, he appears to have launched a general attack on the whole of Peking's policies, on much the same lines as Peng Teh-Huai's ill-fated memorandum in August. This meeting between Mao and Khrushchev would not have been made smoother by the Chinese Party's announcement of Peng's dismissal and disgrace in the middle of September, only a couple of weeks before Khrushchev arrived. It would be surprising if Mao did not let Khrushchev know that he resented such interference in his party's affairs. Khrushchev had to swallow the fact that his efforts to defeat Mao had failed.

At the end of these exchanges, the two leaders did not find it possible or necessary to issue the customary communiqué recording the unity of their views. There was no communiqué at all, and the only brief report that *Pravda* gave of the talks suggested a steady deterioration. *Pravda* said on September 31 that the talks had been 'cordial and amicable', on October 1 that they had been 'cordial', and on October 2 that they had taken place.

The meeting in October 1959 was the last meeting to take

place between Mao Tse-tung and Khrushchev. It seems likely to remain the last. When, in 1963, the possibility of their meeting arose again, each of them took refuge in elaborate evasions to avoid visiting the other's capital. It would doubtless be mistaken to suggest that relations between these two great nations depended entirely upon the personalities of their leaders. But both China and Russia are highly centralised, dictatorial states in which policy is to a considerable extent a reflection of the personal views of the leader. The conflict between Moscow and Peking is also a conflict between Mao Tse-tung and Nikita Khrushchev and it seems unlikely to be resolved so long as both remain in power in their respective countries.

VII

IDEOLOGICAL RUMBLINGS

Are the teachings of Marxism-Leninism now 'out-moded'?
'Red Flag', April 16, 1960*

By the end of 1959, there can have been very few persons of any importance inside the Communist camp who were unaware of the rapid deterioration in Sino-Soviet relations, and it must have been apparent at least to the leaders of the other Communist parties outside the camp. They had already witnessed the conflict of views expressed at the meeting in 1957, and in 1958 they must have realised that there were widely differing views over the Chinese communes and the 'great leap forward'. In 1959 they cannot have failed to understand that the Russians disapproved of China's attitude to India, and they must have known that the meeting between Mao and Khrushchev at the end of 1959 had done nothing to improve relations between the two biggest Communist countries. No thinking Communist, outside the inner circle of policy-makers, can have failed to realise that, on most important issues, there were now two clearly different views: the Russian and the Chinese. It was an entirely novel situation for the new generation of Communist officials.

But this awareness of the developing conflict between Moscow and Peking did not extend outside the Communist movement at that time, and there were good reasons why it did not. For one thing the Chinese and the Russian leaders were equally at pains to conceal the fact and the nature of their differences. Secrecy and conspiracy are of the essence of Communist practice and it was second nature for both sides, even when they were spitting at each other in private, to smile

* From an article in this issue entitled 'Long Live Leninism'.

politely at one another in public. (That was why their failure to issue the usual anodyne statement about the 'identity' of their views after their 1959 meeting was significant of the state of personal relations between Mao and Khrushchev.) When, later, the dispute came into the open, one of the charges which Chinese and Russians hurled at each other was that of first *revealing* the existence of the conflict to the 'enemy': the outside world. But at the end of 1959 they were still playing the game according to Communist rules.

Again, by the end of 1959 neither the Chinese nor the Russians had in fact done anything which could be definitely identified as a sign of conflict. What ever had gone on behind the scenes at the 1957 meeting, Russians and Chinese had produced an agreed 'Declaration'. It was still possible to explain the Russians' change in attitude to Tito without reference to the Chinese. The Chinese seemed to have had Russian backing over the off-shore islands affair. And the Russians' hesitations over the Chinese incursion into India, revealing though they were, were not fully appreciated at the time in the West. Much that can be understood today with the benefit of hindsight and the revelations since made by the parties to the dispute, could be detected in 1959 only through the most painstaking research.

There was, however, another factor tending to obstruct recognition of the dispute between Russian and Chinese Communists. This was a curious reluctance on the part of Western observers to admit even the possibility of a conflict between the Soviet and Chinese leaders. Many competent observers in the West, with no shade of sympathy for Communist views, appeared to assume that, because both the Chinese and the Russians claimed to derive inspiration from Marx and Lenin and to rule in the name of Communism and the 'protelariat', they could not therefore have conflicting interests. There was a strange readiness to accept that, in the Marxist faith and its doctrine of 'proletarian internationalism', the Communists had found something to bind them together more firmly and more lastingly than any other faith had bound any two major powers in the past. This apparent acceptance of the Communist claim to have overcome the claims of nationalism seemed to make many Western commentators more Communist than the Communists themselves, and to allow them to overlook the many signs of conflict between Russian and Chinese national interest already recorded. It also seemed to ignore the experience of the quarrel between the Russian and Yugoslav Communists which was very instructive in this connexion. And, as in the case of this earlier falling-out in the Communist camp, even when there were unmistakable signs of the dispute between Moscow and Peking, many Western observers persisted in the belief that it was just a 'put-up job' designed to fool the Western powers. Was it memories of Stalin and his skill at hoodwinking the West that accounted for this exaggerated esteem for the Communists' ability to pull the wool over Western eyes?

Perhaps a word should be added in excuse of those who doubted the possibility of a rift between Communist China and Communist Russia. After all, not Marxism, but common sense suggested that both Russians and Chinese had every advantage to gain from maintaining a close and friendly alliance even if they had occasional differences. On the face of it, this great Communist alliance bestriding Europe and Asia looked un-beatable. China's vastness and dominating position in Asia, coupled with the economic and military potential of the Soviet Union and its East European allies, seemed capable of sweeping everything before them. It was indeed difficult to believe, at that early stage in their alliance, that Russians or Chinese would allow minor differences to break up their amity. That they did so was a measure of the gravity of the issues that divided them.

If it was not apparent to the world at large at the end of 1959 that all was not well between Moscow and Peking, by the end of 1960 there could no longer be any doubt about the existence of a serious rift. During 1960 there emerged clear evidence of a conflict between Russia and China in their relations with the non-Communist countries, over major questions of East-West policy, in relations between their own two states and govern-ments, over matters of Communist ideology, and in their be-haviour inside the Communist movement. This chapter will consider these developments.

*   *   *

One of Khrushchev's first excursions in what was to be a very full and busy 1960 was another tour of Asia, during which he visited India, Indonesia, Burma and Afghanistan between February 11 and March 5. In the case of India, Indonesia and Afghanistan, Khrushchev's visit resulted in an increase of Soviet economic aid and an apparent development of the friendly relations established on his first trip in 1955. In the case of Burma, the results of the visit were less tangible or certain. The trip as a whole had all the appearance of a quick inspection to see that Russia's new friends in Asia were content and that Russia's grip on Asia was not slipping.

The Chinese appeared to take similar action in the same year. In April Chou En-lai visited Nehru in Delhi, but made little headway over the frontier question. With Burma, on the other hand, the Chinese succeeded in concluding a frontier agreement in January and a treaty of 'friendship and non-aggression' in April. In August, Marshal Chen Yi followed Khrushchev to Afghanistan, concluded a treaty of friendship and non-aggression and on trade, and invited the King to visit China. With Indonesia Peking appeared to be unable to make progress, mainly because of the problem of the 'overseas Chinese' population.

Competition between Russians and Chinese for the friend-ship of non-Communist countries, especially those which had freshly acquired independence, was apparent elsewhere. In May Chou En-lai visited Outer Mongolia (the Mongolian People's Republic) to conclude a treaty of friendship and mutual aid and extend a loan of 200 million roubles. It is perhaps not without significance that in August 1960 Khrushchev's critic, Vyacheslev Molotov, was withdrawn from the Soviet embassy in Ulan Bator. The extension of a $35 million loan by Russia to the new state of Guinea in Africa was followed by one of $25 million from the Chinese. Khrushchev's effort to make a firm friend of Fidel Castro in Cuba by extending economic and military aid were followed by a Chinese undertaking to trade with Cuba and lend her $21 million. Even in the Middle East, an area of predominantly Russian interest, the Chinese were competing for influence, for example in Iraq.

It is difficult to believe that the Russians, who had made a considerable effort to aid the Chinese economically and were already stretching their resources in their efforts to win over the newly independent and neutralist nations, were especially pleased to find the Chinese competing in the same markets. The Chinese, it appeared, had every intention of playing the great power, however poor they might be themselves.

Meanwhile Khrushchev pursued his efforts to reach an understanding with the West: efforts which culminated in the 'summit' encounter in Paris in May. This is not the place to discuss again the reasons for the failure of this excursion into 'summitry' for which so many confused explanations were given in the West. Suffice it to say that the commonly held view that Khrushchev took pleasure in breaking up the Paris summit with the aid of the incident involving the shooting down of the American U2 reconnaissance aircraft over Russia seems to be the reverse of the truth. Khrushchev appeared to continue to place hopes in the summit meeting even after the U2 incident seemed to make it unpropitious. Otherwise he would not have gone to Paris at all. It was only when he was forced to realise that the American President would not accept his conditions for 'writing off' the U2 incident that he was obliged to break up the meeting with all the vigour and colour of which he is capable. But he can have taken no real pleasure in this destruction of the 'Camp David spirit' and of his long-laid plans for an East-West détente. The failure of the Paris summit was a defeat for Khrushchev as much as for those in the West who had placed their hopes in the meeting.

It was no defeat for the Chinese, however, and they made no effort to conceal their satisfaction at the way things turned out. Throughout the early months of 1960, the Chinese press and radio had warned consistently against accepting Western talk of peace at its face value and against the idea that 'imperialism' had changed. The Chinese press had maintained a steady stream of denunciation of President Eisenhower, and in a rare interview with foreign visitors, Mao Tse-tung declared in May that 'our common enemy is US imperialism'.

The U2 incident and the consequent failure of the summit meeting were thus a demonstration of the correctness of the Chinese point of view, as Peking hastened to point out. The

Chinese press was enthusiastic in its support for Khrushchev's stand in Paris, and a mass meeting was staged in Peking to denounce America's 'sabotage of the summit'. The attitude of the Chinese at the time was summed up in a reference* to this episode they later made in 1963:

> In May 1960 the American U2 spy plane intruded into the Soviet Union and the four-power summit meeting in Paris was aborted. *We then hoped that the comrades who had so loudly sung the praises of the so-called spirit of Camp David would draw a lesson from these events*, and would strengthen the unity of the fraternal parties and countries in the common struggle against the US imperialist policies of aggression and war.

Although the Chinese were later to complain that Khrushchev did *not* learn the lesson of the Paris summit, *i.e.*, that he did not subsequently follow Chinese advice in matters of general strategy and relations with the West, the Paris débâcle undoubtedly had the effect of ending Khrushchev's flirtation with President Eisenhower and postponing the improvement of East-West relations for which he had been working. President Eisenhower's visit to the Soviet Union, which had been planned for June 1960, was 'postponed' at Khrushchev's suggestion, and his visit to Japan, which should have taken place at the same time was also abandoned because of Communist-inspired protests in Tokyo. These protests were probably encouraged by the Chinese Communists, whose influence inside the Japanese Communist Party was strong.

Thus the Chinese had demonstrated at the beginning of 1960 that, even though their presence at major East-West exchanges was not accepted, they could exert an influence on the course of those exchanges through their superior understanding of the forces at work in the world. While Peking's friends and allies abroad were given the impression that the Chinese Communists' principal ambition was to occupy China's seat in the United Nations, they themselves were demonstrating that they could play a part in world affairs without representation in such 'capitalist' organisations. At the beginning of 1960 Chen Yi,

* 'Whence the Differences?', *People's Daily*, February 27, 1963.

the Foreign Minister, had defined his government's attitude in the following terms:

> China is ready unhesitatingly to commit itself to international obligations to which it agrees. But any international disarmament which is arrived at without the formal participation of the Chinese People's Republic and the signature of its delegates cannot, of course, have any binding force in China.

The attitude of the Chinese was no help to the Russians in their attempts to reach agreement with the West, especially in matters of disarmament. No agreement which did not also involve China was going to be regarded by the Western powers as a satisfactory one. But while the Russians were ready to support demands for Communist China's representation at UNO and to make general declarations about Communist China's participation being essential to the solution of major problems, they were *not* prepared to make this a *condition* for the holding of East-West talks. The Chinese took pleasure in demonstrating to both Russians and Western powers that they could not reach effective agreements *without* Peking's participation.

The Russians had always been able to give the impression that they were anxious to have the Chinese play a full part in world affairs by their sponsorship of resolutions in the United Nations demanding that the Chinese seat be occupied by the Peking regime. But the relative voting strengths were such that the Russian support for Communist China had never been anything but a formality, and there is reason to believe that the Chinese later rebuked the Russians for not making greater efforts on their behalf.

Khrushchev himself headed the Soviet delegation to the General Assembly of the United Nations in September 1960. In his main speech to the Assembly it was noted that he dismissed the question of Chinese representation in a very few words. It was left to the Albanian delegate to make the most impassioned plea for the Chinese Communists.

Khrushchev's purpose in attending the General Assembly falls outside the scope of this book. It appeared to be part of his campaign to project himself as a world statesman, to extend Soviet influence over the 'non-committed' and neutralist nations, and to continue his reconnaissance of America. It did, however, throw a little indirect light on the situation in the Communist camp. Khrushchev travelled to New York in a Russian ship, accompanied by most of the Communist leaders of Eastern Europe, who also headed their delegations at the Assembly. The leader of the Albanian Communist Party, Enver Hoxha, remained in Tirana, however, and the delegation was headed by Mehmet Shehu, the Prime Minister. It was noticed that he travelled to New York separately and was severely cold-shouldered by Khrushchev and the other leaders, even to the point of a public snubbing. This was one of the first overt signs of the deterioration in Soviet-Albanian relations that had been taking place behind the scenes since Khrushchev's visit to Tirana in 1959 and the meetings of Communist leaders in Bucharest in June 1960.

Equally striking were the ostentatiously friendly talks which Khrushchev had with Tito in the couloirs of the General Assembly. While the Albanian delegate was left severely alone, Tito was seen on several occasions in laughing conversation with Khrushchev. These meetings clearly marked the resumption of better relations between Moscow and Belgrade.

The fifteenth session of the United Nations General Assembly received very different assessments in the Russian and Chinese press. *Pravda* said: 'The Soviet people have noted with unanimity and great satisfaction the tremendous political success of the work of their delegation, led by Comrade Khrushchev, at the 15th session of the United Nations General Assembly.' (*Pravda*, October 27, 1960.) The *People's Daily* said: 'US imperialism . . . has pushed around the socialist camp, headed by the Soviet Union, and all the peoples of the world in a most outrageous way at the 15th session of the General Assembly.' (*People's Daily*, October 19, 1960.)

While these political differences were becoming apparent on the surface, practical relations between Moscow and Peking, had taken a sharp turn for the worse in the middle of 1960. The outward and visible sign of this deterioration was to be found in reports from diplomatists in Peking to the effect that large numbers of Soviet technicians and their families left Peking by train for Moscow in the months of July and August.* No official statement about a withdrawal of Soviet aid was issued at the time in Moscow or Peking, and such unofficial comments as were made tended to depict the departure of the Russians from China as a routine affair. Even later in the year, in conversation with a British Member of Parliament, the Foreign Minister, Chen Yi, while admitting that some but not all of the Russians had left, tried to minimise the significance of their departure. He added, however, that China hoped eventually to do without any Soviet personnel and to dispense with the costly business of training students in Russia. However, the truth, as it later emerged, was that at some point in 1960 the Russians decided drastically to reduce the scale of their aid to China and possibly to end it altogether. As the Chinese later described this development: 'Disregarding international practice, they [the Russians] perfidiously and unilaterally tore up agreements and contracts . . . [which were] to be counted, not in twos or threes or in scores, but in hundreds.'† It is believed that, at the time, only half of the industrial plants being constructed under Soviet direction had been completed. The sudden withdrawal of Soviet assistance obliged the Chinese radically to revise their economic plans, which had already been upset by the 'great leap forward' policy of 1958, and which were further endangered by the crisis which overtook agriculture in 1960.

The sudden reduction of Soviet aid was in fact only a more dramatic step in a process that had already become apparent in economic relations between China on the one hand and the Soviet Union and its East European allies on the other. In 1960 Soviet exports to China dropped to 84.8 per cent, and in 1961 to only 38.1 per cent, of the 1959 level. In 1959 the Russians had exported $600 million worth of machinery to China; in 1961 they sent only $108 million worth. China's initial dependence on the Soviet bloc for economic aid had been reflected in the fact that, in 1955, over three-quarters of her foreign trade was

* *See* Chronology: August 13, 1960.
† 'Whence the Differences?', *People's Daily*, February 27, 1963.

with these countries. But the proportion which this trade constituted of her total foreign business fell from 77 per cent in 1955 to 64 per cent in 1960. Soviet exports to China dropped from 57 per cent of China's imports in 1955 to only 42 per cent in 1960. At the same time, China's capacity to pay for Soviet aid either in goods or money was also declining.

It is not possible to establish whether the curtailment of Russian aid in 1960 was primarily, as the Chinese implied, an attempt to bring economic pressure to bear on Peking for political reasons, or whether it resulted from the Russian economists' belated recognition of the enormity of the task they had assumed and the inability of China ever to repay them. It is estimated that, by the end of 1960, Soviet aid to China amounted to some 13.5 billion roubles which the Chinese were expected to pay off in exports to the Soviet Union. The Russians let it be known early in 1961 that, at the end of 1960, China's debt in agricultural exports to Russia had reached $320 million.

While there can be no doubt that the Russians were finding China an increasingly heavy and unrewarding burden on their own resources, it is important to put the dimensions of the burden into perspective. Russia's 14 billion roubles of aid to China amounted to just over 5 US dollars per head of China's 670,000,000 population. This has to be compared with Western aid to Greece of 271 dollars per head. It is also relevant to recall that Soviet aid to China was only a small fraction of Soviet aid to the more developed (and more obedient) Communist countries of Eastern Europe.

It is possible that the Russians might have been more tolerant of China's economic and political indiscipline if her leaders had not at the same time been playing the generous uncle to their own potential satellites in Asia and elsewhere. Chinese credits extended between 1957 and 1961 to various countries in the world amounted to $1.7 billion, or almost exactly half the amount which the Russians had extended to China. It was one thing for the Russians to be generous: it was quite another for them to see their aid being used to combat their own influence in Asia, Africa and Latin America!

There was a further indication during 1960 that the Chinese leaders were expecting a reduction in Soviet aid and were already seeking alternative sources of essential materials. In the autumn, Chinese officials put out their first feelers in the West for supplies of oil, for which they were almost entirely dependent on Russia.

Thus, by the end of 1960, actual contact between Russia and China had been severely reduced. Economic and probably military advisers had been withdrawn. Exchanges of students had been curtailed. Even diplomatic contacts had been reduced to a lower level with the departure from Peking at the end of 1959 of the Soviet ambassador, Pavel Yudin, and his replacement by S. V. Chervenenko. Yudin was a man of some stature in the Communist movement and of worthy rank in the CPSU. His successor, Chervonenko, was neither a career diplomatist nor a high official of the CPSU. While he probably owed his appointment to personal contact with Khrushchev, his embassy could clearly be no more than a letter-box for communications between Moscow and Peking.

One such communication referred to later (in the Soviet Party's letter of March 30, 1963) served to indicate the coolness of relations between the 'fraternal' parties. The Russians say that in May 1960 they invited Mao to 'spend a holiday in the USSR and familiarise himself with the life of the Soviet people'. But, it appeared, Mao 'could not avail himself' of this invitation.

Some exchanges may have continued between Moscow and Peking behind the scenes during 1960. But the dispute between them now took the public, if esoteric, form of lengthy articles on ideological themes in their party newspapers and journals. Only by implication was it possible to determine what were the real issues in dispute and, since both Russians and Chinese have subsequently made their views clearer and less indirect, there is now less need to enter into the 'ideological' dispute in great detail. Since the 'ideological' form was obviously intended to conceal the true nature of the dispute and the real issues involved, to become too deeply involved in it would not serve the aim of clarity in this account of the dispute.

The opening broadside in the ideological battle was delivered by the Chinese in the form of an article of monumental dimensions, entitled 'Long Live Leninism!', which appeared in the

Chinese Communist Party's journal *Red Flag* on April 16, 1960.* Nominally written to celebrate the ninetieth anniversary of Lenin's birth, it was obviously intended as a complete statement of the Chinese point of view on major policy issues in the Communist camp and in particular as the Chinese reply to the innovations introduced into Marxist thought by Khrushchev at the Twentieth Congress of the CPSU. The Chinese later explained that they had published the article 'for the sake of upholding the Moscow Declaration, defending Marxism-Leninism and enabling the people of the world to understand our point of view on the current international situation.' They also explained why they did not direct their criticisms at the Russians by name: 'Although we had already been under attack for more than half a year, we set store by amity and made imperialism and Yugoslav revisionism the targets of the struggle in our discussion of the erroneous views which contravened the Moscow Declaration.' (This is one of the very few references by either side to the deliberate symbolism used in the debate and to their exploitation of Yugoslavia as a stalking-horse. It is reasonable to suppose that this convention suited the Russians equally well, and that Albania came to serve a similar purpose a little later.)

'Long Live Leninism!' was, as its title suggested, a reaffirmation of certain basic Leninist concepts, and notably those which Khrushchev had revised in 1956. Generally speaking, the Chinese defended the militant revolutionary teachings of Lenin against attempts to water them down in the face of the threat of nuclear war. We have seen that Khrushchev had stressed four main features in the modern world: the greatly increased destructive capacity of modern weapons; the consequent primacy of the fight for peace; the possibility of avoiding war in the modern world; and the possibility of achieving Communism without revolution. The Chinese contested each of these concepts.

They rejected any tampering with Lenin's teaching on war:

> We believe in the absolute correctness of Lenin's thinking: war is an inevitable outcome of exploiting

* *See* Chronology: April 16, 1960.

> systems and the source of modern wars is the imperi-
> alist system. Until the imperialist system and the
> exploiting classes come to an end, wars of one kind
> or another will always occur. They may be wars among
> the imperialists for redivision of the world, or wars of
> aggression and anti-aggression between the imperialists
> and the oppressed nations, or civil wars of revolution
> and counter-revolution between the exploited and
> exploiting classes in the imperialist countries, or, of
> course, wars in which the imperialists attack the
> socialist countries and the socialist countries are
> forced to defend themselves. All these kinds of war
> represent the continuation of the policies of definite
> classes. Marxist-Leninists absolutely must not sink
> into the mire of bourgeois pacificism . . .

This basic teaching on war was unaffected, in the Chinese view, by the development of nuclear weapons: 'certain specific details of technical progress in the present-day world.' They rejoiced in the Soviet Union's achievements in military science which 'further strengthens the position of the proletarian revolution, and of the oppressed nations in their fight against imperialism, and certainly does not weaken it'. But it was 'not technique, but man, the masses of people', that determined the fate of mankind. 'An awakened people will always find new ways to counteract a reactionary superiority in arms and win victory for themselves. This was so in past history, it is so at present, and it will still be so in the future.'

Moreover, the Chinese article continued, if war did come – and that depended on the 'imperialists', not the Communist powers – it would not be the end of everything. It would mean 'the very speedy destruction of these monsters (American or other imperialists) under the encirclement of the people the world over, and the result will certainly not be the annihilation of mankind.' The peoples would have to make 'enormous sacrifices'; but those sacrifices 'would be repaid'. 'On the débris of a dead imperialism the victorious people would create with extreme rapidity a civilisation thousands of times higher than the capitalist system and a truly beautiful future for themselves.' They summed up their faith on this issue in the following words:

> Whichever way you look at it, none of the new techniques like atomic energy, rocketry and so on has changed the basic characteristic of the epoch of imperialism and proletarian revolution pointed out by Lenin, as alleged by the modern revisionists. The capitalist-imperialist system absolutely will not crumble of itself. It will be pushed over by the proletarian revolution within the imperialist country concerned, and by the natural revolution in the colonial and semi-colonial countries. Modern technical progress cannot save the capitalist-imperialist system from its doom but only ring a new death knell for it.

'Long Live Leninism!' enunciated a similarly uncompromising and fundamentalist attitude to the possibility of 'peaceful transition' from capitalism to socialism. It quoted Lenin with approval as saying: 'no serious Marxist will believe it possible to make the transition from capitalism to socialism without a civil war.' If an opportunity for such a 'peaceful' transition occurred, it should be seized. But such opportunities were very rare now; the proletariat must never assume that the bourgeoisie would hand over power peacefully.

The article summarised the Chinese position thus: 'We Communists are struggling for the defence of world peace, for the realisation of the policy of peaceful coexistence. Meanwhile we support the revolutionary wars of the oppressed nations against imperialism. We support revolutionary wars of the oppressed peoples for their own liberation and social progress, because all revolutionary wars are just wars.'

It is not easy to present the Chinese case in brief compass; for a fuller understanding of it the reader is directed to the lengthier extracts from 'Long Live Leninism!' in the appendices. But it would be unfair, for the purposes of what purports to be an objective study of the dispute between Moscow and Peking, to present the Chinese, as Khrushchev had done, as 'cocks craving for a fight'. It is true that they chose to minimise the effect of the advent of nuclear weapons on the devastation that would be wrought by war, and it is also true that they insisted on the continuing validity of the essentially revolutionary teaching of Marx and Lenin. But it cannot be concluded from their statement of their case that they were therefore thirsting for all-out war and bloody revolution. Such a view had been given currency by a statement supposed to have been made by Mao Tse-tung to the effect that, even if China lost 300 million dead in a nuclear war, there would still be 300 million survivors. Whether the Chinese leader really has such a cavalier attitude to nuclear war is not certain. All that can be said with certa nty is that the Chinese view expressed in their polemical writings is less crude than this and does not suggest that they would necessarily pursue revolutionary ends by means of nuclear war if they had the means.

The Chinese attitude is rather that, while much may be true in what the 'revisionists' say about the changing nature of capitalism, the strengthening of the Communist camp, the liberation of colonial peoples, the power of modern weapons and so forth, it is mistaken to rush into an understanding with the 'imperialist' enemy or to abandon the revolutionary struggle. On the contrary, the change in the balance of world forces in favour of the Communist world is, in the Chinese view, a reason for increasing rather than reducing pressure on the rest of the world. Whatever dangers may appear to be inherent in such a doctrine, the Chinese, from the point of view of revolutionary strategy, may well be thought to have a good deal of right on their side. Whatever their motives in crossing swords with the Russians, they were probably not completely frivolous and they may well have believed quite sincerely that Khrushchev and the 'modern revisionists' were indeed disarming the revolution by their doctrinal reforms.

In the months following the appearance of 'Long Live Leninism!', a number of statements were made by Soviet leaders and in the Soviet press* which were in fact replies to the Chinese interpretation of Lenin's teachings. In the exposition of Soviet policy, these statements did not go beyond the lines already

* *See* Chronology: April 22, June 10, June 12, 1960.

laid down by Khrushchev at the Twentieth and Twenty-first Congresses of the CPSU, and there is therefore no point in reproducing their arguments in full. But they added certain glosses to what was already known of Soviet views.

In general, the statements showed that the Soviet pundits were no less diligent than the Chinese in their selection of quotations from Lenin to support their contentions. As the debate developed, it began to appear that Lenin had said and written so much in his lifetime that there was material enough in his works to support a great variety of views. Indeed, the Russians, enjoying the great tactical advantage of being the custodians of Lenin's archives, were, later in the debate, to produce 'hitherto unpublished' writings by Lenin to support their theses when they felt the need.

The first obviously official reaction to the Chinese broadside was contained in a speech made by Otto Kuusinen, the veteran Finnish Communist and member of the Presidium of the CPSU, at the traditional Lenin anniversary meeting in Moscow. Kuusinen stressed, by ample quotations, Lenin's desire for peace and peaceful competition between the Communist and capitalist systems. 'We must demonstrate the importance of Communism practically, by example', Lenin had said. Kuusinen admitted the truth of the Chinese contention that 'aggressiveness is inherent in the nature of capitalism'; but 'one should not dogmatically consider only this aspect of the matter'. Imperialism was on the wane; the forces of socialism were growing.

> Therefore, to be loyal to Marxism-Leninism today, it is not sufficient to repeat the old truth that imperialism is aggressive. The task is to make full use of the new factors operating for peace so as to save humanity from the catastrophe of another war. A dogmatic position is a backward position.

Dealing with the difficult question of the effect of weapons of mass destruction on Marxist teaching, Kuusinen declared firmly: 'The classics of Marxism have never denied the fact that new types of weapons are able, not only to bring about a radical change in the art of war, but also to influence politics.'

To this negative discovery he added a plum dug out of the Lenin archives. Lenin's wife, Krupskaya, was found to have said that Lenin had foreseen the time when war would become 'so destructive as to be impossible'. Lenin, she said, 'passionately wanted war to become impossible'. This seemed to line Lenin up firmly on Khrushchev's side in the nuclear age.

A major contribution to the discussion appeared in *Pravda* in August. It was an article entitled 'Problems of War and Peace in Present-Day Conditions', and written by Yuri Frantsev, one of the CPSU's leading ideologists.* Reaffirming the Khrushchev line in rather more persuasive and reasonable terms, Frantsev added some new points to the argument. He looked forward to the day when the 'camp of socialism' would be so strong as to be able to '*compel* the militant circles of imperialism to abandon their plans for another world war'. He agreed that 'imperialists' remained aggressive but evolved the formula that their opportunities for being aggressive were diminishing. 'Whoever notices only one side of a question and closes his eyes to the other is not a Marxist and cannot correctly understand the present-day international situation.' Frantsev also hit on the impressive argument that people would not be disposed to put much effort into building a new society if they were told in advance that war was inevitable and that the results of their efforts would be destroyed. This argument, and the related argument that nuclear war would mean the end of everything, recurred in several articles. Thus Belyakov and Burlatsky in the CPSU's theoretical journal *Kommunist* (No. 13, 1960) said:

> A world war with the employment of thermo-nuclear weapons would make no distinctions between front and rear. It would lead to the complete destruction of the main centres of civilisation and the wiping out of whole nations, and would bring immeasurable disaster to the whole of humanity. Only madmen could wish for such a catastrophe. . . . It is obvious, therefore, that modern nuclear war of itself could in no way be a factor which would hasten revolution or

* *See* Chronology: August 7, 1960.

bring nearer the victory of socialism. On the contrary, it would throw back humanity, the world revolutionary workers' movement and the cause of building socialism and Communism for many dozens of years.

The impossibility of advancing the cause of revolution by war had never been stated more strongly than this.

VIII

TWO VOICES, 1960

Anyone with a little common sense knows that the question of who is right and who is wrong cannot be determined by the majority or minority at a given moment.
                    'People's Daily', December 15, 1962

However significant the various statements appearing in the Russian and Chinese press in 1960 were for identifying the differences between Moscow and Peking on world strategy, and however carefully they were studied by the policy experts in the two parties – as well as by students of Communism in the West – these abstruse discussions of Lenin's views, and the denunciations of 'dogmatists', 'sectarians' and 'revisionists', made little impression on the rank and file Communists or on the public in general. But, as the two points of view began to crystallise out on the 'ideological' plane, the dispute began also to assume an 'organisational' form, and a larger number of people in the Communist world became aware of it and involved in it. Wherever they had a voice in an international body, the Chinese began to speak out and put forward their views and to criticise those propagated by the Russians and their supporters. In the Communist phrase, the Chinese began to behave as factionalists inside the Communist movement.

The first instance of China's opposing the Soviet 'line' in public occurred in February 1960 at a meeting in Moscow of the Warsaw Pact countries. The meeting was held at a time when Khrushchev's campaign to bring off some form of détente with the Western powers was at its height and it appeared as though he had summoned the meeting with a view to getting the backing of the rest of the camp for his forthcoming excursions into 'summitry'. The last thing the Soviet leader wanted on such an occasion was for anyone to pour cold water on his optimistic plans, and there is some reason to suppose that the Russian hosts were reluctant to have a Chinese 'observer' at the meeting. They certainly assembled representatives of the East European satellites in Moscow for an 'agricultural' meeting before the Warsaw Pact meeting, apparently to give them some preliminary briefing: an act which, in fact, offered one of the first indications that Moscow was having a certain difficulty in keeping its European satellites in order. In the event the meeting was attended by representatives of the eight member-nations and by observers from the three Communist countries of China, North Korea and Mongolia. The Chinese observer was Kang Sheng.

The meeting was able to report the usual 'complete unanimity' of views among the participants and to issue a Declaration* to which, however, the Chinese and other 'observers' did not append their signatures. The significance of this omission became apparent only when Kang Sheng's speech to the meeting was made available by the Chinese; it was given no publicity by the Soviet or East European press.

The Declaration was a remarkably complacent and optimistic document which seemed, in brief, to hold up the prospect of an understanding between East and West as almost an accomplished fact. Recording with satisfaction the growth of 'mutual confidence' between East and West, the Declaration said: 'The world has now entered on a period of negotiations about the settlement of the main international issues in dispute with the aim of establishing a lasting peace, while the advocates of cold war are sustaining a defeat.' It claimed that the situation had already arrived where any attempt by an aggressor would 'lead to the immediate and complete routing of the violator of peace'. War was ruled out; peaceful coexistence, and especially personal encounters between 'leading statesmen', represented the only way to solve the world's problems. Khrushchev's 'historic' meeting with Eisenhower had 'broken the ice of the cold war', his meeting with British Prime Minister Macmillan had improved the international climate; his forthcoming meetings with French and Italián leaders would strengthen world peace; and President Eisenhower's proposed visit to the Soviet Union would further improve relations between Russia and

* *See* Chronology: February 4, 1960.

America, which would be 'an important guarantee of the inviolability of peace throughout the world'. The Declaration recognised that there were still 'influential forces' in the West which were opposing agreement on such major issues as disarmament and the German problem. But it gave the impression that their resistance was doomed to failure, and that the forthcoming 'summit' meeting in Paris would mark a 'turning-point in East-West relations'. It was therefore especially important, the Declaration said, that all countries should do everything in their power to contribute to the success of the talks.

Kang Sheng's speech gave the impression that he had not heard this latter appeal.* He differed from the Declaration in practically every particular, and the general tone of his remarks was indistinguishable from that customary at the height of the cold war. He acknowledged that the international situation was moving in a direction 'favourable to peace', and he recognised 'certain tendencies towards relaxation of the international tension created by imperialism'. Khrushchev's visit to America had been 'successful'. But whatever progress had been made was, in Kang's view: 'the result of repeated struggles waged by the Socialist forces, the national revolutionary forces and the forces of peace and democracy against the imperialist war forces, the result of the East wind prevailing over the West wind.' This theme – that any improvement in the world situation was due, not to a change of heart on the part of 'American imperialism, which still remains the arch enemy of world peace', but to the strength of the Communist camp – was elaborated throughout the speech. Instead of recording points of progress, Kang provided a catalogue of America's 'double-dealing' and 'war plans' in various parts of the world.

In addition to observations that were completely and manifestly out of tune with the Russian-inspired Declaration of policy, Kang made two specifically Chinese points. One was that any international agreement, on disarmament or any other subject, arrived at without the participation of Communist China and not subscribed to by Peking, 'cannot, of course, have any binding force on China'. This was a clear warning

* *See* Chronology: February 4, 1960.

to Khrushchev, and an announcement to the world at large, that the Soviet leader was not speaking on behalf of China in his talks at the summit and that he could not enter into obligations that would bind China. This sharp reminder of China's *independence* of Soviet policy and of the camp could serve only to reduce Khrushchev's chances of reaching agreement with the West.

Kang's second point was in a sense the reverse of the first. It was a reminder that China was *part* of the Communist camp. He recalled the 1957 Moscow meeting and its Declaration, which was 'the charter of solidarity of our Socialist camp'. The Chinese Communists, he said, 'have always taken the safe-guarding of the unity of the Socialist camp as their sacred international duty.' More than that: 'They have always regarded an attack against any Socialist country by the imperi-alists and all reactionaries as an attack against China.'

Kang Sheng's speech illustrated very clearly the essence of the Chinese Communists' attitude towards the 'unity' of the Communist camp and the central issue in their dispute with the Russians. They stood for a closely united bloc of which they were prepared to acknowledge Soviet 'leadership' and they were even eager to assume military obligations towards the other countries of the bloc, with which they had in fact no formal treaty obligations, since they were not members of the Warsaw Pact. On the other hand, the Chinese were *not* content to be silent, non-voting passengers in the Communist machine, merely adding weight to Khrushchev's words and policies without having an effective say in their formation. Their efforts were directed in 1960, as they continued to be in succeed-ing years, to obtaining for China at least an equal say in the formation of policy for the whole Communist world. They wanted both a united camp and one which was moving in the direction they wanted it to go. Their attitudes, both of support for the organisational unity of the camp and of opposition to the 'revisionists' in the camp, can be understood only if their main objective is kept constantly in mind.

There were no doubt many Communist leaders among those gathered at the Warsaw Pact meeting in whom Kang Sheng's words struck a chord of sympathy. Kang's was the authentic voice of the militant revolutionary, talking the sort of language that most of the East European leaders had been listening to and speaking all their lives. Even if, for good reasons of geography, economics and military strategy, they were obliged to put their signatures in February 1960 to the Declaration of what was in effect the Russian point of view, many of the signatories probably did so with doubts heavy in their hearts.

The next opportunity for the Chinese to propagate their views to an international Communist audience came in June 1960, when trade union leaders from all over the world gathered in Peking for a meeting of the General Council of the Communist-sponsored World Federation of Trade Unions. This was, for several reasons, a far more auspicious occasion for the Chinese. The very fact that the meeting was being held in Peking added weight to Chinese views; the Chinese were full members and not just 'observers' of the WFTU with equal rights to express their views; the membership of the WFTU was drawn from the most militant sections of the working-class movement in every part of the world and was therefore a bigger and more receptive audience for Chinese views. And, finally, the fiasco of the Paris summit meeting had surely strengthened the Chinese argument that the imperialists were not to be trusted and that militancy was the only effective weapon.

Chou En-lai, the Chinese Prime Minister, gave the delegates Peking's view of the situation at a banquet on June 6.* The American 'peace fraud', he said, had been exposed. 'The criminal activities of US imperialism, encroaching on the Soviet Union and sabotaging the four-power conference of heads of government, have thoroughly laid bare its vicious and sly gestures. . . . ' He saw a 'storm of opposition' to imperialism developing. The main task of the working-class movement was to 'make full use of the present most favourable situation'. The peoples must 'rise to fight imperialism'. And, in what can only have been a reference to Khrushchev's approach to the problem, Chou said: 'Peace can never be achieved by begging it of imperialism.'

* *See* Chronology: June 5, 1960.

In the conference itself, the Chinese delegate Liu Chang-sheng, Vice-Chairman of the All-China Federation of Trade Unions and also a Vice-Chairman of the WFTU, explained the Chinese attitude to war and peace in greater detail.* It was in direct contradiction to Khrushchev's views. It was wrong, said Liu Chang-sheng, to speak of war in general without distinguishing between one kind of war and another. When Communists talked about the possibility of preventing war they were talking about *world war*, and it was true to say that there was a possibility of preventing the 'imperialists' from unleashing such a war, although 'it is entirely wrong to believe that war can be eliminated for ever while imperialism still exists'. The spreading of such illusions, said Liu, had already had 'evil consequences'.

All other kinds of war: wars between the 'imperialists' and colonial peoples and civil wars in capitalist countries – were unavoidable. To teach otherwise was to condemn the 'oppressed peoples' to permanent enslavement.

As for the prospects of disarmament, the Chinese supported such proposals, but with reservations. 'It is of course inconceivable', Liu Chang-sheng said, 'that imperialism will accept proposals for general and complete disarmament.' The real purpose of putting them forward was to arouse opposition to imperialism and to 'isolate the imperialist bloc led by the United States'.

Though the Chinese line found an echo in the speeches of some of the hotter-headed delegates in Peking, the more moderate Soviet point of view carried the day. Later, in 1963, the Chinese described their disappointment that the Russians appeared still not to have learned the lesson of the Paris affair. 'Contrary to our hopes, at the Peking session of the WFTU . . . certain comrades of fraternal parties still refused to denounce Eisenhower, spread many erroneous views and opposed the correct views put forward by the Chinese comrades.'†

It was thus apparent by the beginning of June 1960 that the Chinese were not engaged in a mere ideological dispute with the Russians: they were making an open bid for support within

* *See* Chronology: June 8, 1960.
† 'Whence the Differences?', p. 14, *People's Daily*, February 27, 1963.

the Communist movement. Though protesting still their loyalty to the idea of the united camp 'headed by the Soviet Union', they were challenging directly the authority of the Soviet leaders within the camp. They flatly rejected Khrushchev's doctrinal innovations on the subjects of war and peace and 'peaceful transition' and they were openly critical of Khrushchev's foreign political strategy and his conduct of diplomatic exchanges with the West. This was an entirely new situation for the Soviet leaders, who had become accustomed under Stalin's rule to the unchallenged exercise of their authority in the Communist movement. Not since the 'twenties had it seriously occurred to any non-Russian Communist leader that ultimate authority rested anywhere else but in Moscow and with the Russian Party. It was true that the CPSU was just one party in a world-wide movement, and that in theory the word of a Russian Communist had no more authority than that of a Chinese or a Czech or an Italian. But a quarter of a century during which the CPSU had been the only *ruling* party, and one moreover with the resources of a great nation behind it which it could use to exert its authority, coupled with Stalin's own authoritarian rule and contempt for the other parties, had left the Soviet leaders with a strongly ingrained habit of leadership. It may, indeed, not have occurred to Khrushchev that when, in his speech at the Twentieth Congress of the CPSU in 1956, he introduced substantial changes into the prevailing doctrine, he was exceeding his rights. He could then have consulted with other Communist leaders on matters of grand strategy and probably have carried them with him on many issues. But, as far as is known, he did not bother to do so. It was this high-handed treatment of the rest of the movement, as much as the actual ideas he put forward, that provoked the Chinese into opposition. By June 1960 it was quite clear that they were determined to fight the issue out.

It appears also that at about the same time Khrushchev and his advisers became aware for the first time of the seriousness of the Chinese challenge and of the threat it constituted to their position in the bloc. They therefore took action to rally support and bring some order into the ranks at least of their immediate neighbours in East Europe. Khrushchev decided, apparently at short notice, to take advantage of the Third Congress of the Rumanian Communist Party, due to take place in Bucharest on June 21, to hold a meeting of the leaders of the Communist bloc. He led the CPSU delegation himself and leaders of the other ruling parties followed suit, with the exception of the Chinese Party, whose delegation was headed by Peng Chen, the lower-ranking, but none the less outspoken, Secretary of the Chinese Party.

There can be little doubt that Khrushchev intended at Bucharest to 'pull a fast one' over the Chinese. He wanted to give this gathering of Communist leaders, among whom he was sure he could win a majority to support him, the authority of an international conference supporting his views. According to the Albanian Communists, Khrushchev approached them before the Congress and tried to persuade them to support him. He probably made similar approaches to the other leaders of parties in East Europe, and a letter setting out the Soviet point of view was certainly circulated to delegations attending the Congress and later, perhaps in revised form, reached the principal parties in the movement. That the Chinese were taken aback by Khrushchev's counter-offensive was confirmed by their later references to the Bucharest meeting:

> It was a fact of particular gravity that late in June 1960 someone went so far as to wave his baton and launch an all-out and converging attack on the Chinese Communist Party at the meeting of the fraternal parties in Bucharest. This action was a crude violation of the principle that questions of common interest should be solved through consultation among fraternal parties. It set an extremly bad precedent for the international Communist movement.*

What went on behind the scenes at the Bucharest meeting can be gathered only by implication from what is known of the Soviet letter to the participants, the published speeches and certain hints thrown out by the Chinese and Albanian Communists. The CPSU's letter was largely a reasoned rejection of Chinese views on the main ideological issues. The Chinese

* 'Whence the Differences?' *loc. cit.*

did not appreciate (it said) the changes that had taken place in the world since Lenin's time, the limits now set to imperialism's opportunities for aggression, and the possibilities of preventing war. The Russians insisted that peaceful coexistence was the 'general line' of the foreign policy of *all* Communist countries, and not just a tactic. Ten or fifteen years of peace would allow the Communist camp so to increase in strength as to make revolutionary struggle easier everywhere. Support for nationalist governments was justified because it weakened 'imperialism'. Progress in disarmament would put obstacles in the way of Western militarism.

However reasonable the CPSU sounded, it revealed that the Russians had been put in something of a quandary by the Chinese criticisms. They were determined, for reasons already considered, to defend their stand on 'peaceful coexistence', but they were none the less anxious not to appear to have lost their 'revolutionary' fire. Nowhere was this clearer than over the question of their attitude to wars other than world war. They rejected the Chinese charge that they were opposed to 'wars of liberation' and similar 'just wars'; but at the same time they argued against the Chinese that any local war could easily become a world war. They were equally ambiguous in their reply to the Chinese charge that they no longer supported the revolutionary overthrow of capitalist régimes. To this the Russian reply was that whether a seizure of power was peaceful or violent depended on the circumstances in the country concerned. These questions, which all derived from the central issue of whether the Russians had abandoned the use of *all* forceful and militant promotion of revolution in the nuclear age, remained unresolved and continued to provide abundant material for endless debate.

The letter from the CPSU appears also to have accused the Chinese for the first time of 'fractional' activities within the Communist camp itself. The letter complained that, whereas the Chinese had first supported the Russians' process of 'de-Stalinisation', they later reversed their attitude and hindered the process in certain parties. A reference to the 'criticism of one party by another behind its back' suggested that the Russians had become aware that the Chinese were making independent approaches to certain parties and trying to win them away from allegiance to Moscow. The basic Chinese tactic was revealed in their complaint: 'while the Chinese say the Soviet Union should be the leader of the socialist camp, they are at the same time attacking and criticising the Soviet Party.'

Other charges levelled against the Chinese appeared in another Soviet letter which was circulated after the Bucharest meeting (and which may have been largely identical with the one circulated at the meeting). That letter referred to Chinese interference in the affairs of two East European Communist parties; to Chinese efforts to obstruct the work of Soviet political instructors among Russians working in China; to Chinese attempts to subvert Soviet Communists in China; to the closing down by the Chinese of a Soviet periodical published in Peking; and to Chinese attempts to 'destroy the unity' of the international 'mass organisations' such as the WFTU and the 'peace movement'.

While these apparently fairly heated debates were going on in private, Khrushchev made a typically spirited defence of the Soviet position in his speech to the Congress.* Once again he based his arguments on the 'incomparably more horrible devastation' that a nuclear war would involve, and told the Communist world for the first time that 'millions of people' would die in the flames of a hydrogen bomb. Then, without at any point naming the Chinese, he affirmed that there would be no retreat from the thesis that war was not inevitable, and he reminded those who relied on Lenin's views on the nature of imperialism to refute the Soviet thesis that:

> Lenin's statements about imperialism were put forward and developed decades ago in the absence of many phenomena which have now become decisive for the development of the historical process and the whole international situation.

It was wrong, said Khrushchev, to 'repeat mechanically' what Lenin had said many decades ago to prove that wars were inevitable so long as socialism had not conquered the whole world:

* *See* Chronology: June 21, 1960.

> [You had] to be able not only to read but to
> understand correctly what you read and to apply it
> to the practical conditions of the time, to take proper
> account of the situation which has developed and the
> actual correlation of forces.

A politician must show that he knew how to 'apply revolutionary teaching creatively'. Khrushchev's defence of his 'creative application' of Leninism was full of vigour and sparkle and evoked a good deal of laughter, as well as 'stormy applause', among the delegates to the Rumanian congress. It was hardly to be expected, especially in view of the linguistic problems involved, that Peng Chen could compete with Khrushchev in public debate. He limited himself to a short speech reaffirming the perfidious nature of imperialism, warning against 'unrealistic illusions' and appealing for unity of the camp.* His speech did not receive much publicity in the Communist world.

The communiqué which the twelve parties of the camp issued at the end of their deliberations did not suggest, however, that the Russians had had it all their own way.† It was, on the whole, an empty document reaffirming the parties' loyalty to the Declaration of 1957. But a reference to imperialism as a continuing source of aggressive wars and to the possibility of revolutions still taking place by 'unpeaceful means' indicated that there was some resistance among the other Communist leaders to giving unqualified support to Khrushchev's interpretation of 'peaceful coexistence'. His shock tactics at Bucharest do not seem to have been entirely successful. Though the Russians tried to give to the Bucharest meeting the same authority as the Moscow meeting of 1957, the Chinese refused to accept this. It seems likely that about this time they began to press for the calling of a world conference of Communist leaders and that the Russians agreed in principle that such a gathering should take place after the traditional anniversary celebrations of the Revolution in Moscow in November.

*   *   *

* *See* Chronology: June 22, 1960.
† *See* Chronology: June 24, 1960.

The next four months were a period of stalemate during which both sides to the dispute appeared to be sharpening their weapons and feeling out the attitude of other parties in the movement. In a speech to graduates of Soviet military academies, Khrushchev appeared to yield somewhat to the Chinese view, acknowledging that the statement that war was not inevitable did not mean that the 'imperialists' could not start one, and stressing that the prevention of war demanded the united efforts of all socialist forces. He also made much of the 'unanimity' which he claimed had been manifested at the Bucharest meeting. This was presumably less a gesture of goodwill than an attempt to take some of the heat out of the dispute: unless it was just careless thinking by the Soviet leader. At all events, there was evidence that both parties were busy instilling the true faith into their own followers. Public polemics, though still highly esoteric, continued in the Communist press; there was a further brush between Russians and Chinese at the Congress of the Vietnamese Communist Party in Hanoi in September. Moreover it was apparently soon after the Bucharest meeting that the Russians decided to withdraw their advisers from China, scale down their trade with the Chinese, and thus bring Sino-Soviet relations down to their lowest level since 1949. This was the heaviest weapon that Khrushchev could use to try to bring the Chinese round to his point of view. But it must be assumed that he wielded it rather in desperation than in the serious hope that Mao would respond to this form of blackmail.

Within the Communist movement, the debate continued through the medium of the letters from the CPSU and CCP which were soon circulating. Such knowledge as we have of the Russians' 84-page document has already been given (pp. 103-5). The Chinese are said to have circulated in reply a letter of some 160 pages answering the Russian charges and reviewing the whole course of Sino-Soviet relations from Stalin's death in 1953. The Chinese said they found the Russians' posthumous treatment of Stalin 'obnoxious' and their attitude towards the Yugoslav Communists 'cringing'. They made it clear that they had not hesitated to criticise Stalin's successors from the outset and that they had charged Khrushchev as early as 1956 with 'distorting Marxism'. They also made the surprising claim that it was only on their insistence that Khrushchev had finally crushed the Hungarian revolt. Describing the dispute at the 1957 meeting, the Chinese asserted that it was only after they had threatened to 'take up the battle against all forms of revisionism' (which meant in effect to split the Communist movement there and then) that the Russians accepted the Chinese amendments to the twelve-party Declaration.

As a result of the circulation of these documents in the Communist movement – though they were treated with the same secrecy as all internal party matters – every responsible official in the world's Communist parties must have had, by July 1960, a fairly full and clear idea of what the dispute was about. The Chinese had apparently gone out of their way to inform as many parties as possible, and the Russians thus had no choice but to reply. But they could have no control over the course of the debate in the many parties, and they presumably came to the conclusion that the best way to restore some order in the ranks of the movement would be to hold a world conference.

August, September and October 1960, were mainly taken up with preparations for this conference. A preparatory commission containing representatives of twenty-six parties, the exact composition of which is not known but which certainly included representatives of Communist parties outside the Soviet bloc (e.g. the Indian Party), was set up under the chairmanship of Mikhail Suslov, a member of the Presidium and secretariat of the CPSU who had long been concerned with the problems of international Communism. The commission considered the various Soviet and Chinese statements as well as contributions from certain other parties and a draft submitted by the CPSU of the declaration to be issued by the forthcoming conference. The commission was said to have met for three and a half weeks in September and October without resolving any of the main issues in dispute.

Such was the situation on the eve of the first full conference of world Communist leaders to be held since the dispute between Moscow and Peking began. Even on the purely 'ideological' level, the Chinese and Russian points of view were as far apart as ever. On the organisational plane tempers were rising and a clear conflict had developed. At the same time relations between the Chinese and Soviet governments were extremely cold. The prospects of agreement in November were not bright: the prospects for debate almost unlimited.

IX

FIGHTING IT OUT IN MOSCOW

*During the meeting we upheld Marxism-Leninism . . . and
opposed the erroneous views put forward by certain comrades; at
the same time we made necessary compromises on certain
questions.*
'People's Daily', February 27, 1963

The conference which took place in Moscow in November
1960 was the first formal meeting of representatives of all the
world's Communist parties to take place since before the
Second World War. The leaders of the Communist movement
in various parts of the world had, it is true, been summoned to
Moscow on previous occasions, notably for the Nineteenth
Congress (Stalin's last) and the Twentieth Congress of the CPSU,
when there had probably been consultation between them.

In Stalin's lifetime, there had been meetings under the aegis of
the Cominform and, since the dissolution of that body, there
had been regional conferences of West European parties.
There had also been meetings of the party leaders of the Warsaw
Pact countries. But on none of these occasions was it seriously
maintained that the party leaders were consulting together to
devise a common policy for the whole Communist movement.
Important changes of strategy and policy had been made at the
Twentieth and Twenty-first Congresses of the CPSU, at which
the foreign Communist leaders had played the part only of
spectators; and this was one of the main sources of Chinese
complaint against the Russians. The 1960 meeting, however,
was clearly designed (though perhaps with some reluctance on
the part of the Russians) to be a genuine conference with a full
exchange of views for the purpose of devising a common
programme for the whole Communist movement. In particular it
was intended to heal or resolve the conflict which had developed

between Moscow and Peking and which was in fact the main reason why the meeting was called. Hitherto Communist 'world strategy', and, indeed, Communist policy at every level and on every issue, had been devised in Moscow and relayed to the other parties. Now, for the first time since Stalin emasculated the Comintern, Communist leaders from all over the world were meeting together, nominally on a basis of complete equality, to lay down the principles which would govern the revolutionary movement for the future.

Despite the importance of the conference and although, as we now know, serious preparation for it had been going on in an international commission throughout September and October, no announcement of the conference appeared in the Communist press before it started or during its progress. While this was probably due in some part to the Communists' usual exaggerated concern for the secrecy of their policy discussions, it must also be regarded as reflecting some doubt about the outcome of the conference and the possibility that no agreement would be reached. It was not until December 2, when the conference was over, that the Soviet press published an announcement that it had been taking place 'in November' and gave the names of the eighty-one parties represented. But from the beginning, the composition of the delegations left no doubt about the importance of the conference, most of them being headed by the first secretary or other senior official of the party concerned. There were two important exceptions to this: the Chinese delegation was not led by Mao Tse-tung but by Liu Shao-chi, the deputy chairman of the CCP; and the Italian delegation was led by Luigi Longo, deputy secretary-general of the Italian CP, and not by Palmiro Togliatti, the party's secretary-general and veteran leader. It may well be that the 'dogmatic' Mao and the 'revisionist' Togliatti thought it wiser to stay out of what was bound to be a stormy meeting involving the risk of some loss of face.

The official communiqué* about the conference said that its participants had 'exchanged experiences and acquainted themselves with each other's views and positions, discussed topical problems of current international development and the Com-

* *See* Chronology: December 2, 1960.

munist movement in the interests of joint struggle for common aims – peace, democracy, national independence and socialism and unanimously adopted a Statement of the Communist and Workers' parties, as well as an appeal to the peoples of the whole world.' The discussion had been conducted, the announcement said, 'in an atmosphere of fraternal friendship on the basis of the immutable principles of Marxism-Leninism and proletarian internationalism.' To judge from the accounts of the proceedings which were later provided by some of the participants, this description of the conference fell somewhat short of the truth.

That the conference was characterised by something less than unanimity was apparent from the length of time it remained in session. Having presumably started work immediately after the November 7 celebrations, it did not succeed in publishing the final Statement until December 6, nearly three months after the preparatory commission had begun to thrash out the issues in dispute. Moreover, an examination of the Statement* itself did not suggest that any approximation of the Russian and Chinese views had taken place, but rather that it represented a papering-over of the differences which remained.

This much could be gathered from a knowledge of the issues in dispute between Moscow and Peking and a study of the final Statement, despite the secrecy that surrounded the proceedings of the conference. But subsequent revelations by officials of the Italian, French and Belgium Communist parties, as well as other apparently trustworthy material from unidentified sources, have thrown much interesting light on the actual debates that took place in Moscow and the real issues which the final Statement often served only to obscure.† It seems unlikely that these unusually revealing 'leaks' were made without Moscow's approval, but neither the Russian nor the Chinese party has yet chosen to publish an account of the 1960 meeting. Indeed, the Chinese have said that they refrained from describing what went on at 'this internal meeting of the fraternal parties' in the interests of the movement. They intended, they said, 'to give the true picture and clarify right and wrong at the proper time and place'.

* *See* Chronology: December 6, 1960.
† *See* Chronology: November 1960.

Before relating what went on at the conference it will be convenient, and perhaps helpful, to review in as simple terms as possible the issues in dispute. With the aid of such a summary it should be easier to assess the speeches at the conference, the terms of the final Statement and subsequent developments in the dispute. It is not maintained that any of these issues, or all of them taken together, was necessarily the *source* or *cause* of the dispute. But they were, and are, the issues over which the Russians and Chinese Communists fight out their battles, which have much deeper, and much less intellectual or 'ideological' roots. The following is merely a description, then, of the battlefield.

Both sides start with a definition of 'the nature of the epoch', from which the rest of their argument stems. To present the Chinese argument first: they contend that the present epoch is still, as it was in Lenin's day, one of imperialism and wars, and that, despite an admitted decline in the power of the imperialist (*i.e.* Western 'capitalist') world and a relative growth in the might of the socialist (*i.e.* Communist) camp, the revolutionary battle between imperialism and Communism is far from won; and, although the ultimate victory is not in question, the battle will be won only if the revolutionary forces intensify their efforts to win it. The world is divided into two mutually antagonistic camps between which there can be no collaboration and ultimately no compromise. Imperialism is the enemy, and the enemy must be defeated; every other consideration is subordinated to the need for carrying the revolution forward wherever and whenever possible.

This attitude determines, in turn, the Chinese view of the advent of nuclear weapons and the prospect of nuclear war. They minimise the devastation that nuclear war would cause and welcome the acquisition of nuclear power by the socialist camp, which they consider enhances the strength of the revolution. They argue that there is no reason to believe that aggressive imperialism will not start a nuclear war, which the socialist camp must aim to win; it is not within the power of the socialist camp to prevent such a war. At the same time, the deterrent power of nuclear weapons can be exploited for the promotion of and assistance to 'local' wars of various kinds. In these circumstances the policy of 'peaceful coexistence' and of seeking a disarmament agreement with the West can be no more than tactical moves and not long-term policy. A policy of direct negotiations with Western statesmen cannot produce results. 'Front' organisations, such as the 'peace movement', the World Federation of Trade Unions and similar bodies, should be kept as narrow as possible, so as to promote revolutionary ends and not dilute the revolutionary spirit. For the same reasons the Communists should be wary of association with other 'socialist' parties who were not committed to revolution. Just as the prospect of avoiding war with imperialism is an illusion, so is the prospect of a 'peaceful' takeover of power from the capitalists.

The Russians differ from the Chinese on every one of these basic theses. They argue that 'imperialism' *has* changed, and that the forces of 'socialism' have grown to such an extent as to be able to restrain the imperialists and complete the revolutionary process by power of superior economic and military strength and the force of example; the use of force is no longer necessary to promote revolution on the international or national plane. A sufficiently large number of influential people in the West, as well as of 'progressive forces' there, recognise the dangers of nuclear war to make it most improbable. The socialist camp has every interest in coming to terms with the West, so as to minimise the chances of war and liberate economic resources for the economic competition with capitalism, especially in the underdeveloped countries. No forceful action should be taken, such as the promotion of 'local' wars, which might lead to major war, since world war would be so destructive as to retard and not advance the progress of the revolution. In these circumstances the Communist governments had every reason to support 'national democracies' which had broken away from the imperialist camp, and Communist parties had interest in allying themselves with other 'socialist' and 'progressive' forces for the purpose of achieving power by democratic means. 'Front' organisations should be used to draw as wide a public as possible under Communist influence.

This was the 'ideological' battlefield. There was also the 'organisational' battlefield, centring around the related and far more practical questions of the 'unity of the international Communist movement' and the form which relations between the Communist parties should take. Here the actual position taken up by the two parties is more difficult to define. The Chinese appear to have taken (and to take still) the view that all parties in the Communist movement have equal rights in the working out of policy and that only policies and doctrines worked out jointly (as in Moscow in 1957) had binding force on the movement as a whole. No one party had the right to impose its views on the whole movement, or to decide what parties should or should not belong to the movement. But, while the Soviet Party could not impose its views on the others, it could be recognised as the 'leader' of the camp. The Chinese favoured both international meetings and the creation of some form of permanent international body or 'secretariat'.

The Russians appeared to be opposed to the setting up of any international organisation and to the naming of the Soviet Union as 'leader' of the Communist world. But they were equally opposed to 'fractional' activities within the movement, *i.e.* attempts by some parties to influence other parties through approaches to their members. This was, in effect, a demand for obedience by all parties to agreed decisions taken at conferences. And, despite their apparent unwillingness to be the 'leader', they wanted the statements of principle made at their Twentieth and Twenty-first Congresses to be accepted as valid additions to Marxism-Leninism.

This question of the 'unity of the movement' was, in fact, the most important and the most complex, because it was the one which came closest to the real issue: how policy for the Communist world was to be decided and by whom. There can be no doubt that, behind all the 'ideological' and 'organisational' issues, was the simple fact that the Russians, owners of the main wealth and the only nuclear power in the Communist world, were not prepared to have others deciding how that wealth and power should be used. At the same time, they did not want to lose the use and control of an international political movement which was an invaluable adjunct to their foreign policy. This was their dilemma: they wanted to be part of a 'united' international movement, but without giving up their exclusive control of their own resources, especially military resources. This dilemma inevitably put them in a difficult position on questions of 'democracy' within the camp. The Chinese, whose aim was simple – to acquire influence over bloc policy – found it easy to exploit the position in which the Russians found themselves.

Two other specific issues remain to be mentioned: those of the attitudes to be adopted to the Yugoslav and to the Albanian Communists. It might perhaps be said of both these parties that if they had not existed both Russians and Chinese would have had to invent them, for they have served very useful purposes in the dispute, enabling both Russians and Chinese to avoid naming each other publicly in the early stages of the dispute. Nor was the use of Yugoslavia and Albania as symbols of 'revisionism' and 'dogmatism' respectively entirely artificial. The Yugoslav Communists *were* revisionist in outlook, because their quarrel with Stalin and their exclusion from the Communist camp had forced them to revise their views of the West, to which they had been obliged to look, not unsuccessfully, for aid. Albanian 'dogmatism', which meant alliance with China, was also something forced on Enver Hoxha by Khrushchev's flirtations with Tito. Just as Tito turned to the West, so Hoxha turned to the Far East, not because he thought Mao a better Marxist than Khrushchev but because China was in practice the *only* country to whom he could turn for support. But the 'ideologies' of Tito and Hoxha were far less important than the practical roles they were to be called upon to play in the Sino-Soviet dispute, and especially in the Moscow conference of 1960. Attitudes towards Yugoslavia and Albania and assessments of the relative dangers of 'dogmatism' and 'revisionism' came to serve as indicators of the relative influence exerted at any moment on a particular party by Russians or Chinese.

It is not clear to what extent Khrushchev himself was directly involved in the work of the conference. He was named as head of the Soviet delegation, but it seems probable that much of the actual negotiating was done by Suslov and the other 'international' officials of the CPSU. Similarly it was Teng Hsiao-ping who did the talking for the Chinese delegation and not Liu Shao-chi. Nor is there any reliable or full account of what Suslov said in his opening speech to the conference, though it seems likely to have followed the general lines of the letter circulated earlier, referred to above. It was certainly a strong reaffirmation of the Soviet line on all issues and, in view of the secrecy which has been observed about it, it was probably outspoken in its criticism of the Chinese. Such information as we have of other speeches makes it clear that there was no attempt inside the conference to conceal the fact that it was primarily a confrontation of the Russian and Chinese views on major issues.

On the eve of the conference the delegations had heard Frol Kozlov, Khrushchev's deputy in the CPSU secretariat, restate the whole Soviet position in unmistakable terms: *

> The time when imperialism ruled everywhere has gone, never to return. The world socialist system, the formation of which is the most important historical event after the victory of the Great October socialist revolution, is now becoming the decisive factor in the development of human society. . . . Developing Marxism-Leninism creatively, the Communist Party of the Soviet Union came to a most important conclusion at its Twentieth Congress. At the present time there is no fatal inevitability of war, and war can be averted. This conclusion received unanimous support from the fraternal Communist and Workers' parties in the programmatic Document – the Declaration of the Moscow Conference . . . in 1957. The propositions of the Moscow Declaration were again confirmed in the communiqué of the Bucharest Conference of Marxist-Leninist parties.

Kozlov even went so far as to assert that the Twenty-first Congress of the CPSU had carried the development of Marxist thought a stage further with its declaration that there was a real possibility of 'excluding war from the life of society' even before the 'complete victory' of socialism on earth. He foresaw the possibility of 'forcing the warlike circles of imperialism to abandon their plans for unleashing another war'.

* *See* Chronology: November 6, 1960.

These and other aspects of the Soviet stand on 'ideological' issues were presumably repeated, possibly more forcibly, by Suslov in his opening speech. The delegates also had the CPSU letter, a commentary on it by Suslov and a draft declaration drawn up by the Russians. In all these documents, it appears, the Russians carried the war into the Chinese camp by accusing them of carrying on anti-Soviet 'fractional' activity in other Communist parties and in the mass organisations. In their draft declaration the Russians certainly proposed a ban on 'fractionalism' and a reference to the Twentieth and Twenty-first Congresses of the CPSU as 'models' for the rest of the movement.

Having thus stated their case and accused the Chinese, the Russians apparently sat back to see what the Chinese would do. Teng Hsiao-ping took up the cudgels early in the conference and used them with vigour throughout the proceedings. From the accounts provided by the European Communist parties it is possible to offer the following reconstruction of Teng's two speeches.

Teng directed the brunt of his attack against Khrushchev's ideological leadership of the Communist camp. He demanded the removal from the draft declaration of a passage describing the decision of the Twentieth and Twenty-first Congresses of the CPSU as 'a model of the positive development of revolutionary theory'. He declared that the Central Committee of the CPSU had, on a number of major questions of principle, 'departed in the most obvious way from the true path of Marxism-Leninism and the Moscow Declaration'. Following the Twentieth Congress, the CPSU had dragged the majority of Communist parties along the path of capitulation to imperialism. Teng rejected the policy of 'destalinisation'; he challenged the view that it was possible or useful to oppose the outbreak of a third world war; he disputed the possibility of 'different paths to socialism' and said the theory that the working-class might seize power in some countries without resort to force was 'utopian'. He appears also to have criticised attempts to establish a common front between Communists and socialists against the 'imperialists'.

On the question of peace and war, Teng declared that peaceful coexistence could be regarded only as a tactic, 'a means of disarming morally the capitalist countries'. Disarmament and coexistence would become possible only when 'socialist' countries alone were left in the world. He argued that 'local wars' did not involve risk of world war.

Some of Teng's sharpest attacks were naturally reserved for the Yugoslav 'revisionists'. He appears to have demanded the inclusion in the Declaration of a passage stating that 'one of the essential tasks of the Communist and Workers' parties is to isolate Yugoslavia from the working-class movement'.

Finally, on the question of the 'unity' of the Communist movement and the relationship between the various parties, Teng rejected the idea that the minority had to accept the general line laid down by the majority in the movement. He admitted more than once that 'practically all' the parties had followed the Russians along the path of revisionism and opportunism, and he appears to have been quite unmoved by finding an over-whelming majority against him. According to Luigi Longo, the Italian delegate, Teng's second speech showed that 'the Chinese comrades are not in the least disposed to take account of the arguments presented and the demands made by the representatives of the fraternal parties'. Teng apparently told the conference that his party would continue after the conference to advocate its own views even if they were not included in the final declaration. The Chinese claimed the right to pursue their 'fractional' activities without restraint. The correctness of their views, Teng said, would be demonstrated by history.

At the same time Teng urged the retention in the Declaration of the concept of a 'leading party' and supported the view that the Communist movement should be 'led by the Communist Party of the Soviet Union'. The Chinese were also presumably among, or behind, the few delegations which proposed the setting up of a permanent secretariat for the international movement.

It seems clear from the accounts of his speeches that Teng did not hesitate to criticise Khrushchev personally and to ridicule ideas especially associated with the Soviet leader. Longo referred to the 'attack of a personal nature on Comrade Khrush-chev and the leaders of the Soviet Party and government', and of 'grave accusations which exceeded all limits'. Teng's reference to humanism as a 'bourgeois concept', and his description of polite relations with Western statesmen as 'kneeling before imperialism', were obviously directed at Khrushchev.

The only delegation which is known to have supported the Chinese with any vigour was the Albanian. All the reports agree in saying that the Albanian delegate, Enver Hoxha, went even further than the Chinese in the content and manner of their attacks on Khrushchev. The Belgian account said:

> The Albanian Party distinguished itself by pressing the expression of its divergent ideas on several occasions to verbal extremes. One has in all truth to say that the Chinese delegation never dissociated itself from this slanging match, even when it became insulting.

Longo said that 'certain insulting insinuations' made by the Albanian delegate about Soviet policy 'sounded in our ears like an offence to the whole gathering'. According to Maurice Thorez, the French Communist leader: 'The members of our delegation listened to [Hoxha's speech] with a feeling of shame. These militant Communists had never heard language like it either in meetings of their own party or in gatherings of the international Communist movement.'

Apart from supporting Chinese ideological criticisms of the Soviet party, Hoxha attacked Khrushchev for his treatment of Albania itself. He objected to the fact that the Russians had entered into negotiations with Tito without first consulting Albania, and he indirectly accused Khrushchev of treating with the Greek politician Sophocles Venizelos at Albania's expense. He revealed that Khrushchev had approached the Albanian Party in August 1960 for support against the Chinese, thus providing the Chinese with material for accusing the Russians of 'fractionalism'. Hoxha clearly implied that the Russians had won over certain elements in the Albanian Party and army and attempted a 'revolution'. He accused Khrushchev of exploiting Albania's economic plight in an attempt to force her into submission:

Albania has suffered earthquakes, floods and a drought of 120 days and has been threatened by famine. Only 15 days' supply of wheat remained in stock. After a delay of 45 days, the USSR promised us 10,000 tons of wheat instead of 50,000 tons or, in other words, 15 days' supply of wheat to be delivered in September or October. These are unbearable pressures. The Soviet rats were able to eat while the Albanian people were dying of hunger, and we were asked to produce gold.

It was this attempt of Hoxha's to 'transform the ideological and political dispute into a disagreement affecting state relations between different Communist countries' which especially offended Longo. Thorez also took exception on this score to Hoxha who, he said, 'devoted the main part of his speech to questions relating to relations between states which have no place at all here, and to a crude attack on the Soviet Union, its Communist party and most particularly on Comrade N. S. Khrushchev'. Thorez considered Hoxha was 'deflecting the discussion from its main purpose'.

Thus the Communists continued, even in the privacy of such a meeting, to maintain a distinction between their ideological and practical relations. It appears that Teng Hsiao-ping also discussed relations between the Soviet and Chinese governments and complained at the reduction of Soviet aid. There can have been little doubt in the minds of the more intelligent delegates that there was a direct connexion between the 'ideological' and the 'economic'. Khrushchev himself does not seem to have tried to maintain the empty distinction and is said to have told Teng simply that 'we shall treat Albania like Yugoslavia'. 'Russia has lost an Albania; the People's' Republic of China has gained an Albania', he is supposed to have said. Hoxha was said to have retorted that whether Albania was in the camp or not did not depend on Khrushchev: a challenge which, coupled with Hoxha's other personal attacks on Khrushchev, may well have accounted for Russia's severing relations with Albania in 1961.

Having committed themselves to the pro-Chinese and anti-

Khrushchev cause, the Albanian leaders were determined to permit no compromise. Khrushchev sought to have a private meeting with Hoxha and Shehu, but at the same time circulated to the conference a document denouncing their 'anti-Soviet' attitude. When the meeting finally took place on November 12, the Albanian leaders indulged in what Khrushchev later described as 'provocations'. The Albanians then walked out of the conference and returned to Tirana. Khrushchev was reported to have said he had found it easier to come to an understanding with Macmillan than with Hoxha.

The debate continued throughout November, in formal sessions and speeches, in private meetings between delegates and in the form of letters and memoranda circulated among the participants. Though Khrushchev himself intervened in the discussions to defend the Soviet point of view, he seems to have left most of the work of refuting the Chinese to other delegates, among whom the Italian, Luigi Longo, and the Frenchman, Maurice Thorez, were certainly prominent and possibly the most outspoken. They and other delegates reaffirmed in now familiar terms the various Soviet 'theses' on coexistence and war. But most interesting for the later development of the dispute was their attitude on the question of relations within the Communist movement.

On the central question of the Russians' ideological leadership of the movement, Longo insisted that the new declaration should include a reference to the international significance of the decisions of the Twentieth and Twenty-first Congresses of the CPSU. It was, he said, a slander to say that the Central Committee of the CPSU had departed from Marxism. 'We regard as very healthy the shock which Comrade Khrushchev, as leader of the Central Committee of the CPSU, has given to Communist ideology and practice.' He added that the Italian Communists and working people cherished for Khrushchev 'a sincere and profound affection that has nothing formal about it'. In a note to Khrushchev towards the end of the conference, the Italians again insisted that there should be no compromise on the question of 'complete approval' for the decisions of the Twentieth Congress of the CPSU.

Similarly Thorez argued that since the CPSU was the most experienced party in every way and since the decisions of the Twentieth and Twenty-first Congresses reflected the experience of the *whole* international movement, they affected all parties and that this should be emphasised in the declaration.

On the issue of 'fractionalism', Longo declared that it was inadmissible that any Communist party should take up a position or undertake a political action 'opposed to the general line laid down by this conference or by any other international conference of our movement'. But the Italians were opposed to the suggestion made by 'some delegations' that 'a secretariat or some permanent body of that kind' should be set up at the end of the conference, and supported Khrushchev in rejecting any recognition of a 'leading party'. Thorez likewise opposed the setting up of a permanent secretariat—'which would turn into a sort of Information bureau [*i.e.* Cominform] which all the parties consider to be no longer applicable to the present state of a movement'. Rejecting any organised 'unity', Thorez hit on a new formula:

> The unity which we hold is a voluntary unity, but a real unity of all sections of our movement around the Communist Party of the Soviet Union. This unity is not and cannot be formal. It rests on a community of principle which experience constantly tests and enriches.

This was a Gallic formula, unlikely to satisfy the hard minds of the Peking Communists. It was Thorez also who devised the formula that the CPSU should be referred to as the 'avant-garde' of the Communist movement instead of the 'leader'. Like Longo, he wanted to see 'fractionalism' properly condemned, and he described some of the Chinese Communists' efforts to involve the French in 'fractional' activity at a meeting of the WFTU.

The question of the attitude to be adopted towards the Yugoslav Communists was dealt with at some length in the Italian note to Khrushchev. The Italians rejected the idea of 'isolating' the Yugoslavs, while still 'severely condemning' their policies. They wanted to avoid offending Yugoslav national feeling, 'which we know from experience is very sensitive', as well as to avoid creating a bad impression among social democrats and public opinion in general.

Thus, apart from the differences between the Russians and Chinese on points of 'ideology', which had been apparent earlier, the conference revealed a number of 'organisational' issues upon which the two sides took up conflicting positions. These issues were: the authority of the Soviet Communist Party in the Communist movement and its right to legislate for the whole movement; Soviet 'leadership' of the Communist movement; the creation of a permanent body to direct the affairs of the movement; the right of individual parties to pursue policies at odds with the 'general line' of the movement; the question of relations with the Yugoslav Communists; and the question of relations with the Albanian Communists. On all these questions the Russians and Chinese took opposed positions and, while the rest of the delegates appeared to line up on one side or the other, certain gradations of opinion emerged, as will later appear.

There is little evidence that Russians or Chinese modified their respective points of view in the course of the conference. But both sides remained sufficiently interested in maintaining at least the superficial 'unity' of the movement for them to be able to make the verbal concessions which made an agreed final 'Statement' possible.

The Statement was, as Mr. Zagoria has said*, a 'masterpiece of ambiguity', which evaded a clear solution of the main issues and wrapped them in a cloak of verbosity from which either side to the dispute could, and did, draw sustenance. On the ideological issues the Statement included most of the Russians' main innovations: that the socialist system 'was becoming the decisive factor in the development of human society', that nuclear war would reduce the world's major centres to ruins, that there was no 'fatal inevitability' of war, that the struggle for peace was the primary task, and that there was a 'real possibility' of excluding war from society altogether. The Statement also affirmed the possibility of a 'peaceful realisation of the socialist revolution'.

* Donald S. Zagoria: *The Sino-Soviet Conflict; see* Bibliography.

On the other hand, the Statement reflected Chinese influence in its lengthy condemnation of American 'imperialism', in its insistence on the continuing danger of war, in its assertion that 'peaceful coexistence' did not mean the abandonment of class struggle or national-liberation wars. On all these theoretical points the Statement was full of contradictions and inconsistencies.

On the practical issues, the distribution of points seemed to be clearer. Thus the contribution to Marxist thought made by the Twentieth and Twenty-first Congresses of the CPSU was acknowledged but somewhat diluted by reference at the same time to the 1957 Declaration and 'documents of other Communist and Workers' parties'. The 'historic' decisions of the Twentieth Congress of the CPSU were recognised, however, to be of significance not only for the Russians and to have 'marked the beginning of a new stage in the international Communist movement and made possible its further development on the basis of Marxism-Leninism'.

Despite the strong views expressed by the French and Italians, the Statement contained no specific condemnation of 'fractionalism', limiting itself to emphasis on the need for amity and for every party to 'observe the assessments and conclusions worked out jointly by the fraternal parties at their conferences'. Such conferences were recognised to be of value for 'working out common positions in the struggle for common aims', though there was no reference to a common 'programme' binding on the parties. The only clear attempt to place some restriction on the freedom of the Chinese to pursue their 'fractional' activities came in the clause:

> When questions arise in one party or the other concerning the activity of another fraternal party, then its leaders approach the leaders of the party concerned; in case of necessity meetings and consultations are conducted.

This was coupled with a Declaration that the parties were all 'independent and equal' and that they worked out their own policies in accordance with conditions in their own countries. There was clearly plenty of room within such formulas for the

Chinese to carry on their independent line. But the absence of any reference to the formation of a permanent international body of any kind showed that the Russians had had their own way on issues which they regarded as essential.

On the question of the status of the Soviet Communist Party, the Statement adopted the Thorez formula. It was declared to be 'the generally recognised avant-garde' of the world Communist movement.

The 'Yugoslav variety of international opportunism' was condemned unanimously and the Yugoslav Communists were said to have 'betrayed Marxism-Leninism', to have devised an 'anti-Leninist, revisionist programme', and to have 'torn their country out of the socialist camp'. But there was no demand that the Yugoslav Communists should be 'isolated', nor were they spoken of in the abusive terms held by the Chinese and Albanians. There was evidence here that the Italian arguments had proved persuasive. Moreover, there was a paragraph devoted to 'dogmatism and sectarianism' which 'can also become the main danger at one or another stage in the development of particular parties'. But that was as far as the Statement got to criticising the Chinese.

That the Statement did, in fact, represent a compromise involving some concessions on both sides was confirmed by several comments that appeared later. The Italians said in a letter to Khrushchev at the end of the conference that they regarded the final text of the Statement as 'excessively verbose' and 'a step backwards compared with the precision and clarity of the Moscow Declaration of 1957 and also by comparison with the draft which you submitted to the meeting in September'. This, they added, was obviously a result of 'the difficulties encountered in trying to draw up a version acceptable to everybody'. The Belgians commented after the conference that it was disturbing to find that:

> after a full-scale discussion lasting a month, preceded by a preparatory discussion lasting even longer, they had managed to sign a declaration so carefully 'balanced' and of such a kind that it would be possible to make use of it to justify the statement, defence and

application of political theses sometimes diametrically opposed and often outrageously divergent.

The Chinese said later* of the 1960 meeting that, while they had 'upheld Marxism-Leninism' and opposed 'erroneous views' held by other parties, they also 'made necessary compromises on certain questions'.

The true significance of this meeting of eighty-one Communist parties in Moscow in November 1961 was that the Russians and Chinese, had failed, after long and exhaustive discussions and despite the presence of many of the best brains in the Communist movement, to compose their differences on the 'ideological' or the 'organisational' plane. Within the movement, indeed, the conference probably served to draw attention to the extent of the rift between Moscow and Peking and to oblige leaders of many parties not previously aware of or involved in the dispute to consider its implications for themselves. The conference marked the beginning, not of agreement between the two sides but of the process of rallying support for each of them, of 'polarisation' in the Communist movement. Some parties, for example, the Poles, the Italians and the French, alarmed by the violence of the Chinese assault, rallied strongly to Khrushchev's side. Others, impressed by the outspokenness of the Chinese, began to turn their eyes more to Peking for leadership, as was the case with the parties in North Korea, Burma and Japan.

Perhaps the most significant feature of the 1960 conference was not the fact that the Russians were able to have their way in most issues (since their voting majority was never in doubt), but that they had to make so many concessions to the Chinese point of view. In theory they could have steam-rollered through a statement in the form they originally proposed. In practice they made obvious concessions to the Chinese over such issues as 'fractionalism' and 'Yugoslav revisionism'. That they did so can mean only that, even among party leaders who were ultimately pro-Russian, there were some who had doubts about Khrushchev's line and who found some reason in

* *People's Daily*, February 27, 1963.

Chinese arguments. This was clearly the case over the question of the attitude to be adopted towards the Yugoslav Communists, about which the French were much less certain than the Italians, and the Czechs less convinced than the Poles.

The really new feature revealed by the 1960 meeting was that, for the first time in thirty years, the leaders of world Communism were faced with real political issues upon which they had to take up position, and it was this that did more than anything else to inject a new political life into the movement. It was a welcome development to the Chinese, but less welcome to the Russians, because it was through such meetings that the Chinese could hope to exert an influence on 'camp policy'. It was probably this consideration that persuaded the Chinese to maintain at all costs the façade of 'unity' and to subscribe to views with which they did not agree. They had no interest in breaking up the movement, in which their word was only just beginning to be heard. Having made their début in the international Communist forum, they were prepared to withdraw and await the next opportunity to advance their cause. The Russians, on the other hand, as they learnt the lesson of 1960, would be reluctant to engage in another encounter of that nature. On the essential 'organisational' issue: that of setting up a permanent international body (with inevitable Chinese representation), Khrushchev had made no hint of a concession. He had not, it is true, succeeded in pushing through a ban on 'fractionalism'. But that was not essential; he knew the Chinese would in any case continue their efforts to win particular parties away from Moscow, and he would simply have to take steps to counter Chinese influence. So long as he could avoid another international gathering on the 1960 model he could hope to isolate the Chinese from the rest of the movement, and this now appeared to be his main objective.

It was typical of the hypocrisy that dominates Communist politics that the Moscow meeting which first clearly revealed the full scope and bitterness of the conflict between the Russians and Chinese for leadership of the Communist world was followed by a carefully staged demonstration of Sino-Soviet 'friendship'. Liu Shao-chi, now heading what was called a Chinese 'party-government' delegation, set off to visit a number of Soviet cities and provide an excuse for the Soviet press to proclaim 'the eternal, indestructible friendship between the great peoples of the USSR and China'. There was in fact little natural warmth to be found in the Russian provincial countryside in December.

X

SHADOW BOXING, 1961

Russia has lost an Albania; China has gained an Albania.
Khrushchev, November 6, 1960

The year 1961 was not eventful for the development of relations between Russia and China. The two contestants for power in the Communist world appeared to have fought themselves to a standstill in November 1960, and had no choice but to retreat to their corners in 1961 and take stock of the situation. The conflict between them was continued, so to speak, by proxy, through the medium of Albania which became the storm-centre in the dispute. One of the main reasons for the relative lull in the Sino-Soviet quarrel in 1961 was undoubtedly the fact that both Russian and Chinese leaders were very much preoccupied during the year with their own domestic problems.

Despite their protestations of 'unity' and 'undying friend-ship' immediately after the Moscow conference, neither the Russians nor the Chinese lost much time in making it clear that they were unchanged in their basic views. As early as December 15, the Chinese theoretical journal *Red Flag* made it clear that there were many issues upon which agreement had not been reached in Moscow. In January 1961 the Central Committee of the Chinese Communist Party heard Teng Hsiao-ping's report on the Moscow meeting and passed a resolution approving the Chinese delegation's work and pointing out what it considered the main significance of the meeting. This was a strictly 'Chinese' interpretation of the Statement, omitting those features with which they disagreed, notably any reference to the authority of the Twentieth Congress of the CPSU and stressing the Chinese 'militant' anti-imperialist view of peaceful coexistence.

On January 6 Khrushchev gave a conference of senior Communist officials in Moscow a review of the Moscow Conference and the problems discussed.* He outlined for them the Soviet view of Communist world strategy, differing in many respects from the Chinese version. In particular he provided a clearer, if still inconclusive, statement of the Soviet position on the 'leadership' of the camp. Explaining the Russians' rejection of the formula 'led by the Soviet Union', Khrushchev said that all parties were completely equal and each was responsible to the whole movement. The merit of the Soviet Union lay in its having 'blazed the trail' to socialism, in being 'the most powerful country' in the camp, in its 'vast positive experience', and in being the first to embark on the 'full-scale building of socialism'. It was the 'universally recognised vanguard'.

But it was 'impossible and unnecessary', said Khrushchev, to lead all the countries and parties 'from a single centre'. There were no rules governing relations between the parties, only a common ideology, loyalty to which was 'the main condition of our solidarity and unity'. The Moscow conference had been an occasion for the various parties to 'set their watches', and the Declaration and Statement were their common timepiece. He concluded by underlining the 'exceptional importance' of close relations between the Russian and Chinese parties.

It is not recorded whether the assembled ideologists found Khrushchev's explanations satisfactory. But it would be strange if among these very serious gentlemen there was none who wondered why, if the various parties were so united and so loyal to common beliefs, they could not have some central office or organisation, not necessarily to direct or 'lead' them but simply to co-ordinate their common activities. Somebody must surely have wondered *why* Khrushchev was so anxious to keep the whole movement free of all organisational forms.

At the end of 1960, the Chinese revealed that their country had been struck by an unprecedented series of 'natural disasters' in which over half China's arable land had been more or less seriously affected. Droughts, floods and disease had had a

* *See* Chronology: January 6, 1961.

disastrous effect on crops, bringing the danger of famine and rendering impossible the fulfilment of the country's over-ambitious economic plans. 1961 was only slightly better than 1960 and did nothing to improve the country's general economic condition. These disasters, and the shortages of foodstuffs and basic raw materials they entailed, forced on the Chinese leaders a change of policy and in particular the abandonment of the 'great leap forward' campaign. Though these economic problems did not, perhaps, at any point bring the stability of the Communist régime or Mao's leadership into question, there can be no doubt that they served to weaken the position of the Chinese, and in particular to make them even more dependent upon Soviet economic aid.

There were, however, no signs that the Russians were disposed to make serious efforts to help the Chinese out of their difficulties. After long-drawn-out talks it was announced in April that the Russians and Chinese had agreed upon their economic exchanges for 1961, that the Russians had agreed to defer repayment of China's debt incurred in 1960 because of the 'great natural disasters', and that they had also promised to 'lend' the Chinese 500,000 tons of sugar interest-free. In June the Russians let it be known that the Chinese had run into debt in their trade with the Soviet Union in 1960 to the extent of $320 million and that they had ceased deliveries of the food-stuffs with which they paid for Soviet goods.

More revealing of the condition of Sino-Soviet 'state' relations, however, was the announcement in February that the Chinese had arranged to purchase about a million tons of wheat and barley from Canada and over 1 million tons of wheat and flour from Australia. By mid-1961 the Chinese had placed orders for a total of 10 million tons of grain with the two countries mentioned and incurred a debt of some $340 million. The political significance of these purchases was even greater than the economic. They indicated that the Russians were sufficiently incensed with the Chinese leaders to try to exploit their economic plight to wring political concessions from them and even to drive home a political lesson. For, however much the plight of the Chinese economy might be due to natural causes, the Communists had practically admitted that their own policies were also largely to blame. After the exaggerated claims they had been making a few years previously, it was a bitter political pill for them to swallow to have to turn to the 'imperialists' for foodstuffs. It has been said in excuse of the Russians that they had their own agricultural problems and that they were therefore in no position to help the Chinese out. But this is difficult to accept. However inefficient Russia's 'collective' agriculture was (and still is), it had succeeded since 1953 in raising substantially the total grain harvest and the Soviet government had certainly by 1961 been able to build up substantial stocks of grain. If Khrushchev had really wanted to ease Mao's lot he could have done so, and thus saved the Chinese precious 'hard' currency. But Krushchev had already warned the Chinese, by his treatment of Albania in 1960, that there was a direct connexion between 'party' and 'state' relations and that political rebels must not expect economic favours. In 1961 he let the Chinese see that he meant business.

Surprisingly enough, China's parlous economic state did not prevent the Chinese government from continuing to act the 'great power' and extending economic aid to countries in Asia and Africa. At the end of 1960, China agreed to extend technical aid and a loan of £30 million to North Korea. In January she extended a similar sum to Burma, with which she also concluded a frontier agreement. Chou En-lai visited Cambodia in May 1961, and a promise of aid was made. Kwame Nkrumah, the President of Ghana, visited China in August to sign a treaty of friendship and received promises of economic aid and trade. In September a technical aid agreeement was signed with Guinea, to whom a loan of £25 million had been granted. Thus the Chinese rulers made it clear that China's own economic problems, and even economic pressure from Russia, would not force them to abandon their efforts to be the friend of the underdeveloped peoples of Asia and Africa.

The Russians could not permit themselves to be outdone in this field. They also concluded aid agreements and treaties with North Korea, Cambodia, Ghana and Guinea, as well as with Afghanistan and Indonesia. Moreover, while the Chinese were unable, on account of the frontier dispute they had provoked, to make friends with Nehru, the Russians were deeply involved in economic aid to India.

But, if the Russians were by no means as hard pressed as the Chinese, they had even more important problems to worry them than their position in Asia, and they too had their economic problems at home.

In February Khrushchev initiated one of his periodic reorganisations of Soviet agriculture which, despite some progress, was far from achieving its target of providing the Soviet population with more and better food than the Americans received. If Khrushchev was sure that the Chinese communes were wrong, he seemed still to be short of finding the right answer to the problem of persuading an expropriated peasantry to work with enthusiasm.

In June Khrushchev had a brief and largely unproductive meeting with President Kennedy, which did not appear to support his view of the value of personal contacts between heads of state, though it enabled him to test at first-hand the quality of the new President. He was able to tell the Soviet people afterwards only that he considered the meeting 'worth while', and to express the hope that President Kennedy would remain aware of the responsibility that rested on him and Khrushchev for a solution of international problems. It seems unlikely that the Chinese leaders were greatly impressed by Khrushchev's renewed venture into 'summitry', and they practically ignored it in their press. Later in the summer the Russians provoked a crisis over the question of Berlin, by allowing a wall to be built cutting East Berlin off from West Berlin. This had the effect of stabilising the Communist régime in East Germany, but could hardly be regarded as a major success for Khrushchev's foreign policy.

In the midst of these events, the Russians published on July 30 their much-delayed new Party Programme. It was intended to be widely discussed by the members of the Party before being submitted to the Twenty-second Congress of the Soviet Party due to be held in October. The proposal to have a new programme to replace the one introduced in 1919 was first made at the Nineteenth Congress in 1952, but Stalin's death and the subsequent changes of men and policies had delayed the production of the document. Its appearance was an event of great importance in the CPSU and the Communist world at large, since the programme contained the quintessence of the wisdom of the best brains in the 'most experienced' party of the movement. Communists the world over would look to the new programme for definite answers to the questions and disputes that were upsetting the movement.

It was in practice a disappointing piece of work: long, verbose and diffuse like all products of the Marxist mind, and it failed singularly to catch the imagination of the people it was aimed at. For the most part it was no more precise on the major 'ideological' issues than the Moscow Statement of 1956 had been, though it naturally gave full weight to the Soviet view of things. It made little impression in the Communist world, though it was hailed dutifully in those parts which looked to Moscow for guidance. It was largely ignored by the Chinese, who have neither reproduced it nor commented on it seriously. Nevertheless, certain sections of it are relevant to the dispute with China for their treatment of the important question of relations within the Communist camp.

Dealing with the nature of the 'world system of socialism' (*i.e.* the Communist countries), the Programme declared that it represented 'a new type of economic and political relations between countries'. What they had in common economically and politically created 'an objective basis for lasting and friendly inter-state relations in the socialist camp', in which '. . . nobody has and nobody can have any special rights or privileges'.

How exactly the Russians expected these friendly relations to work out in practice, especially in the sensitive sphere of economics, was dealt with in a special section on 'the construction of Communism in the USSR and collaboration between socialist countries'. Here the Soviet scholastics were trying to provide an answer to the questions: to what extent did the Soviet Union have to help other countries, including China, to achieve 'Communism'; to what extent should Soviet plans be cut down to enable other Communist countries to catch up; would the Soviet Union inevitably enter 'Communism' first or would all or some countries reach the happy state together? In short, what were the Russians' obligations *as Communists* to help other Communist countries?

The answer was this: the Russians regarded *their* building of Communism (*i.e.* their own economic progress) as part of the progress of the whole 'socialist camp' towards Communism, Different countries would inevitably advance at different rates. but their links with other Communist countries enabled them to cut down the processes and opened up 'the possibility that their transition to Communism would be more or less simultaneous, within the limits of one historic epoch'. This was hardly a precise formulation.

The Russians then went on to remind other Communist countries that 'the raising and levelling up of the general level of the economy of socialist countries is achieved primarily through each country's full use of its own internal resources ...' It was up to the people of each country to create the bases of Communism and thus strengthen the whole 'camp'. This was the Russians' answer to the Chinese contention that it was Russia's 'international duty' to help other Communist countries, and certainly China. This was a question of prime importance in Sino-Soviet relations. The Chinese, with unlimited ambitions and little wealth, argued that the Russians had a *political* and *moral* obligation to help them advance economically. But the Russians saw in China a bottomless pit in which all their own economic progress could easily be lost. While acknowledging a duty to help, they threw the main responsibility back on the Chinese. By the time the Programme was published, the argument was somewhat academic, for the Russians had already substantially reduced their aid to China. It was an interesting example of the way 'ideology' was made to serve practical politics.

The Programme also contained a relatively mild condemnation of the Yugoslavs. Yugoslavia had 'set out on the path to socialism', it said, but its leaders' revisionist policies threatened to lose the 'revolutionary gains'. By the time the Programme was approved in October, this formula too was out of date and Moscow's relations with Belgrade were on the upgrade.

The first and surest sign of Moscow's intention to improve

relations with Yugoslavia, whatever the ideological pundits said, came at the end of March when the Soviet and Yugoslav governments signed a trade agreement which provided for a doubling of their mutual trade by 1965 and for transactions totalling $800 million over the five-year period. The Russians undertook to supply considerable quantities of equipment and raw materials for Yugoslav industry, in exchange for the products of Yugoslavia's shipyards and factories.

Shortly afterwards, an exchange of visits by foreign ministers was agreed, and in July Koça Popović, the Yugoslav Foreign Minister, had talks with Khrushchev, Mikoyan and Gromyko in Moscow. This meeting, which was the first high-level contact between the two governments since the chill came over Soviet-Yugoslav relations at the end of 1957, produced a communiqué saying that the views of the two governments 'are similar or coincide on the major international questions'. Although Gromyko did not visit Belgrade until April 1962, it was quite clear that early in 1961 a decision had been taken in Moscow to restore relations with Yugoslavia whatever the Chinese might think and say and whatever lip-service was paid in policy documents to the need for combating Yugoslav 'revisionism'. By September, Khrushchev was telling an American news-paperman: 'Of course we consider Yugoslavia a socialist country'; a statement utterly at variance with the treatment of the Yugoslav Communists in the Moscow Statement of 1960. Once again, Khrushchev appeared to be courting Tito with greater eagerness than the Yugoslav's charms seemed to justify. Though the Russian leader doubtless had many secondary reasons for wanting better relations with Yugoslavia, it is difficult to avoid the conclusion that his main motive was deliberately to provoke the Chinese. It was Khrushchev's way of trying to force the Chinese to yield or to take action which would condemn them in the eyes of the Communist world.

This unusual technique of conducting a political dispute 'by proxy', through the medium of other countries acting as puppets or stalking-horses, is one of the most interesting aspects of the Sino-Soviet dispute and worthy of deeper study. It applied equally to the Russian and Chinese treatment of Albania and in both cases the use of these two relatively small and unimportant countries provided the main disputants with a means of avoiding direct conflict or situations from which neither of them could retreat with dignity. The Chinese, no less than the Russians, seemed to find this form of indirect conflict more convenient.*

The function of symbol and stalking-horse was even more apparent in the case of Albania. The steady worsening of Soviet relations with Albania, culminating in the de facto severance of relations in the autumn, was the main development in the Sino-Soviet dispute in 1961. By their treatment of the Albanian Communists, the Russians appeared to be demonstrating how far they were prepared to go in the defence of their views in their dispute with Peking, and to be challenging the Chinese to react.

While it was apparent to the serious observer that the Moscow meeting in 1960 had done no more than paper over the cracks in Sino-Soviet relations, and though there were indications in the months following the meeting that relations between Moscow and both Peking and Tirana were strained, the secrecy surrounding political life in the Communist world and the absence of normal sources of information, especially in China and Albania, made it impossible to follow developments closely. It was particularly difficult because the most significant developments were taking place in Albania, where there were only three small Western diplomatic missions (France, Italy and Turkey) and no Western press representation at all.† The few significant events which did reach the Western press (such as the revelations made at the Albanian Communist Party's congress in February and the departure of the Soviet submarines from their base at Vlore in May) were not easy to assess without being able to see the rest of the picture. While the tone of Albanian propaganda left no doubt about the tension in Tirana, it did not reveal what was taking place there. This was

* Albania and Yugoslavia played in the Sino-Soviet conflict a role similar to that played by Cuba in the Soviet-American confrontation at the end of 1962.
† Some West German newspapermen, including Harry Hamm, were allowed to visit Albania as tourists in 1961. I was able to make two similar visits in the spring and autumn of 1962.

learnt only from the revelations made by the Albanians in 1962 and from reports of visitors. The full story has been reconstructed by Professor Griffith in his detailed study* of Albania's part in the Sino-Soviet dispute, to which the following account owes a great deal.

It seems probable that Khrushchev decided, very soon after his stormy meeting with Hoxha during the Moscow meeting in 1960 and Hoxha's precipitate departure from Moscow, that there was no further point in maintaining relations of any kind with Albania. By the end of 1960 Albania was for Russia only an economic burden and represented no asset at all. Khrushchev had tried and failed to remove Hoxha, and Hoxha had demonstrated that he would not align himself with Khrushchev on whom he had made bitter personal attacks. The Russians had no means at their disposal for enforcing their will on the Albanian leaders, and to go on supporting them in economic or other ways would inevitably appear like a defeat for Moscow. This, and the prospect of being able to make an example of Albania in the dispute with China, rather than (as Professor Griffith suggests) a decision to try and bring Albania back into line, would seem to account for the gradual severance of Russian relations with Albania during 1961.

The Albanian economy was extremely backward and progress with the country's industrialisation depended almost entirely upon aid from the Soviet Union and the more advanced Communist countries of Eastern Europe. There had already been evidence of conflict between the Albanian leaders' ambitious plans to turn their country into an industrial power, and the extent to which the Russians were willing or able to subsidise such plans. At the end of 1958 aid had been stepped up, and in 1961 all the main industrial projects in the country were under the direction of Soviet or East European specialists. The Russians now proceeded to withdraw this aid.

The Soviet engineer in charge of building the 'Palace of Culture' (a present from the Russians which was intended to dominate the centre of Tirana) is said to have left for Moscow in October 1960 and to have taken all the working plans with

---

* *Albania and the Sino-Soviet Rift*, William E. Griffith, MIT Press, Cambridge, Mass., 1963.

him. In December the Russians appear to have made the con-clusion of a new trade and credit agreement dependent upon the holding of talks between Khrushchev and Hoxha, which the Albanians rejected in January, as they were presumably expected to do. (The day after the Albanians rejected the Soviet conditions an Albanian trade delegation took off for Peking.) In January the Russians stopped delivering building materials for the 'Palace', ignored a request for the retention of specialists, and told the Albanians they were withdrawing their oil engineers. These actions prompted reaction by the Albanian authorities, including some harassing of the Russians in Albania, and this in turn provided the Russians with grounds for announcing, in a letter dated April 26, the cancellation of all economic aid to Albania.

Relations in other spheres worsened at the same time. Soviet and East European diplomatists in Tirana were subjected to the same rigorous supervision as had previously been reserved for Western representatives. In the summer the size of Communist diplomatic missions was radically reduced and the flow of tourists from Russia and Eastern Europe ceased. At the end of May, the Russian submarines which had been occupying the base on Sasseno island at Vlore were withdrawn. It seems probable that, from July 1961, the only Russians remaining in Albania were a few diplomatists in the embassy in Tirana. From January the embassy had been in the charge of Colonel-General Joseph Shikin, a very senior official in the *apparat* of the CPSU and a former head of the Political Administration of the Soviet armed forces. No diplomatist, he was obviously appointed to supervise the delicate operation of the retreat from Tirana. He left Tirana for good on August 19, being replaced by a chargé d'affaires. The operation was, to all intents and purposes, over.

While the Russians were thus making it clear that they had 'written off' Albania as an ally and were busy winding up their interests in the country, the Chinese proceeded to step into the gap they were leaving. In April the Chinese government granted Albania credits totalling 112.5 million roubles ($123 million) spread over four years, and later in the year they purchased 60,000 tons of wheat from Canada, at a cost of some $3 million, and had it shipped to Albania. The Albanians had found a new friend.

While these moves were taking place behind the scenes, the Albanians' public reaction took the form of increasingly, bitter and outspoken denunciations of Yugoslavia. Articles in the party newspapers, speeches by Albanian leaders at the Fourth Congress of the Albanian Communist Party in February, and charges made at the trial of Admiral Teme Sejku and others in May all depicted Yugoslavia as the chief enemy. It was, however, quite clear that Albanian fury was directed as much against Khrushchev as Tito. In January *Zeri i Popullit* stated, in direct contradiction to Khrushchev's contention, that 'no Communist who holds firmly to the positions of Marxism-Leninism can say that the Tito clique is building socialism in Yugoslavia'. The Albanian leaders denounced Yugoslav 'neutralism', claimed that there was nothing at all in common between the foreign policy of the Communist camp and Yugoslavia, and said the Yugoslav Communists were 'restoring capitalism' and acting as a 'bridgehead of imperialism'. There were no worse charges in the Communist book.

Meanwhile the identification of China and Albania had been made manifest in statements by Albanian and Chinese leaders in February. Abdyll Kellezi, the Albanian spokesman, described the friendship of the Albanian and Chinese peoples as 'great and unbreakable', and aimed against 'American imperialism and its lackey, the Belgrade Tito clique'. Chiang Nan-hsiang, chairman of the Chinese-Albanian Friendship Society, told the Albanians: 'Your victories are our victories . . . serious blows at the imperialist camp headed by US imperialism and modern revisionism represented by the Tito clique of Yugoslavia, are at the same time contributions to the cause of world peace and human progress.' Meanwhile, as the new Peking-Tirana 'axis' was being formed, the Russians were beginning to implement a new trade agreement with Yugoslavia and arranging for talks between their foreign ministers.

The two policies of the Communist world: the left-wing 'dogmatism' of the Chinese Communists, and the right-wing 'revisionism' of the Russians – had thus each acquired by mid-1961 a small country to represent its policy. By withdrawing aid from Albania and extending it to Yugoslavia, the Russians could demonstrate in practice what their policy meant and make clear just how far they were prepared to go in realising it. By stepping up aid to the Albanians in their defiance of Moscow, the Chinese were also able to show that they meant business. When the Albanians, presumably not without reference to Peking, attacked the 'Tito clique', this was equivalent to a Chinese attack on Khrushchev. In this way, the Russian and Chinese Communists were able to continue their conflict without indulging in direct polemics and revealing the depths of their disagreement to the 'enemy' in the West. Among the advantages of this arrangement was the fact that it left both sides to the dispute free to withdraw, if they wished, with a minimum loss of face. The Chinese commitment in Albania and the Russian involvement with Yugoslavia were never so deep that either of them could not have withdrawn and left the official record clean, so far as actual denunciations of the other side were concerned.

XI

TEMPERS RISE

To bring quarrels between fraternal parties and fraternal countries into the open in the face of the enemy cannot be regarded as a serious, Marxist-Leninist approach.

Chou En-lai, October 1961*

The Twenty-second Congress of the Soviet Communist Party, held in Moscow in October 1961, was an event of considerable importance for the Communist movement and for the evolution of the Sino-Soviet dispute, although its significance in this connexion has tended to be ignored. All the preparations for the Congress in 1961 gave the impression that it would consist of little more than the granting of the customary unanimous approval to the new Programme and Rules of the Party: documents of surprisingly little originality which had already been published and discussed. There appeared to be little likelihood that the Twenty-second Congress would provide the sort of dramatic surprises that the Twentieth Congress of 1956 had produced in Khrushchev's unexpected denunciation of Stalin. And yet, in the event, the Twenty-second Congress turned out to be one of the more lively of Communist gatherings and to be no less surprising in its development than the Twentieth.

Though the discussion and approval of the Programme and Rules remained formally the main business of the Congress, the proceedings in fact centred round renewed denunciations of Stalin and the Stalinist 'anti-party group' and of the Albanian Communists. The Twenty-second Congress became in fact – and for no apparent reason – a most vigorous reaffirmation of the decisions of the Twentieth Congress. The principal reason for this surprising development is to be found in the

* Chou En-lai, speech to the Twenty-second Congress, October 19, 1961.

relations between Moscow and Peking. Nothing else can adequately explain the course which the Twenty-second Congress took.

Like previous congresses of the CPSU, it was attended by the leaders of the world's Communist parties, and was clearly intended to have international significance. The Chinese Communist Party's delegation was led, however, by Chou En-lai and not Mao Tse-tung, which was in itself a downgrading of the Congress by the Chinese. The Albanian Party was not represented at all, presumably because the Russians had not invited it to send representatives. All other parties were represented by their acknowledged leaders.

The main political report to the Congress was made on its opening day by Khrushchev,* who presented in already familiar terms a lengthy defence of the policies pursued by the party since 1956. The most significant section of his speech was that in which he dealt again with the Party's attitude towards Stalin and his works, with the 'anti-party group' and with the Albanian Communists.

Khrushchev stated for the first time what had become apparent since 1956: that the CPSU had been deeply and bitterly divided between Stalinists and anti-Stalinists before the Twentieth Congress and that it had been a case of one or the other side gaining the upper hand. Khrushchev had never before put the Stalin issue in such concrete terms. For the party not to have broken with Stalin, he said, would have entailed, among other things, 'a slowing down of the country's economic development, a lowering of the tempo of Communist construction, and consequently a worsening of the material conditions of the working people'. In the field of foreign affairs, he said, failure to have broken with Stalinism 'would have led to a weakening of the Soviet Union's positions in the world arena, and to a worsening of relations with other countries, which would have been fraught with serious consequences'. Having then firmly identified Lenin with the anti-Stalin course, Khrushchev went on to relate how Molotov and his associates had resisted the 'struggle of the new with the old'. But they had

* *See* Chronology: October 17, 1961.

been defeated, and the 'international Communist movement' had warmly approved the line of the Twentieth Congress. This approval, Khrushchev claimed, had been reflected in the Declaration of 1957 and the Statement of 1960, which had declared that the Twentieth Congress had 'opened a new stage in the international Communist movement'.

Having thus extended the significance of the anti-Stalinist line to the whole international movement, Khrushchev turned his attention immediately to the Albanian Communists. They had at first approved the sessions of the Twentieth and Twenty-first Soviet Congresses, but had more recently 'without any reason sharply changed their political course and taken the path of a sudden worsening of relations with our party and with the Soviet Union'. They no longer concealed their disapproval of the decisions of the Twentieth Congress.

But, Khrushchev concluded, the Twentieth Congress course was a 'Leninist course' and 'we cannot yield in such a matter of principle either to the Albanian leaders or to anyone else'. The CPSU would continue undeviatingly to carry out the policies laid down at its Twentieth Congress. 'No one will succeed in deflecting us from the Leninist path!' And if the Albanian leaders wanted friendship with the CPSU and the other parties, 'they must reject their mistaken views and return to the path of unity and close collaboration in the brotherly family of the socialist commonwealth, the path of unity with the whole international Communist movement'.

Khrushchev's treatment of relations with the Albanian Communists in this way, in a section of his speech which was devoted primarily to the political conflicts which had taken place inside the Soviet Communist Party, is of exceptional significance. Since, with the knowledge we now have, it is reasonable to suppose that his remarks were directed more at the Chinese than at the Albanians, it is not unreasonable to read this part of Khrushchev's speech as an accusation that the Chinese leaders were directly associated with the Stalinist opposition inside the CPSU. That there was some connexion between the internal dispute in the CPSU and the conflict between Moscow and Peking was suggested by a number of other developments.

The first was Chou En-lai's reaction to Khrushchev's attack on the Albanians. His only intervention at the Congress was the speech in which he conveyed the Chinese Communist Party's formal greetings.* It was for the most part a carefully worded statement which avoided wholehearted approval of the Khrushchevian line and of the Twentieth Congress while proclaiming loyalty to the decisions of the Moscow meetings of 1957 and 1960 and to the 'cohesion' of the Communist camp. Then, after asserting Albania's continuing membership of the 'socialist camp', he said, in an obvious allusion to Khrushchev's treatment of the Albanian question:

> We consider that, if quarrels and differences of opinion have, unfortunately, arisen between the fraternal parties and fraternal countries, then they should be resolved with patience, in the spirit of proletarian internationalism and the principles of equality and of reaching unity of view by means of consultation. The open, unilateral condemnation of any fraternal party does not promote cohesion and does not contribute to the solution of the question. Openly to reveal in front of enemies quarrels between fraternal parties and fraternal countries cannot be regarded as a serious Marxist-Leninist approach.

Chou En-lai went on to express the hope that the quarrel would be resolved, adding that 'American imperialism and the Yugoslav revisionist grouping' were doing their best to split the Communist movement.

This discreetly, but, for Communist ears, none the less clearly, worded criticism of Khrushchev for his attitude to the Albanians received an uncompromising reply from the lips of the Soviet leader himself in his final speech to the Congress. He took note of Chou En-lai's concern that the Soviet Union's relations with Albania might affect the 'cohesion' of the socialist camp, and commented:

> We share our Chinese friends' anxiety and appreciate their concern for strengthening unity. If the Chinese

---

* *See* Chronology: October 19, 1961.

comrades desire to make an effort to normalise relations between the Albanian Communist Party and the fraternal parties, then there is scarcely anybody who could contribute to a solution of that problem better than the Chinese Communist Party. That would be really good for the Albanian Communist Party and would correspond with the interests of the whole commonwealth of socialist countries.

This remark, which the delegates greeted, according to *Pravda*, with 'prolonged applause', was in effect an accusation that the Chinese were behind the Albanian 'revolt'. It was as near as Khrushchev could get at the time to a public criticism of the Chinese.

Chou spoke on October 19. On October 21 (*i.e.* before Khrushchev administered his rebuke), he left Moscow and the Congress. His move was clearly intended to be understood as a gesture of protest at Khrushchev's treatment of the Albanians, and, through the Albanians, of the Chinese. This was the second event which underlined the relevance of the Sino-Soviet dispute to the Congress.

Before Chou left, he went out of his way to perform what was, in the circumstances, an even more provocative act. This was his visit to the Red Square to lay a wreath at the feet not only of Lenin but also of Stalin: 'the great Marxist-Leninist'. It was this act which, in my opinion, did more than anything else to account for the apparently unnecessary violence of the anti-Stalin speeches and actions later in the Congress. There is little doubt in my mind that the Russians' macabre gesture in removing Stalin's remains from Lenin's tomb and depositing them in a simple grave outside was intended primarily as a reply to Chou En-lai's wreath-laying, and a guarantee that such 'Stalinist' gestures would not be possible in Moscow in future. The otherwise inexplicably violent anti-Stalinist tone which the Twenty-second Congress assumed cannot be understood except in the context of the Russians' dispute with the Chinese.

There is a final aspect of the Congress which may have a more tenuous connexion with the Sino-Soviet dispute but which is none the less worthy of mention. This emerges from the revelations made by Pavel Satyukov, the chief editor of *Pravda*, about the activities of Vyacheslav Molotov, the former Foreign Minister who was ousted by Khrushchev in 1957 as a member of the 'anti-party' opposition. Doubtless because of his part in the October Revolution, Molotov had been allowed after his disgrace to occupy an official position in the Soviet state, first as ambassador to Mongolia and then, from 1960, as Soviet representative on the International Atomic Energy Agency. Satyukov revealed that Molotov, taking advantage of Khrushchev's post-Stalinist leniency, had continued to put forward his highly critical views of the new trend of Soviet policy. On the very eve of the Twenty-second Congress, Satyukov said, Molotov had sent the Central Committee of the CPSU a letter in which he declared that the new Party Programme was 'anti-revolutionary' and lacked co-ordination with 'the prospects of socialist revolution on an international scale'. And this, exclaimed Satyukov, at a time when the Soviet Programme had been approved, not only by the CPSU and Soviet people, but also by the international Communist movement! (Satyukov did not explain how the Programme could have been approved by the international movement *before* it had been submitted to the Congress for approval.)

This revelation was surprising, in that no one had suspected that, however 'liberal' the Soviet system had become, a member of the defeated 'anti-party' opposition to Khrushchev would be allowed to carry on *any* serious political activity. Though it is extremly unlikely that Molotov, or any other member of the 'anti-party' group, still represented an effective political force in the Soviet Union, the fact that he addressed such a letter to the CPSU's Central Committee suggested that he *believed* there still existed some support in the Party for his left-wing views. And, if *he*, with all his inside knowledge of the CPSU believed this, was it unreasonable to suppose that the Chinese should believe that their views would also find an echo among the members of the Soviet Party? Was it impossible that Molotov should have encouraged them in such a belief, perhaps while he was ambassador in Mongolia? At all events, the Molotov incident stressed the Russians' determination to demonstrate to the Chinese the futility of their looking for support within the CPSU. Khrushchev summed up the situation in his final speech.*

> This [the vital importance of peaceful coexistence] is not understood only by the hopeless dogmatists who, having reaffirmed the general formulae about imperialism, turn stubbornly away from reality. It is precisely in such positions that the thick-headed Molotov remains. He and those like him do not understand the changes in the world situation and the new developments in life; they trail along behind events and long ago became a brake on progress, a ballast.

The connexion between Molotov and the 'dogmatists' was clear for Khrushchev.

The close association between the Albanians and the Chinese was further demonstrated in their public reactions to the developments at the Twenty-second Congress. Continuing the treatment of the Albanian affair, the Albanian press now began to attack Khrushchev 'and his group' personally, implying that there were divided counsels in the Kremlin. Then, on November 7, Enver Hoxha made a speech which was a full-scale reply to the charges made by Khrushchev at the Congress. He covered every aspect of Khrushchevian ideology and practice, including his denigration of Stalin, and declared, as Khrushchev himself had said, that they (the Albanians) had been opposed to Khrushchev's Twentieth Congress 'revisionism' all along. Hoxha's speech was couched in the most violent terms yet heard in the dispute and none more violent than when he dealt with the Yugoslavs, whom he now saw as 'a centre of espionage and plots in the service of imperialism against the countries of the socialist camp'. He considered that Stalin's treatment of Tito and his expulsion of Yugoslavia from the Communist camp had been correct.

The Chinese Communists, having already reproduced in

* *See* Chronology: October 27, 1961.

their own press a strongly-worded editorial from *Zeri i Popullit* of November 1, now printed the full text of Hoxha's speech in the Peking *People's Daily*. Though it is not possible, in the absence of knowledge about the contacts between the Albanian and Chinese Communists at the time, to assert that Hoxha's speech had been previously agreed with the Chinese, their reproduction of it after time for careful thought was tantamount to the same thing and was an act of extreme hostility to Khrushchev and to the Soviet leadership in general. The reason for the violence of the Chinese reaction was that the Chinese clearly realised that Khrushchev intended his treatment of the Albanians to be an object-lesson for the Chinese. He had used the Albanians to demonstrate how far he was prepared to go in defence of his policies: in this case to the point of excluding the Albanian Communists from the company of other Communist parties. His next step was to show that he was ready to sever governmental relations as well.

At the end of November 1961, the Russians informed the Albanians that they were withdrawing their ambassador from Tirana, because of the obstacles put in the way of his mission, and that they required the Albanian ambassador in Moscow to leave because he had been distributing objectionable material in the city. (This referred to copies of Albanian criticism of Khrushchev, notably Hoxha's speech.) This meant in practice the severance of all relations between Moscow and Tirana. Relations between Albania and the Communist countries of Eastern Europe were also reduced to a minimum, but not severed completely, while the number of Chinese diplomatists and advisers of various kinds in Albania increased sharply.

The Russians' treatment of Albania was of great significance for relations within the Communist world, for by severing party and state relations with Albania, Khrushchev was in fact arrogating to himself the right to decide unilaterally which country was and which was not 'socialist'. The Albanians and Chinese would claim that this was not a matter subject to someone's subjective judgment; countries were 'socialist' or not by reference to certain objective criteria. But, by refusing to have the Albanians at the Twenty-second Congress in Moscow, by keeping them out of meetings of the Warsaw Pact and

Comecon, and by cutting off all diplomatic and commercial ties, Khrushchev had in fact imposed his will on the camp. However much the Albanians might protest, the fact was that they had been excluded from the company of other 'socialist' states. Thus, in practice, the criterion of whether a country was 'socialist' or not was how it conducted its relations with Moscow. And, just as he had excluded the Albanian Communists for their hostility or lack of subordination, Khrushchev was at the same time drawing the Yugoslavs back into the camp because they were better disposed towards Moscow. This was the real lesson for the Chinese: that the benefits of membership of the 'socialist camp' went to those leaders who, whatever their internal policies, acknowledged Russian primacy in foreign affairs. It was a lesson which the Chinese would find difficult to swallow.

The Twenty-second Congress and the break with Albania were followed by an intensification of polemics between Moscow on the one hand and Tirana and Peking on the other. Both Russians and Chinese restated their positions on the major foreign policy issues, while the Albanians continued with their more personal attacks on Khrushchev, not all of which were reproduced by the Chinese. In April, however, the polemical storm subsided, partly, perhaps, because the two sides had nothing new to say, but more likely because new developments were already taking place behind the scenes.

The conflict between the Russians and Chinese was seen again in practice at meetings of the World Federation of Trade Unions in Moscow and of the World Peace Council in Stockholm, both in December 1961. At both meetings the Chinese delegates, supported wholeheartedly by the Albanians and with varying warmth by other delegates, put forward a point of view distinct from the Russian. In both cases the question of the priority to be given to the 'struggle for peace', compared with more strictly revolutionary activities, was the main issue, and Chinese recalcitrance in Stockholm prevented agreement's being reached on problems discussed at the conference.

Following these meetings and the Twenty-second Congress of the CPSU, it was possible for the first time to establish with some certainty the extent of the support enjoyed by the Chinese in the Communist movement. The stubbornness with which the Chinese pursued their opposition to Moscow, coupled with their powerful propaganda and energetic 'fractional' work among other parties, was beginning to show some results by the end of 1961. Thus Hoxha was able to claim, with some justification that, of the eighty parties which sent delegations to the Twenty-second Congress of the CPSU, thirty-four did not associate themselves publicly with Khrushchev's criticisms of the Albanian Communists or refer to the quarrel between them.

At the WFTU meeting in Moscow and the WPC conference in Stockholm, a considerable number of Asian, African and Latin American delegates took a clearly pro-Chinese line, while the North Korean and North Vietnamese leaders had moved clearly to the Chinese side. It was becoming clear that at any future international gathering of Communists the Chinese would not be isolated, though they and their 'fraction' would still be in a minority.

XII

OPEN STRIFE, 1962

At these congresses, by careful arrangements, a disgusting situation was created with large-scale and systematic attacks made on the Chinese Communist Party and other fraternal parties by name.

'People's Daily', February 27, 1963

If Sino-Soviet polemics were somewhat muted at the beginning of 1962, there were no signs that the Russians had any intention of yielding to the Chinese on practical issues. The year was notable in particular for a further substantial improvement in Soviet -Yugoslav relations. While Khrushchev had been obliged at the Twenty-second Congress of the CPSU to repeat the standard condemnation of the Yugoslav Communists and of 'revisionism, which found expression in the programme of the Yugoslav League of Communists', it was only the Chinese and Albanians who put any fire into their denunciations of the Yugoslavs. The latter, on the other hand, found it possible on November 27, 1961 to describe the decisions of the Twenty-second Congress as a 'significant contribution to the progress of socialism'. In the months following the Congress, Soviet publicists tended to ignore the Yugoslav question and to avoid polemics with the Chinese over it.

Andrei Gromyko, the Soviet Foreign Minister made in April 1962 his planned visit to Belgrade. His talks with Yugoslav leaders resulted in a communiqué which said that favourable conditions existed for an improvement in Soviet-Yugoslav relations 'in all spheres'. In May it was announced that plans had been made for a Yugoslav 'parliamentary' delegation to visit Russia and that President Tito had ben invited to take a holiday there. Before this took place, however, Leonid Brezhnev, the Soviet President and head of state, paid an official visit to

Yugoslavia in September. It appeared (though it was not said) that this visit was demanded by the Yugoslavs to make amends for the cancellation of the Voroshilov visit in 1958. During the visit Tito dismissed 'certain differences' remaining between the Soviet Union and Yugoslavia as being no obstacle to friendship, while Brezhnev said Soviet policy towards Yugoslavia would be based on a statement made in Varna by Khrushchev in May. There, in the course of a generally optimistic comment on the future of Soviet-Yugoslav relations, the Soviet leader gave the following undogmatic definition:

> The position of the Soviet people is that, despite the differences in the way we look at a number of political and ideological questions, we, as a country that is building Communism, will do all we can to bring about good co-operation with Yugoslavia and thereby help her peoples consolidate their socialist positions.

This would benefit all the other Communist countries, he added.

The Russians gave practical evidence of their goodwill in the course of trade talks in July and following Brezhnev's visit in October. Though there was no clear indication whether the Soviet credits suspended in 1958 had been restored, it appeared from the figures published that the Russians had agreed to treble their trade with the Yugoslavs in subsequent years. The Chinese and Albanians, who had followed the exchanges between Moscow and Belgrade in the spring and summer with remarkable restraint, finally resumed their denunciations of the 'modern revisionists' during the Brezhnev visit. On September 17, the Peking *People's Daily* described the Yugoslav Communists as 'out-and-out renegades to Communism' and accused Tito of 'singing in harmony with US imperialism'. At the beginning of October the Chinese Foreign Minister, Marshal Chen Yi, linked the 'Tito clique' with 'imperialists' and 'reactionaries'.* This prompted an official protest by the Yugoslav government.

It was not until this series of exchanges had taken place, and the Yugoslavs were assured of Soviet goodwill, that Marshal

* *See* Chronology: October 1, 1962.

Tito himself agreed to make the pilgrimage to Moscow. He was there accorded exceptional honours for a Communist leader: more, in fact, than any satellite statesman had ever received, including being invited to attend and address a session of the Supreme Soviet.* While admitting that there were still 'certain disagreements' between them, Tito repeated the formula that 'the Soviet and Yugoslav points of view coincide or are very close to each other on all major international questions'. On his return to Yugoslavia, Tito insisted that the new and close relationship established with Russia and the Communist bloc did not in any way restrict Yugoslavia's independence in foreign affairs or represent a departure from her policy of non-participation in any alliance. The main link with the Communist countries, he said, was provided by their common aims: 'the realisation of socialism'.

On the surface, at all events, Tito appeared to have regained his status as a 'socialist' and all the advantages of membership of the 'socialist camp' without making any substantial concessions in return. While remaining outside the Warsaw Pact and the Council for Mutual Economic Aid and retaining freedom of action in foreign affairs, Yugoslavia was in fact accorded the status of a 'socialist' (*i.e.* Communist) country and the Yugoslav League of Communists was given the status of a Communist party. This was made clear beyond any doubt in January, 1963, when a Yugoslav (but not an Albanian) delegation was invited to attend the Congress of the East German Communist Party. And, as a final sign of the Kremlin's blessing on Tito, Khrushchev agreed to spend a 'holiday' in Yugoslavia in 1963.

It is not easy to explain the exceptional efforts made by Khrushchev to draw Tito back into the company of Communist states and parties, almost at any price and despite the fact that the Yugoslavs were still formally 'revisionists'. It seemed as though the restoration of relations with Yugoslavia was an aim to which Khrushchev was deeply committed personally and one from which he would not be deflected at any cost. And yet such a decision, having such far-reaching consequences for relations within the camp, can scarcely have depended on the

* *See* Chronology: December 4, 1962.

whim of one man; it must have been the subject of long and serious debate. It can have escaped no responsible Soviet official that such treatment of Tito was, in the context of the Sino-Soviet dispute, a strong provocation of the Chinese. To oust the Albanians and beckon in the Yugoslavs could serve only to exacerbate relations with China. It was also a policy not easy to explain in 'ideological' terms; for, whatever differences existed between Albania and Yugoslav Communism, it was difficult to show that one was more 'socialist' than the other or more entitled to Soviet friendship.

It might have been thought that, by accepting Yugoslavia as a 'non-paying' member of the 'socialist camp', the Russians intended to 'dilute' the membership. Did they perhaps feel that there was advantage in making membership of the Warsaw Pact and the Council for Mutual Economic Aid less binding and less exacting, especially since the military significance of the pact had declined in the nuclear age? Speculation on these lines was not encouraged, however, by other developments in Eastern Europe organisations in 1962. In June the Council for Mutual Economic Aid met in Moscow, without representatives from China, Albania, North Korea or North Vietnam. Far-reaching reforms of the organisation were proposed to mark 'the entry of the world Socialist system into a new stage of development', and to make the CMEA better able to meet the challenge of the Western European Common Market. Not only were China and her three allies not involved in these plans, but a special decision was taken to enable Mongolia, which had remained faithful to Moscow, to become a member of this hitherto European body. From this it appeared that the needs of China and her allies no longer featured in the long-term economic plans of the Soviet bloc. A possible consequence of this development was the Chinese decision in late summer 1962 to close down all Soviet consulates in China.

One of the reasons for the abatement of public polemics between Moscow and Peking (and consequently Tirana also) at the beginning of 1962 may have been the fact, revealed only in 1963, that the first moves took place at this time for the holding of a meeting to resolve the differences in the Communist movement that were becoming increasingly difficult to control or conceal.* According to a statement made by the CPSU in March 1963 (in its letter to the Chinese Communist Party of March 30, 1963), proposals were made 'at the beginning of 1962' by the (North) Vietnamese, Indonesian, British and Swedish parties and by 'other comrades', for the holding of a 'meeting of fraternal parties of all countries'. From what is known of the views and allegiances of the four parties named it seems probable that their proposal had at least the approval of the Chinese, even if it was not actually initiated by them. Although the Russians later protested their eagerness to have such a meeting, there is reason to suppose that they were in reality something less than enthusiastic about the idea. They recalled that in a letter of February 22, 1962, they had proposed a moratorium on polemics, urging that 'unnecessary arguments be stopped regarding questions on which we have different opinions [and] that public statements capable of aggravating and not smoothing out our differences be given up'. This was at the height of the polemical warfare following the Twenty-second Congress at the end of 1961.

According to their own account, the Chinese sent on April 7, 1962 a letter to the CPSU accepting the idea of a world meeting and setting forth the necessary preliminary steps for such a gathering. 'Many obstacles would have to be overcome and much preparatory work would have to be done' if the meeting were to be a success. The Chinese proposed in particular: that parties and countries which had disputes should try to alleviate them; that 'public attacks' should cease; that bilateral or multilateral talks should be held where necessary; that the Russians should take the initiative to restore normal relations with Albania; and that the CPSU should summon the meeting after consultation with other parties.

The Russians say that they wrote again to the Chinese on May 31, 1962, saying: 'We fully support the proposal for the convening of a meeting of all the fraternal parties.' But, apart from recalling their concern lest the meeting when assembled should aggravate rather than ease the differences, the Russians have not revealed what conditions they then placed on the

* *See* Chronology: April 7, 1962.

summoning of a meeting. It seems hardly possible that they accepted all the Chinese conditions. Nor does it appear that, after having agreed in principle to the idea of having a meeting, they did anything in practice to promote it. To judge from later references to the exchanges on the question of a meeting, the Chinese letter of April 7 and the Russian letter of May 3 were the last moves in this matter in 1962.

The apparent exclusion of China from the sphere of Soviet economic aid, coupled with the steady improvement in Russia's relations with 'revisionist' Yugoslavia, can have left the Chinese in mid-1962 in no doubt regarding Khrushchev's unwillingness to make any serious concessions to Mao Tse-tung. It was probably this, rather than any faith in the possibility of a real improvement in Sino-Soviet relations, that accounted for the lull in the war of words. The Chinese may well have realised in the course of 1962 that, however persuasively they argued their case and however insistently they demanded a meeting of world Communist parties, this alone would not force the Russians to move or to admit the Chinese to the place in Communist councils they considered their due. Their polemical outpourings could embarrass the Russians and could swing a few parties away from Soviet influence; but this could at best result only in the formation of a separate, Chinese-led Communist movement and an end to any hopes of greater Chinese influence over the Communist movement as a whole. It was not easy to see how the Chinese could, in the face of Russian obstinacy, advance their cause further. Khrushchev seemed quite happy to get along without Mao's help and to have forgotten the letter of May 31 agreeing to take steps for another meeting.

In August, however, came an announcement (scarcely recorded by the world's press) which obviously touched the Chinese more nearly than any number of favours to Tito or unpleasantness to Enver Hoxha could have done. It was the claim by Nehru to have been promised deliveries of Soviet jet fighter aircraft. This claim and the statement by the Indian Defence Minister, Krishna Menon, that the Russians had concluded an agreement for the manufacture of MiG fighters in India was carefully recorded in the Peking press on August

17 and 18. This must have seemed to the Chinese an almost perfect issue through which to expose Khrushchev's 'revisionism' in practice. For he was giving, not only substantial economic aid, but military aid as well to a country which did not pretend to be Communist or even an ally of the Communist countries and which, moreover, was in a state of suspended conflict with its neighbour China. Whose side was Khrushchev on?

On October 20, 1962 the Chinese set out to resolve this question by resuming their invasion of Indian territory in the areas of Ladakh and the North-East Frontier Agency. Their action was alarmingly successful, inflicting ignominious defeat on the Indian forces and provoking a major political crisis in India itself. And, though it was less apparent, the Chinese invasion presented the Soviet leaders with no less serious a crisis. Their embarrassment was apparent in the way the Soviet press almost ignored the Sino-Indian conflict although the world's press was full of it at the time, and from the Russians' obvious reluctance to take sides in the dispute. The Indian leaders, who had received promises of increased support from America and Britain, were anxious to have an assurance of continued backing from the Soviet Union as well. But such a public undertaking by the Russians would have lined them up in a military sense alongside the 'imperialists' against a China which was not only Communist but linked to Russia by a treaty of alliance and mutual assistance. The Russians were therefore forced to avoid making any clear pronouncement on the subject of their military deliveries to India. At the same time they could not lightly dissociate themselves from the Indians and come down firmly on the Chinese side in the frontier dispute. That would have destroyed whatever confidence in Russian friendship had been built up in the Indian official mind by many years of diligent Soviet diplomacy and economic aid. For once, the Soviet propagandists (usually so voluble on any topic) found themselves tongue-tied and unable to do much more than urge a 'peaceful' solution of the dispute. It was only some weeks after the cease-fire in November that Nehru was able to say that the MiG fighters were in fact being delivered.

It would, doubtless, be wrong to suggest that the sole aim of the Chinese in provoking the incident on the Indian frontier was to place the Russians in a difficult position and expose the error of their 'revisionist' ways. The Chinese action certainly did much to impress the peoples of Asia with Chinese military prowess and increase China's influence in the Far East. But its effect on Sino-Soviet relations was certainly not the least important factor in the Chinese mind. It was, after all, an impressive demonstration that, while Khrushchev could continue to keep the Chinese out of policy-making councils in the Communist world, he could not prevent them from upsetting his foreign political plans if they so chose. From the Chinese point of view, the Indian frontier conflict provided clear proof that it was not the possession of nuclear weapons or economic wealth that enabled a country to influence world affairs, but a proper understanding of Marxism.

The lesson might have been much clearer and have had more striking results if another, even more important event had not supervened. This was the crisis in Soviet-American relations provoked by the Russians' attempt to mount missile bases in Cuba, which broke on October 22: only two days after the Chinese assault on Indian frontier positions. The 'crisis in the Caribbean', as the Communists chose to label it, had a deep and lasting effect on the Communist world and on Sino-Soviet relations. It was a strange episode in Khrushchev's rule which still awaits full analysis.

His attempt to outwit the American authorities and obtain a nuclear 'edge' on them almost overnight was an extremely risky and expensive operation to be undertaken in the name of 'peaceful coexistence'. It certainly threw new light on Khrushchev's interpretation of that concept. Moreover, his readiness to risk so much to obtain a strategic advantage over America suggested that Russia had no such advantage (though her propaganda often suggested she had) and had no immediate prospect of obtaining it by other, less risky, means. This in turn suggested that Khrushchev's preference for 'peaceful coexistence' was not so much a matter of choice as of force majeure. Had he succeeded in placing his missiles in Cuba, he might have been able to start treating the American 'imperialists' as the 'paper tigers' the Chinese said they were. In the event, he succeeded only in 'giving the show away'. The ultimate effect of this revelation of Russia's relative weakness has yet to be seen.

The immediate effect of the Cuban crisis was to silence Chinese and Albanian criticism of Soviet policy and produce the appearance of a united front with Russia and Cuba in the face of 'imperialist' threats. But this superficial truce did not survive the Russian withdrawal. The Chinese at once intensified their propaganda in support of Fidel Castro and were before long making openly critical comments on the Russian retreat. While the Russians had no alternative but to pose as the saviours of peace, the Chinese saw in their behaviour only an act of 'cowardice', and made no effort to spare Khrushchev's feelings at what was for him an already difficult enough moment. In their public pronouncements in November and in later references to the Cuban affair, they made clear their disapproval both of Khrushchev's attempt to use Cuba for military purposes and of his retreat in the face of American pressure. The former they described as 'the error of adventurism', the latter as 'the error of capitulationism'. Both errors, they said, derived from a 'blind worship' of nuclear weapons. The Chinese journal *Red Flag* referred on November 16 to unnamed persons who were 'scared stiff' of American military strength. On November 18 the *People's Daily* said it was 'pure nonsense' to say that peace had been saved by the withdrawal of the Soviet missiles. And, at a time when the Russians were having some difficulty in readjusting their relations with Castro and reassuring him of their support, the Chinese made a great show of being his only true friend.

Thus in two major international crises, the Russians and Chinese were clearly seen to be at odds, with the Chinese playing a very provocative role and not hesitating to add to Khrushchev's discomfiture when the occasion offered. The effect of both the Sino-Indian and the Cuban affair was appreciably to deepen the rift between Chinese and Russians and to increase the bitterness of their mutual attacks. This became apparent at once in a series of congresses of European Communist parties which took place in November and December 1962, and at which the debate inside the Communist movement was resumed with full vigour.

The congresses took place of the Bulgarian Communist Party on November 5, of the Hungarian Party on November 21, of the Italian Party on December 3, of the Czechoslovak Party on December 4, and of the East German Party on January 16. The pattern of the dispute that emerged at each congress was the same: the delegates from parties loyal to Moscow praised the Soviet policy over Cuba and denounced the activities of the Albanian leaders; the Chinese delegate, Wu Hsiu-chuan (who attended each congress in turn) defended the Albanians and denounced Yugoslav 'revisionism' in such a way as to make it clear that he was including Soviet 'revisionism' in his attacks. Wu took particular exception to the use of the platform of one party to denounce another; this was later to become one of the main complaints of the Chinese, presumably because particular congresses could be 'packed' by the organisers with supporters of their own policies and yet be given the authority of an international meeting. There was clearly a dispute behind the scenes over this very issue prior to the East German Congress, which Khrushchev himself attended and which the Russians declared in advance would be an 'international forum'. In the event, they were forced to drop this claim. The Chinese were determined to prevent a repetition of the Bucharest meeting of 1960 to which the Russians had tried to give the authority of an international conference. They were determined to have a real international meeting, with all the world's Communist leaders present, and it was on that goal that they now concentrated their efforts in the Communist movement. An essential part of their tactics was to make quite clear their differences of opinion with the Russians and those who followed their lead.

Their first move in this direction was at the Czechoslovak Congress in December 1962, at which Wu Hsiu-chuan presented, in addition to his speech, a formal statement* which was read out to the delegates, protesting at the attacks made on the Albanian Communists and on the Chinese Communist Party and proposing 'a Meeting of Representatives of the Communist and Workers' parties of all countries of the world in order to clarify what is right from what is wrong, to strengthen unity and to stand together against the enemy'. With its admission

* *See* Chronology: December 4–8, 1962.

that the Chinese themselves were directly under attack and its only very thinly veiled criticisms of the Russians for their treatment of the Albanians ('After all, who was the first to launch an attack on the Albanian comrades?'), the statement identified and brought very close together for the first time the two main contestants in the dispute. Moreover in its complaints at the 'shouting and hissing' to which the Chinese delegate had been subjected and its comment that 'some parties and some persons are . . . going further and further along the road towards a split', the statement painted a more dramatic picture of the dispute than had previously been admitted. The Chinese were also able to record the acquisition of a further ally in the battle with Moscow: the North Korean Communist Party, which had supported the Chinese in their stand and been censored for so doing. Geography had proved stronger than ideology in the Far East, and the Russians had lost yet another of their means of 'controlling' China.

The full-dress reply to the post-Cuban campaign of criticism by the Chinese and Albanians was made by Khrushchev himself, first at a session of the Supreme Soviet in Moscow on December 12* (at which Tito was present as an honoured guest), and at the East German Party's congress in Berlin on January 16. Both speeches were vigorous and lengthy defences of Soviet policy with regard to Cuba and to relations with the West in general and of reasonableness in everything in preference to the impetuosity of the 'ultra-revolutionaries'. He left his listeners in no doubt that he was replying to Chinese charges, *first* by depicting the Albanians as mere puppets of someone else ('someone has taught them bad language and they use it against the CPSU'), and *secondly* by commenting directly on the Chinese Communists' 'patience' over the continued occupation of Macao and Hong-Kong by the 'imperialists', and on the 'wisdom' of their withdrawal from Indian territory. He showed no such verbal delicacy, however, in his handling of the Albanian Communists, and he carried his defence of Yugoslav 'socialism' a stage further.

Khrushchev was something less than precise in dealing in these speeches with two practical issues concerning the Com-

* *See* Chronology: December 12, 1962.

munist movement. One was the question of the relative rights of Yugoslavia and Albania to belong to the socialist camp. The other was the question of holding an international conference.

After recognising, in his speech to the Supreme Soviet the inevitability of various 'creative' interpretations of Communist doctrine as it was applied to different countries, and consequently of different opinions on many points, Khrushchev said there could be no 'set pattern' for relations between socialist countries, and that it was wrong to 'press for the complete exclusion of any Communist party from our united movement'. Yet this, he said, was the 'bestial morality' which the Albanians wanted to apply with regard to Yugoslavia. After further defence of Yugoslavia's claim to be 'socialist', Khrushchev then launched into a condemnation of the Albanian leaders' 'Stalinist' practices and finally accused them of 'splitting activities'. He stopped short, however, of any explanation of his de facto exclusion of the Albanian Communists from 'our united movement'. He further confused the issue, in his Berlin speech, by declaring that, despite the 'serious differences' between Russians and Albanians, 'we consider that Albania is a socialist country': the essential qualification, in the case of Yugoslavia, for admission to the socialist community. Finally, he asserted that the Albanians had rejected repeated efforts by the Russians to persuade them to discuss their differences, and he declared that if the Albanians wanted 'friendship with the CPSU and with all the fraternal parties' (i.e. if they wanted to be readmitted to the movement), they must 'recant their erroneous views'. The crucial question, he said, was 'the attitude of the Communist party concerned towards the problems of the struggle for the victory of the working-class and socialism'. And he ended with an appeal for unity, tempered with tolerance, moderation, restraint and patience.

There was no way of deciphering from these impressive and often contradictory statements what were the real qualifications for 'friendship' with the Soviet Union, nor why the Albanians were considered unworthy and the Yugoslavs were welcomed. If the Albanians had to abandon their 'erroneous views', why should the Yugoslavs not do the same? If they were both 'socialist' countries, why should they not equally enjoy the benefits of Russian friendship? These were questions that Khrushchev appeared unable to deal with straightforwardly. The only conclusion to emerge clearly from his two speeches was that the decision on which country was and which country was not entitled to the blessings of Soviet friendship was taken in Moscow, without consultation with other parties. It was the Russians who decided whether the 'attitude of the party concerned' towards socialism was the right attitude. It was left to the 'party concerned' to guess what attitude would win Moscow's approval. The Yugoslavs had guessed right; the Albanians were wrong. This issue, left so unclear in Khrushchev's words, was of prime importance in the future discussion of the 'unity' of the Communist movement.

On the other tactical question: that of the convening of an international meeting, Khrushchev only temporised in his Berlin speech. He thought it would be 'useful' to cease polemics between the parties (which the Chinese were already resuming), and to 'allow some time for passions to subside'. But he thought that there was little immediate hope of eliminating differences and that a meeting might therefore lead 'not to a calm and judicious removal of differences but to their aggravation and to the danger of a split'. They must not forget, he said, that 'there is a logic to every struggle and political passions run high'. Time would help them to understand 'who is right and who is wrong'. It was quite apparent to all who followed the progress of events in the Communist movement that the main differences which a conference would discuss were those between the Russians and the Chinese, and Khrushchev's statement was his first clear admission of the gravity of the dispute. At a time when Communist propagandists had been dismissing all suggestion of a conflict in the camp, Khrushchev admitted that differences were so grave that no meeting could resolve them and that there was a possibility of a 'split'. Moreover, the manner of his remarks suggested that his proposal for a cessation of polemics was dictated rather by a desire to silence the Chinese than the prospect of resolving differences. The Chinese proposal for a meeting, made at the Czechoslovak congress, had in fact been rejected.

One final episode remains to be recorded from this series of party congresses at which the Chinese and Russians confronted each other in public. At the earlier congresses, there had already been some outspoken criticism of Wu Hsiu-chuan, the Chinese delegate. At the East German congress in January, by an apparently concerted and directed effort, he was subjected to 'an uproar of booing, whistling and foot-stamping' by the assembled delegates. He was also rebuked for his comments on the Yugoslav Communists and reported by the Soviet newspaper *Izvestia* as having used 'utterly impermissible' language. It was true that Wu Hsiu-chuan had himself ostentatiously refrained from applauding much that the other delegates had found worthy of applause, and he *had* criticised the Yugoslavs, though carefully basing his criticisms on the 'agreed' Moscow Statement. But organised jeers were something new in Communist politics and lent a new bitterness to the dispute. They certainly added strength to Khrushchev's remarks about 'political passions' and about the difficulties of resolving differences.

XIII

RUSSIAN COMMUNISTS AND CHINESE COMMUNISTS, 1963

We publish all the 'masterpieces' in which you rail at us . . .
Do you dare to do the same?

'People's Daily', December 31, 1962

During the first half of 1963, the dispute proceeded on two connected but distinct planes. There was, on the one hand, a great outpouring of material on points of 'ideological' principle from both sides, though mostly from the Chinese. This elaborated and clarified the Chinese position in many respects; but it did not reveal any fundamental change in the Chinese attitude, and it was chiefly remarkable for the steadily increasing force and directness of the Chinese attack. Neither the Chinese nor the Russians gave any indication that they were ready to make concessions on this level.

Parallel with these exchanges, there was the slow, reluctant approach to some form of Communist 'summit' meeting. This was linked primarily with the main actual issues in the dispute: the questions of where the authority lay in the Communist movement; of how relations between the parties should be governed; of the validity of the Moscow agreements of 1957 and 1960; and of the attitude towards Yugoslavia and Albania. This latter question remained the convenient issue around which the tactical exchanges were fought.

To review all the ideological exchanges in detail would demand far greater space than is available here; and it would not add greatly to an understanding of the development of the conflict. Most of the main issues have already been touched on, so that it will suffice here to summarise the latest contributions to the debate, with stress on the new elements that were introduced. The extracts provided in the appendices from the writings referred to in this chapter are full enough to give an adequate picture of the views of both sides.

The Peking *People's Daily* printed on December 31, 1962 an editorial article of monumental proportions on 'The Differences between Comrade Togliatti and Us'* which, on the pretext of refuting ideas advanced by Togliatti and other Italian Communist leaders at their congress in December 1962, set forth the Chinese view on some major points in dispute. The first was the question of the Chinese Communist Party's attitude to nuclear weapons and nuclear warfare, the dangers of which they were commonly believed to underestimate. The article insisted that this was not so and that the Chinese leaders had always held that nuclear war would be 'an unprecedented calamity' for humanity. They had therefore supported demands for the banning of nuclear weapons and for the creation of 'atom-free' zones in the Pacific. Where they disagreed was over the further conclusions to be drawn. They did *not* agree that the development of nuclear weapons had affected the fundamental Marxist teachings on war and peace: there were still 'just' and 'unjust' wars. They did *not* believe that the threat of nuclear war should be an excuse for pessimism or defeatism; they believed that 'the course of history necessarily leads to the destruction of nuclear weapons by mankind and will definitely not lead to the destruction of mankind by nuclear weapons'. Finally, they believed that, while Communists should take account of the destructiveness of nuclear weapons, they should not allow themselves or their followers to be the victims of 'nuclear blackmail'. They advised their critics to 'pull themselves together and take an active part in the great struggle of the masses against the imperialist policy of nuclear blackmail and for the defence of world peace'.

Closely allied with the question of nuclear war was Mao Tse-tung's reported belief that 'imperialists' were all 'paper tigers'. The Chinese were probably aware that Mao's apparent unconcern for the loss of human life did not endear him to Western Communists, and Khrushchev himself had seized on this point to remind the Chinese that, if imperialism was a

* *See* Chronology: December 31, 1962.

paper tiger, it was a paper tiger with nuclear teeth. To this the Chinese replied that Mao's view was a long-term one: that imperialism must be regarded 'strategically' as a paper tiger, doomed to defeat, even though 'tactically' it must be taken seriously. Had not Mao coined the phrase in 1946 when things looked black for the Chinese revolution, and had he not been proved right? Did not the successful wars in Korea, Vietnam, Cuba, and Algeria prove the same point? In what was in effect a direct reply to Khrushchev, the *People's Daily* said:

> No matter what kind of teeth imperialism may have, whether guns, tanks, rocket teeth, nuclear teeth, or any other kind of teeth that modern science and technology may provide, its rotten, decadent and paper-tiger nature cannot change. In the final analysis, neither nuclear teeth nor any other kind of teeth can save imperialism from its fate of inevitable extinction.

Those who objected to Mao's 'paper tiger' concept had 'obviously lost every quality a revolutionary ought to have and instead have become as short-sighted and timid as mice'. These were hard words to address to the leader of the Soviet Communist Party!

The other major question of principle dealt with by the *People's Daily* was that of the correct interpretation of 'peaceful coexistence'. Here again the Chinese protested at the charge that they were opposed to the concept. But their understanding of it was that it meant that Communist countries could establish 'normal' relations with non-Communist countries on terms of equality and mutual respect. They did *not* believe, however, that this state of affairs could be achieved without 'struggle' against 'imperialism'; nor did they accept the view that peaceful coexistence meant the elimination of antagonisms between socialism and capitalism, between countries or between classes. This would be to 'substitute class collaboration for class struggle on a world scale'. Moreover, it was nonsense to pretend that peaceful coexistence could produce a 'world without war'. 'It is one thing to prevent a world war, and another to eliminate all wars.' Peaceful coexistence did not apply at all to relations between oppressed nations and their oppressors or between oppressed classes and their oppressors. From this position, the article went on to a lengthy refutal of Togliatti's (and by implication, Khrushchev's) argument that the Communists could achieve power through the 'structural reform' of capitalism.

Fascinating though these and similar scholastic discussions of Communist principle may be to students of Marxism in its later stages of development, they do not add greatly to our knowledge of the practical issues in dispute between Moscow and Peking. They serve only to confirm the degree of hostility in the minds of the authors of the ideological diatribes, with theoreticians on both sides sufficiently well versed in the classical texts of Marx and Lenin, and in the more recent creations of the 1957 and 1960 Moscow meetings, to be able always to produce chapter and verse in support of their particular interpretation of doctrine. The extent to which this aspect of the debate declined into mere word-juggling can best be illustrated from an exchange on the subject of 'paper tigers'.

Eager to produce the highest support for Mao Tse-tung's description of the 'imperialists' as 'paper tigers', the *People's Daily* compared it with Lenin's description of imperialism as a 'colossus with feet of clay'. Was Lenin not saying the same as Mao? To this *Pravda* replied, in a long editorial article on January 7, 1963, that Lenin's formula 'stresses that imperialism is still strong (it is a colossus) but it stands on an unstable basis and is rent by internal contradictions (it has feet of clay).' Mao's definition, said *Pravda*, 'speaks only of its weakness'. At this point the discussion seemed to be touching the borders of absurdity.

While these issues of high theory appeared to offer almost endless scope for debate and also (if the parties to the dispute wanted it) for compromise, there were other, more immediate and practical issues over which agreement or compromise seemed less possible and which formed the real battleground of the dispute. These will now be considered in direct connection (as they are obviously connected) with the skirmishing that was going on about the calling of a meeting.

The main 'tactical' issue was, as before, whether Yugoslavia was 'socialist' or not. In its argument against Togliatti on December 31, the *People's Daily* took exception to the presence of a delegation from the Yugoslav League of Communists at the Italian Communist Party's congress, seeing in this, no doubt, a move towards the restoration of the Yugoslav Communists to full membership of the 'socialist camp'. The Chinese referred to the condemnation of the Yugoslavs for their 'revisionism' in the Moscow Statement of 1960, and claimed that they had not changed their ways, declaring that 'the Moscow Statement cannot be overturned by anyone, whoever he may be'. In direct contradiction to Khrushchev, the Chinese added: 'Yugoslavia has long ceased to be a socialist country, and the gradual restoration of capitalism in Yugoslavia began long ago.' The main question was, said the Chinese, 'whether the basic principles of Marxism-Leninism are outmoded and whether the Moscow Declaration and the Moscow Statement are out of date'.

Pravda's long editorial contribution to the debate: 'Strengthen the Unity of the Communist Movement for the Victory of Peace and Socialism' (which appeared a week later, on January 7), was largely an unimpressive restatement of Soviet views. Apart from taking understandable exception to an Albanian description of the Russians as enjoying a 'temporary majority' in the movement, the article added little that was new. It stressed the looseness of the ties binding the Communist movement and rejected the idea of there being 'superior' and 'inferior' parties. But at the same time it underlined the need for unity, for devotion to the joint decisions of the Moscow meetings 'which are common and binding for all of them', and of the great enormity of 'splitting activities'.

Almost at the end of the article, with all the appearance of being an after-thought, came the statement that the Yugoslav Communists had 'removed much of what was erroneous and damaging to the cause of building socialism in Yugoslavia' and had moved towards a rapprochement with the other parties. It was a lie to say 'capitalism' had been restored in Yugoslavia. There were still differences on some ideological questions between Russians and Yugoslavs, but these would be overcome through the new and closer relations.

Pravda ended this homily with a brief reference to the practice of 'collective discussion' among the parties. The CPSU was 'deeply convinced' that such discussion would ensure the 'cohesion of the international Communist movement'. This was far too vague a remark to be regarded as a reply to the Chinese Party's formal proposal for a meeting made in their statement to the Czechoslovak congress on December 8, 1962, and repeated in the *People's Daily* of December 15 and December 31. Khrushchev was even more discouraging in his speech to the East German Party congress on January 16 when (as related above) he argued that the time was not ripe for a meeting, and suggested by a reference to the Albanians that the best way for the Chinese to restore unity would be for them to 'recant their erroneous views'.

The position, therefore, in mid-January was that the Chinese were beginning to press for an international conference of Communist parties, while the Russians were ignoring or evading the demand and even putting obstacles in the way of its being held. The Chinese insistence on the holding of a conference was entirely understandable: an international conference of Communist parties was the only organ still generally accepted by everybody, including the Russians, as having the power to legislate for the whole movement. Only a world conference – and not any more limited gathering, and certainly not the 'congress of a fraternal party' – could reach decisions on the disputed questions which might be accepted as binding by all parties. Until such a conference was held, the only possible international authority lay in the documents issued by the Moscow meetings in 1957 and 1960: and these had already been proved to be very ambiguous guides. Moreover, there were already signs that the 'revisionists' intended to throw doubt on the authority of the Moscow documents, for Togliatti had already declared that the 1960 Statement was 'wrong' on the question of Yugoslavia and had been 'corrected'. The continued exclusion and condemnation of the Albanians, and the admission of the Yugoslavs to Communist congresses, were also calculated, in part deliberately by the Russians, to undermine the authority of the 'international' documents on which the Chinese relied. The Chinese saw slipping out of their hands the only levers they could hope to use for retaining an influence over world Communist strategy. Their only hope of obtaining the meeting they so much needed lay in stressing the extent of the differences in the camp and in pressing for a meeting to resolve them.

The Russian reluctance to hold a meeting was equally understandable, given that the central issue was one of authority within the Communist world. Every international meeting tended to create an international authority superior to any of the constituent parties, the CPSU included. Even though the Chinese might not have their own way in such a conclave, the very fact of its being held tended to limit Soviet liberty of action, as, for example, in the case of Moscow's relations with Belgrade. The Russians wanted to be free to choose their own friends, so that the statements they made on 'organisational' questions were deliberately vague and confusing.

At the end of January the Chinese tried to inject a new urgency into the situation by the publication in the *People's Daily* (January 27) of another major editorial article on the dispute. Saying that the dispute had reached a 'new climax' as a result of the 'utterly uncomradely' and 'extremely vulgar' behaviour of the other parties at the East German Party congress, the Chinese declared that the Communist movement was at a 'critical juncture', that its unity was 'under a grave threat', and that it was 'time to rein in on the brink of the precipice'. They then placed the connected questions of the attitude towards the Yugoslav Communists and the validity of the Moscow documents in the centre of the dispute.

The question of Yugoslav revisionism (they said) was 'not a minor but a major question', and was in fact the question of whether or not the two Moscow documents were to be regarded as the basis of 'unity'. Were the documents to be adhered to strictly or to be torn up? With impeccable logic, they then argued: that the Moscow Statement of 1960 had condemned the Yugoslavs, and that therefore efforts needed to be made to protect the Communist movement from Titoist ideas; that the Yugoslav Communists had approved a programme which was incompatible with the Moscow documents and had declared themselves in disagreement with the Moscow Statement; that

Khrushchev himself had condemned the Yugoslav Communists in 1958 for their 'anti-Marxist, anti-Leninist views'; that Tito had declared as late as December 1962 (on his return from Moscow) that talk of Yugoslavia's changing her policies was 'superfluous and ridiculous'; that people who defended the 'Tito clique' were therefore tearing up the Moscow documents; and that all this was tantamount to declaring that the fundamental principles of Marxism-Leninism were obsolete. If this were so, the Chinese asked: 'What possible common basis would there be for unity among the Communist and Workers' parties of all countries? Is this not a deliberate attempt to create a split in the international Communist movement?'

Having made their point with such vigour, the Chinese were still left with the task of framing the demands that followed from their argument. This took the form of yet another appeal to respect the international nature of the Communist movement and the supreme authority of decisions reached unanimously by all the parties, and in particular the two Moscow documents. No party or group of parties, the Chinese said, had the right to change these or to impose their decisions on the movement as a whole. They added, in words with so obvious a personal connotation as to be hardly calculated to improve relations with Khrushchev: 'it is impermissible . . . to require other fraternal parties to obey the irresponsible, self-contradictory statements made by the leader of a party who talks one way today and another tomorrow, as if those statements were imperial decrees.'

In that remark the Chinese seemed to have recognised that, whatever success their campaign inside the movement might have, they were unlikely ever to reach agreement with Khrushchev; they were in fact campaigning for his removal from power. However, they still said they hoped, even 'on the brink of the precipice', that the Russians would 'return to the path of inter-party consultation', and they repeated their demand for the calling of a meeting of representatives of parties 'of all countries'. It remained their only hope of escaping from the increasing isolation into which Khrushchev was pushing them.

A fortnight later, on February 10, *Pravda* replied to the *People's Daily* with a two-page polemic which for the first time grappled at some length with the key question of whether or not the Yugoslav Communists had changed their ways. In view of the strength of the Chinese case and of what Khrushchev and Tito had been recorded as saying on this point, it might have been wiser of the editors of *Pravda* and the theoreticians in the CPSU's Central Committee to leave this question alone. Their arguments were not as persuasive as those of the Chinese. They will be summarised here, both because the Yugoslav issue was at the centre of the dispute and because they provide an interesting example of Communist sophistry.

The differences between the Yugoslav Communists and other parties, said *Pravda*, had begun in 1948, mainly through the fault of Stalin. 'Serious differences' still existed, as had been noted in the Moscow Statement of 1960, though the conference had clearly based its criticism of Yugoslavia on the assumption that it was a 'socialist' country. The CPSU and the Soviet government had tried to help the Yugoslavs' return to the international movement, in accordance with the Moscow Statement's stress on the need for unity. The Yugoslav Communists had 'corrected much of what the international Communist movement considered mistaken and harmful'. Had not Tito and other Yugoslav leaders in July 1962 criticised mistakes they had made, and had Tito not said at the end of 1962 that the Yugoslavs also wanted to 'build socialism and finally Communism'? Had not the Chinese themselves said, in 1957, that the Yugoslavs had had success in building socialism? The CPSU would not try to conceal the existence of differences in some ideological questions; but it considered that other parties ought to work for an improvement in relations between the Yugoslavs and the Communist movement. What would happen, *Pravda* asked blandly, 'if every Communist party arbitrarily cut off other parties from socialism, strove for their exclusion from the ranks of the Communist movement, and even refused whole peoples the right to collaborate in the building of socialism'?

As for the Albanian Communists, *Pravda* went no further than to repeat what Khrushchev had said at the Twenty-second Congress of the CPSU and the East German Party congress: that they must abandon their 'mistaken views' if they wanted to rejoin the movement. They had rejected repeated offers by the Russians for talks.

On the practical question of how the admitted differences were to be eliminated, the *Pravda* article revealed the Russians to be still in a temporising mood. They could not agree that the Communist movement was 'on the brink of a precipice': they thought that the factors linking the Soviet, Chinese and other Communist parties were 'immeasurably greater' than what divided them; they were convinced that the differences were born of 'temporary factors' and should not spread into 'a deep conflict'. The Russians noted the statement by the Chinese that they were ready to create the necessary conditions for the holding of a conference, but regretted that this statement had been accompanied by criticisms of other parties (at the East German congress) and by a 'unilateral interpretation' of the Moscow documents. The Russians would like to believe, said *Pravda*, that the Chinese did not intend to pursue their polemics with other parties.

As for holding a meeting, said *Pravda*, the CPSU was in favour of doing so, if other parties considered it would be useful and if it were properly prepared. Moreover, they thought that bilateral and even larger meetings between parties would be a useful part of such preparation.

There was no mistaking the Russians' reluctance to call a meeting; though they could not flatly oppose the idea, they had, for tactical reasons, to insist on their approval of the idea in principle. The apparently simple question of calling an international meeting was actually far more complicated than appeared on the surface. Since there was, in fact, no 'international Communist organisation', there was no permanent secretariat or other body to which any party or group of parties could address a demand for a meeting to be called. Nor was there any general understanding among the parties about how or when an international meeting should be summoned. Those which *had* taken place since the dissolution of the Comintern and Cominform (the meetings of 1957 and 1960) had been largely on the initiative, and presumably at the invitation, of the Soviet Party. Proposals for the setting up of a permanent secretariat had then been rejected (for reasons which were now becoming apparent) and the only hint of a 'constitution' for the international movement was in very general statements about the desirability of holding meetings. The Declaration of 1957 said that the participants had concluded:

> It is expedient, besides bilateral meetings of leading personnel and exchange of information, to hold, as the need arises, more representative conferences of Communist and Workers' parties to discuss current problems, share experience, study each other's views and attitudes and concert action in the joint struggle for common goals – peace, democracy and socialism.

The Statement of 1960 included a section on relations between the parties in the movement, to which the Chinese later referred as the agreed rules governing their affairs. But its formula was no more precise than that of the 1957 Declaration. It said that conferences between parties were held 'as necessary'; that if questions arose in one party affecting another, their leaders would meet together if necessary; and that meetings on the 1957 and 1960 pattern had proved effective in working out common points of view.

There was nothing in either of these statements establishing any obligation on any body to summon a meeting, nor anything to indicate what procedure was to be followed by any party or group of parties that wanted a meeting. The Chinese claimed, however, that it had been agreed in 1960 that the Soviet Party bore the *responsibility* for calling a meeting. If that was true, then the only way to have a meeting was to persuade the Russians to call one, and this gave the Russians ultimate power of decision in the matter.

There was another, strictly practical, issue involved in this question: only a Communist party in control of a country and with appreciable resources could provide the facilities and the necessary 'security' for an international conference. Since the parties of Eastern Europe were unlikely to summon a conference independently, the *only* alternative hosts to the Russians were the Chinese. But for the Chinese Communists to summon an international conference in Peking (as they

were presumably quite entitled to do) would, since the conference would have inevitably been boycotted by pro-Russian
parties, have been equivalent in effect to declaring a formal
split in the world movement. This was not what the Chinese
wanted, though Khrushchev was in fact daring them to do it.

On February 21, ten days after the appearance of the *Pravda*
article, the CPSU Central Committee wrote to the Chinese
Central Committee a letter proposing the holding of bilateral
talks between the two parties at a 'high level'. These talks, said
the CPSU, would 'also play an important part in preparing
for a meeting of the Marxist-Leninist parties'. The letter
repeated the Russian view that the differences were 'of a
temporary character', urged the Chinese not to forget that
'we are standing on the same side of the barricades', and
agreed that the situation was 'extremely crucial'.

The letter was handed directly to Mao Tse-tung on February
23 by Chervonenko, the Soviet ambassador in Peking: a detail
which suggests that the only remaining channels of communication between the Soviet and Chinese parties were the normal
diplomatic ones. According to the Chinese reply of March 9
(which they published, along with the Soviet letter, on March
14), Mao Tse-tung gave the Soviet ambassador an immediate
acceptance of the proposal, though making it quite clear that
he regarded the Soviet letter as a formal proposal to hold a
meeting of all the parties.

Mao Tse-tung presumably suspected that the Russian proposal for bilateral talks was in reality a device for delaying the
international meeting rather than speeding it. But, since he
could hardly reject the Soviet proposal, he could only insist
on the importance of the international, rather than the bilateral,
gathering. It was apparent even to the outside observer that
the bilateral talks would quickly run into difficulties. The
simple question of which parties should be invited to an international meeting was fraught with difficulties, since the Chinese
would obviously insist that Albanians be invited and the
Russians would insist on inviting the Yugoslavs. There were
no signs that compromise would be easy even on this primary
issue. In fact, an international meeting was not brought
appreciably closer by the Soviet letter or the Chinese reply.

Before the Chinese handed over their reply to Chervonenko in Peking on March 9, along with their undertaking to suspend public polemics, they delivered several more polemical broadsides at the Russians. The most powerful of these was an article entitled 'Whence the Differences?' which appeared in the *People's Daily* on February 27 and which, on the pretext of replying to criticism of the Chinese made by Maurice Thorez, the French Communist leader, reviewed the whole course of the Sino-Soviet dispute from 1956 in strongly anti-Russian terms. The article was in effect a supplement to the Chinese reply, reaffirming a position of no compromise over 'the Tito clique' and denouncing the relationship between the Soviet Party and its adherents as 'feudal and patriarchal'. As if foreseeing the issue that must be faced in the bilateral talks, the Chinese said: 'Some persons now want to oust the fraternal Albanian Party of Labour from the international Communist movement on the one hand and to pull in the renegade Tito clique on the other. We want to tell these people frankly that this is absolutely impossible.'

In the first days of March *Red Flag*, the main theoretical journal of the Chinese Communists, published a 50,000-word article entitled 'More on the Difference between Comrade Togliatti and Us', which was also reprinted in the *People's Daily* in instalments. Consisting for the most part of a highly theoretical discussion along largely familiar lines of the issues in dispute (the more interesting of which will be found in the appendices), the article concluded with the most brazen challenge to the Russians the Chinese had yet made. Accusing them of deliberately provoking a split in the Communist movement, *Red Flag* said:

> The doughty warriors who claim to possess the totality of Marxist-Leninist truth are mortally afraid of the articles written in reply to their attacks by the so-called dogmatists, sectarians, splitters, nationalists, and Trotskyists whom they have so vigorously condemned. They dare not publish these articles in their own newspapers and journals. As cowardly as mice, they are scared to death! They dare not let the

people of their own country read our articles, and they have tried to impose a watertight embargo. They are even using powerful stations to jam our broadcasts and prevent their people from listening to them. Dear friends and comrades, who claim to possess the whole truth! Since you are quite definite that our articles are wrong, why don't you publish all these erroneous articles and then refute them point by point, so as to inculcate hatred among your people against the 'heresies' you call dogmatism, sectarianism and anti-Marxism-Leninism? Why do you lack the courage to do this? Why such a stringent embargo? You fear the truth. The huge spectre you call 'dogmatism', *i.e.* genuine Marxism-Leninism, is haunting the world, and it threatens you. You are divorced from the masses. That is why you fear the truth and carry your fear to such absurd lengths. Friends, comrades! If you are men enough, step forward! Let each side in the debate publish all the articles in which it is criticised by the other side, and let the people in our own countries and the whole world think over and judge who is right and who is wrong. That is what we are doing, and we hope you will follow our example. We are not afraid to publish everything of yours in full. We publish all the 'masterpieces' in which you rail at us. Then, in reply, we either refute them point by point, or refute their main points. Sometimes we publish your articles without a word in answer, leaving the readers to judge for themselves. Isn't that fair and reasonable? You, modern revisionist masters! Do you dare to do the same? If you are men enough, you will. But having a guilty conscience and an unjust case, being fierce of visage but faint of heart, outwardly as tough as bulls but inwardly as timid as mice, you will not dare. We are sure you will not dare. Isn't that so? Please answer!

Nothing could convey more clearly the level to which Sino-Soviet relations had descended than the jeering, provocative and, perhaps, desperate tone of this passage. It scarcely suggested that the forthcoming talks would be easy or successful.

Two other polemical articles squeezed into the Chinese press before March 9 were shorter but no less sharp in tone. The first: 'A Comment on the Statement of the Communist Party of the USA' (*People's Daily*, March 8, 1963) dealt with the 'crisis in the Caribbean' again but also took the opportunity to reply to Khrushchev's comment on the Chinese attitude to the continued foreign occupation of Tai-wan, Hong-Kong and Macao. Saying that they would deal with these problems in due course, the Chinese reminded the Russians that they also regarded themselves as victims of unjust treaties imposed on China by the Tsarist régime. This was the first suggestion that Sino-Soviet rivalry might one day assume a territorial character. The other article: 'A Mirror for Revisionists' (*People's Daily*, March 9, 1963) dealt with the split in the Indian Communist Party and the seizure of control by the 'revisionist' (*i.e.* pro-Moscow) elements.

The publication on March 13 and 14 in Moscow and Peking of the letters exchanged between the two parties did not put an end to public polemics, though they took on a less direct character. The Chinese published criticisms of the Yugoslavs; the Albanians attacked Khrushchev by name; the Russians came mildly to the defence of the American and French Communists. On March 25, the Chinese published the text of a letter addressed to both Soviet and Chinese parties by Aidit, the Indonesian Communist leader, welcoming the prospect of talks and an international meeting: the Chinese liked to have the record clear!

On March 30 the Soviet Party wrote again to the Chinese, welcoming their agreement to hold bilateral talks which, they agreed, would be a step towards an international meeting. Having given the Chinese their views, for the most part un-original, on 'some questions of principle', the Russians proposed a largely non-committal agenda for the talks, while agreeing also to discuss all the points proposed by the Chinese. Only after this did the Russians mention the Albanians and

Yugoslavs, in such a way as to suggest that neither would form an important item on the agenda nor, perhaps, be invited to the subsequent international meeting.

The final public exchange of letters is remarkable for its curious haggling over the persons of Mao and Khrushchev. When Mao saw Chervonenko on February 23 and agreed to bilateral talks, he suggested that Khrushchev should stop in Peking 'while making his visit to Cambodia'. To this the Russians replied in their letter of March 30 with the most elaborate arguments. Khrushchev, they said, was not going to Cambodia: it had been decided (though it had not been announced) on February 12 that Brezhnev, the Soviet President, would make the trip. In any case, said the Russians, Khrushchev had already visited China 'thrice' (they used a pointedly Slav word for this), whereas Mao had visited the Soviet Union only twice. Since the Chinese leader had said he wanted to see more of Russia, and had already received an invitation in May 1960 to come and do so, why then didn't he come in the spring or summer 'which are good seasons of the year in our country'?

It is not easy for an outsider to understand why these two great 'comrades' should pay so much attention to protocol or why they seemed so loath to meet each other. Was it that they did not trust each other? Or that they knew they could never agree?

The Russians had suggested in their letter that the bilateral meeting should take place on May 15. It was not until May 9, however, doubtless after some exchanges behind the scenes, that Chou En-lai finally informed Chervonenko that the Chinese accepted the bilateral talks and would send a delegation headed by Teng Hsiao-ping, the party's General Secretary, and Peng Chen, the secretary of the Peking branch of the party: both 'tough' men whose appointment did not suggest that the Chinese would approach the meeting in a mood for compromise.

The Chinese asked for the meeting to be in mid-June rather than mid-May. After further exchanges it was finally fixed for July 5.

On May 16, *Pravda* published a factual account of the exchanges that had taken place between the Russians and the

Chinese, recorded the agreement to hold a bilateral meeting on July 5, and announced the composition of the Soviet delegation. It was to be led by Mikhail Suslov, the member of the Presidium and Secretariat of the CPSU who for many years had been responsible for the international aspects of Communism and who had, as we have seen, been in the forefront of the earlier negotiations with the Chinese, notably at the 1960 conference. The choice was natural, since Suslov was the man who corresponded most closely in rank and status with Teng Hsiao-ping, apart from Khrushchev himself, who could clearly not enter into talks with anyone less than Mao himself. Suslov was to be supported by three other secretaries of the CPSU: Yuri Andropov and Boris Ponomarev, both leading 'internationalists', and Leonid Ilyichev, head of the CPSU's 'ideological' department. It was a strong and dependable team.

With this agreement reached, it was reasonable to suppose that preparations for the meeting would go on quietly behind the scenes and that both sides would refrain from further public polemics. Indeed, there seemed to be little more that either the Russians or the Chinese could say to make their positions clearer. If, as they both asserted, the talks were going to contribute to a restoration of 'unity' and good relations, they would be better unaccompanied by vociferous polemics.

There were signs that the Russians, for their part, were anxious to avoid the charge that they had broken the truce. On May 18, Tito made an important speech to the Central Committee of the Yugoslav League of Communists, much of which was devoted to a discussion of Yugoslavia's relations with the international Communist movement and to outspoken criticisms of the Chinese Communists. Apart from rebutting some of the Chinese criticisms of Yugoslav Communism in very frank terms, Tito affirmed for the first time his party's place inside the international movement. 'When I stressed that we are on the side of the anti-dogmatic forces in the Communist movement', he said, 'I thereby stressed our place, our duty and the international obligations of the Yugoslav Communist League in the ranks of the international working-class movement.' And, having dismissed the assessment of Yugoslavia in the Moscow Statement of 1960 as 'a thing of the past', Tito said: 'We must concern ourselves especially with events in the international revolutionary working-class movement. We must be aware that we are *a part of that movement and not something outside it*.' (Tito's emphasis.) This was the statement of all statements with which the Chinese were in complete and utter disagreement.

Eight days passed before the Russians published in *Pravda* an account of Tito's speech: a delay which could only mean that the Kremlin was not sure how it was to be handled. In the end *Pravda* printed six whole columns of extracts from the Yugoslav leader's speech, but without including a single one of his criticisms of the Chinese. Indeed, it would not have been apparent to a reader of *Pravda's* version of Tito's speech that he had discussed differences with the Chinese at all. On the other hand, *Pravda* did include his references to Yugoslavia's obligations to and membership of the Communist movement. It also reproduced his list of those European parties with which the Yugoslavs had restored good relations: the Communist parties of Bulgaria, Hungary, East Germany, France and Italy; a list that suggested by its omissions that some outposts of 'Stalinism' in Europe had yet to be overcome.

Pravda's careful editing of Tito suggested that the Russians were at least anxious not to expose themselves to the charge of reopening direct polemics with the Chinese, though to give any publicity at all to Tito's words was Moscow's way of declaring that there would be no retreat on the Yugoslav issue. On the other hand, something that might have been interpreted as a retreat took place over Khrushchev's planned visit to Yugoslavia. This had at one point been announced for some time in June, and the remark in the Soviet statement of May 16 that some of the engagements that made the bilateral meeting impossible in June were 'of an international character', had suggested that Khrushchev intended to make his visit to Tito *before* the meeting with the Chinese took place. (He had no other engagements 'of an international character' in June.) On June 8, however, it was reported from Moscow that the Yugoslav visit had been postponed until the autumn 'or possibly later': a move which suggested that the Russians were at least avoiding obvious provocations to the Chinese.

This comparative calm was then rudely upset by the Chinese Communists' publication in Peking (and by the New China News Agency throughout the world) of their detailed reply to the Russians' letter to them of March 30. This was the full statement of the Chinese position which Chou En-lai had promised when he agreed to bilateral talks on May 9. It bore the unassuming title of 'A Proposal Concerning the General Line of the International Communist Movement'.

The letter of June 14, couched in the usual crisp, didactic style of the Chinese Communists, was a remarkable piece of Marxist-Leninist sophistry. It restated the whole of the 'dogmatic' attitude to questions of war and peace and revolution in more precise terms than before and in some respects carried Mao's 'teachings' a stage further.

Recognising that there were now a 'number of major differences of principle' in the Communist movement, the Chinese set out to explain, in reply to the Russian letter of March 30, what they thought the 'general line' of the international Communist movement should be. They insisted that the Moscow documents of 1957 and 1960 still represented the ' common programme ' of the movement and that the central question was whether its ' revolutionary principles ' were still to be followed. To reduce this programme one-sidedly to such concepts as 'peaceful coexistence', 'peaceful competition' and 'peaceful transition' was to abandon the 'historical mission of proletarian revolution'. The letter then proceeded to apply this basic attitude to every aspect of Communist policy, producing a total of twenty-five distinct points on which the Chinese and Russian views differed.

Many of these points had been aired in previous Chinese writings. But there were some interesting new developments of the Chinese argument. Their sixth point, for example, dealt with the position of the 'socialist camp' which, they said, since it was the result of the struggles of the international proletariat, therefore *belonged* to the international movement as well as to the peoples of the countries of the camp. The obvious implication of this argument was that the Communist parties which had achieved power in the camp were not free to dispose of their resources as they pleased, but were under an obligation to aid the rest of the movement. A similar argument was applied to relations within the Communist camp in point twenty-one, where the Chinese argued that such relations must be based on mutual support on a basis of complete equality. The exercise of economic pressure on other fraternal countries, said the Chinese with apparent feeling, was a manifestation of 'national egoism'.

Another idea, already implied in earlier Chinese arguments but expressed clearly for the first time in their letter of June 14, concerned the exceptional importance of the part played by the 'anti-imperialist' movements in Asia, Africa and Latin America. The Chinese argued that, although 'certain persons' treated these struggles of oppressed peoples with scorn, they were in fact the 'storm centres of the world revolution'. It was in those areas that there were the best prospects of undermining imperialism. 'In a sense, therefore,' the letter said, 'the whole cause of the international proletarian revolution hinges on the outcome of the revolution of the peoples of these areas, who constitute the overwhelming majority of the world's population.' The attitude towards these struggles, said the Chinese, was 'an important criterion for distinguishing between those who want revolution and those who don't'. Here for the first time the Chinese were putting into words the ideological basis for the movement of the revolution Eastwards – the 'Sinification' of the Communist movement. It was also Peking's bid for leadership of the 'have-not' peoples.

A third new argument was produced in points eighteen and nineteen which discussed the apparently uncontroversial questions of the 'dictatorship of the proletariat' and the nature of its party. The Chinese rejected firmly the idea that there could ever be a 'state of the whole people' or a 'party of the entire people'. The one idea was 'a great historical retrogression'; the other was tantamount to 'restoring capitalism'. The point of this argument becomes apparent only when it is realised that both ideas to which the Chinese took exception are closely associated with Khrushchev and represent some of his more recent contributions to Soviet political and constitutional thought. To the Russian Communist the Chinese strictures were equivalent to interference in their own domestic affairs. In so doing the Chinese were undoubtedly out to make the point that the affairs of the Soviet Communist Party *were* also the affair of the whole Communist movement.

The Chinese letter of June 14 was in effect an attack on Soviet policy on all fronts and the most thorough-going challenge to Russian leadership of the Communist movement that had ever been delivered. It was recognised for this by the Russians, who announced that it would not be published in the Soviet press.

Despite its strongly militant and argumentative tone, the Chinese 'Proposal' did not contain many original points or add appreciably to the depth of the rift between Moscow and Peking. Nevertheless the Russians chose to take great exception to it and announced on June 18 that it would not be published in the Soviet Press. Meanwhile the Chinese set out, by means of their world-wide New China News Agency and their diplomatic missions, to give their letter the widest possible distribution in the Communist world and outside.

The Russians justified their refusal to give publicity to the Chinese letter on the grounds that it was a breach of the truce to polemics agreed between the two parties, and that if they published it they would have themselves to reply and thus exacerbate the situation. There was more in this argument, perhaps, than pure sophistry, since it was indeed true that the Russians, unlike the Chinese, had never given their rivals room in their own press nor helped their people to know the substance of the Chinese charges against them. Their refusal to publish the June 14 letter was at least consistent with their previous policy.

A few days later the Central Committee of the Soviet Communist Party met in Moscow nominally for the discussion of internal 'ideological' questions, but in fact for the members of the Committee to hear a full account from Suslov and Khrushchev of the state of Sino-Soviet relations, and to give the Soviet delegation to the talks its full and unanimous backing for a tough and unyielding line with the Chinese. This was put into the form of a resolution affirming the Russians' determination to stick to all the ideas and policies agreed at the Twentieth, Twenty-first and Twenty-second Congresses of the

CPSU, which, they claimed, had been 'unanimously approved by the whole Soviet people and the international Communist movement'.

With this statement it seemed as though the stage were finally set for the meeting on July 5. Each protagonist had girded his loins, stated his uncompromising position and spat defiance at his opponent. It was difficult to see where Teng and Suslov would begin their talks.

Before they met, however, the Russians took another step which set the two sides even further apart and made the prospects for the talks even gloomier. On June 27, only a week before Teng and his delegation were due to arrive in Moscow, the Soviet government addressed a Note to the Chinese embassy in Moscow demanding the immediate recall of three members of the embassy's staff as well as of a post-graduate student and an official of the Chinese institute in Moscow. The reason given by the Russians was that the people concerned had taken part in the distribution of the Chinese letter in Moscow.

Releasing this information in Peking, the Chinese described the Russian action as 'unreasonable and unfriendly' and argued that they were entitled to distribute 'official documents', as the Russians themselves had done with their letter on March 30 in Peking. Significantly, however, the Chinese said that they would not reply in kind against the Russians in China and appealed to the Russians to take no more 'rash steps'.

The importance of this exchange on the very eve of the Sino-Soviet talks cannot be exaggerated. There can be no doubt that the Chinese were right in suggesting, in their comment on the expulsion, that the Russians were trying to 'create obstacles to talks between the Soviet and Chinese parties'. However much the Russians may have resented the Chinese action in distributing their letter in the Communist world, this did not really cause them great harm; they could easily have overlooked it. That they did not suggested that they intended to be deliberately provocative to the Chinese, as, indeed, Khrushchev, had been for many years.

The final episode in this story – though not the final episode in the story of Sino-Soviet relations – covers the beginning of the inter-party talks in Moscow. By then relations between Russia and China had reached as low a level as could be imagined between two great nations and allies. The Chinese had provoked the Russians by their efforts to distribute their letter of June 14 in the Soviet Union and thus evade the ban imposed by the Soviet press on publication. The Russians had insisted that such behaviour was an infringement of Soviet sovereignty and had demanded the recall from Moscow of three Chinese diplomatists and two other Chinese citizens.

From this point the dispute began to take on almost the air of a musical comedy, or tragi-comedy. Display windows outside the Chinese embassy in Moscow were smashed by some Russians, and the Chinese not unnaturally suggested that the incident had been deliberately planned and carried out. The Chinese who had been expelled from Moscow were given almost a hero's welcome when they arrived in Peking: a gesture which the Russians immediately denounced as provocative. Meanwhile the Chinese continued their efforts to have their point of view communicated to the Soviet people by organising 'shock brigades' who scattered copies of their letter of June 14 from the Peking-Moscow express as it sped across the Russian countryside. This led to further recriminations from the Russians.

In the midst of the exchanges, Teng Hsiao-ping and Peng Chen arrived in Moscow on July 5 for the talks. They were received by Suslov with the barest minimum of ceremony and they disappeared at once behind the high walls of a villa on the outskirts of Moscow. The talks began the same day and continued in a desultory manner behind an impenetrable security barrier.

It quickly became apparent, however, that the fact that the talks had begun had not affected the stand taken by either side. Within a few days, on July 13, the Peking *People's Daily* accused the Russians of inflaming feeling against China at meetings throughout the Soviet Union, asked whether the Russians were trying to bring Sino-Soviet relations 'to the brink of rupture ', and said the situation was ' very grave '. Significantly, the paper added: 'If the differences between our two parties cannot be resolved today, we can wait until tomorrow. If not this year, we can wait till next. Our parties can hold further bilateral talks.'

This appeared to be an admission by the Chinese that, for the moment at least, and on the level at which the Russians had chosen to conduct the dispute in its latter stages, they were beaten. Russian tactics appeared to be to submit the Chinese to every possible kind of provocation, in the hope that they would either refuse to come to Moscow or that they would walk out of the meeting when confronted by the Russians' unbending attitude. In effect, the Russians had been daring the Chinese to go off and do their damnedest with whatever resources and whatever following they could muster. The Chinese, recognising that they could not compete with the Russians on those terms, preferred to swallow their pride and to keep the door to the Communist movement open by talking of further talks to come.

There we have to leave the story of the Russians and the Chinese, but not without taking a glance at what Khrushchev, bête-noire of the Chinese Communists, was doing at this time. Just before the Sino-Soviet talks were due to begin in Moscow Khrushchev paid a visit to East Germany and reaffirmed his friendship with Walter Ulbricht, the East German Communist leader. Within a few days of the talks' starting, Janos Kadar, leader of the Hungarian Communist Party, arrived in Moscow to receive an ostentatiously warm welcome. Between these two meetings the Soviet leader managed to have talks with Paul-Henri Spaak, the Belgian statesman, on East-West relations.

Then, on July 16, Khrushchev gave his personal blessing to the Moscow talks with Britain and America for a nuclear test ban by himself attending the opening session.

He ignored the presence of the Chinese delegates in Moscow. This time Mao Tse-tung would not be able to prevent Khrushchev from coming to terms with the West.

XIV

TWO ROMES?

With the opening of the inter-party talks in Moscow in July 1963 to the accompaniment of more mutual recriminations and the Russians' whole-hearted rejection of the Chinese letter of June 14, the two parties to the dispute seemed to have reached the end of the road. There was clearly no prospect of their reaching any real agreement on the issues dividing them. The only question seemed to be whether the Chinese would depart in wrath, having abandoned the hope of working inside a Communist movement dominated by the Russians, to set up their own 'Eastern movement' centred on Peking, or whether they would try to keep the door open for further talks with the Russians.

Whatever decisions were reached in Moscow, however, it should be clear from the preceding account that the prospects of a genuine understanding being reached by the Russians and Chinese, either on matters of high ideology or on matters of immediate practical politics, are very remote. It is no longer possible to believe that the conflict between the Russian and Chinese Communists is simply a difference about the interpretation of a political doctrine or a disagreement over some particular aspect of policy. It is a dispute between two great and proud peoples about their position and power in the world; it affects every aspect of their relationships; and it has tended to grow in scope and bitterness over the last ten years. Whether or not it may ultimately be possible for these two great powers to compose their differences, the process of so doing is unlikely to be short. A rift which is now so deep and has been so long in the making cannot easily be mended. Moreover, both Russians and Chinese appear to have recognised latterly that there is no longer any point in papering over their differences in the interests of preserving the convention of Communist 'unity'.

It will be surprising, therefore, if there has been any fundamental change in relations between Moscow and Peking by the time this book appears in print.

There are certain other factors affecting the likelihood of reconciliation which have appeared in the later stages of the dispute. They derive from personal and national emotions rather than from political ideas and, even if it is clearly wrong to believe that the relationship between two great nations could depend entirely on personalities and personal feelings, there can be no doubt that they play an important part in the Sino-Soviet dispute. It was, in fact, Khrushchev himself who said, with much justice, that such disputes have a logic of their own and that emotions also come into play. They have certainly done so in this case.

It would certainly be mistaken to regard the dispute between Russia and China as mainly a dispute between the two leaders, Khrushchev and Mao Tse-tung. But it would be equally wrong to ignore the extent to which the dispute is a reflection of the conflicting characters of these two men. The régimes over which they hold sway are highly centralised dictatorships in which the personality of the man at the top is of vastly more importance than in the case of the leader of a democratic régime. If the dispute is fundamentally one between two great nations, Russia and China, it must also be stressed that it is a dispute between *Khrushchev's* Russia and *Mao's* China. The direction and policies which each man has implanted on the party and country he rules has served to deepen the basic differences rather than to reduce them. Both Mao and Khrushchev are now deeply engaged in the dispute in a personal way, so that reconciliation must seem unlikely so long as the two men remain in power.

The Chinese have left no thinking person who reads their polemics in any doubt that they regard Khrushchev as being personally responsible for the 'revisionist' direction which Soviet policy has taken. Though they have, it is true, left it to their Albanian friends to make the bitterest attacks on Khrushchev by name, they have cast only the thinnest of veils over their own blows at the Russian leader. When, in their letter of June 14, 1963, the Chinese speak of 'certain persons' who 'a few years ago suddenly claimed Lenin's policy of peaceful coexistence as their own "great discovery"', who 'assert that they have made the greatest creative contributions to revolutionary theory since Lenin and that they alone are correct', and who 'are enormously exaggerating the role of certain individuals, shifting all errors on to others and claiming all credit for themselves' – there can be no doubt what persons, or person, the Chinese have in mind. It is the same person who is depicted in various parts of the Chinese writings as saying one thing one day and another the next, as demanding obedience from other Communist leaders to the waving of his baton, as maintaining feudal and patriarchal relations between Moscow and other parties, and as practising great-nation chauvinism and national egoism. There is a bitter personal quality about these attacks such as has seldom been heard inside the Communist world, where the personalities of 'statesmen' are sacrosanct. The personal attacks on Khrushchev probably accounted more than anything else for the very strained atmosphere in which the Moscow talks began.

In fairness to the Russians, it must be said that their polemics do not contain similar attacks on the person of Mao Tse-tung, though they too have made jibes at 'people who call themselves Marxist-Leninists' and 'certain new-fledged theoreticians'. At the same time an element of national, even racial, feeling has entered into their statements and comments and has also tended to embitter relations. In the later Russian statements there were references to the 'Chinese embassy' and 'Chinese organisations' where in the past 'China' would always have been 'The Chinese People's Republic'. In this way the Soviet publicists have begun to draw attention to the Oriental quality of their ideological and political rivals and thus to feed a little on the Russians' historical fear of and distaste for their neighbour in the East. It is a dangerous path to tread and one, again, from which it may prove difficult to turn back.

Finally, an element of physical conflict and personal bravado entered into the affair with the incidents preceding the opening of the bilateral talks in July 1963. There seems no reason to doubt that the display windows outside the Chinese embassy in Moscow were smashed as the Chinese claim. In Soviet conditions such ' incidents ' do not happen spontaneously, and the authorities now have much experience of producing this type of carefully controlled ' popular indignation ', though it has hitherto been used exclusively against Western governments. It may yet prove, however, that the Western powers are more understanding and forgiving than the Chinese in such matters. They, for their part, have channelled their spirit of adventure into the scattering of their polemical statements from trains speeding across the Russian land. In both cases this type of action introduces an element of directness into the dispute which may be more difficult to smooth over than the differences about Leninism. As Khrushchev said: ' political passions run high '.

But, however much the window-smashing and name-calling may embitter the dispute, they are in the end only one aspect, and perhaps a superficial aspect, of a conflict which, as I hope the account of it I have given has shown, affects every sphere of relations between Russia and China. Most of the forms which the dispute takes have been touched on at some point in the preceding account. Some others, including some of the most important, have been mentioned only fleetingly or by implication, because neither Russians nor Chinese have yet been ready to speak frankly about them. The following is an attempt to review the full scope of the dispute in all its aspects:

Economic: China still belongs to the 'have-nots' of this world; Russia is at least on the threshold of entering the society of the 'haves'. Whatever political system prevails in the country, China cannot be a great power in the modern world until she has achieved a substantial measure of industrialisation, and she cannot hope to do that without considerable aid from outside. The nature of the birth of the present régime in China dictated that the new rulers in Peking could turn *only* to Russia for the aid they needed. The Russians, alone of all industrialised powers, had at least *some* reasons, partly political or 'ideological' and partly of self-interest, for assisting in the enormous task of creating a modern industry for China. Moreover, there is no doubt at all that the Russian Communists accepted this obligation towards the new régime in China and made a considerable effort to set China on the road to economic progress. That they later, in 1960, withdrew their aid and left the Chinese eventually to fend for themselves is at least in part a measure of the lack of wisdom and understanding on the part of the Chinese Communist rulers. Even if the Russians were naturally unlikely ever to subordinate all their many economic objectives to the aid of advancing China's economic might, they were nevertheless conscious of their obligations towards China. Only the conviction, generated by the actions of the Chinese leaders, that they were nurturing a Frankenstein monster that was out to dominate them could have persuaded the Russians to embark on a policy of economic sanctions and isolation which, they must have seen, inevitably involved the risk of China's breaking out of the Communist camp.

The dispute has already gone a very long way on the economic level. It is not a simple matter for aid on the scale of Soviet aid to China to be switched on or off. The Russians' decision to withdraw from China was a major economic step which they are unlikely lightly to reverse: certainly not without some assurance that a new aid programme would not come up against the same obstacles as the first one. Moreover, the Chinese, who were completely orientated towards Russia in all their industrial construction, must soon begin to look in another direction for aid. Feelers have indeed already gone out in various directions in the Western world, for example in connexion with the purchase of civilian aircraft from Britain. If the Chinese are obliged eventually to turn more openly and on a larger scale to the West for aid, this also will be a difficult decision to reverse.

Military: Soviet Russia is one of the world's two great nuclear powers. China's military strength still consists of vast land armies equipped with 'conventional' weapons, and those not of an especially high quality. Despite occasional suggestions in the West that the Chinese are about to explode an atomic bomb, there can in sober truth be not the slightest possibility that Communist China will become a nuclear power in the American or Russian sense, or even in the British or French sense, in the next twenty years. On the other hand, the Russians could, had they so wished, have made China into an effective nuclear power at any time in the last five years. That they chose not to do so is by no means the least of the causes of the Sino-Soviet dispute.

Yet, despite the enormous outpourings of polemics from Moscow and Peking, the question of the sharing of nuclear weapons has never been a subject of public debate. In none of the numerous documents reproduced in this book, with the exception of one unpublished letter, is there the slightest hint that the Chinese resent being kept out of the 'nuclear club' by the Russians. But it is inconceivable that they should not be aggrieved at being deprived of access to such a wonderful short cut to great power status.

When Khrushchev made his second hasty visit to Peking in the summer of 1958 he took with him his Defence Minister, Marshal Rodion Malinovsky, and Malinovsky's Chinese counterpart, Marshal Peng Teh-huai, also took part in the talks. In view of this, and in view of the tension then being worked up in the Straits of Formosa, it was reasonable to suppose that military matters were at the centre of the talks between Mao and Khrushchev. But there is no evidence to suggest that the question of military collaboration between Russia and China remained the principal bone of contention. Indeed, it would be fair to conclude that Khrushchev made it clear as early as 1958 that he had no intention of sharing Russia's nuclear know-how or capacity in the military field with the Chinese. As far as the published record goes, it looks as if the Chinese accepted this position and reconciled themselves to the thought that, if they were ever to become a nuclear power, it would have to be through their own efforts.

The fact that the question of nuclear 'sharing' between Russia and China appeared to have been ruled out and that the dispute moved into the more abstract realm of ideology did not mean, however, that the problems engendered by nuclear power ceased to play a part in the dispute. On the contrary, Russia's status as a nuclear power has been and continues to be the principal factor keeping the dispute alive. It is the fact that Russia has become one of the two powers upon whom the fate of the world depends that made Khrushchev's 'revision' of Communist world strategy inevitable. It is the possession of nuclear power which obliges the Russians to demand a special position in the Communist movement; it is this, rather than their experience or seniority, that sets them apart from the other Communist countries and parties, gives them special responsibilities and requires that those who would be their allies and friends should recognise Russia's special position. It matters very little for this purpose whether Russia is described as the 'leader' or the 'centre' or the 'avant-garde' of the Communist world or movement. What matters is that Russia's allies should recognise, as America's allies also have to recognise, that on certain matters and at certain times the Russians have to take decisions on their own, without consultation with their allies. Khrushchev cannot risk having 'too many fingers on the trigger'.

Diplomatic: Russia is a 'satisfied' power, in the sense that, as a result of the settlements reached at the end of the Second World War, the Soviet régime regained control of all the territory over which Moscow had ever ruled. No territory to which the government in Moscow could possibly lay claim remained in the hands of another power. China, on the other hand, is an 'unsatisfied' power, forced to accept the presence of a rival government, supported by American economic and military resources, on the island of Formosa, and with territorial claims (whether justified or not) against many other powers. The Russians enjoy the full status of a great power in the world today, with representation and a following in the United Nations Organisation and with diplomatic and commercial relations throughout the world. The Communist régime in Peking, however, is excluded from the United Nations, ignored by most of the Western powers, and has diplomatic and trade relations with only a small group of relatively unimportant countries apart from those in the Communist bloc.

This difference in their status in the world is also an important source of friction between Russia and China and a reason for their differing points of view on foreign affairs. Being treated as equals by the Western powers, the Russians can think in terms of East-West agreements and understanding. The Chinese, with their permanent sense of grievance, can see the rest of the world only as the 'enemy' and frame their policies accordingly. To reduce this aspect of the problem to practical issues: it is very difficult for the Chinese to discuss with the Russians the working out of an agreement with the Americans if they know that they will play no part whatsoever in the negotiations of the agreement nor be involved, except passively, in its conclusions.

Two Ages of Revolution: The Russian revolution is nearly half a century old; the Chinese revolution has only a little more than a decade behind it. The Russian revolution has not only come of age; it has reached middle-age, it has acquired status, possessions and responsibilities. The Chinese Communist régime is still directed by people whose main inspiration was genuinely revolutionary, who acquired power and influence through civil war and who have still to recognise the immensely bigger battles they have to fight before the revolution will show the results it promised. The Russian Communists and at least a section of the Russian people have something to lose; the Chinese rulers have nothing to lose but their power.

This distinction also has a profound effect on the way the Russian and Chinese Communists look at their problems. The Chinese tend to think in terms of the further growth and extension of the revolution, and of further 'revolutionary battles'; the Russians tend to look for less exciting and less risky ways of extending their influence in the world.

Two Different Men: Mao Tse-tung is himself a 'great revolutionary leader': he led his people out of the wilderness to the seat of power in Peking. He is, in fact, the greatest living revolutionary leader and, though it may be unwise to exaggerate the profundity of his thought and the originality of his contributions to Marxist revolutionary theory, there can be no questioning of his independent leadership of the Chinese revolution. Nikita Khrushchev, on the other hand, for all his skilful and sometimes courageous handling of post-Stalin Russia, is a much less 'revolutionary' figure. Though he loves to recall his early contact with the revolution and to reaffirm his faith in revolutionary ideals, the greater part of his life has been spent, not in overthrowing an existing régime or fighting revolutions, but in the creation and administration of a new society. What applies to Mao Tse-tung and Khrushchev applies also to those who stand closest to them. Indeed, in the case of Khrushchev, it must be said that there is now a new and even younger generation rising to power for whom the ideas of revolution must have very little appeal at all. It would be difficult to exaggerate the extent to which the different 'ages' of the Chinese and Russian revolutions account for the present differences between Moscow and Peking.

Ideological: The dispute might have been understood sooner and more clearly had Communism, or Marxism-Leninism, not laid claim to be a complete political, philosophical, economic and moral 'ideology' or doctrine. The existence of this ideology, which is supposed to provide the answers to every political problem and to give absolute authority to those who speak and act in its name, has served to conceal rather than clarify the Sino-Soviet differences, at least to the uninitiated. It has tended to give the impression to the non-Communist observer that the Russians and Chinese were arguing about ideas and not about practical politics. Even in the later stages of the dispute, when Russians and Chinese were having their last meetings in Moscow, they were being described in the West as discussing their 'ideological' differences.

In fact – as every Marxist, at least, should have been ready to acknowledge – ideology has always played a secondary role in the dispute. It has done little more than provide the medium through which differences could be aired without spelling them out in terms of day-to-day policies. It would be unrealistic in the extreme to believe that the policies of the Soviet and Chinese governments are determined primarily by reference to some ideological guide. In fact, the dispute has served to demonstrate just how imprecise and misleading Communist doctrine is, providing ample support for any number of conflicting and contradictory views.

The extent to which ideology has played second fiddle to practical politics, on both the Chinese and the Russian side, could be illustrated by a dozen examples. Suffice it here to refer to two of the more striking 'ideological' issues: the question of peace and war, and the question of Yugoslavia.

On the first question it appears at first sight as if the Russians are arguing flatly that nuclear war must be avoided at all costs, while the Chinese declare themselves ready to face the consequences of such a war. But a closer study of Russian and Chinese outpourings on this important topic reveals no such clear picture. It is confused by the Chinese, who declare that they are certainly not advocating the use of nuclear weapons to advance the Communist cause, that they approve of having proper respect for the enemy in 'tactical' terms, and that they were *not* in favour of Khrushchev's attempt to mount nuclear weapons in Cuba, which they describe as 'adventurism'. The issue is confused no less by the Russians who, while stressing the destruction that would be wrought by a nuclear war, proclaim their readiness to deliver a 'crushing blow' on any aggressor and to lend every kind of support to wars of 'national liberation'. There are times when the difference between the Russian and Chinese approach to this question seems to be no more than a matter of words and when an outside observer may be excused for believing that, if it were only a matter of finding the correct 'Marxist' formula for nuclear war, it would not be very difficult for Russians and Chinese to agree, as in fact they managed to agree on paper in 1957 and 1960. The Chinese have on more than one occasion subscribed formally to the Russian 'revisionist' view that war can be prevented.

Nothing could illustrate the secondary nature of ideology better than the question of the Russian and Chinese attitudes to Yugoslavia, where ideology and practical politics go hand in hand. On this question, both Russians and Chinese have made Communist doctrine do their bidding in a most unprincipled way. From the time of Stalin's quarrel with Tito in 1948 until Stalin's death in 1953, Khrushchev was no less outspoken than any other Soviet leader in his condemnation of 'the renegade Tito'. From the time of the attempt at reconciliation in 1955 Tito became a 'comrade' of Khrushchev's and the Yugoslav régime was found to have 'socialist' qualities which had escaped notice in the preceding period. But when in 1956 Tito's role in the Hungarian revolt made the course of rapprochement more difficult, and when in 1957 he refused to join the 'camp', Khrushchev did not let ideology inhibit him in his assessment of the Yugoslav régime. So, in June 1958, Tito became a 'Trojan horse' in the Communist movement and a 'class enemy' in the pay of the imperialists. This did not, however, prevent him from discovering in 1962 that Yugoslavia was a 'socialist' country or from arranging that delegates of the Yugoslav Communist League should be received back into the company of Communist parties. In fairness to the Yugoslavs, it has to be said that all these changes took place without their having apparently made any substantial change either in their own ' doctrine ', embodied in the Programme of their party, or in their domestic or foreign policies – facts the Chinese have been at pains to point out.

But the Chinese have been no more consistent than the Russians, though they have beaten the ideological drum rather louder. They approved publicly of Khrushchev's resumption of relations with Tito in 1955 and themselves appointed an ambassador to Belgrade. Throughout 1956 and 1957 Yugoslavia remained a 'socialist' country and Tito remained a 'comrade'. It was not until May 1958 that the Chinese interpreters of Marxism discovered that Yugoslav Communism was in fact 'revisionism' and proceeded to denounce it on all sides. Even more significant for the 'ideology' was the fact that the article in the Peking *People's Daily* announcing this change of line was reproduced in the Moscow *Pravda* the next day. Once again, Russians and Chinese saw eye to eye.

The purpose of this argument is not to show that ideology is of no significance at all. There can, indeed, be no doubt that it *does* play an important part in the political life of the Communist world, though perhaps less than the Communists would have us believe and less than it did in the earlier years of the revolution. But the part it plays is secondary: it provides a medium for debate and an esoteric means of communication for people who are notoriously shy of discussing real political issues in the full light of day. For the outside observer the 'ideological' dispute is of enormous value as a guide to the real issues at stake, so long as it is remembered that it is *only* a guide and not the essence of the affair.

One final word on ideology. It must be regarded as one of the two main casualties in the Sino-Soviet dispute. It will be difficult for any Communist leader, of whatever persuasion, 'dogmatic' or 'revisionist', ever again to persuade people of the absolute rightness of his interpretation of Communist doctrine. The whole doctrine has in effect been thrown into the melting-pot and it is too early yet to say in what shape it will ultimately emerge.

Organisational: For some forty years, the Russian Communists were the undisputed leaders of the world Communist movement. With the advent, following the Second World War, of other Communist countries and the formation of the Communist camp, the Russians assumed leadership of this too. It was an entirely natural development, since Stalin had long ago turned the 'international movement' into an obedient instrument of his will, and the new Communist countries were a creation of Soviet military strength and not a spontaneous upsurge of the revolutionary movement in the world. It scarcely occurred to anyone – and least of all to those Communist leaders whom the Russians themselves had placed in power – to question Russian leadership. The revolution had been born in Moscow and continued to be directed from Moscow.

Yet there was nothing sacrosanct in theory about Russian leadership of the revolutionary movement; there was nothing in the Communist writ that said that all revolutions were directed from Moscow. Indeed, it was an accident and an anomaly that the revolution had triumphed there first; it might have been Germany, or Hungary, or China. It might have been successful at the beginning in several countries, so that the 'revolutionary movement' would from the outset have been directed by an international committee and not just the government of one country. But that did not happen, and the Russians remained in charge of the Communist movement, primarily because they alone had the facilities and resources to keep it going. And they remained in charge of the 'socialist camp' because they alone had the economic and military means to hold it together.

This situation was bound to be upset by any retreat from Stalinist absolutism in Moscow and by the emergence of

Communist régimes and parties which did not owe their existence to Russian support. The first such upset came with the revolt of Marshal Tito against Stalin's *diktat*. It was solved in a typically Stalinist way with the excision of Yugoslavia from the Communist camp. A far more serious upset was inherent in the seizure of power by the Chinese Communists, though Stalin did not live to see them challenge his authority. The threat to Russian leadership was also apparent in the post-Stalin revolts in Poland and Hungary. It was a problem that had to be faced and solved by Stalin's successors. It is this problem that is at the centre of the Sino-Soviet dispute, and it is still far from solution.

To put it in concrete terms: What *should* be the relationship between two Communist powers and between two Communist parties, if it is not to be merely the relationship of leader and led? In the case of Communist countries, is it to be a *special* relationship, differing from the relationship between those countries and the rest of the world? If so, in what does this special relationship consist? Does it mean that Communist countries share all their resources equally, forming a closely-knit 'Communist camp' expanding as each new Communist party achieves power? Does it mean that the better-off Communist countries trade on special terms with their less fortunate brothers to their own disadvantage? Or does the special relationship mean no more than that Communist countries are well disposed towards each other, acting as loyal allies and sharing a common view of the rest of the world?

Other questions, though of a less pressing nature, arise with regard to the relations between the Soviet Communist Party and those Communist parties which have not achieved power. Have they all an equal say in world policy and in the councils of the world movement? What are their obligations to the 'ruling' parties, and what obligations have the 'ruling' parties to those still in the wilderness?

Strange though it may seem, one of the lessons of the dispute between Moscow and Peking is that the Russians under Khrushchev appear to favour a looser, more flexible relationship between themselves and the other Communist countries and parties. They appear to have decided that they will *not* allow themselves to be used as the industrial base and arsenal of the Communist movement. They will decide themselves on the distribution of their resources, supporting those countries and governments they think deserving and shunning those which upset their plans. They prefer to extend credits to the Yugoslavs who, while continuing to disagree on 'ideological' matters, have shown they can stand on their own feet. They withdrew their aid from the Albanians who, despite the fervency with which they proclaimed their loyalty to Moscow, proved hopelessly inefficient and unreliable.

These 'organisational' problems of relations within the Communist camp and movement would all have existed even if Russia had not acquired nuclear military capacity. But it is this which has made them so crucial. It is this which has made the Russians ready to see the Chinese driven out of the Communist camp and see them setting up a new 'Eastern' international of their own rather than permit them a decisive influence over Soviet policy.

These considerations lie behind the 'organisational' questions which are at the centre of the dispute: whether the Russians 'lead' the movement or not; whether there should be an organised international movement; whether policy is decided at meetings of the international; whether such policies are binding on the constituent parties and so forth. The Russians have made their view clear: there is *no* organisation; there is just a common faith.

This does not mean that Soviet Russia has ceased to be an expansionist power or that the Russian Communists have abandoned their belief that the revolution, or 'socialism', is still on the march and that Communism will score further victories at the expense of 'capitalism'. It certainly does not mean that the Russians have any intention of giving up control of their recently acquired empire in Eastern Europe. Nor does it mean that the Soviet Communist Party has decided to leave the Communist parties throughout the word to their own devices, to fight their own battles without help from Moscow.

The attitude of the Russians in their dispute with the Chinese has shown, however, that they are firmly decided not to accept any arrangement, particularly an organisational arrangement, that involves them in any clear obligation to a world-wide movement. Khrushchev obviously fears any involvement in an organisation which might mean that a small but militant Communist party in Latin America, or a large and successful Communist party in Western Europe, could take decisions and actions which might ultimately force decisions on the Soviet government itself. This was a fear that Stalin himself had and exorcised in his day.

It would be wrong to say that the 'International' is the second major casualty of the Sino-Soviet dispute, since the international Communist movement was in fact destroyed by Stalin. But the dispute with China has made it clear that Stalin's successors are determined that it shall not be revived as a genuine international organisation. Russians do not make good committee members and have always rejected with scorn the idea that a political party or movement should degenerate into a 'sort of debating club'.

The Sino-Soviet Dispute and the Non-Communist World

However real and however deep the rift between the Russian and Chinese Communists, how does it concern the rest of the world? Does it really matter to us? Does the democratic world stand to gain anything from this quarrel between the two Communist giants? What should our attitude be towards the dispute? Should we say 'a plague on both your houses', believing that both Russian and Chinese are equally committed to bringing about the downfall of the democratic world and are arguing only about the best way of doing it? Or does the split in the Communist world demand a revision of Western policies?

These questions do not admit of a simple, unqualified answer. But, in a world still divided into 'capitalist' (a label embracing every conceivable kind of political and economic system, short of Moscow-style Communist) and 'Communist', and polarised around Washington and Moscow, the development of a major rift in the Communist part of the world would seem to be, in the classical sense, a Good Thing rather than the reverse.

It is sufficient to consider for a moment what the situation might have been if Khrushchev and Mao had managed to reach an understanding. The Western world would have been confronted with a 'monolithic' Communist bloc stretching from the Elbe to the Pacific, controlling powerful Communist parties in Western Europe and throughout Asia and Africa. The Moscow-Peking axis would have dominated the Eurasian land-mass and South-east Asia as well. Jointly planned and executed aid programmes in Africa and elsewhere would have enabled the Communists to exploit the retreat from 'colonialism' to the full. Above all, the rest of the world would have been intimidated by the apparent unity and singleness of purpose of the Communist monolith. Even though American nuclear power might still have kept the monster at bay, its capacity to nibble away at the rest of the world would have been considerable.

Instead of this we are faced with a divided Communist world. Communism now speaks with two voices instead of one, and no one is to know which is the more authentic. The clarion call of revolution has been muffled and confused.

Consequently, Communist policy on a world scale lacks the assurance which gained it many victories in the post-war period. The hesitation and vacillation which were noted over the questions of Berlin and Cuba were a result of the lack of confidence in policy-making circles.

The differences between Moscow and Peking have already communicated themselves to other Communist governments and parties. The Communist camp is now clearly divided between those who follow Peking and those who follow Moscow. The Communists of North Korea and Albania are, for vastly different reasons, firmly on the Chinese side. The Communists of North Vietnam, though reluctant to become mere satellites of the Chinese, are forced for reasons of geography to lean in their direction. In Eastern Europe, if the majority of the Communist leaders remain, perforce, loyal to Moscow, the Rumanian Communists have at least tried to exploit the new situation to their own advantage. Meanwhile the Cuban Communists, newest members of the camp, have been persuaded that, if it is the Chinese who talk the language they like to hear, it is the Russians alone who have the resources to make Cuban 'socialism' work.

The situation among the Communist parties outside the camp itself is even more complex. The Indian Communist Party was split in two by the dispute. The Indonesian Party appears to look mainly in the direction of Peking. The two largest West European parties, in France and Italy, are loyal to Moscow. But pro-Chinese factions have been found in the Belgian and Swedish parties. Many smaller parties in Asia, Africa and Latin America are similarly divided.

Communism is thus divided, not only as an ideological appeal and as a world strategy, but also as a practical policy in particular countries. This can hardly help the Communist cause.

To this it may be objected that the Russians and the Chinese can pursue their revolutionary ends in their different ways despite their disagreements. They may even be more successful following independent paths, the Chinese rallying the masses of the 'have-not' peoples against the 'imperialists' and the Russians striving to defeat 'capitalism' through 'peaceful competition'. It might even be argued that the Chinese are freer to push ahead with the revolution in Asia unrestrained by Russia's nuclear fears. It may also be said that the military power of Communism, which rests primarily in Russian nuclear capacity, is quite unaffected by the quarrel with China.

Only experience will show what weight should be attached to these considerations. None of them can overshadow the simple fact that Communism, as an idea, as a policy and as an organisation, is divided, and because it is divided it is weaker.

What should the West do about it? The simple answer can only be: to remain strong, united and ready to defend the democratic way of life wherever it is threatened. It is the economic and military strength of the Western world which forced the Russians on to the path of 'revisionism'. If the West were weak Khrushchev would be less inclined to disagree with Mao, and more willing to pursue a policy of threats and wars.

But to strength – our military, economic and political strength – we must add understanding. The West cannot hope to form a correct policy towards the Communist world without understanding the motives that govern both Russians and

Chinese as well as the real issues that divide them. If we stress today that the quarrel is real and deep, we must not ignore Khrushchev's assurance that it is no more than a family squabble. If the Russians appear often to have taken the initiative in cutting the Chinese off from the rest of the Communist world, we may be sure that Moscow has not abandoned hope of regaining influence over China one day. If it is wise to take advantage of Khrushchev's ' revisionist ' approach to East-West relations, must we necessarily accept his view of China and join with him in banishing the Chinese to outer darkness? The Sino-Soviet split is a serious challenge to Western policy-makers, and one which they have still not taken up.

PART TWO

A CHRONOLOGY OF DOCUMENTS AND SIGNIFICANT EVENTS

Certain passages in these documents have been italicised to draw attention to statements of special importance

1917

April

In one of his 'Theses' submitted to the Bolshevik party on his return to Russia, Lenin said:

It is the task of our party, acting in a country where the revolution has started earlier than in other countries, to take the initiative in creating a third international.

1919

April

The First Congress of the Communist International resolved that:

1. The fight for the dictatorship of the proletariat requires a united, resolute, international organisation of all Communist elements which adopt this platform . . .

3. If the conference now sitting in Moscow were not to found the Third International, the impression would be created that the Communist parties are not at one; this would weaken our position and increase the confusion among the undecided elements of the proletariat in all countries.

4. To constitute the Third International is therefore an unconditional historical imperative which must be put into effect by the international Communist conference now sitting in Moscow.

1943

May 15

The Executive Committee of the Communist International (the 'Comintern') passed the following resolution:

The development of events in the last quarter of a century has shown that the original form of uniting the workers chosen by the First Congress of the Communist International [in 1919] answered the conditions of the first stages of the working-class movement, but has been outdated by the growth of the movement and by the complications of its problems in individual countries, and has even become a drag on the further strengthening of the national working-class parties.

The Presidium of the ECCI submits for the acceptance of sections of the Communist International:

(i) *The Communist International, as directing centre of the international working-class movement, is to be dissolved.*

(ii) The sections of the Communist International are to be freed from the obligations of their rules and regulations and from decisions of the Congress of the Communist International . . .

1945

February 11

Meeting in Yalta in the Crimea, Stalin, Roosevelt and Churchill signed an agreement about the conditions on which the Soviet Union would eventually enter the war against Japan. It was not made public until a year later. The following is the full text:

The leaders of the three Great Powers – the Soviet Union, the United States of America and Great Britain – have agreed that in two or three months after Germany has surrendered and the war in Europe has terminated the Soviet Union shall enter into the war against Japan on the side of the Allies on condition that;

(i) The status quo in Outer Mongolia (The Mongolian People's Republic) shall be preserved;

(ii) The former rights of Russia violated by the treacherous attack of Japan in 1904 shall be restored, viz:

(a) the southern part of Sakhalin as well as all the islands adjacent to it shall be returned to the Soviet Union,

(b) the commercial port of Dairen shall be internationalised, the pre-eminent interests of the Soviet Union in this port being safeguarded and the lease of Port Arthur as a naval base of the USSR restored,

(c) the Chinese-Eastern Railroad and the South-Manchurian Railroad which provides an outlet to Dairen shall be jointly operated by the establishment of a joint Soviet-Chinese Company it being understood that the pre-eminent interests of the Soviet Union shall be safeguarded and that China shall retain full sovereignty in Manchuria;

(iii) The Kurile Islands shall be handed over to the Soviet Union.

It is understood that the agreement concerning Outer Mongolia and the ports and railroads referred to above will require concurrence of Generalissimo Chiang Kai-shek. The President will take measures in order to obtain this concurrence on advice from Marshal Stalin.

The Heads of the three Great Powers have agreed that these claims of the Soviet Union shall be unquestionably fulfilled after Japan has been defeated.

For its part the Soviet Union expresses its readiness to conclude with the National Government of China a pact of friendship and alliance between the USSR and China in order to render assistance to China with its armed forces for the purpose of liberating China from the Japanese yoke.

July and
August

Talks in Moscow between the Kuomintang and the Soviet government resulted in the signature of a treaty of friendship and alliance directed against Japan and of other agreements.

Autumn

At some point, apparently soon after the surrender of Japan, the Chinese leaders went to Moscow to hear Stalin's views on what their policy should be in the new situation. In 1948 Stalin is said to have told Yugoslav leaders in Moscow about this meeting. After telling the Yugoslavs he considered them wrong to want to continue their support of the Greek civil war, he said:

It is true, we also have made mistakes. For instance, after the war we invited the Chinese comrades to come to Moscow and we discussed the situation in China. *We told them bluntly that we considered the development of the uprising in China had no prospects, that the Chinese comrades should seek a modus vivendi with Chiang Kai-shek, and that they should join the Chiang Kai-shek government and dissolve their army.*

The Chinese comrades agreed here in Moscow with the views of the Soviet comrades, but went back to China and acted quite otherwise. They mustered their forces, organised their armies and now, as we see, they are beating Chiang Kai-shek's army. Now, in the case of China, we admit we were wrong. It has proved that the Chinese comrades, and not the Soviet comrades, were right . . . (Vladimir Dedijer, *Tito Speaks*, Weidenfeld and Nicolson, London, 1953)

The same incident has also been related by Milovan Djilas, the former Yugoslav leader now in gaol for opposition to Tito. He was one of the Yugoslav delegates present at the conversation with Stalin.

Someone mentioned the recent successes of the Chinese Communists. But Stalin remained adamant:

'Yes, the Chinese comrades have succeeded, but in Greece there is an entirely different situation. The United States is directly engaged there – the strongest state in the world. China is a different case; relations in the Far East are different. True, we too can make a mistake. Here, when the war with Japan ended, we invited the Chinese comrades to agree on a means of reaching a modus vivendi with Chiang Kai-shek. They agreed with us in word, but in deed they did it their own way when they got home: they mustered their forces and struck. It has been shown that they were right, and we were not. But Greece is a different case – we should not hesitate, but let us put an end to the Greek uprising.' (Milovan Djilas, *Conversations with Stalin*. Rupert Hart-Davis, London, 1962; Harcourt, Brace, New York, 1962)

1947

September

Meeting in Szklarska Poreba (Poland), leaders of the Soviet, Yugoslav, Bulgarian, Rumanian, French, Polish, Czechoslovak and Italian Communist parties agreed to set up an 'Information Bureau of the Communist and Workers' Parties' (the 'Cominform') in the following terms:

2. The Information Bureau shall be charged with the task of organising the exchange of information and, where necessary, with the co-ordination of the activities of the Communist parties on the basis of mutual consent.

3. The Information Bureau shall be composed of representatives of the Central Committees, two from each Central Committee, the delegations to be nominated and, if necessary, replaced by decision of the Central Committees.

4. The Information Bureau shall establish a newspaper . . .

5. The Information Bureau shall be located in Belgrade.

1948

June 28

A meeting in Bucharest of the Cominform parties passed a resolution (the 'Cominform resolution') expelling the Yugoslav Communists from the organisation in the following terms:

The Information Bureau has come to the unanimous conclusion that, by their anti-party and anti-Soviet views, which are incompatible with Marxism-Leninism, and by their refusal to take part in meetings of the Information Bureau, the leaders of the Communist Party of Yugoslavia have placed themselves in opposition to the Communist parties affiliated to the Information Bureau, have taken the path of secession from the united socialist front against imperialism, have taken a course leading to the betrayal of the international solidarity of the working-class and have adopted a nationalistic attitude . . .

The Information Bureau considers that, in view of all this, the Central Committee of the Communist Party of Yugoslavia has put itself and the Yugoslav party outside the family of fraternal Communist parties, outside the united Communist front, and consequently outside the ranks of the Information Bureau.

1949

October 1

Mao Tse-tung announced the formation of the Chinese People's government and declared it to be the only legal government of China.

October 2

The Soviet government decided to withdraw recognition from Kuomintang and recognise the Chinese Communist régime.

February 14

After nearly two months of negotiations in Moscow between Stalin and Mao Tse-tung a 'Treaty of Friendship, Alliance and Mutual Assistance' was signed between the Soviet and Chinese governments, replacing the one concluded with Chiang Kai-shek. It was directed primarily against Japan. The main provisions were:

ARTICLE I

Both High Contracting Parties undertake jointly to take all the necessary measures at their disposal for the purpose of preventing a repetition of aggression and violation of peace on the part of Japan or any other State which should unite with Japan, directly or indirectly, in acts of aggression. In the event of one of the High Contracting Parties being attacked by Japan or States allied with it, and thus being involved in a state of war, the other High Contracting Party *will immediately render military and other assistance with all the means at its disposal.*

ARTICLE III

Both High Contracting Parties undertake not to conclude any alliance directed against the other High Contracting Party, and not to take part in any coalition or in actions or measures directed against the other High Contracting Party.

ARTICLE IV

Both High Contracting Parties will consult each other in regard to all important international problems affecting the common interests of the Soviet Union and China, being guided by the interests of the consolidation of peace and universal security.

Both the High Contracting Parties undertake, in the spirit of friendship and co-operation and in conformity with the principles of equality, mutual interests, and also mutual respect for the State sovereignty and territorial integrity and non-interference in internal affairs of the other High Contracting Party, to develop and consolidate economic and cultural ties between the Soviet Union and China, to render each other every possible economic assistance, and to carry out the necessary economic co-operation.

February 14

During the same talks the two governments agreed on 'a new approach to the question of the Chinese Changchun Railway, Port Arthur and Dalny' and signed a corresponding agreement, of which the following are the essential points:

ARTICLE I

Both High Contracting Parties have agreed that the Soviet Government transfers gratis to the Government of the People's Republic of China all its rights in the joint administration of the Chinese Changchun Railway, with all the property to the Railway. The transfer will be effected immediately upon the of a peace treaty with Japan, but not later than the end of 1952. . . .

ARTICLE II

Both High Contracting Parties have agreed that Soviet troops will be withdrawn from the jointly utilised naval base of Port Arthur and that the installations in this area will be handed over to the Government of the People's Republic of China immediately upon the conclusion of a peace treaty with Japan, but not later than the end of 1952, with the Government of the People's Republic of China compensating the Soviet Union for expenses incurred in the restoration and construction of installation effected by the Soviet Union since 1945. . . .

ARTICLE III

Both High Contracting Parties have agreed that the question of Port Dalny must be further considered upon the conclusion of a peace treaty with Japan. . . .

February 14

The same meeting resulted in the granting of a credit by the Russians to China, which was recorded in an agreement in the following terms:

In connexion with the consent of the Government of the Union of Soviet Socialist Republics to grant the request of the Central People's Government of the People's Republic of China on giving China credits for paying for equipment and other materials which the Soviet Union has agreed to deliver to China, both Governments have agreed upon the following:

ARTICLE I

The Government of the Union of Soviet Socialist Republics grants the Central People's Government of the People's Republic of China credits, calculated in dollars, amounting to 300 million American dollars, taking 35 American dollars to one ounce of fine gold.

In view of the extreme devastation of China as a result of prolonged hostilities on its territory, the Soviet Government has agreed to grant credits on favourable terms of 1 per cent. annual interest.

ARTICLE II

The credits mentioned in Article I will be granted in the course of five years, as from 1st January 1950, in equal portions of one-fifth of the credits in the course of each year, for payments for deliveries from the USSR of equipment and materials, including equipment for electric power stations, metallurgical and engineering plants, equipment for mines, for the production of coal and ores, railway and other transport equipment, rails and other material for the restoration and development of the national economy of China.

The assortment, quantities, prices and dates of deliveries of equipment and materials will be determined under a special agreement of the Parties; prices will be determined on the basis of prices obtaining on the world markets.

Any credits which remain unused in the course of one annual period may be used in subsequent annual periods.

ARTICLE III

The Central People's Government of the People's Republic of China repays the credits mentioned in Article I, as well as interest on them, with deliveries of raw materials, tea, gold, American dollars. Prices for raw materials and tea, quantities and dates of deliveries will be determined on the basis of prices obtaining on the world markets.

Repayment of credits is effected in the course of ten years in equal annual parts – one-tenth yearly of the sum total of received credits not later than 31st December of every year. The first payment is effected not later than 31st December 1954, and the last on 31st December 1963.

Payment of interest on credits, calculated from the day of drawing the respective fraction of the credits, is effected every six months.

1952

September 15

On the eve of the expiry of the agreement on Port Arthur the Chinese were persuaded to 'request' the Soviet government to leave its troops in the port, in the following words:

Following Japan's refusal to conclude an omnilateral peace treaty and the conclusion of a separate treaty with the United States and with certain other countries, in view of which Japan has not, and apparently does not wish to have, a peace treaty with the Chinese People's Republic and the Soviet Union, conditions have arisen which constitute a threat to the cause of peace and favour a recurrence of Japanese aggression. In view of this . . . the Government of the Chinese People's Republic proposes, and requests the Soviet Government to agree, to extend the period laid down by Article II of the Soviet-Chinese Agreement on Port Arthur for the withdrawal of troops from the jointly-used Chinese naval base of Port Arthur, pending the conclusion of peace treaties between the Chinese People's Republic and Japan, and the Soviet Union and Japan . . .

The Soviet government agreed.

October 5

The Nineteenth Congress of the Communist Party of the Soviet Union opened in Moscow in the presence of Stalin. In the course of the main report to the Congress G. M. Malenkov, secretary of the party's Central Committee, said:

On War: The facts of the past must be heeded. These facts are that as a result of the First World War, Russia fell away from the capitalist system, and as a result of the Second World War quite a number of countries in Europe and Asia fell away from the capitalist system. *There is every reason to believe that a third world war will cause the collapse of the world capitalist system.*

On Yugoslavia: As regards such 'free' countries as Greece, Turkey and Yugoslavia, they have already been converted into American colonies, and the rulers of Yugoslavia – all the Titos, Kardeljs, Rankoviches, Djilases, Pijades and others – long ago signed up as American agents and are carrying out against the USSR and the People's Democracies the espionage and sabotage tasks set them by their American 'chiefs'.

October 30

From the slogans issued by the CPSU for the celebration of the 35th anniversary of the 1917 Revolution:

5. Fraternal greetings to the working people of the countries of people's democracy who are successfully building socialism! May the indestructible friendship and collaboration between the people's democratic countries and the Soviet Union flourish and strengthen!

6. Fraternal greetings to the great Chinese people who have achieved new successes in the construction of a mighty popular-democratic Chinese state! May the great friendship between the Chinese People's Republic and the Soviet Union – the solid basis of peace and security in the Far East and the whole world – strengthen and flourish . . .

10. Greetings to the patriots of Yugoslavia who are fighting for the liberation of their country from the fascist yoke of the Tito-Rankovich clique and imperialist slavery!

1953

February 14

Less than three weeks before his death, Stalin sent Mao Tse-tung a telegram on the third anniversay of the signature of the Sino-Soviet Treaty, looking forward to a 'further strengthening' of their friendship. Mao replied in the same terms, adding his 'heartfelt gratitude' for the 'genuinely selfless aid which the Soviet government and the Soviet people have extended to the new China . . .'

February 14

Commenting on this exchange on the same day *Pravda* said:

The alliance and the friendship between the Soviet Union and China are a model of a completely new kind of international relations, unknown and impossible in the capitalist world. These relations are based on the Leninist-Stalinist principles of internationalism, on the principles of equal rights, on close collaboration and mutual aid, and in a common striving for the preservation of peace and the prevention of imperialist aggression . . .

. . . The fraternal indestructible alliance between the Soviet and Chinese peoples – the great possession and hope of the whole of progressive and peace-loving humanity – is called on to play a mighty role in the further strengthening of the camp of peace, democracy and socialism.

March 5

Stalin died

March 9

Chou-En-lai appeared on Lenin's tomb in Red Square, Moscow, along with Soviet leaders at Stalin's funeral.

March 10

Pravda published pictures (a) of Stalin, Mao and Malenkov together and (b) of Chou En-lai among Soviet leaders in Stalin's funeral procession.

March 10

In an article in *Pravda* entitled: 'The Greatest Friendship' Mao Tse-tung wrote:

All the works of Comrade Stalin are an undying contribution to Marxism. His works: *The Foundations of Leninism, History of the All-Union Communist Party – a Short Course,* as well as his last great work *Economic Problems of Socialism in the USSR* – these are an encyclopaedia of Marxism-Leninism, a summary of the experience of the world Communist movement for the last hundred years. His speech at the Nineteenth Congress of the CPSU is a precious testament for the Communists of all the countries of the world.

We Chinese Communists, like Communists of all the countries of the world, find in the great works of Comrade Stalin the way to our victories.

After Lenin's death Comrade Stalin was always the central figure in the world Communist movement. Gathered closely around him we used to receive instructions from him and constantly derived ideological strength from his works. Comrade Stalin cherished the warmest feelings for the oppressed peoples of the East. 'Do not forget the East' – that was the great slogan proclaimed by Stalin after the October Revolution.

It was generally known that Comrade Stalin loved the Chinese people dearly and considered that the forces of the Chinese Revolution were beyond belief. On questions of the Chinese revolution he displayed the very greatest wisdom. Following the teachings of Lenin and Stalin and relying on the support of the great Soviet State, and all the revolutionary forces of all countries, the Chinese Communist Party and the Chinese people achieved a few years ago an historic victory.

Today we have lost a great teacher and a most sincere friend – Comrade Stalin. It is a great misfortune. It is impossible to express in words the grief which this misfortune has evoked . . .

The Communist Party of the Soviet Union is a party trained by Lenin and Stalin and is the most advanced, the most experienced and theoretically the best equipped party in the world; that party was and still is for us a model; it will also remain a model for us in the future. We are deeply assured that the Central Committee of the CPSU and the Soviet government, led by Comrade Malen-

oubtedly be able to continue the work of Comrade Stalin, to move
o develop with brilliance the cause of Communism.

e no doubt but that the camp of peace, democracy and socialism
viet Union will become even more closely united and even more
powerful . . .

The great friendship of the peoples of China and the Soviet Union is indestructible because it is built on the foundation of the great principles of internationalism of Marx, Engels, Lenin and Stalin. The friendship between the
Chinese and the Soviet peoples and the peoples of the countries of people's
democracy, the friendship between all peace-loving, democratic and just peoples
of the whole world is also built on these great principles of internationalism, and
it is therefore also indestructible.

It is clear that forces born of this friendship are unlimited, inexhaustible and
really invincible . . .

May the unfading name of the great Stalin live through the centuries!

April 22

No reference of any kind to Yugoslavia in May Day slogans issued by
CPSU.

April 29

Molotov, Soviet Foreign Minister, received M. Djurich, Yugoslav chargé
d'affaires in Moscow, in first diplomatic contact between Russians and
Yugoslavs since 1949.

May

Soviet government decided to help in construction of 91 additional industrial plants in China.

[See entry for July 5, 1955—Li Fu-ch'un]

May 21

Marshal Tito, Yugoslav President, said about the prospects for relations
between Yugoslavia and the Communist camp:

*Yes, we want normal, tolerable relations with the Soviet Union and neighbouring
countries* and we are not ashamed to tell anybody so to his face. We are an
independent country and we want to establish equal and tolerable relations with
every country in the world if it is at all possible. *But tolerable relations are still
not deeply friendly relations* . . .

June 6

Soviet government proposed resumption of normal diplomatic relations
with Yugoslavia.

June 15

Announced in Belgrade that Yugoslav government had accepted Soviet proposal for resumption of normal diplomatic relations.

September 15

Mao Tse-tung sent letter thanking Soviet government for undertaking to build the 91 additional industrial plants. He said Soviet aid would play 'an extremely significant role in the industrialisation of China, in helping in her transition by stages to socialism, and in strengthening the camp of peace and democracy headed by the Soviet Union'.

1954

March 12

Malenkov, Soviet Prime Minister, said in an election speech:

No thinking person can fail now to reflect on how to ensure the next step forward, how to find a real basis for the lasting consolidation of peace and friendship among the peoples. It is not true that humanity is left only with the choice between two possibilities: either a new world war, or the so-called cold war. The peoples are vitally interested in the lasting consolidation of peace. The Soviet government stands for a further slackening of international tension, for a stable and lasting peace and is resolutely opposed to the policy of cold war, because that policy is a policy of preparing *another world slaughter which, with the present-day means of waging war, would mean the end of world civilisation.*

April 26–July 21

Geneva conference on 'Far Eastern problems'.

June 22–28

Chou En-lai, Prime Minister and Foreign Minister of Chinese People's Republic, visited Delhi for talks with Nehru. In the course of a speech stressing the tradition of friendship between India and China, Chou said:

It is obvious that the position of India is of great significance for safeguarding peace in Asia. All the peoples of Asia want peace. The menace to the peace of Asia comes now from outside, but Asia today is no longer the Asia of yesterday. The age when outside forces could decide at will the fate of Asia has gone for ever. We are confident that the hope of the peace-loving nations and peoples of Asia will frustrate the schemes of the warmongers. I hope that China and India will co-operate ever more closely in the noble aim of safeguarding peace in Asia.

September 29

'Free Yugoslavia' radio station, believed to operate from Rumanian territory, ceased transmissions.

ıgoslav barter agreement signed in Belgrade.

October 14

Yugoslav authorities announced that Soviet 'jamming' of Radio Belgrade's Russian-language broadcasts had stopped.

September 29–October 11

Khrushchev visited Peking for talks with Chinese leaders, resulting in agreement on:

- (a) Soviet restoration of Port Arthur to China by May, 1955;
- (b) Soviet long-term credit to China of 520 million roubles;
- (c) Soviet aid in construction of two new railway links with China; and
- (d) Soviet relinquishment of share in joint-stock companies formed with China.

October 12

On departing from Peking, Khrushchev said:

It is pleasant and joyful to note that during the brief stay of our delegation in the People's Republic of China, decisions have been reached in an atmosphere of complete mutual understanding on all questions discussed, agreements have been concluded directed towards the well-being and happiness of the peoples of the People's Republic of China and the Soviet Union, towards the further development and strengthening of our inviolable friendship, towards strengthening peace throughout the world. These agreements are based on the principles of deep respect for each other, fraternal concern and mutual assistance.

The mutual exchange of opinions and our joint fruitful work have shown once again that there exists between the Soviet Union and the People's Republic of China complete mutual understanding on all questions pertaining to our further development, and on all international questions.

Leaving Peking, we shall continue with greater confidence our common cause directed towards the advance of our countries, the further development of the great friendship between the USSR and the People's Republic of China, and the strengthening of the whole powerful camp of peace, democracy and socialism.

Long live our eternal and tried and tested friend and brother – the great Chinese people!

October 18–28

Indian Prime Minister Nehru paid official visit to China.

November 6

Maxim Saburov, member of Politburo of CPSU, making Revolution anniversary speech in Moscow, called for 'sincere friendship' between Russia and Yugoslavia and said:

Our country's relations with Yugoslavia have improved recently.
obstacles which were holding back the normalisation of relations betv
USSR and Yugoslavia have been removed and steps have been taken
resumption of trade and the organisation of contacts on cultural and other
questions. As for the Soviet government, it considers it useful and in the interests
of the peoples of both countries to make use of all opportunities to establish
normal and friendly links . . . The Soviet government for its part will continue
to promote in all ways the complete normalisation of Soviet-Yugoslav relations,
the strengthening of the ancient friendship between our peoples and the
fraternal peoples of Yugoslavia, and hopes that it will in this meet with complete
mutual understanding from the Yugoslav side.

1955

January 5

Signature of Soviet-Yugoslav commercial and payments agreement for
1955.

February 8

At a meeting of the Supreme Soviet in Moscow, at which the 'resignation' of Malenkov as Prime Minister was announced, Molotov, Foreign
Minister, made a long statement on foreign policy including the following
significant passage:

The most important result of the Second World War was the formation, alongside
the world capitalist camp, of a *world camp of socialism and democracy headed by
the USSR, or, it would be more accurate to say, headed by the Soviet Union and
the Chinese People's Republic.*

April 4

It was announced in Peking that Kao Kang, a deputy Premier in the
Chinese government and the man in charge of the North-East region
(Manchuria) had been expelled from the Communist Party for forming
an 'anti-party faction' and trying to turn Manchuria into an 'independent
kingdom'. He was reported to have committed suicide.

April 18–24

Conference of Asian and African states in Bandung, Indonesia.

May 15

President Tito of Yugoslavia commented at Pula on forthcoming talks with
Soviet leaders:

What sort of relations should there be between our country and the Soviet Union
and the other countries of the East? What sort of relations should there be
between our country and the countries of the West and many other countries?

I think these relations should be the same between all countries. We don't want to belong to any bloc and we don't want to tie ourselves up with any bloc for any purpose whatever. (Tito, *Collected Speeches*, Zagreb, 1959)

May 24, 26

Announced in Peking that Russians had completed the transfer of Port Arthur to Chinese and that all Soviet forces had been evacuated from the base.

May 26–June 3

Khrushchev visited Belgrade for talks with Tito. On arrival Khrushchev said:

The Soviet delegation has arrived in your country in order to determine, together with the Yugoslav government delegation, the future course for the development and consolidation of the friendship and co-operation between our peoples, to discuss our common tasks in the struggle for the progress of our countries, for relieving international tension and strengthening general peace and the security of the nations.

The peoples of our countries are bound by ties of an age-old fraternal friendship and joint struggle against common enemies. This friendship and militant co-operation had been especially strengthened in the hard trials of the struggle against the fascist invaders, in the years of the Second World War.

It will be remembered that those years witnessed the development of the best relations between the peoples of the Soviet Union and Yugoslavia, between our states and our parties. But those good relations were disturbed in the years that followed.

We sincerely regret that, and we resolutely sweep aside all the bitterness of that period.

On our part, we have no doubt about the part played in provoking that bitterness in the relations between Yugoslavia and the USSR by Beria, Abakumov and other exposed enemies of the people. We have thoroughly investigated the materials upon which the grave accusations against and insults to the leaders of Yugoslavia were based at that time. Facts indicate that those materials were fabricated by the enemies of the people, the contemptible agents of imperialism who had fraudulently wormed their way into the ranks of our Party.

We are deeply convinced that the cloudy period in our relations is past. *We, on our part, are prepared to take all the necessary steps in order to remove all the obstacles to making the relations between our states completely normal, to the promotion of friendly relations between our peoples.*

Now that definite headway has been made in making our relations normal, the Soviet delegation voices the conviction that the coming talks will lead to the development and strengthening of political, economic and cultural co-operation between our peoples. All the conditions for this co-operation exist: the age-old historic friendship of the peoples of our countries, the glorious traditions of the revolutionary movement, the necessary economic foundation and community of ideals in the struggle for the peaceful progress and happiness of the working people. . . .

The final Declaration included the following:

During the negotiations, which were held in a spirit of friendship and mutual understanding, views were exchanged on international problems affecting the interests of the USSR and the Federal People's Republic of Yugoslavia, and the political, economic and cultural relations between the two countries were also examined from every aspect.

The two governments have agreed to undertake further measures for the normalisation of their relations and the development of co-operation between the two countries, being confident that this is in line with the interests of the peoples of the two countries and is a contribution to easing tension and also to strengthening world peace. The sincere desire of the governments of the two countries for the further development of all-round co-operation between the USSR and the Federal People's Republic of Yugoslavia has been revealed in the course of the negotiations, which is fully in conformity with the interests of the two countries and also with the interests of peace and socialism, and for which objective conditions exist at the present time. . . .

June 7–23

Nehru paid official visit to Moscow.

July 4–12

Plenary meeting of Central Committee of CPSU in Moscow revealed direct conflict between Khrushchev and Molotov over relations with Yugoslavia. The following account of the meeting was given by Seweryn Bialer, a Polish Communist official who defected to the West:

What was the chief subject of the secret part of the July Plenum? After reading the record carefully I saw that it concerned itself chiefly with the showdown between Khrushchev and the rest of the Soviet Politburo on one hand, and Molotov on the other.

What was the platform of this showdown? The Yugoslav issue; the problem of the attitude of the Soviet Communist Party toward Marshal Tito and the Yugoslav Party. But it would not be fair to restrict the discussion to Tito's case. The fact is that the question of Yugoslav relations was only a point of departure for a long discussion of political and economic problems.

A good deal of space was given to a discussion of coexistence with the capitalist countries, to the problem of political relations between the Russian Party and the Parties of the people's Democracies. The question of the underdeveloped countries was also discussed, as well as the attitude towards Socialist Parties in the West, and toward Stalinism. However, *the most important subject, and the basis for the showdown with Molotov, was the Yugoslav problem.* What follows is based on the shorthand minutes of the secret part of the Plenum about the showdown itself.

In February 1955, at the Supreme Soviet meeting, Molotov's attitude had already been different from the line taken toward the Yugoslav problem by Khrushchev and most of the other Politburo members, and this became clear to me, and to the majority of the political *aktiv* when we heard of the Khrushchev-Bulganin visit to Belgrade. In February, however, Khrushchev did not attack Molotov because he needed him in the showdown with Malenkov. This is proved by the fact that the Soviet Politburo permitted his official address to the Supreme Soviet to express views which opposed those of the majority of the Politburo.

From the stenographic record of the secret part of the Plenum, it seemed that preparations for Molotov's removal began immediately after Malenkov's resignation. In the spring of last year, the Politburo held a meeting at which Molotov was criticised as Minister of Foreign Affairs for his attitude toward the Yugoslav problem and several other international problems. Molotov was accused of having hampered the re-establishing of Soviet-Yugoslav relations by all means.

Before the departure of Khrushchev and Bulganin for Belgrade in May 1955, the Politburo held another meeting at which Molotov opposed the visit. Molotov was for re-establishing international relations with Yugoslavia, but, for ideological reasons, resisted re-establishment of party relations with the Yugoslav Communist Party. What he had in mind was not only Khrushchev's and Bulganin's visit to Belgrade but also the character of their visit.

These facts were given by Khrushchev in his opening speech to the secret part of the July Plenum. As a result of Politburo discussion, Khrushchev said Molotov still had not changed his attitude. The disagreement found its expression in the adoption of two Politburo resolutions. In one, the majority of the Politburo recognised the necessity of the Belgrade visit and the necessity of attempting to reconstitute inter-party relations with Yugoslavia. In the second resolution, Molotov's attitude was described, appraised by Khrushchev and the rest of the Politburo, and a decision was taken to put it up for discussion at the earliest Plenum of the CC of the CPSU.

At the July Plenum, Khrushchev once again charged Molotov with having prevented the re-establishment of international relations with Yugoslavia, and denounced his attitude on this issue as both erroneous and against the party line.

As a result of the violent discussion, Molotov made a short declaration toward the end of the secret meeting, occupying not more than one page of the shorthand minutes, in which in an extremely formal manner he listed Khrushchev's charges and admitted that they were well-founded. He also said that he yielded to the Central Committee's view of the Yugoslav problem.

July 18–23

'Summit' conference of British, American, French and Soviet heads of government in Geneva.

July 5 and 6

Li Fu-ch'un, China's Vice-Premier and Chairman of State Planning

Commission, reported on China's first Five-Year plan to the National People's Congress in Peking. Extracts:

China's First Five-Year Plan covers the period from 1953 to 1957. The work of drawing up the draft plan had already begun in 1951, and, after being repeatedly supplemented and revised, was completed in February 1955, two years after the First Five-Year Plan had actually been put into operation. This was because our natural resources had been insufficiently studied, we had little statistical data on hand, we had to deal with many different forms of economy existing side by side, we lacked experience in drawing up long-term plans, and our experience in construction was very inadequate. Furthermore, taking the situation of our country as a whole, it was not until the end of July 1953 that an armistice was brought about in the war to resist American aggression and aid Korea which had begun in 1950. *The second group of 91 projects constituting the main portion of the 156 industrial projects which the Soviet Union is helping us to build, was not finally decided upon until May 1953.* All this attests to the fact that, in the past two years, the only course was to draw up a long-term plan while we were actually engaged in construction. Nevertheless, no time was lost in construction. This was because we had already completed the restoration of the national economy in 1952, and, starting from 1953, we were already able every year to draw up and execute yearly plans for the development of the national economy. In addition, as early as 1950, a decision was made and construction begun one after another on the first group of 50 projects which the Soviet Union was to help us build. China's First Five-Year Plan stands all the closer to reality and its successful completion is more assured precisely because we have done extensive preparatory work and acquired considerable experience in the course of carrying out the two yearly plans.

It is clear from the foregoing that in order to build socialism, we must make a vigorous effort to bring about socialist industrialisation, and simultaneously, the socialist transformation of agriculture, handicrafts and capitalist industry and commerce. But does this mean that we can complete the work of socialist industrialisation and socialist transformation within the period of the First Five-Year Plan? No. According to Marxism-Leninism, the transition to socialism should be looked upon as a whole historical period. China is a big country with complex conditions; our national economy was originally very backward, with a small-peasant economy embracing over one hundred and ten million households and an enormous amount of handicraft production. Furthermore, capitalist industry and commerce occupy a fairly large proportion of the national economy. That is why the socialist industrialisation and socialist transformation of our country is a Herculean task, requiring a comparatively long time. In the actual conditions of our country, it will take, not counting the three-year rehabilitation period, approximately 15 years, that is, about thee five-year plans, to fulfil this fundamental task of the transition period. As Chairman Mao Tse-tung has said, we may, in the main, attain a socialist society in perhaps 15 years of intense work and arduous construction, *but to build a powerful country with a high degree of socialist industrialisation will require decades of effort, say 40 or 50 years, or the whole second half of this century.*

The general task set by China's First Five-Year Plan was determined in the light of the fundamental task of the state during the transition period.

It may be summarised as follows: We must centre our main efforts on industrial construction; this comprises 694 above-norm construction projects, *the core of which are the 156 projects which the Soviet Union is designing for us, and which will lay the preliminary groundwork for China's socialist industrialisation;* we must foster the growth of agricultural producers' co-operatives, whose system of ownership is partially collective, and handicraft producers' co-operatives, thus laying the preliminary groundwork for the socialist transformation of agriculture and handicrafts; and, in the main, we must incorporate capitalist industry and commerce into various forms of state-capitalism, laying the groundwork for the socialist transformation of private industry and commerce.

Now I wish to speak on the relation between the assistance which the Soviet Union and the People's Democracies are giving us and our construction programme.

Everyone knows that the fact that our country is able to push ahead so rapidly with the First Five-Year Plan for Development of the National Economy is inseparable from the assistance given to us by the Soviet Union and the People's Democracies, and particularly the assistance of the Soviet Union. The 156 industrial construction projects which the Soviet Union is helping us to design form the nucleus of industrial construction in our First Five-Year Plan.

The Soviet Union is giving systematic, all-round assistance to our country's construction. On the 156 industrial projects which the Soviet Union is helping us to build, she is helping us from start to finish of the whole process, beginning with geological surveys, selecting construction sites, collecting basic data for designing, designing itself, supplying equipment, directing the work of construction, installation, and getting into production, and supplying technical information on new types of products, and ending with directing manufacture of the new products. Designs provided by the Soviet Union make extensive use of the most up-to-date technical achievements, and all the equipment supplied to us by the Soviet Union is first-rate and of the latest type. The great Soviet working class, which is helping us with the greatest enthusiasm, is making every effort to produce the best equipment for us as quickly as possible. *The great Soviet government also gives us first priority in supplies of the best equipment.*

The Soviet government has also concluded a scientific and technical agreement with our government, on the basis of which the Soviet Union is giving a great deal of help to the economic construction of our country. The Soviet government has also offered, on its own initiative, to give our country scientific, technical and industrial assistance in promoting research work in the use of atomic energy for peaceful purposes, and has also concluded an agreement with our country on the peaceful use of atomic energy.

In the midst of her own bustling construction for Communism, the Soviet Union has sent large numbers of experts to our country to help us. They supply us with advanced experience gained in the socialist construction of the Soviet Union and give concrete help to us in all kinds of economic work. All of them possess not only a profound knowledge of science and technique and rich experience in practical work, but also a lofty spirit of internationalism and a selfless attitude to work. In industry, agriculture, water conservancy, forestry, railway, transport, posts and telecommunications, building construction, geology, education, public health and other departments, in scientific, technical and cultural co-operation, the Soviet experts faithfully and unreservedly contribute their experience, knowledge and skill. They regard the great cause of socialist construction of our country as their own. The Communist working attitude of Soviet experts has set an example for the people of our country. It must be said that our great achievements in economic construction are inseparable from the help of the Soviet experts.

Tremendous efforts have been made by the Soviet Union to help our country train technical personnel. *The Soviet Union has accepted a large number of students and trainees from our country and provided them with every convenience in their studies and practical training.* This is an important aid to us in mastering modern industrial technique, guaranteeing that our new enterprises go into operation properly and that our scientific level is raised. The Soviet experts who have come to our country have also made big contributions in the training of our technical personnel.

The Soviet Union has extended a great deal of financial aid to our country both by a succession of loans granted us on the most favourable terms and by trade, selling us technical equipment and materials at low prices. Such benefits in loans and trade also help the speedy restoration and development of our country's economy, and particularly our industrial construction.

It is clear from the above that Soviet assistance plays an extremely important part in enabling us to carry on our present construction work on such a large scale, at such high speed, on such a high technical level and, at the same time, avoid many mistakes.

Besides Soviet aid, our work of national construction has also received economic and technical assistance from the People's Democracies such as Poland, Czechoslovakia, Hungary, Rumania and the German Democratic Republic. At the same time, such People's Democracies as Mongolia, Bulgaria and Albania also co-operate with us economically.

The struggle of the heroic Korean and Viet-Namese peoples for the independence and freedom of their countries plays an important part in the world movement for peace and democracy. Their struggle is also of enormous significance for the building of our country.

The Chinese government and people express their heartfelt thanks for the aid of the Soviet Union and the People's Democracies, especially the great, long-term, all-round and unselfish assistance of the Soviet Union. In order to consolidate and advance the socialist industrialisation of our country, we must further consolidate and develop our economic alliance and friendly co-operation with the Soviet Union and the People's Democracies, so as to promote the common economic advance of the socialist camp and strengthen the world forces of peace and democracy.

July 28

Speaking at Karlovac (Croatia) about Yugoslavia's relations with the Communist bloc, Tito revealed that the Russians had written off a pre-1948 Yugoslav debt of $90 million and then said about the attitude of certain Communist leaders to the improvement in Soviet-Yugoslav relations:

There are still people who do not like the normalisation of relations. They dare not speak out, but are acting under cover. They will not recognise what the Soviet leaders have said. They raise objections against Yugoslavia whenever they can, and continue to arrest people who are in favour of friendship with Yugoslavia . . . These men have their hands soaked in blood . . .

August 23–September 1

Talks in Moscow result in substantial expansion of Soviet-Yugoslav trade and of Soviet economic aid to Yugoslavia.

November 18–December 21

Khrushchev visited India, Afghanistan and Burma.

1956

February 14–25

In his main political report to the Twentieth Congress of the Communist Party of the Soviet Union held in Moscow, Khrushchev made the following statement on basic Communist policy:

The Peaceful Coexistence of the Two Systems.

The Leninist principle of *peaceful coexistence of states with different social systems has always been and remains the general line of our country's foreign policy.*

It has been alleged that the Soviet Union puts forward the principle of peaceful coexistence merely out of tactical considerations, considerations of expediency. Yet it is common knowledge that we have always, from the very first years of Soviet power, stood with equal firmness for peaceful coexistence. Hence, *it is not a tactical move, but a fundamental principle of Soviet foreign policy.*

The principle of peaceful coexistence is gaining ever wider international recognition. This principle has become one of the cornerstones of the foreign policy of the Chinese People's Republic and the other people's democracies. It is being actively implemented by the Republic of India, the Union of Burma and a number of other countries. And this is natural, for in present-day conditions there is no other way out. Indeed, *there are only two ways: either peaceful coexistence or the most destructive war in history. There is no third way.*

We believe that countries with differing social systems can do more than exist side by side. It is necessary to proceed further, to improve relations, strengthen confidence between countries and co-operate. The historical significance of the famous five principles, put forward by the Chinese People's Republic and the Republic of India and supported by the Bandung Conference and the world public in general, lies in the fact that they provide the best form for relations between countries with differing social systems in present-day conditions. Why not make these principles the foundation for peaceful relations among all countries in all parts of the world? It would meet the vital interests and demands of the peoples if all countries subscribed to these five principles.

The Possibility of Preventing War in the Present Era.

Millions of people all over the world are asking whether another war is really inevitable, whether mankind, which has already experienced two devastating world wars, must still go through a third one? Marxists must answer this question, taking into consideration the epoch-making changes of the last decades.

There is, of course, a Marxist-Leninist proposition that wars are inevitable as long as imperialism exists. This proposition was evolved at a time when (i) imperialism was an all-embracing world system, and (ii) the social and political forces which did not want war were weak, poorly organised, and hence unable to compel the imperialists to renounce war.

People usually take only one aspect of the question and examine only the economic basis of wars under imperialism. This is not enough. War is not only an economic phenomenon. Whether there is to be a war or not depends in large measure on the correlation of class, political forces, the degree of organisation and the awareness and determination of the people. Moreover, in certain conditions the struggle waged by progressive social and political forces may play a decisive role. Hitherto the state of affairs was such that the forces that did not want war and opposed it were poorly organised and lacked the means to check the schemes of the war-makers.

In that period this precept was absolutely correct. At the present time, however, the situation has changed radically. Now there is a world camp of socialism, which has become a mighty force. In this camp the peace forces find not only the moral, but also the material means to prevent aggression. Moreover, there is a large group of other countries with a population running into many hundreds of millions which are actively working to avert war. The labour movement in the capitalist countries has today become a tremendous force. The movement of peace supporters has sprung up and developed into a powerful factor.

In these circumstances certainly the Leninist precept that so long as imperialism exists, the economic basis giving rise to wars will also be preserved, remains in force. That is why we must display the greatest vigilance. As long as capitalism survives in the world, the reactionary forces representing the interests of the capitalist monopolies will continue their drive towards military gambles and aggression, and may try to unleash war. *But war is not fatalistically inevitable.* Today there are mighty social and political forces possessing formidable means to prevent the imperialists from unleashing war, and if they actually do try to start it, to give a smashing rebuff to the aggressors and frustrate their adventurist plans. In order to be able to do this, all the anti-war forces must be vigilant and prepared, they must act as a united front and never relax their efforts in the battle for peace. The more actively the peoples defend peace, the greater will be the guarantees that there will be no new war.

Forms of Transition to Socialism in Different Countries.

In connexion with the radical changes in the world arena new prospects are also opening up as regards the transition of countries and nations to socialism.

Alongside the Soviet form of reconstructing society on socialist lines, we now have the form of people's democracy.

In Poland, Bulgaria, Czechoslovakia, Albania and the other European people's democracies, this form sprang up and is being utilised in conformity with the concrete historical, social and economic conditions and peculiarities of each of these countries. It has been thoroughly tried and tested in the course of ten years and has fully proved its worth.

Much that is unique in socialist construction is being contributed by the People's Republic of China, whose economy prior to the victory of the revolution was exceedingly backward, semi-feudal and semi-colonial in character. Having taken over the decisive commanding positions, the people's democratic state is using them in the social revolution to implement a policy of peaceful reorganisation of private industry and trade and their gradual transformation into a component of socialist economy.

The leadership of the great cause of socialist reconstruction by the Communist Party of China and the Communist and Workers' parties of the other people's democracies, exercised in keeping with the peculiarities and specific features of each country, is creative Marxism in action.

In the Federal People's Republic of Yugoslavia, where state power belongs to the working people, and society is founded on public ownership of the means of production, specific concrete forms of economic management and organisation of the state apparatus are arising in the process of socialist construction.

It is probable that more forms of transition to socialism will appear. Moreover, the implementation of these forms need not be associated with civil war under all circumstances. Our enemies like to depict us Leninists as advocates of violence always and everywhere. True, we recognise the need for the revolutionary transformation of capitalist society into socialist society. It is this that distinguishes the revolutionary Marxists from the reformists, the opportunists. There is no doubt that in a number of capitalist countries the violent overthrow of the dictatorship of the bourgeoisie and the sharp aggravation of class struggle connected with this are inevitable. But the forms of social revolution vary. *It is not true that we regard violence and civil war as the only way to remake society.*

At the same time the present situation offers the working class in a number of capitalist countries a real opportunity to unite the overwhelming majority of the people under its leadership and to secure the transfer of the basic means of production into the hands of the people.

In the countries where capitalism is still strong and has a huge military and police apparatus at its disposal, the reactionary forces will, of course, inevitably offer serious resistance. There the transition to socialism will be attended by a sharp class, revolutionary struggle.

Whatever the form of transition to socialism, the decisive and indispensable factor is the political leadership of the working class headed by its vanguard. Without this there can be no transition to socialism.

February 25

A closed session of the Congress heard Khrushchev's denunciation of Stalin and passed a resolution on the 'cult of the individual'. It included the following references to the international movement:

The decisions of the Twentieth Congress of the CPSU are regarded by all supporters of peace and socialism, by all democratic and progressive circles, as an inspiring programme of struggle for the consolidation of peace throughout the world, for the interests of the working class, for the triumph of the cause of socialism. . . .

   In the new historical conditions, such international organisations of the working class as the Comintern and the Cominform have ceased their activities. But this in no way means international solidarity has lost its significance and that there is no longer any need for contacts among the fraternal revolutionary parties adhering to the positions of Marxism-Leninism. At the present time, when the forces of socialism and the influence of socialist ideas have immeasurably grown throughout the world, when different means of achieving socialism in the various countries are being revealed, the Marxist working-class parties must naturally preserve and consolidate their ideological unity and fraternal international solidarity in the fight against the threat of a new war, in the fight against the anti-national forces of monopoly capital striving to suppress all the revolutionary and progressive movements. The Communist parties are welded together by the great objective of freeing the working class from the yoke of capital, they are united by their fidelity to the scientific ideology of Marxism-Leninism, to the spirit of proletarian internationalism, by the utmost devotion to the interests of the people.

   In their activity under modern conditions, all the Communist parties base themselves on the national peculiarities and conditions of every country, giving the fullest expression to the national interests of their peoples. At the same time, recognising that the struggle for the interests of the working class, for peace and the national independence of their countries is the cause of the entire international proletariat, they are consolidating their ranks and strengthening their contacts and co-operation among themselves. The ideological consolidation and fraternal solidarity of the Marxist parties of the working class in different countries are the more necessary since the capitalist monopolies are creating their own aggressive international coalitions and blocs.

March 30

The *People's Daily* reproduced a *Pravda* editorial of March 28 on 'Why is the Cult of the Individual Alien to Marxism-Leninism?' in which Stalin was criticised by name. This was the first public reaction by the Chinese to Khrushchev's speech at Twentieth Congress of the CPSU.

April 5

The *People's Daily* published an editorial article entitled 'On the Historical Experience of the Dictatorship of the Proletariat' representing a cautious public reaction by the Chinese Communist Party's Politbureau to the developments at the Twentieth Congress of the CPSU. The following are extracts:

The Twentieth Congress of the Communist Party of the Soviet Union summed up the fresh experience gained both in international relations and domestic construction. It took a series of momentous decisions on the steadfast implementation of Lenin's policy in regard to the possibility of peaceful coexistence between countries with different social systems, on the development of Soviet democracy, on the thorough observance of the Party's principle of collective leadership, on the criticism of shortcomings within the Party, and on the sixth Five-Year Plan for development of the national economy.

The question of combating the cult of the individual occupied an important place in the discussion of the Twentieth Congress.

The Congress very sharply exposed the prevalence of the cult of the individual which, for a long time in Soviet life, had given rise to many errors in work and had led to ill consequences. This courageous self-criticism of its past errors by the Communist Party of the Soviet Union demonstrated the high level of principle in inner-party life and the great vitality of Marxism-Leninism.

For more than a month now, reactionaries throughout the world have been crowing happily over self-criticism by the Communist Party of the Soviet Union with regard to this cult of the individual. They say: Fine! The Communist Party of the Soviet Union, the first to establish a socialist order, made appalling mistakes, and, what is more, it was Stalin himself, that widely renowned and honoured leader, who made them! The reactionaries think they have got hold of something with which to discredit the Communist parties of the Soviet Union and other countries. But they will get nothing for all their pains. Has any leading Marxist ever written that we could never commit mistakes or that it is absolutely impossible for a given Communist to commit mistakes? Isn't it precisely because we Marxist-Leninists deny the existence of a 'demigod' who never makes big or small mistakes that we Communists use criticism and self-criticism in our inner-party life? Moreover, how could it be conceivable that a socialist state which was the first in the world to put the dictatorship of the proletariat into practice, which did not have the benefit of any precedent, should make no mistakes of one kind or another?

Leaders of Communist parties and socialist states in various fields are duty bound to do their utmost to reduce mistakes, avoid serious ones, endeavour to learn lessons from isolated, local and temporary mistakes and make every effort to prevent them from developing into mistakes of a nation-wide or prolonged nature. To do this, every leader must be most prudent and modest, keep close to the masses, consult them on all matters, investigate and study the actual situation again and again and constantly engage in criticism and self-criticism appropriate to the situation and well measured. It was precisely because of his failure to do this that *Stalin, as the chief leader of the Party and the State, made certain serious mistakes in the later years of his work*. He became conceited and imprudent. Subjectivism and one-sidedness developed in his thinking and he made erroneous decisions on certain important questions, which led to serious consequences. . . .

Marxist-Leninists hold that leaders play a big role in history. The people and their parties need forerunners who are able to represent the interests and will of the people, stand in the forefront of their historic struggles and serve as their leaders. But when any leader of the Party or the State places himself over and above the Party and the masses instead of in their midst, when he alienates himself from the masses, he ceases to have an all-round, penetrating insight into the affairs of the state. As long as this was the case, even so outstanding a personality as Stalin could not avoid making unrealistic and erroneous decisions on certain important matters. Stalin failed to draw lessons from isolated, local and temporary mistakes on certain issues and so failed to prevent them from becoming serious mistakes of a nation-wide or prolonged nature. During the latter part of his life, Stalin took more and more pleasure in this cult of the individual, and violated the Party's system of democratic centralism and the principle of combining collective leadership with individual responsibility. *As a result he made some serious mistakes such as the following: he broadened the scope of the suppression of counter-revolution; he lacked the necessary vigilance on the eve of the anti-fascist war; he failed to pay proper attention to the further development of agriculture and the material welfare of the peasantry; he gave certain wrong advice on the international Communist movement, and, in particular, made a wrong decision on the question of Yugoslavia.* On these issues, Stalin fell victim to subjectivism and one-sidedness, and divorced himself from objective reality and from the masses.

The cult of the individual is a foul carry-over from the long history of mankind. The cult of the individual is rooted not only in the exploiting classes but also in the small producers. As is well known, patriarchism is a product of small-producer economy. After the establishment of the dictatorship of the proletariat, even when the exploiting classes are eliminated, when small-producer economy has been replaced by a collective economy and a socialist society has been founded, certain rotten, poisonous ideological survivals of the old society may still remain in people's minds for a very long time. 'The force of habit of millions and tens of millions is a most terrible force.' (Lenin.) . . .

The Chinese Communist Party congratulates the Communist Party of the Soviet Union on its great achievements in this historic struggle against the cult of the individual. The experience of the Chinese revolution, too, testifies that it is only by relying on the wisdom of the masses of the people, on democratic centralism and on the system of combining collective leadership with individual responsibility that our Party can score great victories and do great things in times of revolution and in times of national construction. The Chinese Communist Party, in its revolutionary ranks, has incessantly fought against elevation of the self and against individualist heroism, both of which mean isolation from the masses. Undoubtedly, such things will exist for a long time to come. Even when overcome, they re-emerge. They are found sometimes in one person, sometimes in another. When attention is paid to the role of the individual, the role of the masses and the collective is often ignored. That is why some people easily fall into the mistake of self-conceit or blind faith in themselves or blind worship in others. We must therefore give unremitting attention to opposing elevation of the self, individualist heroism and the cult of the individual. . . .

After the founding of the People's Republic of China, there appeared in our Party in 1953 the anti-Party bloc of Kao Kang and Jao Shu-shih. This anti-party bloc represented the forces of reaction at home and abroad, and its aim was to undermine the revolution. Had the Central Committee not discovered it quickly and smashed it in time, incalculable damage would have been done to the Party and to the revolution.

Communists must adopt an analytical attitude to errors made in the Communist movement. *Some people consider that Stalin was wrong in everything; this is a grave misconception. Stalin was a great Marxist-Leninist, yet at the same time a Marxist-Leninist who committed several gross errors without realising that they were errors.* We should view Stalin from an historical standpoint, make a proper and all-round analysis to see where he was right and where he was wrong, and draw useful lessons therefrom. Both the things he did right and the things he did wrong were phenomena of the international Communist movement and bore the imprint of the times. Taken as a whole, the international Communist movement is only a little over a hundred years old and it is only 39 years since the victory of the October Revolution; experience in many fields of revolutionary work is still inadequate. Great achievements have been made, but there are still short-comings and mistakes. Just as one achievement is followed by another, so one defect or mistake, once overcome, may be followed by another which in turn must be overcome. However, the achievements always exceed the defects, the things which are right always outnumber those which are wrong, and the defects and mistakes are always overcome in the end.

The mark of a good leader is not so much that he makes no mistakes, but that he takes his mistakes seriously. There has never been a man in the world completely free from mistakes.

True to the behest of Lenin, the Communist Party of the Soviet Union is dealing in a serious way both with certain mistakes of a grave nature committed by Stalin in directing the work of building socialism and with the surviving effects of such mistakes. Because of the seriousness of the effects, it is necessary for the Communist Party of the Soviet Union, while affirming the great contributions of Stalin, to sharply expose the essence of his mistakes, to call upon the whole Party to take them as a warning, and to work resolutely to remove their ill consequences.

We Chinese Communists are firmly convinced that as a result of the sharp criticisms made at the Twentieth Congress of the Communist Party of the Soviet Union, all those positive factors which were seriously suppressed in the past as a result of certain mistaken policies will inevitably spring everywhere into life, and the Party and the people of the Soviet Union will become still more firmly united in the struggle to build a great Communist society, such as mankind has never yet seen, and win a lasting world peace.

Reactionary forces the world over are pouring ridicule on this event; they jeer at the fact that we are overcoming mistakes in our camp. But what will come of all this ridicule? There is not the slightest doubt that these scoffers will find themselves facing a still more powerful, for ever invincible, great camp of peace and socialism, headed by the Soviet Union, while the murderous, blood-sucking enterprises of these scoffers will be in a pretty fix.

The Chinese Communists later (in 1963) explained their attitude to the Twentieth Congress of the CPSU in the following terms:

Thorez [Maurice Thorez, leader of the French Communist Party] and other comrades state that these differences arose because the Chinese Communist Party did not accept the theses of the Twentieth Congress of the CPSU. This very statement is a violation of the principles guiding relations among fraternal parties as set forth in the Moscow Declaration (1957) and Statement (1960). According to these two documents which are jointly agreed upon, the fraternal parties are equal and independent in their relations. No one has the right to demand that all fraternal parties should accept the theses of any one party. No resolution of any congress of any one party can be taken as the common line of the international Communist movement or be binding on other fraternal parties. If Thorez and other comrades are willing to accept the viewpoints and resolutions of another party, that is their business. As for the Chinese Communist Party, we have always held that the only common principles of action which can have binding force on us and on all other fraternal parties are Marxism-Leninism and the common documents unanimously agreed upon by the fraternal parties, and not the resolutions of any one fraternal party, or anything else.

As for the Twentieth Congress of the CPSU, it had both its positive and its negative aspects. We have expressed our support for its positive aspects. As for its negative aspects, namely the wrong viewpoints it put forward on certain important questions of principle relating to the international Communist movement, *we have held different views all along*. In talks between the Chinese and Soviet parties and at meetings of fraternal parties, we have made no secret of our views and have clearly set forth our opinions on many occasions. But in the interests of the international Communist movement, we have never publicly discussed this matter, nor do we intend to do so in the present article.

('Whence the Differences? A Reply to Thorez and other Comrades', *People's Daily*, Peking, February 27, 1963.)

April 18

Pravda published a statement announcing the *dissolution of the Cominform*, from which the Yugoslav Communist Party had been expelled in June 1948. (Members were the Communist parties of the Soviet Union, Poland, Czechoslovakia, Rumania, Hungary, Bulgaria, France and Italy, and Yugoslavia.) The dissolution was explained in the following way:

The founding in 1947 of the Information Bureau of the Communist and Workers parties was a positive contribution toward overcoming the lack of co-ordination which developed among Communist parties after the dissolution of the Comintern and was an important force in strengthening proletarian internationalism in the ranks of the international Communist movement and in further uniting the working class and all working people in the struggle for lasting peace, democracy, and socialism.

However, there have been changes in recent years in the international situation: the extension of socialism beyond the boundaries of a single country and its transformation into a world system; the formation of a vast 'peace zone' including both socialist and non-socialist peace-loving countries of Europe and Asia; the growth and consolidation of many Communist parties in capitalist, dependent, and colonial countries and their increased activities in the struggle against the threat of war and reaction, in the struggle for peace, for the vital interests of the working people and their countries' national independence; and, finally, the particularly urgent tasks today of overcoming the division within the working class movement and strengthening the unity of the working class in the interests of a successful struggle for peace and socialism. These changes have provided new conditions for the activities of the Communist and Workers' parties. *The Information Bureau* of the Communist and Workers' parties, in terms both of its make-up and the content of its activity, *no longer meets these new conditions.*

The Central Committees of the Communist and Workers' parties belonging to the Information Bureau, having exchanged views on problems of its activity, *recognised that the Information Bureau which they set up in 1947 had completed its function, and so by mutual agreement they adopted a decision to end the activity of the Information Bureau of the Communist and Workers parties and its newspaper*, '*For a Lasting Peace, for a People's Democracy!*'

The Central Committees of the Communist and Workers' parties which participated in the Information Bureau consider that in the struggle for working class interests, for the cause of peace, democracy and socialism, each party or group of parties will, in the course of developing its work in conformity with the common aims and tasks of Marxist-Leninist parties and the specific national features and conditions of their countries, find new and useful forms of establishing links and contacts among themselves. The Communist and Workers' parties will undoubtedly continue, at their own discretion and taking into account specific conditions of their work, to exchange opinions on general problems of the struggle for peace, democracy and socialism, of defending the interests of the working class and all working people, of mobilising the masses for the struggle against the danger of war, and at the same time will continue to take up problems of co-operating with parties and movements oriented toward socialism and with other organisations striving toward strengthening peace and democracy. All this will reinforce to a still greater degree the spirit of mutual co-operation among Communist and Workers' parties on the basis of the principles of proletarian internationalism and will strengthen the fraternal ties among them in the interests of peace, democracy and socialism.

April 7

Anastas Mikoyan, Soviet First Deputy Prime Minister, had talks in Peking with Mao Tse-tung and concluded an *agreement for increased Soviet economic aid, to provide China with 55 industrial plants in addition* to the 156 already promised.

June 1

It was announced in Moscow that Vyacheslav Molotov, Soviet Foreign Minister since 1953 and lifelong collaborator of Stalin, had been relieved of his duties.

June 2

President Tito of Yugoslavia arrived in Moscow for three-week governmental visit.

June 27

First Chinese ambassador to Yugoslavia, Wu Hsiu-chuan, presented credentials in Belgrade and conveyed personal gifts from Mao Tse-tung to Tito.

July 21–22

Anastas Mikoyan had talks with Tito and other Yugoslav leaders on Brioni (Yugoslavia).

August

Central Committee of CPSU believed to have circulated to other Communist parties a letter on Soviet-Yugoslav relations, critical of the Yugoslav Communists. (No text ever released.)

September 15–27

Eighth Congress of the Chinese Communist Party met in Peking. The main political report was made by Liu Shao-chi, who said inter alia:

What is the international situation in which our country now finds itself? . . .

There was no other socialist country in the world when the people of the Soviet Union embarked upon their socialist construction after the October Revolution, but the conditions are fundamentally different now when the people of our country are carrying on socialist construction. After the Second World War, not only has the Soviet Union become more powerful, but many new socialist countries have come into being in Europe and Asia. The socialist countries, including China, have a combined population of over nine hundred million – one-third of the world's total population, and are geographically linked together as one vast expanse of land, forming a big family of fraternal, socialist countries headed by the Soviet Union. The fraternal friendship, mutual assistance and co-operation that exist among us are being constantly developed and consolidated. The Soviet Union and other socialist countries have re-established friendly relations with the Federal People's Republic of Yugoslavia. *Our country has also established diplomatic relations and developed friendly intercourse with the Federal People's Republic of Yugoslavia.*

The Twentieth Congress of the Communist Party of the Soviet Union, held last February, was an important political event of world significance. It not only drew up the Sixth Five-Year Plan of gigantic proportions, *decided on many important policies and principles for further development of the cause of socialism and repudiated the cult of the individual* which had had grave consequences inside the Party. It also advocated further promotion of peaceful coexistence and international co-operation, making an outstanding contribution to the easing of international tension. . . .

The unity and friendship between China, the great Soviet Union and the other socialist countries, built upon the basis of a community of objectives and mutual assistance, is unbreakable and eternal. To further consolidate and strengthen this unity and friendship is our supreme international duty, and is the basis of our foreign policy.

We must continue to strengthen our fraternal solidarity with the Communist parties and the Workers' parties of all countries; we must continue to learn from the experience of the Communist Party of the Soviet Union and the Communist parties of all other countries in regard to revolution and construction. . . .

The Chinese revolution is part of the world's proletarian revolution. In our achievements are the fruits of the struggle of the working class and working people of all countries. The Central Committee of the Communist Party of China avails itself of this opportunity to extend heartfelt thanks and pay its respects to the fraternal parties of all countries and, through them, to the working class and working people of their countries, and assure them of our lasting solidarity with them.

The Congress also approved proposals from China's Second Five-Year Plan, which included the following passage:

Aid from the Soviet Union and the People's Democracies is an important condition for building socialism in our country. In the course of developing our national economy and building a comprehensive industrial system, we must, therefore, strengthen co-operation with the Soviet Union and the People's Democracies, and expand our economic and cultural exchanges and trade with them so that mutual support and help among these fraternal countries can be promoted. Given this relationship based on division of labour and co-operation in the economic and technical spheres and in scientific research, it is possible to make the fullest, mutually beneficial use of the material resources, latent productive capacity and scientific and technological achievements of these countries, thus accelerating the growth of their national economies and bringing about a common upsurge in the economies and cultures of all the socialist countries with the Soviet Union at their head.

Economic co-operation, trade relations, and cultural and technical exchanges with countries with different social systems, particularly with those in Asia and Africa, should be developed on the principle of equality and mutual benefit to promote the peaceful coexistence and the economic development of the peoples of all lands.

Anastas Mikoyan, chief Soviet delegate to the Chinese Party's Congress, said inter alia:

We are especially happy to learn that the CPSU Central Committee's measures have met with full understanding and support from the great Communist Party of China. Those who shouted about 'confusion' in the ranks of the Communist parties have one more disappointment to live down. No one will ever succeed in shaking the unity and solidarity, the ideological kinship and proletarian solidarity of the Communists!

The international essence of our common cause demands fraternal friendship and mutual understanding, ties and contacts between all Marxist-Leninist parties. What is most valuable is the exchange of experience and the mutual assistance which can be rendered by workers' parties inspired by one great idea and advancing towards one common goal.

The forms of ties and contacts between Marxist parties are not predetermined and are not immutable. They follow from the requirements of the Communist movement at each stage of development and struggle and are determined by the parties themselves in the interest of the victory of the common cause and not, of course, to suit someone in particular.

Neither need the nature and forms of ties and contacts between Marxist-Leninist parties be the same. For example, one cannot deny the special significance of ties between Communist parties in power. The exchange of experience and developing co-operation between the Communist and workers' parties of the countries building socialism allows for taking the best from the experience of all countries that has been tested by life itself and has facilitated the elaboration of the best forms and methods of construction, taking into account both the experience of the building of socialism in the USSR and in other countries, and the distinctive features of each particular country.

The presence of delegates of fraternal Communist parties at your truly historic congress is one of the important forms of contacts, ties and friendship, mutual exchange of experience and opinions.

As for us, Communists of the Soviet Union and Communists of China, our close co-operation and our unbreakable friendship have been tested in the crucible of great historical battles.

Enemies would like it very much if at least a tiny crack were to be formed in our relations, at least a tiny hitch in our friendship. But only the ideologists of imperialism, doomed by history, can dream of this, for they judge friendship on their own example, on their bourgeois relations, when today they are together and tomorrow they are apart, again ready to spring at one another like wolves. But there has been no friendship in the world equal to the friendship of our great peoples, our mighty parties!

September 19

Khrushchev arrived in Yugoslavia for eight-day talks with Tito.

September 27–October 5

Tito went for 'holiday' to Crimea where he had talks with Khrushchev.

October–November

Revolt in Hungary, near-revolt in Poland.

October 30

The Soviet government published a 'Declaration on the Principles of Development and Further Strengthening of Friendship and Co-operation between the Soviet Union and other Socialist States'.

The process of building up the new system and the deep-going revolutionary transformations in social relations met with many difficulties, unsolved problems and direct mistakes, including those in the mutual relations between socialist countries – *violations and mistakes which belittled the principle of equal rights in the relations between the socialist states.* . . .

The Soviet government is ready to discuss jointly with the governments of other socialist states measures such as would ensure the further development and strengthening of the economic ties between the socialist countries so as to remove any possibility of violation of the principle of national sovereignty, mutual benefit and equality in economic relations. . . .

The Soviet government regards it as urgent to examine jointly with the other socialist states the *question of the desirability of the further stay of Soviet advisers in those countries.* . . .

With the aim of safeguarding the mutual security of the socialist countries *the Soviet government is ready to examine with the other socialist countries that are parties to the Warsaw Treaty the question of the Soviet forces stationed in those countries.* . . .

November 1

The Chinese government issued a statement on the Soviet 'Declaration'. Extracts:

The government of the Soviet Union on October 30, 1956, issued a declaration on the foundations of the development and further strengthening of friendship and co-operation between the Soviet Union and other socialist countries. *The government of the People's Republic of China considers this declaration of the government of the Soviet Union to be correct.* This declaration is of great importance in correcting errors in mutual relations between the socialist countries and in strengthening unity among them.

As the declaration of the Soviet government pointed out, the mutual relations between the socialist countries are not without mistakes. These mistakes resulted in misunderstandings and estrangement between certain socialist countries. Some of these countries have been unable to build socialism better in accordance with their historical circumstances and special features because of these mistakes.

As a result of these misunderstandings and estrangement, a tense situation has sometimes occurred which otherwise would not have occurred. The handling of the 1948–49 Yugoslav situation and the recent happenings in Poland and Hungary are enough to illustrate this.

Following the Soviet-Yugoslav joint declaration issued in June 1955, the Soviet government has again taken note of this problem and in its declaration of October 30, 1956, indicated its willingness to solve various problems in mutual relations on the basis of the principles of full equality, respect for territorial integrity, national independence and sovereignty, and non-intervention in each other's internal affairs and by friendly negotiations with other socialist countries. This important step is clearly of value in eliminating estrangement and misunderstandings among the socialist countries. It will help increase their friendship and co-operation.

The government of the People's Republic of China notes that the people of Poland and Hungary in the recent happenings have raised demands that democracy, independence, and equality be strengthened and the material well-being of the people be raised on the basis of developing production. These demands are completely proper. Correct satisfaction of these demands is not only helpful to consolidation of the people's democratic system in these countries but also favourable to unity among the socialist countries.

We note with satisfaction that the people of Poland and their leaders have taken notice of the activities and danger of reactionary elements who attempt to undermine the people's democratic system and unity among socialist countries.

November 1

Yugoslav Communist newspaper *Borba* issued a comment on the Soviet 'Declaration'.

The Soviet government's declaration on relations with socialist countries undoubtedly has great international significance, for it provides a positive basis of principle for the regulation of relations and for the development of co-operation among socialist countries.

The principal significance of this declaration is, above all, the result of three positions which are expressed in it. First, the Soviet government in its declaration notes openly that there were irregularities and mistakes in relations between the socialist countries so far, 'which diminished the principle of socialist equality'. Second, the Soviet government stresses that relations between the socialist countries should be founded on principles of full national independence and equality, and third, the Soviet government supports in its declaration the point of view that in the building of socialism the specific conditions of every individual country must be taken into consideration. . . .

November 11

President Tito addressed members of the Yugoslav League of Communists at Pula and made the following comments on Soviet-Yugoslav relations after the events in Hungary:

As far as we are concerned, we have gone a considerable way in our relations with the Soviet Union. We have improved these relations and have concluded a whole series of economic arrangements, very useful for us, on very favourable terms, and so forth. Two declarations have also been adopted, one in Belgrade and the other in Moscow. Both declarations should in fact be significant not only in our mutual relations but also in relations among all socialist countries. But, unfortunately, they have not been understood in this way. It was thought as follows: good, since the Yugoslavs are so stubborn we will respect and implement these declarations, but they do not concern the others because the situation there is, nevertheless, a little different from what it is in Yugoslavia. Yugoslavia is an organised and disciplined state. The Yugoslavs have proved their worth because they have succeeded in maintaining themselves even in the most difficult times and in not allowing a restoration of the capitalist system, and so forth; that is, they are something different from you in the Eastern countries where we brought you to power. And this was wrong, because those same elements which provoked such resistance on the part of Yugoslavia in 1948 also exist in these Eastern countries, in Poland, Hungary, and in others, in some more and in some less. During the time that we were preparing the declaration in Moscow on our party relations, mainly on the relations between the Yugoslav League of Communists and the CPSU, this was a little difficult to settle. Here we could not completely agree, but, nevertheless, *the declaration was issued which*, *in our opinion, is intended for a wider circle than Yugoslavia and the Soviet Union*. We warned that those tendencies which once provoked such strong resistance in Yugoslavia existed in all countries, and that one day they might find expression in other countries, too, when this would be far more difficult to correct.

December 29

The Peking *People's Daily* published an article entitled 'More on the Historical Experience of the Dictatorship of the Proletariat', containing the Chinese leaders' considered views on relations between the Communist parties in the 'socialist camp'. Extracts:

In April 1956, we discussed the historical experience of the dictatorship of the proletariat in connexion with the question of Stalin. Since then, a further train of events in the international Communist movement has caused concern to the people of our country. The publication in Chinese newspapers of Comrade Tito's speech of November 11, and the comments on that speech by various Communist parties, have led people again to raise many questions which call for an answer. In the present article we shall centre our discussion on the following questions: first, an appraisal of the fundamental course taken by the Soviet Union in its revolution and construction; second, an appraisal of Stalin's merits and faults; third, the struggle against doctrinairism and revisionism; and fourth, the international solidarity of the proletariat of all countries.

In examining *present-day international questions*, we must proceed first of all from the most fundamental fact, the antagonism between the imperialist bloc of aggression and the popular forces in the world. The Chinese people, who have suffered enough from imperialist aggression, can never forget that imperialism has always opposed the liberation of all peoples and the independence of all oppressed nations, that it has always regarded the Communist movement, which stands most resolutely for the people's interests, as a thorn in its flesh. Since the birth of the first socialist state, the Soviet Union, imperialism has tried by every means to wreck it. Following the establishment of a whole group of socialist states, the hostility of the imperialist camp to the socialist camp, and its flagrant acts of sabotage against the latter, have become a still more pronounced feature of world politics. The leader of the imperialist camp, the United States, has been especially vicious and shameless in its interference in the domestic affairs of socialist countries; for many years it has been obstructing China's liberation of its own territory Taiwan,* and for many years it has openly adopted as its official policy the subversion of the East European countries. . . .

Although we have consistently held and still hold that the socialist and capitalist countries should coexist in peace and carry out peaceful competition, the imperialists are always bent on destroying us. *We must therefore never forget the stern struggle with the enemy, i.e. the class struggle on a world scale. . . .*

People ask: Since the basic path of the Soviet Union in revolution and construction was correct, *how did Stalin's mistakes happen?*

We discussed this question in our article published in April of this year. But as a result of recent events in Eastern Europe and other related developments, the question of correctly understanding and dealing with Stalin's mistakes has become a matter of importance affecting developments within the Communist parties of many countries, unity between Communist parties, and the common struggle of the Communist forces of the world against imperialism. So it is necessary to further expound our views on this question.

Stalin made a great contribution to the progress of the Soviet Union and to the development of the international Communist movement.

But Stalin made some serious mistakes in regard to the domestic and foreign policies of the Soviet Union. His arbitrary method of work impaired to a certain extent the principle of democratic centralism both in the life of the Party and in the state system of the Soviet Union, and led to a partial disruption of socialist legality. Because in many fields of work Stalin estranged himself from the masses to a serious extent, and made personal, arbitrary decisions concerning many important policies, it was inevitable that he should have made *grave mistakes*. These mistakes stood out most conspicuously *in the suppression of counterrevolution and in relations with certain foreign countries*. In suppressing counterrevolutionaries, Stalin, on the one hand, punished many counter-revolutionaries whom it was necessary to punish and, in the main, accomplished the tasks on this front; but, on the other hand, he wronged many loyal Communists and honest citizens, and this caused serious losses. On the whole, in relations with brother countries and parties, Stalin took an internationalist stand and helped the struggles of other peoples and the growth of the socialist camp; but in tackling certain concrete questions, he showed a *tendency towards great-nation chauvinism* and himself lacked a spirit of equality, let alone educating the mass of cadres to

* Formosa.

be modest. *Sometimes he even intervened mistakenly, with many grave consequences, in the internal affairs of certain brother countries and parties.*

How are these serious mistakes of Stalin's to be explained?

What is the connexion between these mistakes and the socialist system of the Soviet Union?

Were Stalin's mistakes due to the fact that the socialist economic and political system of the Soviet Union had become outmoded and no longer suited the needs of the development of the Soviet Union? Certainly not. Soviet socialist society is still young; it is not even forty years old. The fact that the Soviet Union has made rapid progress economically proves that its economic system is, in the main, suited to the development of its productive forces; and that its political system is also, in the main, suited to the needs of its economic basis. *Stalin's mistakes did not originate in the socialist system; it therefore follows that it is not necessary to 'correct' the socialist system in order to correct these mistakes.*

The Communist Party of the Soviet Union has already taken measures to correct Stalin's mistakes and eliminate their consequences. These measures are beginning to bear fruit. *The Twentieth Congress of the Communist Party of the Soviet Union showed great determination and courage in doing away with blind faith in Stalin, in exposing the gravity of Stalin's mistakes and in eliminating their effects. . . .*

As is well known, although Stalin committed some grave mistakes in his later years, *his was nevertheless the life of a great Marxist-Leninist revolutionary.* In his youth, Stalin fought against the tsarist system and for the spread of Marxism-Leninism. After he joined the central leading organ of the Party, he took part in the struggle to pave the way for the revolution of 1917. After the October Revolution, he fought to defend its fruits. In the nearly thirty years after Lenin's death, he worked to build socialism, defend the socialist fatherland and advance the world Communist movement. *All in all, Stalin always stood at the head of historical developments and guided the struggle; he was an implacable foe of imperialism.* His tragedy was that even when he made mistakes, he believed what he did was necessary for the defence of the interests of the working people against encroachments by the enemy. . . . *In our opinion Stalin's mistakes take second place to his achievements.*

The attitude taken by Comrade Tito and other leading comrades of the Yugoslav League of Communists towards Stalin's mistakes and other related questions, as their recently stated views indicate, *cannot be regarded by us as well-balanced or objective.* It is understandable that *the Yugoslav comrades* bear a particular resentment against Stalin's mistakes. *In the past, they made worthy efforts to stick to socialism under difficult conditions.* Their experiments in the democratic management of economic enterprises and other social organisations have also attracted attention. *The Chinese people welcome the reconciliation between the Soviet Union and other socialist countries on the one hand, and Yugoslavia on the other*, as well as the establishment and development of friendly relations between China and Yugoslavia. Like the Yugoslav people, the Chinese people hope that Yugoslavia will become ever more prosperous and powerful on the way to socialism. *We also agree with some of the points in Comrade Tito's speech, for instance, his condemnation of the Hungarian counter-revolutionaries, his support for the Worker-Peasant Revolutionary Government of Hungary; his condemnation of Britain, France and Israel for their aggression against Egypt, and his condemnation of the French Socialist party for adopting a policy of aggression.* But we are amazed that, in his speech, he attacked almost all the socialist countries and many of the Communist parties. Comrade Tito made assertions about 'those hard-bitten Stalinist elements who in various parties have still managed to maintain themselves in their posts and who would again wish to consolidate their rule and impose those Stalinist tendencies upon their people, and even others'. Therefore, he declared, 'together with the Polish comrades we shall have to fight such tendencies which crop up in various other parties, whether in the Eastern countries or in the West'. We have not come across any statement put forward by leading comrades of the Polish United Workers' Party saying that it was necessary to adopt such a hostile attitude towards brother parties. We feel it necessary to say in connexion with these views of Comrade Tito's that he took up a wrong attitude when he set up the so-called 'Stalinism', 'Stalinist elements', etc., as objects of attack and maintained that the question now was whether the course 'begun in Yugoslavia' or the so-called 'Stalinist course' would win out. *This can only lead to a split in the Communist movement.*

Clearly, *the Yugoslav comrades are going too far.* Even if some part of their criticism of brother parties is reasonable, the basic stand and the method they have adopted infringes the principles of comradely discussion. We have no wish to interefere in the internal affairs of Yugoslavia, but the matters mentioned above are by no means internal. For the sake of consolidating the unity of the international Communist ranks and avoiding the creation of conditions which the enemy can use to cause confusion and division in our own ranks, we cannot but offer our brotherly advice to the Yugoslav comrades. . . .

The Communist movement has been an international movement from its very inception, because the workers of various countries can throw off joint oppression by the bourgeoisie of various countries and attain their common aim only by joint effort. . . .

During the past thirty-nine years the Soviet Union has been the centre of the international Communist movement, owing to the fact that it is the first country where socialism triumphed, and, after the appearance of the camp of socialism, the most powerful country in the camp, having the richest experience and the means to render the greatest assistance to other socialist countries and to the peoples of various countries in the capitalist world. This is not the result of anyone's arbitrary decision, but the natural outcome of historical conditions. In the interest of the common cause of the proletariat of different countries, of joint resistance to the attack on the socialist cause by the imperialist camp headed by the United States, and of the economic and cultural upsurge common to all socialist countries, *we must continue to strengthen international proletarian solidarity with the Soviet Union at its centre.*

The international solidarity of the Communist parties is a type of relationship entirely new to human history. It is natural that its development cannot be free from difficulties. The Communist parties of all countries must seek unity with each other as well as maintain their respective independence. Historical experience proves that mistakes are bound to occur if there is no proper integration of these two aspects, and one or the other is neglected. If the Communist parties maintain relations of equality among themselves and reach common understanding and take concerted action through genuine, and not nominal, exchange of views, their unity will be strengthened.

Conversely, if, in their mutual relations, one party imposes its views upon others, or if the parties use the method of interference in each other's internal affairs instead of comradely suggestions and criticism, their unity will be impaired.

In the socialist countries, the Communist parties have assumed the responsibility of leadership in the affairs of the state, and relations between them often involve directly the relations between their respective countries and peoples, so the proper handling of such relations has become a problem demanding even greater care. . . .

To strengthen the international solidarity of the socialist countries, the Communist parties of these countries must respect the national interests and sentiments of other countries. This is of special importance for the Communist party of a larger country in its relations with that of a smaller one. To avoid any resentment on the part of the smaller country, the party of a larger country must constantly take care to maintain an attitude of equality.

As we have already said, Stalin displayed certain great-nation chauvinist tendencies in relations with brother parties and countries. The essence of such tendencies lies in being unmindful of the independent and equal status of the Communist parties of various lands and that of the socialist countries within the framework of international bond of union. There are certain historical reasons for such tendencies. The time-worn habits of big countries in their relations with small countries continue to make their influence felt in certain ways, while a series of victories achieved by a party or a country in its revolutionary cause is apt to give rise to a sense of superiority. . . .

As we pointed out above, the foreign policy of the Soviet Union has, in the main, conformed to the interests of the international proletariat, the oppressed nations and the peoples of the world. In the past thirty-nine years, the Soviet people have made tremendous efforts and heroic sacrifices in aiding the cause of the peoples of the various countries. Mistakes committed by Stalin certainly cannot detract from these historic achievements of the great Soviet people.

The Soviet government's efforts to improve relations with Yugoslavia, its declaration of October 30, *1956, and its talks with Poland in November 1956 all manifest the determination of the Communist Party of the Soviet Union and the Soviet government to thoroughly eliminate past mistakes in foreign relations.* These steps by the Soviet Union are an important contribution to the strengthening of the international solidarity of the proletariat.

1957

January 7–18

Chou En-lai visited Moscow, Warsaw and Budapest and subscribed in each capital to statements approving the new relationships established between the Communist countries. A Soviet-Chinese declaration issued on January 18 covered all aspects of foreign affairs, said that 'it is completely possible for Socialist countries in their relations to combine unity and the independence of each country', and reaffirmed the complete equality of all Communist countries.

June 22–29

The Central Committee of CPSU removed Molotov and the 'anti-party' group from power.

July 16

Yugoslav leaders Kardelj and Rankovic visited Moscow for talks with Soviet leaders and met leaders of the Albanian and Bulgarian parties.

August 1–2

Khrushchev met Tito secretly in Rumania.

November 6–20

Mao Tse-tung attended in Moscow the celebration of the fortieth anniversary of the Russian Revolution and the meeting of leaders of Communist parties in power (with the exception of the Yugoslav party). The meeting approved a 'Declaration' (subsequently referred to as the 'Moscow Declaration' of 1957) on all aspects of policy, from which the following extracts are taken:

The exchange of opinions revealed *identity of views of the parties on all the questions examined at the meeting and unanimity in their assessment of the international situation.* In the course of discussion the meeting also touched upon general problems of the *international Communist movement.* In drafting the declaration the participants in the meeting consulted with representatives of the fraternal parties in the capitalist countries. The fraternal parties not present at this meeting will assess and themselves decide what action they should take on the considerations expressed in the Declaration.

1. *The main content of our epoch is the transition from capitalism to socialism* which was begun by the great October socialist revolution in Russia.

The world socialist system, which is growing and becoming stronger, is exerting ever greater influence upon the international situation in the interests of peace and progress and the freedom of the peoples.

The policy of certain aggressive groups in the United States is aimed at rallying around them all the reactionary forces of the capitalist world. Acting in this way they are becoming the centre of world reaction, the sworn enemies of the people. By this policy these anti-popular, aggressive imperialist forces are courting their own ruin, creating their own grave-diggers.

So long as imperialism exists there will always be soil for aggressive wars.

The question of war or peaceful coexistence is now the crucial question of world policy. All the nations must display the utmost vigilance in regard to the war danger created by imperialism.

At present the forces of peace have so grown that there is a real possibility of averting wars as was demonstrated by the collapse of the imperialist designs in Egypt. The imperialist plan to use the counter-revolutionary forces for the overthrow of the People's Democratic system in Hungary failed as well.

The cause of peace is upheld by the powerful forces of our era: the invincible camp of socialist countries headed by the Soviet Union; the peace-loving countries of Asia and Africa, taking an anti-imperialist stand and forming, together with the socialist countries, a broad peace zone; the international working class and above all its vanguard – the Communist parties; the liberation movement of the peoples of the colonies and semi-colonies; the mass peace movement of the peoples; the peoples of the European countries who have proclaimed neutrality, the peoples of Latin America and the masses in the imperialist countries are putting up increasing resistance to the plans for a new war. *The unity of these powerful forces can prevent the outbreak of war.* But should the bellicose imperialist maniacs venture, regardless of anything, to unleash a war, imperialism will doom itself to destruction, for the peoples will not tolerate a system that brings them so much suffering and exacts so many sacrifices.

The Communist and Workers' parties taking part in the meeting declare that the Leninist principles of peaceful coexistence of the two systems, which has been further developed and brought up to date in the decisions of the Twentieth Congress of the CPSU is the sound basis of the foreign policy of the socialist countries and the dependable pillar of peace and friendship among the peoples. The idea of peaceful coexistence coincides with the five principles advanced jointly by the Chinese People's Republic and the Republic of India and with the programme adopted by the Bandung Conference of Afro-Asian countries. Peace and peaceful coexistence have now become the demands of the broad masses in all countries.

The Communist parties regard the struggle for peace as their foremost task. They will do all in their power to prevent war.

2. The meeting considers that in the present situation the *strengthening of the unity and fraternal co-operation of the socialist countries, the Communist and Workers' parties and the solidarity of the international working-class, national liberation and democratic movements acquire special significance.*

The working class, the democratic forces and the working people everywhere are interested in tirelessly strengthening fraternal contacts for the sake of the common cause, in safeguarding from enemy encroachments the historical, political and social gains effected in the Soviet Union – the first and mightiest socialist power – in the Chinese People's Republic and in all the socialist countries in seeing these gains extended and consolidated.

The socialist countries base their relations on principles of complete equality, respect for territorial integrity, state independence and sovereignty and non-interference in one another's affairs. These are vital principles. However, they do not exhaust the essence of relations between them. *Fraternal mutual aid is part and parcel of these relations.* This aid is a striking expression of socialist internationalism.

On a basis of complete equality, mutual benefit and comradely mutual assistance, the socialist states have established between themselves extensive economic and cultural co-operation that plays an important part in promoting the economic and political independence of each socialist country and the socialist commonwealth as a whole. The socialist states will continue to extend and improve economic and cultural co-operation among themselves. . . .

The socialist countries are united in a single community by the fact that they are taking the common socialist road, by the common class essence of the social and economic system and state authority, by the requirements of mutual aid and support, identity of interests and aims in the struggle against imperialism, for the victory of socialism and Communism, by the ideology of Marxism-Leninism, which is common to all. . . .

3. The meeting confirmed the identity of views of the Communist and Workers' parties on the *cardinal problems of the socialist revolution and socialist construction.* The experience of the Soviet Union and the other socialist countries has fully borne out the correctness of the Marxist-Leninist proposition that the processes of the socialist revolution and the building of socialism are governed by a number of basic laws applicable in all countries embarking on a socialist course. These laws manifest themselves everywhere, alongside a great variety of historic national peculiarities and traditions which must by all means be taken into account.

Of vital importance in the present stage is *intensified struggle against opportunist trends in the working class and Communist movement.* The meeting underlines the necessity of resolutely overcoming revisionism and dogmatism in the ranks of the Communist and Workers' parties. Revisionism and dogmatism in the working class and Communist movement are today, as they have been in the past, international phenomena. Dogmatism and sectarianism hinder the development of Marxist-Leninist theory and its creative application in the changing conditions, replace the study of the concrete situation with merely quoting classics and sticking to books, and leads to the isolation of the party from the masses. A party that has withdrawn into the shell of sectarianism and that has lost contact with the masses cannot bring victory to the cause of the working class.

In condemning dogmatism, the Communist parties believe that the *main danger at present is revisionism* or, in other words, right-wing opportunism, which as a manifestation of bourgeois ideology paralyses the revolutionary energy of the working class and demands the preservation or restoration of capitalism. *However, dogmatism and sectarianism can also be the main danger at different phases of development in one party or another.* It is for each Communist party to decide what danger threatens it more at a given time.

Modern revisionism seeks to smear the great teachings of Marxism-Leninism, declares that it is 'outmoded' and alleges that it has lost its significance for social progress. The revisionists try to exorcise the revolutionary spirit of Marxism, to undermine faith in socialism among the working class and the working people in general. They deny the historical necessity for a proletarian revolution and the dictatorship of the proletariat during the period of transition from capitalism to socialism, deny the leading role of the Marxist-Leninist party, reject the principles of proletarian internationalism and call for rejection of the Leninist principles of party organisation and, above all, of democratic centralism, for transforming the Communist party from a militant revolutionary organisation into some kind of a debating society.

4. The Communist and Workers' parties are faced with great historic tasks. The carrying out of these tasks necessitates closer unity not only of the Communist and Workers' parties, but of the entire working class, necessitates cementing the alliance of the working class and peasantry, rallying the working people and progressive mankind, the freedom and peace-loving forces of the world.

The defence of peace is the most important world-wide task of the day. The Communist and Workers' parties in all countries stand for joint action on the broadest possible scale with all forces favouring peace and opposed to war. . . .

Contrary to the absurd assertions of imperialism about a so-called crisis of Communism, the Communist movement is growing and gathering strength. *The historic decisions of the Twentieth Congress of the CPSU are of tremendous importance not only to the CPSU and to the building of Communism in the USSR; they have opened a new stage in the world Communist movement and pushed ahead its further development along Marxist-Leninist lines.* The results of the Congresses of the Communist parties of China, France, Italy and other countries in recent times have clearly demonstrated the unity and solidarity of the party ranks and their loyalty to the principles of proletarian internationalism. This meeting of the representatives of Communist and Workers' parties testifies to the international solidarity of the Communist movement.

After exchanging views, the participants in the meeting arrived at the conclusion that *in present conditions it is expedient besides bilateral meetings of leading personnel and exchange of information, to hold, as the need arises, more representative conferences of Communist and Workers' parties to discuss current problems, share experience, study each others views and attitudes and concert action in the joint struggle for the common goals – peace, democracy and socialism.*

The participants in the meeting unanimously express their firm confidence that, by closing their ranks and thereby rallying the working class and the peoples of all countries, the Communist and Workers' parties will surmount all obstacles in their onward movement and accelerate further big victories for the cause of peace, democracy and socialism.

The Chinese Communists later gave the following assessment of the 1957 meeting:

As is well known, the 1957 Moscow Meeting of Communist and Workers' parties, basing itself on Marxism-Leninism, *eliminated certain differences* among the fraternal parties, reached agreement on the current major issues in the international Communist movement, and produced the Moscow Declaration as a result of comradely consultation and collective effort. The Declaration is the common programme of the international Communist movement. Every fraternal party has proclaimed its acceptance of this programme.

If the Declaration had been strictly adhered to by all the fraternal parties in their practice and had not been violated, the unity of the international Communist movement would have been strengthened and our common struggle advanced.

For some time after the Moscow Meeting of 1957, the Communist and Workers' parties were fairly successful and effective in their united struggle against the common enemy, and above all against US imperialism, and in their struggle against Yugoslav revisionists, who had betrayed Marxism-Leninism.

But, because certain comrades of a fraternal party repeatedly attempted to place the resolutions of the congress of one party above the Moscow Declaration, above the common programme of all the fraternal parties, differences within the international Communist movement inevitably ensued.

('Whence the Differences?', *People's Daily* editorial, February 27, 1963).

1958

March 27

Khrushchev assumed post of Prime Minister in addition to being First Secretary of CPSU.

April 22–26

The Seventh Congress of the Yugoslav League of Communists approved a new Programme.

May 6

Peking *People's Daily* said that the Cominform resolution of 1948 had been 'basically correct' in its attitude to Yugoslavia and that the new Yugoslav Programme was 'a wild attempt to induce the working people to take the path of surrender to capitalism'.

May 9

Pravda reproduced *People's Daily* article of May 6.

May 9

Pravda editorial accused Tito of 'white-washing' the Western Powers and of 'kow-towing' to America, and, in a reference to the Yugoslav charge that some 'socialist' countries were exploited by others, said 'it would be possible to free Yugoslavia from such exploitation'.

May 27

Soviet government informed Yugoslav government of decision to suspend credits granted in 1956. Soviet President Voroshilov's planned visit to Yugoslavia was cancelled at the last minute.

June

In a speech at the Congress of the Bulgarian CP, Khrushchev reviewed at length relations between the CPSU and the Yugoslav Communists:

The draft programme of the League of Communists of Yugoslavia and statements by Yugoslav leaders at the Seventh Congress of the League of Communists, were attempts to accuse other Communist parties of socialist countries of practicism. . . .

Some theoreticians are striving in every way to lower the practical activities of the Communist and Workers' parties in their construction of socialism by disparagingly accusing them of practicism, but, at the same time, *they only exist because of the alms they receive from imperialist countries in the form of left-over goods.* It is clear to everyone that a socialist economy cannot be strengthened by such means. About what successes of socialism can one speak here, what development of Marxist-Leninist theory can be dealt with here? If such poor theoreticians do not understand how much harm the theories they put forward can do to the cause of the working class, the imperialist circles, on the other hand, know full well what they want and do everything in their power to support and encourage that which helps them in their struggle against Communism. I would not wish to offend anyone. But, on the other hand, I cannot refrain from asking the question which deeply concerns all Communists everywhere. Why do the imperialist bosses, while striving to obliterate the socialist states from the face of the earth, and to squash the Communist movement, at the same time finance one of the socialist countries, granting that country credits and free gifts?

Nobody will believe that two socialisms exist in the world – one which bitterly hates universal reaction, and the other acceptable to the imperialists . . .

Everyone knows that the imperialists never give money to anyone without a purpose, just for the sake of 'beautiful eyes'. They invest their capital in those enterprises from which they hope to receive a good profit. If the imperialists agree to give assistance to a socialist state, they do not take such a step so as to strengthen it. One can in no way suspect the monopolistic circles of the United States of America of being interested in strengthening socialism and the development of Marxist-Leninist theory. Representatives of this country assert that we are allegedly deviating from Marxist-Leninist theory. A somewhat curious situation arises: the imperialists want to develop Marxism-Leninism through that country. . . .

Present-day revisionism is in its way a Trojan horse. The revisionists are striving to corrupt the revolutionary parties from within, and to disrupt the unity of Marxist-Leninist theory.

Of all the Communist and Workers' parties, the League of Communists of Yugoslavia alone declared their non-agreement in regard to the Declaration of 1957, and thus stand in opposition to all Marxist-Leninist parties of the world. This position of the Yugoslav leaders is most clearly defined in the draft programme of the League of Communists of Yugoslavia for the work of the Seventh Congress of the League. All Communist and Workers' parties have been unanimous in strongly condemning the revisionist premise – contradictory to Marxism-

Leninism – which is contained in the draft programme of the League of Communists of Yugoslavia, and the depraved position of the Yugoslav leaders.

The relationship between our parties and the League of Communists of Yugoslavia has its own history. Certain important moments in this history must now be recalled. You know that until 1948 good relations existed betwen Yugoslavia and the Soviet Union, which were created during the joint struggle against fascist usurpers during the Second World War and during the first post-war years. In September 1947, when imperialist reaction started intensified attacks against the socialist countries, the Communist parties of the Soviet Union, the European countries, the people's democracies, as well as some Communist parties of capitalist countries of Europe, *organised an Information Bureau of the Communist and Workers' parties, the Informburo,** a working organ which was first located in Belgrade.

Looking back on the past, we must say that the Informburo for a certain period of time played a positive role in the history of the revolutionary Marxist-Leninist movement in rallying the forces of the Communist and Workers' parties on the principles of proletarian internationalism, in the struggle for a stable peace, democracy, and socialism. The Communist Party of Yugoslavia, together with the CPSU and a number of other fraternal parties, was one of the organisers of the Informburo and an active participant in its activity during the first period.

This is how matters were up to 1948. Then came a worsening in relations between the Communist Party of Yugoslavia and other fraternal parties. *In 1948 a Conference of the Informburo issued a Resolution* on the state of affairs in the Communist Party of Yugoslavia, which contained just criticisms of the activity of the Communist Party of Yugoslavia on a number of questions of principle. *This resolution was fundamentally correct,* and corresponded to the interests of the revolutionary movement. Later on, from 1949 to 1953, a conflict arose between the Communist Party of Yugoslavia and other fraternal parties when, in the course of the struggle mistakes were permitted which caused damage to our common cause. Fully conscious of its responsibility in respect of our countries and peoples and the international Communist movement, the Communist Party of the Soviet Union took the initiative to liquidate this conflict and to achieve a normalisation of relations between our countries, and to establish contacts, co-operation, and an alliance of Marxist-Leninist principles.

In this connexion, talks between representatives of the Soviet Union and Yugoslavia were held on our initiative in May and June 1955, which ended with the signing of the Belgrade Declaration. *It is very important to note that during the talks in Belgrade Comrade Tito spoke of forgetting the past and starting our relations on a new basis.* We willingly agreed to this, and on our part did everything to strengthen friendly relations. While doing this, we were conscious that between our parties there were ideological differences on a number of important questions. On our part, much endurance and patience was shown to achieve unity of views on a Marxist-Leninist basis.

Even after the normalisation of relations, the Yugoslav leaders continued to make anti-Soviet statements, and to attack the socialist camp and the fraternal

* Known in the non-Communist world as 'the Cominform'.

Communist parties. Particularly great harm to the cause of socialism was done by the Yugoslav leaders in their public statements and their actions during the Hungarian events. During the counter-revolutionary insurgence in Budapest, the Yugoslav embassy virtually became a centre for those who started the struggle against the people's democratic régime in Hungary, and a sanctuary for the group of capitulants and traitors of Nagy-Losonczy. Just recall the unprecedented speech made by Comrade Tito in which he defended the insurgents in Hungary and described as 'Soviet intervention' the fraternal help by the USSR to the Hungarian people; the speech which contained direct appeals to certain forces in other socialist countries to follow the so-called Yugoslav course. . . .

Subsequently, *on the initiative of the Yugoslav leaders, a meeting of the delegations of the Soviet Union and Yugoslavia was held in Bucharest in August 1957.* During this meeting we candidly explained to the Yugoslav leaders our views concerning the policy of the League of Communists of Yugoslavia as regards the Hungarian and other que tions. As a reul t of negotiation, *agreement was reached on the basic problems of the present international situation, although it was admitted that there existed certain differences between us on ideological questions.*

During the Bucharest meeting, we hoped to find common language and to pave the way for further friendly co-operation. At the same time we openly told the Yugoslav leaders that if in future they should permit themselves to make attacks against the countries of the socialist camp and fraternal parties, such sallies would not remain unanswered.

During the meeting in Bucharest agreement was reached that a delegation of the League of Communists of Yugoslavia would take part in a conference of the fraternal parties of the socialist countries which was being prepared, and in the working out of the draft declaration of that conference.

Subsequent events showed, however, that the Yugoslav leaders deviated from the positions agreed upon. By refusing to ign the Declaration of the Communist and Workers' parties of the Sociali t countries, *the Yugoslav leaders decided to produce their own platform – the draft programme of the League of Communists of Yugoslavia, opposed to the co-ordinated views of the Marxist-Leninist parties, claiming to be a programme document for the international Communist and Workers' movement.*

Of course, the programme of the League of Communi ts of Yugoslavia is an internal affair of Yugoslav Comm units, but a the draft of that programme included tendentious and insulting comments on the other parties of socialist countries, our Pa rty deemed it to be it direct duty to criticise the anti-Marxist theses of that document. The principles and the attitude of our Party, stated in the letters of the Central Committe of the CPSU and in our Party Pre s, have been unanimously supported and approved by all Communist and Workers' parties. . . .

By rejecting comradely criticism on matter of principle offered by the fraternal parties, the Yugoslav leader have once more found themselves in is olation, and continue stubbornly to defend their mitaken and anti-Marxist views. . . . They attack the Communit Party of the Sov iet Union, and *they want somehow to infer that the Chinese Communist Party criticises their mistakes in a peculiar way.* But these attempts to find different shades in the criticism of present-day revisionism on the part of the fraternal parties are in vain. All the fraternal parties are united in this matter. *We consider that the Chinese comrades, just as all the othe parties, very rightly criticise the revisionist statements of the draft pro the League of Communists of Yugoslavia and consistently defend the of Marxism-Leninism.* We fully agree with this principled criticism. . . .

Recently the weekly *Komunist*, organ of the League of Communists of Yugoslavia, published an article devoted to the third anniversary of the signing of the Belgrade Declaration. At first sight it appears that the article is written in quiet tones and seeks to reduce the tension which has arisen between the League of Communists of Yugoslavia and other fraternal parties. But this is far from being so. It tries to justify the mistaken position of the Yugoslav leaders. Thus, for example, *the article contends that the struggle for peace is the main content of the struggle for socialism. One cannot agree with such assertions.* No doubt, those who struggle for socialism also consistently fight for the cause of peace. But many leaders who do not support the principles of socialism also struggle for peace. Even some Conservatives, clergymen, and all kinds of bourgeois public and political leaders are struggling for peace. Naturally we are uniting our efforts in our struggle for peace; thus in the struggle for peace, forces and organisations of various views and political opinions can be united. . . .

We have held and continue to hold the view that it is necessary to strengthen in every way co-operation between all states in the struggle for peace and for the security of nations. We want to maintain such relations with the Federal People's Republic of Yugoslavia. But we, as Communists, would like more than that. *We would like to reach mutual understanding and co-operation on the party plane.*

The Yugoslav Communists have considerable revolutionary experience and great merit in the struggle against our common class enemies. The working class and all the working people of Yugoslavia made a considerable contribution to the struggle against fascism in the years of the Second World War. Of course, if co-operation on the party plane cannot succeed, then we shall support and develop normal relations with Yugoslavia on the state plane. At the same time, we frankly declare that we shall not tolerate deviations on questions of ideology. We shall guard the unity of the Marxist-Leninist parties and struggle for the purity of revolutionary theory.

July 31–August 3

Khrushchev visited Peking and had talks with Mao Tse-tung. A communiqué issued after the talks said that relations between the governments and Communist parties of China and the Soviet Union were 'being developed successfully and becoming more firmly established', and that they were in complete agreement about future policy. The two parties said they would 'wage an uncompromising struggle against revisionism – the main danger in the Communist movement'. Revisionism 'found its clearest manifestation in the Programme of the Yugoslav League of Communists'. During the visit the Russians agreed to undertake the construction of a further 47 industrial plants in China.

August 4

Khrushchev withdrew suggestion for 'summit' meeting with Western powers.

August 29

Chinese Communist Party approved resolution on 'people's communes'.

November 23

Tito said communes had 'nothing in common with Marxism'.

December 1

Khrushchev told American Senator Humphrey that communes were 'old-fashioned'.

November 28–December 10

Mao Tse-tung retired as Chairman of Chinese Republic but remained Chairman of Chinese Communist Party.

December 27

Russians agreed to give substantial additional economic aid to Albania.

1959

January 27–February 5

Twenty-first Congress of the CPSU in Moscow. Khrushchev made the following references to relations inside the Communist movement:

The conferences of representatives of Communist and Workers' parties held in November 1957 demonstrated the complete identity of views of the fraternal parties. The Declaration of the conference, unanimously approved by all Communist and Workers' parties, has become the charter of international unity for the world Communist movement.

The Declaration condemns revisionism as the principal danger, besides condemning dogmatism and sectarianism. The correctness of the Declaration's conclusions has been fully confirmed by reality and we are guided by it at the present time.

The leaders of the League of Yugoslav Communists are trying to pretend that the Marxist-Leninist parties initiated an ideological struggle against them because they refused to sign the Declaration. However, this is an utterly false assertion. It was the Yugoslav leaders themselves who, to counteract the Declaration, came out with their revisionist programme in which the Marxist-Leninist positions of the international Communist movement were attacked. Could Marxists disregard these facts? Of course not! Therefore all parties basing their positions on Marxism-Leninism levelled criticisms of principle against the programme of the League of Yugoslav Communists.

Our position regarding the views of the Yugoslav leaders is clear, and we have repeatedly set it forth in all frankness, but the Yugoslav leaders twist and turn and run from the truth.

The Yugoslav leaders seek to conceal the essence of their differences with Marxist-Leninists. This essence consists in the fact that the *Yugoslav revisionists are denying the necessity of international class solidarity* and are leaving the positions of the working class. They try to persuade everybody *that there exist two blocs in the world, two military camps.* But it is a matter of general knowledge that the socialist camp, comprising the socialist countries of Europe and Asia, is not a military camp but a community of equal peoples joined in the struggle for peace and better life for the working people, for socialism and Communism.

The Yugoslav leaders allege that they stand outside the blocs, that they stand above the camps, but actually they belong to the Balkan bloc comprising Yugoslavia, Turkey and Greece. The latter two countries, as is known, are members of the aggressive NATO bloc, and Turkey is moreover a party to the Baghdad Pact.

The leaders of the League of Yugoslav Communists resent it very much when we tell them that they are sitting on two chairs. They give assurances that they are sitting on their own Yugoslav chairs. But that Yugoslav chair is for some reason eagerly supported by the American monopolies. And this is why *their extra-bloc position and neutrality*, which are advertised so much by the leaders of the League of Yugoslav Communists, *smell strongly of the American monopolies which are feeding Yugoslav socialism.*

The history of the class struggle still lacks a precedent where the bourgeoisie materially or spiritually collaborated with its class enemy and helped to build socialism.

We have the friendliest of feelings toward the brotherly peoples of Yugoslavia and the Yugoslav Communist heroes of the underground partisan struggle. On a number of foreign policy questions we have a common language. We will continue to develop trade with Yugoslavia on a mutually profitable basis; we will strive to collaborate with Yugoslavia on all questions of struggle against imperialism and for peace on which our positions coincide. And *how will matters stand on the party line? Everything will depend on the League of Yugoslav Communists.* Its leaders have isolated themselves from the international Communist movement. Therefore it is up to the League to take a turn in the direction of a rapprochement with the Communist parties on the basis of Marxism-Leninism, which would also be in accord with the interests of the Yugoslav people themselves. . . .

All Communist parties are independent and work out their policy on the basis of the concrete conditions in their given country.

In the same way it is naive to think that it is possible to prescribe to millions of people united in Communist parties, from somewhere without, what they are to think today and what they are to do tomorrow. It is said that the dependence of Communist and Workers' parties on Moscow is confirmed by statements that the CPSU heads the international Communist movement, and reference is made to the well-known thesis of the Declaration of the Moscow conference that the camp of socialist countries is headed by the Soviet Union. Communists of the

Soviet Union and of all other countries consider that this is a tribute to our country and working class, which under the guidance of the Communist Party headed by the great Lenin was the first to carry out a socialist revolution and to take power into its own hands.

In forty-odd years a great and difficult road of struggle and victories has been covered, and a powerful state has been created which is the bulwark of all socialist countries and the world Communist movement. For such an acknowledgment of the historical role of the Soviet Union and the CPSU, we express our sincere gratitude to the fraternal parties.

At the same time it is necessary to stress that in the Communist movement and in the socialist camp *complete equality and independence of all Communist and Workers parties and socialist countries has existed and does exist. The CPSU in reality does not control any other party. The Soviet Union does not control any other country. In the Communist movement there are no superior or subordinate parties. All Communist and Workers' parties are equal and independent and all of them are responsible for the fate of the Communist movement and for its failures and victories*!

Every Communist and Workers' party is responsible to the working class, the working people of its country, and the entire international Workers' and Communist movement. Communist parties, in the struggle for the interests of the working class and for socialism, combine the universal truths of Marxism-Leninism with the concrete historical and national conditions of their countries. . . .

With regard to the Soviet Union, its role, as we know, consists not in controlling other countries but in having been the *first* to blaze mankind's way to socialism, in being *the most powerful* country in the world socialist system, and the *first* to enter a period of expanded construction of Communism. . . .

The Yugoslav leaders by their revisionist policy help in splitting the revolutionary forces of the working class in the struggle for the basic interests of the working people.

But just look at the despicable and provocative methods the Yugoslav revisionists are now resorting to in an attempt to injure the unity of the socialist countries. As was mentioned in the report, the Yugoslav revisionists are compiling all sorts of inventions about differences of opinion that allegedly exist between our Party and the Communist Party of China. In the last few days they have gone still further and, apparently in order to substantiate their inventions, have drawn in a 'substantial witness' and specialist on questions of the 'disagreement between the USSR and the Chinese People's Republic' – the American Senator Hubert Humphrey. . . .

And now the Yugoslav revisionists have taken this fabricator unto themselves as a witness. The very idea that I could have been in any way confidential to a man who himself boasts of his twenty-year struggle against Communism can only serve to raise a laugh. Anybody who has the slightest knowledge of politics, not to speak of a knowledge of Marxism-Leninism, will understand *how unthinkable a confidential talk with Humphrey would be on questions of the policy of the Communist parties, on our relations with our best friends, the leading people in the Communist Party of China.*

Final Resolution of Twenty-first Congress.

The Congress considers that the accomplishment of the Seven-Year Plan and also of the plans of the other socialist countries will create more favourable conditions for solving the principal problem of our time – the preservation of universal peace. The conclusion drawn by the Twentieth Party Congress to the effect that there is no fatal inevitability of war has proved to be perfectly justified. There now exist tremendous forces capable of defending the peace and of delivering a crushing blow to any imperialist aggressor who tries to start a war. An aggression by imperialist states against the socialist camp can have only one outcome – the fall of capitalism.

Fresh successes of the socialist countries will induce an expansion and strengthening of the peace forces throughout the world. The countries working for enduring peace will be joined by ever more countries. The idea that war is intolerable will take ever firmer root in the conscience of nations. Backed by the might of the socialist camp, the peaceful nations will then be able to compel the bellicose imperialist groups to abandon their plans of starting new wars. In this way, *even before the complete victory of socialism in the world, with capitalism still extant in a part of the globe, there will take shape a realistic possibility of excluding world war from human society.* . . .

The Congress notes with satisfaction that the conference of representatives of Communist and Workers' parties in November 1957 demonstrated the *complete unity* of viewpoints of the fraternal parties. *The Declaration of the Conference was unanimously approved by all the Communist and Workers' parties and has become a fighting programme of action for the world Communist movement.* The conclusions of the Declaration were proved completely right by the course of events. . . . Revisionism has been routed ideologically and politically.

The revisionist programme of the League of Communists of Yugoslavia was unanimously condemned by all the Marxist-Leninist parties. The theory and practice of the Yugoslav leadership is a deviation from the positions of the working class, the principles of international proletarian solidarity. The views and policy of the leaders of the League of Communists of Yugoslavia jeopardise the gains of the people's revolution and socialism in Yugoslavia. The Soviet Communists and the whole Soviet people have friendly feelings for the fraternal peoples of Yugoslavia and for the Yugoslav Communists. The Soviet Union will continue to work for *co-operation with Yugoslavia in all questions of the struggle against imperialism for peace in which our positions will coincide.*

While continuing to expose revisionism as the main threat within the Communist movement, *the struggle against dogmatism and sectarianism must go on unabated*, for they impede the creative application of Marxist-Leninist theory and lead away from the masses.

The Congress considers essential the strengthening in every way the might of the socialist camp and the further consolidation of the unity of the international Communist movement in accordance with the principles of the Moscow Declaration. The fraternal co-operation of the Communist and Workers' parties must be developed and extended on the basis of complete independence of each party on the basis of proletarian internationalism, voluntary co-operation and mutual assistance. . . .

January 29

In his speech to the Twenty-first Congress of the CPSU, Chou En-lai reaffirmed policy on 'communes':

Actively supported and guided by the Chinese CP and Comrade Mao Tse-tung, the Chinese people have created the organisational form of large-scale people's communes, which combine industry, agriculture, trade, education and military affairs, and in which government administration and commune management are integrated.

Very rapidly, the mass movement of establishing people's communes spread throughout China. Not long ago, the sixth Plenary Session of the Eighth Congress of the CP of China gave a very high appraisal to the people's communes, considering them the best form for developing socialism under Chinese conditions, the best form for the Chinese rural areas to make the transition from collective ownership to ownership by the whole people, and the best form for China to make the transition from socialism to Communism in future. We are now more confident that we can speed the development of socialist construction. We intend to build China into a socialist country with a highly-developed modern industry, agriculture and science and culture in fifteen or twenty years, or a little longer.

February 7

Russians agree to add another 31 industrial plants to the 47 additional plants they agreed in August 1958, to build for China, making total value of Soviet aid under revised agreement up to 1,250,000,000 dollars, to be repaid by Chinese deliveries of goods to Russia.

May 25–June 4

Khrushchev paid official visit to Albania. Enver Hoxha, leader of the Albanian Communist Party, said on his arrival:

The Albanian people are extremely happy to receive an outstanding leader of the Soviet Communist Party and government, a great son of the Soviet people, a faithful pupil of the great Lenin, the most outstanding leader of the international Communist and Workers' movement, a great fighter for peace, a friend near to their hearts, Nikita Sergeyevich Khrushchev. The close and unbreakable friendship linking the Albanian people with the brotherly Soviet people has deep roots in history; it is strengthened by the blood of the best sons of both our peoples shed in the great liberation war against nazi-fascist aggressors, and it is illumined by the all-conquering ideas of Marxism-Leninism. The Albanian people regard their friendship with the USSR as their most valuable treasure. Everybody in Albania, great and small, ardently loves and is deeply grateful to your glorious homeland; for it is with the USSR that the greatest victories of our people are linked – the victory of the national liberation struggle in the people's revolution, the existence of the People's Republic of Albania as a sovereign and independent State, and the construction of socialism in our country.

Our friendship is firmer than granite and as eternal as our mountains. The

Albanian people, our Party, and our government safeguard the friendship with the Soviet Union as the apple of their eye and regard it as a decisive factor for the freedom and happiness of our people.

Long live the indestructible Albanian-Soviet friendship! Long live the great Soviet Union and its glorious Communist Party! Long live the mighty socialist camp led by the Soviet Union! Glory to Marxism-Leninism! Long live peace! May our dear friend Nikita Sergeyevich Khrushchev live as long as our mountains!

August 3

It was announced that Khrushchev was to meet President Eisenhower.

August 2–16

Lushan Plenum of Central Committee of the Chinese Communist Party. Dismissal of Marshal Peng Teh-huai.

August 7

Chinese incidents on Indian frontier begin.

August–September

Chinese invasion of Indian territory.

September 9

Soviet government issued a statement on Sino-Indian frontier incidents:

TASS STATEMENT

Certain political circles and the press in Western countries have recently worked up a noisy campaign around an incident which took place not long ago on the Sino-Indian frontier in the region of the Himalayas. This campaign was obviously aimed at driving a wedge in between the two largest states of Asia – the Chinese People's Republic and the Republic of India, whose friendship has great significance for ensuring peace and international collaboration in Asia and throughout the world. The people inspiring this campaign are trying to discredit the idea of peaceful coexistence between states with different social systems and to interfere with the strengthening of the solidarity of the Asian peoples in the struggle for consolidating national independence. It is noteworthy that this incident has been seized on by those circles in Western countries, especially in the USA, who are trying to obstruct the slackening of international tension and complicate the situation on the eve of the exchange of visits between the Chairman of the Council of Ministers of the USSR, N. S. Khrushchev, and the President of the USA, D. Eisenhower. By this sort of device they hope to paralyse the growing efforts in Western countries to achieve agreement with the socialist states on questions involved in the cessation of the 'cold war'.

One cannot fail to express regret at the fact that the incident on the Sino-Indian frontier took place. The Soviet Union is in friendly relations both with the Chinese c and the Republic of India. The Chinese and Soviet people are ctible bonds of fraternal friendship, based on the great principles tionalism. Friendly collaboration between the USSR and India ssfully in accordance with the ideas of peaceful coexistence. ...ᴄe use of the incident on the Sino-Indian frontier for the purpose ...ᴜnning the 'cold war' and undermining friendship between the people are worthy of resolute condemnation.

In Soviet ruling circles the assurance is being expressed that the government of the Chinese People's Republic and the government of the Republic of India will not permit this incident to give comfort to those forces who do not want an improvement of the international situation but its worsening, and who are trying not to admit the planned slackening of international tension in relation between states. In the same circles *the assurance is being expressed that both governments will adjust the misunderstanding that has arisen*, taking account of their mutual interests in the spirit of the traditional friendship between the peoples of China and India. This will also contribute to the strengthening of the forces working for peace and international collaboration.

The Chinese later declared that it was this statement by the Russians which first revealed the existence of the Sino-Soviet dispute to the outside world (*see* Chronology: February 27, 1963).

September 15–28

Khrushchev in America – 'Camp David' talks. For Chinese comment, *see* Chronology: February 27, 1963.

September 27

Dismissal of Peng Teh-huai revealed in Peking.

September 30

Khrushchev arrived in Peking for celebrations of the tenth anniversary of the Chinese Republic and talks with Mao Tse-tung. At a banquet in his honour he said:

Comrades! Socialism brings to the people peace – the greatest blessing. The greater the strength of the camp of socialism grows, the greater will be its possibilities for successfully defending the cause of peace on this earth. The forces of socialism are already so great that real possibilities are being created for excluding war as a means of solving international disputes.

In our time the leaders of governments in some capitalist countries have begun to show a certain tendency towards a realistic understanding of the situation that has emerged in the world.

When I spoke with President Eisenhower – and I have just returned from the United States of America – I got the impression that the President of the USA – and not a few people support him – understands the need to relax international tension.

Perhaps not every bourgeois leader can pronounce the words 'peaceful coexistence' well, but they cannot deny that two systems exist in the world – the socialist and the capitalist. The recognition of this fact ran like a red thread through all the talks; this was repeatedly spoken about by the President and other leaders. Therefore we on our part must do all we can to exclude war as a means of settling disputed questions and settle these questions by negotiations.

Already in the first years of the Soviet power the great Lenin defined the general line of our foreign policy as being directed towards the peaceful coexistence of states with different social systems. . . .

Comrades! The socialist countries have achieved great successes in developing their economies and as a consequence have created mighty potential forces on the basis of which they can successfully continue their advance. They have the means to defend themselves from the attacks of the imperialist aggressors if these should attempt by interference in our countries' affairs to force them to leave the socialist path and return to capitalism. That time has gone never to return.

But we must think realistically and understand the contemporary situation correctly. This, of course, does not by any means signify that if we are so strong, then we must test by force the stability of the capitalist system. This would be wrong: the peoples would not understand and would never support those who would think of acting in this way. We have always been against wars of conquest. Marxists have recognised, and recognise, only liberating, just wars; they have always condemned, and condemn, wars of conquest, imperialist wars. This is one of the characteristic features of Marxist-Leninist theory.

It is not at all because capitalism is still strong that the socialist countries speak out against war, and for peaceful coexistence. No, we have no need of war at all. If the people do not want it, even such a noble and progressive system as socialism cannot be imposed by force of arms. The socialist countries therefore, while carrying through a consistently peace-loving policy, concentrate their efforts on peaceful construction, they fire the hearts of men by the force of their example in building socialism, and thus lead them to follow in their footsteps. The question of when this or that country will take the path to socialism is decided by its own people. This, for us, is the holy of holies. . . .

September 30

Khrushchev met Mao. Official report said: 'During the meeting a cordial friendly talk took place.'

October 1

Talk between Khrushchev and Mao was 'cordial'.

October 2

Official report recorded only that Khrushchev and Mao had met.

December 1

Khrushchev said in a speech at the Seventh Congress of the Hungarian Communist Party:

If we get conceited, if we permit mistakes in our leadership, if we distort Marxist-Leninist teaching about the construction of socialism and Communism, these mistakes may be used by the enemies of Communism, as was done in 1956.

Every socialist country individually and the whole socialist camp together are now so powerful that our strength is undefeatable. But it may be repeated once again that this does not in the least mean that enemies will not adopt subversive methods within each country and will not try to set one socialist country against another so as to weaken the forces of socialism. . . . That is why the unchanging principles of proletarian internationalism are the supreme and absolute law of the international Communist movement.

Making intelligent use of the great advantages of the socialist system and strengthening in every way the world socialist camp, we must put into practice consistently and creatively Lenin's teaching about the construction of socialism and Communism, we must be fully qualified Leninists, *not lagging behind and not rushing ahead and, speaking figuratively, set our watches one against the other. If the leadership of one country or another starts giving itself airs, this may play into the hands of the enemy.* In that case the socialist countries themselves and the leaders themselves will be giving help to the enemies in the struggle against socialism and against Communism. And that must not be allowed.

1960

February 4

At the conclusion of a meeting in Moscow the member-states of the Warsaw Pact issued a lengthy statement on foreign policy of which the following concluding passages convey the general tone:

Now, on the eve of crucial talks between statesmen of the East and the West, on the eve of a meeting at the summit, it is especially important, in the opinion of the Warsaw Treaty countries, that all states should do everything in their power to create a situation facilitating the success of the coming talks. The states represented at the present conference declare that they will act precisely in this direction and urge all other countries *to promote the success of East-West talks and to refrain from any steps capable of complicating these negotiations.*

The governments of the Warsaw Treaty countries note with satisfaction that their untiring efforts aimed at the termination of the arms race, the elimination of dangerous seats of international conflicts, and the ending of the cold war, are meeting with ever wider support from the peoples of the world and are yielding positive results. They are unanimous in believing that in our time states do not and cannot have any greater or nobler task than that of contributing to the establishment of lasting peace on earth.

The Chinese later released the text of a speech made at the Warsaw meeting by Kang Sheng, China's observer at the meeting. Extracts:

US President Eisenhower's State of the Union Message recently gave the clearest indication that the new tricks of the United States are designed to gain precisely what it failed to obtain by its old tricks. The actions of the United States prove fully that its imperialist nature will not change. American imperialism still remains the arch-enemy of world peace. All those throughout the world who are working sincerely for peace must maintain their vigilance against US double-dealing. If our socialist camp and the people of all countries in the world continue to strengthen unity, continue to fortify our strength and thoroughly smash all the intrigues and schemes of the enemy of peace, US war plans can be set back even further and even checked, and the cause of defence of peace will certainly win still greater victories. Although US imperialism dare not oppose disarmament in so many words, it has always in fact sabotaged universal disarmament. Whenever certain US proposals were accepted by the Soviet Union, the United States always concocted new pretexts for a retreat from its original position, creating all kinds of difficulties and preventing by every means the reaching of agreement on the disarmament question. US actions prove that it will not abandon its policy of the arms race. Therefore, the struggle for universal disarmament is a long-term and complicated struggle between us and imperialism.

The Chinese government and the Chinese people have always stood for universal disarmament, and actively supported the proposals concerning disarmament made by the Soviet Union and other socialist countries. Since 1951, the Chinese government has on its own initiative again and again reduced its armed forces. The present Chinese armed forces are less than half their original size. We shall continue to work tirelessly for universal disarmament together with the Soviet Union and other socialist countries. We hope that the countries concerned will reach agreement on this question of universal disarmament.

The Chinese government has never hesitated to commit itself to all international obligations with which it agrees. But US imperialism, hostile to the Chinese people, has always adopted a discriminatory attitude against our country in international relations. Therefore, the Chinese government has to declare to the world that *any international agreements which are arrived at without the formal participation of the Chinese People's Republic and the signature of its delegate cannot, of course, have any binding force on China. . . .*

The Chinese Communist Party and the Chinese people have always regarded an attack against any socialist country by the imperialists and all reactionaries as an attack against China. They have always considered that the modern revisionists of Yugoslavia are renegades of the Communist movement, that revisionism is the main danger in the present Communist movement. and that it is necessary to wage a resolute struggle against revisionism. This stand of ours is firm and unshakable.

February 11–March 5

Khrushchev visited India, Burma, Indonesia and Afghanistan.

March 23–April 2

Khrushchev visited France.

April 16

Red Flag, theoretical journal of Chinese CP published '*Long Live Leninism*!' to mark the ninetieth anniversary of Lenin's birth. It marked the beginning of the 'ideological' phase of the dispute. The following extracts are chosen to illuminate the Chinese attitude on the main issues in dispute:

Are the teachings of Marxism-Leninism now 'outmoded'? Does the whole, integrated teaching of Lenin on imperialism, on proletarian revolution and proletarian dictatorship, on war and peace, and on the building of socialism and Communism still retain its vigorous vitality? . . . These questions now confront us and must be answered. . . .

The US imperialists, open representatives of the bourgeoisie in many countries, the modern revisionists represented by the Tito clique, and the right-wing social democrats, in order to mislead the people of the world, do all they can to paint an utterly distorted picture of the contemporary world situation in an attempt to confirm their ravings on how 'Marxism is outmoded', and 'Leninism is outmoded too'.

Tito's speech at the end of last year referred repeatedly to the so-called 'new epoch' of the modern revisionists. . . . This renegade completely writes off the question of class contradictions and class struggle in the world, in an attempt to negate the consistent interpretation of Marxist-Leninists that our epoch is the epoch of imperialism and proletarian revolution, the epoch of the victory of socialism and Communism.

But how do things really stand in the world?

Can the exploited and oppressed people in the imperialist countries 'relax'? Can the peoples of all the colonies and semi-colonies still under imperialist oppression 'relax'? Has the armed intervention led by the US imperialists in Asia, Africa and Latin America become 'tranquil'? Is there 'tranquillity' in our Taiwan Straits when the US imperialists are still occupying our country's Taiwan? Is there 'tranquillity' on the African continent when the people of Algeria and many other parts of Africa are subjected to armed repressions by the French, British and other imperialists? Is there any 'tranquillity' in Latin America when the US imperialists are trying to wreck the people's revolution in Cuba by means of bombing, assassination and subversion?

What kind of 'construction' is meant in saying '[they] devote themselves to their internal construction tasks'? Everyone knows that there are different types of countries in the world today and principally two types of countries with social systems fundamentally different in nature. One type belongs to the socialist world system, the other to the capitalist world system. Is Tito referring to the 'internal construction tasks' of arms expansion which the imperialists are carrying out in order to oppress the peoples of their own countries and oppress the whole world? Or is it the 'internal construction' carried out by socialism for the promotion of the people's happiness and in the pursuit of lasting world peace?

Is the question of war and peace no longer an issue? Is it that imperialism no longer exists, the system of exploitation no longer exists, and therefore the question of war no longer exists? Or is it that there can be no question of war even if imperialism and the system of exploitation are allowed to survive for ever?

The fact is that since the Second World War there has been continuous and unbroken warfare. Do not the imperialist wars to suppress national liberation movements and the imperialist wars of armed intervention against revolutions in various countries count as wars? Even though these wars have not developed into world wars, still do not these local wars count as wars? Even though these wars were not fought with nuclear weapons, still do not wars using so-called conventional weapons count as wars? Does not the US imperialists' allocation of nearly 60 per cent. of the 1960 budget outlay to arms expansion and war preparations count as a bellicose policy on the part of US imperialism?

Will the revival of West German and Japanese militarisms not confront mankind with the danger of a new big war?

What kind of 'co-operation' is meant? Is it 'co-operation' of the proletariat with the bourgeoisie to protect capitalism? Is it 'co-operation' of the colonial and semi-colonial peoples with the imperialists to protect colonialism? Is it 'co-operation' of socialist countries with capitalist countries to protect the imperialist system in its oppression of the peoples in these countries and suppression of national liberation wars?

In a word, the assertions of the modern revisionists about their so-called 'epoch' are so many challenges to Leninism on the foregoing issues. It is their aim to obliterate the contradiction between the masses of people and the monopoly capitalist class in the imperialist countries, the contradiction between the colonial and semi-colonial peoples and the imperialist aggressors, the contradiction between the socialist system and the imperialist system, and the contradiction between the peace-loving people of the world and the warlike imperialist bloc. . . .

In the past few years, the *achievements of the Soviet Union in science and technology have been foremost in the world*. These Soviet achievements are products of the Great October Revolution. These outstanding achievements mark a new era in man's conquest of nature and at the same time play a very important role in defending world peace. But, in the new conditions brought about by the development of modern technology, has the ideological system of Marxism-Leninism been shaken, as Tito says, by the 'rocket on the moon, atomic bombs and the great technical progress' which Marx and Lenin 'did not predict'? Can it be said that the Marxist-Leninist world outlook, social-historical outlook, moral outlook and other basic concepts have therefore become what they call stale 'dogmas' and that the law of class struggle henceforth no longer holds good?

Marx and Lenin did not live to the present day, and of course could not see certain specific details of technological progress in the present-day world. But what, after all, does the development of natural science and the advance of technology augur for the capitalist system? Marx and Lenin held that this could only augur a new social revolution, but could certainly not augur the fading away of social revolution.

At the present time, the socialist Soviet Union clearly holds the upper hand in the development of new techniques. Everybody knows that the rocket that hit the moon was launched by the Soviet Union and not by the United States, the country where capitalism is most developed. This shows that only in the socialist countries can there be unlimited prospects for the large-scale development of new techniques.

The US imperialists and their partners use weapons like atom bombs to threaten war and blackmail the whole world. They declare that anyone who does not submit to the domination of US imperialism will be destroyed. The Tito clique echoes this line, it takes up the US imperialist refrain to spread terror of atomic warfare among the masses. . . .

Marxist-Leninists have always maintained that in world history it is not technique but man, the masses of people, that determine the fate of mankind. There was a theory current for a time among some people in China before and during the War of Resistance to Japanese Aggression, which was known as the 'weapons-mean-everything theory'; from this theory they concluded that since Japan's weapons were new and its techniques advanced while China's weapons were old and its techniques were backward, 'China would inevitably be subjugated'. Comrade Mao Tse-tung in his work *On the Protracted War* published at that time refuted such nonsense. He made the following analysis: the Japanese imperialists' war of aggression against China was bound to fail because it was reactionary, unjust, and being unjust lacked popular support; the Chinese people's war of resistance against Japan would certainly win because it was progressive, just, and being just enjoyed abundant support. Comrade Mao Tse-tung pointed out that the most abundant source of strength in war lay in the masses, and that a people's army organised by awakened and united masses of people would be invincible throughout the world. This is a Marxist-Leninist thesis. And what was the outcome? The outcome was that the Marxist-Leninist thesis triumphed and the 'theory of national subjugation' ended in defeat. During the Korean war after the Second World War, the triumph of the Korean and Chinese peoples over US aggressors far superior in weapons and equipment again bore out this Marxist-Leninist thesis.

An awakened people will always find new ways to counteract a reactionary superiority in arms and win victory for themselves. This was so in past history, it is so at present, and it will still be so in the future. Because the socialist Soviet Union has gained supremacy in military techniques, the US imperialists have lost their monopoly of atomic and nuclear weapons; at the same time, as a result of the awakening of the people in the United States itself, there is now in the world the possibility of concluding an agreement for the banning of atomic and nuclear weapons. We are striving for the conclusion of such an agreement. Unlike the bellicose imperialists, the socialist countries and peace-loving people the world over actively and firmly stand for the banning and destruction of atomic and nuclear weapons and the defence of world peace.

Of course, whether or not the imperialists will unleash a war is not determined by us; we are, after all, not chiefs-of-staff to the imperialists. As long as the people of all countries enhance their awareness and are fully prepared, with the socialist camp also mastering modern weapons, it is certain that if the US or other imperialists refuse to reach an agreement on the banning of atomic and nuclear weapons and should dare to fly in the face of the will of all humanity by launching a war using atomic and nuclear weapons, the result will be the very speedy destruction of these monsters encircled by the peoples of the world, and *the result will certainly not be the annihilation of mankind*. We consistently oppose the launching of criminal wars by imperialism, because imperialist war would impose enormous sacrifices upon the peoples of various countries (including the peoples of the United States and other imperialist countries). But should the imperialists impose such sacrifices on the peoples of various countries, we believe that, just as the experience of the Russian revolution and the Chinese revolution shows, those sacrifices would be repaid. *On the débris of a dead imperialism, the victorious people would create very swiftly a civilisation thousands of times higher than the capitalist system and a truly beautiful future for themselves.* The conclusion can only be this: whichever way you look at it, *none of the new techniques like atomic energy, rocketry and so on has changed,* as alleged by the modern revisionists, *the basic characteristics of the epoch of imperialism and proletarian revolution pointed out by Lenin.* The capitalist-imperialist system absolutely will not crumble of itself. It will be overthrown by the proletarian revolution within the imperialist country concerned, and the national revolution in the colonies and semi-colonies. Contemporary technological progress cannot save the capitalist-imperialist system from its doom but only rings a new death knell for it. . . .

We believe in the absolute correctness of Lenin's thinking: War is an inevitable outcome of systems of exploitation and the source of modern wars is the imperialist system. Until the imperialist system and the exploiting classes come to an end, wars of one kind or another will always occur. They may be wars among the imperialists for redivision of the world, or wars of aggression and anti-aggression between the imperialists and the oppressed nations, or civil wars of revolution and counter-revolution between the exploited and exploiting classes in the imperialist countries, or, of course, wars in which the imperialists attack the socialist countries and the socialist countries are forced to defend themselves. All these kinds of wars represent the continuation of the policies of definite classes.

To attain their aim of plunder and oppression, the imperialists always have two tactics: the tactics of war and the tactics of 'peace'; therefore, the proletariat and the people of all countries must also use two tactics to counter the imperialists: the tactics of thoroughly exposing the imperialists' peace fraud and striving energetically for a genuine world peace, and the tactics of preparing for a just war to end the imperialist unjust war when and if the imperialists should unleash it. . . .

Peaceful coexistence of nations and people's revolutions in various countries are in themselves two different things, not one and the same thing; two different concepts, not one; two different kinds of question, and not one and the same kind of question.

Peaceful coexistence refers to relations between nations, revolution means the overthrow of the oppressors as a class by the oppressed people within each country, while in the case of the colonial and semi-colonial countries, it is first and foremost a question of overthrowing alien oppressors, namely, the imperialists.

When a socialist country, in the face of imperialist aggression is compelled to launch counter-attacks in a defensive war, and goes beyond its own border to pursue and eliminate its enemies from abroad, as the Soviet Union did in the war against Hitler, is this justified? Certainly it is completely justified, absolutely necessary and entirely just. In accordance with the strict principles of Communists, such operations by the socialist countries must be strictly limited to the time when the imperialists launch a war of aggression against them. Socialist countries never permit themselves to send, never should and never will send their troops across their borders unless they are subjected to aggression from a foreign enemy. Since the armed forces of the socialist countries fight for justice, when these forces have to go beyond their borders to counter-attack a foreign enemy, it is only natural that they should exert an influence and have an effect wherever they go; but even then, the emergence of people's revolutions and the establishment of the socialist system in those places and countries where they go will still depend on the will of the masses of the people there.

It would be in the best interests of the people if the proletariat could attain power and carry out the transition to socialism by peaceful means. It would be wrong not to make use of such a possibility when it occurs. . . .

The question is not whether the proletariat is willing to carry out a peaceful transformation; it is rather whether the bourgeoisie will accept such a peaceful transformation. This is the only possible way in which followers of Lenin can approach this question.

So, contrary to the modern revisionists who seek to paralyse the revolutionary will of the people by empty talk about peaceful transition, Marxist-Leninists hold that the question of possible peaceful transition to socialism can be raised only in the light of the specific conditions in each country at a particular time. The proletariat must never allow itself to one-sidedly and groundlessly base its thinking, policy and its whole work on the calculation that the bourgeoisie is willing to accept peaceful transformation. It must, at the same time, prepare for alternatives: one for the peaceful development of the revolution and the other for the non-peaceful development of the revolution. Whether the transition will be carried out through armed uprising or by peaceful means is a question that is fundamentally separate from that of peaceful coexistence between the socialist and capitalist countries; it is an internal affair of each country, one to be determined only by the relation of classes in that country in a given period, a matter to be decided only by the Communists of that country themselves. . . .

'Peace' in the mouths of modern revisionists is intended to whitewash the war preparations of the imperialists, to play again the tune of 'ultra-imperialism' of the old opportunists, which was long since refuted by Lenin, and to distort our Communist policy concerning peaceful coexistence of countries with two different systems into elimination of the people's revolution in various countries. It was that old revisionist Bernstein who made this shameful and notorious statement: The movement is everything, the final aim is nothing. The modern revisionists have a similar statement: The peace movement is everything, the aim is nothing. Therefore, the 'peace' they talk about is in practice limited to the 'peace' which may be acceptable to the imperialists under certain historical conditions. It attempts to lower the revolutionary standards of the peoples of various countries and destroy their revolutionary will.

We Communists are struggling in defence of world peace, for the realisation of the policy of peaceful coexistence. At the same time we support the revolutionary wars of the oppressed nations against imperialism. We support the revolutionary wars of the oppressed people for their own liberation and social progress because all these revolutionary wars are just wars. Naturally, we must continue to explain to the masses Lenin's thesis concerning the capitalist-imperialist system as the source of modern war; we must continue to explain to the masses the Marxist-Leninist thesis on the replacement of capitalist imperialism by socialism and Communism as the final goal of our struggle. We must not hide our principles before the masses. . . .

Marching in the forefront of all the socialist countries and of the whole socialist camp is the great Soviet Union, the first socialist state created by the workers and peasants led by Lenin and their Communist Party. Lenin's ideals have been realised in the Soviet Union: socialism has long since built. Now, under the leadership of the Central Committee of the Communist Party of the Soviet Union and the Soviet government headed by Comrade Khrushchev, a great period of extensive building of Communism is already beginning. The valiant and enormously talented Soviet workers, peasants and intellectuals have brought about a great new labour upsurge in their struggle for the grand goal of building Communism.

We, the Chinese Communists and the Chinese people, cheer every new achievement of the Soviet Union, the native land of Leninism. The Chinese Communist Party, integrating the universal truths of Marxism-Leninism with the concrete practice of the Chinese revolution, has led the people of the entire country in winning great victories in the people's revolution, marching along the broad common road of socialist revolution and socialist construction charted by Lenin, carrying the socialist revolution to full completion and it has already begun to win great victories on the various fronts of socialist construction. The Central Committee of the Chinese Communist Party creatively set down for the Chinese people, in accordance with Lenin's principles and in the light of conditions in China, the correct principles of the general line for building socialism, *the big leap forward and the people's communes*, which have inspired the initiative and revolutionary spirit of the masses throughout the country and are thus day after day bringing about new changes in the face of our country. . . .

Leninism is the complete and integrated revolutionary teaching of the proletariat, it is a complete and integrated revolutionary outlook which, following Marx and Engels, continues to express the thinking of the proletariat. This complete and integrated revolutionary teaching and revolutionary outlook must not be distorted or carved up. We hold the view that the attempts of the modern revisionists to distort and carve up Leninism are nothing but a manifestation of the last ditch struggle of the imperialists facing their doom. In face of continuous victories in building Communism in the Soviet Union, in face of continuous victories in building socialism in the socialist countries, in face of constant strengthening of the unity of the socialist camp headed by the Soviet Union and of the steadfast and valiant struggles being waged by the increasingly awakened peoples of the world seeking to free themselves from the shackles of capitalist imperialism, the revisionist endeavours of Tito and his ilk are completely futile.

Long live great Leninism!

The Chinese later explained why they published '*Long Live Leninism*!' and why they directed the criticism against Tito and the Yugoslav Communists (*see* Chronology: February 27. 1963).

April 22

Otto Kuusinen, speaking at the Lenin anniversary meeting in Moscow, made the following statements:

As for our relations with countries of the socialist camp, with the Chinese People's Republic, the Korean Democratic People's Republic, the Democratic Republic of Viet Nam and the Mongolian People's Republic – those relations have been determined from the very outset by the principles of socialist internationalism. Close alliance and fraternal friendship, mutual assistance and co-operation in building socialism and Communism – that is the foundation of these relations.

But we have a broader understanding of the international duty of our socialist country – we understand it as rendering assistance to those liberated peoples, too, who are not included in the world system of socialism. All-round, disinterested assistance in strengthening their political and economic independence is the foundation of our relations with the newly-created states. Of course, we do not impose assistance on anyone, but we help when we are asked to do so.

The road to the consolidation of the independence of the liberated countries is the road of developing their national economy, promoting the advance of their culture and improving the living standards of the people. Industrialisation is of tremendous importance for such countries. It is precisely here that the young states need support most of all. Understanding this, the Soviet Union is accordingly developing its economic co-operation with them.

The supplying of up-to-date industrial equipment, assistance in building large enterprises, in prospecting for and exploiting natural resources, in training national cadres of specialists – these are the principal aspects of Soviet assistance. The Soviet Union's participation in building the gigantic steel works at Bhilai, in the construction of the Aswan High Dam, a steel works in Indonesia and dozens of other industrial projects accords with the vital interests of the peoples of the East. . . .

Lenin's behest to our Party and all Communists was: Fight tirelessly for peace and work to end wars. He said 'The ending of wars, peace between the nations, the stopping of plunder and violence – it is precisely this that is our ideal.'

In the West at the present time there are glib propagandists who allege that Lenin was against the peaceful coexistence of the two systems. . . .

But then, these gentlemen carefully pass over in silence Lenin's entire policy during the first years of Soviet power, his line towards establishing businesslike co-operation with capitalist states, the line which was clearly expressed in Lenin's directives to the Soviet delegates to the first international conferences, for instance in Geneva in 1922.

In that period Lenin developed his idea of the peaceful economic competition of the two systems. To use Lenin's expression, this is the 'rivalry of two methods, two formations, two kinds of economy – Communist and capitalist'.

The principles of peaceful co-existence, both then and now, form the basis of the whole of Soviet foreign policy. During recent years our Party has been creatively developing this idea of Lenin's. *Of decisive importance in this connexion was the conclusion drawn by the Twentieth and Twenty-first Party Congresses about there being no fatal inevitability of wars in our epoch, about the possibility of preventing wars. By drawing this conclusion, the Party has made a new contribution to Marxism.*

Of course, aggressiveness is inherent in the nature of imperialism. But one should not dogmatically consider only this aspect of the matter. The fact that powerful forces counteracting war have appeared should not be ignored. One should not overlook the fact that the time has gone, never to return, when imperialism had the whole world under its sway. Capitalism can no longer make the whole world follow its laws. A powerful world system of socialism is already in existence; imperialism has been weakened by the collapse of the colonial system; a vast 'zone of peace' has come into being; the forces of peace and democracy are now more closely united and better organised even in the imperialist countries themselves. Don't these powerful factors have practical significance in settling the question of peace and war?

Therefore, in order to be loyal to Marxism-Leninism today it is not sufficient to repeat the old truth that imperialism is aggressive. The task is to make full use of the new factors operating for peace in order to save humanity from the catastrophe of another war. . . .

In its practical activity the Soviet government is widely cultivating *personal contacts with both statesmen and public leaders of bourgeois countries.*

The numerous state visits to foreign countries by the head of the Soviet government, Nikita Khrushchev, have, as we know, acquired tremendous importance. They have been of historic significance in improving the Soviet Union's relations with other states and in improving the international situation as a whole. These visits have confirmed once again that the Leninist policy of the peaceful coexistence of states with different social systems, pursued by our Party and the Soviet government headed by Comrade Nikita Khrushchev, is the only correct and viable policy. All of us remember full well the moving demonstrations of friendship by masses of people during Nikita Khrushchev's stay in the United States of America, India, Indonesia, Burma, Afghanistan and France on his great mission of goodwill.

The change in the balance of forces on the international scene, the growing might of the socialist camp and the obviously disastrous consequences of another war – all this leads to a split in the ruling circles of the imperialist states. There appear, alongside the thick-skulled opponents of peace, sober-minded statesmen who realise that a war with the use of weapons of mass destruction would be madness.

Such are the dialectics of military-engineering progress: a new weapon created for war begins to exert an influence in favour of peace. For Marxists there is nothing mysterious in this. The classics of Marxism have never denied the fact that new types of weapons can not only bring about a radical change in the art of war but can also influence politics.

For instance, Engels wrote about this in *Anti-Dühring*. And Nadezhda Krupskaya tells us that Lenin foresaw that 'the time will come when war will become so destructive as to be impossible'.

Lenin told Krupskaya about his talk with an engineer who had said that an invention was then in the making which would render it possible to destroy a large army from a distance. It would make a war impossible. 'Ilyich,' Krupskaya writes, 'talked about it with great enthusiasm. It was obvious that he passionately wanted war to become impossible.'

May 14–19

Khrushchev in Paris for the abortive 'summit' meeting.

June 5–9

General Council of World Federation of Trade Unions met in Peking. Welcoming the delegates, Chou En-lai said:

Our epoch is one in which the forces of peace prevail over the forces of war, the forces of the people prevail over the forces of reaction, and the forces of socialism prevail over the forces of imperialism. The fundamental task facing the working class of the world and progressive mankind is to make full use of the present most favourable situation to concentrate all our energies to defeat the forces of war and aggression headed by US imperialism, continue to advance the causes of the peoples of various countries for world peace, national independence, democratic liberties and socialism, and attain the noble aim of realising a lasting peace and human progress.

To stop aggressive war and safeguard world peace is the urgent universal desire of the working class and broad masses of all countries. Countless experiences have told us that, in order to realise this desire of the people, *the people themselves must rise to fight imperialism. Peace can never be obtained by begging it of imperialism.* The aggressive and warlike nature of imperialism will never change, but the warlike and aggressive activities of imperialism can be smashed so long as the people of the world wage persistent struggles against them.

Since the Second World War, the imperialist colonialist forces have been compelled to withdraw from many areas of Asia, Africa and Latin America; US imperialism's 'positions of strength' and 'brink of war' policies have continuously been frustrated and its 'peace' fraud has been exposed again and again. The criminal activities of US imperialism, encroaching on the Soviet Union and sabotaging the four-power conference of government heads, have thoroughly laid bare its vicious and sly features, thus arousing the universal indignation of the peace-loving people of the world and landing US imperialism itself in unprecedented isolation.

A storm of opposition to US imperialism is rising and extending. Struggles against US imperialism and its lackeys have broken out even in South Korea, Turkey and Japan, which have been under the tightest control of US imperialism. A general strike on the largest scale since the war was staged by the Japanese workers on June 4, which marked a new upsurge in the Japanese People's anti-US patriotic struggle.

All this proves that the people are the decisive factor. Confronted with powerful people's struggles, the imperialists headed by the USA can be triumphed over. The imperialists, of course, will never be reconciled to their failure. They will carry on disruptive activities so long as they survive. Comrade Mao Tse-tung has said: 'Disrupt, fail, disrupt again, fail again, till their doom – that is the logic of imperialism and all reactionaries in the world. They will certainly not go against this logic.'

The unity of the socialist camp headed by the Soviet Union and the unity of the working class of all countries constitute the surest guarantee for the cause of world peace, the cause of the emancipation of the working class and the cause of the liberation of all oppressed nations. . . .

June 8

The Chinese delegate to the WFTU meeting, Liu Chang-sheng, outlined his government's attitude to questions of war and peace:

As to what attitude we should adopt towards war, we must first of all make a distinction as to its nature. A war between imperialist countries in a scramble for colonies is an unjust war. An imperialist war to suppress the colonial people and the people at home and to commit aggression against other countries is also an unjust war. On the other hand, a revolutionary war waged by the colonial peoples and by the oppressed peoples of the imperialist countries for their own liberation is a just war. Since the imperialists use armed force to suppress the oppressed peoples and nations, the oppressed peoples and nations cannot but take up arms themselves. *We must stand for and uphold just revolutionary wars, and oppose and stop unjust wars. It is wrong to talk indiscriminately about whether or not war should be supported or whether or not it should be opposed, without making a specific analysis of its nature.*

The question of whether or not war can be averted, in our opinion, refers mainly to a world war. As to whether a world war can be averted, it should be pointed out that, on the one hand, under the conditions of the steady growth of the forces of the socialist countries, the forces of the liberation movements in the colonies and semi-colonies, and the forces of the revolutionary movements and peace movements of the peoples of the countries the world over, and the united struggle of these forces, there exists the possibility of stopping the imperialists from unleashing a new world war. But, on the other hand, *so long as there is imperialism the root cause of war remains, the breeding ground of war remains, and the war maniacs remain, and that is why there still exists the danger of imperialism launching a new world war.* If we only talk about the possibility of stopping the imperialists from launching a world war, but not about the danger of imperialism launching a world war, and are not on the alert against the military adventures of the war maniacs, we will only lull ourselves and the people. This will only help imperialism in its arms expansion and war preparations and, once it launches a war, the peoples of various countries, taken off guard, may be thrown into a state of alarm and confusion and even suffer unduly heavy losses. *It is entirely wrong to believe that war can be eliminated for ever while imperialism still exists.** The spreading of such illusions about imperialism among the peoples of all lands will lead to evil consequences of a serious nature and, in fact, we can already see such consequences at present.

* *Cf.* Khrushchev at the Twenty-first Congress of the CPSU: *see* Chronology January 27, 1959.

As for imperialist wars of suppression against colonies and semi-colonies, national liberation wars of the colonial and semi-colonial peoples against imperialism, wars of suppression against the people by the exploiting classes and people's revolutionary wars in the capitalist countries, wars of such nature have always existed in history, and have never stopped in the capitalist world since the Second World War. The wars in Indo-China, in Algeria, over the issue of the Suez Canal and in Cuba are all such wars. In the future, as long as imperialism and the exploiting system are still in existence, *such wars of a different nature will still be unavoidable. The belief that wars of the above-mentioned types can be avoided is entirely wrong and contrary to fact.* Such views will deprive the oppressed peoples of their fighting spirit and in the face of armed suppression by the enemy, prevent them from arming themselves to actively fight the enemy who is armed to the teeth, and to liberate themselves. This will, in effect, keep the oppressed peoples for ever in the state of enslavement. . . .

We support the disarmament proposals put forward by the Soviet Union. *It is of course inconceivable that imperialism will accept proposals for general and complete disarmament. The purpose of putting forward such proposals is to arouse the people throughout the world to unite and oppose the imperialist scheme for arms drive and war preparations, to unmask the aggressive and bellicose nature of imperialism before the peoples of the world in order to isolate the imperialist bloc headed by the United States to the greatest extent, so that they will not dare unleash a war lightly.* But there are people who believe that such proposals can be realised when imperialism still exists and that the 'danger of war can be eliminated' by relying on such proposals. This is an unrealistic illusion. As to the view that, after disarmament, imperialism would use the funds earmarked for war purposes for 'the welfare of the labouring masses' and for 'assisting underdeveloped countries' and that this would 'bring general progress to people as a whole without exception' – this is downright whitewashing and embellishing imperialism, and indeed this is helping imperialism headed by the United States to dupe the people throughout the world.

Only when socialist revolution is victorious throughout the world can there be a world free from war, a world without arms. Such a world is inconceivable while imperialism still exists. This is not a question of whether we want it or not; the question is that the imperialists will never lay down their arms of their own accord. . . .

We hold that the utmost efforts must be made to reach agreement on the banning of nuclear weapons and to prevent the outbreak of a nuclear war in the world. The mastery of nuclear weapons by the Soviet Union has now deprived US imperialism of its atomic monopoly. The Soviet Union and the other socialist countries should continue to develop their lead in the sphere of atomic energy and at the same time the people throughout the world should wage a more extensive struggle against imperialism and against nuclear weapons. Only in these circumstances can such agreement be reached. But even if agreement is reached, imperialism can still tear it to pieces. And even if in their own interests the imperialists dare not unleash a large-scale nuclear war, they still can wage war with the so-called conventional weapons. Therefore, in all circumstances people throughout the world should maintain sharp vigilance against imperialism and should not adopt a naive attitude towards US and other imperialism.

To win world peace, the struggle of the world's peoples and diplomatic negotiations carried out by the socialist countries should go hand in hand. It should not be supposed that, since diplomatic negotiations are needed, the struggle of the peoples can thus be dispensed with. On the contrary, diplomatic negotia- ations must be backed up by the united struggle of the world's peoples. To win world peace, we should mainly rely on the struggles waged by the peoples of various countries. . . .

June 10

Writing in *Sovietskaya Rossiya*, a CPSU theoretician, D. Shevlyagin, discussed the continuing danger of 'dogmatism', 'sectarianism' and various forms of 'leftism' in the Communist movement. His article included the following passage.

Present-day leftism in the Communist movement is also manifested in both concealed and overt resistance to the Communist parties' policy of establishing collaboration with working people in the ranks of the social-democratic, Catholic and various other bourgeois-radical parties and organisations. The policy of achieving peaceful coexistence, of cessation of the arms race and establishing of peace and friendship between peoples of capitalist and socialist countries is interpreted by present-day leftists as a 'deviation' from Marxism-Leninism, and they take the slightest aggravation of the international situation as proof of their sectarian views. Although from the outside they seem 'terribly revolutionary', they do harm to the cause of rallying the working class to the struggle against the aggressive designs of the imperialists, for the cessation of the 'cold war' and the strengthening of peace throughout the world. . . .

June 12

Writing in *Pravda*, another party theoretician, N. Matkovsky, also issued a warning against 'leftism':

Creatively developing Marxist-Leninist theory under the new conditions and generalising the great experience of socialist construction in our country in full accordance with the principles of social development, the Twenty-first Party Congress laid out a well-grounded, full-fledged programme for the transition from socialism to Communism. That programme is the concrete embodiment of the general line of the Communist Party in the present stage.

Characterising the process of transition from socialism to Communism Comrade N. S. Khrushchev told the Twenty-first Party Congress:

'We must not hurry and hastily introduce what has not yet ripened. That would lead to distortions and compromise our cause. But neither must we rest on our laurels because such a course would lead to stagnancy.'

The course of social development is objective. Mistaken and incorrect are the statements of 'leftists' in the international Communist movement to the effect that once you have the power into your hands you can at once introduce Com- munism, by-passing certain historical stages in its development.

Such statements contradict Leninism. Lenin taught us that to try to anticipate the result of a fully developed, fully consolidated and established, fully unfolded and matured Communism amounts to the same thing as to try to teach higher mathematics to a four-year-old child.

The left-sectarian sentiments and tendencies against which Lenin's book was directed find their expression in some places even in our time. Some persons mistakenly consider the course of the achievement of peaceful coexistence of our countries with different political systems, the struggle to halt the arms race and to strengthen peace and friendship among peoples and the talks between leaders of socialist and capitalist countries as some kind of deviation from the positions of Marxism-Leninism.

June 20–25

Third Congress of the Rumanian Communist Party in Bucharest.

June 21

Khrushchev addressed the Rumanian Congress at length on questions of war and peace:

Comrades, questions of international relations, questions of war and peace, have always deeply concerned the mass of the people. That is natural. More than once in history the anti-popular policy of the imperialists, their desire for a redivision of the world, for the seizure of new colonies, have subjected mankind to the horrors of devastating wars. But no matter how terrible wars have been in the past, if the imperialist circles should succeed in unleashing another world war, its calamities would be incomparably more terrible. *For millions of people might burn in the conflagration of hydrogen explosions, and for some states a nuclear war would be literally a catastrophe.* That is why the Marxist-Leninist parties, in all their activity, have always been consistent champions of a reasonable peace-loving policy, of the prevention of another world war. . . .

The Communists are realists; they are aware that in present conditions, when there are two world systems, it is imperative to build mutual relations between them in such a way as will preclude the possibility of war breaking out between states. Only madmen and maniacs can now call for another world war. As for people of sound mind – and they are in the majority even among the most deadly enemies of Communism – they cannot but be aware of the fatal consequences of another war.

All this means that we must still more actively expose the evils of imperialism, its vices. In order to prevent war – including a local war, because a local war might grow into a world war – each people in their own country must bring pressure to bear on their government and force it to adhere to the principles of peaceful coexistence between states with different social systems. . . .

The statesmen now directing United States policy have shown their aggressiveness and irreconcilability. They are so much blinded by hatred of Communism that this does not let them understand correctly the prevailing conditions in the world. The present leaders of the United States are evidently unable to cultivate in the proper way relations between states with differing social systems.

It is not for us, it is for the American people to decide who will be the next President of the United States. But our state, our people, who want to live in peace and friendship with the American people, are naturally interested in the election of such a President and the formation of such a government as would understand and correct the mistakes made by the present government of the United States.

The Soviet Union and the United States are great world powers. History itself has assigned them such a place. On our two powers depends to a large extent how the international situation will develop in the future – along the road of strengthening peace or along the road of straining relations.

We do not intend to yield to provocations and to deviate from the general line of our foreign policy, which was laid down by the Twentieth CPSU Congress and approved in the Declaration of the Communist and Workers' parties, adopted in 1957, during the celebrations of the fortieth anniversary of the Great October Socialist Revolution.

This is a policy of coexistence, a policy of consolidating peace, easing international tension and doing away with the cold war.

The thesis that in our time war is not inevitable proclaimed at the Twentieth and Twenty-first Congresses of our Party has a direct bearing on the policy of peaceful coexistence. Lenin's propositions about imperialism remain in force and are still a lodestar for us in our theory and practice. *But it should not be forgotten that Lenin's propositions on imperialism were advanced and developed decades ago, when many factors that are now decisive for historical development, for the entire international situation, were not present.*

Some of Lenin's propositions on imperialism date back to the period when there was no Soviet Union, when the other socialist countries did not exist.

The powerful Soviet Union, with its enormous economic and military potential, is now growing and gaining in strength; the great socialist camp, which now numbers over 1,000 million people, is growing and gaining in strength; the organisation and political consciousness of the working class have grown, and even in the capitalist countries it is actively fighting for peace. Such factors are in operation now as, for instance, the broad movement of peace champions; the number of countries coming out for peace among nations is increasing. It should also be pointed out that imperialism no longer has such a rear to fall back upon as the colonial system which it had formerly.

Besides, comrades, *one cannot repeat mechanically now on this question what Vladimir Ilyich Lenin said many decades ago about imperialism, and go on asserting that imperialist wars are inevitable until socialism triumphs throughout the world.* [*See* Liu Chang-sheng, Chronology: June 8, 1960.] We are now living in such a period when the forces of socialism are increasingly growing and becoming stronger, where ever-broader masses of the working people are rallying behind the banner of Marxism-Leninism.

History will possibly witness such a time when capitalism is preserved only in a small number of states, maybe states for instance as small as a button on a coat. Well? And even in such conditions would one have to look up in a book what

Vladimir Ilyich Lenin quite correctly said for his time; would one just have to repeat that wars are inevitable since capitalist countries exist? . . .

Therefore *one cannot ignore the specific situation*, the changes in the correlation of forces in the world *and repeat what the great Lenin said in quite different historical conditions. If Lenin could arise from his grave he would take such people, as one says, by the ear and would teach them how one must understand the essence of the matter.*

We live in a time when we have neither Marx, nor Engels, nor Lenin with us. If we act like children who, studying the alphabet, compile words from letters, we shall not go very far. Marx, Engels and Lenin created their immortal works which will not fade away in centuries. They indicated to mankind the road to Communism. And we confidently follow this road. On the basis of the teaching of Marxism-Leninism we must think ourselves, profoundly study life, analyse the present situation and draw the conclusions which benefit the common cause of Communism.

One must not only be able to read but also to understand correctly what one has read and apply it in the specific conditions of the time in which we live, taking into consideration the existing situation, and the real balance of forces. *A political leader acting in this manner shows that he not only can read but can also creatively apply the revolutionary teaching. If he does not do this, he resembles a man about whom people say: 'He looks into a book, but sees nothing!'*

All this gives grounds for saying with confidence that under present conditions war is not inevitable. . . .

Is the possibility of the imperialists' unleashing war under present conditions ruled out? We have said several times and we repeat once again: No, it is not. But the imperialist countries cannot fail to take into account the power of the Soviet Union, the power of the socialist camp as a whole. . . .

Even the crazy Hitler, if he had believed that the war which he launched against the Soviet Union would end in the routing of his fascist hordes and in his hiding in a Berlin shelter in the fifth year of the war and shooting a bullet into his head, he would not have taken such a mad decision on war against our country. That is quite clear!

And if the imperialists do unleash a war, will our socialist camp be in a position to cut it short? Yes, it will. Let me cite an instance. When France, Britain and Israel attacked Egypt in 1956, our intervention put an end to this imperialist war which had been started by the aggressive forces to deprive Egypt of her independence.

Or let us take another example. In 1957 we prevented Syria from being attacked by Turkey, which was incited to this adventure by the United States imperialists. And in 1958, after the revolution in Iraq, the Americans and British concentrated their forces and were preparing to attack Iraq. The American imperialists egged on Turkey, Iran and Pakistan to attack Iraq. But in that case as well they had to stop short and did not dare to start aggression against Iraq in view of the resolute warning served by the Soviet Union and other socialist countries. . . .

June 22

Chinese delegate, Peng Chen, said in his speech at the Rumanian Congress:

US imperialism, the most vicious enemy of the people of the world, is now more isolated than ever. In trying to extricate itself from its plight, it has, in the past few years, taken great pains to play the trick of faking peace while actually preparing for war. It has worked in every way to use peace as a camouflage for its aggression and preparations for a new war. However, it only serves as a good teacher by negative example. Recently the crimes of the United States in intruding into the Soviet air-space and sabotaging the four-power conference of government heads have stripped US imperialism and its head, Eisenhower, of all their disguises and bared the utterly ferocious features of US imperialism. This has provided an instructive lesson to the people of the world. Imperialism is, after all, imperialism and its fine words can never be trusted. . . .

The aggressive and predatory nature of imperialism will never change. US imperialism is the arch enemy of world peace, and the peoples of the world must never entertain any unrealistic illusions about imperialism, especially US imperialism. They must maintain a high degree of vigilance, carry on a persistent struggle against US imperialism and its lackeys and maintain solidarity and mutual support in the struggle.

June 24

Communiqué issued after Bucharest meeting:

Representatives of the Communist and Workers' parties of the socialist countries, attending the Third Congress of the Rumanian Workers' Party . . . decided to take advantage of their stay in Bucharest to exchange opinions on current problems of the present international situation, and the conclusions for the fraternal parties arising from them.

The participants in the conference affirm unanimously that the whole course of all international events and the development of the countries of the world socialist system have fully reaffirmed the correctness of the Marxist-Leninist theses of the Declaration and the Peace Manifesto adopted by the Communist and Workers' parties in Moscow in November 1957.

The participants in the conference reaffirm their allegiance to the principles of the Declaration and Peace Manifesto, which are the charter of the present-day Communist and Workers' movement, the programme of its struggle for peace, democracy and socialism.

The representatives of the Communist and Workers' parties of the socialist countries consider that all the conclusions of the Declaration and the Peace Manifesto – on peaceful coexistence between countries with different social systems, on the possibility of preventing wars in the present epoch, on the need for maintaining vigilance of the peoples with regard to the danger of war, since the existence of imperialism means there is a basis for wars of aggression – are fully applicable in the present situation, too. . . .

The Declaration also draws an important conclusion about the forms of the transition of countries from capitalism to socialism: 'In the present conditions in a number of capitalist countries, the working class, headed by its vanguard, has the possibility . . . of breaking the resistance of reactionary forces and creating the necessary conditions for the peaceful accomplishment of the socialist revolution.' All the same, it is also necessary to take into account the possibility of the working class gaining victory for the socialist revolution by non-peaceful means. . . .

The participants in the Conference declare that the Communist and Workers' parties will continue to strengthen the cohesion of the countries of the world socialist system and defend like the apple of their eye their unity in the struggle for the peace and security of all peoples and for the triumph of the great cause of Marxism-Leninism.

June 28

Khrushchev dealt again with the question of peace and war in a speech in Moscow to graduates of Soviet military academies:

The basic aim of the Communist Party and the Soviet government in the sphere of international relations was, is, and will remain, not war, but peace. . . .

All these radical changes in the disposition of economic, political and class forces mean that it has become possible to avert wars in the present epoch. But, as I have had to say more than once, the proposition that in present conditions war is not inevitable does not mean that the imperialists cannot launch one. Recent facts have shown again and again that the aggressive circles of imperialism are hatching war plans.

In recent years we have more than once held the aggressors back and prevented their plans to launch another war. . . .

To increase vigilance, to expose and destroy aggressive imperialist plans, to strengthen our power and ability to destroy any aggressor – in this our Party and the Soviet government see their sacred duty to the Soviet people and the whole of mankind. And it is this that determines the tasks of the Armed Forces.

We want you to understand correctly and profoundly the policy of the Communist Party and the Soviet government with regard to wars.

I repeat that now, when the mighty camp of socialism has emerged and established itself, when such changes have taken place in the world as make it possible to avert war, war can be averted if all peace-loving peoples make an effort and if the aggressor meets with the unity of the socialist countries.

August 7

Yuri Frantsev, leading CPSU theoretician, said in an article in *Pravda* entitled 'Problems of War and Peace in Present Conditions':

The question arises: In these conditions can the imperialists, as in the old days, arbitrarily drive the peoples into bloody slaughter? Will the bloody primordial horror of war rage over the globe as in the past?

An answer to this most important question was given by the Twentieth Congress of the CPSU, which on the basis of profound Marxist-Leninist analysis of the present day reached the conclusion that *in our time there is no fatal inevitability of war.*

The implementation of the economic plans of the USSR and of all the other socialist countries will introduce still greater changes into the international situation. When the USSR becomes the world's first industrial power, when the Chinese People's Republic becomes a mighty industrial power, and all the socialist countries together turn out more than half the world's industrial production, then the influence of the socialist countries on the strengthening of the peace-loving forces will grow still further. Relying on the might of the camp of socialism, *the peace-loving peoples will then be able to compel the militant circles of imperialism to abandon their plans for a new world war*. These ideas form the basis of the conclusions of the Twenty-first Congress of the CPSU to the effect that even before the complete victory of socialism on the earth and while capitalism continues to exist in part of the world, a real possibility will arise of excluding world war from the life of society.

The Conference of Representatives of the Communist and Workers' parties of socialist countries held *in Bucharest in June 1960 confirmed with fresh force that the Communist and Workers' parties unanimously support the conclusions of the Twentieth and Twenty-first Congresses of the CPSU*, which have exerted a tremendous influence on the international situation in the interests of peace and socialism, and support the principles of the Declaration and Peace Manifesto. The Conference in Bucharest demonstrated the fidelity of the international Communist movement to Marxism-Leninism, the readiness of all the fraternal parties to continue to strengthen the solidarity of the world socialist camp and to preserve like the apple of their eye the unity of the international Communist movement. The July Plenum of the Central Committee of the CPSU adopted unanimously a resolution on the results of the Conference of Representatives of Communist and Workers' parties in Bucharest. The Plenum fully and entirely approved the political line and activity of the CPSU Delegation headed by Comrade N. S. Khrushchev at this Conference and the comminique of the Conference. The Central Committee of the CPSU confirmed its fidelity to the principles of the Declaration and Peace Manifesto and expressed complete solidarity with the statement by the Communist and Workers' parties which participated in the Bucharest Conference to the effect that the struggle for peace remains the cardinal task of the Communist movement. . . .

Is the aggressive nature of imperialism changing in the course of these processes? No, it is not. By its social nature imperialism remains rapacious. But do the imperialists still have their former opportunities to manifest their rapacious nature unimpeded on the world arena? No, these opportunities are diminishing. . . .

The aggressive nature of imperialism remains, but its opportunities are diminishing – this is the peculiarity of the present-day international situation. Whoever notices only one side of a question and closes his eyes to the other is not a Marxist and cannot correctly understand the present international situation.

Contemporary revisionists and reformists close their eyes to the aggressive nature of imperialism and proclaim that imperialism has allegedly changed since the time when the classics of Marxism-Leninism wrote about it, and that the wolves have allegedly been 'transformed' into sheep. The point, the revisionists and reformists preach, is not that it is getting more and more difficult for the wolves to use their teeth, but that the wolves do not have any teeth and no longer have any desire to live at the expense of others. In that case there would be no need to wage the struggle for peace.

On the other hand, the dogmatists and sectarians claim that while imperialism exists it retains its rapacious nature and even now the question of whether there will be a war or not allegedly depends on its whim. In this case, the struggle for peace loses its perspective.

The position of creative, consistent Marxism-Leninism on these questions is different. . . .

At the present time there is no fatal inevitability of wars. But it would be mistaken to suppose that it is possible to ensure lasting peace without a struggle. The issue is decided by the struggle of the masses, in the first place by the assiduous and consistent struggle for peace of the camp of socialism and the world Communist movement. Communists are not fatalists and are not Utopian dreamers. In the struggle for peace they rely on actual possibilities contained in the historical situation and convert these possibilities into reality. The characteristic feature of the present-day international situation consists precisely in the fact that imperialism, without changing its aggressive nature, is forfeiting its former opportunities of lording it in the world arena, while the opportunities of the world socialist system to curb the aggressive aspirations of the imperialists are growing.

In present-day conditions a revival of views like those of the 'left' Communists would merely play into the hands of the imperialists by helping them to spread false stories about the 'aggressiveness of Communism'. A revival of such left sectarian views would merely have a demoralising influence on the builders of the new society: *why construct, build, create, if one knows in advance that all the fruits of one's labour will be destroyed by the tornado of war?* Such views have nothing in common with Communism. Nor can one fail to see that as a result of modern warfare the productive forces, including the main productive force – the working people – would suffer considerably and *mankind would experience tremendous difficulties in erecting the new social system on the ruins remaining after a military catastrophe.* A destructive war would only make difficult the process of constructing a new society.

Now, when there is a great commonwealth of socialist countries forming a mighty bulwark of peace and social progress, it is necessary to approach in a new way the question of the conditions and the possibilities of victorious socialist construction in various countries.

August 13

Agence France Presse reported from Peking:

The departures of Soviet technicians and their families from Peking and from the industrial provinces have increased at such a rate since the end of July that they are now coming to be spoken of openly in diplomatic circles in the Chinese capital as a veritable exodus.

These departures, which appeared to be normal until May, since they coincided with the return to China of Chinese technicians trained in the Soviet Union and the other socialist countries as well as with an increase in the number of students leaving Chinese schools, have now assumed such proportions that it would be difficult not to give them a political significance.

It appears that the 'ideological' discussion which has been going on for some weeks between the Russians and the Chinese Communists is at the root of this exodus which, if it continues, could leave a gap in the Chinese economy and endanger the progress so far made. . . .

The exodus affects at present only the Soviet experts and not those from the people's democracies.

August 16

Another CPSU theoretician, S. Titarenko, hinted at economic sanctions in *Sovietskaya Latvia*:

Now, when there is a great commonwealth of socialist countries forming a mighty bulwark of peace and social progress, it is necessary to approach in a new way the question of the conditions and the possibilities of victorious socialist construction in various countries. In the period when the USSR was the only country of proletarian dictatorship in the world, it did not have the possibility of relying on anybody's direct economic or military aid. The working class and the working peasantry of the USSR could count only on their own strength and resources both in the construction of a socialist economy and in ensuring the country's military security.

The situation is now completely different. The working class of any country knows well that, in the struggle for socialism, it will always receive fraternal support from the Soviet Union and the whole camp of socialism. Lenin's teaching about the victory of socialism in particular countries should now be considered in direct connexion with the successes of the socialist camp.

Could one imagine the successful construction of socialism going on in present day conditions even in so great a country as, let us say, China, if that country were in a state of isolation and could not rely on the collaboration and aid of all other socialist countries? While being subjected to an economic blockade by the capitalist countries such a country would be subjected simultaneously to military blows from outside. It would experience the greatest difficulties even if it succeeded in withstanding the furious attacks of the enemy.

August 17

Explaining in *Sovietskaya Rossiya* why there was no longer a 'fatal inevitability' of war, Titarenko introduced a new argument:

Talking of the possibility of averting another military catastrophe one should bear in mind the nature of modern warfare. The level of military equipment has now reached such a level of development that *war ceases to be a means with the aid of which it is possible to achieve particular political ends* without placing hundreds of millions of people and whole countries under threat of destruction.

It may be said that the imperialists are pushed into war ultimately by objective economic causes and that considerations of a subjective nature do not play an essential role. But that is not so. The political, subjective factors in questions of war have a far from secondary significance. *Even the most inveterate militarist will hardly take the risk of war if he knows for sure that he will himself be destroyed in its fire.*

September 8

Expulsion of Liri Belishova and Kocho Tashko from Albanian Communist leadership announced.

October

Soviet draft statement submitted to 26-party commission preparing for November conference.

November 6

F. R. Kozlov, secretary of CPSU, restated the whole Soviet case in familiar terms in a speech marking the forty-third anniversary of the Russian Revolution. On the relative status of the CPSU Twentieth Congress, the Moscow Declaration of 1957, the CPSU Twenty-first Congress and the Bucharest meeting, he said:

Creatively developing Marxism-Leninism, the Communist Party of the Soviet Union drew an important conclusion at its Twentieth Congress: Today war is not fatally inevitable; war can be averted. This conclusion received the unanimous support of the fraternal Communist and Workers' parties in a document of programmatic importance – in the Declaration of the Moscow conference of representatives of Communist and Workers' parties of the socialist countries. The theses of the Moscow Declaration were reaffirmed in the communiqué of the Bucharest conference of the Marxist-Leninist parties.

A further advance of the theory of Marxism-Leninism was the conclusion of the Twenty-first Congress of the Communist Party of the Soviet Union, which said: 'Even before the complete victory of socialism on earth, given the preservation of capitalism in a part of the world, there is a real possibility of excluding world war from human society.'

November

The Conference of 81 Communist parties met in Moscow after the celebration of the anniversary of the Revolution on November 7 and remained in session throughout the month. A brief communiqué was issued on December 2 and the final Statement was released on December 6. Though the conference was held entirely behind closed doors, documents which have since become available provide a direct impression of the debates that took place. They come, inter alia, from the Italian, Belgian and French Communist parties and the relevant portions are given below. There is no version available of the speeches made at the opening by Khrushchev and Suslov nor of the original draft Statement, though they can be implied from the other speeches and the Statement in its final form. I have therefore given first the account made by the Belgian Communists of Teng Hsiao-ping's contribution to the debate and a summary of Enver Hoxha's speech. These are followed by the various contributions made by Maurice Thorez and Luigi Longo, the French and Italian delegates respectively, in reply to Teng and Hoxha. The order in which the statements are given is not necessarily the order in which they were made.

Belgian Account of Chinese Views

Three leaders of our Party (Ernest Burnelle, Frans Vanden Branden, Jean Blume) took part in the Moscow conference of 1960. On their return they informed the Central Committee of the difficult aspects of the debates in Moscow. They stressed the positive aspects of them, which were in their view dominant, but they also stressed the disturbing features. The first of these, which is apparent to everybody, is certainly not the fact that there was a divergence of views between the majority of the Communist parties present and the Chinese and Albanian parties in first place. What is disturbing is that, after a plenary discussion lasting a month, preceded by an even longer preparatory discussion, a declaration was finally signed that was so 'balanced' and of such a nature that it would be possible to refer to it to justify the presentation, defence and application of political views sometimes diametrically opposed and often outrageously divergent. . . .

What are the controversial factors which brought into question the universal validity of the Statement of the 81 Communist parties? Who introduced these elements of controversy into the debate?

It was unquestionably the Chinese Communist Party which defended most fiercely and most consistently the greatest number of ideas diverging from the ideas adopted by the majority. The Albanian Communist Party distinguished itself above all by carrying to verbal extremes on several occasions the expression of its disagreements. It must be said in truth that the Chinese delegation never dissociated itself from excesses of this kind even when they assumed an insulting character. Let us summarise the *main theses presented by the Chinese CP to the Conference of the 81*:

First Thesis: We must stop referring to the Twentieth Congress of the CPSU as though its teachings were valid for the whole of the world Communist movement. In the opinion of the Chinese delegation it is from the time of the Twentieth Congress that the CPSU has been leading the majority of the Communist parties along the road of capitulation to imperialism. The Albanian Communist Party made this argument more precise by accusing the CPSU of having gone over to revisionism.

Here we have our finger on the key point of difference; they deny altogether the validity and usefulness of the criticism of the cult of personality, they object to the idea that it is possible and useful to prevent the outbreak of a third world conflict, they question the political value of the application of the various paths to socialism, they describe as utopian the theory that the working class in certain countries and certain conditions may take power without bloodshed. Moreover, the essential unity of the working-class movement against the dictatorship of the monopoly capitalists and of militarist forces is relegated to the second place in importance to make room for the verbal denunciation of the social-democrat leaders and their mistakes.

Second Thesis: The struggle for peaceful coexistence can be regarded only as a tactical move, a means of morally disarming the peoples of the capitalist countries and materially disarming the countries themselves. World disarmament and lasting peaceful coexistence will be not possible in practice until there are only socialist countries left in the world. The whole gravity of this sort of attitude is apparent. In the first place it leads to thinking that a third world conflict is inevitable and that the first duty is to prepare to win it at no matter what price in human lives and devastation. From this several theories develop logically. There is the theory that 'local wars' are essentially inoffensive and without risk as far as world peace is concerned. There is the theory of the futility of efforts made by many Communist parties in the capitalist countries to work out plans of action aimed at developing democracy, restricting the power of the monopolies and changing substantially the policy of their countries. There is the theory which describes as 'revisionist' the work of the second Rome conference of the 17 Communist parties of the capitalist countries.

In fact all these theories rest on a deep distrust of the working-class movement of the non-socialist countries and of its advance-guard parties, the Communist parties. The latter are regarded purely and simply as supernumerary forces and not as organisations enjoying full responsibility before the working-class of their own countries and the world working-class. They thus arrive finally at the anti-Marxist conception of 'exported revolution' and it was not by accident that Maurice Thorez had to remind the Chinese comrades that the people do not like 'booted missionaries'.

Third Thesis: In the world Communist movement the minority does not have to take account of the general political line adopted by the whole movement. It has the right to embark on continuous fractional activity with no restrictions whatsoever.

In this connexion the debates assumed a certain bitterness. All the more so since at the Moscow conference the Chinese and Albanian delegations, while opposing the principle of fraternal equality between the parties, clung determinedly to the mistaken concept of the 'leading party', the latter being for the time being the CPSU. It is well said: for the time being. Actually from the moment that one considers that the 'leading party' is mistaken ideologically and politically one is raising the question of its replacement and, consequently, submitting a candidate. In his speech at the Moscow conference our comrade Ernest Burnelle stressed the danger to which this sort of argument exposed the world Communist movement.

We will not linger over the other theses presented by the Chinese and Albanian delegations. For example: Humanism is a bourgeois concept which amounts to presenting the bourgeoisie with something it has not deserved. Or again: To address statesmen of the capitalist countries politely is to 'go on one's knees' to imperialism.

What is apparent is that the Statement of the 81 Communist parties could not, in these conditions, be a completely homogeneous document. It contains original elements of analysis of capital importance. For example: that the third phase of the general crisis of capitalism has come without a world conflict. On the other hand, it is full of what we call 'restrictive clauses'. These are the clauses which allow the Chinese and Albanian parties to make use of the Statement of the 81 parties although they were and they remain opposed to its general orientation. (*Le Drapeau Rouge*, February 22, 1962.)

Enver Hoxha's speech

(The following document consists of notes made on what Hoxha said in direct speech. It is not claimed to be the actual text of his speech, which was made on November 16.)

This is an extremely important conference. Socialism is advancing, imperialism is on the decline, but the nature of imperialism has not changed. Imperialism is preparing for war. The Albanian people is aware of this situation and is working with a gun in one hand and a spade in the other.

Anyone who does not see that imperialism is preparing for war is blind. Anyone who sees it and refuses to recognise it is a traitor.

The socialist camp is encircled and Tito is part of its encirclement.

World war is not fatally inevitable, but we insist that it should be made clear that war will not be wholly rejected until imperialism has disappeared in one or many countries. We must prepare to seize power by violence. It is only in this way that the struggle for peace will be won.

The People's Republics of China and Albania are of course in favour of peaceful coexistence. This presupposes the intensification of the class struggle until we achieve the complete liquidation of imperialism.

Khrushchev has distorted the thesis of Leninism to suit his own purposes; no party has yet seized power without resorting to violence. We shall fight for peace and disarmament on the basis of the Moscow Declaration of 1957 and we shall fight against imperialism, revisionism and dogmatism.

Albania does not wish to separate itself from the socialist camp, but if we think that errors are committed we shall say so. We have joined it not by chance, but thanks to the struggle of the Albanian people, its sacrifices, and the help of socialist countries led by the USSR. We recognise our eternal debt to the USSR.

Some states (Yugoslavia, Greece and Italy) appear to wish that our frontiers should be open to their agents and try to isolate us from the socialist camp by accusing us of being war-mongers. We shall make no territorial concessions.

The unity of the international Communist movement requires the condemnation and rectification of errors committed. At Bucharest we reserved our position, hoping to make it clear at this conference.

On Soviet initiative a conference was hastily started at Bucharest at the time of the Rumanian Party Congress of June 24, 1960. The Chinese Communist Party was accused in front of the other Communist parties on the sole basis of Soviet allegations. We insisted that the Chinese CP should be able to defend itself. Even the parties who were asked to condemn the Chinese CP had no knowledge of the Soviet allegations until a few hours before the debate opened.

We condemned then and we still condemn the Bucharest conference in both its form and its aims. Our Russian comrades have committed an error with regard to the Chinese CP. They tried to drag in other Communist parties to condemn the Chinese CP without communicating the necessary information to them. We are neither neutral nor pro-Chinese. We have pleaded the cause of moderation and level-headedness.

Was it because Khrushchev and the other Soviet leaders lacked confidence in their cause that they had to have recourse to such procedure?

[Hoxha then gave examples of cases where the Russians had used 'pressure and evasion'.]

i. On the Hungarian question decisions were taken without consulting us.

ii. In August 1960 the CPSU sent a letter to the Albanian CP asking it to join a bloc against the Chinese CP. This authorises us to accuse the CPSU of fractionalism. They have asked us to conceal some of their serious errors.

iii. The USSR delivered a surprise attack, made a brutal intervention and put general pressure on some leaders of the Albanian CP to try and set them against the leadership and force them to choose between the 200 million Russians and the 650 million Chinese. Liri Belishova capitulated to the dishonest threats of the USSR.*

iv. The Russian ambassador and the rest of the Russian embassy in Tirana are continuing their attacks against some elements of the leadership of the Albanian Party. These are the corrupt elements that have sown trouble in our Party and gone so far as to precipitate a revolution in the army.

v. Pressure from Moscow continues. Malinovsky† attacked the government and the Party in Albania at a meeting of the chiefs of staff of the Warsaw Pact. Grechko‡ also brought pressure to bear on us by threatening us from the Warsaw Pact.

vi. Khrushchev said to Teng Hsiao-ping: 'We shall treat Albania like Yugoslavia', and he has carried out his threat.

Our only crime is that of being a poor country, but courageous in our views. Albania has suffered earthquakes, floods and a drought of 120 days and has been threatened by famine. Only 15 days' supply of wheat remained in stock. After a delay of 45 days the USSR promised us 10,000 tons of wheat instead of 50,000 tons, or, in other words, 15 days' supply of wheat to be delivered in September and October. These are intolerable pressures. The Soviet rats were able to eat while the Albanian people were dying of hunger. We were asked to produce gold.

On November 6, 1960, Khrushchev said: 'Russia has lost an Albania; the People's Republic of China has gained an Albania'.

If there are people who have behaved like the Yugoslavs, it is you and not we. Albania's membership of or exclusion from the socialist camp does not depend on you but on our people and the Soviet people who sacrificed their blood to liberate us. Our Party believes that friendship should be based on principles.

Yugoslav revisionism should not be blamed on Stalin. The line for which the Cominform and the other parties were responsible was in fact correct. Why then did Khrushchev make his volte-face without informing us? That was a bombshell. In May 1955 we made known our opposition to the unilateral revisionism

---

* See Chronology, September, 8, 1960.
† Marshal Rodion Malinovsky, Soviet Minister of Defence.
‡ Grechko, Soviet Commander of Warsaw Pact forces.

of the Communist parties in their attitude to Yugoslavia. But the Yugoslav comrades were rehabilitated.

The Titoist group in the Albanian Communist Party regarded us as Stalinists in order to liquidate us in the expectation of diversionary attacks by the Yugoslavs.

After the Twentieth Congress of the CPSU, at the time of the Third Congress of the Albanian CP in 1956, false reports were put around about the physical liquidation of Yugoslav agents, including a pregnant woman.* . . .

Tito wished to co-ordinate the counter-revolution in Albania and Hungary, and Khrushchev had more confidence in Tito than in us. How can one explain the immunity enjoyed in Hungary by Titoist bands operating in broad daylight? The reason is that Imre Nagy had the confidence of Khrushchev and Suslov† on the basis of a hypocritical self-criticism. Why so many meetings on Brioni with Tito and not with us? The USSR had no right to take the sole initiative in intervening in Hungary.

Documents are being unearthed to condemn Stalin, but the Russians are going almost as far as decorating Tito and his friends and concealing any documents which compromise him.

The revisionists of Hungary have been unmasked, but not those of Belgrade. No people's democracy except Czechoslovakia has taken a correct attitude to the need for exposing the Titoists.

We do not want a rectification of the Albanian-Yugoslav frontiers, but we demand the protection of the Albanian minority in Yugoslavia, which is one million strong. We have put Sophocles Venizelos in his place.

The cult of personality does not apply only to Stalin. Stalin had world-wide fame and was Lenin's successor.

[Hoxha ended by saying that the Albanian delegation accepted the Statement, except for the passage on 'fractionalism', which he wanted excluded.]

First Speech of Maurice Thorez:

Our attitude was based on the study of texts brought together by the Chinese comrades in their collection 'Long Live Leninism' which was distributed in France and other countries. We had, moreover, the information given to our Central Committee by Comrade Frachon, vice-chairman of the World Federation of Trade Unions and a delegate at the present conference. He had reported to us the activity of a fractional nature which the Chinese embarked on at the time of the meeting of the General Council of the WFTU in Peking. . . .

We have taken note of *the letter sent by the Chinese comrades to the Central Committee of the CPSU, and above all we have here heard the speech of Comrade Teng Hsiao-ping. We are now quite certain that it is not a question of a disagreement limited to two or three points in the Statement proposed to this conference, but of a whole line opposed to that of the international Communist movement.*

We have at the same time confirmation that it is not a question of differences

---

* See Khrushchev, *Chronology:* October, 27, 1961.
† Mikhail Suslov, Member of Presidium and Secretariat of CPSU, responsible for international Communism.

between the Chinese Communist Party and the CPSU but of a profound disagreement between the Chinese comrades and the whole international Communist movement. . . .

We regret that the Chinese comrades considered it their duty to raise the problem of their state relations with the Soviet Union at this conference, the purpose of which is to discuss ideological and political problems of the international Communist movement. This procedure can only lead the discussion astray, and this would prejudice the conference and prevent it from achieving the results we all expect. . . .

The Chinese Comrade has brought up the question of the recent conflict on the Sino-Indian border. I must say frankly that, if we understand and approve the Chinese People's Republic when it rebuffs incursions into its territory by foreign armed forces, we are less able to understand that the question of the frontiers should have been raised at such a moment. We were alarmed at the tense situation that was being generated between the two great states of Asia, both members of the camp of peace, and, like all the workers in France, we welcomed the political wisdom of the Soviet Union on this question. We deplored the fact that Eisenhower had been given the opportunity of having a reception in India which he would not have had in other circumstances. . . .

We must also say that we do not understand the views of the Chinese comrades about the 'paper tiger' which has to be scorned strategically and taken seriously tactically. Such a confused argument cannot enlighten the peoples on the state of the forces of imperialism or on the means of combating them. . . .

The Chinese comrades say that one must not make propaganda about the horrors of atomic war. But atomic war would mean massive extermination. Any attempt to underestimate the effects of a nuclear conflict is difficult to understand . . . How could a better life be born of an atomic hell? How can one present socialism as the 'reward for sacrifices' accepted by the peoples in an atomic war? . . .

The unity of our movement cannot be conceived of apart from the recognition, in deeds as well as in words, of the role of vanguard played by the CPSU. This role of vanguard is not to be explained purely by historical reasons or by the fact that this party led the first victorious socialist revolution and opened the first breach in the imperialist front. This role relates to the present situation, to the fact that the USSR is building a Communist society and is thus placed at the most advanced point of social development. . . .

We reject any point of view which would tend to weaken the unity of the socialist system and the international Communist movement by allowing that they could have several centres. Our Party has always fought against this mistaken point of view. . . .

The Communist Party of the Soviet Union is the most experienced party from every point of view. The Twentieth and Twenty-first Congresses reflected the experience of the whole international Communist movement and they drew general conclusions from it. That is why the lessons of these congresses concern all the parties together. And that should be stressed in the Statement.

We support entirely on this question the amendment put forward by the Polish comrades. And we are surprised that the Chinese comrades no longer accept in 1960 what they admitted three years ago. By opposing this judgment the Chinese comrades demonstrate that it is really the line of principle elaborated at the Twentieth Congress and confirmed by the Declaration of 1957 that they are rejecting, to replace it by their own line.

Recognition of the pre-eminent role of the CPSU seems to us preferable to the formula which says that the CPSU is 'at the head of' the international Communist movement. We approved the attitude taken up on this subject by the Twenty-first Congress of the CPSU. . . . That formula could even be harmful in so far as it offers a pretext for slanderous propaganda by the bourgeoisie against the parties. . . .

Moreover, we see that under cover of such a formula efforts are being made to damage the prestige of the CPSU and the authority of its guidance and of Comrade Khrushchev in particular. One cannot condemn such behaviour too strongly.

The unity we need is voluntary unity, but a real unity, of all the parts of our movement around the CPSU. This unity is not and cannot be formal. It rests on a community of principle which experience is constantly testing and enriching. . . .

This thesis [of the need for applying the principles of Communism correctly to the peculiarities of each country] is deeply correct and had nothing in common with the curious theories defended by the Chinese comrades about the 'Sinification' of Marxism-Leninism or even . . . on the 'adaptation' of Marxism-Leninism to China. What would be left of the universal principles of Marxism-Leninism after its 'Sinification' by some, its 'Francification' by others, or its 'Russification', to repeat the language of the social-democrats against Lenin?

Every Communist party contributes in the conditions of its own country to the enrichment of our theory and not to its 'adaptation', which would mean ultimately its impoverishment, to its narrow limitation to the conditions of one particular country.

Thorez supported the inclusion in the Statement of a paragraph 'calling for the defence of the Marxist-Leninist unity of our movement and the rejection of any fractional activity or group which might sap that unity'.

We approve the amendment put forward on this point by the fraternal parties of Brazil and Cuba.

There would be no longer a single international Communist movement if groups could be formed within it or tendencies could crystallise there.

The view that the movement could accept within itself the presence of a permanent, organised minority, with this minority enjoying the right to carry on activity contrary to the line laid down in documents adopted by the majority, – this idea would involve the unity of the movement.

Some people say that the principles of democratic centralism can no longer be applied on a world scale because there no longer exists a Communist international. . . . The Chinese comrades are apparently no longer in agreement with these elementary ideas. That is why they oppose the condemnation of fractional work. They confuse the right to have their own opinion on problems being discussed with the 'right' to spread their mistaken ideas when the majority of the parties has rejected them.

From the 'Declaration of the French Communist Party':

Our delegation condemns categorically the speech made at the conference by Comrade Enver Hoxha. Neither in the questions dealt with nor in its tone did it serve the ends of our conference.

The members of our delegation listened to him with a feeling of shame. Though they are militant Communists they had never heard language like it either in the meetings of their party nor in meetings of the international Communist movement. . . . Comrade Hoxha devoted the main part of his speech to questions relating to relations between states, which have no place at all here and to a crude attack on the Soviet Union, its Communist Party and most particularly Comrade N. S. Khrushchev. . . .

The delegation from the Albanian Party today opposes all these correct views. Even more: while assuring us that his differences with the international Communist movement date from the Bucharest conference in June 1960, Comrade Enver Hoxha revealed that he was in fact opposed to the essential conclusions of the Twentieth Congress of the CPSU and to the Soviet government from 1953. . . .

Thorez' last appeal:

After having heard the representative of the Chinese CP, Comrade Teng Hsiao-ping, the delegation of the French CP would like particularly to appeal to the Chinese comrades.

In his speech Comrade Teng Hsiao-ping has maintained, on several important problems presented to the conference, ideological and political attitudes which practically all the parties represented here consider mistaken. He has rejected in an absolute and haughty manner all criticisms directed at the Chinese CP. . . .

An abnormal situation, full of dangers, has thus been created; if this situation were to be continued it might result in considerable damage for the world revolutionary movement. Imperialism, though it is weakened, would undoubtedly try to take advantage of it.

Think again, comrades of the Chinese CP. It is not possible that you should take no account at all of the opinion of the overwhelming majority of the parties represented at the conference. . . .

Extracts from first speech by Luigi Longo, delegate from Italian Communist Party:

These problems [of the last three years] are of great significance, as has been rightly stressed in his introductory report by Comrade Suslov and as Comrade Khrushchev has demonstrated in a masterly fashion in his speech, with which we find ourselves in complete agreement. It is by virtue of this appreciation that the Italian delegation wholly approves the statement contained in the new declaration that 'the whole international working-class movement and all the socialist countries have derived powerful support from the decisions of the Twentieth and Twenty-first Congresses of the CPSU, which are a model of the positive development of revolutionary theory'. *The Chinese comrades propose to suppress this paragraph.* . . .

We are very surprised at the statement by the Chinese comrades that the Central Committee of the CPSU has, on a whole number of major questions of principle, strayed 'in the most obvious way from the true path of Marxism-Leninism and the Moscow Declaration'. We think that this charge is unjust and that it is even slanderous, because it is absolutely devoid of foundation and exceeds all bounds of permissible criticism. . . .

Equally inadmissible is the attempt of the Albanian delegate to question the correctness of the condemnation of the cult of the personality and the mistakes of Stalin, as well as the correctness of the effort made in 1955 to bring Yugoslavia back to more correct political positions and in any case to improve state relations between Yugoslavia and the other socialist countries. He wants also to question the correctness of the analysis of the political causes of the Hungarian counter-revolution and the events in Poland. . . .

For the same reason the Italian delegation considers it *inopportune to accept the proposal made by several delegations to set up at the end of our conference a secretariat or some permanent organisation of that kind.* In our opinion such a body would not be of any practical assistance to the Communist parties. To exchange our experiences and co-ordinate our activities it is necessary and sufficient to exchange information and delegations, to summon special meetings between representatives of parties interested in a particular political activity, or to summon a general conference.

Extracts from letter sent by Italian delegation to Khrushchev at the end of the Conference.

We consider that the draft Statement presented to the conference, though excessively verbose, conveys the substance of the valuable theses. But in our opinion the present text represents, on certain points, a step backwards compared with the precision and clarity of the Moscow Declaration of 1957 and compared also with the draft which you submitted to the meeting held in September. This obviously is a result of the difficulties encountered in trying to produce a version acceptable to everyone. . . .

We attach particular importance to that passage of the statement dealing with Yugoslav revisionism. On this point we have already submitted an amendment which we still press for. It expresses rightly a severe condemnation of the ideological and political positions of the Yugolsav leaders and of their practical activity. Our amendment thus does not depart from the basis of the ideas already expressed in the draft statement. But it is written in a less bitter and aggressive tone, so that it should not provoke an irremediable rupture with Yugoslav public opinion. We know from experience that this opinion is very sensitive and that the present leaders of Yugoslavia will not fail to make use of everything that can be presented as an offence to the national feelings of the Yugoslav people. . . . Our amendment rejects completely the view, in our view mistaken, that one of the essential tasks of the Communist parties is to isolate Yugoslavia from the working-class movement.

December 2

The communiqué on the conference said:

In November 1960 there took place in Moscow a Conference of representatives of Communist and Workers' parties which attended the Forty-third anniversary of the Great October Socialist Revolution. [There follows the list of 81 parties.] Participants in the Conference exchanged experiences and acquainted themselves with each other's views and positions, discussed current problems of present-day international developments and of the Communist movement in the interests of joint struggle for common aims – peace, democracy, national independence and socialism – and adopted unanimously a Statement of the Communist and Workers' parties and an Appeal to the peoples of the whole world.

The discussion of all questions was conducted in an atmosphere of fraternal friendship on the basis of the unshakable principles of Marxism-Leninism and proletarian internationalism.

December 6

'Statement' of the Moscow Conference published. Extracts:

Representatives of the Communist and Workers' parties have discussed at this meeting urgent problems of the present international situation and of the further struggle for peace, national independence, democracy and socialism.

The meeting has shown unity of views among the participants on the issues discussed. The Communist and Workers' parties have unanimously reaffirmed their allegiance to the Declaration and Peace Manifesto adopted in 1957. These programme documents of creative Marxism-Leninism determined the fundamental positions of the international Communist movement on the more important issues of our time and contributed in great measure toward uniting the efforts of the Communist and Workers' parties in the struggle to achieve common goals. They remain the banner and guide to action for the whole of the international Communist movement.

The course of events in the past three years has demonstrated the correctness of the analysis of the international situation and the outlook for world development as given in the Declaration and Peace Manifesto, and the great scientific force and effective role of creative Marxism-Leninism.

The chief result of these years is the rapid growth of the might and international influence of the world socialist system, the vigorous process of disintegration of the colonial system under the impact of the national-liberation movement, the intensification of class struggles in the capitalist world, and the continued decline and decay of the world capitalist system. The superiority of the forces of socialism over those of war is becoming ever more marked in the world arena. . . .

I

Our time, whose main content is the transition from capitalism to socialism initiated by the Great October Socialist Revolution, is a time of struggle between the two opposing social systems, a time of socialist revolutions and national-liberation revolutions, a time of the breakdown of imperialism, of the abolition of the colonial system, a time of transition of more peoples to the socialist path, of the triumph of socialism and Communism on a world-wide scale.

It is the principal characteristic of our time that the world socialist system is becoming the decisive factor in the development of society. . . .

Today it is the world socialist system and the forces fighting against imperialism, for a socialist transformation of society, that determine the main content, main trend and main features of the historical development of society. Whatever efforts imperialism makes, it cannot stop the advance of history. A reliable basis has been provided for further decisive victories for socialism. The complete triumph of socialism is inevitable. . . .

US imperialism has become the biggest international exploiter. . . .

International developments in recent years have furnished many new proofs of the fact that US imperialism is the chief bulwark of world reaction and an international gendarme, that it has become an enemy of the peoples of the whole world. . . .

A new stage has begun in the development of the general crisis of capitalism. . . .

All the revolutionary forces are rallying against imperialist oppression and exploitation. The peoples who are building socialism and Communism, the revolutionary movement of the working class in the capitalist countries, the national-liberation struggle of the oppressed peoples and the general democratic movement – these great forces of our time are merging into one powerful current that undermines and destroys the world imperialist system. The central factors of our day are the international working class and its chief creation, the world socialist system. They are an earnest of victory in the struggle for peace, democracy, national liberation, socialism and human progress.

II

A new stage has begun in the development of the world socialist system. The Soviet Union is successfully carrying on the full-scale construction of a Communist society. Other countries of the socialist camp are successfully laying the foundations of socialism, and some of them have already entered the period of construction of a developed socialist society. . . .

Today the restoration of capitalism has been made socially and economically impossible not only in the Soviet Union, but in the other socialist countries as well. The combined forces of the socialist camp reliably safeguard every socialist country against encroachments by imperialist reaction. Thus the rallying of the socialist states in one camp and the growing unity and steadily increasing strength of this camp ensure complete victory for socialism within the entire system. . . .

The socialist camp is a social, economic and political community of free and sovereign peoples united by the close bonds of international socialist solidarity; by common interests and objectives, and following the path of socialism and Communism. It is an inviolable law of the mutual relations between socialist countries strictly to adhere to the principles of Marxism-Leninism and socialist internationalism. Every country in the socialist camp is ensured genuinely equal rights and independence. Guided by the principles of complete equality, mutual advantage and comradely mutual assistance, the socialist states improve their all-round economic, political and cultural co-operation, which meets both the interests of each socialist country and those of the socialist camp as a whole.

One of the greatest achievements of the world socialist system is the practical confirmation of the Marxist-Leninist thesis that national antagonisms diminish with the decline of class antagonisms. In contrast to the laws of the capitalist system, which is characterised by antagonistic contradictions between classes, nations and states leading to armed conflicts, there are no objective causes in the nature of the socialist system for contradictions and conflicts between the peoples and states belonging to it. Its development leads to greater unity among the states and nations and to the consolidation of all the forms of co-operation between them. Under socialism, the development of national economy, culture and statehood goes hand in hand with the strengthening and development of the entire world socialist system, and with an ever greater consolidation of the unity of nations. The interests of the socialist system as a whole and national interests are harmoniously combined. It is on this basis that the moral and political unity of all the peoples of the great socialist community has arisen and has been growing. Fraternal friendship and mutual assistance of peoples, born of the socialist system, have superseded the political isolation and national egoism typical of capitalism....

Manifestations of nationalism and national narrow-mindedness do not disappear automatically with the establishment of the socialist system. If fraternal relations and friendship between the socialist countries are to be strengthened, it is necessary that the Communist and Workers' parties pursue a Marxist-Leninist internationalist policy, that all working people be educated in a spirit of internationalism and patriotism, and that a resolute struggle be waged to eliminate the survivals of bourgeois nationalism and chauvinism.

The Communist and Workers' parties tirelessly educate the working people in the spirit of socialist internationalism and intolerance of all manifestations of nationalism and chauvinism. Solid unity of the Communist and Workers' parties and of the peoples of the socialist countries, and their loyalty to the Marxist-Leninist doctrine are the main source of the strength and invincibility of each socialist country and the socialist camp as a whole. . . .

The time has come when the socialist states have, by forming a world system, become an international force exerting a powerful influence on world development. There are now real opportunities of solving cardinal problems of modern times in a new way, in the interests of peace, democracy and socialism.

III

The problem of war and peace is the most burning problem of our time.

War is a constant companion of capitalism. The system of exploitation of man by man and the system of extermination of man by man are two aspects of the capitalist system. Imperialism has already inflicted two devastating world wars on mankind and now threatens to plunge it into an even more terrible catastrophe. Monstrous means of mass annihilation and destruction have been developed which, if used in a new war, can cause unheard-of destruction to entire countries and reduce key centres of world industry and culture to ruins. Such a war would bring death and suffering to hundreds of millions of people, among them people in countries not involved in it. Imperialism spells grave danger to the whole of mankind.

The peoples must now be more vigilant than ever. As long as imperialism exists there will be soil for wars of aggression.

The peoples of all countries know that the danger of a new world war still persists. US imperialism is the main force of aggression and war. Its policy embodies the ideology of militant reaction. The US imperialists, together with the imperialists of Britain, France and West Germany, have drawn countries into NATO, CENTO, SEATO and other military blocs under the guise of combating the 'Communist menace'; it has enmeshed the so-called 'free world', that is, capitalist countries which depend on them, in a network of military bases spearheaded first and foremost against the socialist countries. The existence of these blocs and bases endangers universal peace and security and not only encroaches upon the sovereignty but also imperils the very life of those countries which put their territory at the disposal of the US militarists. . . .

The aggressive nature of imperialism has not changed. But real forces have appeared that are capable of foiling its plans of aggression. War is not fatally inevitable. Had the imperialists been able to do what they wanted, they would already have plunged mankind into the abyss of the calamities and horrors of a new world war. But the time is past when the imperialists could decide at will whether there should or should not be war. More than once in the past years the imperialists have brought mankind to the brink of world catastrophe by starting local wars. The resolute stand of the Soviet Union, of the other socialist states and of all the peaceful forces put an end to the Anglo-Franco-Israeli intervention in Egypt, and averted a military invasion of Syria, Iraq, and some other countries by the imperialists. The heroic people of Algeria continue their valiant battle for independence and freedom. The peoples of the Congo and Laos are resisting the criminal acts of the imperialists with increasing firmness. Experience shows that it is possible to combat effectively the local wars started by the imperialists, and to stamp out successfully the hotbeds of such wars.

The time has come when the attempts of the imperialist aggressors to start a world war can be curbed. World war can be prevented by the joint efforts of the world socialist camp, the international working class, the national-liberation movement, all the countries opposing war and all peace-loving forces.

The development of international relations in our day is determined by the struggle of the two social systems – the struggle of the forces of socialism, peace and democracy against the forces of imperialism, reaction and aggression – a struggle in which the superiority of the forces of socialism, peace and democracy is becoming increasingly obvious. . . .

The democratic and peace forces today have no task more pressing than that of safeguarding humanity against a global thermo-nuclear disaster. The unprecedented destructive power of modern means of warfare demands that the main actions of the anti-war and peace-loving forces be directed towards preventing war. The struggle against war cannot be put off until war breaks out, for then it may prove too late for many areas of the globe and for their population to combat it. *The struggle against the threat of a new world war must be waged now and not when atom and hydrogen bombs begin to fall, and it must gain in strength from day to day. The important thing is to curb the aggressors in good time, to prevent war, and not to let it break out.* . . .

No political, religious or other differences should be an obstacle to all the forces of the working class uniting against the war danger. The hour has struck to counter the forces of war by the mighty will and joint action of all the contingents and organisations of the world proletariat, to unite its forces to avert world war and safeguard peace.

The Communist parties regard the fight for peace as their prime task. They call on the working class, trade unions, co-operatives, women's and youth leagues and organisations, on all working people, irrespective of their political and religious convictions, firmly to repulse by mass struggles all acts of aggression on the part of the imperialists.

But should the imperialist maniacs start war, the peoples will sweep capitalism out of existence and bury it.

The foreign policy of the socialist countries rests on the firm foundations of the Leninist principle of peaceful coexistence and economic competition between the socialist and capitalist countries. In conditions of peace, the socialist system increasingly reveals its advantages over the capitalist system in all fields of economy, culture, science and technology. The near future will bring the forces of peace and socialism new successes. The USSR will become the leading industrial power of the world. China will become a mighty industrial state. The socialist system will be turning out more than half the world industrial product. The peace zone will expand. The working-class movement in the capitalist countries and the national-liberation movement in the colonies and dependencies will achieve new victories. The disintegration of the colonial system will become completed. The superiority of the forces of socialism and peace will be absolute. *In these conditions a real possibility will have arisen to exclude world war from the life of society even before socialism achieves complete victory on earth, with capitalism still existing in a part of the world.* The victory of socialism all over the world will completely remove the social and national causes of wars.

The Communists of all the world uphold peaceful coexistence unanimously and consistently, and battle resolutely for the prevention of war. The Communists must work untiringly among the masses to prevent under-estimation of the possibility of averting a world war, underestimation of the possibility of peaceful coexistence and, at the same time, underestimation of the danger of war.

In a world divided into two systems, the only correct and reasonable principle of international relations is the principle of peaceful coexistence of states with different social systems advanced by Lenin and further elaborated in the Moscow Declaration and the Peace Manifesto of 1957, in the decisions of the Twentieth and Twenty-first Congresses of the CPSU, and in the documents of other Communist and Workers' parties.

The Five Principles jointly advanced by the Chinese People's Republic and the Republic of India, and the propositions adopted at the Bandung Conference accord with the interests of peace and the peace-loving peoples.

Peaceful coexistence of countries with different systems or destructive war – this is the alternative today. There is no other choice. Communists emphatically reject the US doctrine of 'cold war' and 'brinkmanship', for it is a policy leading to thermo-nuclear catastrophe. By upholding the principle of peaceful coexistence, Communists fight for the complete cessation of the cold war, disbandment of

military blocs, and dismantling of military bases, for general and complete disarmament under international control, the settlement of international disputes
through negotiation, respect for the equality of states and their territorial integrity,
independence and sovereignty, non-interference in each other's internal affairs,
extensive development of trade, cultural and scientific ties between nations. . . .

*The meeting considers that the implementation of the programme for general and
complete disarmament put forward by the Soviet Union would be of historic
importance for the destinies of mankind.* To realise this programme means to
eliminate the very possibility of waging wars between countries. It is not easy to
realise owing to the stubborn resistance of the imperialists. Hence it is essential
to wage an active and determined struggle against the aggressive imperialist forces
with the aim of carrying this programme into practice. It is necessary to wage this
struggle on an increasing scale and to strive perseveringly to achieve tangible
results – the banning of the testing and manufacture of nuclear weapons, the
abolition of military blocs and war bases on foreign soil and a substantial
reduction of armed forces and armaments, all of which should pave the way to
general disarmament. Through an active, determined struggle by the socialist and
other peace-loving countries, by the international working class and the broad
masses in all countries, it is possible to isolate the aggressive circles, foil the arms
race and war preparations, and force the imperialists into an agreement on general
disarmament. . . .

*The Communists regard it as their historical mission not only to abolish exploita-
tion and poverty on a world scale and rule out for all time the possiblity of any kind
of war in the life of human society, but also to deliver mankind from the nightmare
of a new world war already in our time. The Communist parties will devote all their
strength and energy to this great historical mission.*

IV

National-liberation revolutions have triumphed in vast areas of the world.
About forty new sovereign states have arisen in Asia and Africa in the fifteen
post-war years. The victory of the Cuban revolution has powerfully stimulated
the struggle of the Latin-American peoples for complete national independence.
A new historical period has set in in the life of mankind: the peoples of Asia,
Africa and Latin America that have won their freedom have begun to take an
active part in world politics.

*The complete collapse of colonialism is imminent. The breakdown of the system
of colonial slavery under the impact of the national-liberation movement is a
development ranking second in historic importance only to the formation of the
world socialist system.*

The Great October Socialist Revolution aroused the East and drew the colonial
peoples into the common current of the world-wide revolutionary movement.
This development was greatly facilitated by the Soviet Union's victory in the
Second World War, the establishment of people's democracy in a number of
European and Asian countries, the triumph of the socialist revolution in China,
and the formation of the world socialist system. The forces of world socialism
contributed decisively to the struggle of the colonial and dependent peoples for
liberation from imperialist oppression. The socialist system has become a reliable

shield for the independent national development of the peoples who have won freedom. The national-liberation movement receives powerful support from the international working-class movement.

The face of Asia has changed radically. The colonial order is collapsing in Africa. A front of active struggle against imperialism has opened in Latin America. Hundreds of millions of people in Asia, Africa and other parts of the world have won their independence in hard-fought battles with imperialism. Communists have always recognised the progressive, revolutionary significance of national-liberation wars; they are the most active champions of national independence. The existence of the world socialist system and the weakening of the positions of imperialism have provided the oppressed peoples with new opportunities of winning independence.

The peoples of the colonial countries win their independence both through armed struggle and by non-military methods, depending on the specific conditions in the country concerned. They secure durable victory through a powerful national-liberation movement. The colonial powers never bestow freedom on the colonial peoples and never leave of their own free will the countries they are exploiting.

The United States is the mainstay of colonialism today. . . .

The Communist parties are working actively for a consistent completion of the anti-imperialist, anti-feudal, democratic revolution, for the establishment of national democracies, for a radical improvement in the living standard of the people. They support those actions of national governments leading to the consolidation of the gains achieved and undermining the imperialists' positions. At the same time they firmly oppose anti-democratic, anti-popular acts and those measures of the ruling circles which endanger national independence. Communists expose attempts by the reactionary section of the bourgeoisie to represent its selfish, narrow class interests as those of the entire nation. They expose the demagogic use by bourgeois politicians of socialist slogans for the same purpose. They work for a genuine democratisation of social life and rally all the progressive forces to combat despotic régimes or to curb tendencies towards setting up such régimes. . . .

All the socialist countries and the international working-class and Communist movement recognise their duty to render the fullest moral and material assistance to the peoples fighting to free themselves from imperialist and colonial tyranny.

V

The new balance of world forces offers the Communist and Workers' parties new opportunities of carrying out the historic tasks they face in the struggle for peace, national independence, democracy and socialism. . . .

The Communist parties decide on the prospects and tasks of revolution according to the concrete historical and social conditions in their respective countries and with due regard to the international situation.

The working class, peasantry, intellectuals and the petty and middle urban bourgeoisie are vitally interested in the abolition of monopoly domination. Hence there are favourable conditions for rallying these forces.

Communists hold that this unity can be achieved on the basis of the struggle for peace, national independence, the protection and extension of democracy, nationalisation of the key branches of economy and democratisation of their management, the use of the entire economy for peaceful purposes in order to satisfy the needs of the population, implementation of radical agrarian reforms, improvement of the living conditions of the working people, protection of the interests of the peasantry and the small and middle urban bourgeoisie against the tyranny of the monopolies. . . .

Communists regard the struggle for democracy as part of the struggle for socialism. In this struggle they continuously strengthen their bonds with the working people, increase their political consciousness, help them understand the task of the socialist revolution and realise the necessity of accomplishing it. This sets the Marxist-Leninist parties completely apart from the reformists, who consider reforms within the framework of the capitalist system as the ultimate goal and deny the necessity of socialist revolution. Marxist-Leninists are firmly convinced that the peoples in the capitalist countries will in the course of their daily struggle ultimately come to understand that socialism alone is a real way out for them. . . .

The urgent interests of the working-class movement demand that the Communist and Social-Democratic parties take joint action on a national and international scale to bring about the immediate prohibition of the manufacture, testing and use of nuclear weapons, the establishment of atom-free zones, general and complete disarmament under international control, the abolition of military bases on foreign soil and the withdrawal of foreign troops, to assist the national-liberation movement of the peoples of colonial and dependent countries, to safeguard national sovereignty, promote democracy and resist the fascist menace, improve the living standards of the working people, secure a shorter working week without wage cuts, etc. Millions of Social-Democrats and some Social-Democratic parties have already in some form or another come out in favour of solving these problems. It is safe to say that *on overcoming the split in its ranks, on achieving unity of action of all its contingents, the working class of many capitalist countries could deliver a heavy blow to the policy of the ruling circles in the capitalist countries. It could make them stop preparing a new war, repel the offensive of monopoly capital, and have its daily vital and democratic demands met.* . . .

The Communist parties reaffirm the propositions put forward by the Declaration of 1957 on the forms of transition of different countries from capitalism to socialism.

The Declaration points out that the working class and its vanguard – the Marxist-Leninist Party – seek to achieve the socialist revolution by peaceful means. This would accord with the interests of the working class and the people as a whole, with the national interests of the country.

Today in a number of capitalist countries the working class, headed by its vanguard, has the opportunity, given a united working-class and popular front or other workable forms of agreement and political co-operation between the different parties and public organisations, to unite a majority of the people, win state power without civil war and ensure the transfer of the basic means of production to the hands of the people. Relying on the majority of the people and resolutely rebuffing the opportunist elements incapable of relinquishing the policy of compromise with the capitalists and landlords, the working class can defeat the reactionary, anti-popular forces, secure a firm majority in parliament, transform parliament from an instrument serving the class interests of the bourgeoisie into an instrument serving the working people, launch an extra-parliamentary mass struggle, smash the resistance of the reactionary forces and create the necessary conditions for peaceful realisation of the socialist revolution. All this will be possible only by broad and ceaseless development of the class struggle of the workers, peasant masses and the urban middle strata against big monopoly capital, against reaction, for profound social reforms, for peace and socialism.

In the event of the exploiting classes resorting to violence against the people, the possibility of non-peaceful transition to socialism should be borne in mind. Leninism teaches, and experience confirms, that the ruling classes never relinquish power voluntarily. In this case the degree of bitterness and the forms of the class struggle will depend not so much on the proletariat as on the resistance put up by the reactionary circles to the will of the overwhelming majority of the people, on these circles using force at one or other stage of the struggle for socialism.

The actual possibility of the one or the other way of transition to socialism in each individual country depends on the concrete historical conditions. . . .

VI

The world Communist movement has become the most influential political force of our time, a most important factor in social progress. As it fights bitterly against imperialist reaction, for the interests of the working-class and all working people, for peace, national independence, democracy and socialism, the Communist movement is making steady headway, is beoming consolidated and tempered.

There are now Communist parties active in 87 countries of the world. Their total membership exceeds 36,000,000. . . .

The growth of the Communist parties and their organisational consolidation, the victories of the Communist parties in a number of countries in the struggle against deviations, elimination of harmful consequences of the personality cult, and the greater influence of the world Communist movement open new prospects for the successful accomplishment of the tasks facing the Communist parties. . . .

The Communist parties have ideologically defeated the revisionists in their ranks who sought to divert them from the Marxist-Leninist path. Each Communist party and the international Communist movement as a whole have become still stronger, ideologically and organisationally, in the struggle against revisionism, Right-wing opportunism.

The Communist parties have unanimously condemned the Yugoslav variety of international opportunism, a variety of modern revisionist 'theories' in concentrated form. After betraying Marxism-Leninism, which they termed obsolete, the leaders of the League of Communists of Yugoslavia opposed their anti-Leninist revisionist programme to the Declaration of 1957; they set the LCY against the international Communist movement as a whole, severed their country from the socialist camp, made it dependent on so-called 'aid' from US and other imperialists, and thereby exposed the Yugoslav people to the danger of losing the revolutionary gains achieved through a heroic struggle. The Yugoslav revisionists carry on subversive work against the socialist camp and the world Communist movement. Under the pretext of being outside blocs, they engage in activities which prejudice the unity of all the peace-loving forces and countries. Further exposure of the leaders of Yugoslav revisionists and active struggle to safeguard the Communist movement and the working-class movement from the anti-Leninist ideas of the Yugoslav revisionists, remain an essential task of the Marxist-Leninist parties.

The practical struggles of the working class and the entire course of social development have furnished a brilliant new proof of the great all-conquering power and vitality of Marxism-Leninism, and have thoroughly refuted all modern revisionist 'theories'.

The further development of the Communist and working-class movement calls, as stated in the Moscow Declaration of 1957, for continuing a determined struggle on two fronts – against revisionism, which remains the main danger, and against dogmatism and sectarianism.

Revisionism, Right-wing opportunism, which mirrors bourgeois ideology in theory and practice, distorts Marxism-Leninism, robs it of its revolutionary spirit, and thereby paralyses the revolutionary will of the working class. It disarms and demobilises the workers and all working people in their struggle, against oppression by imperialists and exploiters, for peace, democracy and national-liberation, for the triumph of socialism.

Dogmatism and sectarianism in theory and practice can also become the main danger at some stage of development of individual parties, unless combated unrelentingly. They rob revolutionary parties of the ability to develop Marxism-Leninism through scientific analysis and apply it creatively according to the specific conditions. They isolate Communists from the broad masses of the working people, doom them to passive expectation of Leftist, adventurist actions in the revolutionary struggle. They prevent the Communist parties from making a timely and correct estimate of the changing situation and of new experience and using all opportunities to bring about the victory of the working class and all democratic forces in the struggle against imperialism, reaction and the war danger. Thereby they prevent the peoples from achieving victory in their just struggle.

At a time when imperialist reaction is joining forces to fight Communism it is particularly necessary to consolidate the world Communist movement. Unity and solidarity redouble the strength of our movement and provide a reliable guarantee that the great cause of Communism will make victorious progress and all enemy attacks will be effectively repelled.

Communists throughout the world are united by the great doctrine of Marxism-Leninism and by the joint struggle for its realisation. The interests of the Communist movement require solidarity by every Communist party in the observance of the estimates and conclusions on the common tasks in the struggle against imperialism, for peace, democracy and socialism, jointly reached by the fraternal parties at their meetings.

The interests of the struggle for the working-class cause demand of each Communist party and of the great army of Communists of all countries ever closer unity of will and action. It is the supreme internationalist duty of every Marxist-

Leninist party to work continuously for greater unity in the world Communist movement.

A resolute defence of the unity of the world Communist movement on the principles of Marxism-Leninism and proletarian internationalism, and the prevention of any actions which may undermine that unity, are a necessary condition for victory in the struggle for national independence, democracy and peace, for the successful accomplishment of the tasks of the socialist revolution and of the building of socialism and Communism. Violation of these principles would impair the forces of Communism.

All the Marxist-Leninist parties are independent and have equal rights; they shape their policies according to the specific conditions in their respective countries and in keeping with Marxist-Leninist principles, and support each other. The success of the working-class cause in any country is unthinkable without the internationalist solidarity of all Marxist-Leninist parties. Every party is responsible to the working class, to the working people of its country, to the international working-class and Communist movement as a whole.

The Communist and Workers' parties hold meetings whenever necessary to discuss urgent problems, to share experiences, acquaint themselves with each other's views and positions, work out common views through consultations and co-ordinate joint actions in the struggle for common goals.

Whenever a party wants to clear up questions relating to the activities of another fraternal party, its leadership approaches the leadership of the party concerned; if necessary, they hold meetings and consultations.

The experience and results of the meetings of representatives of the Communist parties held in recent years, particularly the results of the two major meetings – that of November 1957 and this meeting – show that in present-day conditions such meetings are an effective form of exchanging views and experience, enriching Marxist-Leninist theory by collective effort and elaborating a common attitude in the struggle for common objectives.

The Communist and Workers' parties unanimously declare that *the Communist Party of the Soviet Union has been, and remains, the universally recognised vanguard of the world Communist movement, being the most experienced and steeled contingent of the international Communist movement.* The experience which the CPSU has gained in the struggle for the victory of the working class, in socialist construction and in the full-scale construction of Communism, is of fundamental significance for the whole of the world Communist movement. The example of the CPSU and its fraternal solidarity inspire all the Communist parties in their struggle for peace and socialism, and represent the revolutionary principles of proletarian internationalism applied in practice. *The historic decisions of the Twentieth Congress of the CPSU are not only of great importance to the CPSU and Communist construction in the USSR, but have initiated a new stage in the world Communist movement, and have promoted its development on the basis of Marxism-Leninism.*

All Communist and Workers' parties contribute to the development of the great theory of Marxism-Leninism. Mutual assistance and support in relations between all the fraternal Marxist-Leninist parties embody the revolutionary principles of proletarian internationalism applied in practice. . . .

The meeting sees the further consolidation of the Communist parties on the basis of Marxism-Leninism, of proletarian internationalism, as a primary condition for the unification of all working-class, democratic and progressive forces, as a guarantee of new victories in the great struggle waged by the world Communist and working-class movement for a happy future for the whole of mankind, for the triumph of the cause of peace and socialism.

1961

January 6

Khrushchev delivered a speech on the Moscow Conference to a general meeting of party organisations in the Higher Party School, the Academy of Social Science and the Institute of Marxism-Leninism in Moscow. Extracts:

Comrades, the Conference of Representatives of 81 Marxist-Leninist parties held in Moscow in November 1960 will go into the history of the world Communist and Workers' movement as one of its vivid pages. This Conference profoundly analysed the present international situation, and worked out common positions for our movement pertaining to the most important questions. . . .

The Statement which was unanimously adopted at the Conference is a militant Marxist-Leninist document of tremendous international importance. It confirms the fidelity of the Communist parties to the Declaration of 1957. At the same time, it makes a profound analysis of new phenomena in the world arena and contains important theoretical and political deductions for the activities of all the Marxist-Leninist parties. The Statement will serve as a true compass in the further struggle for the great aims that confront the Communists, the working-class and progressive people of all countries. . . .

Comrades, questions of war and peace were at the centre of the attention of the Conference. The participants in the Conference were fully aware that *the problem of preventing a world thermo-nuclear war is the most burning and vital problem for mankind.*

Wars have followed the division of society into classes, which means that the outbreak of all wars will be eliminated finally only when the division of the society into hostile and antagonistic classes is abolished. The victory of the working class throughout the world and the victory of socialism will remove all social and national causes of wars and give mankind the opportunity of ridding itself forever of that dreadful plight. *In modern conditions a distinction should be made between the following categories of war: world wars, local wars, liberation wars and popular risings.* This is necessary in order to work out the correct tactics with regard to these wars. Let us begin with the question of *world wars.*

Communists are the most determined opponents of world wars, just as they are general opponents of wars between states. These wars are needed only by imperialists for the purpose of seizing the territories of others, and of enslaving and plundering other peoples. Before the formation of the world socialist camp the working class had no opportunity to make a determining impact on the solution of the question of whether there should or should not be world wars. . . .

Of course, at present, too, there exist among the imperialist countries acute contradictions and antagonisms, as well as the desire to profit at the expense of others who are weaker. But the imperialists now have to keep an eye on the Soviet Union and the whole socialist camp and are afraid of starting wars among themselves.

In present conditions, the most probable wars are the *wars between capitalist and imperialist countries*. But this, too, should not be ruled out; wars are chiefly prepared by imperialists against socialist countries, and in the first place against the Soviet Union as the most powerful among the socialist states. . . . But the unleashing of wars has become a much more complicated business for the imperialists than it was before the emergence of the mighty socialist camp. Imperialists can unleash a war. But they have to think hard about the consequences. . . .

In the conditions where a mighty socialist camp exists, possessing powerful armed forces, the people, by mobilising all their forces for active struggle against the warmongering imperialists, can certainly prevent war and thus ensure peaceful coexistence.

A word or two about *local wars*. A lot is being said nowadays in the imperialist camp about local wars, and they are even making small-calibre atomic weapons for use in such wars; a special 'theory of local wars' has been concocted. Is this fortuitous? Of course not. Certain imperialist circles, fearing that world war might end in the complete collapse of capitalism, are putting their money on the unleashing of local wars. There have been local wars and they may reoccur in the future, but the opportunities for the imperialists to unleash these wars are also becoming fewer. *A small imperialist war, independent of which of the imperialists begins it, may grow into a world thermo-nuclear and rocket war. We must therefore combat both world wars and local wars.*

I have already said that local wars are not excluded in the future. Therefore, our task is to be always on our guard, mobilising both the forces of the socialist camp and the peoples of the world, all the peace-loving forces for the prevention of aggressive wars. . . .

Now a word about *national liberation wars*. The armed struggle of the Vietnamese people or the war of the Algerian people, which is already in its seventh year, serve as the latest examples of such wars. These wars began as an uprising of the colonial peoples against their oppressors and changed into guerilla warfare. Liberation wars still continue to exist as long as imperialism and colonialism exist. These are revolutionary wars. *Such wars are not only admissible but inevitable*, since the colonialists do not grant independence to the peoples voluntarily. Therefore, the peoples can attain their freedom and independence only by means of a struggle, including armed struggle.

How was it that the US imperialists, while wanting to help the French colonialists in every way, nevertheless decided against a direct intervention in the war in Vietnam? They did not intervene because they knew that if they helped France with armed forces Vietnam would get appropriate aid from China, the Soviet Union and other socialist countries, which could lead to a world war. The outcome of the war is known. North Vietnam was victorious. At present a similar war is taking place in Algeria. What kind of war is it? It is a rising of the Arab people in Algeria against the French colonisers. It is being conducted in the form of a partisan war. The imperialists in the USA and Britain assist their French allies with arms. Moreover, they have allowed France, a member of NATO, to transfer her troops from Europe for the struggle against the Algerian people. The Algerian people, too, is receiving assistance from neighbouring and other countries sympathetic towards its peace-loving aspirations. *But it is a liberation war of a people for its independence, it is a holy war. We recognise such wars, we help and will help the peoples striving for their independence. . . .*

Can such wars flare up in the future? They can. Can there be such risings? There can. But these are precisely wars which are national risings. Can there be in other countries such conditions created that a people will lose its patience and rise in arms? There can. What is the attitude of the Marxists to such risings? The most positive one. *These risings must not be identified with wars between states, with local wars,* because the people in these risings are fighting for the implementation of their right to self-determination, for independent social and national development. These are risings against rotten reactionary régimes, against the colonisers. *Communists fully support such just wars* and march in the front ranks of the people waging liberation struggles.

Comrades! Mankind has come close to the historic point where it is able to solve all problems which were beyond the strength of former generations. This concerns also the most vital issue – the prevention of a world war. The working class, which is already leading a large part of the world – and the time will come when it will lead the whole world – cannot allow the forces doomed to ruin to drag hundreds of millions of people with them to the grave. And a world war in the present conditions would be a rocket and nuclear war, the most destructive war in history.

We know that in the event of war it is the working people and their vanguard – the working class – that will suffer most of all. . . .

Forty-one years ago, here in Moscow, the First Congress of the Comintern took place. Communist parties and left-wing socialist organisations from 30 countries were represented at the Congress. If one were to disregard the Communist parties of the Republics which now form a part of the USSR, there existed only five Communist parties in the whole of Europe at that time. In Asia, Africa, Australia and Oceania there were no Communist parties. On the American continent there was only the Communist Party of Argentina. Now, there are Communist and Workers' parties in 87 countries. They unite in their ranks more than 36,000,000 people. The ideas of Communism have captured the minds of millions of people in every corner of the world. This is good, very good, comrades. We are witnesses of the birth of a succession of new Communist parties. . . .

It should be noted that the CPSU delegation at the [1960] Conference set out its viewpoint *concerning the wording that the Soviet Union is at the head of the socialist camp and that the CPSU is at the head of the Communist movement.* Our delegation declared that in this wording we see first of all high praise of the services of our party which was created by Lenin and expressed cordial thanks to all the fraternal parties. Our Party, nurtured by Lenin, has always regarded it as its foremost duty to fulfil international obligations to the international working class. The delegation assured the participants of the Conference that the Party would also in the future bear high the banner of proletarian internationalism and would spare no efforts to fulfil its international obligations. At the same time, *the CPSU delegation proposed that the aforementioned wording should not be included in the Statement or other documents of the Communist movement.*

As regards the principles of mutual relations between the fraternal parties, the CPSU expressed its position on this question most definitely at the Twenty-first Party Congress. From the tribune of the Congress we declared before the whole world that in the Communist movement, just as in the socialist camp, there has existed and exists *complete equality of rights and solidarity of all Communist and Workers' parties and socialist countries.* The Communist Party of the Soviet Union in reality does not exercise leadership over other parties. In the Communist movement there are no parties that are superior or subordinate. All Communist parties are equal and independent. All carry responsibility for the destiny of the Communist movement, for its victories and failures. Each Communist and Workers' party is responsible to the working class, the working people of its own country, to the entire international workers' and Communist movement. The role of the Soviet Union does not lie in the fact that it leads other socialist countries, but in the fact that it was the first to blaze the trail to socialism, is the most powerful country in the world socialist system, has amassed a great deal of positive experience in the struggle for the building of socialism and was the first to enter the period of comprehensive construction of Communism. It is stressed in the Statement that the universally acknowledged vanguard of the world Communist movement has been and still remains the Communist Party of the Soviet Union, as the most experienced and hardened unit of the international Communist movement.

At the moment, when there exists a large group of socialist countries each of which is faced with its own tasks, when there are functioning 87 Communist and Workers' parties, each of which, moreover, is also faced with its own tasks, *it is not possible for leadership over socialist countries and Communist parties to be exercised from any centre at all. This is neither possible nor necessary.* There have grown up in the Communist parties hardened Marxist-Leninist cadres which are capable of leading their own parties, their countries. Moreover, in practice, as is well known, the CPSU does not give directives to any other parties. *If we are called the leader it gives no advantage either to our Party or to other parties. On the contrary it only creates difficulties.*

As is evident from the text of the Statement the fraternal parties agreed with the conclusions of our delegation. The question may arise: will not our international solidarity be weakened by the fact that the aforesaid provision is not written down in the Statement. No, it will not be weakened. *At the present time there is no statute which could regulate relations between parties, but instead we have a common Marxist-Leninist ideology, loyalty to which is the main condition of our solidarity and unity.* It is necessary to be consistently guided by the teaching of Marx, Engels and Lenin and resolutely bring into being the principles of Marxism-Leninism; then the cause of international solidarity of the Communist movement will grow stronger all the time.

Representatives of Communist and Workers' parties exchanged their opinions on the present international situation, discussed the urgent problems of the

Communist and Workers' movements, or, as comrades figuratively sta
Conference, synchronised their watches. Indeed, the socialist countrie
Communist parties must synchronise their watches. . . .

On behalf of the CPSU, our delegation assured those at the Conference that we, on our part, would do everything to strengthen still more the close fraternal bonds with all Communist parties. . . . In this connection, I would like to refer to our unswerving endeavour to strengthen the bonds of fraternal friendship with the Communist Party of China, with the great Chinese people.

In our relations with the Communist Party of China, our Party is always guided by the fact that the friendship of the two great peoples, the cohesion of our two parties – the largest in the international Communist movement – is of exceptional importance in the struggle for the triumph of our common cause. Our Party has always made, and will continue to make, every effort to strengthen this great friendship. With People's China, with Chinese Communists – just as with the Communists of all countries – we share one goal: the safeguarding of peace and the building of Communism; common interests; the happiness and well-being of the working people; and the common basis of firm principles: Marxism-Leninism.

February 2

Canadian government announced £20 million worth of grain sold to China.

February 3

Chinese government granted Albania loan of 500 million (old) roubles.

February 6

Australian government announced sale of 21.6 million tons of grain to China.

February 12

Fourth Congress of the Albanian Communist Party opened in Tirana. Enver Hoxha accused Yugoslavia, Greece, the North Atlantic Treaty Organisation and the US Sixth Fleet of conspiring with a 'group of Albanian traitors' to overthrow his régime.

March 30

Soviet and Yugoslav governments signed a five-year trade agreement providing for the doubling of trade between them by 1965 and for total exchanges to the value of $800 million in five years.

April 27

Chinese government announced it would supply Albania with grain and other foodstuffs and assist in a number of Albanian industrial projects.

May 15–28

Trial in Tirana of Admiral Sejku, Commander-in-chief of Albanian Navy, and other members of anti-Hoxha conspiracy. Sejku executed May 31.

May 27–29

It was reported that a Soviet submarine tender and 8 W-class submarines had left the Vlore (Valona) base in Albania and steamed out through the Mediterranean.

June 3–4

Khrushchev met President Kennedy in Vienna.

July 7–13

Koca Popovich, Yugoslav Foreign Minister, visited Moscow and had talks with Khrushchev, Mikoyan and Gromyko. This was the first high-level contact between the Soviet and Yugoslav governments since 1957.

July

Fortieth anniversary of Chinese CP celebrated in Chinese theoretical journal *Red Flag*:

After the Chinese CP took the lead in the Chinese revolution, a new situation emerged. The CCP, under the leadership of Comrade Mao Tse-tung, creatively applied the universal truth of Marxism-Leninism to the Chinese revolution, surmounted the errors of Right and Left opportunism, and correctly formulated the programme, policies and tactics for the Chinese democratic revolution, guiding it forward along a correct path.

Under the brilliant inspiration of the three Red banners of the general line, the big leap forward and the people's communes, tremendous strides have been made in our country in economic construction, as well as in cultural and economic undertakings. In the past three years, the rate of development of industrial production has been greatly accelerated, the level of industrial production has been raised considerably, and the material and technical foundation of industry greatly strengthened. We have fulfilled the major targets for industrial production under the Second Five-Year Plan ahead of schedule.

In agriculture, the people's communes have developed their immense influence in the past three years; tremendous development has been achieved in farming; and, through popular practice, the 'eight-point charter' for agricultural production has also been enriched in content and developed. All this has not only minimised the losses caused by the serious natural calamities which lasted through 1959 and 1960, but it has also provided favourable conditions for increasing agricultural production henceforth.

The great victory in the Chinese revolution and construction is the outcome of the protracted and strenuous struggle of the Chinese people and is inseparable from the aid from the international revolutionary forces, particularly the assistance of the Soviet Union and other fraternal countries. The victory of the Chinese people has dealt a serious blow to imperialism and it has greatly strengthened the forces of the socialist camp and the forces in defence of world peace, promoted changes in the relative strength in the world in favour of socialism, and forcefully pushed forward the development of the national liberation movement in the world.

The victory of the Chinese revolution and construction is synonymous with the victory of Marxism-Leninism in China, the victory of Mao Tse-tung's thinking, which integrates the universal truth of Marxism-Leninism with the concrete practice in China, and the victory of the CCP's leadership. Under the leadership of Comrade Mao Tse-tung and through the long period of revolutionary struggle our Party has steeled itself into a mature Marxist-Leninist political party. In the practice of the revolutionary struggle, our Party has cultivated and developed its own fine working style and in all its undertakings it has upheld the principle of 'verifying the facts in order to get at the truth', consistently implemented the mass line, maintained close contact with the masses, assumed a humble and cautious attitude in all circumstances, and learned humbly from the masses.

July

By the end of the month the withdrawal of Soviet technicians and advisers from Albania was completed.

July 30

Draft of new Programme of CPSU published.

August 13

Boundary between East and West Berlin closed by the 'Wall'.

October 17

Khrushchev delivered the main political report to the Twenty-second Congress of the CPSU in Moscow. Dealing with the Sino-Soviet dispute he said:

The decisions of the Twentieth Congress, backed by the fraternal parties, added to the great creative power of the Communist movement and helped restore the Leninist spirit and style to the activities of the fraternal parties and the relations between them. The meetings of Communist and Workers' parties held in recent years were important milestones marking the progress of the world Communist movement. *International Communist meetings are one of the forms evolved by the fraterna parties to ensure their militant co-operation.*

It is indisputable to Marxist-Leninists that the fundamental interests of the international Communist movement require consistent unity of action, and the Communist and Workers' parties are loyal to it. Only the leaders of the League of Communists of Yugoslavia, who are plainly affected by national narrow-mindedness, have turned from the straight Marxist-Leninist road on to a winding path which has landed them in the bog of revisionism. The Yugoslav leaders responded to the 1957 Declaration of the fraternal parties, which resounded throughout the world as a charter of Communist unity and solidarity, with a revisionist anti-Leninist programme, which all the Marxist-Leninist parties subjected to a severe and just criticism.

Revisionist ideas pervade both the theory and practice of the leadership of the League of Communists of Yugoslavia. The line they have adopted – that of development in isolation from the world socialist community – is harmful and perilous. It plays into the hands of imperialist reaction, foments nationalist tendencies and may in the end lead to the loss of socialist gains in the country, which has broken away from the friendly and united family of builders of a new world.

Our Party has criticised, and will continue to criticise, the Yugoslav leaders' revisionist concepts. As internationalists, we cannot but feel concern about the destinies of the fraternal peoples of Yugoslavia, who fought selflessly against fascism and, on the achievement of victory, chose the path of socialist construction. . . .

On the eve of the Twentieth Congress the issue facing us was: either the Party would openly, in Leninist fashion, condemn the errors and distortions committed at the time of the cult of Stalin's personality and reject the methods of party and government leadership that had become an obstacle to progress, or the forces which clung to the old and resisted all that was new and creative would gain the upper hand in the Party. *The issue was as crucial as that.*

Was it really necessary to criticise, so scathingly and so frankly, the major errors and grave consequences bound up with the cult of the individual?

Yes, it was. . . . The Central Committee, which was well aware of its responsibility to the Party and the people, could not possibly take the line of concealing or hushing up past errors and distortions. Following Lenin's behests, the Central Committee decided to tell the truth about the abuses of power perpetrated at the time of the cult of the individual. It was a moral requirement, the duty of the Party and its leadership. It was a correct decision and it had tremendous importance for the destiny of the Party and for the building of Communism.

What would have become of the Party and the country had the cult of the individual not been condemned, had its harmful consequences not been removed and the Leninist standards of party and government activity not been restored? . . . In the sphere of international relations, the result would have been a weakening of Soviet positions on the world scene and a worsening of relations with other countries, which would have had dire consequences. . . .

The course adopted by the Twentieth Congress was applauded by the world Communist movement and by the fraternal Marxist-Leninist parties. This found expression in decisions passed by congresses of the fraternal parties, as well as in other records of those parties, and in the documents of the meetings of representatives of the Communist and Workers' parties in 1957 and 1960.

To cite an example, the Statement of the Moscow Meeting of 1960 said: 'The historic decisions of the Twentieth Congress of the CPSU . . . have initiated a new stage in the world Communist movement, and have promoted its development on the basis of Marxism-Leninism'.

I must say, however, that our Party's policy aimed at eliminating the harmful consequences of the cult of the individual did not, as it became obvious afterwards, meet with due understanding on the part of the leaders of the Albanian Party of Labour. Indeed, they began to oppose that policy. . . .

For many years the Albanian leaders signified their complete agreement with the Central Committee of our Party and the Soviet government on all matters pertaining to the world Communist movement. They repeatedly voiced support for the course adopted by the Twentieth Congress. Enver Hoxha, First Secretary of the Central Committee of the Albanian Party of Labour, mentioned this in his speeches at the Twentieth and Twenty-first Congresses of our Party. The Third Congress of the Albanian Party of Labour, held shortly after the Twentieth Congress, fully approved of the criticism levelled at the cult of the individual, as well as of the steps taken to eliminate the harmful consequences of that cult.

We Soviet people believed the Albanian leaders and held that there was mutual understanding and unity of views between our Party and the Albanian Party of Labour.

The facts show, however, that the Albanian leaders have lately reversed their policy for no apparent reason, despite their previous assurances and contrary to the decisions of the congress of their own party, and have set out to worsen seriously their relations with our Party, with our country. They have begun to depart from the common agreed line of the Communist movement of the whole world on major issues of today, something which became particularly noticeable in the middle of last year.

The Albanian leaders no longer conceal their disapproval of the course adopted by our Party with a view to eliminating completely the harmful consequences of the cult of Stalin's personality, severely condemning abuses of power and re-establishing the Leninist standards of party and government activity.

It would appear that in their hearts the Albanian leaders disagreed with the conclusions of the 1957 and 1960 meetings of the fraternal parties, which, as we all know, approved of the decisions of the Twentieth Congress and our Party's policy directed towards eliminating the harmful consequences of the cult of the individual. This stand of the Albanian leaders is due to the fact that, to our deep regret, they are themselves using the same methods as were current in our country at the time of the cult of the individual. . . .

We are deeply concerned about the situation and have never stopped our earnest search for ways and means of overcoming the divergences that have arisen.

The policy elaborated by the Twentieth Congress of our Party is a Leninist policy, and we cannot make a concession on this fundamental point either to the Albanian leaders or to anyone else. To depart from the course adopted by the Twentieth Congress would amount to ignoring the wise directions of Lenin, who discerned the danger of a cult of Stalin's personality when it was still in embryo. It would amount to disregarding the costly lessons of history and forgetting the price which our Party had to pay because it had not acted in good time on the warning given by its great leader.

The Albanian leaders, who oppose the course adopted by the Twentieth Congress, are now trying to pull our Party back to practices which they like but which will never recur in our country. Our Party will press forward with determination the policy of its Twentieth Congress, a policy which has withstood the test of time. *No one can divert us from the Leninist road.*

If the Albanian leaders hold dear the interests of their own people and of socialist construction in Albania, and if they really want friendship with the CPSU and the other fraternal parties, *they must renounce their erroneous views* and revert to the path of unity and close co-operation within the fraternal family which is the socialist community, they must revert to the path of unity with the world Communist movement as a whole.

As regards our Party, it will continue, in keeping with its internationalist duty, to do all in its power for Albania to march shoulder to shoulder with all the socialist countries.

October

Chou En-lai placed wreath on the tomb of Stalin as well as on Lenin's.

October 19

Chou En-lai, leading the Chinese delegation, spoke at the CPSU's Twenty-second Congress. In an apparent reference to the absence of an Albanian delegation and to Khrushchev's comments on the Albanian leaders, he said:

. . . The Declaration and the Statement point out that the unity of the socialist camp, the unity of the international Communist movement, is the nucleus of all broader world unity. This unity of ours is cemented by common ideals and by a common cause; it has been strengthened and developed in joint struggles against our common enemy and it is based on Marxism-Leninism and proletarian internationalism. This unity of ours has stood the test of time; no force can destroy it. *Our socialist camp, comprising 12 fraternal countries, is a single entity, from the Korean Democratic People's Republic to the German Democratic Republic, from the Democratic Republic of Vietnam to the Albanian People's Republic. . . .*

We hold that if a dispute or difference unfortunately arises between fraternal parties or fraternal countries, it should be resolved patiently in the spirit of proletarian internationalism and on the principles of equality and unanimity through consultation. *Any public, one-sided censure of any fraternal party does not help unity and is not helpful to resolving problems. To lay bare a dispute between fraternal parties or fraternal countries openly in the face of the enemy cannot be regarded as a serious Marxist-Leninist attitude.* Such an attitude will only grieve those near and dear to us and gladden our enemies. The CCP sincerely hopes that fraternal parties which have disputes or differences will unite afresh on the basis of Marxism-Leninism and on the basis of mutual respect, independence and equality. This, in my opinion, is the position which we Communists ought to take on this question. (Applause.) . . .

Profound friendship has long existed between the peoples of China and the Soviet Union. Both in revolution and in construction, the Chinese people have enjoyed support and assistance from the people and the CPSU. For this, we again express our heartfelt gratitude. *This great unity and friendship of the people of our two countries will flow on eternally like the Yangtse and the Volga.*

October 20

Albanian Communist Party issued a statement replying to Khrushchev's charges and for the first time criticising him by name:

Khrushchev's anti-Marxist lies and attacks serve only the enemies of Communism and of the Albanian People's Republic, the imperialists and the Yugoslav revisionists. By revealing to the enemy *the misunderstandings which have existed for a long time between the leaders of the Soviet Communist Party and the Albanian Party of Labour*, Khrushchev has violated brutally the Moscow Statement of 1960 which stresses that misunderstandings between fraternal parties must be settled patiently in the spirit of proletarian internationalism, on the basis of the principle of equality and by consultation. By attacking the Albanian party before the whole world, Nikita Khrushchev has in effect launched an open attack on the unity of the international Communist movement and on the unity of the socialist camp....

The Albanian Party received favourably the statement by Comrade Chou En-lai, pointing out that one-sided criticism and public revelation of misunderstandings between fraternal parties cannot be regarded as a serious Marxist-Leninist attitude.

October 23

Chou En-lai left Moscow.

October 27

In his closing speech to the CPSU Congress Khrushchev said:

In our time the might of the world system of socialism has grown as never before. It now already unites over one-third of mankind and its forces are rapidly expanding; it is a great bastion of world peace. The principle of peaceful coexistence between states with differing social systems assumes vital importance in contemporary conditions.

This is not understood only by hopeless dogmatists who, repeating general formulas about imperialism, obstinately turn away from life. It is precisely on such positions that the last-ditcher Molotov still stands. He and his like do not understand the changes in the world situation, the new features in life; they are lagging behind events, have long since become a brake, become ballast.

Comrades, the Central Committee's report, as well as the speeches by delegates to this congress, have dealt with the erroneous stand of the leaders of the Albanian Party of Labour, who have set out to fight the course adopted by the Twentieth Congress of our Party and to undermine the friendship with the Soviet Union and other socialist countries.

The representatives of fraternal parties who have spoken here have said that they share our concern over the state of affairs in the Albanian Party of Labour and emphatically condemn the dangerous actions of its leaders, which prejudice the basic interests of the Albanian people and the unity of the socialist common-wealth as a whole. The speeches made by the delegates and by representatives of fraternal parties show plainly that the Central Committee of our Party was abso-lutely correct in reporting to this congress, frankly and from a principled stand-point, that the situation with regard to Soviet-Albanian relations is abnormal.

It was our duty to do so because our numerous attempts to normalise relations with the Albanian Party of Labour unfortunately yielded no results. I should like to stress that the Central Committee of our Party showed the utmost patience and did all in its power to restore good relations between our parties.

Members of the presidium of CPSU Central Committee made repeated attempts to meet the Albanian leaders to discuss the controversies that had arisen. *As far back as in August 1960 we twice made a proposal for a meeting to the Albanian leaders, but they evaded it. They were just as obstinate in rejecting talks with us during the Moscow meeting of fraternal parties in November 1960.*

When a meeting was finally arranged, at the insistence of the CPSU Central Committee, Enver Hoxha and Mehmet Shehu frustrated it and resorted to actions which can only be described as provocative. The leaders of the Albanian Party of Labour ostentatiously withdrew from the November meeting, thus showing that they refused to take account of the collective opinion of the fraternal parties. They rudely turned down our subsequent proposals for getting together, exchang-ing views and removing differences, and stepped up their campaign of slanderous attacks against our Party and its Central Committee. . . .

Albania is the only country in the socialist community that has not published the full text of the draft programme of the CPSU.

We are aware of why the Albanian leaders are concealing the programme of the CPSU from their Party and their people. They are scared stiff of the truth. The party programme is sacred to us; it is our lodestar in Communist construction.

Had the Albanian leaders published it in full, Albania's working people would have seen who was slandering and who was speaking the truth, would have seen that the entire activity of our Party and all its plans are in keeping with the vital interests of the peoples, including the interests of the friendly Albanian people.

Our great Party has more than once been a target for fierce and foul attacks on the part of overt and covert enemies of Communism. But it must be said bluntly that we do not recall anyone passing at such breakneck speed from protestations and vows of everlasting friendship to unbridled anti-Soviet calumny in the way the Albanian leaders have done.

They apparently expect in this manner to clear the ground for winning the right to receive hand-outs from the imperialists. The imperialists are always prepared to pay thirty pieces of silver to those who split the Communist ranks. But pieces of silver have never brought anyone anything but dishonour and ignominy.

Obviously, the Central Committee of our Party could not fail to tell this congress the whole truth about the pernicious stand of the leadership of the Albanian Party of Labour. Had we not done so, the Albanian leaders would have gone on making out that the Central Committee of the Soviet Communist Party was afraid of informing the congress of the differences it had with the leadership of the Albanian Party of Labour. Our Party and the Soviet people should know about the conduct of the Albanian leaders. And let this congress, which is entitled to speak on behalf of the entire Party, take its stand on the matter, let it pass its weighty judgement. . . .

Comrade Chou En-lai, the leader of the delegation of the Communist Party of China, expressed in his speech concern over the open discussion at this congress of the issue of Albanian-Soviet relations. The main point in his statement, as we see it, was anxiety lest the present state of our relations with the Albanian Party of Labour might affect the unity of the socialist camp.

We share the anxiety expressed by our Chinese friends, and appreciate their concern for greater unity. If the Chinese comrades wish to make efforts towards normalising the relations between the Albanian Party of Labour and the fraternal parties, there is hardly anyone who could contribute more to the solution of this problem than the Communist Party of China. That would really benefit the Albanian Party of Labour, and would meet the interests of the entire socialist commonwealth. . . .

Why did the Albanian leaders launch a campaign against the decisions of the Twentieth Congress of our Party? What is the heresy they espy in them?

To begin with, the Albanian leaders disapprove of the resolute condemnation of the cult of Stalin's personality and its harmful consequences. They disapprove of our having firmly condemned the arbitrary methods and the abuses of power which affected many innocent people, including prominent representatives of the old guard who, together with Lenin, founded the world's first proletarian state! . . .

All that was bad in our country at the time of the cult of the individual manifests itself in even worse form in the Albanian Party of Labour. It is no longer a secret to anyone that the Albanian leaders stay in power by resorting to violence and arbitrary actions.

An abnormal, pernicious situation has long been prevailing in the Albanian Party of Labour, where each person the leadership dislikes can be subjected to brutal reprisals.

Where now are those Albanian Communists who founded the Party, who fought against the Italian and German fascist invaders? Almost all of them have fallen victim to the bloody atrocities perpetrated by Mehmet Shehu and Enver Hoxha.

The Albanian leaders reproach us, alleging interference in the internal affairs of the Albanian Party of Labour. I should like to explain what this so-called interference consisted of.

Several years ago, the Central Committee of the CPSU interceded with the Albanian leaders for the former member of the political bureau of the Central Committee of the Albanian Party of Labour, Liri Gega, who had been sentenced to death together with her husband. For several years she had served in the leading bodies of the Albanian Party of Labour, taking part in the Albanian peoples struggle for liberation. In approaching the Albanian leaders at that time, we proceeded from considerations of humanity, from a desire to prevent the execution of a woman, and an expectant mother at that.

We believed and continue to believe that as a fraternal party we had the right to express our opinion on this. For even during the most sinister times of rampant reaction the Tsarist satraps, who tormented revolutionaries, did not dare to execute expectant mothers. And there, in a socialist country, a death sentence was passed on an expectant mother and she was executed – a display of utterly unjustified brutality.

Honest people are now being victimised in Albania, only because they have dared to come out in defence of Soviet-Albanian friendship, of which the Albanian leaders like to speak so pompously and bombastically.

Comrades Liri Belishova and Kocho Tashko, prominent leaders of the Albanian Party of Labour, have not only been removed from the Central Committee of the Albanian Party of Labour but are now openly called enemies of the Party and the people. And all this for the sole reason that Liri Belishova and Kocho Tashko have had the courage to voice openly and honestly their disagreement with the policy of the Albanian leaders, have come out for Albanian's unity with the Soviet Union and the other socialist countries.

Those who today stand for friendship with the Soviet Union, with the CPSU are regarded as enemies by the Albanian leaders.

How can all this be reconciled with the pledges and assurances given by Shehu and Hoxha about friendly sentiments for the CPSU and the Soviet Union? It is evident that all their prattling about friendship is only hypocrisy and deceit.

That is the situation prevailing in the Albanian Party of Labour; that is why the Albanian leaders are opposing the Leninist course of the Twentieth Congress of the Party. *For to end the personality cult would virtually mean for Shehu, Hoxha and others to resign their leading positions in the Party and the state.* This they do not want to do. But we are confident that the time will come when the Albanian Communists and the Albanian people will have their say and the Albanian leaders will then be held responsible for the damage they have inflicted on their country, their people and the cause of building socialism in Albania. . . .

October 30

Congress approved resolution calling for the removal of Stalin's remains from the Mausoleum in Red Square.

October 31

Stalin's remains removed to simple grave near the Kremlin wall.

November 7

Enver Hoxha criticised Khrushchev's treatment of Albania in the following terms:

Khrushchev was compelled to accept the results of the Moscow Conference of November 1960, at which correct debates took place during which it became clearly evident that his views did not find enthusiastic support. . . .

The Soviet leaders are trying to impose their opportunist conceptions on all the Communist parties, not hesitating to use the most brutal pressure, blackmail and attacks on fraternal parties and their leaders who do not agree with his revisionist theses. . . .

As a result of pressures in the economic, political and military spheres, relations between our country and the USSR have been greatly worsened. *All the credits granted by the USSR to our country for the third Five-year Plan were cut off, with the object of sabotaging our economic plans.*Without any reason all Soviet specialists working in Albania were withdrawn arbitrarily, though we had asked them to stay. By demanding the repayment of old loans, the Soviet side has almost completely broken off commercial relations. All Albanian students studying in the USSR have been deprived of their scholarships. Economic pressure was accompanied by pressures and restrictive measures in the military sphere. . . .

Moreover Khrushchev launched an open appeal from the platform of the Twenty-second Congress for the overthrow of the leaders of the Albanian Party and for the liquidation of the Party – something he refrains from doing even in the case of governments of capitalist countries.

November 25

The Soviet government informed the Albanian chargé d'affaires in Moscow of its decision to withdraw the Soviet ambassador from Tirana and demanded that the Albanian ambassador be withdrawn from Moscow.

December 5

The Soviet government announced the recall of the whole staff of the Soviet embassy in Tirana.

December 14

Albanian embassy staff left Moscow.

December 16–19

Meeting of World Peace Council in Stockholm turned into heated debate between Russian-led majority and Chinese-led minority over title to be given to 1962 Peace Congress. Final voting was 166 delegates for Russian view and 24 for the Chinese.

December 26

Chinese and Albanian governments agreed to set up joint shipping company.

1962

January 9

The Albanian Communist Party's newspaper *Zeri i Popullit*, in an article entitled 'Deeper and Deeper into the Morass of Anti-Marxism', attacked Khrushchev and said:

When we say that the Soviet Union is at the head of the socialist camp we certainly do not want to be understood as saying that the USSR and the CPSU are the supreme authority.

January

At the beginning of 1962 the Vietnamese, Indonesian, British, Swedish 'and other comrades' proposed 'the convocation of a meeting of fraternal parties of all countries'.

February 12–16

Meeting of Afro-Asian writers in Cairo.

February 22

CPSU sent letter to Chinese CP suggesting that 'unnecessary arguments be stopped regarding questions on which we have different opinions, that public statements capable of aggravating and not smoothing out our differences be given up'.

March 5

Replying to unspecified critics abroad at a meeting of the Central Committee of the CPSU, Khrushchev said, in reference to the question of Soviet economic aid:

The construction of Communism in our country is tantamount to the fulfilment of our international duty to all the revolutionary forces in the world.

March

The Soviet journal *International Affairs* said:

The view that, having completed the construction of socialism ahead of other countries, the Soviet Union should wait for the levelling up of the general economic development of the socialist countries is strange. It has nothing in common with Marxism-Leninism or the interests of the international solidarity of the working people.

April 16–21

Gromyko, Soviet Foreign Minister, on an official visit to Yugoslavia, agreed that conditions were favourable for further improvements in relations.

April 7

Chinese CP proposed calling of international meeting:

In its desire to uphold the principles guiding the mutual relations of fraternal parties and countries and to strengthen unity, the Chinese CP in April 1962 gave its active support to proposal made by some fraternal parties for easing relations and improving the atmosphere, and, in a letter to the fraternal party concerned [clearly the CPSU – DF] formally expressed its opinion that a meeting of representatives of the Communist and Workers' parties of all countries should be convened to iron out differences and strengthen unity through comradely discussion and consultation. We also pointed out that, prior to such a meeting, all fraternal parties should make extensive preparations, including the cessation of radio and press attacks on another fraternal party, in order to create favourable conditions for the meeting and ensure its success. [*See* Chronology: January 27, 1963.]

May 18

On visit to Bulgaria Khrushchev said the Soviet Union must do everything to help the Yugoslavs 'consolidate their socialist positions'.

May 23

Supreme Soviet of USSR invited a Yugoslav 'parliamentary' delegation to visit the Soviet Union.

May 28

Soviet government announced its invitation to Tito to visit the Soviet Union for holiday.

May 31

CPSU wrote to Chinese CP about an international meeting:

As you are well aware, our Party has always been in favour and is still in favour of the collective discussion of vital problems of the world Communist movement. The Central Committee of the CPSU was the sponsor of the meetings of fraternal parties in 1957 and 1960. In both cases these meetings were connected with serious changes in the international situation and the need for working out corresponding tactics for the Communist movement. On this occasion too we fully support the proposal for convening a meeting of all the fraternal parties.

June 6–7

Meeting of leaders of Comecon countries in Moscow admitted Mongolia to membership of the organisation, though Albania was not invited.

July 6

An agreement signed in Moscow provided for a considerable increase in Soviet-Yugoslav trade above the volume agreed in 1961.

August 17

Nehru's claim to have Soviet military aircraft reported in Peking.

August 18

Peking reported statement by Krishna Menon, Indian Defence Minister, on agreement reached for manufacture of Soviet jet fighters in India.

September 19

Albanian newspaper *Zeri i Popullit* attacks Khrushchev:

Tito once more shows his true face as a renegade from Marxism-Leninism and a lackey and seasoned agent of American imperialism in the struggle against Communism, against the national liberation movement, and against world peace, as the imperialist intermediary attached to the revisionist group of N. Khrushchev. . . .

The N. Khrushchev group and its toadies have resolutely followed Tito's path, never hesitating to use every means and method, from demagogy and intrigue to plots, interference, pressure, blackmail and undisguised threats. . . . Tito takes on the role of interpreter of the views of N. Khrushchev to the imperialists. . . . This proves that the Tito clique and the N. Khrushchev group are following the same path.

September 24–October 4

Soviet President Leonid Brezhnev paid official visit to Yugoslavia, reaffirmed Soviet–Yugoslav declaration of 1955 and stressed 'identity or proximity' of views on foreign affairs.

October 1

Chen Yi, Chinese Foreign Minister, spoke of Tito in the following terms:

The imperialists need the help of reactionaries in various countries and the latter are serving imperialism in a less disguised way. The modern revisionists represented by the Tito clique precisely meet these needs. . . .

The fighting peoples of the world can in no way be lulled into inaction. The reaction of various countries and the Yugoslav modern revisionists will only further reveal their ugly features. . . .

The imperialists, the reactionaries of various countries and the modern revisionists gloated over the difficulties encountered by our country. They have attempted by every means to vilify, sabotage, subvert, and invade our great motherland. . . . But all their wishful thinking has come to naught. The criminal activities of the imperialists and their running dogs against the People's Republic of China, far from overwhelming the Chinese people, have heightened their revolutionary fervour in building and defending the motherland.

October 15

Albanian paper *Zeri i Popullit* described Brezhnev's visit to Yugoslavia as:

. . . a link in the chain of N. Khrushchev's aims to achieve rapprochement with the Yugoslav revisionists, to co-ordinate with them a new revisionist split the socialist camp and liquidate socialism.

The masses of Communists and workers are more and more aware o betrayal of the revisionists who are renegades to Communism and are beyond repair.

Those Communists who are wading in the mud of N. Khrushchev should find the energy and the courage to stop and detach themselves from the revisionists.

October 20

Chinese begin invasion of India.

October 22–28

Crisis in Soviet-American relations over Cuba.

November 5

Speaking at Congress in Sofia of Bulgarian Communist Party, Chinese delegate Wu Hsui-chuan defended Albanian Communists against criticisms. Todor Zhivkov, First Secretary of Bulgarian Party, said:

We cannot tolerate the slanderous campaign of the Albanian leaders against the Soviet Union, the Soviet Party and Khrushchev. This campaign only helps the enemies of Communism.

November 18

Summing up critical propaganda campaign on Soviet reaction to Cuban crisis, *People's Daily* said:

It is pure nonsense to say that 'peace has been saved' by withdrawing Soviet missiles.

November 18

Pravda said in an editorial:

Neither bourgeois propagandists nor other falsifiers can conceal the main fact that Soviet policy saved world peace and preserved the Cuban revolutionary movement.

November 21

Opening the Congress of Hungarian Communist Party in Budapest, First Secretary Janos Kadar said:

It follows that we profoundly condemn the anti-party Enver Hoxha and his followers and all the parties and sectarian symptoms making their appearance in other parties of the international Communist movement. . . . The disruption of unity can benefit only our enemies who have pinned their hopes on the disintegration of Communism. . . . We consider it our task to develop our relations with Yugoslavia into a truly smooth and neighbourly relation.

December 3

Frol Kozlov, secretary of the CPSU Central Committee, said in a speech to Congress of Italian Communist Party in Rome:

Peace-loving men are looking with keen concern [on the Chinese-Indian conflict], which is seriously harming the interests of both the brotherly Chinese people and the friendly Indian people. We all want the controversial border dispute between these two great powers of Asia to be solved through peaceful means. Those who are certain of their historic future have no need to play with thermo-nuclear fire and endanger all the achievements of civilisation. . . . Whether there is war or peace does not depend on noisy and useless phrases like those of the Albanian leaders.

December 4–8

Twelfth Congress of Czechoslovak Communist Party in Prague. Referring to the Albanian Communist leaders, First Secretary Antonin Novotny said:

We cannot accept their conduct or the support they are given by the Chinese Communist Party.

December 8

The Chinese delegate Wu Hsiu-chuan handed Novotny a 'Statement' which was read to the Congress:

. . . It has been most unfortunate and contrary to our expectations that at your congress some comrades of the Communist Party of Czechoslovakia and the comrades from some other fraternal parties have made use of the platform of this congress to continue attacking the Albanian Party of Labour and to deliver unbridled attacks on the Communist Party of China. A practice of this kind is not in conformity with the Moscow Declaration and the Moscow Statement, is not in the interest of the unity of the socialist camp and the unity of the international Communist movement, is not in the interest of the struggle against imperialism, is not in the interest of the struggle for world peace and is not in conformity with the fundamental interests of the people of the socialist countries. We cannot but express the deepest regret at such actions which are contrary to Marxism-Leninism and proletarian internationalism. . . .

Some people have glibly said that the Albanian Party of Labour made charges against some comrades of a certain fraternal party, and that the Albanian comrades are to blame for the distressing situation which exists today in the international Communist movement. Going farther, they distort the facts and accuse the Albanian comrades of being 'anti-Soviet'. Why don't these people give a little thought to the question of who should be held responsible for such a situation? After all, who was the first to launch an attack at its own party congress against another fraternal party, while the party attacked does not have even the right to reply? Is it possible that the launching of an attack on a fraternal party is to be called 'Marxist-Leninist' and conforming to the Moscow Declaration and the Moscow Statement, but that the reply by the attacked party is to be branded as 'sectarianism', 'splittism', 'dogmatism' and a violation of the Moscow Declaration and the Moscow Statement? If the replies of the Albanian comrades are to be called 'anti-Soviet', then, may we ask, what name should be given to those who first attacked the Albanian comrades and arbitrarily levelled a whole series of charges against them? On important questions like these, Marxist Leninists should distinguish between right and wrong and not distort the truth. We hold that the differences among fraternal parties can only be settled in accordance with the principles of independence, of equality and of unanimity through consultation, as set forth in the Moscow Declaration and the Moscow Statement, and by the party which made the first attack taking the initiative. Once again, we sincerely make this appeal. . . .

We hold that the employment of a congress of one party to attack another party or parties and the recourse to such unusual manners as shouting and hissing can hardly prove that one is right and furthermore cannot be helpful in settling any problems.

With the object of settling the differences in the international Communist movement on certain important questions of principle, *the Communist Party of China and a number of other fraternal parties have proposed the convening of a Meeting of Representatives of the Communist and Workers' parties of all countries of the world in order to clarify what is right from what is wrong*, to strengthen unity and to stand together against the enemy. We consider that this is the only correct method of settling problems. The Communists of the whole world have a common enemy, a common cause and a common objective; there is no reason whatsoever why we should not unite. . . .

December 4–20

Tito paid official visit to the Soviet Union, where in an address to the Supreme Soviet on December 13, he said:

We agree in the main with what Comrade Nikita Sergeyevich said about relations between our two countries. I should not like to speak about the past, but in so far as there are still certain disagreements we shall remove them jointly through constructive co-operation.

December 12

Khrushchev delivered a long speech on foreign policy to the Supreme Soviet. Extracts:

Comrade Deputies, it should be said that during the peaceful adjustment of the conflict in the Caribbean shrill voices of discontent could also be heard from another side – from people who even call themselves Marxist-Leninists, even if their actions have nothing in common with Marxism-Leninism. I refer specifically to the Albanian leaders. Their criticism of the Soviet Union in effect echoed that coming from the most reactionary, bellicose circles in the West. Why is it that the loudest shouts today come from the Albanian leaders? . . .

The Albanian leaders are like . . . silly boys. Someone has taught them foul language, and they go about and use it against the Communist Party of the Soviet Union, and yet it is their mother; and for using this foul language they get the promised three copecks; and if they use stronger and cruder language they get another five copecks and praise. What do they want, these people who call themselves Marxist-Leninists? Why are they attempting the same thing, in fact, as Adenauer - *i.e.*, to push us into conflicts and into aggravating the international situation? It is a true saying that if you go to the left you'll find yourself on the right. Objectively speaking, they acted during the Cuban crisis – well, like people out to provoke a conflict. They really wanted to set the Soviet Union and the USA on a collision course. Yet what does it mean to set these two great world powers on a collision course? It means to provoke a world thermonuclear war. The only interesting thing is how they themselves would behave in such a war. I do not think that they would want to join in it. Apparently they would prefer to sit it out. But the question arises: what are they out for? Can it be that they want the blood of the peoples of the Soviet Union and other socialist countries to flow? The Albanian leaders, to judge by their statements, are obviously dissatisfied with the termination of the Cuban crisis. They call the solution reached a retreat, and have gone so far as to allege that the Soviet Union capitulated to imperialism. One may ask: how have we retreated? Socialist Cuba exists. Cuba remains a beacon of Marxist-Leninist ideas in the Western Hemisphere. The strength of her revolutionary example will increase. The US government has undertaken on behalf of its country not to invade Cuba. The threat of a thermonuclear war has been averted. Is this really a retreat by us? . . .

Macao is situated at the mouth of the Chu Chiang river, on the coast of China. It is a small territory and not easily spotted on the map. The Portuguese leased it as far back as the middle of the sixteenth century, and in 1887 wrested it completely from China and made it their colony. There is also the British colony of Hongkong there; it lies in the delta of the Hsi Chiang river, literally below the heart of such an important town as Canton. The smell coming from these places is by no means sweeter than that released by colonialism in Goa. But no one will denounce the Chinese People's Republic for leaving intact these fragments of colonialism. *It would be wrong to prod China into any kind of actions which she considers untimely.* If the government of the Chinese People's Republic tolerates Macao and Hongkong, it clearly has good reasons for doing so. Therefore, it would be ridiculous to level against it the accusation that this is a concession to Britain and Portuguese colonialists, that this is appeasement.

But maybe this is a retreat from Marxism-Leninism? Nothing of the kind. It means that the government of the Chinese People's Republic takes into account the realities, the actual possibilities. And this is by no means because the Chinese are less sensitive to colonialism than the Indians, or that they are more tolerant towards Salazar than is India. No; our Chinese friends hate colonialism, just as every revolutionary does. But they clearly proceed from their conditions and act on their own understanding, and display patience. But does that mean that we must condemn them for it, or contend that they have retreated from Marxism-Leninism? No, it does not. That would be foolish.

In consequence of a number of circumstances one sometimes has to live not among fragrant roses but amidst thorns, and sometimes even in close proximity to the colonialists' latrine. But the hour will come and our Chinese friends will find this position intolerable and tell the colonialists in a loud voice: 'Get out!' And we shall welcome such a step. . . .

And what would have happened, had we, during the events over Cuba, failed to display due restraint but heeded the shrill promptings of the ultra-revolutionaries? We would have sunk into the morass of a new world war, a thermo-nuclear war. Of course, our vast country would have held out, but tens upon tens of millions of people would have perished! As to Cuba, as a result of a thermo-nuclear war it probably would have simply ceased to exist. Other densely populated countries, lacking broad expanses, involved in the conflict would also have completely perished. The consequences of atomic radiation would have brought untold suffering also on the survivors and on future generations. . . .

And so it happens that, on the one hand, war is eagerly desired by the aggressive adventurist forces of imperialism, those madmen who have lost the hope that capitalism can hold its own in peaceful competition with socialism, and, on the other hand, attempts are made to push developments in the same direction by people who call themselves Marxist-Leninists but who in fact are dogmatists who do not believe in the possibility of the victory of socialism and Communism under conditions of peaceful coexistence with capitalism. Both the former and the latter want to prod history towards a new war, to decide the issue of the victory of Communism or capitalism by means of war, in a way in which millions upon millions of people would be killed. These people, it would seem, are poles apart in their thinking, and yet their positions coincide, and they hold the same views and act in the same way in this vitally important question.

Comrade Deputies, in examining the current international situation, one cannot overlook the *regrettable events which have occurred in the area of the Indian-Chinese border*. As is known, it was not a week or a month ago that the border conflict began, but as far back as 1959. Recently this conflict has grown more acute and developed into armed clashes, in which thousands have died on both sides.

The Soviet Union's position in relation to the Indian-Chinese border conflict was stated as far back as 1959 in the well-known Tass statement. The statement expressed the hope that the government of the Chinese People's Republic and the government of India would not allow the forces averse to relaxation of international tension to profit from their border incidents, and that the two governments would settle the misunderstanding which had arisen between them with due consideration for mutual interests and in the spirit of the traditional friendship between the peoples of China and India. The Soviet Union expressed great regret at the incident which had arisen. We sincerely hoped that the governments of the two countries would quickly find a way to a peaceful solution of the dispute. To this day we regret that the sides did not avail themselves in time of the possibilities of nipping the incipient conflict in the bud.

It is especially painful to us that the blood of the sons of the fraternal Chinese People's Republic and of our friend, the Republic of India, has been shed. For the first time a situation has arisen in which a border dispute between a socialist country and a country which has started on the road of independent development and follows a policy of non-alighment has led to armed clashes. . . .

There are, however, forces in the world, the international imperialist circles, which rejoice at the aggravation of the Indian-Chinese conflict. They link far-reaching provocative plans with it. They hasten to offer to deliver arms so that Indians and Chinese may kill each other. The imperialist powers are ready to loosen their purse strings and show 'generosity', to provide arms 'free', as a 'gift'. To the imperialists this conflict is a godsend. . . .

Therefore, we regard as reasonable the step taken by the government of the Chinese People's Republic when it announced that it was unilaterally effecting a cease-fire and would begin withdrawing its troops on December 1. We are most happy about this and welcome such actions by our Chinese comrades. It might be said: How can you maintain that this is a reasonable step, when it was taken after so many lives had been lost and so much blood shed? *Would it not have been better if both sides refrained from resorting to arms in general? Of course, it would have been better.* We have said so on many occasions and we repeat it again. But if it was not possible to avert such a course of events, it is better to show courage now and stop the clashes. Is that not wisdom worthy of statesmen?

Of course, there might be some who would say: See, the Chinese People's Republic is now withdrawing its troops in fact to the line at which this conflict broke out. *Would it not have been better not to advance from the positions where these troops were at the time?* Such reasoning is understandable. It shows that people are concerned and regret what has happened.

But, comrades, there are also people who try to put a different interpretation on the decision taken by the government of the Chinese People's Republic. They say: Is it not a retreat? They also pose the following question: Is it not a concession on the part of the Chinese comrades? Of course, such questions are asked and apparently will be dragged out by cavillers to hurt the feelings of one side or the other, to fan hostility between India and China and warm their hands at it. We believe in the widom of the leaders of China and India and hope that they will not be deceived by such provocations and will ensure a reasonable settlement of the conflict.

There are some who are already alleging that China desisted from hostilities apparently because India had begun receiving support from the American and British imperialists who are supplying her with arms. Therefore, such people say, the Chinese People's Republic realised that, if the armed conflict continued to develop, it might turn into a large-scale war, which would result in even greater numbers of victims. Yes, apparently our Chinese friends took the situation into account and this also shows their wisdom and their understanding of the fact that, when a war breaks out between friendly neighbouring peoples, the imperialists always try to profit from it. . . .

It is indisputable that the actions of the government of the Chinese People's Republic will be assessed at their true value by the peace-loving peoples. Indeed, why wage war? Has China ever set itself the aim of invading India? No. We reject such assertions as slanderous and, of course, *we also absolutely disavow the thought that India wanted to start a war with China.* That is precisely why we sincerely welcome the steps taken by the government of People's China and in no way consider that it has made some sort of retreat. No, the government of the Chinese People's Republic has shown wisdom and a correct understanding of the situation and has made efforts to stop the military clash and to normalise the situation. . . .

Comrade Deputies, I would like to dwell in somewhat greater detail on the question of *the mutual relations between our country and the Federal People's Republic of Yugoslavia.* You know that the friendship between the peoples of our countries has its roots in the distant past. In the period of the Second World War the fraternal relations between the peoples of our two countries were sealed by the blood shed in the struggle against the common foe. The peoples of Yugoslavia, under the leadership of their Communist party headed by Comrade Tito, displayed wonders of heroism in the battle against the fascist invaders. They made a big contribution to the cause of routing Hitler's Germany.

Unfortunately, friendly relations between the Soviet Union and Yugoslavia were spoilt soon after the end of the Second World War. I will not speak about the reasons for the deterioration in these relations. As is known, the Yugoslav comrades believe that the responsibility for this lies entirely with Stalin. In his time Stalin accused the Yugoslavs of everything. We have our own definite opinion on this matter. We have already said and we repeat again that the main part of the responsibility for the deterioration in Soviet-Yugoslav relations is undoubtedly borne by Stalin, who allowed gross and absolutely unjustified arbitrary action to be taken with regard to Yugoslavia. However, we would not be quite sincere if we did not say that the Yugoslav comrades also must bear their share of the responsibility for what happened to relations between our countries and our parties in that period.

That was the situation in the past. But we are Communists and must look ahead and think of the future of our peoples. At present our relations with Yugoslavia are good. Comrade Tito and Comrades Rankovic, Veselinov and others accompanying him are now on holiday in our country at our invitation – and, indeed, are present here. We have met them as friends and have already had several useful talks with them which have produced a great deal for better mutual understanding. We see that the Yugoslav leaders, like ourselves, are applying efforts to eliminate disagreements and are striving for an improvement of relations with our country. I must say that it has been confirmed once again that on many international problems, on questions of state and economic relations, we have a common understanding and common views. . . .

As to our attitude on the question of developing relations with the League of Communists of Yugoslavia, it follows completely from the course that was determined by the Twentieth and Twenty-second Congresses of the CPSU. This course aims at strengthening the unity between the CPSU and all fraternal parties and consolidating all forces of the anti-imperialist front.

In the past the Yugoslavs abused us and we replied in kind. At present we and the Yugoslav Communists are advancing on the road of improving our relations. It cannot be said that all the troubles and difficulties which existed in the relations between the CPSU and the League of Communists of Yugoslavia have been eliminated. There were and still are serious differences on a number of ideological questions reflected in the Programme of the League of Communists of Yugoslavia, as was noted in the Declaration of the Conference of fraternal parties. We, on our part, are ready to do everything to overcome these differences.

This does not depend only on us, but also on the attitude of the League of Communists of Yugoslavia and its leadership. . . .

It would be wrong to work out a set pattern and to adhere to it in the relations with other socialist countries. It would be a mistake to brand as renegades all who do not conform with the pattern. Should we really press for the complete exclusion of any Communist party from our united movement? How can we ignore the fact that the people of such a country are building socialism? Or are we to shut our eyes to the very fact of the existence of such a people and fight against it? To act like this would be to adopt the bestial laws of the capitalist world and apply them to the mutual relations between Communist parties and socialist countries. Yet it is precisely such a bestial morality that the Albanian sectarians and splitters want us to adopt in relations with Yugoslavia. They are literally ready to tear the Yugoslav Communists to pieces for their mistakes, although they themselves are retreating much further from Marxism-Leninism than those whom they accuse. Such a morality is alien to us as Communists. . . .

It must be said that steps taken recently by the Yugoslav Communists, and their leaders, both in internal and in foreign policy, *have eliminated many things which we considered erroneous and harmful to the cause of building socialism in Yugoslavia.* This has been reflected in a number of decisions of the League of Communists of Yugoslavia and in speeches by Comrades Tito, Rankovic and other Yugoslav leaders. If, so far, we still have not reached complete understanding on certain questions, this does not mean at all that in building our relations we must start from the remnants of differences, that we must close our eyes to the steps taken by the Communists of Yugoslavia towards rapprochement and unity with the whole international Communist movement. This would be a policy aimed not at unification but at disunity. Furthermore, it would be erroneous to extend the differences which still exist to the sphere of relations between our states. On the contrary, the strengthening and development of economic ties, of relations along state and public lines between our countries, pave the way for rapprochement on ideological questions also.

The Albanian sectarians and dogmatists are striving to prevent an improvement in the socialist countries' relations with Yugoslavia. They have been squealing particularly loudly now, when Comrades Tito, Rankovic, Veselinov and other Yugoslav leaders have come to the USSR. It is obviously not to the liking of the Albanian splitters that we should welcome the Yugoslav comrades in a fraternal manner.

We are told that it is reprehensible to have good relations with Yugoslavia along government lines in the field of economics until certain ideological differences with the League of Communists of Yugoslavia are fully overcome. And this is said by people who call themselves Marxist-Leninists. But this is stupid, for even imperialists are trying to overcome and to iron out their differences in order to survive in the struggle against the advancing forces of the Communist, workers, and national liberation movement. They are feverishly strengthening and expanding the association of the Common Market countries, despite differences between the member-countries. But we, in our camp, have people who want to split our forces. This is not our policy, nor is it a Marxist-Leninist policy.

Some people contend that Yugoslavia is not a socialist country. In that case, allow me to ask, what kind of a country is it? . . .

It is known that in Yugoslavia there have for a long time been no landlords and capitalists, no private capital, no private enterprises or private estates, and no private banks. We see also that the Yugoslav Communists and their leaders are directing their efforts to the development of the economy, the consolidation of the conquests of socialism. Therefore, if one is to proceed from objective laws, from the teaching of Marxism-Leninism, *it is impossible to deny that Yugoslavia is a socialist country.* . . .

Now the Albanian leaders are clinging precisely to what was the most negative in Stalin's activity, that characterised his retreat from Marxism-Leninism. They are attracted most of all by the methods of repression and crude administrative pressure used by Stalin which are alien to the very spirit of a socialist state. You see, they want to become the pillars of the international Communist movement, the infallible guardians of Marxism-Leninism. But these attempts are like those of the proverbial frog. You remember how in the well-known fable the frog wanted to become as big as an ox. Everybody knows the result: the frog burst and nothing remained but a damp spot. . . .

The contemporary left-wing opportunists and sectarians, the most outspoken mouthpieces of whom are the Albanian leaders, disguise their struggle against the Leninist policy of peace and peaceful coexistence by shrill pseudo-revolutionary phrases. As has already been said, they have slid down to a Trotskyite position. It is not difficult to see that such a policy undermines the unity of forces opposing imperialism and plays into the hands of the most aggressive imperialist circles of the Western Powers, encouraging their anti-Communist designs.

Such a leftist dogmatic policy has been properly appraised at the Congresses of the Communist and Workers' parties of Bulgaria, Hungary, Czechoslovakia and Italy. This provocative policy was exposed and sharply denounced in the speeches of representatives of fraternal parties who addressed these Congresses. If one scratches these loud-mouthed leftist dogmatists, one can easily discover that behind their brave façade lies nothing but fear of imperialism and lack of faith in the possibility of beating the capitalist system in peaceful economic competition. . . .

December 15

The *People's Daily* published an editorial article entitled 'Workers of All Countries Unite, Oppose Our Common Enemy', in which the Chinese replied to their critics on the main issues and repeated their proposal for a meeting. Extracts:

. . . It is distressing to find an adverse current appearing in the ranks of the international Communist movement, a current which is opposed to Marxism-Leninism opposed to the Communist Party of China and other Marxist-Leninist parties, and which is disrupting the unity of the international Communist movement.

In the past month or so, the Eighth Congress of the Bulgarian Communist Party, the Eighth Congress of the Hungarian Socialist Workers' Party, the Tenth Congress of the Italian Communist Party, and the Twelfth Congress of the Czechoslovak Communist Party were held in Europe one after another. Unfortunately, the rostrums of these party congresses were used as platforms for attacking fraternal parties. This adverse current, which is disrupting unity and creating splits, reached a new high at the Italian and Czechoslovak Communist Party Congresses. Comrades of certain fraternal parties not only continued their attacks on the Albanian Party of Labour, but *also openly attacked the Communist Party of China by name*, and they even censured the Korean Workers' Party for disagreeing with the attacks on the Chinese Communist Party. This is an utterly outrageous violation of the 1957 Moscow Declaration and the 1960 Moscow Statement, which had been unanimously adopted by the Communist and Workers' parties of all countries. It is an event of the utmost gravity in the international Communist movement. . . .

The erroneous practice of using the congress of one party to launch an attack on another fraternal party first emerged a year ago at the Twenty-second Congress of the Communist Party of the Soviet Union. The Chinese Communist Party resolutely opposed this erroneous practice at that time. At that congress and subsequently too, the Chinese Communist Party made many earnest appeals to the fraternal parties having disagreements and differences to reunite on the basis of Marxism-Leninism and on the basis of respect for each other's independence and equality, and made the special point that *the party which launched the first attack ought to take the initiative*. However, it is to be regretted that this sincere effort on our part has not succeeded in preventing a continued deterioration in the situation. Instead of giving thought to changing this erroneous practice, the leaders of certain fraternal parties have intensified it and gone further along the road towards a split, and as a result this erroneous practice recently occurred at four successive congresses of fraternal parties in Europe.

Here we wish to say something about what happened at the *Congress of the Czechoslovak Communist Party*. At that congress, some comrades of the Czechoslovak Party and comrades from certain other fraternal parties wantonly vilified and attacked the Communist Party of China for its 'adventurism', 'sectarianism', 'splittism', 'nationalism' and 'dogmatism'. The Chinese Communist Party delegation in its statement resolutely opposed this practice that creates splits. . . .

However, the attitude of the Chinese Communist Party, an attitude treasuring unity, has not yet succeeded in causing a change of heart in those persons who are persisting in this erroneous practice. . . . In these circumstances, we have no alternative but to make the necessary reply.

Some comrades of the Czechoslovak Communist Party and comrades from certain fraternal parties attacked the Chinese Communist Party for having committed what they called errors of 'adventurism'. They charged that on the Cuban question China had opposed a 'sensible compromise' and wanted the whole world 'plunged into a thermonuclear war'. Are matters really as they charged?

On the question of *how to deal with imperialism and all reactionaries, the Chinese*

Communist Party has always maintained that one should despise them strategically but take full account of them tactically. That is to say, in the final analysis, strategically, with regard to the long term and to the whole, imperialism and all reactionaries are sure to fail, and the masses of the people are sure to triumph. Without this kind of understanding, it would not be possible to encourage the masses of the people to wage resolute revolutionary struggles against imperialism and the reactionaries with full confidence; nor would it be possible to lead the revolution to victory. On the other hand, tactically, on each immediate, specific problem, it is necessary to deal seriously with imperialism and the reactionaries, be prudent and carefully study and perfect the art of struggle. Without such understanding, it is impossible to wage successful revolutionary struggles, there is the danger of incurring setbacks and defeats and, again, it is impossible to lead the revolution to victory. This viewpoint of despising the enemy strategically and taking full account of him tactically, which the Chinese Communist Party has adhered to throughout its history, is precisely our oft-stated viewpoint that the imperialists and all reactionaries are paper tigers; it is entirely Marxist-Leninist. We are opposed both to capitulationism and to adventurism. Everyone who wants to make a revolution and win victory must adopt this attitude, and no other, when dealing with the enemy. The reason is that if one does not dare despise the enemy strategically, one will inevitably commit the error of capitulationism. And if one is heedless, and reckless tactically in any specific struggle, one will inevitably commit the error of adventurism. If one dares not despise the enemy strategically and, at the same time, one is heedless and reckless tactically, then one will commit both the error of capitulationism in strategy and the error of adventurism in tactics.

As far as the question of *how to cope with nuclear weapons is concerned*, we Chinese Communists have always stood for a complete ban on nuclear weapons, which are enormously destructive, and have always opposed the imperialists' criminal policy of nuclear war. We have always held that in a situation in which the socialist camp enjoys great superiority, it is possible to reach an agreement on banning nuclear weapons through negotiations and through the constant exposures of and struggle against US imperialism. But Marxist-Leninist and revolutionary people have never been paralysed with fear by the nuclear weapons in the imperialists' hands and so abandoned their struggle against imperialism and its lackeys. *We Marxist-Leninists do not believe either in the theory that weapons decide everything, nor do we believe in the theory that nuclear weapons decide everything.* We have never believed that nuclear weapons can determine man's fate. We are convinced that it is the masses of the people who are the decisive force in history. It is they alone who can decide the course of history. We are firmly opposed to the imperialist policy of nuclear blackmail. We also hold that there is no need whatsoever for socialist countries to use nuclear weapons as counter for gambling or as means of intimidation. To do so is really committing the error of adventurism. If one blindly worships nuclear weapons, does not recognise or trust in the strength of the masses of people, and so becomes scared out of one's wits when confronted by the imperialists' nuclear blackmail, then one may jump from one extreme to the other and commit the error of capitula-tionism. We maintain that in their struggle against US imperialism the heroic

Cuban people have committed neither the error of capitulationism nor the error of adventurism. . . .

If China's support for the Cuban people's just struggle against US aggressors is 'adventurism', we would like to ask: Does this mean that the only way for the Chinese people not to be called 'adventurist' is to abstain from doing everything in their power to support Cuba in its struggle against US imperialist aggression? Does this mean that the only way to avoid being called adventurist and capitulationist would have been to force Cuba to surrender its sovereignty and independence and to give up its five just demands? The whole world has seen that *we neither requested the transport of nuclear weapons to Cuba nor obstructed the withdrawal of 'offensive weapons' from that country*. Therefore, as far as we are concerned, there can be absolutely no question of 'adventurism', still less of 'plunging [the whole world] into thermo-nuclear war'.

Some people have censured *China's correct position on the Sino-Indian boundary question* as if China had precipitated a disaster. But what are the facts? . . . In dealing with the vain attempts of the Indian reactionary group to alter the situation on the Sino-Indian frontier by force and in dealing with their ever-increasing encroachment on China's border territories, the Chinese people have for years exercised forbearance, striving time and time again to find a fair and reasonable solution through peaceful negotiation.

Confronted with the massive attacks of the Indian troops, China launched a counter-attack in self-defence; this was a minimum, legitimate measure that any other sovereign state would have taken. Having repulsed the attacks of the Indian forces, China immediately proposed the cessation of fighting, disengagement and the reopening of negotiations, and then, on her own initiative, ceased fire and withdrew her troops. . . .

Those who accuse China of having pushed the Nehru government to the West are exactly reversing cause and effect. Throughout the Sino-Indian boundary dispute, these people have failed to distinguish right from wrong, have pretended to be 'neutral', and have called China 'brother' in words, while actually regarding the Indian reactionary group as their kinsmen. Should not these people examine their conscience and ask themselves what has become of their Marxism-Leninism and what has become of their proletarian internationalism? . . .

The principles for guiding the relations among fraternal parties and countries set forth in the Moscow Declaration and the Moscow Statement did not grant to any party, large or small, any right whatsoever to launch an attack at its own congress on another fraternal party. If such an erroneous practice is accepted, then one party can attack another party – this party today and that party tomorrow. *If this continues, what will become of the unity of the international Communist movement?*

The principles guiding the relations among fraternal parties and countries set forth in the Moscow Declaration and the Moscow Statement are the very embodiment of the principles of proletarian internationalism concerning relations among fraternal parties and fraternal countries. If these guiding principles are violated, one will inevitably fall into the quagmire of great-nation chauvinism or other forms of bourgeois nationalism. But have those very people who have accused the Chinese Communist Party of committing the error of 'nationalism' ever given a thought to the question of the position in which they have been placing themselves in their relations with fraternal parties and countries? It is obviously they who have violated the principles guiding relations among fraternal parties and countries, who have launched attacks on another fraternal party and fraternal country and have followed the erroneous practices of nationalism and great-nation chauvinism. Yet they insist that everybody else should do as they do, and those who do not listen and follow the conductor's baton are accused of 'nationalism'. Can it be that this conforms with the principles of proletarian internationalism? Is not such an erroneous practice exactly what splittism and sectarianism are? Is not this erroneous practice the worst manifestation of nationalism and great-nation chauvinism? . . .

For a Communist the minimum requirement is that he should make a clear distinction between the enemy and ourselves, that he should be ruthless towards the enemy and kind to his own comrades. But there are people who just turn this upside-down. For imperialism it is all 'accommodation' and 'mutual concessions', for the fraternal parties and fraternal countries it is only implacable hostility. These people are able to adopt an attitude of 'sensible compromise' and 'moderation' towards the sabre-rattling enemy, but are unwilling to adopt a conciliatory attitude towards fraternal parties and fraternal countries. To be so 'kind' to the enemy and so 'ruthless' towards fraternal parties and countries is certainly not the stand a Marxist-Leninist should take. . . .

These people think that if they just put up the signboard of 'anti-dogmatism' and bellow about what they call 'creativeness', they can distort Marxism-Leninism and tamper with the Moscow Declaration and the Moscow Statement as they like.

This is absolutely impermissible. We would like to question these people: Are these two historic documents of the international Communist movement, unanimously adopted and signed by all the Communist and Workers' parties, still valid? Do they still have to be observed?

Some people say: 'We are the majority and you are the minority. Therefore we are creative Marxist-Leninists and you are dogmatists; we are right and you are wrong.' But anyone with a little common sense knows that the question of who is right and who is wrong, and who represents the truth, *cannot be determined by the majority or minority at a given moment,* cannot turn falsehood into truth; nor can the minority at a given moment make truth turn into falsehood. History abounds with instances in which, at certain times and on certain occasions, truth was not on the side of the majority, but on the side of the minority.

Their 'majority' is only a fictitious, superficial phenomenon, and in essence they are in the minority, while the 'minority' they are attacking is, in essence, the majority. . . .

The erroneous practice of creating splits which has appeared in the international Communist movement can be beneficial only to the imperialists and the reactionaries. Don't you see that the imperialists, the reactionaries of all countries and the modern revisionists of Yugoslavia are applauding, gloating over misfortunes and looking forward to a split in the international Communist movement?

Communists of all countries share the same great ideal and the same noble cause and face a common enemy; we have a thousand and one reasons to unite, but not a single reason to create splits. Those comrades who are creating splits should come to their senses.

December (late)

A confidential memorandum, not published in the Communist press, was sent by the Chinese Communist Party to the eleven ruling parties of the 'socialist camp'. The following is a description of the letter:

The memorandum, beginning with comradely greetings to the whole socialist camp, is divided into seven parts. The first part accuses the Soviet government of not assisting the Chinese Communists in the pre-war period, but of supporting Chiang-Kai-shek even after he broke away from the united front with the Communists. Several examples of this are given, the chief being the Soviet refusal in 1936 to grant asylum to a number of Chinese Communists who were subsequently executed. Mention is also made of several notes requesting military aid in 1948 and 1949 which were rejected on the grounds that the USSR was unable to help so soon after the end of the war. It is admitted that a certain amount of aid was given, but this was not decisive for victory. The Chinese people liberated themselves on their own.

The second part deals with relations between China and countries of the 'socialist camp' in the period 1949–1956. The tremendous help of the USSR and other socialist countries in the building of 'the largest socialist country' is recognised. At the same time, however, the accusation is made that on orders from certain people in Moscow the full development of China's potential was impeded because certain misguided people in Moscow and elsewhere were haunted by the numerical superiority of the Chinese people. Stalin did not know about these deviations; he was the genuine friend of the Chinese people.

The accusation is made that, though some aid was given to China's industry, the inventions of the last two decades were kept secret and the Chinese were excluded from obtaining military information, though they themselves always told their socialist allies of any military knowledge they gained, for instance from Japan.

After Stalin's death a deliberate campaign started against the Chinese, the memorandum says.

It is not China's business to enquire into the accusations made against Stalin, but the point is made that many of those who are denigrating him held high office during his lifetime.

Suddenly China is being accused of wanting to dominate other Communist parties and of regarding itself as the only leading Communist party or the only one respecting Marxism-Leninism. While this accusation is false it is true that the 700 million Chinese liberated themselves not only from their own capitalists but also from the British and American imperialists and that, without wanting to dominate anybody, China has one of the leading positions in the socialist bloc. Consequently China has a perfect right to express its opinions on certain international agreements between the socialist and capitalist countries and to voice its disapproval if these agreements harm Chinese interests. It was not China who made these differences public for the benefit of capitalist propaganda.

The third part accuses all socialist countries who are members of the United Nations of failing to do their best to secure for China her rightful place in UNO.

Part four concerns Yugoslavia. The Yugoslav CP is described in strong words, as not a Communist but a Trotsykite party with right-wing leanings. The country is completely in the hands of the Anglo-American capitalists. Figures are given of direct and indirect aid received by Yugoslavia. Yugoslavia is a classic example of the Anglo-American technique of driving a wedge in the socialist camp, the memorandum says.

Part five deals with Albania. The USSR is accused of being ready to let the country fall into the hands of the capitalists and attempting to control Albania by stopping deliveries and by withdrawing technicians and specialists. China, it is asserted, will continue to render Albanian aid of every kind to enable her to develop in a socialist way. Is it true that the USSR has given Tito a free hand in Albania?

Part six concerns India. Twenty-one pages are devoted to arguing that there was no aggression against India. The Chinese government was forced to start military operations because demands for the return of purely Chinese territory proved unsuccessful. China is prepared to negotiate but only on the basis of the return of Chinese territory. A strong attack is made on the USSR because, together with the US and UK, it is supporting India with guns and aeroplanes. This puts the USSR on the side of the imperialists. India is neither a neutral nor a pseudo-socialist country. The Indian government takes orders from Washington and London. Soviet aid to India is equivalent to direct military aid to India against China. China will shortly suggest to India negotiations on summit level and will not object to the presence of representatives of neutral Asian countries.

Part seven accuses the USSR of cowardice and of falling for American bluff. The Soviet retreat undermined the socialist system in Cuba and thereby also South America's confidence in the socialist countries.

The USSR led other European socialist countries in ordering the cessation of supplies to China and thereby endangered the fulfilment of China's economic plan. The false slogan of 'peaceful coexistence' leads to the weakening of the USSR and facilitates imperialist attacks on the world socialist system.

The USSR refuses to give China atomic weapons although it well knows that the Germans will get them from the US.

The memorandum ends with a proposal for convening a conference of all socialist countries, including Albania and Yugoslavia.

China is the only country that unflinchingly and undeviatingly follows the flag of Marx and Lenin.

There can be no reconciliation with capitalism or imperialism, and China if need be will carry on the struggle single-handed since only an uncompromising attitude of the Communists towards the capitalists will achieve the victory of socialism.

December 31

A *People's Daily* editorial entitled 'The Differences Between Comrade Togliatti and Us' dealt at length with the Chinese view on the main 'ideological' issues. Extracts:

In accordance with its consistent stand of strengthening friendship with fraternal parties, the Communist Party of China sent its representative to attend the *Tenth Congress of the Communist Party of Italy*, which was held in early December, at the latter's invitation.

At this congress, to our regret and against our hopes, Comrade Togliatti and certain other leaders of the CPI rudely attacked the Communist Party of China and other fraternal parties on a series of important questions of principle.

In such circumstances, we cannot remain silent but must publicly answer the attacks on us by Comrade Togliatti and other comrades. . . . We wish to say frankly that on a number of fundamental questions of Marxism-Leninism there exist differences of principle between Comrade Togliatti and certain other CPI leaders on the one hand and ourselves on the other. . . .

Although Comrade Togliatti and certain others have, as usual, covered up their real views by using obscure, ambiguous and scarcely intelligible language, the essence of their views becomes clear once this flimsy veil is removed. . . .

In the final analysis, the stand taken by Togliatti and certain other CPI leaders boils down to this – *the people of the capitalist countries should not make revolutions, the oppressed nations should not wage struggles to win liberation, and the people of the world should not fight against imperialism.* Actually, all this exactly suits the needs of imperialists and the reactionaries.

Comrade Togliatti and certain other comrades differ with us, first of all, on *the question of war and peace.* In his general report to the Tenth Congress of the Communist Party of Italy, Togliatti declared: 'This problem was widely discussed at the Conference of the Communist and Workers' parties held in Moscow in the autumn of 1960. The Chinese comrades put forward some views, which were rejected by the meeting.'

This accusation levelled against the Communist Party of China by Comrade Togliatti and certain other comrades is completely groundless and trumped up. . . .

Since Togliatti and certain other comrades know perfectly well where the Communist Party of China stands on the problem of war and peace, why do they keep on distorting and attacking this stand? *What are the real differences between them and us?*

They are manifested mainly on the following three questions:

Firstly, *the Communist Party of China holds that the source of modern war is imperialism.* The chief force for aggression and war is US imperialism, the most vicious enemy of all the peoples of the world. . . . In order to defend world peace, it is necessary to expose the imperialist policies of aggression and war unceasingly and thoroughly, so as to make the people of the world to maintain a high degree of vigilance. The fact that the forces of socialism, of national liberation, of people's revolution and of world peace have surpassed the forces of imperialism and war has not changed the aggressive nature of imperialism and cannot possibly change it. The imperialist bloc headed by the United States is engaged in frenzied arms expansion and war preparations and is menacing world peace. . . .

It will be recalled that three years ago, following the 'Camp David talks', some persons in the international Communist movement talked a great deal about Eisenhower's sincere desire for peace, saying that this ring-leader of US imperialism was just as concerned about peace as we were . . . .

Now we again hear some people saying that Kennedy is even more concerned about world peace than Eisenhower was and that Kennedy showed his concern for the maintenance of peace during the Caribbean crisis.

One would like to ask: Is this way of embellishing US imperialism the correct policy for defending world peace? And are not those people who try time and again to prettify imperialism deliberately deceiving the people of the world? . . .

Secondly, the Communist Party of China holds that world peace can only be securely safeguarded in the resolute struggle against imperialism headed by the United States, by constantly strengthening the socialist camp, by constantly strengthening the national and democratic movements in Asia, Africa and Latin America, and by constantly strengthening the people's revolutionary struggles in various countries and the movement to defend world peace. In order to achieve world peace it is necessary to rely mainly on the strength of the masses of the people of the world and on their struggles. In the course of the struggle to defend world peace, it is necessary to enter into negotiations on one issue or another with the governments of the imperialist countries, including the government of the United States, for the purpose of easing international tension, reaching some kind of compromise and arriving at certain agreements, subject to the principle that such compromises and agreements must not damage the fundamental interests of the people. However, world peace can never be achieved by negotiations alone, and in no circumstances must we pin our hopes on imperialism and divorce ourselves from the struggles of the masses.

Thirdly, the Communist Party of China holds that the struggle for the defence of world peace supports, is supported by, and indeed is inseparable from, the national-liberation movements and the peoples' revolutionary struggles in various countries. . . .

On the question of *nuclear weapons and nuclear war*, the first difference between us and those who attack the Communist Party of China is whether or not the fundamental Marxist-Leninist principles on war and peace have become 'out of date' since the emergence of nuclear weapons.

Togliatti and certain others believe that the emergence of nuclear weapons 'has changed the nature of war' and that 'one should add other considerations to the definition of the just character of a war'. Actually, they hold that war is no longer the continuation of politics, and that there is no longer any distinction between just and unjust wars. Thus they completely deny the fundamental Marxist-Leninist principles on war and peace. We hold that *the emergence of nuclear weapons has not changed and cannot change the fundamental Marxist-Leninist principles with regard to war and peace.*

On the question of nuclear weapons and nuclear war, the second difference between us and those who attack the Communist Party of China is whether one should view the future of mankind with pessimism or with revolutionary optimism.

Togliatti and certain others talk volubly about 'the suicide of mankind' and the 'total destruction' of mankind. They believe that 'it is idle even to discuss what might be the outlook for such remnants of the human race with regard to the social order'. *We are firmly opposed to such pessimistic and despairing tunes.* We believe that it is possible to attain a complete ban on nuclear weapons in the following circumstances: the socialist camp has a great nuclear superiority, the peoples' struggles in various countries against nuclear weapons and nuclear war become broader and deeper; having further forfeited their nuclear superiority, the imperialists are compelled to realise that their policy of nuclear blackmail is no longer effective and that their launching of a nuclear war would only accelerate their own extinction.

If, after we have done everything possible to prevent a nuclear war, imperialism should nevertheless unleash nuclear war, without regard to any of the consequences, it would only result in the extinction of imperialism and definitely not in the extinction of mankind. The Moscow Statement points out that 'should the imperialist maniacs start war, the peoples will sweep capitalism out of existence and bury it'. All Marxist-Leninists firmly believe that the course of history necessarily leads to the destruction of nuclear weapons by mankind, and will definitely not lead to the destruction of mankind by nuclear weapons. . . .

On the question of nuclear weapons and nuclear war, the third difference between us and those who attack the Communist Party of China concerns the policy to be adopted in order successfully to reach the goal of *outlawing nuclear weapons, and preventing a nuclear war*.

Togliatti and certain others zealously advertise the dreadful nature of nuclear weapons and blatantly declare that 'it is justified' to 'shudder' with fear in the face of the nuclear blackmail when US imperialism parades it. Togliatti has also said that 'war must be avoided at any cost'. According to what he and certain others say, should not the only way of dealing with the US imperialist policy of nuclear threats and blackmail be unconditional surrender and the complete abandonment of all revolutionary ideals and all revolutionary principles? Can this be the kind of stand a Communist should take? Can a nuclear war really be prevented in this way?

Comrade Mao Tse-tung's analysis of imperialism and all reactionaries is completely in accord with Lenin's analysis. In 1919 Lenin compared the 'allpowerful' Anglo-French imperialism to a 'colossus with feet of clay'.

Isn't the reasoning of Lenin in his description of the 'colossus with feet of clay' the same as that of Comrade Mao Tse-tung in his reference to the 'paper tiger'? We ask, what is wrong with Lenin's proposition? Is this proposition of Lenin's 'outmoded'? . . .

History has proved that even when imperialism is armed with nuclear weapons it cannot frighten into submission a revolutionary people who dare to fight. The victory of the Chinese revolution and the great victories of the peoples of Korea, Vietnam, Cuba, Algeria and other countries in their revolutionary struggles, were all won at a time when US imperialism possessed nuclear weapons. Imperialism has always been armed to the teeth and has always been out for the blood of the people. No matter what kind of teeth imperialism may have, whether guns, tanks, rocket teeth, nuclear teeth or any other kind of teeth that modern science and technology may provide, its rotten, decadent and paper-tiger nature cannot change. In the final analysis, neither nuclear teeth nor any other kind of teeth can save imperialism from its fate of inevitable extinction. In the end the nuclear teeth of imperialism, and whatever other teeth it may have, will be consigned by the people of the world to the museum of history, together with imperialism itself. . . .

But Comrade Togliatti and those who attack China hold that through 'peaceful coexistence' it is possible to 'renovate the structure of the whole world' and to establish 'a new world order'.

In taking this stand, Comrade Togliatti and other comrades have completely revised Lenin's principles for peaceful coexistence and discarded the Marxist-Leninist doctrine of class struggle; in reality they are substituting class collaboration for class struggles on a world scale, advocating a fusion of the socialist and capitalist systems.

Even more absurd is the allegation that 'a world without war' can be achieved through peaceful coexistence. In the present situation, it is possible to prevent imperialism from launching a new world war if all the peace-loving forces of the world unite into a broad international anti-imperialist united front and fight together. *But it is one thing to prevent a world war and another to eliminate all wars.* . . .

The extent to which Comrade Togliatti and certain other comrades have departed from Marxism-Leninism and from the Moscow Declaration and the Moscow Statement, is more clearly revealed by their recent ardent flirtation with the Yugoslav revisionist group.

A representative of the Tito group, who are renegades from Marxism-Leninism, was invited to the recent Congress of the Italian Communist Party and was given a platform from which to denounce China. At the same congress, Comrade Togliatti and certain other comrades publicly defended the Tito group and lavishly praised them for 'the value of what they have done and are doing'.

We wish to ask Comrade Togliatti and certain other comrades: Do you still recognise the Moscow Statement as binding on you? The 1960 Moscow Statement states unequivocally:

'The Communist parties have unanimously condemned the Yugoslav variety of international opportunism, a variety of modern revisionist 'theories' in concentrated form. After betraying Marxism-Leninism, which they termed obsolete, the leaders of the League of Communists of Yugoslavia opposed their anti-Leninist revisionist programme to the Declaration of 1957; they set the League of Communists of Yugoslavia against the international Communist movement as a whole . . .'

Can it be that this condemnation of the Tito group is a mistake? Is the resolution which was unanimously adopted by the Communist parties of all countries to be thrown overboard at the whim or will of any individual or individuals?

After all, facts are facts and renegades to Communism remain renegades to Communism. The judgement arrived at in the Moscow Statement cannot be overturned by anyone, whoever he may be.

Far from giving up their thoroughly revisionist programme, the Titoists have stuck to it in the draft Yugoslav Constitution which they published not long ago.

With the development of the Tito group's revisionist line and their increasing dependence upon US imperialism, *Yugoslavia has long ceased to be a socialist country*, and the gradual restoration of capitalism in Yugoslavia began long ago. . . .

In the final analysis our differences on a whole series of problems with Comrade Togliatti and certain other comrades who hold similar views involve the fundamental question of *whether the basic principles of Marxism-Leninism are outmoded, and whether the Moscow Declaration and the Moscow Statement are out of date....*

On several occasions, we have suggested the holding of a representative conference of the Communist and Workers' parties of all countries to settle the current differences in the international Communist movement. We hold that Communists of all countries should take to heart the common interests of the struggle against the enemy and the cause of proletarian revolution, should abide by the principles guiding relations among fraternal parties as set forth in the Moscow Declaration and the Moscow Statement, and should eliminate their differences and strengthen their unity on the basis of Marxism-Leninism and proletarian internationalism. This is the hope of the working class and of people throughout the world.

1963

January 5

The theoretical journal of the Chinese CP, *Red Flag*, published a long article on 'Leninism and Modern Revisionism', expounding the Chinese view on all aspects of revisionism. Extracts:

. . . Like the revisionism-opportunism of the Second International, modern revisionism-opportunism is trying hard to cover up the contradictions of capitalism and imperialism and to deny that imperialism is moribund, decaying capitalism whose days are numbered. It has gone so far as to describe modern imperialism as 'peaceful' and 'democratic supra-imperialism'. *But they never have a single word to say about the need, in the transition from capitalism to socialism, to make a revolution that will smash the bourgeois state machine and to replace bourgeois dictatorship with proletarian dictatorship . . . .*

For without such a revolution, all talk about socialist transformation will be meaningless, and state-monopoly capitalism will remain capitalism and nothing else. . . . Herein lies a fundamental difference in the appraisal of our epoch. When Marxist-Leninists say that 'the main content of our epoch is the transition from capitalism to socialism which was begun by the Great October Socialist Revolution in Russia',* they base themselves on the viewpoint of proletarian revolution and proletarian dictatorship, and on the fundamental experience of the Great October Socialist Revolution. But the modern revisionists, shunning this viewpoint like the plague, distort the experience of the October Revolution and avoid referring to the road of the October Revolution as the common road leading to the emancipation of mankind. As a matter of fact, they regard our epoch as one of 'capitalism growing into socialism peacefully'.

On the question of the fight for world peace and peaceful coexistence, too, the modern revisionists have vulgarised Leninism in the extreme and have completely adulterated it. . . .

The attempt of the modern revisionists to restrict, weaken and even negate the revolutionary struggles of the oppressed people and oppressed nations by hypo-

* Declaration of the Meeting of Representatives of the Communist and Workers' parties of the Socialist Countries, held in Moscow, November 14–16, 1957.

critical appeals for 'peace' and 'peaceful coexistence' fits in entirely with the wishes of the imperialists and the reactionaries of various countries and is most damaging to the struggle for peace and for peaceful coexistence between countries with different social systems. . . .

Moreover, the modern revisionists give voice to pure inventions, such as that the revolutionary Marxist-Leninists, whom they call 'dogmatists', 'reject' certain necessary compromises. We would like to tell these modern revisionists that no serious-minded Marxist-Leninist rejects all compromises indiscriminately. In the course of our protracted revolutionary struggle, we Chinese Communists have reached compromises on many occasions with our enemies, internal and external. For example, we came to a compromise with the reactionary Chiang Kai-shek clique. We came to a compromise, too, with the US imperialists, in the struggle to aid Korea and resist US aggression. For Marxist-Leninists, the question is what kind of a compromise to arrive at, the nature of the compromise, and how to bring about a compromise. . . .

In April 1946, Comrade Mao Tse-tung wrote in his article 'Some Points in Appraisal of the Present International Situation' that it was possible for the socialist countries to reach agreement with the imperialist countries through peaceful negotiation and make necessary compromise on some issues, including certain important ones. Comrade Mao Tse-tung holds that 'such compromise . . . can be the outcome only of resolute, effective struggles by all the democratic forces of the world against the reactionary forces of the United States, Britain and France'. He then adds: 'Such compromise does not require the people in the countries of the capitalist world to follow suit and make compromises at home. The people in those countries will continue to wage different struggles in accordance with their different conditions.'* This analysis advanced by Comrade Mao Tse-tung is scientific; it is a Marxist and Leninist analysis. . . . In the eyes of the modern revisionists, any revolution and any action that supports revolution runs counter to the 'logic of survival', now that nuclear weapons and similar military techniques exist. In fact, what they call the 'logic of survival' is the logic of slaves, a logic that would paralyse the revolutionary will of the people of all countries, bind them up hand and foot and make them the submissive slaves of imperialism and of the reactionaries of various countries. The Marxist-Leninists are firmly against this slave logic and maintain that the people should emancipate themselves and build a happy, new life as their own masters. . . . *The modern revisionists believe that, under the present historical conditions, it would be good enough just to muddle along.* So what point is there in differentiating classes, differentiating the proletariat from the bourgeoisie, imperialism from the oppressed nations, capitalism from socialism, just wars from unjust wars, and revolution from counter-revolution? To them, all these differentiations have lost their significance for the present 'epoch' and are 'dogmatist'. In short, *they have actually thrown to the winds all the teachings of Marxism, all the teachings of Leninism.* At the same time, they insist that whoever does not speak and act in response to their baton is 'violating' Marxism-Leninism, 'denying' the creativeness of Marxism-Leninism, 'attacking' the policy of peaceful coexistence, and is a 'pseudo-

* Mao Tse-tung: *Selected Works*, Foreign Languages Press, Peking, 1961. Vol. IV, p. 87.

revolutionary', a 'left adventurist', a 'dogmatist', a 'sectarian', a 'nationalist' and so on and so forth. . . .

Revisionism is an opium to anaesthetise the people; it is a beguiling music for the consolation of slaves. As a political grouping, revisionism constitutes a detachment of the bourgeoisie within the working-class movement, an important social prop for the bourgeoisie and for imperialism. As a trend of thought, revisionism will never fail to appear in varying guises at different times so long as capitalism and imperialism exist in the world. In fact, shortly after Lenin's death a serious struggle between Marxist-Leninists and anti-Marxist-Leninists arose in the international Communist movement. That was the struggle between, on the one hand, the Leninists headed by Stalin and, on the other hand, Trotsky, Bukharin and other 'left' adventurists and right opportunists. . . . Today the dark clouds of revisionism hang over the international working-class movement. *The modern revisionists are openly engaged in splitting activities.* The emergence of modern revisionism is, of course, a bad thing. But as its emergence was inevitable and as its existence is an objective reality, its public appearance enables people to see, discern and understand the harm it does. Thus the bad thing will be turned to good account. . . .

January 7

Pravda printed a two-page unsigned editorial article entitled 'Strengthen the Unity of the Communist Movement for the Triumph of Peace and Socialism', which replied to Chinese criticisms on all main points and *for the first time named the Chinese Communists as the opponents in the dispute.* The article defended the Yugoslav Communists and the policy of rapprochement with Yugoslavia. Extracts:

. . . The main result of the foreign policy of the Soviet Union and the other countries of socialism, the heroic struggle of the Cuban people and all the peace-loving forces in the past year, was that the attack on Cuba, carefully prepared by the aggressive imperialist circles of the United States, was thwarted. Socialist Cuba has been defended and is confidently continuing her triumphant advance. The threat of a world thermo-nuclear war has been warded off from mankind. It has been proved once again that the forces of socialism and peace are capable of curbing imperialist aggressors. . . .

Unfortunately, views are being spread in the ranks of the international Communist movement which are directed against a number of the principal propositions of Marxism-Leninism and are designed to undermine the cohesion of the fraternal parties. The most outspoken exponents of these dogmatic, splitting views, which are profoundly hostile to Leninism, are the top leadership of the Albanian Party of Labour. . . .

At the Twenty-second Congress of the Communist Party of the Soviet Union, and subsequently at the congresses of the Communist and Workers' parties of Bulgaria, Hungary, Italy and Czechoslavakia, the *delegation of the Communist Party of China claimed that it was a mistake to criticise openly the line of the Albanian leaders, and tried to place on the fraternal parties the responsibility for the differences which had arisen.* Making such claims, however, means going against irrefutable facts and absolving from responsibility those who are in fact fighting against the common line of the Marxist-Leninist parties.

The international Communist movement knows that the Albanian leaders openly attacked the line of the Twentieth Congress of the CPSU and the propositions of the 1957 Declaration at the meeting of 81 Communist parties in November 1960. Already at that time they expressed their disagreement with the policy of the peaceful coexistence of states with different social systems, with the struggle for disarmament and the peaceful settlement of disputed questions through negotiation, with the proposition concerning the variety of forms of transition to socialism.

The 1960 meeting administered a vigorous rebuff to the anti-Leninist line of the leadership of the Albanian Party of Labour. The Albanian leaders, however, did not heed the voice of reason. Instead of paying attention to the warnings of experienced, tried and tested Marxist-Leninist parties, the leadership of the Albanian Party of Labour launched an open and violent campaign against Marxism-Leninism, against the Statement of the 81 parties, and showered the fraternal parties with slander and fabrications which even many open anti-Communists are not employing at the present time. . . .

The stand taken by the leadership of the Albanian Party of Labour caused great concern in the Communist Party of the Soviet Union, in all the Communist parties which hold dear the unity of our ranks. Firmly abiding by the principle that disputes in the international Communist movement should be settled through an exchange of views and mutual consultations between parties, *the Central Committee of the CPSU, as early as August 1960, twice approached the Central Committee of the Albanian Party of Labour proposing that a meeting be arranged* between representatives of the two parties. In a letter to the Central Committee of the Albanian Party of Labour of August 13, 1960, the Central Committee of the CPSU wrote in part:

> It would be right to extinguish in good time the spark of misunderstanding that has arisen so as to prevent its kindling. . . . If the Central Committee of the Albanian Party of Labour shares our view and does not object to an exchange of opinions, we are prepared to meet a delegation of your party at any level, at a time convenient to you.

The Albanian leaders turned down these proposals. They rejected all attempts by the Central Committee of the CPSU to normalise relations. . . .

The Albanian leaders – for instance, Enver Hoxha – boast that they do not agree with those who 'regard peaceful coexistence as the general line of the foreign policy of the socialist countries'.

But what, then, is the general line? War? If so, where then is the difference between such an approach to the solution of the question of the victory of Communism or capitalism and the point of view held by the adventurist circles of imperialism? In point of fact, the only difference is that the frenzied imperialists have lost faith in the ability of capitalism to hold its own in the competition with socialism, while the dogmatists do not believe in the possibility of the victory of Communism in the conditions of peaceful competition between states with different social systems. But would any Marxist-Leninist agree that the way to the victory of Communism lies through thermo-nuclear war? . . .

In contrast to these propositions, the dogmatists insist that nuclear war is not to be feared, that modern weapons are monstrous only 'in the view of the imperialists and reactionaries', and that 'the atom bomb is a paper tiger'. This is nothing but a renunciation of the main goal in the struggle for peace indicated in the Statement, a renunciation of the whole policy of peaceful coexistence. . . .

The peoples know that the active struggle of the Soviet Union, its strength, have played a decisive role in preventing the world war which bellicose imperialist circles have tried to touch off many times in recent years, and also in promoting the liberation struggle against imperialism.

Who was it that extinguished the raging flames of war in the Suez Canal zone in 1956 by compelling the British-French-Israeli aggressors to beat a retreat? Who was it that in 1957 prevented the invasion of Syria which the imperialists had prepared? Who was it that in 1958 prevented war from flaring up in the Middle East and in the area of Taiwan Strait?* It was the Soviet Union and all the countries of the socialist camp, the forces of peace. They – and, above all, the strength and vigorous actions of the USSR – compelled the imperialist war-mongers to retreat. . . .

The postwar years have not seen a sharper international crisis, fraught with the danger of thermo-nuclear world conflagration, than the recent crisis American imperialism created in the area of the Caribbean Sea. What was the position assumed in that crucial hour by those who shout from Tirana? Did they support the Soviet Union, which was the main force defending revolutionary Cuba and barring the road against the atomic maniacs? No, they didn't do that. What is more, they actually helped the imperialist instigators to kindle the conflict, to set the USSR and the United States at loggerheads, thereby pushing the entire world towards the abyss of war.

Fortunately for mankind, however, this did not happen. The all-devouring holocaust of atomic and hydrogen bombs did not hit the peoples. The whole world admits that credit for this goes to the Soviet Union. The firm and flexible policy of the Soviet government and of its leader, Comrade Nikita Khrushchev, which prevented a thermo-nuclear catastrophe, is highly valued by a grateful mankind as an example of wisdom, reason, a genuine love of peace and concern for the destinies of the peoples.

The dogmatists disagree with this. Now that the height of the crisis is behind us, purveyors of 'leftist phrases' are slanderously striving to present the case as if the Soviet Union had capitulated to imperialism and had even agreed to a 'second Munich'. But everyone who analyses the results of the elimination of the crisis in the area of the Caribbean Sea without bias sees that there is not a grain of truth in the accusations of the dogmatists and that the phrases they utter are actually calculated to provoke war.

A modern war cannot be approached with the old yardsticks. A world war, if we fail to prevent it, will immediately become a thermo-nuclear conflict, will lead to the death of millions upon millions of people, to the destruction of tremendous material values and to the devastation of whole countries. Those who do not consider the consequences of a modern war, who underestimate or

* The Straits of Formosa.

simply discount nuclear weapons as being something secondary to manpower, are making a big mistake.

Can there be any doubt that, if the socialist camp had not had mighty weapons, and, above all, nuclear rocket weapons, its position in the modern world would have been absolutely different? What would the security of socialism be based upon in that case? Not, surely, on some magic incantations? Is it not clear that even those who now revile the Soviet Union so vehemently would not have held out without its backing, without its might, against imperialism which is armed to the teeth? . . .

To impose on the Communist movement their definition of modern imperialism and to ignore its atomic fangs, some people claim that the 'paper tiger' thesis is tantamount to Lenin's definition of imperialism as 'a colossus with feet of clay'. It is common knowledge, however, that the figurative expression does not cover or substitute for the whole substance of Lenin's all-round definition of imperialism. Moreover, this expression stresses that imperialism is still strong, ('colossus'), but it stands on an unstable basis and is rent by internal contradictions ('with feet of clay'). The 'paper tiger' definition of imperialism speaks only of its weakness. The main point, however, is that what we need are not paper definitions, stubbornly thrust upon us, but a genuine analysis of contemporary imperialism: the disclosure of its vices, weaknesses and laws which lead to its ruin, and at the same time a sober assessment of its forces, including its huge atomic and other military potential. The expression 'paper tiger' actually leads to the demobilisation of the masses, because it conditions them to the thought that the strength of imperialism is a myth and must not be taken into account. Such phrases can only sow complacency among the peoples, and blunt their vigilance. The sowers of these phrases also say that it is necessary to despise the enemy from the strategic point of view, and approach him with all seriousness from the tactical point of view. But this 'double entry' is in contradiction with Marxism-Leninism. From the Marxist viewpoint, strategy and tactics are linked by a profound unity. Tactics are called upon to serve the purpose of achieving the strategic goal; strategy is not in contradiction with tactics, but is aimed at achieving more important historical goals. . . .

If a war is forced upon us, the Soviet Union will be able to stand up for itself and for its allies. No one can have any doubts about that. . . .

The Soviet Union does its best to promote the development of revolutions of national liberation and to achieve the earliest abolition of the shameful colonial system. It has invariably extended as it is doing now, a helping hand to all peoples rising up against imperialism and colonialism. The programme of the CPSU says that the Party and the entire Soviet people 'regard it as their duty to support the sacred struggle of the oppressed peoples, their just wars of liberation against imperialism'. And this is real, not just verbal, support. The USSR is rendering considerable political, diplomatic and economic assistance, including aid in arms, to states which ask for support in the struggle against the imperialists and colonialists, in the struggle to consolidate their independence . . .

Communists cannot but feel gravely concerned over the thesis launched recently that there is a 'temporary majority' in the international Communist movement which 'persists in its mistakes', and a 'temporary minority' which 'boldly and resolutely upholds the truth'. To insist on this thesis would in effect mean to lead matters to the fragmentation of the international Communist movement, to undermine the ideological and organisational principles on which it is built and which have provided the foundation for the historic victories of socialism. This thesis only serves to justify a split in the Communist movement and the abandonment of the common positions of the Marxist-Leninist parties.

This contention is especially harmful in that it is associated with an incredible pretension to proclaim one party the true heir of Lenin, and all other parties to be apostates from Marxism-Leninism. . . . Who has the right to put himself in the place of the great Lenin who upheld the principles of revolutionary Marxism and raised high the banner of struggle against opportunism? There is no doubt that the Communist parties will reject these inordinate pretensions of people to put themselves in the place of Lenin, and to proclaim themselves to be the sole guardians of the 'truth'. These pretensions are not only basically wrong, but absolutely unwarranted. . . . It also reveals incredible arrogance, a complete absence of any sense of respect or desire to heed the unanimous view and the appeals of the overwhelming majority of the fraternal parties, each of which has done great services to the international proletariat, and has great revolutionary experience. . . .

In the opinion of the Albanian 'theoreticians', only 'cliques of revisionists' now remain in the world Communist movement. In vain they appeal to the 'rank and file Communists', now of this, now of that Communist party, urging them to 'overthrow' these 'cliques'. And there are people who offer their services to distribute such writings throughout the world. . . .

Is there anything in common between this Marxist-Leninist provision and the thesis about a 'temporary majority', and 'a minority defending truth'? Absolutely nothing. This thesis, unworthy of Communists, means an unceremonious attack on the unity of the Communist movement, means banking on disunity in the ranks of our movement, on splitting it. The authors of this anti-Marxist and anti-internationalist thesis, against facts, are trying to assure everybody, that they are defending the Declaration and the Statement! . . .

The pretension of a single Communist party to lay claim to infallibility and to ignore at the same time the opinion of other Communist parties is entirely wrong and damaging to the interests of the Communist movement. . . .

The positions of the Communist movement of the whole world on these questions are set forth in the documents of the 1957 and 1960 Moscow meetings. Every Communist party must fully take into consideration and stand by this unanimous opinion of the world Communist movement. There is no other way. . . .

The Communist parties do not have rules common for all, but they do have the decisions of the Moscow meetings, which are common and binding for all of them. Devotion to these decisions is an international duty of every Communist party. Not to carry out in the present conditions the collectively drafted decisions of the Moscow meetings would mean to disrupt the unity of the Communist movement, to withdraw each into its own 'national house', would mean, in the final analysis, to help imperialism in carrying out its plans and to put a brake on the liberation struggle of the peoples. . . .

It is impermissible to separate from one another these closely interconnected laws of our movement. Splitting activities must not be tolerated in the ranks of the international Communist movement. Disregard of this demand is tantamount to undermining the very foundations of the fraternal unity of the Communist parties, to encroaching on the very principles of proletarian internationalism. It may lead, first of all, to the appearance of a 'minority' trend and then to the emergence of the danger of a split in the international Communist movement, to the joy of its common enemy – international imperialism.

The course of the CPSU defined by its Twentieth and Twenty-second Congresses, is a course aimed at rallying all the forces of socialism, at consolidating the unity of all the fraternal parties, and at rallying all the forces of the anti-imperialist front. This course underlies our position in the development of our relations with socialist Yugoslavia.

The steps taken recently by the Yugoslav Communists and their leaders in their home and foreign policy have removed much of what was erroneous and damaging to the cause of building socialism in Yugoslavia. The Yugoslav Communists have taken steps towards rapprochement and unity with the entire world Communist movement. Those who allege that 'capitalism has been restored' in Yugoslavia, that 'new bourgeois elements' have occupied a dominant position there, are deliberately lying, refusing to analyse facts and phenomena, substituting fabrications for them, and trying to expel the people of a whole country from the ranks of the fighters for socialism. The CPSU declares openly that there still exist differences with the League of Communists of Yugoslavia on a number of ideological questions. But the rapprochement between Yugoslavia and the country that is building Communism can, without doubt, help to overcome the differences on a number of ideological questions much more quickly. . . .

There are no 'superior' and 'inferior' parties in the Communist movement. The Communist parties are fraternal parties. They have one and the same ideology – Marxism-Leninism; one and the same aim – struggle against imperialism for the triumph of Communism. All Communist parties are equal and independent. All are responsible for the destinies of the Communist movement, for its victories and setbacks. Our Party was the first to put forward these propositions. The other documents of the Communist movement should not say that the Soviet Union stands at the head of the socialist camp, or the CPSU at the head of the Communist movement. This is but one of the indications of how scrupulously the CPSU observes the principles of the equality and solidarity of the fraternal parties, how boundlessly loyal it is to the principles of proletarian internationalism. . . .

January 12

The Communist Party of Great Britain issued a statement outlining its position in the dispute. Extracts:

All Communist parties are independent and have equal rights. They make their own decisions based on Marxism-Leninism. At the same time, however, the 81 parties assembled in Moscow, recognised that there must be established rules of conduct and a recognition of the internationalist duties of the parties. We all declared then that the 'supreme internationalist duty' of every Marxist-Leninist party was to work continuously for the greater unity of the world Communist movement. This was the essential precondition for our common victory. . . .

Our meetings further declared and we all unanimously agreed, that 'the interests of the Communist movement require solidarity by every Communist party in the observance of the estimates and conclusions on the common tasks in the struggle against imperialism, for peace, democracy and socialism, jointly reached by the fraternal parties at their meetings'. This, in our view, is the essential basis for restoring the unity of the international Communist movement. Unity is the burning need, not division into 'minorities' and 'majorities' of parties in our movement. This brings no solution and is fraught with danger.

If the road to public debate is not the solution to our differences, what is? What now must be considered is the preparation for a further international conference to promote the unity of our movement. Our Soviet comrades in their *Pravda* article wrote that the Communist parties have a tested method of settling contentious issues by way of collective discussion. The CPSU has always advocated this method. Our Chinese comrades have also suggested that the issues be settled by international conference.

In addition, the CPSU has made approaches to our Chinese comrades for joint discussion. To our regret they have not taken this up. We hope it will yet be considered. What is at issue is not the principle of international consultation, which is common to all parties, but the approach to international discussion in the present position in our movement.

A further international conference must be dedicated to promoting the unity of our movement and be approached and governed by that spirit. To assemble in a spirit of perpetuating division would be worse than useless. In such a case it would be better if no conference took place. In the light of this we think that the following provisions are vital if an international conference is to succeed in this task:

First, the present public polemic between parties should stop and be replaced by serious internal preparation for such a conference.

Second, completely adequate time must be taken to prepare the conference. This matter cannot be hurried if success is to result. We need as much preparation as is necessary calmly and in a Communist fashion to examine and weigh up honestly held differences; to assess how far, in fact, they exist and what are the possible lines of solution. Only the preparation itself will show how much time we need. . . .

January 15–21

Sixth Congress of East German Communist Party in Berlin.

January 16

Khrushchev addressed the German Congress, making a number of references to the dispute with the Chinese and Albanian Communists. He rejected the idea of holding a meeting immediately on the grounds that it would only exacerbate differences and might lead to a 'split', and he proposed a truce on polemics. Extracts:

Some people assert that Cuba and the Soviet Union were defeated in the Caribbean conflict. But theirs is a strange logic, for how does it come about that revolutionary Cuba is there and is growing stronger, if it is true that we have been defeated?

Who really retreated and who benefited from the conflict? . . . It will be recalled that the US President, in his message to the Soviet government, gave the pledge before the world that the United States would not invade Cuba and would stop its allies from doing so. Thereby the US government virtually had to renounce armed intervention against the Republic of Cuba.

This was a failure of the policy of the more aggressive imperialist circles and a victory for the policy of peaceful coexistence, of fighting against imperialism; it was a triumph for the policy aimed at preventing the export of counter-revolution. . . .

Some people who consider themselves Marxists say that the struggle against imperialism does not imply that we must above all else build up the economic power of the socialist countries – a real factor with which our enemies reckon. These people have invented a new method of waging this struggle, a method that is supposedly the cheapest. This method, you see, does not depend on the economic level of a country or on the quality and quantity of armaments; it is nothing but abuse. Those people imagine that to fling interminable curses at imperialism means precisely doing what will help the socialist countries more than anything else.

But cursing is not the strongest means of fighting your enemies. It runs off like water from a duck's back. That is why we must not fight imperialism by cursing. We must compete with imperialism, with capitalism, on an economic basis. And to have a firm foundation for competition, we must develop the economic potential of the socialist countries and have actual strength, nuclear rocket forces, which would be a warning to the imperialists: If you poke your nose in here, you will lose your head! This is the language the imperialists understand. . . .

Today some people who call themselves Marxist-Leninists allege that the defence of peace and the struggle against the war danger are contrary to the spirit of Marxism-Leninism and hamper the progress of the revolutionary movement. . . .

If the Communists were to be guided by a 'theory' such as that, this would repel the masses instead of attracting them. This 'theory' is all the more repellent in this rocket and nuclear age. . . . Foreign scientists and military experts estimate that the United States now has roughly 40,000 hydrogen bombs and warheads. Everyone knows that the Soviet Union, too, has more than enough of this stuff.

What would happen if all these nuclear weapons were brought down on people? Scientists estimate that the first blow alone would take a toll of 700 to 800 million human lives. All the big cities would be wiped out or destroyed – not only in the two leading nuclear countries, the United States and the USSR, but in France, Britain, Germany, Italy, China, Japan and many other countries of the world. The effects of a nuclear war would continue to tell throughout the lifetime of many generations, causing disease and death and the worst deformities in the development of people. I am not saying these things to frighten anyone. I am simply citing data at the disposal of science. These data cannot but be reckoned with.

There can be no doubt that *a world nuclear war, if started by the imperialist maniacs, would inevitably result in the downfall of the capitalist system, a system breeding wars. But would the socialist countries and the cause of socialism all over the world benefit from a world nuclear disaster?* Only people who deliberately shut their eyes to the facts can think so. As for Marxist-Leninists, they cannot propose to establish a Communist civilisation on the ruins of centres of world culture, on land laid waste and contaminated by nuclear fall-out. We need hardly add that in the case of many peoples, the question of socialism would be eliminated altogether, because they would have disappeared bodily from our planet.

I shall let you into a secret: our scientists have developed a 100-megaton bomb. But a 100-megaton bomb, our military men hold, cannot be dropped on Europe, if our probable adversary unleashes a war. Where can we drop it here – on Western Germany or France? But the explosion of such a bomb on this territory would also destroy you and certain other countries. *That is why this weapon can be used by us, apparently, only outside Western Europe.* I say this only to give you a clearer idea of the terrible means of destruction that now exist. . . .

To use a familiar phrase: 'Blessed is he who talks about war without knowing what he is talking about.' The Albanian leaders talk a lot about rocket and nuclear war but nobody is worried by their talk. Everyone knows that they have nothing to their name but idle talk, and that they have no real possibilities. As you see our positions on these questions and our responsibilities are different. . . . The advocates of the so-called theory of the victory of socialism through war also deny that socialism can win by peaceful means, saying that this is a departure from Marxism. We must say for the edification of these admirers of the cult of Stalin that it was none other than Stalin, who in an interview with British Communists after the Second World War, spoke of using the peaceful, parliamentary way to bring about the victory of socialism, and this is recorded in the programme of the Communist Party of Great Britain. The leaders of the British Communist party know that this wording was proposed by Stalin.

The Albanian leaders persist in the allegation that the Communist Party of the Soviet Union advocates only the peaceful road and rules out the method of armed struggle. One may well ask them: can they cite an example of a Communist party maintaining that there was a revolutionary situation in its country and wanting to begin a revolt, when the CPSU was opposed to using the method of armed struggle? Can the Albanians cite such an example by any chance? No, they cannot, because no such example exists. . . .

As for the CPSU, ours is a Marxist-Leninist position. Specific preconditions are required for a revolution to be victorious. If there is a revolutionary situation, the working class led by its vanguard must use it to win power. Should exploiter classes resort to the use of force against the people, the people have the right to take the most drastic measures, including armed struggle, in the interests of the victory of socialism. . . .

Even if we diverge over certain ideological questions, possibly including rather important ones, we must try to ensure that these questions are properly understood. In so doing we must not go to extremes, must not take a subjective stand in appraising the general situation in a particular country. We must not, for example, assess the political system of this or that socialist country only by the erroneous views of leaders, views which have prevailed for a while. It is objective and not subjective factors that should be taken as the principal indications. And this implies, first of all, the question of who owns the means of production, who holds the power and on what lines the state is developing.

If we disagreed on certain questions and quarrelled, and then said at once that the socialist country whose leaders differed with us on something was not socialist, we would be demonstrating subjectivism pure and simple. It would be as in the case of the Church: when a person ceases to keep religious vows and perform religious rites, he is excommunicated and anathematised. It does not befit us to proceed like churchmen and engage in 'excommunications' from socialism.

To cite an example: we differ with Yugoslavia on certain ideological issues. But this in itself does not warrant the claim that that country is not socialist. We cannot claim such a thing because the objective indications and the system existing there are socialist. The means of production and state power in Yugoslavia, which its peoples have won by heroic struggle, are held by the working people. There are no landlords, bankers or capitalists there. The peoples of Yugoslavia are engaged in building socialism and Communism. That being so, what grounds are there for 'excommunicating' Yugoslavia from socialism and expelling it from the ranks of the socialist countries?

There are serious differences between the leaders of the Albanian Party of Labour and ourselves. *Must we therefore declare, for subjective reasons, that Albania is not a socialist country? It would be an incorrect, a subjective approach.* Although the Albanian leaders show incomprehension of a number of highly important issues and we are combating that, we consider that Albania is a socialist country and that its people have displayed genuine heroism in the struggle for the victory of socialism. . . .

Even today we are prepared to repeat what we said in the report of the Central Committee of the CPSU to the Twenty-second Congress of the Party: if the Albanian leaders cherish the interests of their people and the cause of socialist construction in Albania, and if they want friendship with the CPSU and with all the fraternal parties, they must recant their erroneous views and revert to the path of unity and close co-operation in the fraternal family that is the socialist commonwealth, to the path of unity with the entire world Communist movement.

The Central Committee of our Party would consider it useful now to *call a halt to polemics* between Communist parties, to stop criticising other parties inside one's own party, and allow some time for the passions to subside.

Some comrades suggest calling *a meeting of all the fraternal parties to discuss the questions that are ripe for it.* Our Party has always favoured such meetings. *We believe, however, that if we convene that meeting immediately there will probably be little hope of successfully eliminating the existing differences. Such a meeting would lead, not to a calm and judicious removal of differences, but to their aggravation and to the danger of a split. We must not forget that there is a logic to every struggle and that political passions run high.*

The Soviet Communists are true and resolute adherents of the unity of all the Communist and Workers' parties, and of the consolidation of our common forces on the basis of Marxism-Leninism. This is why we consider that it would be more reasonable, in the interests of the working class and our future, to stop now the polemics in the press on the disputed questions. Let us give time a chance to work for us. It will help us understand who is right and who is wrong. Moreover during this time we should get rid of all that is extraneous and accidental.

January 18

Chinese delegate Wu Hsiu-chuan addressed East German Congress: Extracts:

Kennedy talks profusely about peace but is actually pursuing a more cunning and more adventurous global strategy of counter-revolution. One must not entertain any unrealistic illusions about this chieftain of the US monopoly capitalist class. . . .

Recently, the situation in Cuba has provided the revolutionary people of the world with extraordinarily rich and vivid lessons. This situation proves that man is the decisive factor in the struggle against imperialism. It was the heroic Cuban people who mobilised themselves and rallied around their revolutionary leader, Comrade Fidel Castro, persevered in the five just demands for the safeguarding of Cuba's independence and sovereignty, waged an unswerving struggle against US imperialism and, with the sympathy and support of the peoples of Latin America and the world, won a great victory in defence of Cuba's independence, sovereignty and the fruits of her revolution, thus making a great contribution to the cause of world peace. . . .

The Communist Party of China sincerely hopes that fraternal parties which have disputes of differences between them will unite afresh on the basis of Marxism-Leninism and on the basis of mutual respect for independence and equality. However, it is to be regretted that this sincere advice on our part has not succeeded in preventing a deterioration in the situation. Actuated by its desire to uphold the principles guiding the mutual relations of fraternal countries and parties and to strengthen unity, *in April 1962 the Communist Party of China energetically supported the suggestions put forward by a number of fraternal parties for easing relations and improving the atmosphere, and formally proposed to the fraternal party concerned that a meeting of representatives of all Communist and Workers' parties should be convened to iron out differences and strengthen unity through comradely discussions and consultations.* We also pointed out that, pending the convening of such a conference, all parties should stop attacking each other over the radio and in the press, so as to create conditions favourable to the convening of the conference. We cannot but point out that to our distress such efforts on the part of the Communist Party of China and some other fraternal parties have not evoked a response from the fraternal party concerned. On the contrary, the practice which violates the principles guiding relations among fraternal countries and parties has been steadily intensified, so much so that the recent series of congresses of a number of fraternal parties have been used as platforms for further attacks on other fraternal parties. At these congresses, comrades of some fraternal parties continued their attacks on the Albanian Party of Labour and attacked the Communist Party of China and another fraternal party by name. In addition, they have extensively mobilised their newspapers and other propaganda media to make large-scale attacks and slanders against the Communist Party of China. It is completely justified that many fraternal parties have expressed deep anxiety and worry at this grave adverse current which is disrupting unity and creating a split. . . .

January 17–19

Leaders of other East European delegations spoke to East German Congress. Extracts:

Wladyslaw Gomulka (First Secretary of the Polish Communist Party): We are fully in agreement with the proposition put forward by Comrade Khrushchev that, irrespective of the differences between the CPSU and the vast majority of the Communist parties on the one side and the leadership of certain Communist parties on the other, *public polemics and arguments should be stopped*. These differences should be removed quietly and patiently by means of internal discussions.

The public polemics and irresponsible attacks on the CPSU by the leaders of certain Communist parties, which are harming the cause of the unity of the international Communist movement, increased during the crisis in the Caribbean. The leaders of those parties do not want to admit that it was thanks to the calm and reasonable policy of the Soviet Union, which was inspired by a deep sense of responsibility, that that crisis was resolved favourably for Cuba and for the cause of socialism. . . .

The Soviet Union is the main and decisive force in the socialist camp without which not a single Socialist State could stand up for itself in the struggle with imperialism. This must never be forgotten by any Communist party, especially the parties of the socialist countries. The enormous strength of the Soviet Union, its military nuclear might and its central position in the socialist camp place on the CPSU and the Soviet government great responsibility for every step, for every political undertaking in the international sphere and for the fate of mankind. *No other party and no other socialist country bears such responsibility*. . . .

Where it is a matter of war or peace, every Communist party must be extremely careful not to make mistakes in its policy. This principle acquires a special quality and a special sense when it concerns the CPSU and the Soviet government. And when it comes to such a testing time as happened in the days of the Caribbean crisis, when it was being decided whether there should be peace or war, the leaders of the CPSU simply must not make a mistake. The whole world and all the peoples are deeply grateful to the Soviet Union, to the Soviet government and especially to Comrade Khrushchev that in the critical days of the Caribbean crisis they courageously took a decision that saved the world from nuclear catastrophe. . . .

Todor Zhivkov (First Secretary of the Bulgarian Communist Party) said: Our Party resolutely condemns the line taken by the leaders of the Albanian Communist Party which slanders the Soviet Union and the great party of Lenin. . . .

To slander the Soviet Union means undermining the authority of *the only centre and advance-guard of the international Communist movement and the authority of the party from which all Marxist-Leninist parties have learnt and continue to learn Leninism and draw revolutionary experience.* To slander the Soviet Union means undermining *the principal guarantee of the existence and the prosperity of the socialist countries* and to undermine *the main and decisive force of peace and socialism,* which is leading the attack on the forces of imperialism and war.

We associate ourselves without qualification with the words already pronounced at this Congress to the effect that *the main criterion of the internationalism of every Marxist-Leninist party and of every Communist is their attitude to the Soviet Union and to the CPSU.* . . . We support the proposal of the Central Committee of the CPSU to stop public polemics between Communist parties on controversial questions and wait until passions have cooled. We share the opinion that if a meeting of fraternal parties were to be called at once it would at the present moment not contribute to the successful liquidation of existing difficulties. . . .

January 27

People's Daily published editorial entitled 'Let Us Unite on the Basis of the Moscow Declaration and Statement', the greater part of which was devoted to criticism of the Yugoslav Communists. The editorial again called for an international meeting. Extracts:

The outstanding features of the East German Communists' Congress were that while much was said about stopping attacks and strengthening unity among the fraternal parties, extremely crude attacks were continued against the Chinese Communist Party and other fraternal parties, attacks which further widen differences and damage unity, and that while much was said about supporting the Moscow Declaration and the Moscow Statement, *brazen attempts,* which were in open violation of the Moscow Declaration and the Moscow Statement, *were made to reverse the verdict passed on the Tito clique of renegades to Marxism-Leninism.*

When in the course of his speech the head of the Chinese Communist Party Delegation, which attended the Congress by invitation, quoted and discussed the criticisms of Yugoslav revisionism made in the Moscow Statement, the executive chairman of the Congress repeatedly stopped him. Prompted by this cue, there was an uproar of booing, whistling and foot-stamping in the congress hall. It is indeed strange and almost incredible for such a phenomenon to occur in the international Communist movement. When the delegate of the Chinese Communist Party ended his speech, the executive chairman of the Congress went so far as to protest. He stated that he 'most decidedly rejected' the criticism of Yugoslav revisionism made by the delegate of the Communist Party of China and described it as 'contradicting all the norms prevailing among Communist and revolutionary Workers' parties'. Following this, the Soviet newspaper *Izvestia* attacked the delegate of the Communist Party of China for his criticism of Yugoslav revisionism, stating that it was 'utterly impermissible'.

This Congress of the Socialist Unity Party of Germany has posed the following vitally important questions to the Communists of the whole world: are the ranks of the international Communist movement to be united or not? Is there to be genuine unity or sham unity? On what basis is there to be unity – is there to be unity on the basis of the Moscow Declaration and the Moscow Statement, or 'unity' on the basis of the Yugoslav revisionist programme or on some other basis? In other words, are differences to be ironed out and unity strengthened, or are differences to be widened and a split created? . . .

The Communist Party of China has consistently worked to uphold and strengthen the unity of the socialist camp and of the international Communist movement. . . . Through their joint efforts and full consultations at the 1957 and 1960 Moscow meetings, the other fraternal parties and the Chinese Communist Party formulated a common line for the international Communist movement and established common princples guiding the mutual relations of fraternal parties and countries. *At these two meetings, we conducted a necessary struggle against certain wrong tendencies detrimental to unity and also made necessary compromises on certain matters, thus contributing to the unanimous agreement reached at the meetings.*

At the Twenty-second Congress of the Communist Party of the Soviet Union in 1961, when there occurred the first serious incident in which one party at its own congress made an open attack by name on another fraternal party, that is, on the Albanian Party of Labour, the delegation of the Chinese Communist Party voiced firm opposition and proffered sincere advice.

In its desire to uphold the principles guiding the mutual relations of fraternal parties and countries and to strengthen unity, the Chinese Communist Party *in April 1962* gave its active support to the *proposals made by some fraternal parties for easing relations and improving the atmosphere*, and, in a letter to the fraternal party concerned, formally expressed its opinion that *a meeting of representatives of the Communist and Workers' parties of all countries should be convened* to iron out differences and strengthen unity through comradely discussion and consultation. We also pointed out that, prior to such a meeting, all fraternal parties should make extensive preparations, including the cessation of radio and press attacks on another fraternal party, in order to create favourable conditions for the meeting and ensure its success.

To our great distress, these positive proposals of the Communist Party of China and some other fraternal parties have not evoked a corresponding response from the fraternal party concerned. On the contrary, the practice of violating the principles guiding relations among fraternal parties and countries, and especially the vicious practice of openly attacking other fraternal parties by name at a party congress, has gone from bad to worse. At every one of the recent congresses of fraternal parties the attacks on the Albanian Party of Labour were continued and attacks were made against the Communist Party of China, while at one congress the Korean Workers' Party, too, was attacked. This adverse current, which runs counter to the Moscow Declaration and the Moscow Statement and which is disrupting the unity of the international Communist movement, reached a new climax at the Sixth Congress of the Socialist Unity Party of Germany. There, the Yugoslav revisionist clique was shielded in many ways, while the fraternal party delegate who criticised Yugoslav revisionism in accordance with the Moscow Statement was treated in an utterly uncomradely and rude manner. *Such behaviour is extremely vulgar as well as completely futile.* In the view of certain comrades, adherence to the principles of the Moscow Statement, which had been unanimously agreed upon by the fraternal parties, was utterly impermissible and illegitimate, while the Yugoslav revisionism condemned by the Moscow Statement was to be welcomed and was legitimate. On the one hand, they wantonly attacked comrades who adhere to Marxism-Leninism, and on the other, they talked volubly of uniting with out-and-out revisionists. On the one hand, they used every conceivable method to deprive delegates of fraternal parties opposing Yugoslav revisionism of the opportunity to speak, and on the other, they applauded the betrayals of Marxism-Leninism. This outrageous practice was all the more serious because it was carefully planned.

Here we must state in all seriousness that the international Communist movement is at a critical juncture. The Moscow Declaration and the Moscow Statement – the common basis of the unity of the Communist and Workers' parties of all countries – are in great danger of being publicly torn up. *The unity of the socialist camp and of the international Communist movement is under a grave threat.* In the international Communist movement of today, one's attitude towards Yugoslav revisionism is not a minor but a major question; it is a question that concerns not just one detail or another but the whole. It is a question of whether to adhere to Marxism-Leninism or to wallow in the mire with the Yugoslav revisionists, whether to take the Moscow Declaration and the Moscow Statement as the foundation of unity or to take the Yugoslav revisionist programme or something else as the foundation of 'unity', and whether genuinely to strengthen unity or merely to pay lip service to unity while in fact creating a split. In the final analysis, it is a question of whether to adhere strictly to the Moscow Declaration and the Moscow Statement or to tear them up. . . .

Is it or is it not right to criticise Yugoslav revisionism? There should have been no doubt about this in the international Communist ranks. The principled stand taken by the Chinese Communist Party in firmly opposing Yugoslav revisionism was approved by the other fraternal parties. We may all recall that, at the Seventh Congress of the Bulgarian Communist Party in June 1958, Comrade Khrushchev said that 'the Chinese comrades and also the other fraternal parties are rightly and profoundly criticising the revisionist propositions of the draft programme of the League of Communists of Yugoslavia'.

We also remember that at the previous Congress of the Socialist Unity Party of Germany, that is, at its Fifth Congress held in July 1958, there was no difference of opinion among Communist and Workers' parties on whether Yugoslav revisionism should be criticised. Comrade Khrushchev then said:

> 'The anti-Marxist, anti-Leninist views of the Yugoslav leaders were subjected to thorough-going, principled criticism by the Communist Party of China, the Socialist Unity Party of Germany and all the other fraternal parties. In decisions taken by their leading bodies and in articles in the party press, all the parties took a clear-cut position and condemned those views, paying considerable attention to a critical analysis of them. And this was correct'. . .

We cannot understand why some comrades, who formerly took the correct stand of criticising Yugoslav revisionism, should have now made an about-turn of 180 degrees. It has been claimed that this was because 'the Yugoslav leaders have removed very much of what was considered erroneous'. Unfortunately, the Tito clique themselves have never admitted to having made any mistakes, let alone removed them. It is indeed subjectivism pure and simple to assert that the Tito clique have 'removed' their mistakes. We would ask the apologists for the Tito clique to listen to the Titoists' own statements. . . . Only recently, in December 1962, the moment he alighted from the train on his return from the Soviet Union, Tito said in Belgrade: 'Discussions . . . about how Yugoslavia will now change her policy are simply superfluous and ridiculous. We have no need to change our policy.' He added a few days later: 'I said there (in the Soviet Union) that there is no possibility of Yugoslavia's changing her foreign policy'. What were the apologists for the Tito clique doing if not lying when they said that the Tito clique 'have removed very much of what was considered erroneous'. . . . *

Certain people have lately been talking a lot about how their views on many problems are coming closer to or agreeing with those of the Tito clique. We would ask, since there has not been any change in the revisionist line and policies of the Tito clique, does it not follow that the makers of these statements are themselves moving closer to the revisionist line and policies of the Tito clique?

Here we should like to emphasise that those who are zealously engaged in reversing the verdict on the Tito clique are trying to make a breach in the Moscow Declaration and the Moscow Statement on the Yugoslav issue and *then to tear them up completely*. Were their scheme to succeed, it would be tantamount to declaring that the criticisms of Yugoslav revisionism made by all Communist and Workers' parties over these years are wrong and the traitorous Tito clique is right, that the fundamental principles of Marxism-Leninism have become obsolete and modern revisionism can no longer be opposed, still less be treated as the main danger in the international Communist movement, and that we should all follow at the heels of the Tito clique and 'join forces with Karl Kautsky's offspring – his son Benedict'.

Were this to happen, the strategy and tactics of the international Communist movement would have to be completely changed and the revolutionary line of Marxism-Leninism would have to be replaced by the capitulationist line of revisionism. Were this to happen, what possible common basis would there be for unity among the Communist and Workers' parties of all countries? *Is this not a deliberate attempt to create a split in the international Communist movement*? . . .

The primary test of a Communist's sincerity in upholding the unity of the international Communist movement is whether he conscientiously abides by the principles guiding relations among fraternal parties and countries.

The Moscow Declaration and the Moscow Statement, the two international documents unanimously agreed upon by the Communist and Workers' parties *are binding on all the fraternal parties. These parties have the obligation to abide by them and have absolutely no right to wreck them. No single party or group of parties has the right to change them or to declare them null and void. In the international Communist movement, the resolutions of any one fraternal party, whether*

* *See* Khrushchev, Speech to Supreme Soviet: Chronology, Dec. 12, 1962.

right or wrong and however important the place and the role of that party, can be binding on that party alone. According to the principles laid down in the Moscow Declaration and the Moscow Statement, it is impermissible to impose the programme, resolutions, line or policies of any one party on other fraternal parties, or to require other fraternal parties to obey the irresponsible self-contradictory statements made by the leader of a party who talks one way today and another tomorrow, as if those statements were imperial decrees; and it is more impermissible for one or more parties wantonly to kick out one or another fraternal party from the international Communist movement or pull in renegades to Marxism-Leninism. . . .

Better a single good deed contributing to unity than a thousand empty words about unity. *It is time to rein in on the brink of the precipice*! To do so late in the day is better than not to do it at all. We sincerely hope that the fraternal party which launched the first attack will suit its action to its words, take the initiative, and return to the path of inter-party consultation on the basis of equality, to the principles guiding relations among fraternal parties and countries as set forth in the Moscow Declaration and the Moscow Statement. . . .

The Communist Party of China has advocated on more than one occasion, and still advocates, the convening of a meeting of representatives of the Communist and Workers' parties of all countries at which all can sit down calmly, and, through adequate and comradely discussion, harmonise their viewpoints, iron out their differences and strengthen their unity on a new basis. Together with all other fraternal parties, we desire to take every possible step towards easing relations and strengthening unity, in order to improve the atmosphere and create the conditions necessary for convening the meeting of fraternal parties.

January (late)

Towards the end of the month the CPSU sent out a confidential letter to all the parties in the 'socialist camp' replying to the charges made in the Chinese confidential letter of December 1962 (*See* Chronology). The following are extracts from the summary of the letter:

I. The whole of the first part deals with the question of *Russo-Chinese relations before the last war*. The accusation that the Russians did not aid the Chinese is sharply and emphatically rejected. Reference is made to the big deliveries of arms, munitions and foodstuffs in the 'thirties, and to the training of Chinese military personnel in Russia and to the despatch of military personnel to China into territory held by the revolutionaries. Without aid from the USSR, which was at that time encircled by all the capitalist states, the letter says, the Chinese partisans would have found it difficult to hold on to eight complete provinces for more than a decade.

Concerning the civil war, nobody doubts the bravery of the Chinese comrades, but to say that no aid was given is at the very least a crude exaggeration. China not only received every kind of military equipment which the Soviet Union could afford to give after the last war but also received similar aid from other socialist states. Between 1947 and 1949 the Soviet Union also had to reconstruct its terribly damaged industry, mainly the arms industry. The Soviet Union had no agricultural surpluses and the harvest of 1947 was catastrophic for the socialist states. But in spite of this *the USSR and the other socialist states supplied material to the value of 2.5 billion roubles during the years of the war for China's freedom.*

In the diplomatic sphere the USSR had always striven and would continue to strive for the proper defence of China's interests. The Soviet Union and the other socialist members of UNO would continue to press for China's acceptance into UNO, and it was only a matter of time until this justified step was realised. The USSR had for a whole decade only its own voice and that of the socialist states in UNO and was thus always automatically outvoted. This was changed only in the last few years by the entry of the Asian and African countries into UNO, and no one will be happier than the USSR when China occupies her rightful place in UNO side by side with the USSR and the other socialist states. Only when China becomes a member of UNO will that organisation become a world instrument for peace and an organisation which will bring about that peace.

II. It is at the very least a distortion of the entire situation when China says that the USSR and other socialist states have not done everything to help China stand on her own feet both in the military and the economic sense. Aid to China in the years from 1950 to 1961 amounted to over 34 billion roubles, and aid from the other socialist states in the same period came to 7 billion roubles. Attention is drawn to the tremendous and effective aid during the Korean war when the USSR, the Czechoslovak Socialist Republic and other socialist states actually supplied everything from guns to boot-laces. [A long list of what was then delivered to China is given: tanks, machine-guns, artillery, munitions, aircraft, uniforms, boots, foodstuffs, medicaments and auxiliary military and medical personnel.]

Where would China and the Korean Republic be today without that aid? Have the Chinese comrades forgotten how far the American army got?

With the aid of the USSR and the other socialist states in the last decade there have been completed – and financed solely by – the Soviet Union and the other socialist states:

14 aircraft factories.

39 munition factories and other armaments plants.

7 factories producing lorries and passenger cars.

19 railway automatic plants.

Over 90 sugar refineries.

Factories for boots, clothes and tinned goods, and many others.

The aid was given unselfishly. Experts and specialists were sent from all the socialist states to live in China side by side with the Chinese people for many long years and work hand in hand with the Chinese comrades for a happy and socialist future for the Chinese People's Republic. Thousands of students from China benefited from instruction in the colleges and specialised centres of the USSR....

All accusations hinting at racial prejudice on the part of the USSR are rejected and very sharply. China had always been regarded as a brother of the USSR with whom the latter must share everything.

The letter refers to *the famine in China in 1954 and 1958*, which was concealed from the capitalists by the spontaneous and speedy help of the USSR.

At the Twentieth Congress of the CPSU in 1956 a clear statement was made of what was the main task of the socialist states. In those plans China played a large role. Although China agreed with everything that was discussed in public and private meetings at the time, she began, at an extraordinarily difficult time for the USSR, to sabotage every step taken by the USSR and at the same time demanded the same, and even more, aid from the USSR and the other socialist states, without paying the slightest attention to the economic situation of those countries or what they needed for their advancement. *That very same China, which received every kind of aid from the USSR and others, began to make propaganda gifts from that aid to other states and by so doing harmed its own deficit economy.*

The slogan 'Peace and Coexistence' was worked out once and for all in Lenin's principles. Lenin foresaw the tremendous scientific and economic development of all the Great Powers and for that reason proposed even in his time the coexistence of all states in the interests of peace and economic progress. But at that time the USSR was a weak and underdeveloped country, so that the capitalists jeered at it. Today the USSR is the first Communist Great Power, recognised and respected even by the most reactionary capitalist opposition. *But this important position was achieved only in the years after 1956*, and that was through getting rid of the personal cult of Stalin, which obstructed the economic and political development not only of the USSR but also of other socialist states, and also destroyed faith in the USSR among Communists in the capitalist countries.

In the manner of open Marxist-Leninist criticism, the mistakes of that period had to be and must be removed, and they must not only be removed, but citizens and Communists must be set an example so that these departures from the only right party line shall not be repeated again.

Thousands of genuine Communists died in Stalin's prisons and those of his helpers; the reconstruction of the country suffered terribly; faith in the USSR was completely destroyed; and every country not only recognised this but drew from it the appropriate conclusions, except China and Albania.

For genuine aid from the USSR, China had only contempt which has recently developed into ridiculous ideas of greatness. In agricultural policy China ignored sincere Soviet advice about the need for gradual collectivisation. She went her own way, and that evoked justifiable opposition from the middle peasant and the agricultural worker, and China still has today an agricultural policy which might be justified in the times of the commune of the French Revolution but not in the twentieth century. But that was not the most important – for China claimed to have invented her own Chinese Communism which is based on the principle that everything Chinese is good while everything that comes from the USSR is bad.

The USSR is in no way currying favour with the USA. But the USA is willy-nilly a Great Power, with a strength of which there can be no doubt. We have to reconcile ourselves to this fact and to the fact that with the present advancement of military science war is suicide for the aggressor and the victim, and we must learn to live with this thought. The USSR continues to develop its industry and to extend its foreign trade with all countries of the world on a peaceful basis without reference to their political system.

In a few years the USSR will be the most powerful country in the production of consumer goods as well, and only then will begin the socialist competition for the well-being of the whole world in which, whether they like it or capitalist states will have to join.

Let China not bother herself about the problem of Germany. We are ~~~~ solving it to the advantage of all Germans and ourselves. We don't involve ourselves in the question whether the Chinese eat their rice with forks or chopsticks, but we want to eat our *shashlyk* in our own way. The USSR and its allies are fighting consistently for one and the same objective: the liberation of the proletariat of the whole world from the capitalist yoke, the destruction of the class enemy and the creation of a classless society in the spirit of Marx, Engels and Lenin.

China has returned to a short-sighted reactionary policy of territorial acquisitions of rule by terror and government without the participation of the Chinese people. Chinese policy in recent years is very similar to the policy of the Japanese imperialists in the last decade before the last war.

Asia for the Asians: we all remember this dangerous slogan and what it led to, and today it leads to direct attacks by the CPR on the USSR, while the Soviet Union has for the last three years been patiently hoping that the Chinese comrades will recognise the just position of the USSR and self-critically admit their mistakes. However big these mistakes are, still the Soviet Communists will receive the CPR back into the family of socialist states with the greatest pleasure and eagerness and will put right everything that has been upset by the malice of individuals and their yearning for personal power.

But if the CPR continues its attacks on the USSR and its allies, then the USSR sees no alternative but to break off all economic relations with the CPR, because these attacks and deliberate insults are damaging to the USSR and its allies and undermine their international negotiations. The USSR reserves to itself the right to take all necessary steps to defend its international positions and to maintain among the countries of the Far East a peace such as the underdeveloped peoples of these countries need for the development of their countries.

Albania: We shall not concern ourselves here with the slanderous and petty attacks of the so-called Albanian Communists, who are nothing but political adventurers. If it were not for the USSR there would be no Albania: this is known by the whole socialist world. China, who herself needs aid, supports the reactionary Albanians only so that she can point at least to one ally. But Albania also has her place at the Communist table and it is there for her when she takes it again.

Yugoslavia: It seems as though the Yugoslav comrades have lost nothing in health or spirits as a result of the vile attacks which China has now been making for many long months. It is true that over a long period Yugoslavia received great aid from the capitalist great powers, but that is not our affair. If we go to the heart of the matter, perhaps the reason why this aid was given lay with us and not with Yugoslavia. The Yugoslav comrades do not see things as we might perhaps wish. But they are building the road of peace-loving socialism in their own way and it is up to us to help them with everything we have and not as in Stalin's time to drive them into the imperialist capitalist camp. We hope sincerely that the Chinese People's Republic will one day again sit down to eat with us, and it will be an honour for us that we should also invite representatives of Yugoslavia to meet with them and to clinch that cordial friendship which is so necessary for the development of the socialist society.

India: China invaded India without even informing the USSR beforehand, though the latter had many times willingly offered to mediate in this delicate question. India was willing to negotiate, and the USSR supported China in all the preceding negotiations. But China entered these talks only to gain time for aggressive actions. That unprovoked aggression put the USSR in a very difficult position.

There is no doubt that the MacMahon line is artificial, and it is not based on the national distribution of the population there. But this was no reason for provoking military operations which were bound to throw India into the arms of the capitalists, as was always emphasised in talks with China. The policies of India and the USSR have much in common. India tried genuinely to find the path to neutral absolute independence, and there were many socialist elements which it was worth encouraging. Moreover, from 1956 there were between the USSR and India truly friendly relations, advantageous economic agreements and negotiations, and, most important, the Indians followed with gratitude the sincere efforts of the USSR to construct in their country the basis for the future well-being of many millions of Indians, who live after a century of colonial occupation in the very worst living conditions.

The establishment of this state of mutual trust required many years of difficult negotiations and patience before the fruits of mutual confidence and friendship were apparent.

In what position did the Soviet Union find itself? Its ally – though unfaithful, still an ally – was invading a country which was bound to the USSR by strong friendly relations, strengthened by several treaties of non-aggression, economic collaboration and non-interference. China was aware of the USSR's relationship with India, the contents of our treaty, and, inter alia, that it was the USSR which was supplying India with the means of self-defence, which represented a tremendous victory over the United States and England. *Then that same China requested from the USSR aid in the invasion which it had itself provoked.* How could the USSR act differently from the way it did in this case?

We begged – yes, we begged – the Chinese to stop their military operations immediately and we offered immediate mediation, for which India was ready. We wanted to prevent India from being forced to turn for military aid to the United States and Great Britain, who had been waiting for such an opportunity from the Chinese, who call themselves Communists.

Thus years of hard striving for Indian friendship and Indian neutrality went for nothing. Not only that – and let us be straight – today the capitalists are supplying arms to India because Chinese aggression forced them to do so. The Chinese aggression also had the consequence that we lost one of our most faithful friends among the Indian leaders, and that because he relied on our help.

The USSR had only one way out and we took it: during the Chinese aggression we stopped all deliveries of military material to India. When finally, but too late, the CPR stopped the aggression, because it was obvious that she had lost the sympathy even of the Asian peoples, both socialist and others, so for good material reasons the USSR came to the conclusion that there were no grounds for not fulfilling its commitments to friendly India, and it informed the Indian government that it would carry out all its treaty obligations, both civilian construction investment and military. This announcement was received with gratitude and pleasure by all sections of the Indian people.

The USSR is now fulfilling those economic commitments and will continue to fulfil them, and only hopes that China will leave aggression to the capitalists and conduct its talks with India in a peace-loving way on a basis of equality as ally with ally and as Great Power with Great Power.

Is it not clear to China that in the case of another attack India will be flooded with American and British military aid?

Before this treacherous attack India was, thanks to our untiring efforts, genuinely neutral. Her neighbour is a member of the aggressive SEATO pact. But with this appendage of the capitalists the CPR is now negotiating a pact of friendship.

February 10

Pravda published a two-page unsigned editorial entitled 'For Marxist-Leninist Unity of the Communist Movement, for Close Relations between the Countries of Socialism', which was mainly a reply to the *People's Daily* article of January 27. It took up the defence of the Yugoslav Communists and expressed a preference for bilateral meetings while accepting the necessity for a world-wide meeting. Extracts:

. . . The question of relations with Yugoslavia is a serious and fundamental question. In effect, it is a question of the line to be followed in relations between the Communist parties of socialist countries and of the principles on which relations between these countries are based. It is a question of objective appraisal of processes taking place in one socialist country or another and of the purpose of criticism by fraternal parties of mistakes made at definite times and in definite conditions and of the methods and forms of struggle for the cohesion of all the forces of Communism. What is needed is not a subjective, but a genuinely scientific Marxist-Leninist approach to this question. . . .

The League of Communists of Yugoslavia had serious differences with the world Communist movement on a number of ideological questions. This found concentrated expression in the Programme of the League of Communists of Yugoslavia. This was noted in the Statement of the Moscow meeting of 1960, which stressed that the revisionist mistakes made by the leadership of the League of Communists of Yugoslavia 'created the danger of the loss of revolutionary gains, achieved by the heroic struggle of the Yugoslav people'. Every unbiased person, reading this thesis, sees that *the meeting*, subjecting to principled criticism the erroneous conceptions of the Programme of the League of Communists of Yugoslavia, *proceeded at the same time on the assumption of Yugoslavia's being a socialist country*. The international Communist movement pursued the purpose of helping Yugoslavia and its leaders to rectify the existing mistakes – to return them to the road of unity with the world socialist system, with the fraternal parties. Precisely this approach underlies the policy of the Soviet State and the CPSU with regard to Yugoslavia and the League of Communists of Yugoslavia. . . .

It is seen from this that the CPSU's line was not to cut off Yugoslavia from the countries of socialism; not to perpetuate the departure of the League of Communists of Yugoslavia from the international Communist movement, but to help it rectify its mistakes and take its place in the ranks of our movement. The steps of our Party and the Soviet government, taken with regard to Yugoslavia, fully conform to the idea of the statement that it is necessary to rally together all the forces of peace and socialism, and reckon with the processes occurring in Yugoslavia itself. . . .

The steps taken of late by *the leadership of the League of Communists of Yugoslavia* in the sphere of party life, economy, home and foreign policy, *have rectified much of what the international Communist movement regarded as erroneous and harmful to the cause of building socialism in Yugoslavia.* This is an indisputable and very positive fact. Some comrades try to convince us that the Yugoslav leaders have never themselves admitted that they have made any mistakes 'and hence there is no reason to speak of the so-called correction of blunders'.* But those who study the processes occurring in Yugoslavia cannot but note that. . . . Comrades Josip Tito, Aleksandar Rankovic and other leaders of the League of Communists of Yugoslavia [have] criticised in several of their speeches the mistakes that were made and the existing shortcomings, and set forth practical steps for their rectification.

Addressing a meeting in Split on May 6, 1962, Comrade Tito pointed out: 'If we now have objective difficulties, objective shortcomings, this is the result of subjective mistakes primarily by our leading people', a result of the fact that the Communists 'let the guiding role slip from their hands'. The Central Committee of the League of Communists of Yugoslavia took measures to strengthen the guiding role of the Party in all spheres of the country's life. Steps are being taken in Yugoslavia to strengthen the centralised planning principle in the management of the economy, to put in order foreign trade, to step up efforts for the socialist reorganisation of agriculture. The League of Communists of Yugoslavia stresses the need for improving the education of the working people in the spirit of socialism. . . .

Yugoslavia's stand on the main international problems – war and peace, peaceful coexistence, disarmament, abolition of colonialism, the German problem and a number of other questions – is identical with, or close to, the positions of the USSR and the other socialist countries. The Yugoslav leaders are taking steps to strengthen the economic, cultural and political contacts with the countries of socialism.

Speaking in the town of Zeleznik late last year, Comrade Tito emphasised that the Yugoslav working class has great friends in the Soviet working men and women. 'And it cannot be otherwise,' he said, 'for we have common aims – the building of socialism and ultimately Communism. These are our aims, and they must be the main trend of our foreign policy – especially in our relations with them.' If one analyses the facts, one cannot but draw the conclusion that positive processes are taking place in the League of Communists of Yugoslavia, in the Federal People's Republic of Yugoslavia, towards a rapprochement with the socialist community, with the world Communist movement. One can only

* *See People's Daily* article. Chronology, Jan. 27, 1963.

wonder that voices are heard just now alleging that 'capitalism has been restored' in Yugoslavia, and saying that its leaders must be anathematised.

We would like to recall the appraisal which the *People's Daily* gave to the nature of the social order in Yugoslavia. Here is, for instance, what an editorial article of the newspaper of September 12, 1957, devoted to the arrival in China of a Yugoslav delegation, said:

> Now the peoples of our countries are advancing along the road to building socialism. We all have the same approach to many international problems. Unity on these fundamental problems furnishes a foundation for friendly co-operation between our countries. . . . For cohesion we must, above all, ascertain what we have in common in the approach to the main problems, must respect each other's achievements and each country's experience in building socialism in different historical conditions.

The article pointed out that 'Yugoslavia achieved important successes in socialist construction. At the same time Yugoslavia is also active in international affairs'. This was written six years ago. How can one now, in the light of the above-cited facts, which attest to positive changes in Yugoslavia, allege that its socialist achievements have been lost? . . .

The CPSU has not concealed, and does not conceal, that in the relations with the League of Communists of Yugoslavia there are still divergences on a number of ideological questions which found expression in the Programme of the League of Communists of Yugoslavia. This was frankly mentioned by Comrade Nikita Khrushchev at the session of the Supreme Soviet of the USSR. The CPSU criticised, and will criticise, the attempts of some leaders of the League of Communists of Yugoslavia to identify the community of the socialist countries with a military bloc and, in effect, to put the sign of equality between it and NATO: for such identification means a departure from the class positions of Marxism-Leninism.

At the same time, the CPSU holds that the socialist countries must contribute to the consolidation of socialism's positions in Yugoslavia, to the improvement of relations of the League of Communists of Yugoslavia with the international Communist movement on the Marxist-Leninist basis. It goes without saying that the development of this process depends, above all, on the position of the League of Communists of Yugoslavia, on its leadership. There can be no doubt that improvement of relations between Yugoslavia and the other socialist countries strengthens the position of socialism in Yugoslavia, and the forces of the socialist system, and meets the interests of all the countries of socialism.

What would have happened if each Communist party, at its own discretion, excommunicated other Communist parties from socialism, strove to expel them from the ranks of the Communist movement, and – what is more – refused whole nations the right to co-operate in the building of socialism? This would inevitably put a serious brake on the world revolutionary process, on the cause of struggle for the victory of the new system, for the creation of a new society. . . .

The CPSU has put an end for ever in its ranks to the Stalinist methods of cutting off those who are sincerely fighting for Communism, even though they make a few mistakes. Our Party, remaining uncompromising on principled fundamental questions of theory and practice of the Communist movement, at the same time has done and will do everything to persuade people who are vacillating or have made mistakes, to draw them into the ranks of the champions of the cause of socialism. Of course, *this refers to those who correct their mistakes. If people continue to follow their erroneous line, insist on their mistakes and even aggravate them and increasingly depart from Marxism-Leninism, it is imperative to continue and even step up the decisive struggle against them.*

If one adheres to the Leninist line in rallying the Communist movement on a principled basis, then there are all the necessary conditions to overcome any difficulties and differences that may arise. We cannot agree to the allegation that the Communist movement is 'on the brink of an abyss'. There are no reasons for such an appraisal. Of course, the CPSU, like the other fraternal parties, is deeply pained to see the differences within the ranks of the Communist movement on some important questions. But are these differences really insurmountable? *It is our profound belief that what unites the Communist Party of the Soviet Union, the Communist Party of China, all Marxist-Leninist parties, is incomparably bigger and more significant than existing differences.*

The speeches of the Chinese comrades emphasise that they adhere to the principles set out in the Declaration and the Statement of representatives of the Communist and Workers' parties; that the Chinese Communist Party is striving to avert another world war and believes in the feasibility of achieving this, advocates peaceful coexistence between states with differing social systems, and admits the possibility of using peaceful forms as well as the armed forms of struggle for the establishment of the dictatorship of the proletariat.

If the Chinese comrades agree with the CPSU and the other fraternal parties on such fundamental problems of our time, then is it not obvious that the necessary conditions exist to settle the outstanding differences? . . .

We are convinced that the differences that have arisen in the Communist movement have been generated by temporary factors, and must not turn into a profound conflict. If goodwill for a settlement of differences is displayed, no difficulties can prevent us from marching shoulder-to-shoulder along the common road to a single goal.

Everybody knows how much patience and restraint was displayed by the CPSU with regard to the leadership of the Albanian Workers' Party. Although it assumed a frankly hostile position with regard to the CPSU from the very outset, when the differences came to light, our Party repeatedly displayed initiative in the holding of negotiations to settle the disputed questions. However, the Albanian leaders rejected all our proposals. They went further and further along the road to apostasy of Marxism-Leninism and the principles of proletatian internationalism. Yet despite this, N. S. Khrushchev again repeated at the Sixth Congress of the Socialist Unity Party of Germany what he stated in the report of the CPSU Central Committee to the Twenty-second Congress of the Party: If the Albanian leaders hold dear the interests of their own people and of socialist construction in Albania, and if they really want friendship with the CPSU and the other fraternal parties, *they must renounce their erroneous views* and revert to the path of unity and close co-operation within the fraternal family, which is the socialist community, to the path of unity with the world Communist movement as a whole. Thereby, it was shown that our Party leaves the doors open for the settlement of differences with the leadership of the Albanian Workers' Party. . . .

The practice of the development of the world Communist movement has worked out various forms and methods of overcoming differences and drawing up a common line: bilateral and multilateral meetings, mutual consultations, exchange of party delegations and party information, personal contacts of party leaders, mutual participation in the work of congresses and conferences, joint scientific-theoretical and publishing work. *The most important form of the exchange of experience among Marxist-Leninist parties, of working out identical views on pressing questions of our time, enrichment of the revolutionary theory, are international meetings of Marxist-Leninist parties. The Communist Party of the Soviet Union was the initiator of both Moscow meetings.*

Now, too, the CPSU is in favour of calling a new meeting if the fraternal parties deem it expedient. Our Party, like the other Marxist-Leninist parties, is convinced that the success of the meeting would be promoted by the necessary preparatory work. Precisely this is what prompted the initiative of the CPSU Central Committee to *end open polemics* among the fraternal parties. The CPSU proceeds from the fact that it is necessary to give time a chance to do its work. It will help us to see who is right and who is wrong, to clear away all the extraneous, irrelevant stuff heaped up in the passion of polemics, to make clear the views which really require discussion and agreement. We are convinced that this is an important condition for the preparation of a meeting of Communist and Workers' parties. *Our Party deems it expedient to hold bilateral and broader meetings*, which would permit the creation of better conditions for a meeting of all the fraternal parties. The CPSU states: If in reply to this initiative of ours, some party, regardless of how substantial the differences between us may be, displays interest in a bilateral meeting, our Party is ready to have such a meeting, at any level and at any time acceptable to both sides. We come out for the genuine overcoming of existing differences, and the achievement of real unity.

February 21

People's Daily published full text of Khrushchev's Supreme Soviet speech of December 12, 1962.

February 23

Chervenkov, Soviet ambassador in Peking, handed to Mao Tse-tung a letter from the Central Committee of the CPSU dated February 21. Slightly shortened text:

Dear Comrades,

The Central Committee of the Communist Party of the Soviet Union, guided by the supreme interests of our common cause, has decided to write this letter to you in order to express our considerations concerning the need to make a common effort to strengthen the unity of the world Communist movement in accordance with the principles of Marxism-Leninism, proletarian internationalism, and the Declaration and the Statement of the Moscow meetings. We are addressing you, being deeply convinced that in the present conditions there is no task more important for the Marxist-Leninist parties than the struggle for the cohesion of our ranks, for strengthening the unity of all the socialist countries.

All who treasure the great cause of peace and socialism cannot but feel serious concern over the situation which has arisen recently in the Communist movement. The open, ever-sharpening polemics are shaking the unity of fraternal parties and doing serious damage to our common interests. The disputes which have arisen within the ranks of the international Communist movement are hindering the successful struggle against imperialism, weakening the efforts of the socialist countries in the international arena and adversely affecting the activities of fraternal parties, especially the parties of those capitalist countries where a complicated internal political situation has arisen.

The enemies of socialism are striving to take advantage of the differences that have arisen within the Communist movement in order to divide the socialist countries, to split the national liberation movement and to strengthen their own position.

. . . The direct duty of Marxist-Leninist parties, *and above all the biggest parties like the Communist Party of the Soviet Union and the Communist Party of China*, is not to permit events to develop in a direction that would confront the Communist movement with serious difficulties, and to do everything possible in order to eliminate the present abnormal situation and achieve unity in the ranks of the Communist movement and the cohesion of the socialist community.

We are deeply convinced that the difficulties now being experienced by the Communist movement are transient and can certainly be overcome. We possess everything needed to strengthen our unity and cohesion. In assessing the present situation from the point of view of the historical prospects for the development of world socialism, one cannot fail to come to the conclusion that what we have in common, the main things that unite the Communist Party of the Soviet Union, the Communist Party of China, and all the Marxist-Leninist parties, are immeasurably higher and more significant than the existing differences.

We are welded together by the unity of the class interests of the proletariat, of the working people of the whole world, by the great Marxist-Leninist teaching. No matter how serious our differences might seem today, it cannot be forgotten that in the great historical struggle of the forces of socialism against capitalism, *we stand together with you on the same side of the barricade.* . . .

The Marxist-Leninist parties are in possession of jointly worked out programmatic documents – the Declaration and the Statement of the Moscow meetings – loyalty to which they invariably stress. Steadfastly carrying out the common line agreed upon by the world Communist movement, the Communist Party of the Soviet Union is waging an active struggle against imperialism, for the triumph of the great ideals of socialism and Communism all over the globe. . . . The successes of Communist construction in the Soviet Union are a contribution on the part of our people to the cause of strengthening world socialism, increasing its authority and its power of attraction. The Communist Party of China, for its part, has continually declared that it firmly stands by the positions of the Declaration and the Statement and adheres to the conclusions and propositions contained therein, and that its main aim is to struggle against imperialism for the triumph of socialism and Communism all over the world. The Communist Party of China stresses its adherence to the policy of the peaceful coexistence of states with different social systems and acknowledges the correctness of the conclusion of the Statement concerning the possibility of preventing a new world war. The Central Committee of the Communist Party of China recognises that the principle of proletarian internationalism remains the main principle guiding mutual relations among the Communist parties and the socialist countries, and affirms its loyalty to the slogan 'Workers of all countries, unite!'

Common positions on such paramount questions are a good basis for increasing cohesion and overcoming the difficulties that have arisen. *Given firm adherence to the documents of the Moscow meetings, there is no substantial reason for exacerbating the existing differences, because a correct solution can be found to them.* . . .

In view of all this, the Central Committee of the CPSU considers that it is especially important *to take immediate concrete practical steps* to ensure our unity and to improve the atmosphere in the relations between all fraternal parties. It was these considerations that guided the first secretary of the Central Committee of the CPSU, Comrade N. S. Khrushchev, when speaking at the Sixth Congress of the Socialist Unity Party of Germany, he proposed on behalf of our Party that *polemics among Communist parties be discontinued, as well as criticism of other parties within one's own party.* As is well known, this proposal has met with a wide response and support in the world Communist movement. In writing this letter, the Central Committee of the CPSU wants to take a new step towards overcoming the difficulties that have arisen. In the interests of strengthening our friendship and better mutual understanding *we propose to the Central Committee of the Communist Party of China that a bilateral meeting be held of representatives of the CPSU and the Communist Party of China.*

Taking into consideration the importance of this meeting, and in order to be more sure of achieving its aims, we would rather have the aforementioned meeting held *at a high level.* During the talks it would be possible to take up point by point all the major questions of interest to both parties, especially those relating to the common tasks of our struggle. As for the problems on which different viewpoints actually prove to exist, agreement should be reached on measures that would help to bring our position closer to each other. If you agree to such a meeting, the place and time for holding it could be settled additionally. A meeting of representatives of the Communist Party of the Soviet Union and the Communist Party of China, the significance of which is obvious to everyone, would *also play an important role in preparing a conference of Marxist-Leninist parties and in creating the favourable climate without which it would not work successfully.*

The CPSU, like many other fraternal parties, has advocated, as it does now, the calling of the conference, considering that there are sufficiently serious grounds for this. As we see it, the attention of the conference should be centred on the common tasks of the struggle against imperialism and its aggressive plans, for the further advancement of the liberation movement of the peoples, for the rallying and all-round development of the world socialist community and for increasing its influence throughout the world, for strengthening the unity of the Communist movement.

We have already set out our view concerning the need to call a conference in our letter to you of May 31, 1962, and we now confirm it again. It is our common duty to do everything in our power to ensure that the conference leads to the further rallying of the Marxist-Leninist parties and to greater unity. We are prepared to study carefully and support any initiative aimed at overcoming the existing difficulties. The main thing needed now is good will to settle, on the basis of Marxism-Leninism, the problems that have arisen, and not to permit any actions that might hinder the strengthening of our unity.

Dear comrades, all Marxist-Leninist parties are aware that a very important moment has arrived in the development of the world Communist movement. *Upon us, upon our parties, upon the correctness of our policy depends whether we shall continue marching further together in the same ranks, or whether we shall allow ourselves to become involved in a hard and unnecessary struggle which could only lead to mutual estrangement, to the weakening of the forces of socialism, and to the undermining of the unity of the world Communist movement.*

On our parties rests the historical responsibility for enabling the Soviet and Chinese peoples to live as brothers. The unity of the CPSU and the Communist Party of China is of tremendous importance to the socialist community and to the entire Communist movement. . . .

History has placed on the first detachments of the new revolutionary movement, which have wrested their countries from the yoke of capitalism, the great task of establishing and developing relations of a new type, fraternal and friendly relations between peoples, and of creating a prototype of the future socialist society for all mankind. Our parties are in duty bound to find a way out of the existing situation and courageously and resolutely sweep away that which hinders our friendship. This is the only road that Marxist-Leninists can and must take.

We are profoundly convinced that the overcoming of the differences that have arisen would be in keeping, not only with the interests of the CPSU and the Communist Party of China, but also with the basic aims of the common struggle of the international Communist movement for peace, national independence, democracy and socialism.

It is only necessary to display good will and a profound understanding of the aims and interests of our struggle; then no obstacle can prevent us from strengthening and developing our friendship and the cohesion of the international Communist movement.

With Communist greetings,

Central Committee of the Communist Party of the Soviet Union
Moscow, February 21, 1963.

February 27

People's Daily published editorial entitled 'Whence the Differences? – A Reply to Comrade Thorez and Other Comrades'. It contained the first full account of the dispute from its beginnings, repeated the demand for an international meeting and agreed on desirability of ceasing polemics and holding bilateral meetings as necessary preparatory steps. Extracts:

Comrade Thorez, General Secretary of the French Communist Party, and certain other members of the CPF, have a prominent place in the present adverse current of attacks on the Chinese Communist Party and other fraternal parties, a current which is undermining the unity of the international Communist movement.

Since the latter part of November 1962, they have made numerous statements in quick succession attacking the Chinese Communist Party and other fraternal parties and published many related inner-party documents. . . .

. . . It is evident from these statements that in the recent anti-Chinese chorus and in the emulation campaign against the Chinese Communist Party, Thorez and other comrades have been particularly energetic, and have outdone many other comrades in assailing the Chinese Communist Party. Besides their assaults on us, Thorez and other comrades have levelled malevolent attacks at the Albanian Party of Labour, censured the fraternal parties of Korea, Burma, Malaya, Thailand, Indonesia, Vietnam and Japan, and even gone so far as to assail the national liberation movement, which is heroically fighting imperialism and colonialism. They have slanderously alleged that the 'sectarian and adventurist' positions taken by the Chinese Communist Party 'have found some echoes in certain Communist parties, particularly in Asia, and within nationalist movements', and that they 'feed the "leftism" which exists at times in these parties and movements'. The attitude of certain French comrades towards the revolutionary cause of the oppressed nations is indeed shocking. They have truly gone too far in disrupting the unity of the international Communist movement. . . .

We should like to tell those comrades who have wantonly attacked the Chinese Communist Party and other fraternal parties: the fraternal parties are equal. Since you have publicly lashed out at the Chinese Communist Party, you have no right to demand that we should refrain from publicly answering you. Similarly, since you have made public and vicious attacks on the Albanian Party of Labour, the Albanian comrades have the full and equal right to answer you publicly. At present, certain comrades of fraternal parties, while talking about a halt to the public polemics, are themselves continuing to attack the Chinese Communist Party and other fraternal parties. This double-faced attitude actually implies that only you are permitted to attack others and that it is impermissible for others to reply. This will never work. In the words of an old Chinese saying: 'Courtesy demands reciprocity. It is discourteous not to give after receiving.' In all seriousness we feel it necessary to bring this point to the attention of those who have been assailing the Chinese Communist Party. . . .

Since Thorez and other comrades have brought up the question of who is responsible for the emergence of differences in the international Communist movement, let us discuss it. *Whence the differences in the international Communist movement?* Thorez and other comrades state that these differences arose because the Chinese Communist Party did not accept the theses of the Twentieth Congress of the CPSU. This very statement is a violation of the principles guiding relations among fraternal parties as set forth in the Moscow Declaration and Statement. According to these two documents which were jointly agreed upon, the fraternal parties are equal and independent in their relations. *No one has the right to demand that all fraternal parties should accept the theses of any one party. No resolution of any congress of any one party can be taken as the common line of the international Communist movement or be binding on other fraternal parties.* If Thorez and other comrades are willing to accept the viewpoints and resolutions of another party, that is their business. As for the Chinese Communist Party, we have always held that the only common principles of action which can have binding force on us and on all other fraternal parties are Marxism-Leninism and the common documents unanimously agreed upon by the fraternal parties, and not the resolutions of the congress of any one fraternal party, or anything else.

As for the Twentieth Congress of the CPSU, it had both its positive and negative aspects. We have expressed our support for its positive aspects. *As for its negative aspects, namely, the wrong viewpoints it put forward on certain important questions of principle relating to the international Communist movement, we have held different views all along.* In talks between the Chinese and Soviet parties and at meetings of fraternal parties, we have made no secret of our views and have clearly set forth our opinions on many occasions. But in the interests of the international Communist movement, we have never publicly discussed this matter, nor do we intend to do so in the present article.

The facts are clear. The differences in the international Communist movement in recent years arose entirely because certain comrades of a fraternal party had violated the Moscow Declaration which was unanimously agreed upon by all the Communist and Workers' parties.

As is well known, the 1957 Moscow Meeting of Communist and Workers' parties, basing itself on Marxism-Leninism, eliminated certain differences among the fraternal parties, reached agreement on the current major issues in the international Communist movement, and produced the Moscow Declaration as a result of comradely consultation and collective effort. *The Declaration is the common programme of the international Communist movement.* Every fraternal party has proclaimed its acceptance of this programme. . . .

For some time after the Moscow Meeting of 1957, the Communist and Workers' parties were fairly successful and effective in their united struggle against the common enemy, and above all against US imperialism, and in their struggle against the Yugoslav revisionists, renegades from Marxism-Leninism. But, because certain comrades of a fraternal party repeatedly attempted to place the resolutions of the congress of one party above the Moscow Declaration, above the common programme of all the fraternal parties, differences within the international Communist movement inevitably ensued. Particularly around the time of the Camp David talks in September 1959, certain comrades of a fraternal party put forward a series of erroneous views on many important issues relating to the international situation and the international Communist movement, views which departed from Marxism-Leninism and violated the Moscow Declaration.

They contravened the Moscow Declaration's scientific thesis that imperialism is the source of modern wars, and that 'so long as imperialism exists there will always be soil for aggressive wars'. They incessantly proclaimed that, even while the imperialist system and the system of exploitation and oppression of man by man continue to exist in the greater part of the world: 'already in our times, the practical possibility is being created of banishing war from the life of society finally and for ever',* and 'a world without weapons, without armed forces and

* Khrushchev at Twenty-first Congress of CPSU.

without wars' can be brought into being. They also predicted that 1960 would 'go down in history as a year in which the long-cherished hope of mankind about a world without weapons and armed forces and a world without wars begins to come true.'

They contravened the thesis of the Moscow Declaration that in order to prevent another world war we should rely on the joint struggle of the socialist camp, the national liberation movement, the international working class and the mass movement of the peoples for peace. *They pinned their hopes for defending world peace on the 'wisdom' of the heads of the major powers, holding that the historical fate of the present epoch is actually decided by individual 'great men' and their 'wisdom', and that summit meetings of the major powers can determine and change the course of history.* They made such statements as: 'We have already said more than once that it is only the heads of governments who are invested with great powers, who are able to settle the most complicated international questions.' They portrayed the Camp David talks as a 'new stage', a 'new era' in international relations, and even 'a turning point in the history of mankind'.

They contravened the thesis of the Moscow Declaration that the US imperialists 'are becoming the centre of world reaction, the sworn enemies of the people'. They were especially ardent in lauding Dwight Eisenhower, the chieftain of US imperialism, as one who had 'a sincere desire for peace', who 'sincerely wishes to put an end to the state of "cold war"', and who 'also worries about ensuring peace just as we do'. . . .

They contravened the thesis of the Moscow Declaration that US imperialism vigorously seeks 'to enmesh the liberated peoples in new forms of colonialism', and proclaimed far and wide that imperialism could help the underdeveloped countries to develop their economies on an unprecedented scale, thus virtually denying that it is the nature of imperialism to plunder the underdeveloped countries. They made such statements as: 'General and complete disarmament would also create entirely new opportunities for aid to the countries whose economies are still underdeveloped and need assistance on the part of more developed countries. Even if only a small part of the money released by the termination of the military expenditures of the great powers were devoted to such aid, it could open up literally a new epoch in the economic development of Asia, Africa and Latin America.'

They contravened the thesis of the Moscow Declaration that in our day the liberation movement of the colonial and semi-colonial peoples and the revolutionary struggle of the working class of various countries are powerful forces for the defence of world peace, and counterposed the national liberation movement and the people's revolutionary struggle in various countries to the struggle for the defence of world peace. Although they occasionally spoke of the necessity of supporting national liberation wars and people's revolutionary wars, they repeatedly stressed that 'a war under contemporary conditions would inevitably become a world war', that 'even a tiny spark can cause a world conflagration' and that it was necessary to 'oppose all kinds of wars'. This amounts to making no distinction between just and unjust wars and to opposing wars of national liberation, people's revolutionary wars and just wars of all kinds on the pretext of preventing a world war.

They contravened the thesis of the Moscow Declaration that there are two possibilities, peaceful and non-peaceful, with regard to the transition from capitalism to socialism, and that 'the ruling classes will never relinquish power voluntarily', and laid a one-sided stress on the 'growing immediate possibility' of peaceful transition, alleging that peaceful transition 'is already a realistic perspective in a number of countries'. From this series of erroneous views, one can only draw the conclusions that the nature of imperialism has changed, that all its insuperable inherent contradictions no longer exist, that Marxism-Leninism is outmoded and that the Moscow Declaration should be cast aside.

But no matter what pretexts they may resort to, whether 'diplomatic language' or 'flexibility', the comrades of a fraternal party who spread these erroneous views cannot cover up their deviations from Marxism-Leninism and from the principles of the 1957 Moscow Declaration or absolve themselves from their responsibility for the creation of differences in the international Communist movement.

Such is the origin of the differences in the international Communist movement which have arisen in recent years. *How did these differences come to be exposed before the enemy?*

Thorez and other comrades allege that the differences were brought into the open with 'the Chinese Communist Party's publication of the pamphlet *Long Live Leninism* in all languages in the summer of 1960'. But what are the actual facts?

The truth is that *the internal differences among the fraternal parties were first brought into the open, not in the summer of 1960, but on the eve of the Camp David talks in September 1959 – on September 9, 1959, to be exact.* On that day a socialist country, turning a deaf ear to China's repeated explanations of the true situation and to China's advice, hastily issued a statement on a Sino-Indian border incident through its official news agency. Making no distinction between right and wrong, the statement expressed 'regret' over the border clash and in reality condemned China's correct stand. They even said that it was 'sad' and 'stupid'. Here is the first instance in history in which a socialist country, instead of condemning the armed provocations of the reactionaries of a capitalist country, condemned another fraternal socialist country when it was confronted with such armed provocation. The imperialists and reactionaries immediately sensed that there were differences among the socialist countries, and they made venomous use of this erroneous statement to sow dissension. The bourgeois propaganda machines at the time made a great deal of it, saying that the statement was like a 'diplomatic rocket launched at China' and that 'the language of the statement was to some extent like that of a stern father coldly rebuking a child and telling him to behave himself'.

After the Camp David talks, the heads of certain comrades were turned and they became more and more intemperate in their public attacks on the foreign and domestic policies of the Chinese Communist Party. They publicly abused the Chinese Communist Party as attempting 'to test by force the stability of the capitalist system', and as 'craving for war like a cock for a fight'. They also attacked the Chinese Communist Party for its general line of socialist construction, its big leap forward and its people's communes, and they spread the slander that the Chinese Party was carrying out an 'adventurist' policy in its direction of the state.

For a long time these comrades have eagerly propagated their erroneous views and attacked the Chinese Communist Party, banishing the Moscow Declaration from their minds. They have thus created confusion within the international Communist movement and placed the peoples of the world in danger of losing their bearings in the struggle against imperialism. Comrade Thorez can no doubt recall what was vigorously propagated at the time in the organ of the French Communist party, *L'Humanité*: 'Between Washington and Moscow a common language has been found, that of peaceful coexistence. America has taken the turning.' It was in those circumstances and for the sake of upholding the Moscow Declaration, defending Marxism-Leninism and enabling the people of the world to understand our point of view on the current international situation that the Chinese Communist Party published, on the ninetieth anniversary of Lenin's birth, the three articles, 'Long Live Leninism!', 'Forward Along the Path of the Great Lenin!', and 'Unite Under Lenin's Revolutionary Banner!'. Although we had already been under attack for more than half a year, *we set store by unity and made imperialism and Yugoslav revisionism the targets of the struggle in our discussion of the erroneous views which contravened the Moscow Declaration.*

Thorez and other comrades turned the truth upside down when they alleged that the publication of the three articles was the point at which the differences in the international Communist movement were brought into the open.

In May 1960, the American U2 spy plane intruded into the Soviet Union, and the four-power summit meeting in Paris was aborted. We then hoped that the comrades who had so loudly sung the praises of the so-called spirit of Camp David would draw a lesson from these events, and would strengthen the unity of the fraternal parties and countries in the common struggle against the US imperialist policies of aggression and war. But, contrary to our hopes, at the General Council Meeting of the World Federation of Trade Unions held in Peking early in June of the same year, certain comrades of fraternal parties still refused to denounce Eisenhower, spread many erroneous views and opposed the correct views put forward by the Chinese comrades.

It was a fact of particular gravity that late in June 1960 some one went so far as to wave his baton and launch an all-out and converging surprise attack on the Chinese Communist Party at the meeting of the fraternal parties in Bucharest. This action was a crude violation of the principle that questions of common interest should be solved through consultation among fraternal parties. It set an extremely bad precedent for the international Communist movement.

Thorez and other comrades have alleged that the delegate of the Albanian Party of Labour 'attacked the Communist Party of the Soviet Union' at the meeting in Bucharest. But all the comrades who attended the meeting are very well aware that the Albanian comrade did not attack anyone during the meeting. *All he did was to adhere to his own views, disobey the baton and take exception to the attack on China.* In the eyes of those who regard the relations between fraternal parties as those between patriarchal father and son, it was indeed an appalling act of impudent insubordination for tiny Albania to dare to disobey the baton. From that time on, they harboured a grudge againt the Albanian comrades, employed all kinds of base devices against them and would not rest content until they had destroyed them.

After the Bucharest meeting, some comrades who had attacked the Chinese Communist Party lost no time in taking a series of grave steps to apply *economic and political pressure*, even to the extent of *perfidiously and unilaterally tearing up agreements and contracts* they had concluded with a fraternal country, in disregard of international practice. These agreements and contracts are to be counted, not in twos or threes or in scores, but in hundreds. These malicious acts, which extended ideological differences to state relations, were out-and-out violations of proletarian internationalism and of the principles guiding relations among fraternal socialist countries as set forth in the Moscow Declaration. Instead of criticising their own errors of great-power chauvinism, these comrades charged the Chinese Communist Party with the errors of 'going it alone', 'sectarianism', 'splitting', 'national communism', etc. Does this accord with Communist ethics? Thorez and other comrades were aware of the facts, yet they dared not criticise those who actually committed the error of extending political and ideological disputes to the damage of state relations, but on the contrary charged the Chinese comrades with 'mixing problems of state with ideological and political questions'. This attitude, which confuses right and wrong and makes black white and white black, is indeed sad.

It is clear from the foregoing facts that the aggravation of differences in the international Communist movement after the Moscow Meeting of 1957 was due entirely to the fact that, with respect to a series of important issues, certain comrades of fraternal parties committed increasingly serious violations of the common line unanimously agreed upon by the fraternal parties and of the principles guiding relations among fraternal parties and countries.

The fact that Comrade Thorez disregards the facts and perverts the truth is also strikingly manifested in his distortion of *what actually happened at the 1960 Moscow Meeting*. He has charged that the Chinese Communist Party 'did not approve the line of the international working-class movement . . . and thus created a difficult situation' for the meeting.

For the good of the international Communist movement, we prefer not to go into detail here about what went on at this internal meeting of the fraternal parties; we intend to give the true picture and clarify right and wrong at the proper time and place. It must be pointed out here, however, that *the Chinese Communist Party was an initiator of the 1960 Meeting of all the Communist and Workers' parties of the world. We made great efforts to bring about its convocation*. During the meeting, we upheld Marxism-Leninism and the Moscow Declaration of 1957 and opposed the erroneous views put forward by certain comrades of fraternal parties; *at the same time, we made necessary compromises on certain questions*. Together with other fraternal parties, we made concerted efforts to overcome a variety of difficulties and enabled the meeting to achieve positive results, reach unanimous agreement and issue the Moscow Statement. These facts alone give the lie to Thorez and certain other comrades. . . . Since the Moscow Meeting of 1960, who is it that has committed increasingly serious violations of the Moscow Declaration and Statement with respect to a number of issues?

Shortly after the Moscow Meeting there was a further deterioration in the *relations between the Soviet Union and Albania*. Comrade Thorez has tried to shift the responsibility for this deterioration onto the Chinese Communist Party. He has accused China of failing 'to use its influence to bring the leaders of the Albanian Party of Labour to a more correct understanding of their duty'. . . .

We have offered our advice to the Soviet comrades many times, stating that the larger party and the larger country should take the initiative in improving Soviet-Albanian relations and settle the differences through inter-party consultation on an equal footing, and that even if it were not possible to settle some differences for the time being, they should exercise patience instead of taking any steps that might worsen relations. Accordingly, the Central Committee of the Chinese Communist party wrote to the Central Committee of the Soviet Communist Party, expressing the hope that the question of Soviet-Albanian relations would be resolved through consultation.

But no consideration was given to our sincere efforts. A number of incidents occurred: the withdrawal of naval vessels from the naval base of Vlore, the recall of experts from Albania, the cessation of aid to Albania, interference in her internal affairs, etc.

The Chinese Communist Party was pained by these crude violations of the principles guiding relations among fraternal countries. On the eve of the Twenty-second Congress of the CPSU, the leaders of the Chinese Communist Party once again gave the Soviet comrades comradely advice concerning the improvement of Soviet-Albanian relations. But to our surprise, at the Twenty-second Congress there occurred the grave incident in which the Albanian Party of Labour was publicly named and attacked, and *the odious precedent was thus created of one party using its own congress to make a public attack on another fraternal party*. . . .

It is a matter for regret that this serious and just attitude of ours should have been censured. One comrade* even said: 'If the Chinese comrades wish to contribute to normalising relations between the Albanian Party of Labour and fraternal parties, there is hardly anyone who could do more than the Communist Party of China to help solve this problem.' What did this remark mean? If it meant to hold the Chinese comrades responsible for the deterioration of Soviet-Albanian relations, that was shirking one's own responsibility and trying to impute it to others. If it meant that the Chinese comrades should help to bring about an improvement in Soviet-Albanian relations, we would point out that some comrades actually deprived other fraternal parties of the possibility of effectively contributing to the improvement of those relations by completely ignoring our repeated advice and by obdurately exacerbating Soviet-Albanian relations even to the length of openly calling for a change in the leadership of the Albanian party and state. After the CPSU Congress, these comrades broke off the Soviet Union's diplomatic relations with the fraternal socialist country of Albania without any scruples. Did this not convincingly demonstrate that they had not the slightest desire to improve relations between the Soviet Union and Albania?

Thorez and other comrades have blamed the Chinese press for 'spreading the erroneous propositions of the Albanian leaders'. We must point out that *the*

* *i.e.* Khrushchev.

Chinese Communist Party has always opposed bringing inter-party differences into the open and that it was certain comrades of a fraternal party who insisted on doing this and maintained, moreover, that not to do so was inconsistent with the Marxist-Leninist stand. In these circumstances, when the differences between the Soviet Union and Albania came into the open, we simultaneously published some of the material on both sides of the controversy in order to let the Chinese people understand how matters actually stood. Can it possibly be considered right that certain comrades of a fraternal party may repeatedly and freely condemn another fraternal party, may say that its leaders are anti-Leninist, that those leaders want to earn the privilege of receiving an imperialist hand-out of thirty pieces of silver, that they are executioners with blood on their hands, and so on and so forth, while this fraternal party is not allowed to defend itself, and other fraternal parties are not allowed to publish material on both sides of the controversy simultaneously? *Those who claim to be 'completely correct' have published one article after another attacking Albania, but they are mortally afraid of the Albanian comrades' replies, they dare not publish them and are afraid of others doing so.* It simply shows that justice is not on their side and that they have a guilty conscience.

Furthermore, Comrade Thorez and other comrades *accuse the Chinese Communist Party of having 'transferred into the mass movements the differences which may exist or arise among Communists'*, referring especially to the Stockholm Conference of the World Peace Council in December 1961, where, they say, the Chinese Communist 'counterposed the struggle for national liberation to the struggle for disarmament and peace'.

But the truth is just the reverse. It is not the Chinese comrades but certain comrades of a fraternal party who have injected the differences between fraternal parties into the international democratic organisations. . . .

. . . At the Stockholm Conference of the World Peace Council in December 1961, the demand made by certain persons . . . was that colonial and semi-colonial peoples living under the bayonets of imperialism and colonialism should wait until the imperialists and colonialists accept general and complete disarmament, renounce their armed suppression of the national independence movement and help the underdeveloped countries with the money saved from disarmament. . . . Proceeding from precisely this absurd 'theory', these persons have vilified the national independence movement as a 'movement for piling up corpses'. It is these persons, and not the Chinese comrades, who violated the Moscow Declaration and the Moscow Statement.

The two most recent major issues in the international situation were *the Caribbean crisis* and *the Sino-Indian border conflict*. The stand taken by the Chinese Communist Party on these issues conforms entirely with Marxism-Leninism and with the Moscow Declaration and the Moscow Statement. Yet in this connexion Thorez and other comrades have made vicious attacks on the Chinese Communist Party.

With regard to the Caribbean crisis, Thorez and the other comrades have accused China of wanting to 'bring on a war between the Soviet Union and the United States and so plunge the world into a thermonuclear catastrophe'. Do the facts bear out this charge? What did the Chinese people do during the Caribbean crisis? They firmly condemned the acts of aggression perpetrated by US imperialism, they firmly supported the five demands of the Cuban people in defence of their independence and sovereignty, and they firmly opposed the attempt to impose 'international inspection' on Cuba which was made for the sake of an unprincipled compromise. In all this, what exactly did we do that was wrong? . . .

We should like to say to Thorez and the other comrades that the eyes of the people of the world are clear; it is not we but you who have committed mistakes in connexion with the Caribbean crisis. For you have tried to help out the Kennedy Administration, which provoked the crisis in the Caribbean, by insisting that people should believe the US promise not to attack Cuba, although the Kennedy Administration has itself denied having made any such promise. You have defended those comrades who committed both the error of adventurism and the error of capitulationism. You have defended infringements upon the sovereignty of a fraternal country. And you are making the fight against the Chinese Communist Party and other Marxist-Leninist parties, rather than the fight against US imperialism, your prime concern.

On *the Sino-Indian boundary question*, Thorez and other comrades have accused China of lacking the 'minimum of goodwill' for a settlement of the dispute. This charge is ludicrous. . . . The surprising thing is that when a fraternal socialist country was facing the Nehru government's provocations and attacks, certain self-styled Marxist-Leninists should abandon the principle of proletarian inter-nationalism and assume a 'neutral' stand. In practice, they have not only been giving political support to the anti-China policy of the Nehru government, but have been supplying that government with war material. Instead of condemning these wrong actions, Thorez and other comrades have described them as a 'sensible policy'. What has happened to your Marxism-Leninism and your proletarian internationalism? . . .

Several fraternal European parties held their congresses between November 1962 and January 1963. At these congresses, by careful arrangements, a disgusting situation was created in which large-scale and systematic public attacks were made on the Chinese Communist Party and other fraternal parties by name. In particular, at the recent congress of the German Socialist Unity Party, this adverse current reached a new high in the attacks on the Chinese Communist Party and other fraternal parties and the disruption of the unity of the inter-national Communist movement. At this congress, certain comrades, while talking about ending the attacks, continued violently to assail the Chinese Communist Party and other fraternal parties and, moreover, they openly tried to reverse the verdict on the traitorous Tito clique. Can these comrades deceive anybody by their double-dealing? Obviously not. Such double-dealing just shows that they are not sincere about stopping the polemics and restoring unity.

In particular, it must be pointed out that *the question of how to treat the Tito clique is a major question of principle*. It is not a question of how to interpret the Moscow Statement but of whether to defend it or tear it up. It is not a question of helping comrades to rectify the mistakes they have made, but of unmasking and denouncing enemies of Marxism-Leninism and the Moscow Statement. The Chinese Communist Party will never allow the common agreement of the fraternal parties to be either doctored or scrapped, will never allow traitors to be pulled into our ranks, and will never agree to any trading in Marxist-Leninist principles or bartering away of the interests of the international Communist movement. . . .

If Thorez and the other comrades dare to face the facts and believe themselves to be right, they ought to publish the material of the Chinese Communist Party which explains its views, including the relevant articles we have published recently, and let all the members of the French Communist Party and the French working class learn the truth and decide for themselves what is right and what is wrong. Comrade Thorez and the other comrades! *We have already published your statements accusing us. Will you do the same? Do you have that kind of statesmanship? Do you have that kind of courage?* Comrade Thorez and certain other comrades of the French Communist Party have distorted facts and reversed right and wrong to an extent that is really astonishing and yet they keep on calling themselves 'creative Marxist-Leninists'. Very well, let us look at this kind of 'creativeness'.

We note that, prior to 1959, Thorez and the other comrades rightly pointed out that US imperialism was the leader of the forces of aggression and that they denounced the US government's policies of aggression and war. But on the eve of the Camp David talks someone* said that Eisenhower hoped for 'the elimination of tension in the relations between states', and so Thorez and the others decided that the elected municipal and general councillors of the French Communist Party should welcome this 'peace emissary'. *This was a complete turn of 180 degrees in response to the baton.*

We also note that, in September 1959, after de Gaulle had issued a statement about 'self-determination' for Algeria in which he totally refused to recognise her independence and sovereignty, the Political Bureau of the Central Committee of the French Communist Party issued a statement which rightly exposed this as a 'purely demagogic manoeuvre'. At that time Comrade Thorez himself said that it was 'nothing but a political manoeuvre'. But in little more than a month, as soon as a foreign comrade said that de Gaulle's statement had 'great significance', Comrade Thorez severely criticised the Political Bureau of the Central Committee of the French Communist Party for having made a 'false appreciation', declaring that the Political Bureau's original statement had been 'hasty, precipitate'. *This was another complete turn of 180 degrees in response to the baton.*

We note further that in the past Thorez and the other comrades correctly denounced the revisionist programme of the Yugoslav Tito clique, saying that the Tito clique was accepting 'the subsidies of the American capitalists', and that these 'capitalists clearly do not bestow them in order to facilitate the construction of socialism'. But recently someone spoke of 'helping' the Tito clique 'to resume its place in the great family of all fraternal parties', and so Thorez and other comrades began to talk a great deal about 'helping the League of Yugoslav Communists to return once again to the fold of the great Communist family'. *This was another complete turn of 180 degrees in response to the baton.*

We also note that a year or so ago when the Chinese Communist Party opposed the practice of one party publicly attacking another fraternal party at its own congress, someone condemned this as being 'contrary to the Marxist-Leninist

* *i.e.* Khrushchev.

stand'. And then, Comrade Thorez followed him by saying that the Chinese comrades were 'wrong' to take such an attitude, which was 'not right'. Recently, someone continued the attacks while saying that open polemics should halt, and so certain comrades of the French Communist Party again followed suit and said this was 'sensible, Leninist'. This was still another turn in response to the baton.

Instances of this sort are too numerous to mention. Turning about in this way and following the baton so unconditionally cannot possibly be regarded as indicative of the normal relationship of independence and equality that should exist among fraternal parties, but rather of *abnormal, feudal, patriarchal relationships*. . . .

In order to eliminate differences and strengthen unity, the Chinese Communist Party has many times proposed, and still holds today, that *a meeting of representatives of the Communist and Workers' parties of all countries should be convened*; moreover, the Chinese Communist Party is ready to take the necessary steps together with all the fraternal parties to prepare the conditions for the convening of such a meeting.

One of the preparatory steps for such a meeting is *the cessation of the public polemics* which are still going on. The Chinese Communist Party made this proposal long ago. We are of the opinion that in ceasing public polemics the actions must suit the words, and that the cessation must be mutual and general. While professing to terminate these polemics, some persons have continued to make attacks. Actually they want to forbid you to strike back after they have beaten you up. This will not do. Not only must attacks on the Chinese Communist Party cease; *the attacks levelled at the Albanian Party of Labour and other fraternal parties must also stop. Moreover, it is absolutely impermissible to use the pretext of stopping polemics in order to forbid the exposure and condemnation of Yugoslav revisionism, because this violates the provision of the Moscow Statement* on the obligation to expose further the revisionist leaders of Yugoslavia. Some persons now want to oust the fraternal Albanian Party of Labour from the international Communist movement on the one hand, and to pull in the renegade Tito clique on the other. *We want to tell these people frankly that this is absolutely impossible.*

A necessary step for preparing such a meeting is to hold bilateral and multilateral talks among the fraternal parties. This was proposed by the Chinese Communist Party as far back as ten months ago. We have always been willing to have talks with all the fraternal parties which share our desire to eliminate differences and strengthen unity. . . .

February (end)

CPSU approached Albanian Communists with proposal for bilateral talks.

March 1–4

People's Daily published by instalments the full 50,000-word text of *Red Flag* article entitled 'More on the Differences between Comrade Togliatti and Us – Some Important Problems of Leninism in the Modern World'.

It reviewed all the main issues in the dispute and challenged the Russians to publish the Chinese articles in their press. Extracts:

The current great debate was first provoked by the Tito clique of Yugoslavia through its open betrayal of Marxism-Leninism. The Tito clique had taken the road of revisionism long ago. In the winter of 1956, it took advantage of the anti-Soviet and anti-Communist campaign launched by the imperialists to conduct propaganda against Marxism-Leninism on the one hand and, on the other, to carry out subversive activities within the socialist countries in co-ordination with imperialist schemes. Such propaganda and sabotage reached a climax in the counter-revolutionary rebellion in Hungary. It was then that Tito made his notorious Pula speech. . . .

The Communists of all countries waged a stern struggle against this treacherous attack by the Tito clique. We had published the article 'On the Historical Experience of the Dictatorship of the Proletariat' in April 1956. Towards the end of December 1956, aiming directly at the Titoist attack, we published another article 'More on the Historical Experience of the Dictatorship of the Proletariat'. In 1957, the Meeting of Representatives of the Communist and Workers' parties of the socialist countries adopted the famous Moscow Declaration. This Declaration explicitly singled out revisionism as the main danger in the present international Communist movement. It denounced the modern revisionists because they 'seek to smear the great teaching of Marxism-Leninism, declare that it is "outmoded" and allege that it has lost its significance for social progress'. The Tito clique refused to sign the Declaration, and in 1958 put forward their out-and-out revisionist programme, which they counterposed to the Moscow Declaration. Their programme was unanimously repudiated by the Communists of all countries. But in the ensuing period, especially *from 1959 onwards, the leaders of certain Communist parties went back on the joint agreement they had signed and endorsed, and made Tito-like statements.* Subsequently, these persons found it increasingly hard to contain themselves; their language became more and more akin to Tito's, and they did their best to prettify the US imperialists. They turned the spearhead of their struggle against the fraternal parties which firmly uphold Marxism-Leninism and the revolutionary principles laid down in the Moscow Declaration, and made unbridled attacks on them. After consultation on an equal footing at the 1960 Meeting of Representatives of Communist and Workers' parties, agreement was reached on many differences that had arisen between the fraternal parties. The Moscow Statement issued by this meeting severely condemned the leaders of the Yugoslav League of Communists for their betrayal of Marxism-Leninism. We heartily welcomed the agreement reached by the fraternal parties at this meeting, and in our own actions have strictly adhered to and defended the agreement. But *not long afterwards, the leaders of certain fraternal parties again went back on the joint agreement* they had signed and endorsed, and they made public attacks on other fraternal parties at their own party congresses, laying bare before the enemy the differences in the international Communist movement. While assailing fraternal parties, they extravagantly praised the Tito clique and wilfully wallowed in the mire with it.

Events have shown that the modern revisionist trend is a product, under new conditions, of the policies of imperialism. Inevitably, therefore, this trend is international in character, and, like the previous debates, the present debate between Marxist-Leninists and the modern revisionists is inevitably developing into an international one.

After launching and organising a series of preposterous attacks on the Chinese Communist Party and other fraternal parties, certain people have suddenly begun to strike up the tune of 'unity'. But what they call unity consists of giving themselves permission to abuse others, while not allowing the others to reason with them. By 'calling a halt to open polemics', they mean permission for themselves to attack others as they please, while the others are forbidden to make whatever reply is called for. While talking of unity, they continue to undermine unity! While talking of calling a halt to open polemics, they continue their open attacks. What is more, they say threateningly that unless those whom they attack keep their mouths shut, it will be 'imperative to continue and even step up decisive struggle against them'.

But when it comes to the Tito clique, these people really seek unity. Their desire is unity with the Tito clique, not the unity of the international Communist movement; they desire unity on the basis of modern revisionism as represented by the Tito clique, or unity on the basis of the baton of certain people, and not unity on the basis of Marxism-Leninism, of the Moscow Declaration and the Moscow Statement. In practice, therefore, their unity is a pseudonym for split. Using unity as a smokescreen, they are trying to cover up their actual splitting activities. . . .

There are people who are *working frantically to create a split* by resorting to many dishonest tricks, spreading rumours, slinging mud and sowing dissension. But the overwhelming majority of the people of the world want unity in the international Communist movement and are opposed to a split. . . . Historically, none of the splitters who betrayed Marxism-Leninism ever came to a good end. We have already advised those who are working to create a split to 'rein in at the brink of the precipice', but certain people are unwilling to take our advice. They believe they are not yet at the 'brink', and they are not ready 'to rein in'. Apparently they are very much interested in continuing their splitting activities. Let them go on creating trouble if they must. The masses, and history, will pass judgement on them. . . .

Something very interesting is happening today on a wide scale in the international Communist movement. What is this interesting phenomenon? The doughty warriors who claim to possess the totality of Marxist-Leninist truth are mortally afraid of the articles written in reply to their attacks by the so-called dogmatists, sectarians, splitters, nationalists and Trotskyites whom they have so vigorously condemned. They dare not publish these articles in their own newspapers and journals. As cowardly as mice, they are scared to death. They dare not let the people of their own countries read our articles, and they have tried to impose a watertight embargo. They are even using powerful stations to jam our broadcasts and prevent their people from listening to them.

Dear friends and comrades, who claim to possess the whole truth! Since you are quite definite that our articles are wrong, why don't you publish all these erroneous articles and then refute them point by point, so as to inculcate hatred among your people against the 'heresies' you call dogmatism, sectarianism and anti-Marxism-Leninism? Why do you lack the courage to do this? Why such a stringent embargo? You fear the truth. The huge spectre you call 'dogmatism', *i.e.* genuine Marxism-Leninism, is haunting the world, and it threatens you. You have no faith in the people, and the people have no faith in you. You are divorced from the masses. That is why you fear the truth and carry your fear to such absurd lengths.

Friends, comrades! If you are men enough, step forward! Let each side in the debate publish all the articles in which it is criticised by the other side, and let the people in our own countries and the whole world think over and judge who is right and who is wrong. That is what we are doing, and we hope you will follow our example. We are not afraid to publish everything of yours in full. We publish all the 'masterpieces' in which you rail at us. Then, in reply we either refute them point by point, or refute their main points. Sometimes we publish your articles without a word in answer, leaving the readers to judge for themselves. Isn't that fair and reasonable? You, modern revisionist masters! Do you dare to do the same? If you are men enough, you will. *But having a guilty conscience and an unjust case, being fierce of visage but faint of heart, outwardly as tough as bulls but inwardly as timid as mice, you will not dare.* We are sure you will not dare. Isn't that so? Please answer! . . .

March 8

People's Daily published an editorial entitled 'A Comment on the Statement of the Communist Party of the USA', defending the Chinese attitude to the Cuban crisis and mentioning for the first time 'unequal treaties' imposed by Tsarist Russia on China.

With an ulterior purpose, the statement of the CPUSA referred to Taiwan, Hongkong and Macao. It said that the Chinese comrades were 'correctly, not following the adventurous policy in Taiwan, Hongkong and Macao that they advocate for others. Why this double standard approach?' *We know from what quarter they have learned this ridiculous charge. And we know, too, the purpose of the person who manufactured it.*

Here we should like to answer all those who have raised this matter. For us there never has been a question of a 'double standard'. We have only one standard, whether in dealing with the question of Taiwan, whether in dealing with the questions of Hongkong and Macao, or whether in dealing with all international questions, and that standard is Marxism-Leninism, proletarian internationalism, the interests of the Chinese people and of the people of the world, the interests of world peace and the revolutionary cause of the people of all countries. In international struggles we are opposed both to adventurism and to capitulationism. These two hats can never fit our heads. Inasmuch as some persons have mentioned Taiwan, Hongkong and Macao, we are obliged to discuss a little of the history of imperialist aggression against China.

In the hundred years or so prior to the victory of the Chinese revolution, the imperialist and colonial powers – the United States, Britain, France, Tsarist Russia, Germany, Japan, Italy, Austria, Belgium, the Netherlands, Spain and Portugal – carried out unbridled aggression against China. They compelled the governments of old China to sign a large number of unequal treaties: the Treaty of Nanking in 1842, the Treaty of Aigun in 1858, the Treaty of Tientsin of 1858, the Treaty of Peking of 1860, the Treaty of Ili of 1881, the Protocol of Lisbon of 1887, the Treaty of Shimonoseki of 1895, the Convention for the Extension of Hongkong of 1898, the Treaty of 1901, etc. By virtue of these unequal treaties, they annexed Chinese territory in the north, south, east and west and held leased territories on the seaboard and in the hinterland of China. Some seized Taiwan and the Penghu Islands, some occupied Hongkong and forcibly leased Kowloon, some put Macao under perpetual occupation, etc., etc.

At the time the People's Republic of China was inaugurated, our government declared that it would examine the treaties concluded by previous Chinese governments with foreign governments, treaties that had been left over by history, and would recognise, abrogate, revise or renegotiate them according to their respective contents. In this respect, our policy towards the socialist countries is fundamentally different from our policy towards the imperialist countries. When we deal with various imperialist countries, we take differing circumstances into consideration and make distinctions in our policy. As a matter of fact, many of these treaties concluded in the past either have lost their validity, or have been abrogated or have been replaced by new ones. With regard to the outstanding issues, which are a legacy from the past, we have always held that, when conditions are ripe, they should be settled peacefully through negotiations and that, pending a settlement, the status quo should be maintained. Within this category are the questions of Hongkong, Kowloon and Macao and the questions of all those boundaries which have not been formally delimited by the parties concerned in each case. As for Taiwan and the Penghu Islands, they were restored to China in 1945, and the question now is the US imperialist invasion and occupation of them and US imperialist interference in China's internal affairs. We Chinese people are determined to exercise our sovereign right to liberate our own territory of Taiwan; at the same time, through the ambassadorial talks between China and the United States in Warsaw, we are striving to solve the question of effecting the withdrawal of US armed forces from Taiwan and the Taiwan Straits. Our position as described above accords not only with the interests of the Chinese people but also with the interests of the people of the socialist camp and the people of the whole world.

Why is it that after the Caribbean crisis this correct policy of ours suddenly became a topic of discussion among certain persons and a theme for their anti-China campaign? These heroes are apparently very pleased with themselves for having picked up a stone from a cesspool, with which they believe they can instantly fell the Chinese. But whom has this filthy stone really hit? . . .

We know very well, and you know too, that you are, to put it plainly, bringing up the questions of Hongkong and Macao merely as a fig-leaf to hide your disgraceful performance in the Caribbean crisis. But all this is futile. There is an objective criterion for truth, just as there is for error. What is right cannot be made to look wrong, nor can wrong be made to look right. To glory in your disgraceful performance will not add to your prestige. How can the correct policy of the Chinese people on the questions of Hongkong and Macao be mentioned in the same breath with your erroneous policy on the Caribbean crisis? How can such a comparison help you to whitewash yourselves? Our resolute defence of our sovereignty in the matter of Taiwan is completely consistent with our resolute support of the Cuban people in defending their sovereignty during the Caribbean crisis. How can this be described as having a 'double standard'? We say to these friends who are acting the hero, it is you, and not we, who really have a 'double standard'. With regard to the US imperialists, one day you call them pirates and the next you say they are concerned for peace. As for revolutionary Cuba, you say that you support her five demands for safeguarding her independence and sovereignty, but on the other hand, you try to impose 'international inspection' on her. With regard to the Sino-Indian boundary dispute, you speak of 'fraternal China' and 'friendly India' on the one hand, but on the other you maliciously attack China and support the Indian reactionaries in divers ways. As for Hong-kong and Macao, while you ostensibly speak for China, you are actually stabbing her in the back. Are you not applying a 'double standard' in all your actions? Is this not a manifestation of dual personality?

March 9

Teng Hsiao-ping, General Secretary of Chinese CP handed the Soviet ambassador, Chervonenko, his party's reply to the CPSU letter of February 21. Shortened text:

Dear Comrades,

The Central Committee of the Communist Party of China has received the letter of the Central Committee of the Communist Party of the Soviet Union dated February 21, 1963.

Comrade Mao Tse-tung has already set forth our appraisal of your letter during the talk with the Soviet ambassador to China, Comrade Chervonenko, on February 23.

We welcome your letter. We welcome the desire for unity and cohesion. We welcome the normal attitude of equality towards fraternal parties shown in it. *We welcome your definite approval of the proposal for convening a conference of representatives of Communist and Workers' parties of the world. . . .*

We ought to face the fact that at present there are serious differences in the international Communist movement on a series of important questions of principle. As for the causes of these differences, which your letter says 'can be explained by the different conditions in which this or that detachment of the world Communist movement is working', the more important factor, in our opinion, is the question of how Marxism-Leninism is understood and what attitude is taken towards it, and the question of how the Moscow Declaration and the Moscow Statement are understood and what attitude is taken towards them.

The Chinese Communist Party has always advocated that, when differences on questions of principle arise between fraternal parties, the fraternal parties should start with the desire for unity, carry on comradely discussion and mutual criticism so as to distinguish right from wrong, and reach the goal of unity on the basis of Marxism-Leninism. . . .

The Chinese Communist Party is and always has been opposed to public exposure of differences between fraternal parties before the enemy. We are even more strongly opposed to the inflammation of debate and the complication of matters by the use of such methods as the convening of party congresses, the issuing of resolutions or statements by party central committees, and the publication of articles and speeches by party and state leaders. . . .

The international Communist movement has indeed reached a critical juncture. The time has indeed come when the differences among the fraternal parties have to be settled.

We have before us a very good international situation, one that is most favourable for revolution in the world. . . .

In this situation, what is of decisive significance for the international cause of the proletariat as a whole is the struggle against imperialism, headed by the United States, and the support for the revolutionary struggles of the oppressed nations and peoples of Asia, Africa and Latin America. . . .

The Moscow Declaration and Statement set forth the common line, course and policies for our common struggle. . . .

In our words and deeds, we Chinese Communists have unswervingly followed and maintained this correct line, this correct course and these correct policies. We are very glad that the Soviet comrades, too, have in their letter expressed their loyalty to these two programmatic documents. . . .

With the purpose of eliminating differences and strengthening unity, the Central Committee of the Chinese Communist Party wrote a letter to the Central Committee of the CPSU on April 7, 1962.

In that letter, the Central Committee of the Chinese Communist Party expressed its support for the proposal to convene a meeting of the fraternal parties put forward by the Communist Party of Indonesia, the Workers' Party of Vietnam, the Communist Party of Sweden, the Communist Party of Great Britain and the Communist Party of New Zealand, and explicitly proposed that a meeting of representatives of the Communist and Workers' parties of all countries be convened to discuss problems of common concern. We are very glad that in its recent letter the Central Committee of the CPSU also favours calling a meeting of representatives of the Communist and Workers' parties.

In our letter of April 7, 1962, we also pointed out that in order to convene and make a success of a meeting of the fraternal parties, many obstacles would have to be overcome beforehand and much preparatory work would have to be done. At the same time *we advanced the following points:*

1. The fraternal parties and fraternal countries which have disputes between them should take steps, however small, that will help to ease relations and restore unity so as to improve the atmosphere and prepare the conditions for the convening and the success of a meeting of the fraternal parties.

2. We support the proposal of the Workers' Party of Vietnam that public attacks should cease.

3. Where needed, certain fraternal parties should hold bilateral or multilateral talks to exchange opinions.

4. We sincerely hope that the Soviet comrades and the Albanian comrades will both take positive steps to remove their differences and restore normal

relations between the two parties and the two countries. In this connexion it seems necessary for the Soviet comrades to take the initiative.

5. *According to the decision of the meeting of the fraternal parties in 1957, the CPSU is responsible for convening meetings of representatives of the Communist and Workers' parties after consultation with fraternal parties.*

At present, we still hold that the foregoing points are important for the success of a meeting of the fraternal parties. We are very glad that in its recent letter the Central Committee of the CPSU has also advanced valuable proposals for making the meeting of the fraternal parties successful. We agree with you that 'it is especially important to take immediate concrete practical steps to ensure our unity and to improve the atmosphere in the relations between all fraternal parties'.

In order to create a favourable atmosphere for the convening of the meeting of the fraternal parties, we have decided that, apart from the articles which we have already published as replies, *we will from now on temporarily suspend public replies in our newspapers and periodicals to the public attacks which were directed by name against the Chinese Communist Party by comrades of the CPSU and other fraternal parties.* It goes without saying that, basing ourselves on the principle of equality and reciprocity between fraternal parties, we reserve the right to make public replies to all the statements of fraternal parties which publicly attacked the Chinese Communist Party by name. On the suspension of public polemics, it is also necessary that our two parties and the fraternal parties concerned should have some discussion and reach an agreement that is fair and acceptable to all.

We welcome the proposal in your letter that talks be held between the Chinese and Soviet parties. We hold that such talks constitute a necessary preparatory step for the convening of a meeting of representatives of the Communist and Workers' parties of all countries. *In his conversation with Comrade Chervonenko, Comrade Mao Tse-tung expressed the hope that Comrade Khrushchev, while making his visit to Cambodia, would stop over in Peking for talks between our two parties and an exchange of views.* If this is not convenient for you, the Central Committee of the CPSU can send to Peking a delegation headed by another responsible comrade or we can send a delegation to Moscow.

We agree with your view that 'during the talks it would be possible to take up point by point all the major questions of interest to both parties, especially those relating to the common tasks of our struggle'. We hold that the questions that need to be discussed in the talks between the Chinese and Soviet parties are also the questions that need to be discussed at the meeting of representatives of the Communist and Workers' parties of all countries, and that they are, first of all, the following: *the question of the strategy and tactics of revolution in the contemporary world, the question of opposing imperialism and defending world peace, the question of the liberation struggles of the oppressed nations and people, the question of strengthening the power and unity of the socialist camp, the question of strengthening the unity of the international Communist movement, and other questions of common interest.*

All these questions ought to be discussed in a comradely way, point by point, to the full and in detail, in accordance with the fundamental teachings of Marxism-Leninism and with the revolutionary principles set forth in the Moscow

Declaration and Statement and the consultation ought not to be a mere formality but should be conducted on a footing of real equality.

Whatever is agreed upon by both sides can be settled at once and agreement can be concluded. Existing differences that cannot be settled immediately may be laid aside, pending later settlement. We propose that if we cannot finish our discussions in one session, *several* should be held, or that our parties should hold further bilateral talks.

It is the common desire of the people of China and the Soviet Union, of all the people in the socialist camp, of the Communists in all countries and of all the oppressed people the world over to strengthen the unity of the international Communist movement, to strengthen the unity of the socialist camp, and especially to strengthen the unity between our two parties and countries.

We are conscious of the responsibility that falls on our two parties. We must not disappoint these expectations. Let us unite on the basis of Marxism-Leninism, on the basis of proletarian internationalism and on the basis of the Moscow Declaration and the Moscow Statement.

With Communist greetings,

Central Committee of the Communist Party of China
March 9, 1963.

March 9

People's Daily published an editorial entitled 'A Mirror for Revisionists' condemning the attitude of the 'Dange clique' in the Indian Communist Party. Extracts:

In the past twelve months, the revisionist clique headed by Dange have seized the leadership of the Communist Party of India by taking advantage of the large-scale campaign launched by the ruling groups of the Indian big bourgeoisie and big landlords against China, against Communism and against the Indian people. They have betrayed Marxism-Leninism and proletarian internationalism, betrayed the revolutionary cause of the Indian proletariat and the Indian people and embarked on the road of national chauvinism and class capitulationism, thus creating complete chaos in the Indian Communist Party. Their intention is to turn the Indian Communist Party into an appendage of India's big bourgeoisie and big landlords and a lackey of the Nehru government.

How low have Dange and company sunk? Let us first look at Dange's letter of greetings to Nehru, dated November 14, 1962, on the occasion of the latter's birthday. Here is the full text:

My dear Panditji,

Allow me to convey our heartfelt congratulations to you on behalf of the Communist Party of India on your 73rd birthday. You have inspired and led heroically the Indian nation in its struggle for national freedom. In the post-independence period you have laid the foundations of a new Indian nation pledged to the policies of planned development, democracy, socialism, peace, non-alignment and anti-colonialism.

Today, in this hour of grave crisis created by the Chinese aggression, the nation has mustered around you as a man to safeguard its honour, integrity and sovereignty. The Communist Party of India pledges its unqualified support to your policies of national defence and national unity. May you live long to realise your ideals of building a prosperous and socialist India.

Yours sincerely,

S. A. Dange,

Chairman CPI

This is not an ordinary courtesy letter. In his letter, (1) Dange completely sides with the Indian reactionaries and violently opposes socialist China; (2) Dange pledges the Indian Communist Party's support to the Nehru government's 'policies of national defence and national unity' which are directed against China, against Communism and against the Indian people, and what is more, he pledges, not support in general, but 'unqualified support', and (3) Dange places his reliance on Nehru, the representative of the big bourgeoisie and big landlords, to bring about socialism in India.

This letter is the Dange clique's political oath of betrayal of the Indian proletariat; it is an indenture by which they sell themselves to the Indian big bourgeoisie and big landlords and the Nehru government. . . .

Since World War II, revisionist trends have afflicted the Communist parties of a number of countries. Renegades from Marxism-Leninism, like Browder and Gates in the United States, Larsen in Denmark and Shojiro Kasuga in Japan have appeared in a good many parties. And it is not only in Communist parties of capitalist countries that such renegades have made their appearance; in Yugoslavia where the proletariat once held power, there emerged the revisionist Tito clique which betrayed Marxism-Leninism. It is important for Communists throughout the world to draw lessons from the damage these traitorous cliques have inflicted on the cause of Communism. . . .

The Tito clique provides a mirror. It reveals how a group of renegades following a revisionist line corrupt a party and cause a socialist country to degenerate into a capitalist country.

The Dange clique provides another mirror. It reveals how the leaders of a Communist party in a capitalist country take the road of revisionism, slide down it and end up as the servants and the tail of the bourgeoisie. . . .

March 16

New China News Agency released the text of a speech by Liao Cheng-chi attacking Yugoslav Communists.

March 17

Pravda published a cautious defence of American Communists, replying in effect to *People's Daily* editorial of March 8.

March 18

Pravda published an article containing high praise of Maurice Thorez, thus replying in effect to the Chinese criticisms of his stand.

March 20

Enver Hoxha, Albanian leader, made a strongly anti-Khrushchev speech.

March 21

People's Daily started publication of statements made by foreign Communist leaders in criticism of the Chinese Communist Party.

March 25

New China News Agency released text of letter addressed simultaneously to the Soviet and Chinese Communist parties by Aidit, Chairman of the Indonesian Communist Party, welcoming the exchange of letters between Moscow and Peking and the decision to hold talks.

April 2

Russians released the text of a letter from CPSU to Chinese CP, dated March 30, proposing bilateral talks in Moscow in mid-May and setting out their views of main questions. Extracts:

Dear Comrades,

The Central Committee of the Communist Party of the Soviet Union notes with satisfaction that our proposals on measures aimed at strengthening the unity and solidarity of the ranks of the Communist movement have met with favourable response on the part of the Central Committee of the Communist Party of China. *We welcome your agreement to the holding of a meeting between representatives of the Communist Party of the Soviet Union and the Communist Party of China.* This meeting is called upon to play an important part in creating a favourable atmosphere in relations between the fraternal parties and in smoothing out the differences which have arisen in recent times in the world Communist movement. *We would like to hope that as a result of this meeting it will be possible to carry out a number of constructive measures to surmount existing difficulties.*

In its letter, the Central Committee of the Communist Party of China invites Comrade N. S. Khrushchev to visit Peking en route to Cambodia. The Central Committee of the Communist Party of the Soviet Union and Comrade N. S. Khrushchev express gratitude for this invitation. Comrade N. S. Khrushchev would with great pleasure visit the People's Republic of China, and meet the leadership of the Communist Party of China to exchange views on urgent questions of the international situation and the Communist movement with the object of achieving common understanding of our tasks and strengthening solidarity between our parties. *However, Comrade N. S. Khrushchev's Cambodian tour, which you mention in your letter, is not planned.* The fact is that, in conformity with a decision passed by our leading bodies on February 12, 1963, Comrade L. I. Brezhnev, President of the Presidium of the USSR Supreme Soviet, will travel to Cambodia. The Cambodian government has already been notified of this and it has been announced in the press. *Comrade N. S. Khrushchev, who has already visited the People's Republic of China thrice*, still hopes to avail himself of your kind invitation in the future to visit China and meet the Chinese comrades.

We remember that, during his stay in Moscow in 1957, Comrade Mao Tse-tung said that he had been in the USSR only twice and had visited only Moscow and Leningrad. He expressed the desire to visit the Soviet Union again to become better acquainted with our country. He said then that he would like to travel from the far eastern borders of our country to the western, and from the northern to the southern borders. We welcomed this desire of Comrade Mao Tse-tung.

The CPSU's Central Committee sent a letter to Comrade Mao Tse-tung on May 12, 1960, inviting him to come and spend a holiday in the USSR and familiarise himself with the life of the Soviet people. Unfortunately, Comrade Mao Tse-tung at that time could not avail himself of our invitation. *The Central Committee of the CPSU would welcome a visit by Mao Tse-tung. The best time for such a visit would be the approaching spring or summer, which are good seasons of the year in our country.* We are also ready at any other time to give a worthy reception to Comrade Mao Tse-tung as a representative of a fraternal party and of the fraternal Chinese people. In this tour of our country Comrade Mao Tse-tung, of course, would not be alone. Comrades from the leadership of our Party would travel with him, and there would be a fine opportunity for an exchange of opinion on different questions. Comrade Mao Tse-tung would be able to see how the Soviet peoples are working, and what successes they have scored in the construction of Communism and in the implementation of the programme of our Party.

If a visit by Comrade Mao Tse-tung to Moscow cannot take place at present, we are ready to hear your considerations on a top-level meeting between representatives of the CPSU and the Communist Party of China in Moscow. *We believe that a meeting of this kind could take place around May 15, 1963*, if this date is acceptable to you.

We are very pleased that the Chinese comrades, like ourselves, regard the forthcoming meeting of representatives of the CPC and the CPSU as a 'necessary step in preparing for the meeting of representatives of Communist and Workers' parties of all countries'. Indeed, without violating the principle of equality and without infringing upon the interests of other fraternal parties, this meeting must facilitate better preparation for and convening of the meeting. Without such a meeting, as well as without putting an end to open polemics in the press, and to the criticism within one's own party of other fraternal parties, preparation for the meeting and achievement of the main aim – the strengthening of the unity of the international Communist movement – would be made difficult. Precisely for this reason the Central Committee of the CPSU, while agreeing with the proposals made by the Vietnamese, Indonesian, British, Swedish and other comrades at the beginning of 1962 regarding the convocation of a meeting of fraternal parties of all countries, at the same time stressed the need for taking such measures as would create a favourable atmosphere for the work of the world Communist forum. . . .

In their pronouncements many of the leaders of fraternal parties have recently been justly expressing the same point of view on the necessity to take a number of steps before the meeting to create a normal situation in the Communist movement and to place conflicts of opinions within the permissible bounds of a comradely party discussion. Now you also agree with us, as is seen from your letter, and it can be said that certain progress has been made in the preparation of the forth-coming meeting. *It goes without saying that when our two parties are discussing questions concerning all fraternal parties, such discussion can only be of a pre-liminary nature.* The 1957 and 1960 meetings have shown that the elaboration of the policy of the international Communist movement can be successful only if all fraternal parties collectively take part in it and if due consideration is taken of the extensive experience of all its component parts.

We have attentively studied your considerations concerning the range of questions which could be discussed at the meeting of representatives of the Com-munist Party of the Soviet Union and the Communist Party of China. These are important questions, and we are ready to discuss them. In our turn, we would like to dwell in this letter on some questions of principle, which, in our opinion, are in the centre of attention of the fraternal parties and their struggle for our common cause. We do not mean, of course, an exhaustive statement of our views on these questions. We only wish to note that which is of paramount importance and by which we are guided in our policy in the international arena and in our relations with fraternal parties.

We hope that such a statement of our views will help to define the range of questions requiring an exchange of opinions at a bilateral meeting and will contribute to overcoming the existing differences. We are doing this so as to stress once again our determination firmly and consistently to uphold the ideological platform of the entire world Communist movement and its general line which has found its expression in the Declaration and the Statement.

During the time that has passed since the adoption of the Statement, life has not only not impaired any of its main conclusions, but, on the contrary, has fully confirmed the correctness of the course taken by the world Communist movement worked out jointly through generalisation of the present day experience and creative development of Marxism-Leninism. . . .

. . . In the Communist movement, there are no 'higher ranking' and 'sub-ordinated' parties. And it cannot be otherwise. The domination of any party or the manifestation of any hegemony whatsoever, does no good to the international Communist and Workers' movement; on the contrary, it can only do it harm. All Communist parties are independent and equal. All bear responsibility for the destiny of the Communist movement, for its victories and setbacks, all must build their relations on the basis of proletarian internationalism and mutual assistance.

We also proceed from the consideration that proletarian internationalism places equal demands on all parties, big and small, but makes no exceptions for anyone. All fraternal parties must be equally concerned to ensure that their activities are based on Marxist-Leninist principles, in accord with the interests of strengthening the unity of the socialist countries and of the entire world Communist and working-class movement.

The formation and development of the world socialist system lend special significance to the question of correct relations between Marxist-Leninist parties. *Communist and Workers' parties in the countries of socialism are ruling parties. They bear responsibility for the destiny of the states, for the destiny of their peoples.* Under these conditions the violation of Marxist-Leninist principles in the relations between parties can affect not only party interests but the interests of the wide masses of the people. . . .

We declare with full responsibility that the Communist Party of the Soviet Union has never taken and will never take a single step that could sow hostility among the peoples of our country towards the fraternal Chinese people or other peoples. On the contrary, in all circumstances our Party has steadily and consistently been propagating the ideas of internationalism and warm friendship with the peoples of the socialist countries and all peoples of the world. We consider it important to stress this and hope that the Central Committee of the Communist Party of China shares this view. . . .

While being firmly convinced that the present policy of the international Communist movement, which found its expression in the Declaration and Statement of the fraternal parties, is the only correct one, we believe that at the forthcoming meeting between the representatives of the CPSU and CP of China *it would be desirable to discuss the following, most urgent, problems:*

(a) *Questions concerning the struggle for the further strengthening of the might of the world socialist system and its conversion into the decisive factor of the development of human society, which is the main distinguishing feature of our era.* We could jointly discuss how to secure a victory for the socialist countries faster and better in peaceful economic competition with capitalism;

(b) *Questions concerning the struggle for peace and peaceful coexistence.* The need to pool the efforts of all peace-loving forces for the struggle to prevent a new thermo-nuclear world war. The creation and strengthening of the broadest united front of peace supporters. The exposure of the reactionary essence of imperialism, enhancement of vigilance, and mobilisation of the broad masses to fight against the preparations by the imperialists for a new world war, frustrate the aggressive schemes of the imperialists, and isolate the forces of reaction and war. Assertion in international relations of the Leninist principle of peaceful coexistence of states with different social systems. The struggle for general and complete disarmament and for the elimination of the vestiges of the Second World War;

(c) *Questions concerning the struggle against imperialism headed by the United States.* The use, in the interest of our cause, of the weakening positions of capitalism and growing instability of the entire capitalist system of world economy, the aggravation of contradictions of capitalism, and, above all, contradictions between labour and capital, and the deep crisis of bourgeois ideology and policies. Support of the class and revolutionary struggle of the working people of the capitalist countries against the monopolies, for their social liberation, for the destruction of exploitation of man by man, for the extension of the democratic rights and freedoms of the peoples;

(d) *Questions concerning the national liberation movement.* The support and utmost development of the national liberation movement of the peoples. The struggle for the complete and final liquidation of colonialism and neo-colonialism in all its forms. The rendering of support to peoples fighting against colonialism, and also to countries which have achieved their national liberation. The development of economic and cultural co-operation with these countries;

(e) *Questions concerning the consolidation of the unity and cohesion of the socialist community and of the ranks of the Communist movement.* The need for consolidating in every way the international Communist movement which is the most influential political force of our times, particularly in conditions when the imperialist reactionaries have joined forces for a struggle against Communism. The prevention of any actions which can undermine this unity, the united adherence by each fraternal party to the assessments and conclusions worked out jointly. The continuation of the struggle against revisionism and dogmatism, as an indispensable condition for the defence of the purity of Marxism-Leninism and upholding of its creative development, and of further successes of the Communist movement. The development of relations among the fraternal parties on the basis of the principles of proletarian internationalism, mutual aid and support. The elaboration of joint measures for intensifying the ideological and political struggle against imperialism and reaction.

During the talks it would be possible to discuss all the questions mentioned in your letter, questions of common interests which stem from the struggle for the implementation of the decisions of the Moscow meetings. A great role could be played by the discussion of the questions connected with the consolidation of solidarity between the USSR and the People's Republic of China.

In your letter you deal among other things with *the Albanian and Yugoslav questions*. We have already written to you that *these questions, though of a basic nature, cannot and should not eclipse the main problems of our times which call for discussion at our meeting*.

Our Party, having condemned the splitting activities of the Albanian leaders, has been at the same time taking a number of steps necessary for normalising the relations between the Albanian Party of Labour and the CPSU and other fraternal parties. In spite of the fact that of late the leaders of the Albanian Party of Labour have been coming out with calumniatory attacks against our Party and the Soviet people, we, being guided by supreme interests, do not relinquish the thought that the relations between the CPSU and the Albanian Party of Labour can be improved. At the end of February this year the Central Committee of the CPSU once again took the initiative and suggested to the Central Committee of the Albanian Party of Labour that a bilateral meeting be held of the representatives of our two parties. However, this comradely step of ours also did not meet with due response on the part of the Albanian leadership. *The leaders of the Albanian Party of Labour did not even deem it necessary to accept our letter with the CPSU Central Committee's proposal about the bilateral meeting. Later, having obviously come to their senses, the Albanian leaders sent us a letter in which, after making some reservations and stipulations, they speak of such a meeting*. If real desire is actually shown, we are ready to have a meeting.

As far as Yugoslavia is concerned, we maintain, proceeding from an analysis and assessment of the objective economic and political conditions in that country, *that it is a socialist country*, and in our relations with it we strive to establish closer relations between it and the socialist commonwealth, as being in accord with the policy pursued by the fraternal parties of cementing together all the anti-imperialist forces in the world. We also take into consideration the definite positive tendencies evident of late in Yugoslavia's economic and socio-political life. Meanwhile the CPSU is aware of the serious differences that there are with the League of Communists of Yugoslavia on several ideological points, and deems it necessary to tell the Yugoslav comrades so outright, criticising those views of theirs which it finds wrong. . . .

Our Party does not succumb to the heat of the polemic struggle but, aware of our common responsibility to the world Communist movement, wants to stop the dangerous process of sliding down to a new series of discussions. . . .

We know that this meeting is being looked forward to by our friends in all the countries of the world, who pin great hopes on it. On us, on our will and reason depends whether results gladdening our friends and disappointing the enemies of Communism will be achieved at the meeting. This will be our common contribution to the cause of the struggle for the liberation of all the oppressed, for the victory of peace and socialism on earth, for the triumph of the great revolutionary doctrine of Marxism-Leninism.

With Communist greetings,

The Central Committee of the Communist Party of the Soviet Union.
March 30, 1963.

April 17

Albanian Communists published strong personal attacks on Khrushchev in *Zeri i Popullit*. Extracts:

On March 30 last, the Central Committee of the CPSU sent a letter to the Central Committee of the Chinese Communist Party; this letter was published in *Zeri i Popullit* on April 17, 1963. This letter deals, inter alia, with questions concerning the organising of bilateral conversations between representatives of the CPSU and the CCP on their mutual relations and the preparation of an international meeting of Communist and Workers' parties.

However, since in this letter N. Khrushchev, whilst pressing on with the public polemics with the Albanian Workers' Party – which once more shows that his assertions at the Sixth Congress of the German Socialist Unity Party that an end ought to be put to polemics, etc. were only bluff and hypocrisy – attacks and slanders it in a tendentious manner, whilst at the same time endeavouring in a demagogic fashion to present himself and his attitudes as being entirely compatible with the doctrines of Marxism-Leninism and the Moscow Declaration, we are replying to him. . . .

[Then follows a quotation from the CPSU's letter to the CCP of March 30, 1963.]

As you can see, the N. Khrushchev group in this passage, too, combines hatred, slander and attacks on the Albanian Workers' Party with deception and demagogy. It endeavours at any price to make others responsible for its faults, it tries to shift responsibility on to the Albanian Workers' Party for the undesirable state of Soviet-Albanian relations. Thus, once again, it tries to hoodwink the whole Communist movement and international public opinion. . . .

This happened at the Bucharest meeting in June 1960 and at the meeting of the 81 Communist and Workers' parties in Moscow in November of the same year, when the Albanian Workers' Party and other fraternal parties firmly opposed N. Khrushchev's schismatic efforts, attacked the anti-Marxist-Leninist views, positions and intrigues, and courageously defended the Marxist-Leninist line of the international Communist movement and the question of its unity. It was then that, by way of reaction, N. Khrushchev made public the ideological divergencies between the Albanian Workers' Party and his group; it was then that the open and unprincipled struggle of N. Khrushchev's group and its supporters against the Albanian Workers' Party began, a struggle which became more and more violent and fierce, reaching its climax in the public attacks from the rostrum of the Twenty-second Congress of the CPSU and later in the press and at the congresses of certain other parties.

In this way, the alleged 'Albanian question' originated as an aspect of the struggle between Marxism-Leninism and revisionism, between the parties standing on revolutionary positions and the modern revisionists – the N. Khrushchev group and its supporters. It is thus, in fact, a question concerning the general line of the international Communist movement with which N. Khrushchev has always been at variance either covertly or openly; it concerns the question as to what road the development of this movement should take; the road of Marxism-Leninism or that of revisionism. . . .

N. Khrushchev is very well aware of the colossal importance of the affair of J. V. Stalin not only for the USSR, but also for international Communism and Marxism-Leninism itself. He thought that he had liquidated and surmounted these questions. He thought that he had created such a terrible 'bogey' that no one would dare to defend Stalin, or indeed dare to pronounce the name of Stalin. But the opposite has happened. Marxist-Leninists, true revolutionaries, peoples, are coming to understand that *the affair of J. V. Stalin is an important matter of principle* in the struggle against the non-Marxists and the revisionists; for it concerns the defence of Leninism, since without restoring Stalin and his work in the revolutionary movement, the cause of Marxism-Leninism cannot advance. . .

In view of all this, what need has N. Khrushchev to put on the same plane, even if formally, the Yugoslav question and the so-called 'Albanian question'?

To us it is perfectly clear that he makes this manoeuvre to link and make interdependent two matters and to impose upon the Marxist-Leninist parties the acceptance of Yugoslavia as a socialist country and of the League of Communists of Yugoslavia as a fraternal party, while 'compensating' this by the recognition of Albania as a socialist country.

In other words: either you, Marxist-Leninist parties, accept Yugoslavia as a socialist country and the League of Communists of Yugoslavia as a fraternal party, and therefore renounce the struggle to expose the Titoist clique, while we, on our part – i.e. the group of N. Khrushchev – accept, 'in compensation', to consider Albania as a socialist country and to renounce public attacks against the Albanian Workers' Party and its leaders; or: if you continue the struggle against the Yugoslav revisionists, we shall continue the struggle against the Albanian Workers' Party and the People's Republic of Albania and we will demand their exclusion from the Communist movement and from the socialist camp. Or, finally: we shall relegate into the background both the Yugoslav question and the 'Albanian question', and let time solve them.

But N. Khrushchev forgets one 'small detail': the revisionist clique of Tito stands unanimously condemned by the international Communist and Workers' movement as a traitor of Marxism-Leninism. The Albanian Workers' Party, being a Marxist-Leninist party, and the Albanian People's Republic, being a member of the socialist camp, it is impossible to make a comparison with the League of Communists of Yugoslavia and Titoist Yugoslavia, and one cannot relegate this into the background when discussing the solution of problems touching the international Communist and Workers' movement. . . .

. . . As far as we are concerned, taking into account the fact that the exchange of correspondence between our two parties at the beginning of March 1963 is being employed by Khrushchev for new slanders against the Albanian Workers' Party, we here quote the complete text of our reply, addressed to the CPSU Central Committee of March 13, 1963:

On March 11, 1963, Miroslav Holub, chargé d'affaires of the Czechoslovak Socialist Republic in Tirana, was received at his request at the Albanian Workers' Party Central Committee. [Since the break in diplomatic relations with the Albanian People's Republic, the Czechoslovak embassy in Tirana protects the interests of the USSR in Albania.] The chargé d'affaires of the Czechoslovak Socialist Republic, on the recommendation of the CPSU Central Committee, passed for information a letter of the CPSU Central Committee addressed to the Central Committee of the Chinese Communist Party, together with a letter addressed to the Albanian Workers' Party Central Committee, containing only a few lines, in which the CPSU Central Committee, claiming that its letter addressed to a third party constitutes a basis for the normalisation of Soviet-Albanian relations, proposes, in passing, 'to organise bilateral talks between the CPSU and Albanian Workers' Party'.

The Albanian Workers' Party Central Committee considers that such a démarche by the CPSU Central Committee – made in such a way, taking for pretext the CPSU Central Committee's letter to the Central Committee of the Chinese Communist Party which contained arguments and considerations regarding relations and the necessity of talks between the CPSU and the Chinese Communist Party – in fact presents the Albanian Workers' Party as being the dependant of another party, a fact which can only be considered as a disparagement and as contempt for the Albanian Workers' Party, as a violation of the principle of equality and mutual respect – an elementary principle in contacts and relations between Communist and Workers' parties. It is for this reason that the above-mentioned letter of the CPSU Central Committee, being unacceptable, has not been taken into consideration.

The Albanian Workers' Party Central Committee cannot help thinking that the CPSU Central Committee has shown once more the lack of a sincere desire for a normalisation of relations between our two parties, and that it appears to be seeking a false pretext: that, allegedly, the Albanian Workers' Party has not accepted bilateral talks.

The Albanian Workers' Party Central Committee, which in its relations with fraternal parties follows the Leninist norms of mutual respect, was and is ready to accept and study with attention any letter and any proposal that the CPSU Central Committee may address to our Party; but it will reject

all attempts to discredit the Albanian Workers' Party, to violate its independence and its equal rights in the international Communist and Workers'
movement. The Albanian Workers' Party was and remains ever ready for
bilateral talks with the CPSU when the CPSU Central Committee creates
all the conditions of total equality. . . .

Neither have we ever slandered N. Khrushchev's group. We have always
spoken the truth, referring to real facts, to the attitudes and actions of N.
Khrushchev. We have said, and are saying, that it is N. Khrushchev who was
the first to make public our differences at the Twenty-second CPSU Congress,
thus giving a weapon to our enemies and creating a dangerous precedent in the
international Communist movement by using a party congress as a rostrum for
attacking and arbitrarily condemning other parties. We affirm that N.
Khrushchev's group stopped all credits, withdrew Soviet specialists from Albania,
expelled Albanian students from educational establishments in the Soviet Union,
denounced all trade, cultural and military agreements and even broke diplomatic
relations, thus establishing a total blockade of the Albanian People's Republic.
We affirm that N. Khrushchev's group has slanderously called the leaders of the
Albanian Workers' Party agents of imperialism who had sold themselves for
thirty pieces of silver. We affirm that N. Khrushchev and his henchmen have
openly taken under their protection the enemies of our people's rule – sentenced
as traitors to the motherland and agents of espionage services – as well as various
anti-party elements, and they at the same time have called for the overthrow of
the leadership of the Party and the State in Albania thus grossly interfering in the
internal affairs of our Party and our country. All this is proclaimed by
documents. . . .

April 22

In a speech marking the anniversary of Lenin's death, Ponomarev spoke
of the 'forthcoming world-wide forum of Communists'.

May 9

Chou En-lai informed Chervonenko, the Soviet ambassador in Peking,
that the CPC agreed to the Soviet proposal for bilateral talks and that Teng
Hsiao-ping and Peng Chen would lead the Chinese delegation. But the
Chinese preferred mid-June to mid-May. A detailed reply to the CPSU
letter of March 30 would follow.

May 10

People's Daily declares capitalism restored in Yugoslavia.

May 11

Chervonenko called on Yang Shang-kun, a CPC official, and proposed
July 5 for talks.

May 13

Russians announced the postponement of the Plenum of CPSU Central Committee from end of May to end of June.

May 14

Yang Shang-kun informed Chervonenko that the CCP agreed to June 5 as date for talks in Moscow.

May 16

CPSU issued statement on exchanges with CCP and named Suslov to lead CPSU delegation in talks.

May 18

In a speech to the Central Committee of the Yugoslav League of Communists, Tito stressed Yugoslavia's links with the Communist movement and accused the Chinese of 'Trotskyism'. Extracts:

The leaders of the Chinese Communist Party and certain others persist in their dogmatic positions on relations within, and the further development of, the Communist movement. They deny the possibility of progressive forces coming to power in certain countries by any way other than an armed struggle in a new war, regardless of the consequences. They deny the possibility of solving disputed international problems by peaceful means and consider that this can be achieved only by force. They reject peaceful and active coexistence among states and nations with differing social systems and consider this a concession to the capitalist world and abandonment of revolutionary struggle. They confuse the revolutionary struggle of the working class in every country with the coexistence of states and nations which is imperative – as I have said so many times – if we are to avoid plunging into disaster in a devastating nuclear world war. Apparently, they cannot grasp that peaceful coexistence among states does not mean ideological compromise or preservation of class antagonisms and class struggle in the capitalist countries. They are fighting against de-Stalinisation and resurrecting Stalinist relationships and methods in the world Communist movement and in the development of socialism. . . .

Thanks to Comrade Khrushchev and his associates, we have succeeded in gradually, though slowly, improving our relations with the Soviet Union and other socialist countries. This improvement in relations with the USSR and other socialist countries is of profound, far-reaching and positive significance not only for Yugoslavia and for the socialist countries concerned, but also for the revolutionary working class and progressive movements in general. For it strengthens the unity, not only of the socialist, but also of all progressive forces in the struggle for peace and for constructive, active and peaceful coexistence.

Good relations and co-operation with the Soviet Union and other socialist countries are not inconsistent with the policy we have been pursuing, a policy of co-operation with all countries which are ready to co-operate with us on a basis of equality. . . .

. . . When I said that we are on the side of the anti-dogmatic forces in the Communist movement, *I thereby stressed our place, our duty, and the international obligations of the League of Communists of Yugoslavia in the international working-class movement.*

We profoundly regret that such deep differences of principle have arisen in the international revolutionary movement which can lead to a cleavage in that movement and to a weakening of the struggle of progressive forces, and particularly the struggle of the working class. I still believe that matters will not go so far, but in order to prevent this from happening it is necessary *to be active, to participate, in a principled way, in clearing up the disagreements among the Communist parties.* Any compromise or unprincipled agreements at the expense of others, or at the expense of the fundamental principles upon which the contemporary struggle for socialism rests, would do great harm to the working-class movement in general. . . .

In speaking earlier on about the need to solve misunderstandings in the Communist movement in a principled manner, I also had in mind the recent past. *The decisions made by the 81 parties at the Moscow consultations of 1960, in connexion with Yugoslavia, did not correspond to the facts and therefore, naturally, could not have been principled either. That is now a thing of the past, and we Communists must look to the present and the future.* One should not, because of that past, go on harbouring feelings like distrust against the Soviet Union and other socialist countries and parties. What matters is the present relationship of these parties with us, and their attitude to the most important international problems. . . .

We hailed the victory of the Chinese revolution. It was our desire to develop comprehensive co-operation with the CPR. We made great efforts to build up such relations on a sound, principled foundation. We took a determined stand against the policy of blockades and the isolation of China in international relations, manifested particularly in the organisation of the UN. The Chinese Communist Party was one of the first parties, after 1948, to invite a delegation of the League of Communists of Yugoslavia, to attend its Eighth Congress, where this delegation was very warmly and cordially received and welcomed. The development of mutual relations gave no cause for the change which took place in 1958. The reasons for that change lie outside of the policy of the League of Communists and outside of the bilateral relations between socialist Yugoslavia and the CPR. It is well known to everyone that the policy of impairing relations with other countries is alien to us even where there are profound differences or disagreements. Obviously, there was an about-turn in the policy of the Chinese Communist Party, a change resulting from certain positions on internal problems, certain specific dogmatic attitudes towards the tasks of international policy as a whole and concepts at odds with the positions not only of the League of Communists of Yugoslavia, but also of other Communist parties and working class movements. . . .

The Chinese leaders have, however, proclaimed that China 'is the only country in which Marxism-Leninism is developing properly'. The only concession made is to Enver Hoxha. Taking these positions as a point of departure, it is not difficult to go one step further towards provoking factional strife and interference in the internal affairs of other parties and countries when various kinds of pamphlets and materials with a dogmatic content, materials containing slanders and distortions of the truth are persistently handed out and disseminated in other countries, against other parties and their leaders. Having achieved a certain degree of temporary success in their factional activities, especially among certain Asian Communist parties, the leaders of the Chinese Communist Party have taken pains to give their activities an ideological and political veneer and to continue the offensive. Hence their intensified attacks on all those forces within the working-class movement to which these methods of factional activity and hypocritical policy are alien. . . .

Pursuing such a policy, *certain Chinese leaders conceived the idea that the centre of revolution has shifted.* Having interpreted Lenin's thesis on the shifting of the centre of revolution from West to East in their own way – literally, geographically and mechanically – these leaders actually wish to conceal their aspirations to hegemony and an ideological monopoly in the working-class movement *by claiming that now the centre of revolution has moved even further east – to China.* This concept of the eastward shift of the centre of revolution has given rise to the further idea that the international working-class movement must demonstrate its solidarity with the policy and ideology of the new centre. According to the logic of some of the Chinese Communist Party leaders, the only proletarian solidarity today is that which supports the Party's policy and positions without reservation, regardless of whether they are good or bad. The consistency with which they apply this policy is reflected in their proclamation of Enver Hoxha as the staunchest revolutionary and a great Marxist. . . .

Nationalism of the worst possible kind can develop on such a foundation. It appears that it is in the process of developing in China. This is also reflected in the attitude of the Chinese leaders to the European working-class movement, in the policy of setting the peoples of Asia, Africa and Latin America against the peoples of Europe and the developed countries. . . .

During the celebration of their last National Day in October, the Chinese leaders publicly proclaimed the slogan of a 'Permanent Offensive'. It appears that this is the Chinese variation of Trotsky's theory of the 'Permanent Revolution'.

May 26

Pravda printed a carefully edited version of Tito's speech of May 18.

June 15

Chinese delivered to the CPSU a letter dated June 14 and entitled 'A Proposal Concerning the General Line of the International Communist Movement' in reply to the CPSU letter of March 30. Extracts:

The Central Committee of the Communist Party of China has studied the letter of the Central Committee of the Communist Party of the Soviet Union of March 30, 1963. All who have the unity of the socialist camp and the international Communist movement at heart are deeply concerned about the talks between the Chinese and Soviet parties and hope that our talks will help to eliminate differences, strengthen unity and create favourable conditions for convening a meeting of representatives of all the Communist and Workers' parties.

It is the common and sacred duty of the Communist and Workers' parties of all countries to uphold and strengthen the unity of the international Communist movement. *The Chinese and Soviet parties bear a heavier responsibility for the unity of the entire socialist camp and international Communist movement and should of course make commensurately greater efforts.*

A number of major differences of principle now exist in the international Communist movement. But however serious these differences, we should exercise sufficient patience and find ways to eliminate them so that we can unite our forces and strengthen the struggle against our common enemy.

It is with this sincere desire that the Central Committee of the Communist Party of China approaches the forthcoming talks between the Chinese and Soviet parties.

In its letter of March 30, the Central Committee of the CPSU systematically presents its views on questions that need to be discussed in the talks between the Chinese and Soviet parties, and in particular raises the question of the general line of the international Communist movement. In this letter we too would like to express our views, which constitute *our proposal on the general line of the international Communist movement and on some related questions of principle.*

We hope that this exposition of views will be conducive to mutual understanding by our two parties and to a detailed point-by-point discussion in the talks.

We also hope that this will be conducive to the understanding of our views by the fraternal parties and to a full exchange of ideas at an international meeting of fraternal parties.

(1) *The general line of the international Communist movement must take as its guiding principle the Marxist-Leninist revolutionary theory concerning the historical mission of the proletariat and must not depart from it.* The Moscow meetings of 1957 and 1960 adopted the *Declaration* and *Statement* respectively after a full exchange of views and in accordance with the principle of reaching unanimity through consultation. The two documents point out the characteristics of our epoch and the common laws of socialist revolution and socialist construction, and lay down the common line of all the Communist and Workers' parties. *They are the common programme of the international Communist movement.*

It is true that for several years there have been differences within the international Communist movement in the understanding of, and the attitude towards, the Declaration of 1957 and the Statement of 1960. *The central issue here is whether or not to accept the revolutionary principles of the Declaration and the Statement.* In the last analysis, it is a question of whether or not to accept the universal truth of Marxism-Leninism, whether or not to recognise the universal significance of the road of the October Revolution, whether or not to accept the fact that the people still living under the imperialist and capitalist system, who comprise two-thirds of the world's population, need to make revolution, and whether or not to accept the fact that the people already on the socialist road, who comprise one-third of the world's population, need to carry their revolution forward to the end . . . .

(2) *What are the revolutionary principles of the Declaration and the Statement?* They may be summarised as follows:

Workers of all countries, unite; workers of the world, unite with the oppressed peoples and oppressed nations; oppose imperialism and reaction in all countries; strive for world peace, national liberation, people's democracy and socialism; consolidate and expand the socialist camp; bring the proletarian world revolution step by step to complete victory; and establish a new world without imperialism, without capitalism and without the exploitation of man by man.

This, in our view, is the general line of the international Communist movement at the present stage.

(3) This general line proceeds from the actual world situation taken as a whole and from a class analysis of the fundamental contradictions in the contemporary world, and is directed against the counter-revolutionary global strategy of US imperialism.

This general line is one of forming a broad united front, with the socialist camp and the international proletariat as its nucleus, to oppose the imperialists and reactionaries headed by the United States; it is a line of boldly arousing the masses, expanding the revolutionary forces, winning over the middle forces and isolating the reactionary forces. This general line is one of *resolute revolutionary struggle* by the people of all countries and of carrying the proletarian world revolution forward to the end; it is the line that most effectively combats imperialism and defends world peace.

If the general line of the international Communist movement is one-sidedly reduced to 'peaceful coexistence', 'peaceful competition' and 'peaceful transition', this is to violate the revolutionary principles of the 1957 Declaration and the 1960 Statement, to discard the historical mission of proletarian world revolution, and to depart from the revolutionary teachings of Marxism-Leninism. . . .

(4) In defining the general line of the international Communist movement, *the starting point is the concrete class analysis of* world politics and economics as a whole and of actual world conditions, that is to say, of *the fundamental contradictions in the contemporary world.* . . . *What are the fundamental contradictions in the contemporary world?* Marxist-Leninists consistently hold that they are:

The contradiction *between the proletariat and the bourgeoisie* in the capitalist countries; the contradiction *between the oppressed nations and imperialism*; and the contradictions *among imperialist countries* and *among monopoly capitalist groups.* . . .

It is inevitable that these contradictions will give rise to popular revolutions, which alone can resolve them.

(5) *The following erroneous views should be repudiated* on the question of the fundamental contradictions in the contemporary world:

(a) The view which blots out the class content of the contradiction between the socialist and the imperialist camps and fails to see this contradiction as one between states under the dictatorship of the proletariat and states under the dictatorship of the monopoly capitalists;

(b) The view which recognises only the contradiction between the socialist and the imperialist camps, while neglecting or underestimating the contradictions between the proletariat and the bourgeoisie in the capitalist world, between the oppressed nations and imperialism, among the imperialist countries and among the monopoly capitalist groups, and the struggles to which these contradictions give rise;

(c) The view which maintains with regard to the capitalist world that the contradiction between the proletariat and the bourgeoisie can be resolved without a proletarian revolution in each country and that the contradiction between the oppressed nations and imperialism can be resolved without revolution by the oppressed nations;

(d) The view which denies that the development of the inherent contradictions in the contemporary capitalist world inevitably leads to a new situation in which the imperialist countries are locked in an intense struggle, and asserts that the contradictions among the imperialist countries can be reconciled, or even eliminated, by 'international agreements among the big monopolies'; and

(e) The view which maintains that the contradiction between the two world systems of socialism and capitalism will automatically disappear in the course of 'economic competition', that the other fundamental world contradictions will automatically do so with the disappearance of the contradiction between the two systems, and that a 'world without wars', a new world of 'all-round co-operation', will appear.

It is obvious that these erroneous views inevitably lead to erroneous and harmful policies and hence to setbacks and losses of one kind or another to the cause of the people and of socialism.

(6) The balance of forces between imperialism and socialism has undergone a fundamental change since World War II. The main indication of this change is that the world now has not just one main socialist country but a number of socialist countries forming the mighty socialist camp, and that the people who have taken the socialist road now number not two hundred million but a thousand million, or a third of the world's population. *The socialist camp is the outcome of the struggles of the international proletariat and working people. It belongs to the international proletariat and working people as well as to the people of the socialist countries.* . . .

The question of what is the correct attitude towards the socialist camp is a most important question of principle confronting all Communist and Workers' parties. It is under new historical conditions that the Communist and Workers' parties are now carrying on the task of the proletarian internationalist unity and struggle. *When only one socialist country existed* and when this country was faced with hostility and jeopardised by all the imperialists and reactionaries because it firmly pursued the correct Marxist-Leninist line and policies, *the touchstone of proletarian internationalism for every Communist party was whether or not it resolutely defended the only socialist country.*

Now there is a socialist camp consisting of thirteen countries: Albania, Bulgaria, China, Cuba, Czechoslovakia, the German Democratic Republic, Hungary, the Democratic People's Republic of Korea, Mongolia, Poland, Rumania, the Soviet Union and the Democratic Republic of Vietnam. Under these circumstances, *the touchstone of proletarian internationalism for every Communist party is whether or not it resolutely defends the whole of the socialist camp,* whether or not it defends the unity of all the countries in the camp, on the basis of Marxism-Leninism and whether or not it defends the Marxist-Leninist line and policies which the socialist countries ought to pursue. . . .

(7) Taking advantage of the situation after World War II, the US imperialists stepped into the shoes of the German, Italian and Japanese Fascists, and have been trying to erect a huge world empire such as has never been known before. The strategic objectives of US imperialism have been *to grab and dominate the inter-mediate zone* lying between the United States and the socialist camp, put down the revolutions of the oppressed peoples and nations, proceed to destroy the socialist countries, and thus to subject all the peoples and countries of the world, including its allies, to domination and enslavement by US monopoly capital. . . .

The realistic and correct course is to entrust the fate of the people and of mankind to the unity and struggle of the world proletariat and to the unity and struggle of the people in all countries.

Conversely, to make no distinction between enemies, friends and ourselves and to entrust the fate of the people and of mankind to collaboration with US imperialism, is to lead people astray. The events of the last few years have exploded this illusion.

(8) *The various types of contradictions in the contemporary world are concentrated in the vast areas of Asia, Africa and Latin America;* these are the most vulnerable areas under imperialist rule and the storm-centres of world revolution dealing direct blows at imperialism. *The national democratic revolution in these areas is an important component of the contemporary proletarian world revolution.*

The anti-imperialist revolutionary struggles of the people in Asia, Africa and Latin America are pounding and undermining the foundations of the rule of imperialism and colonialism, old and new, and are now a mighty force in defence of world peace.

In a sense, therefore, the whole cause of the international proletarian revolution hinges on the outcome of the revolutionary struggles of the people of these areas, who constitute the overwhelming majority of the world's population. . . .

Certain persons in the international Communist movement are now taking a passive or scornful or negative attitude towards the struggles of the oppressed nations for liberation. They are in fact protecting the interests of monopoly capital, betraying those of the proletariat, and degenerating into social democrats.

The attitude taken towards the revolutionary struggles of the people in the Asian, African and Latin American countries is an important criterion for differentiating those who want revolution from those who do not and those who are truly defending world peace from those who are abetting the forces of aggression and war.

(9) The oppressed nations and peoples of Asia, Africa and Latin America are faced with the urgent task of fighting imperialism and its lackeys.

History has entrusted to the proletarian parties in these areas the glorious mission of holding high the banner of struggle against imperialism, against old and new colonialism and for national independence and people's democracy, of standing in the forefront of the national democratic revolutionary movement and striving for a socialist future. . . .

In the course of the revolutionary struggles of the oppressed nations and peoples, *the proletarian party must put forward a programme of its own which is thoroughly against imperialism and domestic reaction* and for national independence and people's democracy. . . .

(10) *In the imperialist and the capitalist countries, the proletarian revolution and the dictatorship of the proletariat are essential for the thorough resolution of the contradictions of capitalist society.*

In striving to accomplish this task the proletarian party must under the present circumstances actively lead the working class and the working people in struggles to oppose monopoly capital, to defend democratic rights, to oppose the menace of fascism, to improve living conditions, to oppose imperialist arms expansion and war preparations, to defend world peace and actively to support the revolutionary struggles of the oppressed nations. . . .

In order to lead the proletariat and working people in revolution, Marxist-Leninist parties must master all forms of struggle and be able to substitute one form for another quickly as the conditions of struggle change. . . . It is wrong to refuse to use parliamentary and other legal forms of struggle when they can and should be used. However, if a Marxist-Leninist party falls into legalism or parliamentary cretinism, confining the struggle within the limits permitted by the bourgeoisie, this will inevitably lead to renouncing the proletarian revolution and the dictatorship of the proletariat.

(11) On the question of *transition from capitalism to socialism*, the proletarian party must proceed from the stand of class struggle and revolution and base itself on the Marxist-Leninist teachings concerning the proletarian revolution and the dictatorship of the proletariat.

Communists would always prefer to bring about the transition to socialism by peaceful means, but *can peaceful transition be made into a new world-wide strategic principle for the international Communist movement? Absolutely not.* . . . As a matter of fact, there is no historical precedent for peaceful transition from capitalism to socialism. . . .

Whoever considers a revolution can be made only if everything is plain sailing, only if there is an advance guarantee against sacrifices and failure, is certainly non-revolutionary.

However difficult the conditions and whatever sacrifices and defeats the revolution may suffer, proletarian revolutionaries should educate the masses in the spirit of revolution and hold aloft the banner of revolution and not abandon it.

It would be 'left' adventurism if the proletarian party should rashly launch a revolution before the objective conditions are ripe. But it would be 'right' opportunism if the proletarian party should not dare to lead a revolution and to seize state power when the objective conditions are ripe. . . .

There are *certain persons who assert that they have made the greatest creative contributions to revolutionary theory since Lenin and that they alone are correct.* But it is very dubious whether they have ever really given consideration to the extensive experience of the entire world Communist movement, whether they have ever really considered the interests, the goal and tasks of the international proletarian movement as a whole, and *whether they really have a general line for the international Communist movement which conforms with Marxism-Leninism.* . . .

(13) *The socialist countries and the revolutionary struggles of the oppressed peoples and nations support and assist each other.*

The national liberation movements of Asia, Africa and Latin America and the revolutionary movements of the people in the capitalist countries are a strong support to the socialist countries. It is completely wrong to deny this. . . .

Certain persons have one-sidedly exaggerated the role of peaceful competition between socialist and imperialist countries in their attempt to substitute peaceful competition for the revolutionary struggles of the oppressed peoples and nations. According to their preaching, it would seem that imperialism will automatically collapse in the course of this peaceful competition and that the only thing the oppressed peoples and nations have to do is to wait quietly for the advent of this day. What does this have in common with the Marxist-Leninist views? Moreover, certain persons have concocted the strange tale that China and some other socialist countries want 'to unleash wars' and to spread socialism by 'wars between states'. As the Statement of 1960 points out, such tales are nothing but imperialist and reactionary slanders. To put it bluntly, the purpose of those who repeat these slanders is to hide the fact that *they are opposed to revolutions by the oppressed peoples and nations of the world and opposed to others supporting such revolutions.*

(14) In the last few years much – in fact a great deal – has been said on *the question of war and peace.* Our views and policies on this question are known to the world, and no one can distort them.

It is a pity that, although certain persons in the international Communist movement talk about how much they love peace and hate war, they are unwilling to acquire even a faint understanding of the simple truth on war pointed out by Lenin. . . .

As Marxist-Leninists see it, war is the continuation of politics by other means, and every war is inseparable from the political system and the political struggles which give rise to it. If one departs from this scientific Marxist-Leninist proposition which has been confirmed by the entire history of class struggle, one will never be able to understand either the question of war or the question of peace. There are different types of peace and different types of war. Marxist-Leninists must be clear about what type of peace or what type of war is in question. Lumping just wars and unjust wars together and opposing all of them indiscriminately is a bourgeois pacifist and not a Marxist-Leninist approach. . . .

In recent years, certain persons have been spreading the argument that a single spark from *a war of national liberation* or from a *revolutionary people's war* will lead to a world conflagration destroying the whole of mankind. What are the facts? Contrary to what these persons say, the wars of national liberation and the revolutionary people's wars that have occurred since World War II have not led to world war. The victory of these revolutionary wars has directly weakened the forces of imperialism and greatly strengthened the forces which prevent the imperialists from launching a world war and which defend world peace. Do not the facts demonstrate the absurdity of this argument?

The emergence of *nuclear weapons* can neither arrest the progress of human history nor save the imperialist system from its doom, any more than the emergence of new techniques could save the old systems from their doom in the past.

The emergence of nuclear weapons does not and cannot resolve the fundamental contradictions in the contemporary world, does not and cannot alter the law of class stuggle, and does not and cannot change the nature of imperialism and reaction.

(16) It was Lenin who advanced the thesis that it is possible for the socialist countries to practise *peaceful coexistence with the capitalist countries*. It is well known that after the great Soviet people had repulsed foreign armed intervention the Communist Party of the Soviet Union and the Soviet government, led first by Lenin and then by Stalin, consistently pursued the policy of peaceful coexistence and that they were forced to wage a war of self-defence only when attacked by the German imperialists.

Since its founding, the People's Republic of China too has consistently pursued the policy of peaceful coexistence with the countries having different social systems, and it is China which initiated the five principles of peaceful coexistence.

However, *a few years ago certain persons suddenly claimed Lenin's policy of peaceful coexistence as their own 'great discovery'*. They maintain that they have a monopoly on the interpretation of this policy. They treat 'peaceful coexistence' as if it were an all-inclusive, mystical book from Heaven and attribute to it every success the people of the world achieve by struggle. What is more, they label all who disagree with their distortions of Lenin's views as opponents of peaceful coexistence, as people completely ignorant of Lenin and Leninism, and as heretics deserving to be burnt at the stake. How can the Chinese Communists agree with this view and practice? They cannot, it is impossible.

Lenin's principle of peaceful coexistence is very clear and readily comprehensible by ordinary people. Peaceful coexistence designates a relationship between countries with different social systems, and must not be interpreted as one pleases. *It should never be extended to apply to the relations between oppressed and oppressor nations, between oppressed and oppressor countries, or between oppressed and oppressor classes, and never be described as the main content of the transition from capitalism to socialism*, still less should it be asserted that peaceful coexistence is mankind's road to socialism. . . .

It is necessary for the socialist countries to engage in negotiations of one kind or another with the imperialist countries. It is possible to reach certain agreements through negotiation by relying on the correct policies of the socialist countries and on the pressure of the people of all countries. But necessary compromises between the socialist countries and the imperialist countries do not require the oppressed peoples and nations to follow suit and compromise with imperialism and its lackeys. No one should ever demand in the name of peaceful coexistence that the oppressed peoples and nations should give up their revolutionary struggles.

The application of the policy of peaceful coexistence by the socialist countries is advantageous for achieving a peaceful international environment for socialist construction, for exposing the imperialist policies of aggression and war and for isolating the imperialist forces of aggression and war. But if the general line of the foreign policy of the socialist countries is confined to peaceful coexistence, then it is impossible to handle correctly either the relations between socialist countries or those between the socialist countries and the oppressed peoples and nations. Therefore it is wrong to make peaceful coexistence the general line of the foreign policy of the socialist countries.

In our view, *the general line of the foreign policy of the socialist countries should have the following content:* to develop relations of friendship, mutual assistance and co-operation among the countries in the socialist camp in accordance with the principle of proletarian internationalism; to strive for peaceful coexistence on the basis of the five principles with countries having different social systems and oppose the imperialist policies of aggression and war; and to support and assist the revolutionary struggles of all the oppressed peoples and nations. These three aspects are interrelated and indivisible, and not a single one can be omitted.

(17) *For a very long historical period after the proletariat takes power, class struggle continues as an objective law independent of man's will, differing only in form from what it was before the taking of power.* . . . To deny the existence of class struggle in the period of the dictatorship of the proletariat and the necessity of thoroughly completing the socialist revolution on the economic, political and ideological fronts is wrong, does not correspond to objective reality and violates Marxism-Leninism.

(18) Both Marx and Lenin maintained that *the entire period before the advent of the higher stage of Communist society is the period of transition from capitalism to Communism, the period of dictatorship of the proletariat.* In this transition period, the dictatorship of the proletariat, that is to say, the proletarian state, goes through the dialectical process of establishment, consolidation, strengthening and withering away. . . .

Can there be a 'state of the whole people'? Is it possible to replace the state of the dictatorship of the proletariat by a 'state of the whole people'?

This is not a question about the internal affairs of any particular country but a fundamental problem involving the universal truth of Marxism-Leninism.

In the view of Marxist-Leninists, there is no such thing as a non-class or supra-class state. So long as the state remains a state, it must bear a class character; so long as the state exists, it cannot be a state of the 'whole people'. As soon as society becomes classless, there will no longer be a state. . . .

In calling a socialist state the 'state of the whole people', is one trying to replace the Marxist-Leninist theory of the state by the bourgeois theory of the state? Is one trying to replace the state of the dictatorship of the proletariat by a state of a different character? If that is the case, it is nothing but a great historical retrogression. The degeneration of the social system in Yugoslavia is a grave lesson.

(19) Leninism holds that *the proletarian party must exist together with the dictatorship of the proletariat in socialist countries.* The party of the proletariat is indispensable for the entire historical period of the dictatorship of the proletariat. The reason is that the dictatorship of the proletariat has to struggle against the enemies of the proletariat and of the peoples, remould the peasants and other small producers, constantly consolidate the proletarian ranks, build socialism and effect the transition to Communism; none of these things can be done without the leadership of the party of the proletariat.

Can there be a 'party of the entire people'? Is it possible to replace the party which is the vanguard of the proletariat by a 'party of the entire people'? This, too, is not a question about the internal affairs of any particular party, but a fundamental problem involving the universal truth of Marxism-Leninism.

In the view of Marxist-Leninists, there is *no such thing as a non-class or supra-class political party*. All political parties have a class character. Party spirit is the concentrated expression of class character. . . .

What will happen if it is announced halfway before entering the higher stage of Communist society that the party of the proletariat has become a 'party of the entire people' and if its proletarian class character is repudiated? Does this not fundamentally conflict with the teachings of Marx and Lenin on the party of the proletariat? Does this not disarm the proletariat and all the working people, organisationally and ideologically, and is it not tantamount to helping restore capitalism? Is it not 'going south by driving the chariot north' to talk about any transition to Communist society in such circumstances?

(20) Over the past few years, certain persons have violated Lenin's integral teachings about the inter-relationship of leaders, party, class and masses, and *raised the issue of 'combating the cult of the individual'; this is erroneous and harmful*. . . .

The party of the proletariat is the headquarters of the proletariat in revolution and struggle. Every proletarian party must practise centralism based on democracy and establish a strong Marxist-Leninist leadership before it can become an organised and battle-worthy vanguard. *To raise the question of 'combating the cult of the individual' is actually to counterpose the leaders to the masses, undermine the party's unified leadership which is based on democratic centralism, dissipate its fighting strength and disintegrate its ranks*.

Lenin criticised the erroneous views which counterpose the leaders to the masses. He called them 'ridiculously absurd and stupid'.

The Communist Party of China has always disapproved of exaggerating the role of the individual, has advocated and persistently practised democratic centralism within the party and advocated the linking of the leadership with the masses, maintaining that correct leadership must know how to concentrate the views of the masses.

While loudly combating the so-called 'cult of the individual', certain persons are in reality doing their best to defame the proletarian party and the dictatorship of the proletariat. At the same time, *they are enormously exaggerating the role of certain individuals, shifting all errors on to others and claiming all credit for themselves*. What is more serious is that, under the pretext of 'combating the cult of the individual', certain persons are crudely interfering in the internal affairs of other fraternal parties and fraternal countries and forcing other fraternal parties to change their leadership in order to impose their own wrong line on these parties. What is all this if not great-power chauvinism, sectarianism and splittism? What is all this if not subversion?

It is high time to propagate seriously and comprehensively Lenin's integral teachings on the inter-relations of leaders, party, class and masses.

(21) *Relations between socialist countries are international relations of a new type*. Relations between socialist countries, whether large or small, and whether more developed or less developed, economically, must be based on the principles of *complete equality, respect for territorial integrity, sovereignty and independence*,

and non-interference in each other's internal affairs, and must also be based on the principles of *mutual support and mutual assistance in accordance with proletarian internationalism.* . . .

If, proceeding only from its own partial interests, any socialist country unilaterally demands that other fraternal countries submit to its needs, and used the pretext of opposing what they call 'going it alone' and 'nationalism' to prevent other fraternal countries from applying the principle of relying mainly on their own efforts in their construction and from developing their economies on the basis of independence, or *even goes to the length of putting economic pressure on other fraternal countries – then these are pure manifestations of national egoism.*

It is absolutely necessary for socialist countries to practise mutual economic assistance and co-operation and exchange. Such economic co-operation must be based on the principles of complete equality, mutual benefit and comradely mutual assistance. . . .

(22) *The 1957 Declaration and the 1960 Statement lay down the principles guiding relations among fraternal parties.* These are the principle of solidarity, the principle of mutual support and mutual assistance, the principle of independence and equality and the principle of reaching unanimity through consultation – all on the basis of Marxism-Leninism and proletarian internationalism. . . . .

If the principle of independence and equality is accepted in relations among fraternal parties, then it is *impermissible for any party to place itself above others, to interfere in their internal affairs, and to adopt patriarchal ways in relations with them.* If it is accepted that there are no 'superiors' and 'subordinates' in relations among fraternal parties, then it is *impermissible to impose the programme, resolutions, and line of one's own party on other fraternal parties as the 'common' programme of the international Communist movement.*

If the principle of reaching unanimity through consultation is accepted in relations among fraternal parties, then *one should not emphasise 'who is in the majority' or 'who is in the minority' and bank on a so-called majority in order to force through one's own erroneous line and carry out sectarian and splitting policies.*

If it is agreed that differences between fraternal parties should be settled through inter-party consultation, then other fraternal parties should not be attacked publicly and by name at one's own congress or at other party congresses, in speeches by party leaders, resolutions, statements, etc.; and still less should the ideological differences among fraternal parties be extended into the sphere of state relations. . . .

How to treat the Marxist-Leninist fraternal Albanian Party of Labour is one question. How to treat the Yugoslav revisionist clique of traitors to Marxism-Leninism is quite another question. These two essentially different questions must on no account be placed on a par.

Your letter says that you 'do not relinquish the hope that the relations between the CPSU and the Albanian Party of Labour may be improved', but at the same time you continue to attack the Albanian comrades for what you call 'splitting activities'. Clearly this is self-contradictory and in no way contributes to resolving the problem of Soviet-Albanian relations.

Who is it that has taken splitting actions in Soviet-Albanian relations? Who is it that has extended the ideological differences between the Soviet and Albanian parties to state relations? Who is it that has brought the divergences between the Soviet and Albanian parties and between the two countries into the open before the enemy? Who is it that has openly called for a change in the Albanian party and state leadership?

All this is plain and clear to the whole world. Is it possible that the leading comrades of the CPSU do not really feel their responsibility for the fact that Soviet-Albanian relations have so seriously deteriorated? We once again express our sincere hope that the leading comrades of the CPSU will observe the principles guiding relations among fraternal parties and countries and take the initiative in seeking an effective way to improve Soviet-Albanian relations. . . .

. . . The comrades of the CPSU state in their letter that 'the Communist Party of the Soviet Union has never taken and will never take a single step that could sow hostility among the peoples of our country towards the fraternal Chinese people or other peoples'. Here we do not desire to go back and enumerate the many unpleasant events that have occurred in the past, and we only wish that the comrades of the CPSU will strictly abide by this statement in their future actions.

During the past few years, *our party members and our people have exercised the greatest restraint in the face of a series of grave incidents which were in violation of the principles guiding relations among fraternal parties and countries and despite the many difficulties and losses which have been imposed on us.* The spirit of proletarian internationalism of the Chinese Communists and the Chinese people has stood a severe test. . . .

(23) In order to carry out the common programme of the international Communist movement unanimously agreed upon by the fraternal parties, an *uncompromising struggle must be waged against all forms of opportunism*, which is a deviation from Marxism-Leninism.

The Declaration and the Statement point out that *revisionism, or, in other words, right opportunism, is the main danger in the international Communist movement. Yugoslav revisionism typifies modern revisionism.* . . .

. . . It is completely groundless and out of keeping with the facts to assert that Yugoslavia is showing 'definite positive tendencies', that it is a 'socialist country', and that the Tito clique is an 'anti-imperialist force'. Certain persons are now attempting to introduce the Yugoslav revisionist clique into the socialist community and the international Communist ranks. This is openly to tear up the agreement unanimously reached at the 1960 meeting of the fraternal parties and is absolutely impermissible. . . .

(24) A most important lesson from the experience of the international Communist movement is that the development and victory of a revolution depend on the existence of a revolutionary proletarian party.

There must be a revolutionary party. There must be a revolutionary party built according to the revolutionary theory and revolutionary style of Marxism-Leninism. There must be a revolutionary party able to integrate the universal truth of Marxism-Leninism with the concrete practice of the revolution in its own country. There must be a revolutionary party able to link the leadership closely with the broad masses of the peoples. There must be a revolutionary party that perseveres in the truth, corrects its errors and knows how to conduct criticism and self-criticism.

Only such a revolutionary party can lead the proletariat and the broad masses of the people in defeating imperialism and its lackeys, winning a thorough victory in the national democratic revolution and winning the socialist revolution.

If a party is not a proletarian revolutionary party but a bourgeois reformist party;

If it is not a Marxist-Leninist party but a revisionist party;

If it is not a vanguard party of the proletariat but a party tailing after the bourgeoisie;

If it is not a party representing the interests of the proletariat and all the working people but a party representing the interests of the labour aristocracy;

If it is not an international party but a nationalist party;

If it is not a party that can use its brains to think for itself and acquire an accurate knowledge of the trends of the different classes in its own country through serious investigation and study, and knows how to apply the universal truth of Marxism-Leninism and integrate it with the concrete practice of its own country, but instead is a party that parrots the words of others, copies foreign experience without analysis, runs hither and thither in response to the baton of certain persons abroad, and has become a hodgepodge of revisionism, dogmatism and everything but Marxist-Leninist principle;

Then *such a party is absolutely incapable of leading the proletariat and the masses in revolutionary struggle, absolutely incapable of winning the revolution and absolutely incapable of fulfilling the great historical mission of the proletariat.*

This is a question all Marxist-Leninists, all class-conscious workers and all progressive people everywhere need to ponder deeply.

(25) It is the duty of Marxist-Leninists to distinguish between truth and false-hood with respect to *the differences that have arisen in the international Communist movement.* In the common interest of the unity for struggle against the enemy, we have always advocated solving problems through inter-party consultations and opposed bringing differences into the open before the enemy. As the comrades of the CPSU know, *the public polemics in the international Communist movement have been provoked by certain fraternal party leaders and forced on us.* Since a public debate has been provoked, it ought to be conducted on the basis of equality among fraternal parties and of democracy, and by presenting the facts and reasoning things out.

Since certain party leaders have publicly attacked other fraternal parties and provoked a public debate, it is our opinion that they have no reason or right to forbid the fraternal parties attacked to make public replies. Since certain party leaders have published innumerable articles attacking other fraternal parties, why do they not publish in their own press the articles those parties have written in reply?

Latterly, the Communist Party of China has been subjected to preposterous attacks. The attackers have raised a great hue and cry and, disregarding the facts, have fabricated many charges against us. We have published these articles and speeches attacking us in our own press. . . .

Presumably, you are referring to these articles when, towards the end of your letter of March 30, you accuse the Chinese press of making 'groundless attacks' on the CPSU. It is turning things upside down to describe articles replying to our attackers as 'attacks'. Since you describe our articles as 'groundless' and as so very bad, why do you not publish all seven of these 'groundless attacks', in the same way as we have published your articles, and let all the Soviet comrades and Soviet people think for themselves and judge who is right and who wrong? You are of course entitled to make a point-by-point refutation of these articles you consider 'groundless attacks'.

Although you call our articles 'groundless' and our arguments wrong, you do not tell the Soviet people what our arguments actually are. This practice can hardly be described as showing a serious attitude towards the discussion of problems by fraternal parties, towards the truth or towards the masses. We hope that the public debate among fraternal parties can be stopped. This is a problem that has to be dealt with in accordance with the principles of independence, of equality and of reaching unanimity through consultation among fraternal parties. In the international Communist movement, no one has the right to launch attacks whenever he wants, or to order the 'ending of open polemics' whenever he wants to prevent the other side from replying. It is known to the comrades of the CPSU that, in order to create a favourable atmosphere for convening the meeting of the fraternal parties, we have decided temporarily to suspend, as from March 9 1963, public replies to the public attacks directed by name against us by comrades of fraternal parties. We reserve the right of public reply. In our letter of March 9, we said that on the question of suspending public debate: 'It is necessary that our two parties and the fraternal parties concerned should have some discussion and reach an agreement that is fair and acceptable to all'.

The *foregoing are our views regarding the general line of the international Communist movement and some related questions of principle. . . .*

In addition, there are *other questions* of common concern, *such as the criticism of Stalin* and *some important matters of principle regarding the international Communist movement which were raised at the Twentieth and Twenty-second Congresses of the CPSU,* and we hope that on these questions, too, there will be a frank exchange of opinion in the talks.

With regard to the talks between our two parties, in our letter of March 9 we proposed that Comrade Khrushchev come to Peking; if this was not convenient, we proposed that another responsible comrade of the Central Committee of the CPSU lead a delegation to Peking or that we send a delegation to Moscow. Since you have stated in your letter of March 30 that Comrade Khrushchev cannot come to China, and since you have not expressed a desire to send a delegation to China, the *Central Committee of the Communist Party of China has decided to send a delegation to Moscow.*

In your letter of March 30, you invited Comrade Mao Tse-tung to visit the Soviet Union. *As early as February 23, Comrade Mao Tse-tung in his conversation with the Soviet ambassador to China clearly stated the reason why he was not prepared to visit the Soviet Union at the present time. You were well aware of this.*

When a responsible comrade of the Central Committee of the Communist Party of China received the Soviet ambassador to China on May 9, he informed you that we would send a delegation to Moscow in the middle of June. Later, in compliance with the request of the Central Committee of the CPSU, we agreed to postpone the talks between our two parties to July 5.

We sincerely hope that the talks between the Chinese and Soviet parties will yield positive results *and contribute to the preparations for convening the meeting of all Communist and Workers' parties.*

Workers of all countries, unite!

Workers and oppressed peoples and nations of the world, unite!

Oppose our common enemy!

With Communist Greetings,

The Central Committee of the Communist Party of China.

June 14, 1963.

June 18

TASS statement that the letter of the CCP would not be published in the Soviet press because of its polemical nature.

It will be recalled that the CPSU Central Committee in January 1963, at the Sixth Congress of the Socialist Unity Party of Germany, made a proposal for halting open polemics within the ranks of the international Communist movement. This proposal won broad support from fraternal parties. On March 9 this year the CPSU Central Committee received a letter from the Central Committee of the Communist Party of China expressing agreement with our proposals on the discontinuance of open polemics and the holding of a meeting between representatives of the CPSU and the Chinese Communist Party.

On March 30 this year the Central Committee of the CPSU sent a letter to the Central Committee of the Chinese Communist Party which, in a positive form, expounded its views in connexion with the coming bilateral meeting. In the opinion of the CPSU Central Committee, such a meeting must promote better understanding between our parties on major problems of present world development, the creation of a favourable climate for preparing and holding a meeting of representatives of all Communist and Workers' parties.

The letter of the CPSU Central Committee emphasised the determination, firmly and consistently, to uphold the platform of the world Communist movement, its general line, which found an expression in the Declaration and Statement of the Moscow meetings of Marxist-Leninist parties. In full conformity with these programme documents, the CPSU Central Committee in its letter of March 30 this year set out its views on the major problems of our time, the strategy and tactics of the international Communist movement. The Central Committee of the CPSU urged the Central Committee of the Chinese Communist Party to overcome the existing divergences through a comradely exchange of opinion, to concentrate efforts on the exploration of avenues leading to the consolidation of the unity of all fraternal parties, the strengthening of Soviet-Chinese friendship and co-operation.

Comrade Pan Tzu-li, the ambassador of the People's Republic of China to the Soviet Union, was received at the CPSU Central Committee by Comrades M. A. Suslov, O. V. Kuusinen, Y. V. Andropov, and B. N. Ponomarev on June 15, 1963. The ambassador handed the CPSU Central Committee one more letter from the Central Committee of the Chinese Communist Party, dated June 14. *This letter gives an arbitrary interpretation of the Declaration and Statement of the*

Moscow Conferences of Marxist-Leninist parties, distorts the major theses of these historic documents, contains unwarranted attacks on the CPSU and other fraternal parties. All this gives rise to deep regret.

The CPSU Central Committee believes that the publication at present in the Soviet press of the letter of the Central Committee of the Chinese Communist party, dated June 14, 1963, would call for a public reply which *would lead to a further aggravation of polemics, would not accord with the understanding reached, and would run counter to the opinion of the fraternal parties on this question.* This should not be done, all the more, in view of the forthcoming meeting between representatives of the CPSU and the Chinese Communist Party on July 5, this year. The CPSU Central Committee once again expresses the hope that the Chinese comrades, in the interest of strengthening the unity of the ranks of the world Communist movement, will display readiness to concentrate efforts on what unites the CPSU and the Chinese Communist Party, and all fraternal parties, in their great struggle against imperialism, for the victory of socialism and Communism throughout the world.

June 20

The Rumanian Communist Party, alone of all the parties of Eastern Europe, published extracts from the Chinese Communist Party's letter of June 14.

June 21

At a plenary meeting of the Central Committee of the CPSU in Moscow Suslov, Ponomarev and Andropov 'explained the differences between the Central Committee of the Chinese CP, on the one hand, and the CPSU and other fraternal parties on the other.... The Central Committee of the CPSU had to do this because the leaders of the Chinese CP did not keep to the agreement reached about stopping open polemics by publishing its letter of June 14.' Copies of the Chinese letter were distributed to those attending the Plenum, at which Khrushchev made a 'long and brilliant speech'. The Plenum also approved a resolution concerning the forthcoming bilateral talks between the Russians and Chinese. Shortened text of Resolution:

1. The Plenum of the CC of the CPSU fully and unanimously approves the political work of the Presidium of the CC of the CPSU, of the First Secretary of the CC of the CPSU, the Chairman of the Council of Ministers of the USSR, Comrade Khrushchev, Nikita Sergeyevich, directed towards more closely uniting the forces of the world Communist movement, and also all the practical steps and measures taken by the Presidium of the CC of the CPSU in mutual relations with the Central Committee of the Communist Party of China.

The Plenum notes with approval that the Presidium of the CC of the CPSU, headed by Comrade Khrushchev, N. S., has consistently and unswervingly carried out and is carrying out the decisions unanimously approved at the Moscow meetings of Communist and Workers' parties in 1957 and 1960.

2. The statement of the CC of the CPSU of June 18, 1963, regarding the letter of the CC of the CPC is approved.

3. The Presidium of the CC of the CPSU is instructed at the forthcoming meeting with representatives of the CC of the CPC to be governed by the following:

To carry out unflinchingly the line accepted by our Party at the Twentieth, Twenty-first and Twenty-second Congresses of the CPSU, at meetings of Communist parties and expressed in the Declaration and Statement, which has been fully confirmed by experience, by the practical development of the international Communist movement and the course of international events. . . . The CC of the CPSU rejects categorically, as groundless and slanderous, the attacks by the CC of the CPC on our Party and other Communist parties, on the decisions of the Twentieth, Twenty-first and Twenty-second Congresses of the CPSU, on the Programme of the CPSU, which was worked out on the basis of Marxist-Leninist theory, of the practical experience of socialist construction in the USSR and of the international revolutionary movement. The decisions of the congresses, the new Programme of the CPSU, unanimously approved by the whole Soviet people and the international Communist movement, were a tremendous mobilising force in our country. The CC of the CPSU has assumed and will continue to assume that open polemics should not be carried on in the Communist movement, and expresses the hope that the CC of the CPC will on its part keep, not in words but deeds, to the agreement reached about ceasing open polemics.

To set forth and defend in the talks the position of the CPSU on the main questions of principle of the international Communist and working-class movement, and also explain the position of the CPSU on fundamental questions of the Communist construction in the USSR, confirmed by life itself and unanimously approved by the fraternal Communist parties.

June 26

Chinese delegates to the Congress of the International Federation of Women in Moscow read out long extracts from the Chinese CP letter of June 14, provoking incidents between themselves and other delegates.

June 27

The Soviet Ministry of Foreign Affairs sent a Note to the Chinese embassy in Moscow demanding the recall of five Chinese citizens said to have distributed the Chinese CP letter of June 14.

June 29

The Chinese Ministry of Foreign Affairs reported the Soviet expulsion of Chinese citizens from Moscow and issued a statement from which the following are extracts:

A spokesman of the Chinese Ministry of Foreign Affairs points out that this demand of the Soviet government is unreasonable and its excuse untenable. It is normal and unimpeachable for the Chinese embassy and Chinese personnel in the Soviet Union to distribute official documents of the Central Committee of the CCP. The Soviet establishments and personnel in China have always been doing the same and no objection has ever been raised by the Chinese government. On April 3, before China made public the letter of the Central Committee of the CPSU of March 30 to the Central Committee of the CCP, the Soviet establishments and personnel in China had already distributed it. Since the Soviet establishments and personnel can do and have always done this in China, why cannot the Chinese establishments and personnel do the same in the Soviet Union? What justification has the Soviet government to lodge a protest with the Chinese embassy in the Soviet Union in this connexion? What justification has it to demand that the Chinese government recall the said Chinese personnel?

One cannot but ask: What is the Soviet Union aiming at in putting such an unreasonable demand to the Chinese government on such an untenable excuse? One is also fully justified to ask this: In taking this step, which is unprecedented in the history of the relations between the two socialist countries of China and the Soviet Union, on the eve of the talks between the Chinese and Soviet parties, whether or not the Soviet government is deliberately trying to undermine Sino-Soviet unity, vitiate the relations between the two states and create obstacles to the talks between the Chinese and Soviet parties?

The Chinese government has always conducted its relations with the Soviet Union in accordance with the principle of proletarian internationalism. Despite the fact that the Soviet government has taken such an unreasonable and unfriendly action, the Chinese government will continue to act in a principled way and will not take a corresponding measure with regard to the Soviet establishments and personnel in China. The Chinese governement hopes that the Soviet government will not take further rash steps detrimental to Sino-Soviet unity and the relations between the two states, but will, together with the Chinese government, uphold and strengthen unity on the basis of Marxism-Leninism and proletarian internationalism and strive for the common goal of the Chinese and the Soviet peoples.

July 1

New China News Agency reported that display cabinets in front of the Chinese embassy in Moscow had been smashed on June 27 by Russian youths and that Russians had made an official apology.

July 1

The Central Committee of the Chinese Communist Party announced the composition of their delegation to the Moscow talks and declared:

The Central Committee of the CCP has instructed the delegation of the CCP, that, in the talks with the delegation of the CPSU, it should adhere to our Party's consistent stand of persevering in principle and in unity; *it should expound our Party's views on the general line of the international Communist movement and on some related questions of principle in accordance with the letter of June 14 of the Central Committee of the CCP in reply to the Central Committee of the CPSU;* it should firmly defend the fundamental principles of Marxism-Leninism and the revolutionary principles of the Declaration of 1957 and the Statement of 1960; it should safeguard the unity of the socialist camp and the international Communist movement; and it should defend the interests of the cause of the liberation of the oppressed peoples and nations, the cause of opposition to imperialism and of the struggle for world peace, and the cause of the proletarian world revolution. . . .

The letter of the Central Committee of the CCP of June 14 was a reply to the letter of the Central Committee of the CPSU of March 30. . . . It is highly regrettable that, contrary to the way the Central Committee of the CCP has acted, the Central Committee of the CPSU has not published the letter of the other side in its newspapers and has not let its party members and people learn the views of the CCP. The statement of the Central Committee of the CPSU of June 18, the resolution of the plenary meeting of the Central Committee of the CPSU on June 21 and Comrade Khrushchev's speech at the plenary meeting of the Central Committee of the CPSU described the constructive views of the Central Committee of the CCP as 'groundless and slanderous attacks', announced that they 'categorically rejected' them, and launched direct and unreasonable attacks on the CCP. Subsequently, the government of the Soviet Union demanded the immediate recall of five persons – staff members of the Chinese embassy in the Soviet Union or Chinese research students there, thus extending the ideological differences between the two parties to the sphere of state relations. . . .

Despite the steps taken by the Central Committee and leaders of the CPSU in further worsening the relations between the Chinese and Soviet parties and between the two countries, the *Central Committee of the CCP will still send its delegation to Moscow* as scheduled to take part in the talks between the Chinese and Soviet parties.

July 2

Chou En-lai received the five Chinese expelled from Moscow, congratulated them for having done their work well and for their 'sense of responsibility'.

July 4

CPSU statement in *Pravda* accusing CCP of interfering in CPSU internal affairs and of expanding party differences to state relations. Extract:

On July 1 the Central Committee of the CCP issued a statement depicting in a false light the motives which had prompted the CC of the CPSU not to publish at present in the Soviet press the [June 14] letter of the CC of the CCP. From the statement of the CC of the CCP it was apparent that the leaders of the CCP do not want to stop the polemics and overcome the existing differences. Moreover, various Chinese officials, including officials of the Chinese embassy in Moscow, grossly infringing the existing regulations in the USSR, are trying to distribute the letter of the CC of the CCP of June 14. In this way Chinese organisations are interfering in the internal affairs of our Party and are transferring differences from the sphere of party relations to relations between states.

Thus instead of seeking a way of bringing our two parties closer together, the Chinese leadership is moving towards a sharpening of relations. Trying to shift the blame on to someone else, the CC of the CCP tries in its statement to attribute to the CPSU actions allegedly aimed at 'a further worsening of Soviet-Chinese relations and the creation of a split in the international Communist movement'.

The CC of the CPSU resolutely rejects this slander. Since the CC of the CCP shows no interest in stopping the polemics and continues to give wide distribution to its letter and to issue statements against our Party, the CC of the CPSU has decided in the interests of a correct understanding of the questions in dispute and for the purpose of defending Marxism-Leninism, to make a public reply in its own time to the letter of the CC of the CCP.

July 4

The Soviet Ministry of Foreign Affairs published a statement on the expulsion of the Chinese in *Izvestia*, organ of the Soviet government. Extract:

Why was the USSR Foreign Ministry compelled to resort to this measure? Here are a few facts.

As from June 16 of this year, members of the staff of the Chinese embassy in Moscow and certain Chinese citizens, in an arbitrary way and without the knowledge of Soviet organs, began disseminating illegally by different ways and means and with growing persistence and importunity, the above-mentioned letter, specially printed in a large edition in the Russian language, in Soviet offices, at airports, at railway stations and in other places.

The text of the letter was at the same time taken by members of the embassy staff to various institutions in Moscow in a number of cars, mailed to Soviet citizens and delivered to their homes, and taken by officials, specially sent from Moscow, to other towns, including Leningrad, Kiev, Odessa, Dubna, etc.

This not only astonished Soviet people but also aroused a feeling of justified protest. The Ministry of Foreign Affairs and other Soviet organisations began to receive many letters and statements from Soviet citizens, who drew attention to the impermissible actions of the Chinese representatives and asked why they were behaving in the Soviet Union as if they were in one of the provinces of China. Soviet people demanded that the necessary measures be taken to put a stop to these activities.

Striving from the very outset to prevent this issue from causing unnecessary aggravation, the USSR Foreign Ministry, as long ago as June 17, made an appropriate oral representation to the ambassador of the Chinese People's Republic in the USSR, insisting that the Chinese embassy should cease this activity, unheard of in diplomatic practice – activity which was obviously incompatible with the status and functions of a diplomatic representation.

The Chinese side did not draw the necessary conclusions. In view of this, the USSR Foreign Ministry stated once again to the Chinese ambassador on June 24 that such actions by members of the staff of the Chinese embassy and other Chinese citizens staying in the USSR and enjoying its hospitality, could not be regarded otherwise than as a violation of the Soviet Union's sovereignty, as flagrant disregard for the rules and regulations operating in the USSR and established for foreign diplomatic representations and foreign citizens.

But even after this second representation of the USSR Foreign Ministry, the distribution of the materials continued and assumed an even wider scale. It went so far that the Chinese crews of the Moscow-Peking trains scattered the text of the letter in the Russian language from the windows of coaches at railway stations. The text of the letter was transmitted through the public address system of trains during their stops. When Soviet people politely told the Chinese citizens that their actions were impermissible, the latter in many cases behaved in a defiant way. For instance, the above-mentioned Yao impudently told Soviet people that the Chinese workers 'will not ask anybody's permission' to disseminate materials of this kind.

In these circumstances the Soviet side was compelled to declare that the stay in the USSR of the afore-mentioned three members of the embassy staff and of the two other Chinese citizens, was undesirable and that it was necessary for them to leave immediately.

Such are the facts. . . .

July 4

Chinese CP issued statement on coming talks. Extract:

The Central Committee of the CCP has learned of the statement issued on July 4 by the Central Committee of the CPSU. The Central Committee of the CCP cannot agree to the distortions, accusations and attacks which are made in this statement by the Central Committee of the CPSU against the statement of July 1 by the Central Committee of the CCP.

Since the delegation of the CCP is about to leave for Moscow for the talks between the Chinese and Soviet parties, the Central Committee of the CCP has instructed the delegation to make the necessary comments at the talks with regard to the distortions, accusations and attacks by the Central Committee of the CPSU.

Despite the fact that, on July 4, the Central Committee of the CPSU has once again issued this kind of statement, the Central Committee of the CCP, in accordnance with its consistent stand of perseverance in principle, the strengthening of unity and the elimination of differences in the interests of the common struggle against the enemy, *has instructed the delegation to exercise the greatest patience* and make the greatest efforts at the talks to strengthen the unity of the Chinese and Soviet parties and of the two countries, the unity of the socialist camp and that of the international Communist movement on the basis of Marxism-Leninism and proletarian internationalism and the 1957 Declaration and the 1960 Statement.

The Central Committee of the CCP hopes that the outcome of the talks between the Chinese and Soviet parties will be advantageous to the preparations for convening a meeting of representatives of all the Communist and Workers' parties and advantageous to the great struggle of the people the world over against imperialism and for world peace, national liberation, people's democracy and socialism.

July 5

Chinese published the text of a Note sent to the Soviet Ministry of Foreign Affairs about the expulsion of Chinese from Moscow. Extracts:

The Note of the Soviet Foreign Ministry said that distribution by staff members of the Chinese embassy and Chinese citizens in the Soviet Union of the CCP Central Committee's reply to the CPSU Central Committee is 'illegal' and 'incompatible' with the status of the embassy, and shows 'disrespect for the sovereignty of the Soviet state'. Such charges are completely unwarranted.

It is perfectly normal for the official organs and personnel of one socialist country in another socialist country to distribute the published documents of their own government and party. This has always been done by the Soviet organs and personnel in China. In the past half year, the Soviet organs and personnel in China have distributed the following documents; Comrade Khrushchev's report at the session of the Supreme Soviet on December 12, 1962; the article by the editorial department of *Pravda* dated January 7, 1963; Comrade Khrushchev's speech at the Sixth Congress of the German Socialist Unity Party on January 16, 1963; and the article by the *Pravda* editorial department on February 10, 1963.

What particularly needs to be pointed out with emphasis is the fact that the Soviet organs and personnel in China had distributed the letter of March 30, 1963 of the CPSU Central Committee to the CCP Central Committee before it was published in the Chinese press.

Since the Soviet organs and personnel in China could distribute Soviet government and party documents in China, why then cannot the Chinese organs and personnel in the Soviet Union distribute the official documents of the Chinese government and Party? The principle of reciprocity must be unanimously observed by countries concerned and must in no circumstances be violated at will by any one side. It is utterly untenable to justify the Soviet Union's one-sided, unreasonable demand by certain decisions made by the Soviet government. . . .

The letter of the Central Committee of the CCP of June 14 is a reply to the letter of the Central Committee of the CPSU dated March 30. The Soviet Union should have published in its press this reply letter of the Central Committee of the CCP, as China has done with respect to the letter of the Central Committee of the CPSU dated March 30. However, instead of doing so, the Soviet Union has obstructed the normal activity of the Chinese embassy in distributing the reply letter of the Central Committee of the CCP and has even demanded the recall of Chinese personnel. Thus, the Soviet Union has extended the ideological differences between the two parties to the relations between the two countries, and created new obstacles to the bilateral party talks. In spite of this, the Chinese government still acts in accordance with the principle of proletarian internationalism and is not prepared to take corresponding measures against Soviet organs and personnel in China.

July 5

The Chinese delegation, headed by Teng Hsiao-ping, arrived in Moscow. Opening session held.

July 6

First working session of Sino-Soviet party talks in Moscow.

July 7

Mass meeting in Peking, attended by Chinese Foreign Minister, Chen Yi, to welcome the five Chinese expelled from Moscow.

July 9

Statement by CC of CPSU. Extracts:

At the meeting in Peking [on July 7] statements were again made, and this time in a demonstrative manner, that the Chinese comrades continue to consider it their right to distribute in the USSR the letter of the CC of the CCP of June 14 and they approved these actions.

But such a 'right' as the Chinese comrades want to assume in fact leads to a sharpening of relations between Communist parties at a moment when we have already agreed to stop open polemics. We have agreed on more than that – that representatives of the CPSU and CCP should meet, and this meeting has already begun in Moscow. Before and during this meeting, it would seem that no steps should be taken which would interfere with the creation of the conditions necessary for the consideration of questions in dispute. . . . But the Chinese comrades undertake measures of an opposite character. The very fact of calling such a meeting and the speeches made at it by Chinese officials can be asssesed only as an attempt to inflame unfriendly feelings towards the USSR in the fraternal Chinese people and to worsen the situation during the talks between representatives of the CPSU and CPP. . . .

July 10

Chinese CP statement in reply to Russian criticism of Peking meeting. Extracts:

The talks between the CCP and the CPSU are now in progress, and people are justified in hoping that the Sino-Soviet differences will be discussed calmly at the talks. Certainly, we did not expect that the Central Committee of the CPSU would consider it necessary to unleash a new public attack on the CCP and thus force us to make a public reply. We cannot but regret this state of affairs. The accusation in the statement by the Central Committee of the CPSU against the CCP is totally unjustified. Communists must respect the facts and be reasonable. Who is it that has taken a series of measures to worsen Sino-Soviet relations before and during the Sino-Soviet talks, thus aggravating the situation with regard to the talks? . . .

The CCP and the CPSU are equals, and no genuine unity can be achieved by adopting an attitude of 'allowing the magistrate to burn down houses, while forbidding the common people even to light lamps'. The consistent stand of the CCP regarding the Sino-Soviet differences is: persevere in principle, strengthen unity, eliminate differences and wage a common struggle against the enemy. We practise what we preach, and our deeds are at one with our words. The cause for concern at present is rather the fact that the CC of the CPSU has not only extended the ideological differences between the two parties of China and the Soviet Union to the sphere of state relations, but is also whipping up a campaign against the CCP all over the Soviet Union through meetings and resolutions of party organisations at various levels and through innumerable speeches and articles. People cannot help asking: how far are the comrades of the CPSU prepared to extend the Sino-Soviet differences?

July 13

People's Daily published an editorial entitled 'We Want Unity, Not a Split'. Extracts:

Our letter of June 14 is earnest in its attitude. We maintain that it is correct in its contents. However one looks at our letter, it is certainly not a dreadful monster and is nothing for any revolutionary to be afraid of. Is there any reason to raise such an uproar over it? Eventually, what is false cannot stand up. People can tell right from wrong. Since the Central Committee of the CPSU believes our letter to be totally wrong, we still do not understand why it has not published our letter for the members of the Soviet Party and the Soviet people to read, so as to prove that the CCP is wrong and the CPSU is right.

While the Central Committee of the CCP disagrees with the views of the Central Committee of the CPSU on the general line of the international Communist movement, we do not regard them simply as attacks on us and reject them on this ground. Discussion is essential just because views diverge. *If one peremptorily dismisses the other's views before discussion takes place, what is there to discuss?* It is unfortunate that on the eve of the Sino-Soviet talks the Central Committee of the CPSU impetuously declared that it 'categorically rejected' the views of the Central Committee of the CCP on the general line of the international Communist movement. Does not such an action mean closing the door on negotiations before they start? Though we would prefer to believe this not to be the case, we cannot help pointing out that this action by the Central Committee of the CPSU was an extremely serious one. . . . We sent our delegation to Moscow for the talks at the appointed time. We hoped that all the differences between the CCP and the CPSU would be discussed calmly and that Sino-Soviet relations would be eased as the talks began.

But we now have to point out with heavy hearts that events have gone contrary to our hopes. Since the start of the Sino-Soviet talks, the Central Committee of the CPSU has not ceased its public attacks on the CCP. Still more disturbing is the fact that, although we, on our part, have published the successive statements and decision of the Central Committee of the CPSU censuring us, it has refused to publish the corresponding statements of the Central Committee of the CCP thus preventing the members of the CPSU and the people of the Soviet Union from learning the facts. Also, taking advantage of this state of affairs, the Central Committee of the CPSU is conducting a campaign against the CCP throughout the Soviet Union and inflaming feeling against China among the Soviet people through meetings and resolutions in party organisations at various levels and through numerous articles in the press. Seeing this, people are fully justified in worrying *whether the Central Committee of the CPSU wants to push Sino-Soviet relations to the brink of rupture.*

It must be frankly pointed out that *the present situation is very grave* as a result of the steps taken by the Central Committee of the CPSU to worsen Sino-Soviet relations. We sincerely hope that the comrades of the CPSU will treasure Sino-Soviet unity, will refrain from rash actions and will not push things to the extreme. One should realise that ideas cannot be blockaded and that it is impossible to resolve ideological differences by dictates or commands. To consider one's own words as final and refuse to let others speak will not work. There were many people who committed such follies in the past, and they all failed. Can anything good come of repeating such errors?

We are Marxist-Leninists. The differences between the CCP and the CPSU will eventually be resolved if one truly follows the fundamental principles of Marxism-Leninism and the revolutionary principles of the Declaration and the Statement instead of going counter to them, and if one really treats the other as an equal instead of trying to impose on him. *If the differences cannot be resolved today, they can wait until tomorrow. If they cannot be resolved this year, they can wait until next year.*

The CCP takes the whole situation into consideration. In the interests of the proletarian world revolution, we are unsparing in our efforts. The CCP is patient. We have already stated in all seriousness that the questions needing to be discussed between the CCP and the CPSU should all be covered in a comradely way, point by point, to the full and in detail. Whatever is agreed upon by both parties can be settled at once and an agreement can be concluded. Differences that cannot be settled immediately may be laid aside, pending later settlement. If we cannot finish our discussions in one session, several can be held, and our parties can hold further bilateral talks. As in the past, the CCP will never do anything detrimental to Sino-Soviet unity. . . .

July 14

Pravda published text of Chinese CP's letter of June 14, along with 15,000-word text of 'Open Letter from CC of CPSU to Party Organisations and all Communists in the Soviet Union'. Extracts:

Dear Comrades,

The Central Committee of the CPSU deems it necessary to address this open letter to you in order to set out our position on the fundamental questions of the international Communist movement in connexion with the letter of the Central Committee of the Communist Party of China of June 14, 1963.

The Soviet people are well aware that our Party and government, expressing as they do the will of the entire Soviet people, spare no effort to strengthen fraternal friendship with the peoples of all socialist countries, and with the Chinese people. We are united by a common struggle for the victory of Communism. We have the same aim, the same aspirations and hopes.

For many years the relations between our parties were good, but some time ago serious differences came to light between the CCP on the one hand and the CPSU and other fraternal parties on the other. At the present time the Central Committee of the CPSU feels increasingly concerned over statements and actions by the leadership of the CCP undermining the cohesion of our parties and the friendship of our peoples. . . .

Unfortunately, the events of the past period have shown that the Chinese comrades interpret our restraint in their own way. They depict our sincere striving to avoid a sharpening of the polemics in the Communist movement as all but an intention to hide the views of the Chinese leaders from the Communists and from the Soviet people. Mistaking our restraint for weakness, the Chinese comrades, contrary to the standards of friendly relations between fraternal socialist countries, began, with increasing importunity and persistence, to spread unlawfully in Moscow and other Soviet cities the letter of the CCP Central Committee of June 14, which was brought out in Russian in a mass printing. Not content with this, the Chinese comrades began sedulously to propagate and spread this letter and other documents directed against our Party throughout the world, not scrupling to use imperialist publishing houses and agencies for their distribution. . . .

On July 13 in a leading article in the *People's Daily* attacks are made again and again on our Party and the fact that the letter of the CC of the CCP of June 14 was not published in the Soviet press is depicted in a false light. The openly unfriendly actions of the leaders of the CCP, their persistent efforts to sharpen the polemics in the international Communist movement, the deliberate distortion of the position of our Party and the incorrect interpretation of the motives which prompted us temporarily to refrain from publication impel us to publish the letter of the CC of the CCP of June 14, 1963, and give our appraisal of this document.

All who read the letter of the CCP Central Committee will see behind the bombastic phrases about unity and cohesion unfriendly, slanderous attacks on our Party and the Soviet country, a striving to play down the historic significance of our people's struggle for the victory of Communism in the USSR, for the triumph of peace and socialism throughout the world. The document is crammed with charges – overt and covert – against the CPSU and the Soviet Union. The authors of the letter permit themselves unworthy fabrications – insulting to Communists – about 'betrayal of the interests of the entire international proletariat and all the peoples of the world', about 'departure from Marxism-Leninism and proletarian internationalism' and hint at 'cowardice in face of the imperialists', 'a step back in the course of historical development', and even 'organisational and moral disarming of the proletariat and all the working people', tantamount to 'doing a service to the restoration of capitalism' in our country.

How can they say such a thing about the Party of the great Lenin, about the motherland of socialism, about the people which, the first in the world, accomplished a socialist revolution, upheld its great gains in violent battles against international imperialism and domestic counter revolution, and displayed miracles of heroism and dedication in the struggle for the building of Communism, honestly fulfilling its internationalist duty to the working people of the world?

I

For nearly half a century the Soviet country under the leadership of the Communist Party, has been conducting a struggle for the triumph of the ideas of

Marxism-Leninism, in the name of the freedom and happiness of the working people of the whole world. From the very first days of the existence of the Soviet State, when the great Lenin stood at the helm of our country, up to the present day our people has rendered and is rendering tremendous disinterested aid to all the peoples fighting for their liberation from the yoke of imperialism and colonialism, for building up of a new life.

World history knows no other example of one country rendering such extensive aid to other countries in developing their economy, science and technology. The working people of China, the Chinese Communists, have felt in full measure the fraternal solidarity of the Soviet people and of our Party, both in the period of their revolutionary struggle for the liberation of their homeland and in the years of the construction of socialism. Immediately after the forming of the Chinese People's Republic (CPR) the Soviet government signed with the government of People's China a Treaty on Friendship, Alliance and Mutual Assistance, which is a mighty means of rebuffing the encroachments of imperialism, a factor consolidating peace in the Far East and the whole world. . . .

The Soviet people generously shared with its Chinese brothers all its many years' long experience in socialist construction, its achievements in the field of science and technology. Our country has rendered and is rendering substantial aid to the development of the economy of People's China. *With the active assistance of the Soviet Union, People's China built 198 industrial enterprises, work-shops and other projects equipped with up-to-date machinery.* With the assistance of our country such new branches of industry as the automobile, tractor, aircraft manufacturing and others were created in China. The Soviet Union handed over to the CPR over 21,000 sets of scientific-technical documentation, including more than 1,400 blueprints of big enterprises. We have invariably assisted China in consolidating the defence of the country and in the creation of a modern defence industry. Thousands of Chinese specialists and workers have been trained in Soviet establishments of higher education and at our enterprises. *Now, too, the Soviet Union continues rendering technical assistance to the CPR in the construction of 88 industrial enterprises and projects.* We speak about all this not to brag, but only because the leaders of the CCP are striving of late to belittle the significance of Soviet aid, and we do not forget that the Soviet Union, in its turn, received goods it needed from the CPR. . . .

This was how matters stood until the Chinese leaders began retreating from the general line of the world Communist movement.

In April 1960 the Chinese comrades openly revealed their differences with the world Communist movement by publishing a collection of articles called 'Long Live Leninism!'. This collection, based on distortions and truncated and incorrectly interpreted theses of well-known works by Lenin, contained propositions actually directed against the foundations of the Declaration of the Moscow meeting of 1957, which was signed on behalf of the CCP by Comrade Mao Tse-tung, against the policy of peaceful coexistence of states with different social systems, against the possibility of preventing a world war in the present epoch, against the use of both the peaceful and non-peaceful road of the development of socialist revolutions. The leaders of the CCP began imposing their views on all the fraternal parties. In June 1960, during the session of the General Council of the

World Federation of Trade Unions in Peking the Chinese leaders, without the knowledge of the leaderships of the fraternal parties, called a meeting of representatives of several parties which were then in Peking and started criticising openly the positions of the CPSU and other Marxist-Leninist parties and the Declaration adopted by the Moscow meeting in 1957. Furthermore the Chinese comrades made their differences with the CPSU and other fraternal parties the subject of an open discussion in a non-party organisation. . . .

Striving to prevent such a development of events, *the CPSU Central Committee came out with a proposal to hold talks with the Central Committee of the CCP. These negotiations took place in Moscow in September 1960;* but even then it was impossible to overcome the differences that had arisen due to the stubborn unwillingness of the CCP delegation to heed the opinion of the fraternal party. At the meeting of representatives of 81 Communist and Workers' parties which took place in November 1960, the overwhelming majority of the fraternal parties rejected the incorrect views and concepts of the CCP leadership. The Chinese delegation at this meeting stubbornly upheld its own particular views and signed the Statement only when the danger arose of its complete isolation.

Today it has become absolutely obvious that the CCP leaders were only manoeuvring when they affixed their signatures to the 1960 Statement. Shortly after the meeting they resumed propaganda for their course, using as mouthpiece the leadership of the Albanian Party of Labour. Behind the back of our Party they launched a campaign against the CPSU Central Committee and the Soviet government.

In October 1961, the CPSU Central Committee undertook new attempts to normalise relations with the CCP. Comrades N. S. Khrushchev, F. R. Kozlov and A. I. Mikoyan had talks with Comrades Chou En-lai, Peng Chen and other leading officials who came to the Twenty-second CPSU Congress. Comrade N. S. Khrushchev set forth to the Chinese delegation in detail the position of the CPSU Central Committee on the questions of principle which were discussed at the Twenty-second Congress and stressed our invariable desire to strengthen friendship and co-operation with the CCP.

In its letters of February 22 and May 31, 1962, the CPSU Central Committee drew the attention of the CCP Central Committee to the dangerous consequences for our common cause which could be brought about by the weakening of the unity of the Communist movement. We then proposed to the Chinese comrades to take steps so as not to give the imperialists an opportunity to use in their interests the difficulties which arose in Soviet-Chinese mutual relations. The CPSU Central Committee also moved to take more effective measures on such questions as exchange of internal political information, co-ordination of the positions of fraternal parties in the international democratic organisations and in other spheres. However, these letters and the other steps aimed at improving relations with the CCP and the CPR along all lines did not meet with response in Peking.

In the autumn of last year, before the departure from Moscow of the former CPR ambassador in the Soviet Union, Comrade Liu Hsiao, the Presidium of the CPSU Central Committee had a lengthy talk with him. In the course of this conversation the members of the Presidium of the Central Committee once again displayed initiative in the matter of strengthening Chinese-Soviet friendship.

Comrade N. S. Khrushchev asked Comrade Liu Hsiao to forward to Comrade Mao Tse-tung our proposal 'to put aside all disputes and differences, not to try and establish who is right and who is wrong, not to rake up the past, but to start our relations with a clean page'. But we have not even received an answer to this sincere call. . . .

Deepening their ideological differences with the fraternal parties, the leaders of the CCP began carrying them over into inter-state relations. *Chinese organs began curtailing the CPR's economic and trade relations with the Soviet Union and other socialist countries. On the initiative of the CPR government the volume of China's trade with the Soviet Union has been cut to almost a third in the past three years; deliveries of industrial plant dropped to a fortieth. This reduction took place on the initiative of the Chinese leaders.* We regret that the CPR leadership has embarked on such a road. We have always believed and we believe now that it is necessary to go on developing Soviet-Chinese relations, to develop co-operation. This would have been mutually beneficial for both sides, and above all to People's China, which has received great assistance from the Soviet Union and other socialist countries. The Soviet Union developed extensive relations with China before and it is today still in favour of their expansion and not their curtailment. One would have thought that the leadership of the CCP would have been concerned primarily to develop economic relations with the socialist countries. But it started working in the opposite direction, disregarding the harm caused to the economy of the Chinese People's Republic by such actions. . . .

From the end of 1961 Chinese representatives in international democratic organisations began openly imposing their mistaken views. In December 1961 at the Stockholm session of the World Peace Council the Chinese delegation came out against the convocation of a World Congress for Peace and Disarmament. In the course of 1962 the activities of the World Federation of Trade Unions, the world movement of peace champions, the Afro-Asian solidarity movement, the World Federation of Democratic Youth, the Women's International Democratic Federation and many other organisations were endangered as a result of the splitting activities of the Chinese representatives. They came out against the participation of representatives of the Afro-Asian solidarity committees of the European socialist countries in the third solidarity conference of the peoples of Asian and African countries in Moshi. The leader of the Chinese delegation told the Soviet representatives that 'the whites have nothing to do here'. At the journalists' conference in Jakarta the Chinese representatives followed a line towards preventing Soviet journalists from participating as fully-fledged delegates on the plea that the Soviet Union does not belong to the countries of Asia. . . .

Such is, in brief, the history of the differences which the Chinese leadership has with the CPSU and other fraternal parties. It shows that the leaders of the CCP are setting their own special line against the general course of the Communist movement and trying to impose on it their own *diktat* and their deeply mistaken views on the fundamental problems of the present day.

II

What is the essence of the differences between the CCP on the one hand and the CPSU and the international Communist movement on the other hand? This question, undoubtedly, is asked by anyone who familiarises himself with the letter of the CCP Central Committee of June 14. . . .

If this method of the Chinese comrades is not taken into consideration, it may even seem from outside that the dispute has acquired a scholastic nature and that individual formulas far removed from vital problems are the points at issue. *In point of fact, however, questions which bear on vital interests of the peoples are in the centre of the dispute. These are the questions of war and peace, the question of the role and development of the world socialist system, the questions of the struggle against the ideology and practice of the 'personality cult'; these are the questions of strategy and tactics of the world labour movement and the national liberation struggle.* . . .

In the appraisal of the problems of war and peace and in the approach to their solution there can be no uncertainties or reservations, for this involves the destinies of peoples, the future of all mankind. The CPSU Central Committee believes it is its duty to tell the Party and the people with all frankness that in questions of war and peace the CCP leadership has cardinal differences of principle with us and with the world Communist movement. The essence of these differences lies in the diametrically opposite approach to such vital problems as the possibility of averting world thermonuclear war, peaceful coexistence of states with different social systems and the inter-connexion between the struggle for peace and the development of the world revolutionary movement. . . .

The Chinese comrades obviously underestimate all the dangers of thermo-nuclear war. 'The atomic bomb is a paper tiger'; it 'is not terrible at all', they contend. The main thing, don't you see, is to put an end to imperialism as quickly as possible, but how, and with what losses, this will be achieved seems to be a secondary question. To whom, it is right to ask, is it secondary? To the hundreds of millions of people who are doomed to death in the event of the unleashing of a thermonuclear war? To the states that will be erased from the face of the earth in the very first hours of such a war?

It is permissible to ask the Chinese comrades whether they realise what sort of 'ruins' a world nuclear rocket war would leave behind? The CPSU Central Committee – and we are convinced that our entire Party and the whole Soviet people unanimously support us in this – cannot share the views of the Chinese leadership about the creation of 'a thousand-times greater civilisation' on the corpses of hundreds of millions of people. Such views are in crying contradiction with the ideas of Marxism-Leninism.

It is permissible to ask the Chinese comrades: What means do they propose for the destruction of imperialism? We fully stand for the destruction of imperialism and capitalism. We not only believe in the inevitable destruction of capitalism, but we are also doing everything for this to be accomplished by way of the class struggle and as soon as possible. Who must decide this historic question? First of all the working class led by its vanguard, the Marxist-Leninist party, the working people of each country.

The Chinese comrades propose another thing. They straightforwardly say: 'On the ruins of destroyed imperialism', in other words, as a result of the unleashing of war, 'a bright future will be built'. If we agree to this then, indeed, there is no need for the principle of peaceful coexistence or for the struggle for the strengthening of peace. We cannot agree to such an adventurist road, which contradicts the nature of Marxism-Leninism.

We would like to ask the Chinese comrades, who suggest building a bright future on the ruins of the old world destroyed by a thermonuclear war, whether they consulted the working class of the countries where imperialism dominates? The working class of the capitalist countries would be sure to tell them: Do we ask you to trigger-off a war and destroy our countries while annihilating imperialists? Is it not a fact that the monopolists and the imperialists are only a comparatively small group, while the bulk of the population of the capitalist countries consists of the working class, working peasantry and working intelligentsia? The atomic bomb does not distinguish between imperialists and working people. It hits big areas, and therefore millions of workers would be destroyed for each monopolist. The working class, the working people, will ask such 'revolutionaries': What right have you to settle for us the questions of our existence and our class struggle? – we, too, are in favour of socialism, but we want to gain it through the class struggle and not by unleashing a world war.

Such a posing of the question by the Chinese comrades may engender well-justified suspicions that this is no longer a class approach in the struggle for the abolition of capitalism, but some entirely different aim. If both the exploiters and the exploited are buried under the ruins of the old world, who will build the 'bright future'?

In this connexion it is impossible not to note the fact that instead of the class internationalist approach expressed in the call 'Workers of the World, Unite' the Chinese comrades stubbornly propagate the slogan deprived of any class meaning: 'The Wind from the East prevails over the Wind from the West'.

The CCP leaders have such weak arguments in the struggle against the CPSU and other fraternal parties that they have to resort to all sorts of ruses. They begin by ascribing to us absolutely groundless views of their own invention, and then they accuse us and fight against our exposing these views. Such precisely is the case with their absurd allegations that the CPSU and other fraternal parties renounce revolution and substitute peaceful coexistence for class struggle. In any political circle in our country, it is well known that when we speak of peaceful coexistence, we mean the inter-state relations of the socialist countries with the countries of capitalism. The principle of peaceful coexistence, naturally, can in no way be applied to the relations between the antagonistic classes inside the capitalist states. It is impermissible to apply it to the struggle of the working class for its class interests against the bourgeoisie or to the struggle of the oppressed peoples against the colonialists. The CPSU resolutely comes out against peaceful coexistence in the ideological sphere. This is a simple truth which all who regard themselves as Marxist-Leninists should have mastered long ago.

III

There are serious difficulties between the CCP and the CPSU and other Marxist-Leninist parties on *the question of struggle against the consequences of the Stalin personality cult*. The CCP leaders have taken upon themselves the role of the defenders of the personality cult, the propagators of Stalin's faulty ideas. They are trying to thrust upon other parties the practices, the ideology and morals the forms and methods of leadership which flourished in the period of the personality cult. We must say outright that this is an unenviable role, which will bring them neither honour nor glory. No one will succeed in embroiling the Marxist-Leninists, progressive people, into defending the personality cult! The Soviet people and the world Communist movement duly appreciated the courage and boldness, the truly Leninist firmness of principle demonstrated in the struggle against the consequences of the personality cult by our Party, and by its Central Committee headed by Comrade Nikita Khrushchev. Everybody knows that our Party did this in order to remove the heavy burden that fettered the powerful forces of the working people, and thus to speed up the development of the Soviet society. Our Party did this in order to free the ideals of socialism bequeathed to us by great Lenin from the stigma of abuses of personal power and arbitrariness. Our Party did this in order to prevent the recurrence of the tragic events that accompanied the personality cult and to make all fighters for socialism derive lessons from our experience. . . .

Soviet people find it strange and outrageous that the Chinese comrades are trying to besmirch the CPSU programme, this majestic plan for the creation of a Communist society. Alluding to the fact that our Party proclaims as its task the struggle for the better life for the people, the CCP leaders hint at some sort of 'bourgeoisisation' and 'degeneration' of Soviet society. If one pursued their line of thinking it would be found that if a people walks in bast sandals, eats watery soup out of a common bowl, that is Communism; but that if a working man lives well and wants to live even better tomorrow, that is nearly tantamount to a restoration of capitalism! And they want to present this philosophy to us as the latest revelation in Marxism-Leninism! This fully discloses the promoters of such 'theories' as people who do not believe in the strength and capabilities of the working class, which took power into its own hands and created its own socialist state. . . .

If one is to extract the genuine content of all the mass of pseudo-theoretical discourses contained in the letter of the CCP Central Committee on these questions, it boils down to the following: the Chinese comrades come out against the CPSU line aimed at developing socialist democracy, which was proclaimed with such force in the decisions of the Twentieth, Twenty-first and Twenty-second Congresses of our Party and in the CPSU Programme. It is not fortuitous that nowhere in their long letter did they find place even for a mere mention of the development of democracy in conditions of socialism and in conditions of construction of Communism. . . .

Of course, the struggle against the personality cult was never regarded by our Party, or the other Marxist-Leninist parties, as a negation of the authority of party and governmental leaders. The CPSU has stressed time and again, including at the Twentieth and Twenty-second Congresses, that the Party cherishes the authority of its leadership and that while debunking the personality cult and fighting against its consequences, the Party puts high those leaders who really express the interests of the people and give all their strength to the struggle for the victory of Communism and for this reason enjoy deserved prestige.

IV

The next important question on which we differ is that of *the ways and methods of the revolutionary struggle of the working class in the countries of capitalism, the struggle for national liberation, the ways of the transition of all mankind to socialism.*

As depicted by the Chinese comrades, the differences on this question appear as follows: one side – they themselves – stands for the world revolution, while the other – the CPSU and the Marxist-Leninist parties – have forgotten the revolution, even, 'fear' it, and instead of revolutionary struggle, are concerned with such things, 'unworthy' of a real revolutionary, as peace, the economic development of the socialist countries and improvement of the living standards of their people, or the struggle for the democratic rights and vital interests of the working people of the capitalist countries.

Actually, the dividing line between the views of the CCP and the views of the international Communist movement lies in an entirely different plane: some – namely the leaders of the CCP – talk about world revolution in and out of place, sport the phrase 'revolutionary' on any occasion, and sometimes without it, while others – precisely those whom the Chinese comrades criticise – approach the question of the revolution with utmost seriousness and, instead of phrasemongering, work hard, seeking to find the best ways to the victory of socialism, ways which conform best with the present conditions, who fight hard for national independence, democracy and socialism. . . .

Further, what situation is more propitious to the revolutionary struggle of the working class in the capitalist countries: the situation of peace and peaceful coexistence or the situation of permanent international tension and the cold war? There is no doubt as to the answer to this question. Who does not know that the ruling circles of the imperialist states exploit the situation of the cold war to whip up chauvinism, war hysteria and unbridled anti-Communism, to put in power the most rabid reactionaries and pro-fascists, to suspend democracy and to do away with political parties, trade unions and other mass organisations of the working class? The struggle of the Communists for peace greatly consolidates their ties with the masses and their authority and influence, and, consequently, helps to build up what is called the political army of the revolution. The struggle for peace and peaceful coexistence of states with different social systems, far from hindering, far from delaying, makes it possible to develop in full measure the struggle for the attainment of the ultimate aims of the international working class.

It is hard to believe that the Chinese comrades, who are experienced men and have themselves accomplished a revolution, do not understand the main thing: that world revolution today comes both through consolidation of the world system of socialism, and through the revolutionary class struggle of the workers in the capitalist countries, through the struggle for national liberation, the strengthening of political and economic independence of newly-liberated countries of Asia and Africa, through the struggle for peace, against war of aggression, through the anti-monopoly struggle of the masses, and in many other ways which should not be opposed to each other but united and directed toward the same goal: to overthrow the rule of imperialism. . . .

The Chinese comrades have disagreed with the world Communist movement also concerning the *forms of the transition of different countries to socialism*. It is common knowledge that the CPSU and the other Marxist-Leninist parties, as is clearly pointed out in the documents of the Moscow meetings and in the programme of the CPSU, proceed from the possibility of a peaceful and a non-peaceful transition to socialism. Despite this the Chinese comrades stubbornly ascribe to our Party and the other fraternal parties the recognition of the peaceful method alone. . . .

And what is the position of the Chinese comrades on this question? It keynotes all their statements and the letter of the CCP Central Committee of June 14. The Chinese comrades regard as the main criterion of revolutionary spirit the recognition of an armed uprising always, in everything, and everywhere. Thereby the Chinese comrades actually deny the possibility of using peaceful forms of struggle for the victory of the socialist revolution. Whereas Marxism-Leninism teaches that the Communists must master all forms of revolutionary class struggle – both violent and non-violent.

Yet another important question is that of *the relationship between the struggle of the international working class and the national liberation movement of the peoples of Asia, Africa and Latin America.* The international revolutionary working-class movement, represented today by the world system of socialism and the Communist parties of the capitalist countries, and the national liberation movement of the peoples of Asia, Africa and Latin America: these are the great forces of our epoch. Correct co-ordination among them constitutes one of the main requisites for victory over imperialism.

How do the Chinese comrades solve this question? This is seen from their new 'theory', according to which the main contradiction of our time is, you see, contradiction not between socialism and imperialism, but between the national liberation movement and imperialism. The decisive force in the struggle against imperialism, the Chinese comrades hold, is not the world system of socialism, not the struggle of the international working class, but again the national liberation movement. Through this the Chinese comrades, apparently, wish to win in the easiest way popularity among the peoples of Asia, Africa and Latin America. But let nobody be deceived by this 'theory'. Whether the Chinese theoreticians want it or not, this theory essentially means the isolation of the national liberation movement from the international working class and its offspring – the world system of socialism. But this would have constituted a tremendous danger to the national liberation movement itself. . . .

The question arises: what is the explanation for the incorrect propositions of the CCP leadership on the basic problems of our time? It is either the complete divorce of the Chinese comrades from actual reality, a dogmatic, bookish approach to the problems of war, peace and revolution, their lack of understanding of the concrete conditions of the modern epoch. *Or it is the fact that behind the rumpus about 'world revolution' raised by the Chinese comrades are other aims which have nothing in common with revolution.*

All this shows the erroneous and disastrous nature of the course which the CCP leadership tried to impose on the world Communist movement. What the Chinese leaders propose under the guise of a 'general line' is nothing else but an enumeration of the most general tasks of the working class, made without due consideration for time and the concrete correlations of class forces or for the peculiarities of the present stage of history. . . .

The Marxist-Leninist parties have determined their line, the main provisions of which come down to the following:

The nature and substance of the world revolutionary process in the modern epoch is determined by the merging into one stream of the struggle against imperialism waged by the peoples that are building up socialism and Communism, by the revolutionary movement of the working class in the capitalist countries, the national liberation struggle of the oppressed peoples and the democratic movements in general. In the alliance of the anti-imperialist revolutionary forces the decisive role belongs to the international working class and its main offspring: *the world system of socialism, which exerts the principal influence on the development of the world socialist system by the force of example, and by its economic construction.*

In view of the prevailing objective historical conditions (maximum growth of the aggressiveness of imperialism, emergence of weapons of tremendous destructive power, etc.) the central place among all the tasks facing the anti-imperialist forces in the modern epoch is held by the struggle to prevent a thermonuclear war. *The primary task of the Communist parties is to rally together all the peace-loving forces in the defence of peace, and to save mankind from a nuclear catastrophe.*

The socialist revolution takes place as a result of the internal development of the class struggle in every country, and its form and ways are determined by the concrete conditions of each given nation. The general rule is the revolutionary overthrow of the power of capital and the establishment of a proletarian dictatorship in this or that form. It is the task of the working class and the Communist parties *to make maximum use of the opportunities now available for the peaceful way to socialist revolution, not involving civil war, and to be at the same time ready for the armed suppression of the resistance of the bourgeoisie; the general democratic struggle is an indispensable part of the struggle for socialism.*

The goals of the working class and the Communist parties in the national liberation movement are *to carry through the tasks of the anti-imperialist democratic revolution,* to develop and consolidate the national front, based on the alliance with the peasantry and the patriotically-minded national bourgeoisie, and to prepare conditions for the setting up of a state of national democracy and the transition to the non-capitalist road of development.

Relations of co-operation and mutual assistance between the socialist countries, *the cohesion and unity of the international Communist and labour movement,* loyalty to the positions and appraisals worked out jointly and to Leninist principles in the life of the parties and the relations between them, these are the necessary conditions for a successful solution of the historical tasks facing the Communists.

Such, in our epoch, are the main ways of the development of the world revolutionary process. Such are the basic provisions of the general line of the international Communist movement at the present stage. *The struggle for peace, democracy, national independence and socialism: such is in brief the essence of this general line.* Consistent realisation of this line in practice is the earnest of the successes of the world Communist movement.

V

The erroneous views of the CCP leaders on the cardinal political and theoretical questions of our time are inseparably linked with *their practical activities directed towards undermining the unity of the world socialist camp and the international Communist movement*. The Chinese comrades recognise in oratory that the unity of the USSR and the CPR is a mainstay of the entire socialist community, but in fact they are undermining contacts with our Party and with our country in all directions.

The leadership often speaks of its loyalty to the comity of the socialist countries but the attitude of the Chinese comrades to this comity refutes their high-sounding declarations. *Statistics show that in the past three years the CPR cut the volume of its trade with countries of the socialist community by more than 50 per cent.* Some socialist countries felt the results of this line of the Chinese comrades with particular sharpness. The actions of the Chinese leadership stand in glaring contradiction not only to the principles of mutual relations between socialist countries but in many cases even to the generally recognised rules and norms which should be observed by all states. The flouting of agreements signed earlier inflicted serious damage on the national economy of some socialist states. It is quite understandable that the economy of China also suffered tangibly from the curtailment of its economic contacts.

In an effort to justify its actions in the eyes of the popular masses the CCP leadership recently advanced a theory of 'reliance on one's own forces'. Generally speaking, to build socialism in every country relying primarily on the efforts of its people, with the best utilisation of the internal resources of the country, is the correct way of creating a material and technical basis for socialism. The construction of socialism in every country is primarily a matter of concern for the people of that country, its working class and the Communist party. . . .

The CCP leadership organises and supports various anti-party groups of renegades who come out against the Communist parties in the USA, Brazil, Italy, Belgium, Australia and India. For instance in Belgium the CCP is rendering support to the group of Grippa, expelled from the Party at the last Congress. . . .

The Soviet Union, which was the first country of socialism, had to build socialism relying only on its own forces and using its internal resources. And although there is now a system of socialist countries, this in no way means that the people of some country may sit with folded arms and rely exclusively on the assistance of other countries of socialism. The Communist party of every socialist country regards it as its duty to mobilise all internal reserves for successful economic development. Therefore, the statement of the CCP Central Committee about the construction of socialism mainly by its own forces would, in its direct meaning, give rise to no objections.

However, as shown by the whole text of the letter of the CCP Central Committee and the numerous statements in the Chinese press, this thesis is actually given an interpretation with which it is impossible to agree. The formula of the 'socialist construction mainly by one's own forces' conceals the concept of creating self-sufficient national economies in which the economic contacts with other countries are restricted to trade only. The Chinese comrades are trying to impose this approach on other socialist countries, too. The proclamation of the course of 'reliance on one's own forces' apparently was needed by the CCP leadership in order to weaken the bonds of close friendship between the socialist countries. This policy, of course, has nothing in common with the principles of socialist internationalism. It cannot be regarded otherwise than as an attempt to undermine the unity of the socialist community.

Parallel to the line of curtailing economic contacts, *the CCP leadership took a number of measures aimed at aggravating relations with the Soviet Union.* The Chinese leaders are undermining the unity not only of the socialist camp but also of the entire world Communist movement, trampling under foot the principles of proletarian internationalism and grossly violating the norms of relations between fraternal parties. . . .

Representatives of the CCP left the editorial board of the magazine *Problems of Peace and Socialism*, the collective theoretical and information organ of Communist and Workers' parties, and stopped the publication of this magazine in the Chinese language, striving thus to deprive Chinese Communists of an objective source of information on the activity of the international Communist movement. . . .

One of the patent examples of the special line of the CCP leadership in the socialist camp and the international Communist movement is its position on the Albanian question. As is known, in the second half of 1960 the Albanian leaders openly came out with a left-wing opportunist platform on the main questions of our times and began promoting a hostile policy in respect of the CPSU and other fraternal parties. The Albanian leadership started an anti-Soviet campaign in the country which led to a rupture of political, economic and cultural ties with the Soviet Union. The overwhelming majority of Communist and Workers' parties resolutely condemned this anti-Leninist activity of the Albanian leaders. The CCP leaders took an absolutely different position and did everything to use the Albanian leaders as their mouthpiece. It is now known that the Chinese comrades openly pushed them to the road of overt struggle against the Soviet Union and the other socialist countries and fraternal parties. . . .

In their attacks on the CPSU and other Marxist-Leninist parties the CCP leaders assign a special place to the Yugoslav question. They try to present matters in such a way as though difficulties in the Communist movement were caused by an improvement in relations between the Soviet Union and the other socialist countries and Yugoslavia. Contrary to the facts, they stubbornly contend that Yugoslavia allegedly is not a socialist country. . . .

Why then have the Chinese leaders so drastically changed their position on the Yugoslav question? It is hard to find an explanation other than that they saw in this an advantageous pretext, in their opinion, to discredit the policy of the CPSU and other Marxist-Leninist parties. . . .

At present there are 14 socialist countries in the world.* We are profoundly convinced that in the near future their number will be considerably greater. The range of questions encountered by the fraternal parties that stand at the helm of state is increasing. Besides, each of the fraternal parties is working in different conditions. It is not surprising that in these circumstances the fraternal parties

---

* *i.e.*, USSR, China, East Germany, Poland, Czechoslovakia, Hungary, Rumania, Bulgaria, Albania, Yugoslavia, North Korea, North Vietnam, Mongolia, Cuba.

may develop different approaches to the solution of this or that problem. How should Marxist-Leninists act in this case? Declare that this or that socialist country, whose leaders do not agree with them, is no longer a socialist country? This would be real arbitrariness. This method has nothing in common with Marxism-Leninism.

If we were to follow the example of the Chinese leaders then, because of our serious differences with the leaders of the Albanian Workers' Party, we should long ago have proclaimed Albania to be a non-socialist country. But this would be an erroneous, subjectivist approach. Despite our differences with the Albanian leaders, the Soviet Communists regard Albania as a socialist country and, for their part, do everything to prevent Albania from being split away from the socialist community.

We watch with regret how the leaders of the CCP undermine the traditional Soviet-Chinese friendship and weaken the unity of the socialist countries. The CPSU stands and will stand for the unity and cohesion of the socialist community and of the entire world Communist movement.

VI

Let us recapitulate. Since the adoption of the Statement of 1960 time has fully confirmed the correctness of the Marxist-Leninist programme of the world Communist and working class movement. . . .

All this shows that the Statement of 1960 set correctly the general line of the world Communist movement. The task now is to act in conformity with this general line, to develop and specify it as applied to the conditions in which each given Communist party operates. Therefore, all attempts to impose some new general line on the world Communist and working class movement, as was done in the letter of the CCP Central Committee of June 14, are insolvent and harmful. To accept such a 'general line' would be to depart from the Statement of 1960, to agree to programmatic theses contrary to this Statement which was adopted by 81 parties. Our Party will not do this. . . .

The CPSU has stood and stands for close friendship with the CCP. There are serious differences between us and the leaders of the CCP, but we hold that the relations between the two parties and between our two peoples should be built on the fact that we have the same aim: the building of a new Communist society; and that we have the same enemy: imperialism. United, the two great powers, the Soviet Union and the Chinese People's Republic, can do much for the triumph of Communism. This is well known to our friends and enemies.

A meeting of the delegations of the CPSU and the CCP is being held in Moscow at present. Unfortunately, the CCP representatives at the meeting continue to aggravate the situation. Despite this, the delegation of the CPSU is displaying the utmost patience and self-control, and working for a successful outcome of the negotiations. The near future will show whether the Chinese comrades agree to build our relations on the basis of what unites us and not on what divides us and on the basis of the principles of Marxism-Leninism. . . .

The Central Committee of the CPSU declares with utmost responsibility before the Party and the entire Soviet people that we have done and will do everything within our power to strengthen unity with the CCP, to rally the world Communist movement under the banner of Lenin, to rally the countries of the world system of socialism, to provide effective aid to all peoples fighting against colonialism, to strengthen the cause of peace and to ensure the victory of the great ideas of Communism throughout the world.

All working people of the Soviet Union will rally even closer around their own Communist party and its Leninist Central Committee and will devote all their energy to fulfilling the majestic programme of building Communism.

(Signed) **The Central Committee of the CPSU.**

July 20

The Chinese delegates, headed by Teng Hsiao-ping, left Moscow by air for Peking. They were seen off by Suslov and other members of the Soviet delegation to the inter-party talks. They were welcomed at Peking airport by Mao Tse-tung and a crowd of 5,000.

Before their departure the Chinese delegates were entertained to dinner by the Presidium of the CC of the CPSU. The dinner was said to have taken place in a 'friendly atmosphere' and Khrushchev and Teng Hsiao-ping exchanged toasts.

July 21

A communiqué published simultaneously in Moscow and Peking said that during the talks 'both sides set forth their views and positions on a whole series of important questions of principal affecting current changes in the world situation, the international Communist movement and Soviet-Chinese relations'. At the suggestion of the Chinese delegation it had been agreed to suspend the talks for the time being. The time and place at which the meeting would be continued would be agreed later between the two parties.

BIBLIOGRAPHY

The following is a list of books which may be found illuminating by those who wish to delve deeper into the dispute between Russia and China. It includes all the sources from which I have drawn material for the documentation. But it makes no pretence to being exhaustive. Mr. Donald Zagoria has included an immensely useful bibliography in his *The Sino-Soviet Conflict, 1956–1961.* (Princeton and Oxford University Presses, 1962).

Bass, Robert and Marbury, Elizabeth (eds.). *The Soviet-Yugoslav Controversy, 1948–58: A Documentary Record.* (Prospect Books, New York, 1959).

Beloff, Max. *The Foreign Policy of Soviet Russia, 1929–1941.* (Oxford University Press, 1949).
Soviet Policy in the Far East, 1944–1951. (Oxford University Press, 1953).

Boorman, Howard, L. and others. *Moscow-Peking Axis: Strengths and Strains.* (Harper and Brothers, 1957).

Bowie, Robert R. and Fairbank, John K. (eds.). *Communist China, 1955–1959: Policy Documents with Analysis.* (Harvard University Press, Cambridge, Mass, 1962).

Brzezinski, Zbigniew K. *The Soviet Bloc: Unity and Conflict.* (Frederick A. Praeger, New York, 1961).
Ideology and Power in Soviet Politics. (Frederick A. Praeger, New York, 1962; Thames and Hudson, London, 1962).

Crankshaw, Edward. *The New Cold War: Moscow v. Peking.* (Penguin Books, London and New York, 1963).

Dallin, David J. *The Rise of Russia in Asia.* (Hollis and Carter, London, 1950).
Soviet Foreign Policy After Stalin. (J. B. Lippincott Company, Philadelphia, 1961; Methuen, London, 1962).

Daniels, Robert V. (ed.). *A Documentary History of Communism.* (Random House, New York, 1960).

Dedijer, Vladimir. *Tito Speaks.* (Weidenfeld and Nicolson, London, 1953).

Degras, Jane (ed.). *The Communist International 1919–1943. Documents. Vol. I.* (Oxford University Press, London, 1956).

Djilas, Milovan. *Conversations With Stalin.* (Harcourt, Bruce and Co., New York, 1962; Hart-Davis, London, 1962).

Florinsky, Michael T. *Russia: A History and an Interpretation.* (The Macmillan Company, New York, 1947).

Griffith, William E. *The November 1960 Meeting: A Preliminary Reconstruction.* (The China Quarterly, London, 1962).

Albania and the Sino-Soviet Rift. (The M.I.T. Press, Cambridge, Mass, 1963).

Hsieh, Alice Langley. *Communist China's Strategy in the Nuclear Era.* (Prentice-Hall, Inc., New Jersey, 1962).

Hudson, G. F., Lowenthal, Richard and MacFarquhar, Roderick. *The Sino-Soviet Dispute* [*Documents and Commentaries*]. (The China Quarterly, London, 1961; Frederick A. Praeger, New York, 1961).

Jackson, W. A. Douglas. *The Russo-Chinese Borderlands: Zone of Peaceful Contact or Potential Conflict?* (D. Van Nostrand Company, Inc., New York, 1962).

Kardelj, Edvard. *Socialism and War.* (Methuen, London, 1961).

Kuusinen, O. V. and others. *Osnovy Marksizma-Leninizma: Uchebnoye Posobiye.* [*The Fundamentals of Marxism-Leninism: A Textbook*]. (State Publisher for Political Literature, Moscow, 1959).

MacFarquhar, Roderick. *The Hundred Flowers Campaign and the Chinese Intellectual.* (Frederick A. Praeger, New York, 1960).

Mackintosh, J. M. *Strategy and Tactics of Soviet Foreign Policy.* (Oxford University Press, London, 1962).

Nollau, Günther. *International Communism and World Revolution: History and Methods.* (Frederick A. Praeger, New York, 1961; Hollis and Carter, London, 1961).

North, Robert C. *Moscow and the Chinese Communists.* (Stanford University Press, Stanford, Calif., 1953).

Rostow, W. W. and others. *The Prospects for Communist China.* Published jointly by The Technology Press of the Massachusetts Institute of Technology and John Wiley and Sons, Inc., New York. (Chapman and Hall, Ltd., London, 1954).

Royal Institute of International Affairs (ed.). *The Soviet-Yugoslav Dispute* [*Texts of Documents.*] (London, 1948).

Russian Institute, Columbia University. *The Anti-Stalin Campaign and International Communism.* [*A Selection of Documents*]. (Columbia University Press, New York, 1956).

Schapiro, Leonard (ed.). *The USSR and the Future: An Analysis of the New Program of the CPSU.* (Frederick A. Praeger, New York and London, 1963).

Schwartz, Benjamin I. *Chinese Communism and the Rise of Mao.* (Harvard University Press, Cambridge, Mass., 1951).

Tito, Josip Broz. *Govori i Clanci.* [*Collected Speeches and Articles*]. (Naprijed, Zagreb, 1959).

Ulam, Adam B. *The New Face of Soviet Totalitarianism.* (Harvard University Press, Cambridge, Mass., 1963).

Zagoria, Donald S. *The Sino-Soviet Conflict 1956–1961.* (Princeton University Press, New Jersey, 1962).

Zinner, Paul E. *National Communism and Popular Revolt in Eastern Europe*. (Columbia University Press, New York, 1956).

The following journals dealing with the Communist world have all contained many articles on various aspects of the Sino-Soviet dispute in the last few years:

Bulletin. Institute for the Study of the USSR, Mannhardtstrasse, 6, Munich, 6, Germany.

China Quarterly. (Editor: Roderick MacFarquhar), Ilford House, 133, Oxford Street, London, W.1.

Est et Ouest. (Bulletin de l'Association d'Etudes et d'Informations Politiques Internationales), Rédaction et Administration, 86 Bd. Haussman, Paris, 8-e.

International Affairs. Royal Institute of International Affairs, Chatham House, St. James's Square, London, S. W. 1.

Problems of Communism. The United States Information Agency, 1776 Pennsylvania Avenue, N.W., Washington, 25, D.C.

Survey (Editor: Walter Laqueur). Summit House, 1–2 Langham Place, London, W.1.

World Marxist Review. ('Problems of Peace and Socialism'), Central Books Ltd., 37 Gray's Inn Road, London, W.C.1.

For the texts of speeches and articles by Russian politicians and publicists I have relied mainly on the versions of them given in the Soviet press at the time or, in the case of the party congresses, on the versions later published in book form. But for reasons of haste I have not invariably been able to make my own translations for the purposes of inclusion in the *Chronology*, where I have been forced to make use of existing 'official' translations. For the texts of Chinese statements (which I am not able to read in the original) I have relied either on the English text issued by the New China News Agency in London or on the versions later made available in the Peking Review (Pai Wan Chuang, Peking (37), China) or by the Foreign Languages Press in Peking.

INDEX TO PART ONE

INDEX TO PART TWO